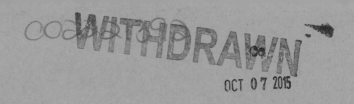

THE EMPIRE TRAP

THE EMPIRE TRAP

THE RISE AND FALL
OF U.S. INTERVENTION TO PROTECT
AMERICAN PROPERTY OVERSEAS,
1893–2013

Noel Maurer

PRINCETON UNIVERSITY PRESS

Princeton and Oxford

press.princeton.edu

All Rights Reserved

ISBN: 978-0-691-15582-1

Library of Congress Control Number: 2013933598

British Library Cataloging-in-Publication Data is available

This book has been composed in Sabon and Trade Gothic

Printed on acid-free paper. ∞

Printed in the United States of America

1 3 5 7 9 10 8 6 4 2

CONTENTS

ACKNOWLEDGMENTS

It is wonderful to have the opportunity to pursue the answers to a big and puzzling question. This book may address a big question but it grew from two small seeds. The first was a case I wrote with Aldo Musacchio in 2005 about Argentina. The case introduced me to the vast legal infrastructure designed to protect foreign investors against expropriation. The second was a discussion in a California café with Kris Mitchener about his work (with Marc Weidenmier) on the economic impact of the Roosevelt Corollary. Kris and I never wrote the paper we talked about, but the seeds of the idea that became this book had been planted. For that, I owe them both a debt of thanks.

Several of the ideas in this book were originally presented in various working papers. I owe thanks to my coauthors on one of those working papers: Faisal Ahmed and Laura Alfaro. I also owe thanks to the participants in the workshops and conferences at which I presented those papers, including Columbia University, the Fletcher School, Rutgers, UCLA, the Zicklin School of Business, the London School of Economics, and the Council on Foreign Affairs. The feedback received at those conferences proved invaluable. I owe particular debts to Michael Bordo, Leah Boustan, Jonathan Brookfield, Alan Dye, Susan Franck, Naomi Lamoreaux, Carolyn Moehling, Lilach Nachum, Clint Peinhardt, Lauge Poulson, Jeswald Salacuse, Rajeev Sawant, Mark Wasserman, Eugene White, Mark Wright, and Jason Yackee.

This book would not have been possible without ample support from the Harvard Business School. I would like to thank the dean of HBS, Nitin Nohria, for the generous research support given during the writing and research process. In addition, many of my colleagues at Harvard, on both sides of the river, gave support and assistance above and beyond the call of duty. Several read and commented upon entire drafts of the manuscript: Rawi Abdelal, David Moss, James Robinson, Gunnar Trumbull, Dick Vietor, and Lou Wells were particularly helpful. Rawi Abdelal provided very useful advice about the book's overall theme and David Moss gave invaluable feedback concerning the archival evidence in the first few chapters. Lou Wells deserves special mention: he read *multiple* drafts and provided detailed comments. This book would have been far different, and far lesser, without his help. In addition, Niall Ferguson was always willing to discuss ideas and helped focus many of the arguments. Gustavo Herrero gave irreplaceable assistance for my field research in Argentina. Zac Pelleriti and Tremana White provided support in Boston, without which this book would have been impossible to complete.

Outside Harvard, I owe particular debts to Stephen Haber and Suresh Naidu. Both gave amply of their time and intellect. They helped me solve several puzzles that might have proved otherwise intractable and I am in debt to both of them. I would also like to thank Leticia Arroyo and Francisco Monaldi for their feedback and support. In addition, this book would have been impossible without superlative research assistance from Caitlin Anderson, Andrew Novo, and Carlos Yu.

Numerous people gave generously of their time to help make this book happen. I would in particular like to thank Mark Bellis, Beth Clevenger, Seth Ditchik, Will Hively, and Theresa Liu. I would also like to thank the anonymous referees from Princeton University Press for their incisive and very helpful reviews of an earlier draft of the book. Any flaws and errors that remain are, of course, wholly my own.

I have dedicated this book to my immediate family for their unflinching and unfailing support. My wife, Amma Nzinga Maurer, read the entire manuscript on more than one occasion and never failed to keep me motivated and on track. Our little boy, Seretse Hilario Maurer, came into the world as I was finishing the manuscript and never failed to provide me with immense amounts of joy as he discovered all the neat new things in this wide wide world. Finally, my father, Leon Maurer, passed away in 2011: he never got a chance to read this book, but I like to think that it honors his memory.

one
Introduction

An extraordinary act in the history of the civilized nations, without precedent, without possible justification, a barbarous act because it is an attack on the most rudimentary principles of international law, an ignoble act because it is the fruit of an immoral and cowardly collusion of force and betrayal.
—*Cipriano Castro, 1902*

This is the great threat, the biggest threat that the planet faces today. The Yankee empire.
—*Hugo Chávez, 2010*

In 1900, Venezuelan president Cipriano Castro seized properties belonging to the American asphalt trust. Venezuelan troops forcibly ousted the trust's employees and occupied its facilities on the shores of Lake Bermúdez, one of the largest natural tar pits in the world. The McKinley administration protested, and the Navy Department ordered three warships to the scene, but the United States did not intervene. Dissatisfied with the official response, the asphalt trust immediately set out arming a rebellion to overthrow Castro's government. American corporate support for the rebels led Castro to seize British-flagged vessels carrying weapons for Castro's opponents. That in turn provoked a confrontation between Castro and the United Kingdom, which caused the German government to get involved on the British side. The Anglo-German alliance shelled La Güaira, sank two Venezuelan vessels, blockaded several ports, and threatened invasion. The U.S. government was dragged back into the dispute, where it brokered a state-to-state settlement at the International Tribunal at the Hague. The imbroglio was confused, politicized, and violent. But it was not unique. From the confrontation between the Hawaiian sugar planters and Queen Liliuokalani in 1893 to the "dollar diplomacy" of the 1920s, the U.S. government found itself drawn again and again into disputes between American investors and foreign governments over their property rights.

In 2007, Venezuelan president Hugo Chávez seized properties belonging to the American oil giants ExxonMobil and ConocoPhillips. When asked, a State Department official stated, "The government of Venezuela, like any other government, has the right to make these kinds of decisions to change ownership rules. The standard has always been that we want to see them meet their international commitments in terms of providing fair and just compensation."[1] The oil giants then sued Venezuela's state-owned oil company at the International Chamber of Commerce (ICC) and the Venezuelan government at the International Centre for Settlement of Investment Disputes (ICSID). The U.S. government was not involved in the suits. The ICC decided that Venezuela owed ExxonMobil $907.6 million in compensation. Chávez blustered, but paid. The dispute was legalistic and relatively orderly. But it was not unique. By 2007, it was perfectly normal for American companies to sue foreign governments in international tribunals over violations of their perceived property rights—and, at least sometimes, to win and to collect.

The Empire Trap is about the shift from politicized confrontations like the imbroglio of 1900 to legalized disputes like the more orderly affair of 2007. It advances four basic findings. First, American government intervention on behalf of U.S. foreign investors was astoundingly successful at extracting compensation through the *1980s*. Second, American domestic interests trumped strategic concerns again and again, for small economic gains relative to the U.S. economy and the potential strategic losses. Third, the United States proved unable to impose institutional reform in Latin America and West Africa *even while American agents were in place*, let alone afterward. Finally, the technology that the U.S. government used to protect American property rights overseas changed radically over time—and ultimately, in a case of unintended consequences, gave U.S. investors a set of tools that they could employ against foreign governments *without* explicitly calling on the power of the American executive to protect them.

The first finding—that the U.S. government intervened often and intervened *successfully* on behalf of American overseas direct investors from the 1890s through the 1980s—is particularly true for natural resources. State Department reports provide data on every investment dispute brought to its attention between 1900 and 1987. For investors in oil and hard-rock natural resources, the number of cases in which countries unequivocally managed to avoid paying full compensation—defined as the market value of foregone future income—was almost entirely limited to countries openly allied to the Soviet Union.[2] In only six non-Soviet cases (out of 130) did investors unambiguously receive less than the value of their investment as a going concern: Venezuela in 1900, Bolivia in 1952 and 1969, Ecuador in 1972, Kuwait in 1975, and Iran in 1979.[3] In other words, once you look at the data, one of the major stylized facts about the foreign expropriation of American assets disappears: investors in natural resources rarely suffered economic damage from expropriation. And this was because the U.S. government actively defended the owners and their interests, almost regardless of the strategic situation or ideological preferences.

The implication is that domestic interests trumped strategic imperatives, over and over again—which is the second finding of this book. This result is surprising considering the relative unimportance of foreign direct investment (FDI) to the American economy. FDI was never a significant part of total American investment, and the returns from FDI were never a significant part of national income. The United States did have strategic interests in securing foreign supplies of raw materials—but never did such security hinge on the *de jure* ownership of foreign wells and mines. Foreign portfolio investment was slightly more important—but only beginning in the 1970s. From the 1890s to the early 1970s, American investment in sovereign debt was neither a significant proportion of American overseas portfolio investment nor systematically important to the health of the financial system. Nevertheless, American administrations again and again went to bat for private interests in their conflicts with foreign governments. This held true even when the rise of the Axis and the Cold War with the Communists sent the potential strategic costs of such conflicts into the stratosphere. After the Cuban Revolution of 1958, many within the State Department feared that it was the American hard line on expropriation that drove Castro into the arms of the Soviet Union—yet the United States ran such strategic risks again and again and again, in Indonesia and Peru and Ethiopia and elsewhere. Simply put, no U.S. president could afford to take a Solomonic view and ignore the immense pressures that private interests could bring to bear to insist upon the defense of their property rights.

To be sure, some presidents needed more persuasion than others. Theodore Roosevelt and Richard Nixon needed little convincing to punish foreign governments that threatened American-owned property. William Howard Taft and Calvin Coolidge did not require a great deal more persuasion to intervene on behalf of investors. Warren Harding, Harry Truman, Dwight Eisenhower, and John Kennedy, on the other hand, were relatively reluctant. Finally, some presidents needed to be dragged kicking and screaming into intervention. Woodrow Wilson, Franklin Roosevelt, Lyndon Johnson, and Jimmy Carter had little interest in using American power to protect wealthy Americans from foreign governments—but did so nonetheless.

The third finding is that the United States proved incapable of fixing what it believed to be the underlying factors that made property rights insecure in Latin America and elsewhere. Early twentieth-century economic orthodoxy held that political insta-bility, insecure property rights, poor infrastructure, and what today would be called "underdevelopment" all stemmed from a single, common root: poor revenue collection caused by internal corruption. The inability to collect taxes and tariffs, in this view, trapped states in a vicious cycle. Governments needed to pay tax collectors in order to collect taxes; so without the admin-istrative capacity to raise revenue there was no way to create the administrative capacity to raise revenue! Low revenues, in turn, meant there were few resources to spend on public goods: armies to maintain order, courts to enforce contracts, and infra-structure to move goods and improve health. The result was po-litical instability: without the ability to tax, governments would resort to expropriating private property (including that of for-eign investors)—which would in turn mobilize violent opposi-tion. Foreign borrowing could in theory square the circle. The problem was that the borrowing states lacked the ability to tax any resulting increase in economic activity. The result would be *at best* a cycle of default. At worst, a country would find itself cut off from foreign capital markets and plagued by rampant instability. Neighboring countries could be destabilized as well, and promising investment opportunities would be lost.

The above diagnosis of the problem offered an obvious solu-tion: appoint American officials to manage a country's revenue institutions. U.S. managers, with the power to hire and fire and enforce new administrative rules, could reduce corruption and enhance efficiency. Revenue would rise. Higher revenue would allow more expenditure on public goods. It would also decrease the chance of default, thereby lowering borrowing costs—enabling even more expenditure on public goods. That would reduce political instability and promote growth, which would in turn attract foreign direct investment, which would in turn create more growth. The end result would be stable prosperous polities in which American investment would be safe.

The only problem with the theory was that it did not work. The United States imposed eight "fiscal receiverships," most with the cooperation (even enthusiasm) of the foreign government. Except for the first, in the Dominican Republic, none managed to raise more revenue than the country had previously collected. In the Dominican Republic, the receivership raised revenues not because the Americans reduced corruption, wrote better rules, or brought innovative management, but because Dominican insurgents stopped attacking the customhouses once American officials were in place. Elsewhere, putting executive authority in American hands (and in many cases rewriting legislation) was not enough to change entrenched cultures of corruption. Fiscal receiverships failed even when the United States ultimately took over *all* government functions, as in Cuba and Haiti. Moreover, with the exception of the first intervention, markets reacted badly to the announcement of a receivership. Bond yields on the debt of *other* Latin American nations jumped several hundred basis points in the month a receivership was announced. Rather than showing reassurance that the Americans stood ready to improve institutions, investors acted as if the receiverships reminded them of what a risky place Latin America really was.

The fourth finding is that the *technology* of intervention to compel compensation changed dramatically over time. In order to defend the property rights of Americans (or at least the value of the income streams those rights generated) in conflicts with foreign governments, the United States needed to do one of three things: bribe the foreign government, threaten the foreign government, or change the foreign government. The most obvious way to protect American investors in foreign territory was to make the territory no longer foreign—that is, bring the area into the United States under the purview of the Constitution. That strategy ran into trouble when Americans began investing in areas with largely nonwhite populations: racist voters would not accept full annexation, which the Fourteenth Amendment ensured would also bring citizenship. Hawaii was the exception for a variety of special circumstances not to be repeated.

The first new "technology" to be introduced was annexation without the Constitution—as in, for example, imperial rule.

The U.S. Supreme Court, in the infamous "Insular Cases," allowed annexation without citizenship or the full protection of the Constitution. Unfortunately for investors, that in turn also proved problematic. Democratic anti-imperialists in Congress deliberately wrote rules that restricted private American investment in the two largest and most economically important U.S. possessions: the Philippine Islands and occupied Cuba. That left informal imperialism: carrots and sticks to be rolled out against nominally independent governments. From 1904 to the Great Depression, the stick was military force (usually via the threat of blockades) and the carrot was access to the American credit market. In the 1930s the set of carrots and sticks broadened: Franklin Roosevelt added public loans, foreign aid, and access to U.S. markets to the carrots, and the threat of denial became a stick. Later, during World War II, the United States developed an entire branch of government dedicated to covert action against foreign states. It became only natural that the new tool would be repurposed to defend the private property rights of Americans abroad.

Beginning in the third quarter of the twentieth century, a series of mostly—but not entirely—unplanned innovations removed the concept of absolute sovereign immunity from legal action and gave investors direct access to international arbitration without the need to get their home governments to "espouse" the complaint. Other changes allowed the resulting decisions to be enforced in national courts. The changes gave investors a third option between cooperation with the foreign government and convincing Washington to back them in confrontation. The new option had the salubrious side effect of depoliticizing investment disputes and freed the U.S. government from the domestic pressures that had dragged it again and again into conflict with foreign states.

The Empire Trap

The above findings suggest the possibility of an "empire trap," in which one American administration's promise to intervene on behalf of U.S. investors makes it harder for future administrations to refrain from such intervention. If a president credibly commits to use the power of the United States to defend property rights in a foreign country, the perceived risk of investing in that country will fall. More capital will flow in, increasing the political pull of investors in that area. In addition, investors (as a matter of historical fact) will perceive that the promise applies to similar countries—in fact, for such countries to become more attractive, investors need only perceive the *possibility* that the promise applies. More American capital will flow in. Future administrations can default on the implicit promise—but only if they are willing to confront the owners of those investments. That entails political costs, the more so the more wealth that investors have at risk. In short, successful intervention on behalf of overseas investors begets more overseas investment, which creates more pressure to intervene when those investments come under threat. The result is an "empire trap," where U.S. administrations find it difficult to resist pressures to defend American overseas property rights.

The rub for investors is that American presidents have multiple reasons to refrain from exercising American power on their behalf. Interventions bear domestic political costs. Voters do not necessarily think that the interests of private investors are the same as the national interest. Some may oppose intervention for ideological reasons. Others oppose intervention because it fails a perceived cost-benefit test. After all, the benefits to voters from overseas investments are generally small given the immense size of the U.S. economy. The costs of getting involved in a foreign quagmire, on the other hand, can loom large. Such quagmires do not have to be military. For example, an economic confrontation with an expropriating government might cause that government to collapse, requiring expensive aid flows to stabilize its successor. Similarly, covert action can engender terrorism or other forms of blowback. Finally, the public might oppose intervention because it lacks sympathy for the co-nationals who lost their property. For example, the bankers and bondholders who held Latin American debt in 1929 enjoyed little to no public sympathy—and moves to support them incurred high domestic political costs.

Presidents also have strategic reasons to refrain from intervention. The United States has many interests, and defending private property rights can endanger those interests. For example, applying sanctions against a government that expropriates U.S.-owned property risks pushing that nation's government to ally with a hostile power. Military intervention can be expensive, trigger nationalist reaction in the target country, and tie up forces needed elsewhere. Nonmilitary intervention risks angering otherwise friendly governments and igniting popular anger against all U.S. businesses operating in or dealing with the target nation. Worse still, intervention of any type risks igniting popular anger *outside the target state*. The small value of foreign investment set against the massive size of the U.S. economy and the multiplicity of American strategic interests militates against intervention.

American investors abroad therefore confronted the flip side of the classic collective action problem: the U.S. government was powerful enough to protect them, but their interests were small relative to the overall welfare of the United States. (These two facts were related: the reason why the U.S. government could protect them was that the United States was so much more powerful than the countries in which they invested.) They therefore needed to convince the government to use its power on their behalf despite the fact that they were a small minority and that such actions generated political and strategic costs.

As an empirical matter, American investors in the twentieth century generally succeeded in trumping domestic opposition and strategic interest. The particular political strategies they employed changed over time. In the early twentieth century, overseas investors mostly used individual political connections to influence policy. This became easier as the dynamics of the empire trap set in. Later on, in the 1930s, investors began to employ more sophisticated strategies, linking the defense of their interests to other interests valued by the government of the day. After World War II, they mobilized public and congressional opinion to pressure the executive branch. Companies tied national interests such as anticommunism to the protection of their property rights and argued that the preservation of their income streams had the salubrious effect of denying such streams to hostile governments. Segments of the U.S. public considered the expropriation of their fellow citizens' property to be an attack against the nation. Others feared that if one expropriation were allowed, others might follow, so that at some point the economic damage might become large enough to affect their well-being. Such fears did not have to be realistic; they only had to be believed. In all these strategies, overseas investors benefited from the fact that the costs of intervention tended to be diffuse and spread over the entire society. Similarly, private investors benefited from changes in the technology of intervention: the political costs of denying aid or employing covert action were (at least in the short term) lower than the costs of blockading harbors or installing a fiscal receivership.

Cycles of Empire

The empire trap was not an ineluctable or monotonic process. Investors did not always get their way. Investor desires for greater property rights protection (and the strategies they employed to get their way) interacted with the American political system, voter preferences, and the technology of intervention to produce cycles of expansion and withdrawal. Note that these cycles involved only the use of American power to protect American *property*—they were not about the expansion of democracy, or the containment of the Soviet Union, or the prevention of genocide, or the search for weapons of mass destruction, or any of the other reasons why the U.S. government has projected power.

Chapter 2 of this book, "Avoiding the Trap," examines how the Democratic opponents of imperial expansion prevented the emergence of an empire trap in the Philippines and occupied Cuba. The McKinley administration annexed the Philippines for strategic reasons, but anti-imperialists used their blocking power in the Senate to restrict American investment in the islands *deliberately in order to prevent the emergence of a domestic interest group favoring the islands' retention as U.S. territory.* Similar laws were passed for Cuba as long as a U.S. occupation government remained. The anti-imperialists failed to grant the Philippines immediate independence, but they did succeed in retarding U.S. investment. As a result, no "Philippine lobby" ever emerged to support the permanent retention of the archipelago.

Chapter 3, "Setting the Trap," recounts the development of an informal American empire in the circum-Caribbean. Formal imperialism was off the table once it became clear that Congress could not be trusted to support investor interests in colonized territories, but the property rights of Americans continued to come under threat from a combination of feckless foreign governments and political instability. Under pressure from a coalition of direct investors in tropical enterprises and creditors to Latin American governments, Theodore Roosevelt used instability in the Dominican Republic to proclaim a de facto intervention sphere within which the United States would in cases of "chronic wrongdoing, or an impotence which results in a general loosening of the ties of civilized society" exercise "an international police power." The chapter shows how markets reacted to Roosevelt's declarations, factoring in American protection. It also shows, however, that when the interests of American investors were *not* aligned—as in Venezuela in 1900, where President Castro carefully designed a strategy to pit the interests of some American investors against others—the United States would not act.

The United States could cajole and threaten foreign governments into protecting American property. It proved less capable, however, of fixing the problems that led to instability, default, and expropriation. Chapter 4, "The Trap Closes," recounts the failures of the early fiscal receiverships. Even the Dominican Republic fell back into civil war by 1912. In fact, the Dominican state entirely collapsed in 1916, forcing a full-scale American occupation to reestablish a modicum of order. Anti-imperialist Woodrow Wilson wound up presiding over a deepening of America's informal empire.

Republican administrations after 1920 continued the intervention policy, even though Warren Harding openly campaigned against it in his 1920 presidential run. Chapter 5, "Banana Republicanism," shows how Harding tried and failed to extricate the United States from the interventions and receiverships in Central America, the Caribbean, and Liberia. Calvin Coolidge succeeded Harding after his death in 1923, and the Coolidge administration was equally ambivalent. Nevertheless, Coolidge failed to resist pressure to intervene on behalf of U.S. investors. By 1927, he would publicly state that "there is a distinct and binding obligation on the part of self-respecting governments to afford protection to the persons and property of their citizens, wherever they may be."

The Great Depression did what Woodrow Wilson and Warren Harding could not: it allowed Herbert Hoover and Franklin Roosevelt to pull back from Theodore Roosevelt's imperial commitment. Chapter 6, "Escaping by Accident," shows how the Depression facilitated the end of the first American empire by breaking up the coalition between creditors and direct investors. When times were good, Latin American governments could usually manage to make debt payments while collecting enough revenues to maintain a functioning state. Under Depression conditions, however, governments faced a painful bind: they could maintain payments on their foreign debt at the cost of austerity measures that undermined political stability; or they could impose tax hikes that directly impinged upon the profitability of foreign direct investments; or they could default. Creditors wanted governments to do everything possible to earn enough revenue to continue servicing their debt. Owners of direct investments disagreed: taxes and austerity measures ate into their profits and reduced the value of their investments. Ultimately, such measures had the potential to generate instability that threatened the very survival of their investments. In the battle between bondholders and direct investors, the direct investors won: the Depression had devastated the domestic influence of the financiers.

Accordingly, the great wave of Latin American defaults began in 1931 when the *Americans* who controlled Bolivian government finances signed off on default—which they had in fact been actively pushing for over a year. A similar story played out across America's other financial protectorates. In Cuba, however, President Gerardo Machado refused to default, even in the face of economic meltdown. Not unlike the Romanian Communist dictator Nicolae Ceaușescu, Machado preferred to raise taxes to confiscatory levels and stop paying government officials. The end result was the extraordinary spectacle of the Roosevelt administration orchestrating the overthrow of a Cuban president because he *refused* to default on his debts to American investors.

The underlying logic of the empire trap, however, continued to hold. The players were different: bondholders were no longer important, since the Great Depression destroyed most of the sovereign debt market. (It would not revive in any serious way until the syndicated bank loans of the 1970s.) Direct investors were now primary, and policy revolved around dissuading expropriation or obtaining adequate compensation afterward. The tools were also different. Under Franklin Roosevelt, the United States began to provide foreign aid (in the form of grants and loans) and rolled out perhaps the first case of modern covert action against the government of Cuba. Both tools were perfected during the Second World War, which saw the creation of entire agencies of government dedicated to providing official transfers and covertly manipulating the affairs of foreign states. In addition, the development of sophisticated trade controls allowed targeted action against the exports of other nations; for example, after 1948 the United States could attempt to influence certain Latin American governments by granting or withholding quotas for sugar. These new tools reduced the political cost of intervention—making it easier for American administrations to fall back into the empire trap. Chapter 7, "Falling Back In," shows how the return to the empire trap played out, starting with Franklin Roosevelt in Mexico through Eisenhower in Guatemala and faraway Iran.

Chapter 8, "The Empire Trap and the Cold War," shows how the empire trap continued to drive policy in the context of the worldwide contest with the Soviet Union. The Cold War had two opposing effects on the empire trap. On one hand, it raised the strategic cost of intervention. American pressure on a foreign government, if unsuccessful, could push that country into the Soviet bloc. (Many in the U.S. government, for example, believed that it was precisely the American reaction to Fidel Castro's nationalizations that drove him into the arms of the Soviets.) On the other hand, the advent of the Cold War also raised the domestic costs of acquiescing to foreign nationalizations. Private interests rapidly learned that the fear of communist expansion made it easier to manipulate intelligence and mobilize public and congressional opinion. The Kennedy administration tried to ignore Third World expropriations, only to have Congress *mandate* the imposition of crushing sanctions in the event. Nixon sanctioned Peru and, at great strategic risk, took hard positions with Arab oil nations that were closely allied to the United States. Carter launched severe sanctions against Ethiopia, despite being warned that the target country might move into the Soviet bloc as a result—which, in fact, it did.

However challenging and frustrating this new world might be for American policymakers, it was on the whole quite good for American investors. Chapter 9 shows how American pressure obtained fair compensation for the vast majority of natural resource investors.[4] There was, of course, one other difference between the Cold War–era empire and its pre-Depression predecessor: in the second empire, the United States essentially gave up trying to directly alter the domestic institutions of foreign countries. There would be massive aid programs, and American advisers would become omnipresent in places like South Vietnam, but once the occupation governments were withdrawn from Germany, Austria, Japan, and Korea there would be no more "fiscal receiverships" or occupations—save for a few brief months in the Dominican Republic and mere *days* in Grenada and Panama.[5] Where the United States did take a more active role, it had little to do with the protection of American property rights and more to do with the containment of Communist expansion.

Beneath the surface, however, the tectonic plates governing investor-state interactions were shifting. Chapter 10, "Escaping by Design?" recounts how over the course of the 1950s, 1960s, and 1970s a series of small legal and political innovations began to allow private investors to use international tribunals to sue foreign governments *and then use American and European courts to enforce the decisions*. Before 1945, the doctrine of absolute sovereign immunity held that no state could be held accountable for its actions in the courts of another state. (This led to some ironies. In 1938, the Mexican government expropriated American and British oil companies. When the Mexicans docked some expropriated tankers in Mobile, Alabama, an *Alabama state judge* blocked the Mexican Eagle Oil Company from repossessing its own expropriated tankers.)[6] After 1945, reforms began to chip away at sovereign immunity. At first, the changes were driven by the rise of state-owned companies: how could Air France do business in Italy if it enjoyed absolute immunity by dint of its ownership? Later, reforms arose from efforts to depoliticize investment disputes: first by giving private investors the right to take foreign governments to arbitration without the need to have their home government "espouse" the claim; then by giving national courts the right to enforce arbitration judgments against foreign governments. These changes were not mere window dressing. They meant that in the case of the expropriation of export-oriented assets, investors could demand compensation, enjoy an element of due process in its determination, and then *use national courts in other countries to enforce a blockade of production from the expropriated assets* if the foreign government reneged on compensation.

These developments were not seen as dramatically game changing at the time. As far as the investors of the 1960s and 1970s were concerned, the old system of sanctions still worked. Moreover, the Soviet Union stood ready to provide an alternative market for nations allied with it, weakening the efficacy of the new systems. But the new institutions were quietly working a revolution: they reduced the political costs that the American executive branch would incur by *not* acting on behalf of investors. Combined with the development of political risk insurance, these new institutions fundamentally changed the nature of international property rights. By the 1990s, American managers faced with a foreign investment dispute had a third option beyond acquiescing to the demands of the local government or asking the United States for help: they could sue in international tribunals—and more often than not, if they won, they could collect.

In presenting these findings, this book shamelessly trespasses across the social sciences. It employs a form of the "analytic narrative" pioneered by Bates, Greif, Levi, Rosenthal, and Weingast.[7] There is a vast and almost bewildering amount of economic, institutional, and historical data available about the history of the United States' attempts to protect the property rights of its citizens outside its boundaries. Analytic narrative allows placement of these data within a theoretical context to move forward from specific to more general conclusions, reasoning from the "thick" to the "thin," as the method's authors described it. *The Empire Trap* offers an account that diverges at several points from the received view. Its traipsing across different fields means that something should be said about the implications of its findings for each one.

Political Science

A major portion of the trespassing of this book is through territory that has traditionally been the province of political scientists. Political scientists have long recognized that the U.S. government went to bat for American investors in conflicts with foreign states. Examples include the work of Jessica Einhorn, George Ingram, Paul Sigmund, and Sidney Weintraub.[8] What these authors have not fully recognized, however, is the *success* the government achieved in obtaining compensation for U.S. investors that equaled or exceeded the value of their investments as going concerns. Moreover, the United States generally managed to retain the strategic advantages that came from access to raw materials.

In *Defending the National Interest*, Stephen Krasner explicitly rejected the "liberal" interest group model. Rather, he adopted the view that the nation itself had interests and ideologies that it acted upon. Krasner hypothesized that one of the primary objectives for the United States was to maintain a secure supply of raw materials.[9] In his view, corporations followed the lead of the state.[10] The "pivot of the state"—the White House and the State Department—was "insulated from specific societal pressures."[11] The analysis was based on a stylized fact: when American strategic interest conflicted with the economic interest of American investors in foreign raw materials whose property had been expropriated, strategic interests won.[12]

The Empire Trap takes direct issue with Krasner's interpretation. First, the United States was remarkably successful in obtaining compensation for its nationals, *especially in natural resources*. Second, the U.S. government was consistently willing to run large geopolitical risks to do so. To give one example, when Indonesia nationalized American property, Lyndon Johnson said, "If we cut off all assistance, Sukarno will probably turn to the Russians"—and then proceeded to cut off assistance and watch Sukarno turn to the Russians. There is overwhelming evidence of private interests pressuring the U.S. government to obtain compensation and the government running large strategic risks in order to obtain it.

In contrast, Charles Lipson in *Standing Guard* (1985) proposed a rather less apocalyptic view of investment disputes. Lipson believed that over the twentieth century, host country development catalyzed a shift from an international regime that favored investor rights to a new regime based on sovereign rights.[13] Lipson argued that investors lacked the political "concentration" to restrain expropriations. Investors instead petitioned the U.S. government to finance political risk insurance schemes to protect them against further takings.[14] He predicted further expansion in the use of the Calvo Doctrine, which held that jurisdiction in international investment disputes lay solely with the host country.[15]

The ending of the Cold War falsified part of Lipson's model. Instead of seeing a hundred Calvo Doctrines bloom, the world saw a rapid convergence to a new set of international legal norms for investors. Lipson's oversight was to view the Soviet Union as the primary example of an expropriating host country, rather than as the actor lurking behind the curtains in any "bilateral" negotiation between the United States and an expropriating country in the postwar period. After the Soviet Union disintegrated, institutions designed to depoliticize investment disputes became more effective, not less. In addition, Lipson missed two other factors. U.S. presidents did make great efforts to avoid invoking laws that mandated American retaliation for expropriation—*but only by dint of imposing the sanctions those laws mandated anyway*. Second, Lipson gave short shrift to the creation of the modern system of investor-state arbitration—which Congress explicitly discussed in terms of "settling investment disputes discreetly so that friendly political relations might continue."[16] The findings here are, however, consistent with two of Lipson's hypotheses: (1) that the U.S. government was not autonomous, and corporate preference mattered; and (2) "What were once international clashes [became] businesslike negotiations over the distribution of future economic gains."

Jeffry Frieden reintroduced economics as the causal variable in the political science literature on intervention. "The most relevant considerations in this regard are the potential costs of imperial intervention in enhancing the return to metropolitan economic interests, and the potential benefits that intervention might bring to these interests."[17] Frieden argued that colonial-style intervention became less attractive because of a shift in investment away from primary products toward government debt and local-oriented manufacturing and services.[18] The findings in *The Empire Trap* run against some of Frieden's empirical assertions—but have the paradoxical effect of strengthening his overall argument. The United States did not become less likely to protect American-owned property after the Second World War, but protection was easier to obtain for natural resource investments than for utilities or sovereign debt.

Most recently, Michael Tomz has argued that retaliation is not important in sovereign debt markets.[19] In work with Mark Wright, he also documented that expropriation and default occurred in alternating (rather than coincident) waves—countries in default did not expropriate, and countries in the midst of expropriation rarely defaulted.[20] The evidence presented here is consistent with Tomz's argument about sovereign debt—Tomz does not address most of the episodes discussed in this book. In addition, the evidence presented here may explain Tomz's finding about alternating waves of default and expropriation. U.S. debt policy during the 1980s was actually *more* hard-line than it was during the 1930s, but Washington in the 1980s helped Latin American economies adjust by providing official credit. As Peru under Alan García discovered, such credit would not be forthcoming if American property rights were disrespected. In other words, the alternating pattern may be endogenous: countries in default were less likely to expropriate because they needed American official credit.

Economics

One of the contributions that historians can make to economics is to convert stylized facts—that is, facts accepted as true for the purpose of argument—into real facts, verified by data and evidence. The evidence mustered in *The Empire Trap* contradicts the accepted stylized facts of expropriation. In the stylized version of the "obsolescing bargain," a sovereign government and an investor strike a deal. Once the investors sink their capital, however, the government has incentives to renege on the initial deal—and it does so. Empirically, however, even using a rigorous standard, it appears that almost all the major nationalizations of American-owned resource investments were fairly compensated. The implication is that foreign investment in extractive industries (at least for Americans) was (and is) far less risky than most economists assumed. This fact may also explain investors' apparent short memories in the wake of expropriation.

In analyzing expropriation, economists also generally assume that foreign retaliation is a decision variable for the government. This ignores the panoply of international institutions, backed by a large body of domestic law in most Western countries (and many non-Western ones) and designed to prevent expropriation without compensation. It is incorrect to assume that states are free from judicial penalties when violating the property rights of foreigners. These mechanisms, however, are very slow—by design—and empirical attempts to analyze expropriation disputes need to take those delays into account.

Finally, the failed record of America's fiscal receiverships casts some doubt on the feasibility of Paul Romer's "charter city" concept as a means to improve governance and promote growth. Romer's concept rests on the assumption (almost certainly correct!) that poor countries are poor because of badly designed institutions that encourage corruption, monopolies, and inefficiency. The idea behind a charter city is that a country creates a greenfield locale in which better foreign rules apply. The country would retain sovereignty, but foreigners or a foreign government would act as "guarantors" in order to ensure "that the charter will be respected and enforced for decades into the future."[21] Honduras recently made provisions for a charter city on the country's Atlantic coast (although its supreme court declared the provisions void and the project is now in limbo). Under the Honduran plan, the charter city will have its own public administration, tax system, legal regime, police, and "the power to sign treaties and international agreements concerning trade and cooperation in matters under their control, subject to the ratification of the national Congress."[22] The rules will be enforced by a "Transparency Commission" of five foreigners: two American economics professors, the former head of the INCAE Business School in Costa Rica, a former International Academy of Business Disciplines vice president, and a former Singaporean general.[23] Jurisdictional conflicts with Honduran law will be settled by an arbitration panel of three judges selected from a pre-assigned list of forty people, half selected by the Honduran Congress and half selected by the Transparency Commission.[24]

The American fiscal receiverships paralleled the charter cities concept, in the sense that the host nations retained sovereignty but American managers took over state functions. The Americans had the ability to hire and fire and rewrite internal regulations and processes. In some cases, they recommended changes to the tax and customs code; in others, changes were a prerequisite to the receivership. Unlike other forms of foreign intervention, the fiscal receiverships had the advantage that their success or failure was easy to measure: either revenue increased (against various counterfactuals), or it did not. They can now serve, therefore, as a partial test of the viability of the charter cities concept.

The American fiscal receiverships failed. For all save one, revenue did not increase. In Panama the American receivers were corrupted; in Peru, they were threatened by their subordinates (despite the vocal support of Peru's president). The one time they succeeded, in the Dominican Republic in 1905, it was because the U.S. presence dissuaded insurgents from attacking the customhouses, not because of lowered corruption or higher efficiency. (In other words, the Dominican receivership succeeded because it was akin to a modern U.N. peacekeeping mission, not a charter city.) The American experience does not, of course, invalidate the concept, but it does imply that it may be more difficult to alter institutions than current proponents of charter cities hope.

History

The Empire Trap's primary contribution is to make concrete what was previously vague. It quantifies the fiscal and market effects of American intervention in Latin America, the extent of the American sanction regime that began in the 1930s, and its success for investors. It also documents that American anti-imperialist politicians were very well aware of the political dynamics of the empire trap in 1898 when they limited American investment in the new possessions.

The Empire Trap offers a nuanced picture of the American stance on overseas property rights. Many accounts rely on an exaggerated caricature of Theodore Roosevelt's pugnacious defense of American interests. Yet, as Michael Tomz has indicated, and this book has confirmed, early interventions were not uncompromisingly focused on debt collection. In fact, the United States *encouraged* Latin American countries to default on their sovereign debt during the early years of the Depression. When bondholders and direct investors were pitted against one another, direct investors won handily.

The evidence gathered on compensation payments contradicts the standard narratives about Latin American economic nationalism. The canonical Mexican oil expropriation of 1938 in particular looks vastly different when measured against the available data. The standard story is that the Mexicans paid much less than the value of the assets. That is false: Mexico paid far more than the *market* value of the assets and did so in order to avoid American economic sanctions. Two other near-canonical stories of economic nationalism—the dozen-plus firms expropriated in Peru by the Revolutionary Military Government in 1968–74 and Venezuela's oil nationalization of 1975—also look quite different in light of the data. Economic nationalism had many effects, but transferring value from American shareholders to Latin American governments was not one of them.

The analysis also suggests a new periodization of American economic imperialism. Rather than shifting with each presidential election, America's informal empire rose and fell in two distinct waves over the twentieth century. The first empire emerged when political pressures compelled the U.S. government to defend its nationals' overseas interests in the 1900s. That informal empire then ended when the Great Depression destroyed the political coalitions that sustained it. The second wave of economically motivated intervention arose during the late 1930s and lasted through the 1980s. It was geographically much larger, was influenced by aggressive anticommunism, and was much less likely to involve direct military intervention; but the second "empire" (like the first) saw investors manipulating the U.S. political system, often with considerable success, either to protect their investments or to ensure that they were compensated for losses. The second empire did not so much end as be superseded by the development of judicialized dispute resolution mechanisms that private investors found as attractive as asking Washington for support.

Finally, this book makes a methodological statement about history and the social sciences. The social sciences are fundamentally about the study of social processes—the ways that human beings interact, and the institutions that structure those interactions over time. Thus, social scientists do not really have a choice regarding the use of history—their interest in change over time gives them little choice but to make historical arguments. The real choice for social scientists is whether the historical arguments they make are supported by systematically gathered and carefully analyzed evidence, or whether they are supported by "stylized facts."

At the same time, coherent history requires a theoretical framework and a set of analytic tools that draws from the social sciences. Historians do not really have a choice regarding the use of quantitative evidence and the analytic tools necessary to analyze that evidence. At some point, the construction of historical narratives requires discussion of trends, frequencies, and distributions. The real choice they confront is whether the inferences they draw are the product of systematic methods or vague impressions. Similarly, historians do not really have a choice regarding the use of theory. Writing a coherent narrative requires them to adopt a scheme by which to order facts and events, and explain the causal relationships among them. Whether they realize it or not, the scheme they employ to do this constitutes a theory. The real choice historians face is whether the theory they employ is implicit or explicit, vague or clearly specified, confused or logically consistent. In sum, the study of social processes requires the integration of tools and methods taken from what have come to be thought of as distinct disciplines. There is much to be gained by the integration of these disciplines into a single, coherent approach to historical social science.

two

Avoiding the Trap

The very theory of the bill is to leave the people of the Philippines to pass their own laws for the regulation of their own land ownership. It contains no regulation as to franchises, either; we leave that question to the people of the islands. It contains no regulation as to banks; we leave them self-government there. It contains no regulation as to coinage; if they are capable of any sort of self-government at all, they must pass their own coinage laws. Nor do we give away, or prepare to give away, their franchises. It would be contrary to the Democratic theory if we made the slightest preparation for that, because every vested interest which we plant in the Philippine Islands is one more strong voice enlisted in favor of their permanent retention—a vested interest pleading not to be left.

—*Representative John Williams (D-Mississippi)*

In 1898, the United States expanded into Hawaii, Puerto Rico, and the Philippines. Afterward, however, formal expansion essentially ceased save a few small exceptions. Moreover, none of those exceptions were driven by the demands of U.S. investors.[1]

Why was America's burst of formal overseas expansion so short-lived? After all, in theory one of the best ways to protect your country's investments in a foreign area is to make that area no longer foreign. Britain, France, Italy, Japan, Germany, and the Soviet Union continued to annex foreign territories until the end of the Second World War. There was no sea change in international norms concerning annexation around the time the United States essentially gave up the practice.

From the point of view of American investors circa 1898, the extension of the U.S. Constitution provided the best protection for their property rights. Home governments could of course cajole foreign governments, issue warnings, apply sanctions (usually in the form of what was called a "pacific blockade"), or use force.[2] Full annexation went far beyond these tools and extended the American legal system, federal judiciary, and executive agencies. In terms of the various "technologies" at the disposal of firms and governments, the extension of the U.S. Constitution was quite possibly the most powerful imaginable.

When the Kingdom of Hawaii threatened the rights of resident U.S. investors, those investors enlisted help from the U.S. government, used that help to overthrow the kingdom in 1893, and then immediately petitioned for annexation. The rub was that Hawaii was mostly populated by *Hawaiians*, and not white American settlers. The coup therefore ignited a firestorm of controversy in the United States. The outgoing Harrison administration aided and approved it, but the incoming Cleveland administration refused to recognize the new government. In fact, Cleveland condemned the settlers. They had to wait until 1897, when another sympathetic Republican administration (William McKinley's) took office. The settlers were then able to leverage their personal and family links with the GOP to push through annexation.

The confluence of circumstances leading to Hawaii's annexation as a fully incorporated territory of the United States was close-run and not to be repeated. First, the investors there considered themselves to be permanent settlers. Second, they possessed close business and family links with prominent Republican politicians, particularly from New England. Third, the native Hawaiian population was in decline, and the Japanese and Chinese workers in the archipelago were overwhelmingly male and considered to be temporary.[3] The Asian population, therefore, was considered to pose little "threat" to the racial balance on the mainland. Fourth, the fastest-growing segment of the Hawaiian population in 1898 was made up of Portuguese immigrants and their children, whom Congress considered white enough to be acceptable. Fifth, the islands' strategic location meant that the United States could neither countenance their possession by any other power nor give up its rights to use Pearl Harbor as a naval base. Nowhere else met this combination. Even when the United States made later strategic acquisitions (for example, the Virgin Islands in 1917, or the Pacific territories taken from Japan in 1945), they would not be made incorporated territories of the United States. Racial attitudes meant that the Constitution was not going to be extended to areas populated by nonwhite people.

There existed a second option to protect American property: imperial rule. The United States could extend its legal system and executive authority *without* granting citizenship to the local population. In theory, imperial rule would simultaneously protect American investors abroad and assuage racist concerns at home. The Spanish-American War provided an opportunity to test this option. The United States did not go to war for the Philippines, but once the islands fell into American hands the McKinley administration felt that it needed to retain them for strategic purposes. President McKinley therefore decided to do something new: he annexed the islands *without* incorporating them into the United States. The Constitution would no longer follow the flag.

The problem was that the Democratic opposition (and one Republican, Senator George Hoar of Massachusetts) did not approve of imperial expansion. The reasons for opposition fell into three general categories. The first was principled ideological objection to the imposition of alien rule over a foreign people. The second was a fear that once U.S. companies invested in Philippine industries (mostly in agricultural products, but there was also, perhaps surprisingly, a fear of manufacturing) it would be impossible to keep the Philippine Islands outside the U.S. tariff wall. The third was that many Democrats feared that it would prove impossible in the long run to keep Filipinos (and Chinese residents in the Philippines) from emigrating to the continental United States.

The Democrats understood the dynamics of the empire trap, and they moved to circumvent it. They failed to stop annexation, because voting against annexation would have meant rejecting the Treaty of Paris that ended the Spanish-American War. The Democrats did, however, succeed in using their blocking power in Congress to pass amendments to other bills that restricted the ability of Americans to invest in the islands. The limitations were not airtight, but the result was a remarkably low level of American investment in the Philippine archipelago. The Democrats also demonstrated, however, that formal imperial rule by the United States *without the benefit of the Constitution* was a bad deal for American investors, because a minority of senators could impose policies that hurt American business interests. From the point of view of U.S. investors, the restrictions proved that formal imperial rule (at least from Washington) was not in their best interests.[4]

The end result was that investor sentiment in favor of formal expansion evaporated. Congress could and would limit investors' ability to invest in areas that were under the formal control of the United States but without the protection of the Constitution. American racial politics, however, ensured that the Constitution would not be extended to any place where the descendants of Europeans did not make up a majority. As a result, U.S. overseas intervention on behalf of American investors after 1898 would not follow the example of the British Empire. Rather, it would take on a new form.

The Hawaiian Coup d'État and Union with the United States

> The ownership of Hawaii was tendered to us by a provisional government set up to succeed the constitutional ruler of the islands, who had been dethroned, and it did not appear that such provisional government had the sanction of either popular revolution or suffrage.
>
> *—President Grover Cleveland*

> In a country where there is no power of the law to protect the citizens of the United States there can be no law of nations nor any rule of comity that can rightfully prevent our flag from giving shelter to them under the protection of our arms, and this without reference to any distress it may give to the Queen who generated the confusion, or any advantage it might give to the people who are disputing her right to resume or to hold her regal powers.
>
> *—Senator John Morgan (D-Alabama)*

At first glance, the expansion of the United States into Hawaii seemed to follow the stylized pattern set by the long expansion across North America. Settlers would arrive in an area, displace the local population, and ultimately formalize their political connection to the rest of the United States. The area would then assume territorial status as established by the Northwest Ordinance of 1784.[5] There was, however, one key difference between Hawaii and previous areas of expansion: the American settler population in Hawaii was a small minority *and* showed very little sign of becoming a majority in the near future.[6]

In the 1840s, U.S. policy toward Hawaii centered on the desire to keep the islands out of British or French hands.[7] Subsequent U.S.-Hawaii relations centered on sugar. Hawaii wanted access to the American market; domestic interests wanted to keep it out. In 1855 and again in 1867, the Senate rejected treaties that would have allowed Hawaiian sugar to enter duty free. The treaty of 1855 was rejected because of opposition by Louisiana sugar planters. In 1867, Louisiana was not a factor—the state was under federal occupation after the Civil War—but the Senate nonetheless rejected the treaty over worries about lost tariff revenue. In 1875, the Senate finally approved a reciprocity treaty by a vote of 51 to 12, in return for a clause preventing Hawaii from disposing of any "port, harbor, or other territory" to any foreign country. Domestic sugar interests accepted the agreement because the United States imported 90% of its sugar at the time, with only 2% coming from Hawaii. Legislators therefore expected that the increases in Hawaiian imports would come at the expense of foreign competitors, not domestic production.[8]

The 1875 treaty triggered a wave of American investment. The value of American sugar holdings in Hawaii rose from $25 million in 1870 (in 2011 dollars) to $80 million in 1880 and $259 million in 1890.[9] Since the Hawaiian disease environment was benign compared with that of other tropical areas, some of the owners of these investments chose to follow their money. The U.S.-born community reached 1,928 by 1890.[10]

These emigrants, however, did not make up a sizable proportion of the Hawaiian population. The Americans living in the islands made up only 2.6% of the total 1890 population of 89,990.[11] By 1896, the number of American emigrants had risen to 2,266, but as a proportion had fallen to 2.1% of Hawaii's total population. The 1896 census recorded 820 Hawaiian-born children with an American father, but including them raised the American proportion of Hawaii's population to only 2.8%.[12] Nor did the emigrants seem likely to make up a majority in the near future. The ethnic Hawaiian population was in decline, falling from around 70,036 in 1853 to 39,504 in 1896, but it was replaced by laborers from Japan, China, and Portugal often recruited by the boatload to work on the Americans' sugar and pineapple plantations—in 1896, these immigrants (and their Hawaiian-born children) made up respectively 22%, 20%, and 14% of the population.[13] (After a spirited debate over whether the Portuguese should be considered white, annexationists took some solace in the fact that the Portuguese population was sex-balanced, unlike the Chinese and Japanese, and therefore enjoyed a much higher birthrate.)[14]

In 1893 the American settlers launched a coup. The proximate cause was Queen Liliuokalani's decision to implement a new constitution that would weaken legislative limits on her power. (The previous, investor-friendly constitution had been forced on the monarchy in 1887 by an armed militia consisting primarily of American settlers.)[15] The settlers feared that allowing the queen to promulgate a new constitution would set a precedent that would effectively remove *all* constraints on the government. A thirteen-member American-dominated "Committee of Safety," headed by the Hawaiian-born Sanford Dole—an older cousin to future pineapple magnate James Dole—then asked the resident U.S. minister in Honolulu for support. On January 16, 1893, the minister ordered U.S. Marines on board the USS *Boston* to land in order to "protect American lives and property." The Committee of Safety occupied government offices the next day, and Queen Liliuokalani yielded power. Dole became president of the Provisional Government, which requested annexation to the United States.

Unfortunately for the Provisional Government, the coup took place *after* President Benjamin Harrison's defeat in the November 1892 elections. The lame-duck president, a Republican, submitted an annexation treaty to the Senate, but opponents held up ratification. It was still bottled up in March 1893 when Grover Cleveland, a Democrat, took the oath of office. President Cleveland met personally with Queen Liliuokalani and ordered that the Stars and Stripes be taken down. Cleveland then threw his support behind a congressional investigation into the coup. The investigation concluded that the coup would have failed without U.S. intervention. President Cleveland thundered, "The provisional government owes its existence to an armed invasion by the United States. By an act of war, committed with the participation of a diplomatic representative of the United States and without authority of Congress . . . a substantial wrong has been done."[16] In his State of the Union address, Cleveland added, "It seemed to me the only honorable course for our government to pursue was to undo the wrong that had been done by those representing us and to restore as far as practicable the status existing at the time of our forcible intervention."[17] The Provisional Government remained in power, but as an unrecognized, illegal regime in the eyes of the United States.

Congress had other ideas. Within Cleveland's own party, Senator John Morgan (D-Alabama) commissioned a separate report that exonerated the United States and the coup plotters. (It would not be the last time the legislative branch would seek to undermine the executive branch's anti-interventionist intentions.) After massive House gains in the 1894 midterm elections, the Republican Party decided to include an annexationist plank in its 1896 platform. The Republican presidential candidate, William McKinley, won the 1896 election against William Jennings Bryan. Negotiations between the United States and the Republic of Hawaii resumed after McKinley's inauguration in March 1897.

The annexation of Hawaii encountered opposition from mainland sugar interests, even though Hawaii was a small producer and *already* enjoyed access to the American market. Choosing his battles wisely, President McKinley waited until the end of the Spanish-American War before submitting an annexation bill to Congress. Rather than take the chance on a treaty, which required a two-thirds vote in the Senate, McKinley convinced Representative Francis Newlands (R-Nevada) to introduce a joint resolution for annexation on May 4, 1898. House Speaker Thomas Reed (R-Maine), however, had contested McKinley for the Republican nomination in 1896 and opposed both the war with Spain and the annexation of Hawaii. Reed tried to keep the bill from coming to a vote, but supporters managed to get it through the Foreign Affairs Committee. Reed decided not to split the Republican caucus, so he allowed the bill to come to the floor, and the House voted in favor by a lopsided count of 209 to 91 on June 15, 1898. Unsurprisingly, the Louisiana and Colorado delegations both voted against the resolution—Louisiana was the largest grower of sugarcane within the United States, and Colorado was one of the few states at the time with significant beet sugar production. The Republican delegations from states with nascent beet sugar industries—Minnesota, Wisconsin, and Utah—split their votes.

The Newlands resolution then went to the Senate. Sanford Dole, the Hawaiian president, was not above directly lobbying key senators, including George Frisbie Hoar (R-Massachusetts), with whom Dole met privately in the White House. (Much of the Dole family, not coincidently, had emigrated to Hawaii directly from Massachusetts.)[18] Hoar was one of the strongest opponents of the Spanish-American War and imperial expansion, and he contemplated opposing the resolution. His meeting with Dole, however, plus pressure from President McKinley and fears that Japan might annex the islands ultimately persuaded him to support the resolution.[19] On July 6, 1898, the resolution passed the Senate 42 to 21, with 26 abstentions. President McKinley signed it into law the following day. Hawaii became a fully incorporated territory: the Constitution applied, and its residents became American citizens.[20]

The Hawaiian case exhibits the domestic politics of the empire trap in full force. A vocal population of resident Americans with strong political connections and a great deal of wealth led to American acceptance of an unconstitutional coup d'état in the Kingdom of Hawaii. The underlying political logic was the logic of collective action: the small minority of Americans who lived on the islands or owned investments in them benefited massively from American involvement, while the costs were spread over the entire American sugar industry. In terms of the result, the annexation of Hawaii was a one-off. In terms of the underlying political dynamics, however, Hawaii was a bellwether.

The Restriction of U.S. Investment
in the Philippines

> If old Dewey had just sailed away when he smashed
> the Spanish fleet, what a lot of trouble he would have
> saved us.
>
> *—President William McKinley*

The United States did in fact extend its Pacific boundaries past
Hawaii, but the reason was *not* to protect the interests of American
investors. Rather, the American annexation of the Philippines
was an unintended outcome of the Spanish-American
War. Once in possession of the archipelago, President William
McKinley decided to retain it for strategic reasons, namely, its
proximity to China.

The Democratic opposition to the annexation of the Philippines,
however, understood the logic of the empire trap. Both
Democrats and Republicans expected annexation to produce
a large flow of American capital to the islands. The Democrats
feared that a large enough flow would create a domestic group
with an interest in the archipelago's permanent retention. With
annexation a fait accompli—few Democrats wanted to pay the
political costs of delaying the ratification of the Treaty of Paris
that ended the war—the Democrats' legislative goal became
the creation of strict barriers against *American* private investment
in the new territory. In addition, the anti-imperialists
mobilized protectionist sentiment—something contrary to the
Democrats' ordinary stance in favor of lower tariffs—to keep
the Philippines outside the U.S. tariff wall. The territory did
not fully enter the American customs area until 1912, and U.S.
investment would remain restricted until de jure independence
in 1946. (Democratic opposition to permanent retention of
the Philippines, it should be noted, had its roots in racial anxieties
over the addition of 7 million "Malays" to the United
States.)

President McKinley's address to Congress on April 11, 1898, mentioned only Cuba.[21] The resulting authorization to use force, passed April 20, did not mention the Philippines:

> Resolved: First, that the people of the Island of Cuba are, and of right ought to be, free and independent. Second, that it is the duty of the United States to demand, and the government of the United States does hereby demand, that the government of Spain at once relinquish its authority and government in the island of Cuba and withdraw its land and naval forces from Cuba and Cuban waters. Third, that the President of the United States be, and he hereby is, directed and empowered to use the entire land and naval forces of the United States, and to call into the actual service of the United States the militia of the several States, to such extent as may be necessary to carry these resolutions into effect.[22]

After hostilities began on April 25, the Asiatic Squadron—then stationed in Hong Kong—received the following terse order from Secretary of the Navy John Long: "Proceed at once to the Philippine Islands. Commence operations at once, particularly against the Spanish fleet. You must capture vessels or destroy. Use utmost endeavors."[23] Commanded by Commodore George Dewey, the squadron sailed into Manila Bay on May 1, 1898, and destroyed the Spanish fleet. The only American death was due to a heart attack suffered during the battle.[24]

When Dewey arrived in Manila, the Philippines were at the tail end of a two-year-old rebellion led by Emilio Aguinaldo against Spanish rule. In December 1897, the Spanish government concluded an armistice with the rebel leadership, sending Aguinaldo into exile in Hong Kong. Guerrilla warfare, however, continued throughout parts of Luzon. Lacking instructions to the contrary, Dewey proceeded to supply arms to the Philippine guerrillas operating in nearby Cavite. He also sent a cruiser to fetch Aguinaldo from Hong Kong. Once word of Dewey's de facto alliance with the rebels reached Washington, however, it countermanded Dewey's decision, instructing him to avoid "political alliances with the insurgents."[25]

McKinley's problem was that his administration had no preexisting policy for the Philippines. Once Dewey sank the Spanish fleet, the navy argued that the United States—dependent on British goodwill to base the Asiatic Squadron at Hong Kong—needed naval facilities near China in order to defend American interests. The retention of a Guantánamo-style base in the Philippines, therefore, emerged as an American goal. The navy feared, however, that a base in Manila or Subic Bay would be indefensible without control of Luzon, the chief island of the archipelago. The reason was that naval planners doubted Aguinaldo's ability to establish a stable government. Civil disorder on Luzon would open the way for foreign infiltration and make the U.S. naval facilities vulnerable to land-based attacks. By the time the war ended on August 12, 1898, therefore, President McKinley had shifted his position to favoring the annexation of Luzon.[26]

McKinley's political advisers, however, reported that such a partial annexation would too closely resemble European-style imperialism and would be impossible to sell to the American public.[27] The Treaty of Paris, signed on December 10, 1898, therefore, transferred all the Philippines Islands, along with Guam and Puerto Rico, to the United States. (Spain gave up sovereignty over Cuba, but it did not transfer the island to the United States.) By then, the McKinley administration had decided that it would retain Guam and Puerto Rico permanently and occupy Cuba until a stable government could be established, but it *still* had no Philippine policy. Democrats were vocal in their opposition to annexing the Philippines; Democratic senators voted to ratify the treaty only because (like most treaties) it was presented to the Senate as a fait accompli for an up-or-down vote.

After ten days of dithering, McKinley declared that American policy in the Philippines was one of "benevolent assimilation, substituting the mild sway of justice and right for arbitrary rule."[28] Unsurprisingly, Aguinaldo and the other independence leaders opposed the decision. In January 1899, they established a government at the town of Malolos, on the rail line northeast of Manila, and launched an armed insurgency. Fighting began on February 4, 1899. U.S. force levels rapidly grew from 12,000 to a peak of 68,816 in October 1900.[29] By most metrics, the war (fought by a small all-volunteer army) was as intense as the Iraq War—proportional to the U.S. population, the peak force represented a per capita commitment twice as large as the peak Iraq deployments in 2008.[30] The combat casualty rate, meanwhile (excluding deaths from disease) ran at 596 per 100,000 troops in 1900 (a bit less than two per day), almost exactly matching the 2004–7 rate of 608 in Iraq.[31]

The Philippine War became one of the signature issues of the 1900 presidential election, with the Democrats declaring their opposition and the Republicans their support. The insurgents paid close attention to American politics and designed their strategy around the election.[32] When the anti-imperialist Democratic candidate, William Jennings Bryan, lost to McKinley, insurgent morale collapsed, and surrenders multiplied. After his capture, Aguinaldo accepted an amnesty in March 1901 and subsequently called on his followers to lay down their arms. Some Malolos loyalists continued fighting until April 1902, when General Miguel Malvar surrendered his forces. On July 2, 1902, the secretary of war pronounced the Philippine insurrection over, although violence continued in outlying areas, particularly Mindanao. Aguinaldo and other former rebel leaders received large tracts of land and, later, political offices.

In the meantime, the McKinley administration needed Congress to grant the authority to establish civil government in the Philippines. Without civil government, the United States would be legally unable to sell public land, issue mining concessions, or otherwise alter Spanish law. On January 11, 1900, Senator John Spooner (R-Wisconsin) introduced a bill to give the president such authority. Democratic opposition, however, kept the bill from coming to a vote. The Democratic minority would accept a civil government bill only if it restricted American capital from entering the Philippine Islands. That was unacceptable to the McKinley administration, of course: the reason it wanted civil government was precisely to allow capital to flow. On January 24, 1900, Secretary of War Elihu Root made this clear in a cable to President McKinley:

> Passage of Spooner bill at present session greatly needed to secure best result from improving conditions. Until its passage no purely central civil government can be established, no public franchises of any kind granted, and no substantial investment of private capital in internal improvements possible. . . . Sale of public lands and allowance of mining claims impossible until Spooner bill. Hundreds of American miners on ground awaiting law to perfect claims. More coming. Good element in pacification. . . . The Army has brought the Philippines to the point where they offer a ready and attractive field for investment and enterprise, but to make this possible there must be mining laws, homestead and lands laws, general transportation laws, and banking and currency laws.[33]

Democratic stalling tactics—and the continuation of combat operations in the Philippines—killed the Spooner bill. It was not until January 1902 that Senator Henry Cabot Lodge (R-Massachusetts), the chairman of the Senate Committee on the Philippines, managed to introduce a new bill to provide for a civil government.

Republicans had 55 seats in the 90-seat Senate, but their actual majority for the purposes of the Lodge bill was only one vote. Once again, sugar was a key issue. Four states—California, Colorado, Michigan, and Utah—accounted for 87% of U.S. beet sugar production in 1902.[34] California and Michigan had fully Republican Senate delegations, and all four senators from those states supported legislation to prevent the establishment American-owned sugar plantations in the Philippines.[35] Utah's lone Republican senator, Thomas Kearns, chose not to take a public position on the issue. Colorado's delegation, meanwhile, consisted of Democrats.[36] The Democrats managed to convince two additional Republicans from states with nascent beet sugar industries to support restrictions on U.S. investment in the islands—Henry Hansbrough (R-North Dakota) and Charles Dietrich (R-Nebraska)—as well as, somewhat mysteriously, William Stewart (R-Nevada).[37] Finally, despite his party affiliation, George Hoar (R-Massachusetts) had been an outspoken critic of the Philippine War from the start, and he was unlikely to support *any* Philippine bill that did not establish a rapid timetable for independence. That left the GOP with only 46 votes for the Lodge bill.

Under normal circumstances, the Republican leadership might have been willing to take the time to apply pressure (or offer concessions) to its wayward members or try to push the bill through with a two-vote margin despite the risk of a filibuster. Unfortunately for the Republican leadership, circumstances in 1902 were not normal. Beginning in January 1902, in the wake of the end of major combat operations, Democratic senators (joined by the antiwar Republican, George Hoar) conducted hearings into accusations of widespread human rights violations by the U.S. Army in the Philippines.[38] The most contentious issue was the "water cure," in which American soldiers poured water down the throats of captured Filipino insurgents in order to get them to reveal information. The water cure induced in the victim a sensation of drowning, much like the waterboarding of a later era.[39] The investigations were deliberately timed to interfere with the passage of the Lodge bill. Senator Thomas Patterson (D-Colorado) went so far as to introduce motions to subpoena U.S. military officers then serving in the Philippines when consideration of the civil government bill came up.[40] Republicans hit back, accusing the Democrats of "slandering" the army. In response, Senator George Turner

(F-Washington; Turner had been elected on a fusion ticket[41]) held a filibuster in which he called U.S. General Jacob Smith "a monster in human form."[42]

Senator Edmund Pettus (D-Alabama), a former Confederate general, unfavorably compared the Lodge bill to Reconstruction:

> Most of the Senators never lived under a carpetbag government; but those of you who have been governed by carpetbaggers cannot fail to see what will be the effect of this bill [the Republican version of the Organic Act, without investment restrictions] when enacted. If this bill be enacted, and you could and did give to the real carpetbagger his choice to go to heaven or the Philippine Islands, he would not hesitate. "I will go to the Philippines."[43]

Pettus was oblique, but other Democrats made clear that they did not want to allow American capital into the islands for fear that it would lead to the creation of a domestic group with a vested interest in their permanent retention. Senator Fred Dubois (D-Idaho) laid out the logic:

> I have tried, in what I have said, to be temperate in language. I have endeavored to argue the question presented by this majority bill fairly, with good temper, and honestly. I do not think it will be easy to get out of the Philippine Islands, should future events demonstrate the wisdom and necessity of doing so, after American capital has gone there and is being employed under the tempting opportunities presented by this bill.
>
> Do they not know, if this bill passes, the difficulties in our path will be multiplied many times, provided in the future it is deemed patriotic and wise to allow the Filipinos their own independent government? The granting of these extra privileges and unusual inducements which are offered to corporations and syndicates, it seems to me,

contemplates a fixed purpose on the part of the advocates of this bill to retain the islands for all time to come as a colony, as a dependency of the United States.[44]

Senator Benjamin Tillman (D-South Carolina), best known for assaulting a fellow solon on the floor of the Senate, concurred. "It is unjust for us to defer the time when these people shall have any voice in their local affairs to 1904 and in the meantime grant Taft and his crowd the right to occupy the whole field and grant franchises which will become vested interests."[45]

The Republicans introduced a version of the Lodge bill into the House, where it attracted Democratic opposition also based on the fear that American investment in the Philippine Islands would trap the United States into holding the archipelago forever. Representative Allan McDermott (D-New Jersey), using a disrespectful diminutive for the GOP that was common around the turn of the last century, stated, "This bill settles the policy of the Republic Party [sic]. It is to be continuing possession and occupancy with unlimited additions to our bonded debt. This bill means that we are to permanently hold the Philippine Islands, and I predict the holding will prove a plague to ourselves and our children."[46] McDermott's colleague John Robinson (D-Nebraska) laid out the mechanism by which the bill would lead to permanent retention:

> The bill which is now before the House provides for the organization of corporations to carry on all branches of business. It provides for the issuance of bonds by the Philippine government and certain of the cities of those islands. It invites the investment of capital, and in the future capital so invested in the Philippines, held by our own and citizens of other countries, will urge their claims to our protection with a stronger voice, and clamor more loudly than ever, that in honor we must not leave their interests unprotected in these islands: but that we must continue to hold down these people by force of arms. We must continue to spend millions

of dollars annually to maintain an army there. We must continue to send the flower of our youth to these tropical islands, in order that foreign investors, seeking only worldly gain may continue to exploit this unfortunate people.

An argument such as this, Mr. Chairman, would mean that the time will never come when we can withdraw our forces from these islands. It would mean that the reasons which prevent us now from granting these people their independence would become stronger with each passing year, and that at no time could we hope to withdraw our jurisdiction and leave these people in liberty and peace.[47]

David de Armond (D-Missouri) railed against the way the Spooner bill would give American business interests the resources to purchase undue political influence:

Civil government for the Filipinos! Civil government in which the Filipinos do not participate; civil government in which the Filipinos have no part; civil government which the Filipinos do not desire; civil government, not for the benefit of the American citizen, but for the American promoter, the American syndicate organizer, the American capitalist, the American boss, the American contributor to campaign funds, used to corrupt the needy voter, to overcome the judgment of the honest element of American citizens, and win victories by false pretenses and more positive wrong. [Applause on the Democratic side.][48]

Democrats did not only fear that a "Philippine lobby" would make Philippine independence impossible; they also feared that such an interest group would press for free trade and changes in the U.S. immigration laws. In the Senate, Benjamin Tillman (D-South Carolina) argued that allowing investment would make it impossible to keep the Philippines outside the American tariff wall:

After the vested interests of Americans have become sufficiently great and potent in this body and the other end of the Capitol, then these people will be given the same free trade of which Porto Rico now boasts. This pretense of protecting! What is the tariff for? The pretense now is that you want to raise revenue for the Philippine government. But after that government shall, as I said, have made it possible for American capital to go there and become invested, the cry will go up: "You are taxing our people. These are Americans against whom you are discriminating. We must have free trade between the Philippines and the United States."[49]

Senator Joseph Rawlins (D-Utah) was in turn concerned about the beet sugar industry. "We have started an industry in the United States called the beet sugar industry, which is doing very well. . . . We can compete with any part of the world in sugar production, Cuba not excepted. We cannot do it now, but in ten or fifteen years, I think, we shall be able to do it. . . . No corporation should be allowed to buy an acre of land [in the Philippines] unless it be for a building or for the immediate necessities of some business that it is carrying on."[50]

Senator Dubois (D-Idaho) went further, worrying that the Philippines would develop a manufacturing sector based on low-wage Chinese and Japanese labor:

The capitalists who will be invited to go to the Philippines will establish great factories. They will establish, for instance, a cotton factory. They will employ a great many Chinese hands, because there are 400,000,000 Chinamen at their doors, for laborers. They will make goods as well as any other people can, under our guidance and superintendency, and put those goods in competition with us here. It will be so in regard to wool. They will get it from Australia and the Mongolian plains. It will be so in regard to iron. Gentlemen may say that by this bill you have demonstrated that you can put a tax on their goods and keep them out of this country. When they are at work there, if you keep the goods out of this country by law, you can not exclude them by law from other countries, and their goods will be in competition with ours either here in the United States or else in the other markets of the world, and especially in China. I say you can not exploit those islands without Chinese and Japanese labor, and, further, that the next step will be to allow them to come in here.[51]

Dubois later reiterated his fear that an American-owned Philippine agricultural and manufacturing sector would lobby to allow Chinese immigration: "There is not a Senator on this floor who does not know that when our capitalists go to the Philippines and start up these great industries, of the factories and of the field, their demands for labor will be so incessant that they will be heard. There was a strong sentiment, and there is a growing sentiment among the leaders of the Republican party against rigid laws for Chinese exclusion, even in the United States."[52] In the House, James "Champ" Clark (D-Missouri) also worried about low-wage Filipino labor. "Our retention of the Philippines means a reduction of wages to the Asiatic level. That is one of the main reasons why I was opposed to acquiring them and why I am dead against keeping them. Let no man hug to his breast the delusion that Asiatics can work only as unskilled laborers, for the evidence in the case flatly contradicts that theory . . . they will not only compete with unskilled laborers but also with those of all degrees of skill, even unto the highest."[53] The Democrats introduced an alternate civil government bill in the House that would ban *all* American investment in the archipelago. (Representative Williams's comments about the Democratic bill are in the opening epigraph to this chapter.)

The continual drip of adverse publicity from the war crimes hearings made the administration—now in the hands of Theodore Roosevelt, following McKinley's assassination on September 6, 1901—increasingly eager to pass *any* civil government bill. In June of 1902, Senator Lodge agreed to place a ceiling of 2,530 acres on the size of nonresident Americans' (and all corporations') owned or leased lands in the Philippines.[54] The revised bill also limited the size of mineral claims to 300 × 300 meters and prohibited any one nonresident person or corporation from holding more than one claim on the same lode. This provision effectively banned large-scale American mining.[55] Lodge later claimed that he switched positions because he believed that limiting American "speculation" in the Philippines would "in the long run" be "more just to the people of the islands and more for their ultimate peace, prosperity, and good government."[56] William Howard Taft, the head of the American civil administration in the Philippines, thought Lodge switched positions to save face: "He does not hesitate to surrender something of real interest to the Islands in order to avoid adverse criticism provided he can carry his bill."[57]

The final version of the Philippine Organic Act of 1902 banned Americans and American companies from owning more than 1,024 hectares (2,500 acres) of land. It limited mining claims to one claim of 1,000 × 1,000 feet per lode. It prevented the adoption of the U.S. dollar in the Philippines, and subsequent legislation created a gold-backed Philippine peso linked to the dollar at a two-to-one ratio. The U.S. national banking system was not extended to the archipelago.[58]

The Republicans immediately began to chip away at the Democratic victory. A 1905 act allowed the insular government to issue railroad concessions. Later acts allowed American companies to invest in public utilities, and there were no limitations on U.S. investment in retail and wholesale distribution (see table 2.1). Nor did the Democrats manage to keep the Philippines outside the American customs area. In 1908, president-elect William Howard Taft—who had served as the first governor-general of the Philippine Islands, where he developed a strong personal interest in their welfare—struck an agreement with

Table 2.1

U.S. direct investment in the Philippine Islands, millions of 2010 dollars

	1897	1908	1914	1919	1924	1929	1935
Utilities		$284.8	$269.5	$166.3	$199.6	$292.9	$406.1
Sugar			$50.5	$59.0	$105.6	$162.2	$216.2
Petroleum distribution						$108.6	$143.8
Sales and distribution						$94.6	$98.4
Railroads			$176.9	$101.4	$70.8	$59.6	$64.2
Other agriculture			$16.8	$19.7	$31.7	$41.8	$59.0
Manufacturing						$40.8	$120.8
Rubber						$5.2	
Mining							
TOTAL	$0.0	$284.8	$513.7	$346.4	$407.7	$805.8	$1,108.4

Source: Cleona Lewis, *America's Stake in International Investments* (Washington, D.C.: Brookings Institution, 1938), pp. 590–91 and 602–3; and U.S. Department of Commerce, *American Direct Investments in Foreign Countries* (Washington, D.C.: GPO, 1930), p. 26.
Note: American investment in railroads fell after 1914 because most of the lines proved unprofitable and were purchased by the Philippine insular government. Nominal values deflated using the U.S. GDP deflator.

Charles Warren, the head of the Michigan Beet Sugar Association. Warren agreed to support legislation allowing the free entry of 300,000 tons of Philippine sugar in exchange for a promise that Taft would maintain the tariff on foreign sugar. The legislation passed a year later in July 1909. Three years later, President Taft met with Senator Nelson Aldrich (R-Rhode Island) to hash out a tariff bill. At the beginning of the negotiations, Taft and Aldrich disagreed over five hundred separate items. We do not know what concessions Taft offered, but he succeeded in getting Aldrich to agree to a generous quota on Philippine tobacco as well as sugar.[59] Later negotiations resulted in the complete removal of the quotas on Philippine exports. Ironically, the Revenue Act of 1913 was a *Democratic* measure that generally lowered tariff rates and implemented a federal income tax under the authority granted by the recently ratified Sixteenth Amendment. Bringing the Philippines fully inside the American tariff wall was a small concession to make to achieve those two long-standing Democratic goals—especially given that the 1909 quotas had proved too high to be binding.

Did the restrictions on American investment in the Philippines have their desired effect? The answer appears to be yes (see table 2.1). American investment in Philippine agriculture was risible until the Revenue Act of 1913 brought the islands inside the U.S. customs area. Even then, investment remained small. By 1929, U.S. investment in Philippine agriculture was worth only $20 million in nominal terms. This was not a great deal in a sector whose *production* was worth $70.4 million in that same year.[60] The apparent growth in the value of U.S. sugar investment between 1929 and 1935 is an artifact of a 20% decline in the U.S. price level: nominal investment rose only 6%. Investment in other agricultural industries also remained small relative to the growing output of Philippine tobacco, copra, and other tropical products.

The American presence in agriculture was greater in sugar production than in other agriculture, because Americans were allowed to invest in the downstream processing of agricultural products. In 1935, the Philippine Department of Agriculture and Commerce published data on investment in agricultural export industries. (The Philippine figures are not compatible with the U.S. Commerce Department estimates used in table 2.1, because they also recorded investments owned by U.S. citizens resident in the Philippine Islands.)[61] Of the $265.4 million invested in the sugar sector, $181.3 million was in land and land improvements, and $84.1 million in mills and refineries. American investors owned only 3.0% of the investment in land; Filipinos owned 94.0%. Americans did, however, own 26.7% of the investments in sugar *mills* (see table 2.2).

The figures from other Philippine export industries tell a similar story: American investors (except in tobacco) gained a position by investing in processing plants, but their inability to invest in large-scale land ownership prevented them from dominating most industries. Filipinos controlled 79% of the total investment in sugar, 88% of the investment in coconuts (used to make

Table 2.2
Investment in Philippine export industries by nationality, 1935

Industry	Investors	Millions of 2010 dollars Land and improvements	Mills, refineries, etc.	TOTAL	Percent of value owned Land	Mills	TOTAL
Sugar							
	Filipinos	$2,232.9	$522.0	$2,754.9	94%	47%	79%
	Americans	$71.4	$294.1	$364.8	3%	27%	10%
	Spanish	$47.8	$262.0	$309.8	2%	24%	9%
	Others	$23.6	$23.6	$47.2	1%	2%	1%
	TOTAL	$2,375.0	$1,101.1	$3,476.1			
	Filipinos	$2,549.9	$11.8	$2,561.7	93%	8%	88%
	Americans	$110.0	$72.7	$182.1	4%	47%	6%
	Spanish	$55.0	$7.2	$61.6	2%	5%	2%
	British	$0.0	$45.9	$45.9	0%	29%	2%
	Others	$27.5	$19.0	$45.9	1%	12%	2%
	TOTAL	$2,741.8	$155.9	$2,897.7			
Manila hemp							
	Filipinos	$2,308.9	$13.1	$2,322.0	94%	13%	91%
	Americans	$72.1	$51.7	$123.8	3%	51%	5%
	Japanese	$47.8	$9.8	$57.6	2%	10%	2%
	British	$0.0	$18.3	$18.3	0%	18%	1%
	Others	$24.2	$9.2	$33.4	1%	9%	1%
	TOTAL	$2,453.0	$102.2	$2,555.2			
Tobacco							
	Filipinos	$266.6	$1.3	$267.9	97%	1%	68%
	Spanish	$5.2	$79.3	$84.5	2%	65%	21%
	Others	$2.6	$40.6	$43.2	1%	34%	11%
	TOTAL	$275.1	$121.2	$396.3			

Source: Philippine Commonwealth, Department of Agriculture and Commerce, *The Philippine Statistical Review*, vol. 3, no. 4 (1936), p. 310.

coconut oil products, such as margarine), 91% of the investment in Manila hemp, and 68% of the investment in tobacco.

The investment restrictions meant that the Philippine rubber industry died practically stillborn. Rubber could not be grown in the continental United States. The greatly increasing demand by American industry created great interest in securing a source under U.S. control. In fact, a 1922 boom in rubber prices led to massive lobbying by American rubber interests to allow their entry into the Philippines. These efforts failed owing to a combination of Governor-General Leonard Wood's impressive lack of political skills and persistent Democratic opposition in Washington.

The price boom was a product of British imperial machinations. The world price of rubber had fallen sharply in 1920. In 1922, the British secretary of state for the colonies, Winston Churchill, called a committee of inquiry to investigate possible solutions to the "crisis" of falling rubber prices. The committee, under Sir James Stevenson—a man most famous for having created the whiskey advertising slogan "Johnny Walker: Born in 1820, still going strong"—created an export restriction scheme that restricted rubber exports from Ceylon and (more important) the Federated Malay States.[62] The Stevenson Plan caused rubber prices to skyrocket from a low of 11.5 cents per pound in early 1922 to an incredible $1.03 per pound by mid-1925[63] (See figure 2.1.)

The Philippines seemed poised to take advantage of the boom in rubber prices. Governor-General Leonard Wood proposed a law for the consideration of the elected Philippine legislature that would allow American corporations to lease public lands for twenty-five years in plantations up to 20,000 hectares (49,421 acres). Unfortunately, Wood was not a man known for his diplomatic skills. In an astounding display of political tone-deafness, Wood included clauses liberalizing the mining laws and allowing the immigration of Chinese labor, two hot-button issues overwhelmingly opposed by the members of the Filipino elite who served in the legislature. As a result, Wood failed to find a single Philippine legislator willing to introduce his proposed bill.[64]

With the Philippine legislature blocking liberalization of its land laws, the Firestone Tire and Rubber Company decided to try appealing directly to Washington. In 1925, the company unveiled a study demonstrating that the Philippines were perfect

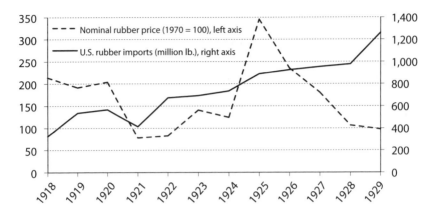

Figure 2.1 U.S. rubber prices and imports, 1918–29
Source: Index of Rubber Market Prices (1970 = 100): Figures for 1900–1986 are from Ocampo and Parra, "Los Términos de Intercambio de los Productos Básicos en el Siglo XX," *Revista de la CEPAL,* vol. 79 (2003), pp. 7–35, with data from the World Bank. U.S. crude rubber imports: National Bureau of Economic Research series 07044, cumulative 12-month period ending in December.

for rubber production. Firestone had the southern frontier island of Mindanao specifically in mind. In January 1926, Harvey Firestone himself testified before the U.S. House of Representatives. "Because of the land laws now in force in the Philippines and the attitude of the native government, our investigators advised against then attempting any large rubber developments in the Philippines. Surely it is practicable to recommend that our government take active steps to remove those existing laws?"[65] Four months later, in May 1926, Representative Robert Bacon (R-New York) introduced a bill that would split Mindanao from the rest of the Philippines, making it a separate unincorporated territory. Bacon justified his bill on the basis of Muslim-Catholic tensions in the archipelago, but he also suggested that the legislation would "liberate" the United States from dependence on imported rubber.[66] Democratic objections prevented the bill from advancing.[67]

In response to the congressional defeat, the Coolidge administration sent Colonel Carmia Thompson to the Philippines to try to convince the insular legislature to open the "vast rubber fields."[68] The Philippine legislature was more than willing to negotiate. Manuel Quezon, the Philippine legislative leader, wined and dined Thompson, suggesting that he would be happy to open the rubber fields if the United States would grant "concessions tending towards complete independence, or at least complete autonomy."[69] In public, Quezon claimed to want independence, but he privately admitted that he preferred "autonomy," which meant the abolition of the office of governor-general and the devolution of executive powers. Quezon, like most of the Filipino elite, preferred to remain in a common market and defense union with the United States, but naturally resented an appointed foreigner exercising executive power. Thompson returned to the United States, having been clearly charmed by Quezon—his report had more to say about Leonard Wood's obstreperousness and his unnecessary confrontations with the Philippine legislature than it did about the land laws. A month after Thompson's departure, Quezon reiterated his desire to negotiate autonomy in return for the liberalization of foreign investment.[70] Unfortunately, by 1926 the price of rubber was in free fall. Firestone abandoned its plans.[71] No more than a few experimental rubber plantations ever opened, and all had been liquidated by 1935.

American legislation also kept U.S.-based firms out of Philippine mining. This is not to say that there was no Philippine mining industry, or that Americans were completely uninvolved in its development. In 1938, Philippine mining operations were estimated to be worth approximately $100,000,000. Of that, Americans owned $37.9 million.[72] They were not, however, officially counted as such by the Department of Commerce.[73] The reason was that 81% of the U.S.-owned mining industry consisted of a minority stake in the operations of the Benguet Consolidated Mining Company—and that stake was owned by an American who had settled permanently on Luzon.[74] The legal barriers forced American investors to *physically* move to the islands if they wanted to participate in the mining industry in any significant way.

Benguet Consolidated was the only significant U.S.-owned mining operation in the Philippines under American rule. The enterprise dated back to the Spanish period, and was Filipino-owned in 1898. In 1911, however, a typhoon flooded its mining properties. As a result, the Bank of the Philippine Islands (a Filipino-owned institution) took possession of the company's properties. John Haussermann, a former U.S. Army officer and the Benguet mine's chief counsel before the flood, convinced the Bank of the Philippine Islands to lend him $75,000 to rehabilitate the enterprise. He used the loan as capital to sell shares in Manila, the revenues from which he used to pay off the bank loan and put the mine back into operation. Haussermann built the operation into, quite literally, a gold mine, of which he owned 30%—approximately $30 million.[75]

The Restriction of U.S. Investment in Occupied Cuba

> No property, franchise, or concessions shall be granted by the United States or by any military or other authority whatever in the Island of Cuba during the occupation thereof by the United States.
>
> *—The Foraker Amendment, 1899*

The United States entered the Spanish-American War having officially disavowed all intention of annexing Cuba. In April 1898, with war fever growing, Senator Henry Teller (D-Colorado, which was not coincidentally a beet sugar state) introduced an amendment to the congressional authorization to use force. It read: "The United States hereby disclaims any disposition or intention to exercise sovereignty, jurisdiction, or control over said island [Cuba] except for the pacification thereof, and asserts its determination, when that is accomplished, to leave the government and control of the island to its people." The amendment passed the Senate 42 to 35, and the House 311 to 6.

The Treaty of Paris that formally ended the war stipulated that Spain would relinquish all sovereignty over Cuba, but it did not transfer that sovereignty to the United States. Rather, Article 1 of the treaty read, "Spain relinquishes all claim of sovereignty over and title to Cuba. And as the island is, upon its evacuation by Spain, to be occupied by the United States, the United States will, so long as such occupation shall last, assume and discharge the obligations that may under international law result from the fact of its occupation, for the protection of life and property."[76]

It was not clear that the United States would, in fact, give up its hold over Cuba. Significant annexationist sentiment existed on the island.[77] In addition, there were American voices calling for its retention and it was common knowledge that the military governor of Cuba, General Leonard Wood, favored annexation.[78]

The Republican Party was divided over the annexation of Cuba, unlike that of the Philippines. On February 10, 1899, Senator Joseph Foraker (R-Ohio), an opponent of annexation, received news that President McKinley had created a board to issue franchises and concessions. He immediately introduced an amendment to an appropriations bill that prevented U.S. occupation authorities from issuing any such authorizations.[79] His logic was the logic of the empire trap. If the United States "granted franchises of the character specified, and thus authorized and induced the investment of the large amounts of money that would necessarily follow, it would probably postpone for several years, at least, our withdrawal. . . . It means the granting of a franchise to build a railroad or some other kind of highway, I imagine, across that island; and if so, then I am opposed to the United States entering into any such business in the island of Cuba, where our occupation is supposed to be temporary. In other words, if that kind of a programme is to be entered upon, it means that the United States will not get out of Cuba in a hundred years."[80] The amendment passed 47 to 11.[81]

The Foraker Amendment proved easy to circumvent—but only by committing the United States to ending its occupation. On April 25, 1900, several prominent magnates established the Cuba Company, with the aim of building a railroad across the island. The principals included William Cornelius Van Horne (former head of the Canadian Pacific Railroad), Levi Morton (president of the Morton Trust Company), E. H. Harriman (chairman of the Union Pacific Railroad), Henry Flagler (president of Standard Oil and future founder of Miami, Florida), Henry Walters (chairman of the Atlantic Coast Railroad), four members of the W. C. Whitney tobacco trust, Charles Barney (whose banking firm became half of Smith Barney in 1938), and a law firm in which President McKinley's second secretary of state, William Day, was a partner.[82]

Van Horne worked with General Wood and a group of Cuban lawyers to devise a way around the Foraker Amendment. As a stopgap measure, they used a clause in Cuban land law that allowed for "revocable permits" to be issued for the construction of private railroads on private land.[83] The problem was that the revocable permits would not allow the railroad to cross *public* lands; nor did Cuban law enable the military government to use eminent domain to purchase land from holdouts. As a second stopgap, therefore, Wood allowed county governments to approve passage through the public lands in their jurisdictions.[84] These measures enabled the Cuba Company to begin land acquisition, but they did not permit full construction.

In September 1900, Van Horne and Wood met to design a permanent workaround to the Foraker Amendment. The ploy they devised depended on the existence of a convention to create an independent Cuban government. The plan was for Van Horne to draft a railroad law, which Wood would then implement and submit to the Cuban convention for approval. By the time any opponents could bring legal action, Cuba would be under the control of an independent government free from the strictures of the Foraker Amendment. After the meeting, Van Horne immediately got to work building relationships with members of the Cuban Revolutionary Party and other convention delegates.[85] The strategy worked. The Cuba Company got its concession, but *because* Cuba was slated for independence, not in spite of it.

It would be too much to claim that the Foraker Amendment was key in keeping Cuba from becoming part of the United States. By 1898, the domestic beet sugar lobby opposed annexation. The lobby, however, was not all-powerful, and the United States retained the option of ruling Cuba as an "unincorporated territory," like the Philippines, thereby keeping the island outside the American customs area. The Foraker Amendment caused businesses that would have otherwise supported annexation (like the Cuba Company) to switch their preference to an independent state under U.S. protection. As a second-best option, independence beat imperial rule.

Investors nonetheless had little desire to be left at the mercy of an independent Cuban republic. As a result, they lobbied Congress to insist upon clauses in the Cuban Constitution that would allow them to call on the U.S. government to protect their interests. The result was the Platt Amendment to the Cuban Constitution. From the point of view of American investors in Cuba, the Platt Amendment had two key features. First, Article 2 of the amendment limited the ability of the Cuban government to borrow without U.S. approval. (A later treaty with the United States gave the United States a veto over all Cuban debt issues.) Second, Article 3 proclaimed "that the government of Cuba consents that the United States may exercise the right to intervene for the preservation of Cuban independence, the maintenance of a government adequate for the protection of life, property, and individual liberty, and for discharging the obligations with respect to Cuba imposed by the Treaty of Paris on the United States."[86]

Conclusion

Opposition to the imperial project made it difficult for Americans to make direct investments in the Philippine Islands, in order to short-circuit the emergence of a "Philippine lobby" that might resist the dissolution of political ties. Congress was able to restrict investment because the Philippine Islands were not a full territory of the United States but rather an "unincorporated" possession. The reason the Philippines was denied incorporation was the racial hysteria engendered by the prospect of millions of "Malay" citizens of the United States, which prompted the McKinley administration to declare that the U.S. Constitution did not apply to the territories seized from Spain. In a series of 5 to 4 decisions, the Supreme Court mostly agreed. It was therefore the Philippines' anomalous position—under American sovereignty, but populated by "citizens of the Philippine Islands" and free from the dictates of the commerce clause—that allowed congressional anti-imperialists to limit the entry of American plantations, mines, and banks into what was formally a territory of the United States.

Congress could not impose investment restrictions on territories under the sway of the Constitution (like Hawaii and Alaska) any more than it could impose investment restrictions on New Hampshire. Nor could Congress ban Americans from investing in de jure foreign territories in the absence of a direct threat to the United States. (Such a ban would be legal, but politically impossible.) Since expansion under the Constitution was politically impossible in territories with large nonwhite populations, but Congress without the Constitution could not be trusted to facilitate investment, investor support for formal imperial expansion rapidly dried up. The United States would attempt formal expansion after 1900 only for strategic reasons: successfully in the Virgin Islands (1917) and Micronesia (1945), unsuccessfully in Trinidad and Bermuda (1931), and temporarily in the Panama Canal Zone (1903–79) and Okinawa (1945–72).

Americans would risk their capital overseas, and Americans would ask their government for political support against hostile or unstable foreign governments. The question now would be, in the absence of formal expansion, how American governments would respond to those requests. Could new methods and strategies be devised to protect the property rights of American citizens outside the boundaries of the United States?

three
Setting the Trap

If a nation shows that it knows how to act with reasonable efficiency and decency in social and political matters, if it keeps order and pays its obligations, it need fear no interference from the United States. Chronic wrongdoing, or an impotence which results in a general loosening of the ties of civilized society, may in America, as elsewhere, ultimately require intervention by some civilized nation, and in the Western Hemisphere the adherence of the United States to the Monroe Doctrine may force the United States, however reluctantly, in flagrant cases of such wrongdoing or impotence, to the exercise of an international police power.

—*President Theodore Roosevelt*

Formal imperialism was off the table after 1900, but the property rights of Americans continued to come under threat from a combination of feckless foreign governments and political instability. Governments in Venezuela and the Dominican Republic confiscated American direct investments, while other Latin American governments defaulted on their debts to American creditors. After the 1893 intervention in Hawaii, the 1895 resolution of the Venezuela-Guyana boundary dispute, the 1898 Spanish-American War, and the 1903 machinations that cleaved Panama from Colombia, it would be hard for any American administration to argue that it did not have the power to intervene on behalf of American investors.

U.S. administrations may have had the power to intervene on behalf of private interests, but their willingness to intervene depended on both the character of the president and the strength of the pressures brought upon him. When investor groups lined up the same way *and* could make a credible case that intervention served strategic interests, then intervention became more likely. Conversely, if investor groups were divided and there was no strategic interest, then intervention would be practically impossible.

In 1904, as instability threatened American direct investments, President Theodore Roosevelt was under pressure to intervene in the Dominican Republic, but he waited to build political support. In fact, he waited until the *Dominican* government joined bondholders and direct investors in requesting intervention. Roosevelt then proclaimed his intervention in terms of broad principles. The United States would exercise an "international police power" across the entire Western Hemisphere should Latin American governments engage in "chronic wrongdoing" or collapse into chaos.

By phrasing his reasons in the broadest possible terms, Roosevelt effectively committed his successors to the protection of American property rights across the circum-Caribbean. With Roosevelt's declaration, risk premiums fell on all sovereign debt issues across the circum-Caribbean (that is, all countries with a Caribbean coastline, plus El Salvador), not just those of the Dominican Republic. A future president could not back down from that commitment without risking a strong adverse market reaction. In fact, when crises emerged in the U.S. intervention sphere, markets *did* react adversely until the administration of the day showed its willingness to act.

A corollary of the argument that intervention was likely when the interests of investors were aligned is that intervention was not likely when the interests of investors were divided. Such a situation in fact occurred in Venezuela in 1902. President

Cipriano Castro confiscated the assets of an American asphalt company. Castro, however, carefully designed his expropriation around conflicting claims between *two* American asphalt interests—and the interests that benefited from Castro's actions were closely connected to powerful Republican politicians. Castro therefore managed to forestall an American reaction. He did not prevent the aggrieved asphalt interests from *privately* funding a revolt against his government, but he did keep the United States from using its power against him.

Roosevelt Makes a Corollary

Theodore Roosevelt was not usually a man to choose inaction when action was an option. He nevertheless moved slowly in declaring hegemony over the Americas. It took an unfortunate and extended series of events in the Dominican Republic to get the American president to declare that the United States would exercise an "international police power" over the hemisphere.

The Dominican Republic had been chronically unstable since independence from Haiti in 1844. The republic suffered armed revolts in 1849 and 1857. Fearing a Haitian invasion (and hoping to stabilize his government), President Pedro Santana agreed to annexation by Spain in 1861. Spain, unfortunately, proved unable to bring stability: after four years of civil war, Madrid withdrew in 1865. In 1870, President Buenaventura Báez invited the United States to assume sovereignty. President Ulysses Grant signed an annexation treaty that promised Santo Domingo territorial status and eventual statehood, but race-based opposition against the admission of a "Negro republic" into the Union caused the treaty to fail on a 28 to 28 vote on the Senate floor.[1]

Dominican political instability translated into financial instability. In 1869, the Dominican government contracted £757,000 ($89.7 million in 2011 dollars) in debt on the London market. The government promptly defaulted. In 1888, the Dominican government arranged a new issue worth £770,000.[2] It used

£142,820 to pay off the defaulted 1869 debt—at 45 pence to the pound—and the rest to finance the government.[3] As security, the Dominican government placed the customhouses under the formal control of the underwriter, Westendorps & Co., a Dutch company, which sent managers from Europe to the republic. Two years later, in 1890, Westendorps underwrote a £615,000 issue intended to build a forty-two-mile railroad across the mountainous terrain between Santiago and Puerto Plata on the coast. The issue failed, and Westendorps assumed the debt.[4] By 1892, eleven miles of railroad had been completed, at which point the Dominican government forcibly took back control of the customhouses and again defaulted on its debt. The Dutch government protested, but it had no legal recourse and took no action.[5]

In 1892, a newly incorporated American firm bought out Westendorps's interest. It sold the debt at 65 cents on the dollar to the San Domingo Improvement Company (SDIC), headquartered in New York. The SDIC gained "control" over the customhouses, but its managers understood that they could do little if Santo Domingo decided to revoke their privileges. As security, therefore, the SDIC wrote into the contract that, in the case of default, the governments of Belgium, France, the Netherlands, the United Kingdom, and the United States would appoint a "financial commission" to take direct control of Santo Domingo's finances. SDIC refinanced the Dominican Republic's existing debt and issued new bonds to finish the construction of the railroad.[6]

The Dominican Republic's precarious politics continued to threaten foreign interests. In 1892, President Ulises Heureaux obtained a court order against the French-owned Banque Nationale de Saint Domingue and seized its assets.[7] France dispatched gunboats, but they did not engage. The dispute went to arbitration by the Spanish government, but the hearings ended fruitlessly, and in 1895 the French government threatened to seize the customhouses.[8] Heureaux appealed to SDIC headquarters in New York for help against the French. The SDIC responded by forwarding the issue to Secretary of State Walter Gresham. The United States dispatched warships to Dominican waters. President Cleveland and Gresham then arranged a deal in which the SDIC would purchase the Banque Nationale for $750,000—at a time when the bank's assets consisted entirely of $19,200 in cash, "several loans to the Dominican government, and the claim for damages resulting from the action of President Heureaux."[9] In effect, the Cleveland administration brokered an agreement under which the SDIC paid the French in exchange for Dominican paper of questionable value. Paying off the French was in the SDIC's interest, since it controlled the customhouses that the French wished to take over. The SDIC thanked Gresham personally for "the manner in which you have treated us and defended the rights of our company—an American company, composed of American citizens."[10]

In 1896, the Dominican government once again went into default. The problem was that the SDIC's control over the customhouses was weak to nonexistent. Dominican officials, not SDIC appointees, inspected goods and determined the duties payable. The SDIC director's job was to participate in the inspection (if he so desired), cosign the necessary documents, and gather the funds the government collectors turned over to the SDIC.[11] This system was easily gamed at both the lowest and the highest levels. At the lowest level, corrupt officials underinvoiced shipments in the customhouses in return for bribes from the importers. At the highest level, President Heureaux granted temporary personal exemptions from duties to prominent merchants and plantation owners in return for loans or "political services."[12] At times, Heureaux dispensed with formal exemptions and simply ordered that merchandise be reclassified from a high-duty category to a lower one. These reclassifications could be blatantly fraudulent: on one occasion, President Heureaux told inspectors to reclassify flour as cement.[13]

On July 26, 1899, Ramón Cáceres, a prominent landowner—and a future Dominican president—shot and killed President Heureaux outside the town of Moca. The assassination plunged the country into civil war. General Horacio Vásquez proclaimed himself provisional president. After poorly organized elections (against a backdrop of violence) Vásquez stepped down in favor of Juan Isidro Jiménez on November 15. Jiménez faced down multiple threats to his rule and stayed in office until April 1902, when a second revolt by Vásquez dislodged him. Vásquez then assumed the presidency in May, this time unprovisionally.

Vásquez's revolt had the unfortunate effect of dividing the army and elites. A counter-coup forced Vásquez from office on March 23, 1903, and Alejandro Woss y Gil became president. The fighting did not stop—between April 1 and April 19, 1903, disorder forced the United States to land marines from the USS *Atlanta* in order to protect the U.S. consulate in Santo Domingo.[14] On December 6, 1903, Woss y Gil fell to an armed movement led by the governor of Puerto Plata Province, Carlos Morales. Morales then became president, whatever that meant in the context of an ongoing civil war. The United States kept warships offshore.

Each new Dominican government tried and failed to reestablish payments on the debt. On March 20, 1900, President Jiménez promised to use 32% of customs revenue for payments on foreign and domestic debt, beginning on April 1, rising to 37% over the next two years. French and Belgian bondholders protested that their debts should have priority, and the agreement failed. Eight months later, on January 10, 1901, Jiménez unceremoniously ejected the SDIC from the customhouses and expropriated the Santiago–Puerto Plata railroad.[15] SDIC's shareholders complained to the State Department. The United States advised Jiménez to negotiate with the company. In March 1901 he reached an agreement under which the SDIC would sell the railroads, the Banque Nationale, and all Dominican debt in its hands back to the Dominican government for a sum to be determined in arbitration.[16] In June 1901 the Dominican government worked out a favorable arrangement with its Belgian and French creditors, who agreed to give the Dominican Republic the option to retire any portion of its debt at one-half its face value over the next two decades, while a one-time payment of $50,000 would cover past-due interest. In return, President Jiménez pledged to allocate 15% of the customs revenue or $300,000 to debt service, whichever was greater.[17]

The Dominican government failed, however, to meet the terms of its agreements. Between June 1901 and June 1903 (during which three different presidents sat in Santo Domingo) payments to Franco-Belgian creditors totaled $327,000, rather less than the $750,000 that was due.[18] The Dominican government also failed to live up to its promises to the SDIC. On January 31, 1903, President Vásquez offered to pay the SDIC $4.5 million for its properties, including the Santiago–Puerto Plata railroad. (The SDIC demanded $11 million.) The exact terms were left to arbitration, but the government agreed to pay $225,000 per year in the interim.[19] In February, the Dominican Republic managed a single monthly payment of $18,750. Vásquez fell to Woss y Gil a month later, after which no more money was forthcoming.[20]

After Woss y Gil in turn fell in December 1903, American owners of direct investments in the Dominican Republic began to lobby the Roosevelt administration. On December 12, 1903, W. L. Bass, the owner of the largest sugar plantations in the Dominican Republic, wrote the U.S. minister in Santo Domingo urging the United States to intervene. On January 2, 1904, A. F. Suárez of the Central Ansonia Sugar Company added his voice. "Mr. Secretary," wrote Suárez to Secretary of State Hay from the company's New York offices, "surely it cannot be the purpose of the United States to abandon its citizens and their interests much longer to such a condition as exists in Santo Domingo!"[21] Suárez was persuasive: the day after he wrote to Hay, marines from the USS *Columbia* and *Newark* landed in San Pedro de Macoris and Santo Domingo. They joined a small force of British Royal Marines to prevent fighting in Puerto Plata, San Pedro de Macoris, and Santo Domingo.[22]

The U.S. Marines departed on February 11, 1904, after only a little over a month. In fact, the presence of the marines accomplished little from the point of view of American investors.

On January 23, for example, Hugh Kelly and Company, a sugar producer, wrote the State Department that their properties were "at the mercy of hordes of untrained and unintelligent mobs . . . likely at any moment to commit outrage upon person and property." Violence also blocked the ports at harvest time. In addition, Hugh Kelly and Company's lawyer personally asked Secretary of State Hay to stop the Morales government from reimposing an export tax on sugar. On February 10 and 17, representatives of the New Jersey–headquartered Central Dominican Railroad Company asked the State Department to defend their property against the government. On February 15, 1904, the owner of the Clyde Steamship Company, whose 1895 trading contract signed under Heureaux gave him "practical control of the trade with Santo Domingo," requested that the State Department prevent the Morales government from nullifying the contract. On July 9, 1904, the president of the Santo Domingo Southern Railway Company asked the United States for protection. Two days later, J. L. Robertson, who owned "large property interests in Santo Domingo," added his voice, asking Francis Loomis, now assistant secretary of state, for "reasonable assurance of protection."[23]

The United States had a second reason to worry about Dominican instability: fear of Germany. The worry was *not* that Berlin might use force to try to collect debts. Rather, the fear was that a penurious Dominican government might offer the Germans the use of naval bases at Samaná or Manzanillo Bay in return for financial and military support. The U.S. minister in Santo Domingo reported several times in 1903 that President Woss y Gil's foreign minister, Jesús Galván, supported just such a scheme. (Galván was also a vocal supporter of a bill that would deprive the Clyde Steamship Company of its privileges.) That fear receded after Carlos Morales replaced Woss y Gil, but it was replaced by a new worry that Germany might provide military aid to insurgents backing former president Juan Isidro Jiménez. That fear was far from baseless. In February 1904, the United States captured a letter from a Jimenista general, Demetrio Rodríguez, to the German consul in Santo Domingo that openly requested German support. In response, Captain James Miller of the U.S. Navy invited Rodríguez on board his ship to explain that this was a bad idea: "The revolution must close . . . neither he nor anyone must think for a moment that Germany or any other foreign power could be situated in any portion of the Dominican territory . . . the United States would not for a moment sanction it."[24]

In February 1904, President Roosevelt decided to try to force a truce on the warring Dominican factions. The cruisers USS *Newark* and *Columbia* and the training boat *Hartford* bombarded the rebel-controlled towns of Duarte and Pajarito and demanded that the warring factions sit down to work out their differences.[25] The factions signed a peace agreement in June 1904.[26] As part of the agreement, President Morales promised to restart payments on the government's debts in November.[27] Unfortunately, it was less than clear how the Dominican Republic could pay its debts, no matter how much Morales might want to. Dominican revenues ran $1.85 million (at an annualized rate) in the second half of 1904, while the government had $1.3 million in annual operating expenses. Unfortunately, the country faced $0.9 million in arrears and obligations of $1.7 million set to come due in 1905. Had the country attempted to pay just its obligations (ignoring the arrears), it would have been left with only $150,000 to meet operating expenses of $1.3 million—operating expenses that included, of course, the military. American officials did not think that the Dominican Republic could possibly comply with the schedule.[28] Worse yet, the peace agreement was not holding: Americans with investments on the island continued to complain about insurgent violence and government predation.[29]

President Morales faced a dilemma. He desperately needed revenues to maintain the loyalty of the army and defeat the rebellion. The problem was that he could not borrow. Nor could he effectively collect customs revenues. Part of the problem, of course, was widespread corruption—but a bigger problem came from the fact that armed factions regularly seized the custom-houses for their revenue. In the words of an official report to President Roosevelt: "A Dominican revolution might be briefly defined as the attempt of a bandit guerrilla to seize a custom-house. In the background, acting as a moving force, will ordinarily be found a political malcontent, ambitious to overthrow the dictator President in power and to succeed in control, to his own profit. But the customhouse and the insurgent chief are the real keys to the situation."[30]

Morales's solution was simple: turn customs over to the United States. *Private* foreign management of the customhouses had failed miserably, but what about *public* foreign management? Uncorrupt American managers could, in theory, collect more revenue. Moreover, the presence of American officials would dissuade armed rebels from attacking the customhouses.[31] The result, Morales hoped, would be a virtuous circle. Revenues would go up, providing money to restart debt payments. Expenses would go down, as the government would have less to fear from armed rebellion and could therefore spend less on defense. Steady debt payments would lower borrowing costs. That, in turn, would permit the debt to be refunded at lower interest rates, freeing up yet more revenue. Morales therefore entreated the United States to take control of the customhouses on the condition that the U.S. government would agree to remit sufficient revenue to Santo Domingo to keep the Dominican government operational.[32]

American agents in Santo Domingo urged the United States to accept Morales's invitation. They worried that European governments might blockade the country . . . a counterproductive move that the agents believed would only worsen the chaos that had already killed several Americans.[33] They also worried that European powers might attempt to secure their interests by supplying weapons to various factions in the civil war.[34] These fears were not unfounded: in April, President Morales settled his debts with Italian creditors, using funds pledged to French and Belgian bondholders—in effect, robbing Pierre to pay Paolo.[35]

U.S. officials on the ground went so far as to suggest to their superiors that they be allowed to take over the customs of their own accord.[36]

Roosevelt thought the notion of taking control of Dominican finances was sound, but he also felt that he needed to build domestic support before acting. There was very limited support in the United States in 1904 for foreign entanglements in rebellious countries. Memories of the brutal war in the Philippines were fresh, and U.S. troops were still engaged in combat operations in Mindanao. Roosevelt preferred to "put off the action until the necessity became so clear that even the blindest can see it."[37]

On May 20, 1904, Roosevelt proclaimed the Roosevelt Corollary to the Monroe Doctrine in a letter to Secretary of War Elihu Root. Roosevelt asked Root to read the letter aloud at a dinner banquet celebrating the second anniversary of Cuban independence at the Waldorf-Astoria in New York City.[38] The letter set the tone for American diplomacy in the Dominican Republic that summer. U.S. naval officers and diplomatic personnel brokered a second peace agreement between the Dominican warring factions, who signed a peace agreement in June.[39] President Morales promised to restart debt payments by November. Unfortunately, with the Dominican government unable to meet its basic expenses, it seemed highly unlikely that it would be able to comply.[40]

In fact, the Dominican Republic's fiscal position worsened considerably on July 14, 1904, when arbiters ruled that the Dominican government would need to pay the SDIC $450,000 per year for two years and $500,000 thereafter. The SDIC would regain control of the Santiago–Puerto Plata railroad until $1,500,000 had been paid.[41] In the event of nonpayment, an agent appointed by the U.S. government would take control of the Puerto Plata customhouse—with the right to assume control of other northern ports should the Dominican Republic still fail to pay. Given the failure of the SDIC to manage the customhouses, the company considered it vital that the agent be a U.S.

official. "In order that the terms of the protocol may be fulfilled, two things are absolutely necessary," wrote the SDIC's chief counsel. "First, the United States must be represented in the collection and control of the requisite revenues; and secondly, the representatives of the United States must have physical possession of the security."[42]

The Dominican government's initial reaction to the ruling was dismay at the size of the compensation. The finance minister stated that it was impossible for the Dominican Republic to discharge the additional obligation.[43] President Morales called it, with some hyperbole, "The most serious problem that the Republic has experienced since its foundation."[44] Upon reflection, however, Morales decided that he was not going to reject a customs receivership—*an idea he had supported*—simply because of the size of the SDIC compensation. In fact, he stated, the biggest problem with the arbitration panel's solution was that it didn't go far enough. Why hand over just one customhouse? He asked the United States to take control of *all* the country's customhouses, again with the caveat that it guarantee enough revenue to keep the Dominican government operational.[45]

On Christmas Eve of 1904, the Italian government gave Roosevelt the pretext he needed to accept Morales's invitation. Rome insisted that the United States either pay Italian claims against the Dominican Republic or permit Rome to "collect the quota due her directly from the customhouses of the Republic."[46] Italy posed little threat, but Roosevelt believed that the Italian statement would help focus minds in Washington. He immediately opened negotiations with Morales, and on January 20, 1905, he concluded an agreement under which U.S. officials would assume control over the customs agency, reporting only to the Dominican president. The Americans would have control over personnel and procedures. The United States would guarantee the Dominican government 45% of revenue, the remainder to be used for debt payments. Santo Domingo would not change tariffs without U.S. approval.[47] The United States pledged to defend the republic against foreign threats.

Roosevelt submitted the agreement to the Senate on February 7, 1905. He justified it as contributing to stability across the circum-Caribbean. "It is supremely to our interest that all the communities immediately south of us should be or become prosperous and stable, and therefore not merely in name, but in fact independent and self-governing."[48] The Senate, however, rejected the treaty. A major objection, raised primarily by Republicans, was that the treaty did not prevent the Dominican Republic from contracting new debt. Democratic senators in turn objected to the defense clause. To address these concerns, Roosevelt changed the wording from a U.S. promise "to undertake the adjustment" of the Dominican Republic's debt to one that would only "attempt the adjustment." Roosevelt also removed the defense clause. The revisions failed to satisfy Senate objections.[49]

The *Dominican* finance minister then proposed that Roosevelt simply take over customs without a treaty.[50] Frustrated with Congress, Roosevelt accepted the proposal. On March 31, 1905, a retired colonel named George Colton took over the administration of the Dominican Republic's customs agency.[51] "The Constitution did not explicitly give me the power to bring about the necessary agreement with Santo Domingo," said Roosevelt, "but the Constitution did not forbid my doing what I did."[52] Roosevelt may or may not have realized it at the time, but the subversion of legislative intentions by the executive (and vice versa) would become a hallmark of American imperial diplomacy. Investors would use whichever branch of government was most amenable to protecting their interests.

The Barber of Santo Domingo

The implementation of the Roosevelt Corollary in the Dominican Republic had three objectives: first, stabilizing the Dominican Republic's finances; second, reassuring investors across the rest of the circum-Caribbean that the United States stood ready to defend their property rights; and third, stabilizing the Dominican Republic's politics. Did the implementation of the Roosevelt Corollary succeed in meeting these objectives? On that score, Roosevelt's new policy was an absolute success in stabilizing the Dominican Republic's finances, a qualified success in reassuring investors, and a failure in changing Dominican politics. This chapter will take up the first two points; the third is addressed in chapter 4.

The Americans took physical control of the Dominican Republic's customs service on March 31, 1905.[53] The new administrators found that the 150-mile Haitian border was entirely unpatrolled, "leaving, as it were, the back door open."[54] The Americans therefore organized a customs and frontier service. The new force consisted of 118 armed and mounted Dominican servicemen and five American commanders. The guards doubled as a postal service in the frontier area. The Americans also constructed a small border post and began construction of a second post at a cost of $5,750 ($117,000 in 2011 dollars).[55] The total expense of the guard came to $103,923 ($2.12 million in 2011 dollars) in its first twenty months of operation.[56] Enlisted personnel (100 out of the force's complement of 150) received $300 per year ($7,910 in 2011 dollars[57])—an excellent wage in the Dominican Republic of 1905, where soldiers in the Dominican Army received only $97 per year and police officers $133.[58] (Sugar plantations usually offered one dollar a day to their plantation workers, but only during the harvest season.)[59] Customs service duty was dangerous: two Americans died in an incident in Las Matas, when they engaged armed smugglers. (The smugglers escaped into Haiti, where two of them were apprehended and turned over to the United States. The wife of one of the dead Americans received $5,563 in compensation from the Dominican government; she returned to her parents' home in Puerto Rico with their three children.)[60]

The Americans also needed to create a Dominican revenue-cutter service. "The customs service was found without water transportation of any kind," reported the new administration. The receivership contracted for four gasoline-powered 75-foot cutters from New York, each armed with a Hotchkiss rapid-fire weapon to the front and an automatic 30-caliber rifle to the rear.

The cost of constructing, transporting, and readying the boats came to $73,489 ($1.36 million in 2011 dollars).[61]

The Americans revamped the system for verifying cargoes. Deputy receivers were ordered to immediately send samples of all cargoes to the central office for verification. Under Dominican law, importers who objected to their assessments were entitled to an automatic appeal to the tariff court. They could then withhold their payments until the verdict. Since the court usually took six months to a year to render decisions, and the amounts owed accrued no interest, there was an obvious incentive to delay payments. The new system did not speed things up, but it did increase the prevalence of positive decisions: of thirty-six rulings in the first twenty months of the receivership, only one went against the American administration.[62]

Finally, the American presence effectively halted insurgent attacks against the customhouses. The Americans did not need to station marines in order to deter attacks. Rather, the belief that retaliation would come quickly was sufficient. In fact, the Americans had already demonstrated their ability to deter from the sea: the naval bombardment in February 1904 succeeded in disrupting just such an assault. Customs collections skyrocketed (see figure 3.1). In the first year of the receivership's operation, collections leaped 44%. Most of the increase went to debt repayment; the net revenue of the Dominican government remained essentially unchanged.

Despite the increase in revenue, bondholders still had to accept substantial haircuts when the United States brokered a debt restructuring in February 1907. Excluding the expropriation compensation due the SDIC, the average haircut was 57%, and no creditor took less than 50%. (Some of the country's domestic creditors accepted a 90% haircut.) Bonds issued on the French and Belgian markets received past-due interest, but other creditors did not (see table 3.1.)

An American appointee, Jacob Hollander (an economics professor at Johns Hopkins University) negotiated the settlement on behalf of the Dominican Republic. Hollander's obvi-

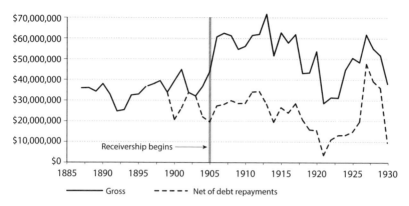

Figure 3.1 Dominican customs collections, 1887–1930, 2009 dollars
Source: Maurer and Mitchener, "Customs Receiverships and Crown Agents," unpublished working paper.

ous competitor for the job was John Moore, the SDIC's chief counsel; Moore's rejection was a sign that Roosevelt was sensitive to accusations of favoritism. Roosevelt had reasons to be concerned. The *Chicago Tribune* wrote that the customs receivership "shall displace and obliterate the most sinister feature of the whole affair—the special precedence given to the $4,500,000 claim of the ever mysterious 'Santo Domingo Improvement Company of New York.' "[63]

Once it became clear that Hollander intended to impose large haircuts on the Dominican Republic's creditors, the SDIC found itself in the strange position of appealing to the *British* government, via its connections with the British Council of Foreign Bondholders, for help against the possible intentions of the *American* government.[64] An exasperated State Department finally had to write to SDIC officials, "The President is unable to recognize any special rights and privileges of the said companies over any other creditors, American or foreign."[65] Nonetheless, the SDIC did relatively well in the settlement, getting 90% of what it had previously agreed to, although its principals continued to publicly claim that its expropriated assets were worth $11 million.[66]

Table 3.1
Dominican debt settlement, 1907

	Amount (thousands of dollars)	Haircut	Includes unpaid interest?	New amount (thousands of dollars)
SDIC	$4,493	10%	na	$4,044
French Belgian bonds	$15,975	50%	Yes	$7,988
Sala claim	$352	50%	Yes	$176
Bancalari claim, 1904 contract	$89	50%	No	$45
Italian protocol	$188	50%	No	$94
Bancalari protocol	$100	50%	No	$50
Spanish-German protocol	$100	50%	No	$50
Ros claim	$37	50%	No	$19
Old foreign debt	$351	50%	No	$176
Consolidated interior debt	$1,760	50%	No	$880
Interior debt held by Vicini estate	$1,621	50%	No	$811
Treasury contracts	$240	50%	No	$120
Vicini estate claim of 1903	$250	50%	No	$125
Certificates of contaduría, dated	$468	60%	No	$187
A. Font & Co.	$44	60%	No	$18
West Indian public works	$122	70%	No	$37
National bank notes	$1,575	70%	No	$473
Deferred debt	$1,029	80%	No	$206
Certificates of contaduría, undated	$1,038	90%	No	$104
Other	$2,000	90%	No	$200
TOTAL	$31,832	50%		$15,799
TOTAL without SDIC	$27,339	57%		$11,755

Source: William Wynne, *State Insolvency and Foreign Bondholders: Selected Case Histories of Governmental Foreign Bond Defaults and Debt Readjustments* (Yale University Press: New Haven, 1951), p. 258.

Note: The French Belgian bonds and the Sala claim include past-due interest in the amounts.

Once the creditors signed on, the settlement was enshrined in a treaty between the United States and the Dominican Republic. The new treaty encountered opposition in the Senate, particularly from southern senators, but on the whole opposition was muted. Many anti-imperialist papers categorized the receivership as a *progressive* measure, helping to bring good government to benighted nations. The *Philadelphia Ledger* wrote,

"President Roosevelt has undertaken to give the island of Santo Domingo an honest government, economically administered. Philadelphia next!"[67] The treaty included two clauses that eased opposition. First, it explicitly relieved the United States from any responsibility for the Dominican Republic's debt. Second, it prohibited the Dominican Republic from issuing any new debt without American approval.[68]

On February 25, 1907, the Senate ratified the agreement 43 to 19. Passage through the Dominican Congress was somewhat stormier, but it ratified the treaty on May 3. Ultimately, the Dominican Republic issued $20 million in new bonds, which generated $19.7 million in cash. $15.8 million of the revenues were used to refinance the restructured debt, with the remainder applied to public works. The interest rate on the nominal value of the new debt was 5%; the effective rate was 5.1%.[69]

Creating a Sphere

It was by no means obvious that investors in other Latin American countries would react positively to the declaration of the Roosevelt Corollary. First, the situation in the Dominican Republic was unique. An American company ran the customhouses and owned the principal bank and railway line, and Americans owned much of the sugar industry; the intervention was more about the protection of those direct investments than about foreign bondholders. Second, the geopolitical context was unique. The Dominican Republic enjoyed an unusually strategic location that the United States wanted to deny to other powers. Third, when in control of Dominican finances, the United States forced creditors to accept haircuts averaging 57%. Finally, the U.S. Senate was explicitly unwilling to guarantee the Dominican Republic's debt issues.

As an empirical matter, however, the markets reacted very favorably to the February intervention against rebel attacks on the Dominican customhouses.[70] Bond yields on the debt of *other*

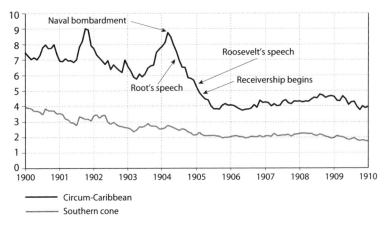

Figure 3.2 Average bond spreads over 10-year Treasuries, 1900–10 (excluding the Dominican Republic)

Source: Data on coupons and bond prices from *Investor's Monthly Manual* (available at http://icf.som.yale.edu/london-stock-exchange-investor-monthly-manual-1869-1929) and the *Wall Street Journal*, various issues.

circum-Caribbean nations fell precipitously. The bombardment drove yields down to their precrisis levels; they continued to fall as the administration took more actions (see figure 3.2). On April 5, 1905, James Cooper, the secretary of the Corporation of Foreign Bondholders, reported, "The securities of South and Central American republics . . . which a short time ago were spoken of as rubbish and to be carefully avoided by all but the most hardened speculators are now apparently regarded as rapidly approaching the position of gilt edged securities." Cooper went on to attribute the rise in bond prices to American actions. "The rises that have occurred appear to be largely due to the idea that the United States is going to intervene in some way so as to make all these defaulting countries pay their debts . . . the recent action of the United States executive in Santo Domingo was regarded as confirmation of this idea."[71]

The rise in investor confidence did not extend to all Latin American sovereign debt, much less sovereign debt in general.

The yields of the Southern Cone countries—Argentina, Brazil, and Chile—were not affected by American actions. This was *not* because the three countries were free from political or default risk. All three had histories of default, most recently in the aftermath of the Barings crisis of 1890.[72] What those countries were free from, at least until the 1930s, was American hegemony. They were modern states, with modern militaries. Argentina in 1912 possessed a navy consisting of nine armored cruisers of various types, seven destroyers, twenty-one torpedo boats, and a submarine. Argentina also had two battleships under construction in Quincy, Massachusetts, and twelve destroyers being built in yards divided between Britain, France, and Germany.[73] Brazil began a large naval buildup in 1904: by 1910, the program had produced two dreadnoughts, two scout cruisers, and ten destroyers with more under way.[74] The Chilean navy in 1912 consisted of two battleships, one armored cruiser, two torpedo cruisers, seven destroyers, and five torpedo boats. The Chilean warships dated from the 1890s, but as of 1912 the country had two modern dreadnoughts, six destroyers, and two submarines under construction.[75]

None of the Southern Cone countries could defeat the United States in a straight-up naval conflict, but any attempt to use gunboats to protect the rights of foreign investors would have involved a real *war*, with all the risks that entailed.[76] (In mid-1914, the U.S. Navy consisted of eight dreadnoughts, twenty-two battleships, twenty-five cruisers, fifty-one destroyers, thirteen torpedo boats, and thirty submarines spread over two oceans.)[77] An American war with any of those countries would also have had the effect of pushing them into an alliance with Germany. The United States was particularly worried about Berlin's links with Brazil, which had experienced significant German immigration.[78] The United States, therefore, was not "practically sovereign" in the Southern Cone of the American continent the way that it was on the lands and islands of the Caribbean or the Pacific coast down to Peru.[79]

Hegemony in Action

The U.S. government had made a broad pledge to investors. It would prevent default, expropriation, and the violent destruction of American assets. In essence, it extended the Platt Amendment to the entire circum-Caribbean. The markets appeared to believe the U.S. pledge. The question was whether the United States would follow through.

The American response to the collapse of Cuba in 1906—the only nation in the U.S. sphere of influence to implode before Roosevelt left office—confirmed the faith of the bond markets. The fraudulent reelection of President Tomás Estrada triggered riots, which grew into armed revolt. When the U.S. consul cabled Roosevelt, "Government forces are unable to quell rebellion," Roosevelt's personal reaction was to say to a friend, "I am so angry with that infernal little Cuban republic that I would like to wipe its people off the face of the earth." Roosevelt, however, used more temperate language in a cable to the consul: "Perhaps you do not yourself appreciate the reluctance with which this country would intervene." Upon hearing of Roosevelt's reluctance, President Estrada threatened to resign, "and therefore," wrote U.S. officials, "the prevailing state of anarchy will continue." In response, Roosevelt dispatched Secretary of War Taft to Havana, with orders to take all necessary measures. (He also dispatched nine warships to Cuban harbors.) When Taft discovered that the Cuban government had essentially lost control of everything save a few cities, he printed up his own letterhead reading "Office of the Governor, Republic of Cuba, under the Provisional Administration of the United States" and ordered the marines to land. The Americans remained until 1909.[80]

Had Roosevelt stood aside as Cuba collapsed into chaos, then it would have been clear that the Dominican situation was a one-off. (In Cuba, unlike the Dominican Republic, few strategic interests were at stake: there is no evidence that foreign powers sought to take advantage of the unrest.) Instead, Roosevelt reaffirmed that the Corollary would be upheld. It is true that Cuba (along

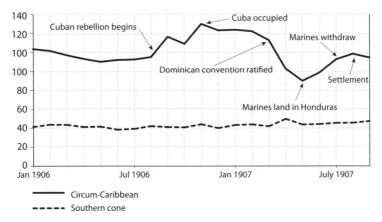

Figure 3.3 Bond spreads over 10-year Treasuries, 1906–7 (excluding Cuba and the Dominican Republic)

Source: Data on coupons and bond prices from *Investor's Monthly Manual* (available at http://icf.som.yale.edu/london-stock-exchange-investor-monthly-manual-1869-1929) and the *Wall Street Journal*, various issues.

Note: Circum-Caribbean bond yields do not include Cuba or Honduras.

with Panama) was a formal protectorate of the United States. It also appears to be true, however, that after the Dominican actions of 1904–5, the markets believed that U.S. pledges applied just as much to its informal protectorates. When instability broke out in Cuba, yields on the debt of *all* countries inside the American intervention sphere rose (see figure 3.3). That is, the violence in Cuba affected the perceived risk of *all* countries subject to the Roosevelt Corollary.[81] When it became clear that the United States would intervene, yields stabilized. This result is not consistent with the hypothesis that the United States enjoyed a special relationship with the Republic of Cuba. In the Cuban case, the markets relaxed once it became clear that the Cuban intervention would not interfere with the U.S. commitments elsewhere, symbolized by the Senate's ratification of the Dominican convention.

The markets may have taken confidence in the American hegemon, but they never gained full confidence in its ability or willingness to handle crises. Yields continued to leap across the intervention sphere whenever the United States intervened, almost as if American actions reminded investors just how risky the place was rather than reassuring them that Washington had things under control. The jump in yields seen during the Cuban intervention repeated itself when Nicaragua invaded Honduras in 1907 with the goal of overthrowing the government of President Manuel Bonilla. The Nicaraguan Army crossed the border on February 18, and the United States landed marines at Puerto Cortés on the Caribbean to protect American banana investments. The U.S. Navy then entered the Gulf of Fonseca and used its guns to stop Nicaraguan forces from advancing on Bonilla's position. Bonilla fled on the USS *Chicago*. The U.S. chargé d'affaires actively brokered a settlement that installed General Miguel Dávila in the Honduran presidential palace, after which the marines withdrew.[82]

In fact, the pattern held with subsequent U.S. interventions through the start of the Great Depression. Every time the United States intervened within its sphere, bond spreads for *other* circum-Caribbean countries jumped by more than 200 basis points in the run-up (see table 3.2). Yields then slowly dropped back to normal; it generally took three months. This pattern was not seen in the bonds of the Southern Cone countries, although it did show up in the stock of United Fruit and the overseas sugar companies. The upshot was that American administrations faced a very real risk of meltdown in the market for Latin American sovereign debt—and, by extension, great political pressure from investors—should it fail to intervene.

Abetting Economic Nationalism in Venezuela

If the declaration of an American intervention sphere was driven by an alignment of interests among investors, then one would expect the United States to refrain from intervention when such interests were not aligned. Such an event occurred in 1901, when President Cipriano Castro of Venezuela expropriated the properties of the New York and Bermúdez Company (NY&B). Castro had advisers who understood very well American poli-

Table 3.2

Bond spreads over 10-year Treasuries, 1905–28

Dependent variable: difference in percentage annual yield on central government bonds for Latin American countries over U.S. 10-year treasuries, adjusted for term

	(1)	(2)
Preintervention	0.006	−0.001
	(0.04)	(0.05)
Intervention	0.13	0.13
	(0.07)*	(0.07)
Postintervention	0.19	0.19
	(0.08)**	(0.08)**
Number of observations	2,982	2,982
R-sq	0.53	0.73
Country dummies	yes	yes
Period dummies	yes	yes
Period trend × Country dummies	no	yes

Source: Author's calculations, based on data from *Investor's Monthly Manual* (available at http://icf.som.yale.edu/london-stock-exchange-investor-monthly-manual-1869-1929) and the *Wall Street Journal*, various issues.

Note: Coefficients that are significantly different from zero are denoted as * 5% and ** 1%.

tics. He couched his expropriation as a dispute between two different U.S. companies and carefully ensured that the company he helped would be one with very influential friends within the Republican administration. Faced with what appeared to be a fight between two sets of Americans, McKinley (and later Roosevelt) chose to do nothing.

Cipriano Castro came to power by violence during a civil war. On May 23, 1899, rebel forces under his leadership crossed from their Colombian sanctuaries into the Venezuelan state of Táchira. After a chaotic and violent advance, Castro proclaimed himself president on October 20. He entered Caracas on November 2. Stability did not ensue—Castro, like later Venezuelan presidents, proved unable to resist meddling in the civil wars besetting his neighbors. Since Liberal forces in Colombia had provided him sanctuary, Castro decided to return the favor in the Liberals' war against Colombia's Conservative government. He allowed Liberal forces to mobilize on Venezuelan soil and equipped them with roughly ten thousand imported rifles.

Two could play at that game, however—the Conservative government in Bogotá, under President José Manuel Marroquín, organized a 4,000-man force of Venezuelan counterrevolutionaries. Under the slogan "Down with the Reds," the counterrevolutionaries crossed the Colombian-Venezuelan border on July 26, 1900. They pillaged border towns before engaging Venezuelan government forces on July 28.[83]

Castro defeated the rebel incursion but decided to retaliate by ordering an ill-fated invasion of Colombia on August 4, 1900. Venezuelan troops advanced along the Caribbean coast, where they were met by a Colombian force at the town of Riohacha, about 190 miles east of Cartagena. French warships intervened to stop the Venezuelan advance, putatively to allow French soldiers to evacuate foreign nationals. The Colombian army used the respite to land 1,200 soldiers and force the Venezuelans down the coast, where they were ambushed and destroyed as an organized fighting force.[84]

The result was a bankrupt Venezuelan government. Desperate for revenues—and imbued with nationalist fervor—Castro decided to squeeze the NY&B, an American-owned asphalt company. The NY&B's initial concession had gone to an Irish-American from Manhattan named Horatio Hamilton. Hamilton, "a small thin man with a large nose and a full beard," traveled from New York to Caracas in the early 1880s as a vendor for the Vanderveer and Holmes biscuit company. Once there, he fell in love with a Venezuelan woman named Mercedes Smith. Hamilton chose his bride well: the Smith family had close ties to Venezuela's then-president, Antonio Guzmán Blanco, who chose to reward the happy couple with exclusive rights to exploit the asphalt deposits in what was then called the state of Bermúdez. (In 1909, the state was renamed Sucre.)[85] Hamilton contacted a trio of New York entrepreneurs, the Thomas brothers (William and Thomas) and their partner, Ambrose Carner. The three formed the New York and Bermúdez Company using $100,000 from the Thomas brothers and a $10,000 loan. Hamilton then sold the Bermúdez concession to the NY&B in return for a 90% stake in the company on November 16, 1885.[86]

By the 1890s the Bermúdez concession was producing only 18,000 tons of asphalt per year, compared with 220,000 tons from the Pitch Lake in southwest Trinidad. Pitch Lake was owned by the Trinidad Asphalt Company of New Jersey, which was in turn owned by Amzi Lorenzo Barber of New York. In 1893, Barber acquired an 85% stake in the NY&B. In 1897, Barber upped his stake to 99.8%, incorporating it into a new company, the London-registered (but American-owned) New Trinidad Lake Asphalt Company. In 1899, in response to a downturn in the asphalt market, Barber merged the New Trinidad Lake Asphalt Company into the Asphalt Company of America with the assistance of General Francis Greene, a war hero from the Philippines and a prominent Republican.[87] The asphalt trust had been born.

It was the entire asphalt trust of the United States, therefore, that Cipriano Castro chose to take on. The NY&B paid a production tax to Venezuela of 40 cents per ton in 1900, amounting to 7.9% of the company's revenue.[88] Castro needed more, and so he extorted the NY&B over a series of concession disputes. From Castro's point of view, the best thing about these disputes was that *they involved another American company*. This was not a coincidence, but a situation Castro deliberately contrived, in order to keep the United States neutral. In 1900, Castro invited representatives of the Warner-Quinlan Asphalt Company of Syracuse, New York, to Caracas. (Warner-Quinlan needed sources of asphalt outside the control of the trust.) Castro pointed them in the direction of properties inside the NY&B's concession, which the NY&B had left largely undeveloped. (The NY&B appears to have left most of its concession undeveloped.) Agents of Castro then sold the properties (without clear ownership) for $40,000.[89] The dispute immediately and unsurprisingly went into litigation.

Castro's plan to prevent American intervention worked. That is not to say that the United States did not voice loud protests—after all, General Greene was a personal associate of President McKinley and had served with Theodore Roosevelt on the New York City Board of Police Commissioners. Senator Boies Penrose (R-Pennsylvania) personally argued NY&B's case in the Senate. Warner-Quinlan, however, did not lack for Republican political connections. Charles Warner himself contacted Representative Michael Driscoll (R-New York, from Syracuse) and former senator Frank Hancock (R-New York). They arranged a personal meeting with Secretary of State John Hay to argue Warner-Quinlan's case. After the meeting, Hay instructed the U.S. minister in Venezuela, Francis Loomis, to remain neutral.[90]

Castro's pathway to extortion was now open. In December 1900, a Venezuelan court ruled against the NY&B, which did not help its case by getting caught attempting to bribe two judges with $10,000 in gold. With the moral high ground and American neutrality in hand, Castro's attorney general offered to resolve the NY&B's troubles for $400,000 and a 33% stake in the company. When the NY&B balked, the attorney general, Fabricio Conde, demanded $400,000 for the government and a $50,000 "commission" for himself. Ambrose Carner, the NY&B's man in Venezuela, countered with $250,000 but said he needed to contact New York for approval.[91] Instead of New York, however, Carner contacted the American minister, Loomis, who went ballistic. Loomis recommended that the United States dispatch gunboats.[92] Washington did, in fact, dispatch three warships to the Venezuelan coast—the USS *Hartford*, USS *Scorpion*, and USS *Buffalo*—but a second round of persuasive lobbying from Frank Hancock ensured that no demands were attached to the ships' arrival.[93] Castro happily ignored the warships off his coast: in fact, he began to expropriate other foreign companies in Venezuela. He used the same divide-and-conquer tactics against the Orinoco Iron Company, siding with another American in a legal dispute. He then commandeered the ships of the Orinoco Steamship Company, which other American companies hated for its hammerlock over shipping.[94] With (well connected!) Americans on all sides of Castro's expropriations, Washington had no incentive to act.

The United States did eventually intervene in Venezuela, but it was not to protect American investors. Rather, it was to stop a war between Venezuela and a British-German coalition. The conflict began because the asphalt trust decided to fund a violent rebellion against Castro. The trust shipped arms to Venezuela using British-flagged vessels, which Venezuela, not unreasonably, began to seize. The rebels also used a small U.K.-claimed island near Trinidad as a staging area, which Castro, again not unreasonably, occupied with Venezuelan troops. London's initial reaction, however, was to threaten Venezuela rather than crack down on the arms smuggling. Germany joined Britain because it feared the consequences of a unilateral British victory. Neither member of the coalition particularly wanted to go to war, but they bombarded Venezuela nonetheless in 1902 when Castro refused to accede to their demands. As a result, the United States was dragged into the conflict as a mediator.

The Roosevelt administration ultimately brokered a settlement that was exceedingly generous to *Venezuelan* interests. At the personal suggestion of U.S. secretary of state John Hay, President Castro appointed an American, Herbert Bowen, to negotiate on Venezuela's behalf.[95] The settlement considered only expropriation and war damage—sovereign debt was not included. American direct investors received an almost risible 0.5% on their claims; investors from other nations received 21.3%.[96]

Resisting Economic Nationalism in Mexico

When American interests were divided the United States did not act—but when they were united, U.S. presidents rarely hesitated. Consider the very different reaction by President William Howard

Taft to Mexico's attempt to expropriate foreign miners in 1907–9. In most matters political, President Porfirio Díaz was far more skilled than his Venezuelan counterpart. When it came to manipulating the U.S. political system, however, he was a piker in comparison with Castro. Díaz wanted to redistribute foreign mining assets to his political cronies, but he failed to split the American interests. As a result, the Taft administration threatened economic sanctions that would ensure that the assets Díaz wanted to redistribute would have no value. The technology of Taft's intervention—trade sanctions—was different from the dispatch of gunboats, but the effect was the same: Díaz backed down, and the miners kept their properties.

In 1907, Porfirio Díaz proposed to reform of the property rights governing foreign-owned mines. The first draft of the reform, written by a committee appointed by Development Minister Olegario Molina, was made public in February. Molina worked on it for another year, during which time Díaz secured permission from the Congress of Mexico to enact the law by decree, regardless of how the initial draft might be revised. A new draft, presented in 1908, contained several dramatic changes to the mining laws. First, the bill prohibited foreign individuals from acquiring mining properties in the northern border states. Second, it banned foreign corporations from acquiring mining properties *anywhere* in the Mexican republic. (The law allowed President Díaz to grant exemptions to foreign individuals, but not foreign companies.)[97] Since the vast majority of industrial metal production took place in the border states, and because almost all foreign investment in mining elsewhere came from corporations, the law essentially banned foreigners from participating in the mining sector. The only way around the ban would be for foreign companies to reincorporate in Mexico, which would require them to appoint Mexican nationals to their boards, providing Díaz with a useful source of patronage.

Virtually all of Mexico's industrial metal production was exported to the United States. This meant that all the U.S. government had to do to sanction Mexico was apply a retaliatory tariff, thereby killing the industry and taking the tax revenues of the Mexican government with it. In 1907 the United States imposed a 20% ad valorem duty on Mexican zinc ores. The tariff effectively killed the Mexican zinc-mining industry. It made a powerful warning to Díaz's government.[98]

The exact details of the negotiations among the miners, Porfirio Díaz, and President Taft are not available. Doubtless much of it took place in smoke-filled rooms. We do know, however, that the Taft administration protested against the proposed law. It was joined in this by the Chamber of Mines, which represented both foreign and domestic producers.[99] Díaz began to backpedal: he had the authority to enact the law by decree, but he chose not to do so.[100] He then, after meeting with his cabinet, chose to drop the article that made it unlawful for foreign corporations to acquire mines in Mexico.[101] He also relaxed the provisions of the bill that conditioned the circumstances under which foreign individuals could acquire property in frontier states.[102] Díaz then delayed the bill's passage through Congress in order that he could travel to El Paso to personally meet with Taft.[103] The Senate did not approve the law until November 20, 1909, and it did not go into effect until January 1, 1910—without the clauses limiting the activities of foreigners. The only restriction that remained was the eighty-kilometer exclusion zone along the border, in which foreign corporations could not hold mining titles. Foreign individuals could hold titles in this zone, but only with the explicit permission of the president. This restriction, however, had been a provision of Mexican mining law since 1856.[104] Finally, we know that Díaz granted these exemptions. The Mining Act of 1909 specified that existing foreign claims in the exclusion zone that did not obtain special presidential permission would be auctioned off.[105] None were. In short, the foreign miners, with the support of the Taft administration, forced Díaz to beat a strategic retreat.

The Creation of the First American Empire

Investors took the declaration of the Roosevelt Corollary as a credible commitment that the United States would, within limits, protect their property against political instability or predatory governments. The era saw a large and sustained drop in the bond spreads of the countries inside the American intervention sphere. Theodore Roosevelt's swift response to the collapse of Cuba in 1906 confirmed the interpretation of the bond markets: the United States was now in the empire business.

The problem was that once the United States took on the task of protecting property rights abroad, pressures at home made it difficult to stop. The markets (and the wealthy people and institutions that invested in them) priced in the expectation of American intervention. Domestic politics made it difficult for the United States to withdraw its promise to defend American property rights inside its intervention sphere; it also made it difficult for the government to delimit the boundaries of its intervention sphere. Wherever and whenever the United States was *capable* of intervening at limited cost, the pressures would be on to *actually* intervene. The intervention sphere that Teddy Roosevelt initiated would grow both wider and deeper.

four
The Trap Closes

True stability is best established not by military but by economic and social forces. Financial stability contributes perhaps more than any other one factor to political stability.

—*Secretary of State Philander Knox, June 15, 1910*

At the turn of the twentieth century, the leaders of American foreign policy believed they had identified poor fiscal conditions as *the* key factor destabilizing the nations of Latin America. In January of 1900, General Leonard Wood, the American military governor of Cuba, wrote to U.S. secretary of war Elihu Root: "When people ask me what I mean by stable government, I tell them that when money can be borrowed at a reasonable rate of interest and when capital is willing to invest in the island, a condition of stability will be reached."[1]

General Wood was an unusually flat-footed diplomat, but as a trained physician he diagnosed a relationship between fiscal health and political stability in America's satellites. Wood's diagnosis was shared by other political leaders. William Howard Taft's secretary of state, Philander Knox, believed that the root cause of default and expropriation was political instability—and that the root cause of political instability was poor tax collection. Knox, a corporate lawyer from Pittsburgh, had previously served as attorney general in the Republican administrations of William McKinley and Theodore Roosevelt. Together,

Taft and Knox crafted an approach that became known as dollar diplomacy. The government encouraged U.S. banks to extend loans to foreign regimes, with American nationals (or the U.S. Supreme Court) specified to oversee repayment or arbitrate disputes. In the event of default, the United States would roll out the solution that it believed had worked in the Dominican Republic: direct U.S. control over local fiscal institutions. With Americans in charge, revenues would increase, borrowing costs would go down, and political stability would result.

It was not clear, however, that the markets shared Leonard Wood's diagnosis. We do know that the market reacted very positively to the declaration of the Roosevelt Corollary.[2] Two possible channels could explain the reaction. The first possible channel is that investors believed that the United States would now step in and fix fiscal institutions. In this view, confidence came from the promise that American fiscal intervention would increase revenues and with that the security of property rights. The second possible channel is that investors believed that the United States would now sanction leaders that behaved badly. In this view, it did not matter whether American fiscal intervention worked to increase revenue. Rather, all that mattered was that foreign leaders viewed it as politically unpalatable—a punishment akin to a naval bombardment or landing marines. A fiscal takeover did not have to *work*; it merely needed to be unpleasant.

History can resolve the dispute. *Every* fiscal intervention failed to raise revenues, save the first one in the Dominican Republic. The Dominican success was due to the fact that rebel forces regularly sacked customhouses before the arrival of the Americans. Once U.S. officials were on the ground, rebel factions ceased most of their attacks on the customhouses. Moreover, the increase in government revenue failed to generate any of the hypothesized positive political effects. Greater revenue did not produce less corruption or greater political stability. Deprived of access to the customhouses, Dominican insurgents proved quite capable of raising revenues from the countryside.

The country soon relapsed into civil war, and the United States was forced to choose between allowing the Dominican state to collapse entirely and moving to a full-fledged occupation.

Fiscal interventions failed to increase revenue in Nicaragua, Liberia, Haiti, and Panama. Nor did they contribute to political stability. In the Haitian case, the situation became so bad that the United States had to take over the entire government. In Nicaragua, the United States never formally occupied the nation, but the marines spent years engaged in counterinsurgency campaigns in support of a government that was supposed to have become self-sufficient with the customs receivership. In Panama, American troops periodically had to leave their redoubts in the Canal Zone in order to restore order. Elsewhere states did not collapse, but the simple fact of placing American officials in charge did not alter the underlying dynamic of the countries' institutions.

The problem for American politicians became one of credibility. Powerful creditors believed that American fiscal takeovers were valuable because they humiliated the local government and thereby encouraged other governments to do what was necessary to avoid them. (This belief was not unfounded despite the negative short-term market reaction to the receiverships—the yields on debt issued by countries within the U.S. intervention sphere did not return to their pre-1904 levels until the onset of the Great Depression.) If an American administration refused to exercise its authority inside the intervention sphere, then it risked a meltdown in the value of American investments across the sphere. While such investments amounted to very little in proportion to domestic U.S. investments, they were owned by very wealthy and well-connected financiers who were quite capable of bringing political pressure to bear to defend them. As long as the political costs of American intervention remained low, U.S. administrations would continue to intervene.

Thus the anti-interventionist administration of Woodrow Wilson continued the policies of Theodore Roosevelt and William Howard Taft. Woodrow Wilson abhorred the notion that might makes right; respect for human rights and national integrity, not commercial or financial interests, should determine a nation's foreign policy. Eight years later, Republican Warren Harding campaigned for president by promising to abandon the foreign entanglements that Wilson found himself unable to avoid; he even struck a populist note by refusing to countenance an informal empire to protect wealthy bankers. Had either president been free to conduct his foreign policy as he liked, the first American empire would have withered away.

Yet the inexorable political logic of the empire trap meant that neither man was free to obey the dictates of his conscience—or even fulfill his campaign promises. The story of U.S. imperialism in the 1910s is a tale of attempted but failed withdrawals. Thanks to the American inability to break the vicious cycle of instability and fiscal misgovernment in its satellite states, efforts to retreat from the circum-Caribbean during the 1920s were a dismal failure. The "first American empire" created by Roosevelt's Corollary spread horizontally into more countries and vertically to become more interventionist inside Nicaragua, Haiti, Liberia, and the Dominican Republic. The constellation of domestic and overseas political forces that led Roosevelt and Taft to intervene was strong enough to overrule the ideological objections and campaign promises of their successors. Nor did the consistent failure of American intervention to fix foreign fiscal institutions have any effect on the growth of the empire.

Dominican Politics under the Receivership

We do not want to take them for ourselves. We do not want any foreign nations to take them for themselves. We want to help them.
—*Secretary of State Elihu Root, January 14, 1907*

In financial terms, the creation of the Dominican customs receivership was a resounding success. Government revenues leapt upward, the island's debt burden fell, the Haitian border came under control, and the Dominican Republic received $3.9 million ($74.9 million in 2011 dollars) in new lending. Revenues jumped because insurgents ceased their attacks on the customhouses—an effective way of improving the quality of governance, but one contingent on armed attacks being a problem in the first place. The United States hoped that by taking the customhouses out of contention, it would end the cycle of civil war. Three months into the receivership, Thomas Dawson (the chief U.S. representative to the Dominican government) wrote that there had been "a cessation of active plotting against the established government."[3]

Dawson was overoptimistic. Bouts of unrest occurred throughout the summer and early autumn of 1905, breaking into open rebellion in November. President Morales lost the support of his own cabinet. Fearing for his life, he fled the capital on Christmas Eve and joined forces with insurgents in the interior. In the words of Otto Schoenrich, "It was the anomalous spectacle of a president leading an insurrection against his own government."[4] In December, with order collapsing and coup rumors proliferating, Dawson asked for permission to land troops. To Dawson's evident surprise, Secretary of State Elihu Root vetoed the idea. "No troops are to be landed except when absolutely necessary to protect life and property of American citizens." Root took the opportunity to make it clear that the United States was there only because the Dominican government had invited them in. "Such protection . . . will extend to the peaceful performance of duty by the Americans who are collecting revenue in the customhouses so long as the Dominican government desires them to continue their service. If the Dominican government determines to end the *modus vivendi* with the United States, protection will extend to their safe withdrawal with their property."[5] In January 1906, Dominican insurgents attacked Puerto Plata, but the attack was halfhearted and repulsed before they could threaten the customs installations. (The rebel general Demetrio Rodríguez, who had earlier sought German support for the insurgency, died in the assault.) Morales, suffering from a broken leg, gave himself up to the American legation. On January 12, 1906, Morales left for Puerto Rico on a U.S. naval vessel. Ramón Cáceres, Heureaux's assassin, took over the presidency.[6] Fighting continued for several months in the northwest, but the Cáceres government soon gained control.

The events of 1905–6 convinced Dawson that his initial inclination had been correct—the receivership had increased political stability. In February 1906 he wrote, "The political leaders, knowing or thinking that by violence they cannot get control of the central government, that control of provincial governments would not be decisive under the present arrangement, and that they cannot get their hands on the customhouses, do not excite the local 'jefes' and professional fighters to take up arms."[7]

Within a few months, however, Dawson began once again to show doubts. "The longer I live in this country the more confident I am that the danger from the professional revolutionary class can be temporarily eliminated by keeping the customhouses out of their reach. But back of the danger from this class is the possibility of a revolution caused by sheer poverty."[8] This time, Dawson's prognostications proved correct. Gunmen ambushed President Cáceres's horse-drawn carriage on November 19, 1911. Cáceres died in the shootout. The ambushers, led by General Luis Tejera, fled in an automobile. During their escape, the conspirators managed to drive their car into a river. Tejera had been shot in the leg during the firefight with Cáceres; after rescuing him from the river, his coconspirators abandoned him in a hut by the road. The Dominican authorities soon caught up to Tejera, and he was summarily executed.[9]

Tejera's rapid capture and execution did not calm the political situation. With no constitutionally designated successor to Cáceres, the commander of the army, Alfredo Victoria, seized power. Victoria then convinced the Dominican Congress to install his uncle, Eladio Victoria, in the presidency. Victoria's election was widely viewed as having been secured by bribery, and the situation "relapsed with incredible rapidity into a state of complete anarchy."[10] Ex-president Horacio Vásquez organized an insurgency against the government, and by December the country was again in civil war. The violence prompted the United States to abandon the customhouses along the Haitian frontier (although they were not directly attacked), leading to questions about the United States' obligations to protect the Dominican customs service.[11]

Why did Dawson's initial hopes for political stability prove wrong? The first problem was that armed men and weapons moved freely across the Haitian border, and the Haitian government had an interest in promoting Dominican instability. On April 15, 1912, for example, the American legation reported, "The government has a well-equipped force in the field and could soon put down the rebellion on the northwestern frontier were it not for the effective aid they claim the Haitian government is giving it."[12] The United States had been able to control smuggling with a small frontier force, but preventing the movement of large armed forces was quite another feat. As mentioned above, the United States pulled its personnel and abandoned its posts on the Haitian frontier as the violence worsened, turning responsibility for the area over to the Dominican Army.[13]

This fed into the second, and larger, problem: the Dominican Army was badly organized and vastly corrupt. Officers routinely pocketed the pay due their men and plundered the areas where they operated. A depressing report from the U.S. legation on August 3, 1912, bluntly stated, "The revolutionists are no nearer to overthrowing the government than they were eight months ago, and the government is still spending enormous sums in military operations against the revolutionists. It is pretty generally admitted now that this condition of affairs is being purposely prolonged by the government military chiefs, who are enriching themselves at the expense of the troops."[14]

Finally, Dominican insurgents proved capable of extracting resources from the countryside; there was no need to seize the customhouses. Revenue came from loans, forced and otherwise, extracted from rural towns and plantations. These income sources probably would not have been enough to sustain a rebellion against a well-organized government, but the Dominican Republic did not enjoy such a government. By November 13, 1912, a special investigatory commission sent by President Taft reported, "The government, now thoroughly discredited and wholly unable longer to withstand the rebels unless materially assisted, desires to hold on to its present lucrative position as long as possible at any cost. On the other hand, the revolution, now stronger than ever and confident of ultimate success, is disinclined to make any terms with the government."[15]

The 1912 civil war in the Dominican Republic ended via *active* American intervention, backed by the threat of force. In November 1912, the Taft administration cut off the funds that it had been advancing to the Dominican government above the 45% floor established by the terms of the customs receivership. The United States then openly threatened to cut off the Dominican government from all funds *and begin funding the rebels itself* unless President Victoria stepped down.[16] The threat was reinforced by the presence of 750 marines just offshore.[17] On November 26, 1912, Victoria resigned. American representatives met with Vásquez and smoothed the selection of Monsignor Adolfo Nouel as provisional president.[18] The marines never disembarked.[19]

The American receivership could stabilize Dominican finances but not Dominican politics. Revenues went up because the Americans ended the attacks on the customhouses, but there was no way to get the government to spend the funds wisely or effectively. Corruption in the armed services ate away at the government's ability to combat rebellion. The countryside, meanwhile, provided rebels with ample sources of manpower and funds, while weapons and staging areas were readily available over the Haitian border.

The United States, however, could not easily walk away from the Dominican Republic. First, the rebellion threatened to turn into a war with Haiti—the Haitian government actively aided the rebels, and Dominican and Haitian troops clashed on multiple occasions. Second, politically influential Americans owned Dominican bonds, railways, banks, and plantations, all of which would be harmed by the collapse of the Dominican state. Finally, America's credibility was on the line. If the Dominican economy collapsed under the pressure of civil war, then there would be little trade for the customhouses to tax, under American administration or otherwise. And if that caused the Dominican Republic to default again, or prompted a new government to emulate Cipriano Castro and begin confiscating American investments, the effects would reverberate across the *entire* circum-Caribbean area. The empire trap, at least in the Dominican Republic, had closed.

The Path to Occupation

> The United States will never again seek one additional foot of territory by conquest.
>
> —*President Woodrow Wilson, speaking in Mobile, Alabama, 1913*

Monsignor Adolfo Nouel's accession to the Dominican presidency temporarily satisfied the various factions. The archbishop, however, found the duties of the executive distressing and wished to resign after two weeks in office. Only the entreaties of the American minister in Santo Domingo convinced him to stay on. Nouel attempted to buy off the competing factions. This strategy took its toll on the already depleted Dominican treasury, which in turn required the government to borrow more money from American banks. The Taft administration approved a $1.5 million loan from National City Bank on March 1, 1913[20] ($26 million in 2011 dollars, using the GDP deflator). The loan eased the fiscal burden on the treasury but did nothing to ease the physical burden on President Nouel. Despite a personal plea from president-elect Wilson, Nouel, in broken health, resigned shortly after Wilson's inauguration.[21]

The new provisional president, José Bordas, immediately faced a revolt launched by his own political allies. Secretary of State Bryan took a hard line with Bordas's opponents, stating that "should the revolution succeed, this Government [of the United States], in view of the President's declaration of policy, would withhold recognition of the *de facto* government, and consequently withhold the portions of the customs collections belonging to Santo Domingo as long as an unrecognized *de facto* government should exist."[22] Bryan succeeded in cobbling together a fragile settlement. As part of the agreement, and over President Bordas's strong objections, the United States insisted on supervising elections for a constitutional convention to be held on December 1913.[23] American observers failed to prevent Bordas from arresting six leaders of the opposition on charges of conspiracy on the second day of the election. Nevertheless, the opposition managed to win a large majority at the convention—but not enough for a quorum, which enabled Bordas's supporters to block progress on a new constitution.[24]

The political drama did not help Dominican finances, which rapidly fell into deficit as Bordas tried to buy off opposition. The U.S. State Department suggested that the Dominican government meet current expenses with $1.2 million ($20.8 million in 2011 dollars) left over from a 1907 bond sale intended for public works. The opposition-controlled Dominican Congress blocked this idea. As a stopgap, the American general receiver of the customhouses began to give the Bordas government daily advances to pay pressing claims and back salaries. This was the atmosphere in which Bordas decided to declare himself a candidate in the 1914 elections. Predictably, the opposition reacted violently. Bordas, desperate for money, agreed to appoint an American financial administrator to control spending in return for further advances.[25] (What the administrator was supposed to accomplish in light of the U.S. decision to abet Bordas's deficit spending was not clear.)

The Americans did not help their position by switching horses midstream. The Wilson administration realized that Bordas's position was untenable once violent opposition emerged. In the best tradition of American foreign policy, the United States then managed to work itself into the worst possible position by ordering the U.S. Navy to fire on Bordas's troops when it appeared they might attack the insurgent-held city of Puerto Plata. By mid-1914, the United States had retreated into a position of de facto neutrality in the Dominican civil war, not from a sense of idealism, but in because the U.S. Navy and Marine Corps found themselves overextended by other commitments, most notably the occupation of Veracruz, Mexico.[26]

President Wilson now chose to directly resolve the chaotic situation in the Dominican Republic. The "Wilson Plan," penned by the president himself, mandated that all factions lay down their arms and agree to a new provisional president. Failing that, the United States would appoint its own candidate. The provisional president would then hold elections, monitored by the United States. Wilson specified that Bordas would receive no special consideration.[27]

The Wilson Plan, at first, appeared to be a success. Within a week, all the major factional leaders had agreed to the plan, with the exception of Desiderio Arias, whose base on the northwest frontier near the Haitian border made his fiefdom practically independent. Two American commissioners left for the Dominican Republic in August, with a detachment of marines in the harbor in Santo Domingo.[28] The new provisional president, Ramón Báez, agreed to leave Arias's fief alone (against Secretary Bryan's wishes) in return for recognition of Báez's provisional presidency. Elections were held on October 25, 1914, with two American observers stationed at each polling place. The victor was an old name in Dominican politics: Juan Isidro Jiménez. Jiménez won a bare majority of the popular vote; his leading opponent, Horacio Vásquez, sued to block Jiménez's inauguration until personally called to task by Secretary of State Bryan. Jiménez took the oath of office on December 5, 1914.[29]

The Jiménez administration attempted to evade American supervision. Jiménez was reluctant to ratify the position of the American financial controller. Twice Jiménez put the controller's position up to a vote in Congress, and twice Congress rejected it. Jiménez consequently ruled that the controller had no authority to dictate Dominican finances.[30] (Jiménez's position is consistent with the view that local leaders considered foreign financial control to be politically damaging and something to be avoided.)

The United States, under Wilson's new secretary of state, Robert Lansing, responded negatively to Jiménez's decision. Whereas Bryan had been willing to let the Dominican Republic's financial duties under the 1907 treaty slide in the interest of political stability, Lansing believed that Jiménez's refusal to control spending merited action. The State Department proposed amending the treaty of 1907 to include a financial "adviser" with *full* control over the Dominican budget, an American-run constabulary, and American public health officials. The proposal, unsurprisingly, was politically toxic to Jiménez, who informed the State Department that the Dominican people were unanimously opposed.[31] Jiménez himself, however, was old and in poor health. He suffered a breakdown in the summer of 1915, leaving his divided cabinet to govern.[32]

The stalemate between the United States and the Dominican Republic remained until mid-April 1916, when Jiménez returned to duty. This precipitated a conflict, the immediate cause of which was Jiménez's decision to act against Desiderio Arias, who was now minister of war—but still in control of his own geographic fiefdom. Arias had accumulated power during Jiménez's illness, and his congressional supporters began impeachment proceedings against Jiménez. Jiménez, therefore, arrested Arias's chief lieutenants. Arias's supporters protested violently—it helped that Arias controlled the armed services—

and Arias himself holed up in an armed compound in the capital city. Jiménez in turn dismissed Arias and moved to extract him from his fortress.

The United States quickly got drawn in into the struggle between Arias and Jiménez. Small-arms fire struck the American legation. The American minister requested protection by U.S. Marines. On May 6, 1916, Jiménez's forces ran out of ammunition, at which point Jiménez requested American military support. The following day, Jiménez changed his mind—he withdrew his request and resigned as president. Arias's supporters in the Dominican Congress then attempted to elect Arias president, but opponents prevented them from reaching a quorum. At this point, the American minister believed military intervention was inevitable. On May 13, U.S. Navy admiral William Caperton, fresh from his duties in Haiti, threatened to occupy the capital city and disarm Arias by force. That evening, Arias abandoned Santo Domingo. U.S. Marines landed without opposition the next day.[33] The occupation of the Dominican Republic took less than two months. U.S. Marines took Arias's last stronghold in Santiago without firing a shot on July 6, 1916.[34]

Anti-American sentiment ran high, however, and the Dominican leadership failed to create a government and a role for the United States that the occupying power would accept. The Dominican Congress came close to electing Federico Henríquez y Carbajal, the chief justice of the Dominican Supreme Court. The problem was that Henríquez opposed any new treaties with the United States. The American minister unhelpfully suggested that the marines arrest some Dominican senators for supporting Henríquez's election. (Washington dismissed this suggestion.) On July 25, Congress elected as provisional president Federico Henríquez's brother, Francisco, instead of Federico. This fig leaf did not impress the United States, which cut off all revenues to the Dominican government.[35] President Francisco Henríquez proposed a compromise in which the United States would appoint an unofficial adviser and be permitted to station troops in the country. (The proposal had the benefit of committing the United States to support the Henríquez brothers against their armed opponents.) Admiral Charles Pond, who replaced Caperton in July as the chief U.S. military authority in the Dominican Republic, believed that the plan had merit. The State Department, however, vetoed it. The putative reason was fear that Henríquez would undercut any "unofficial" American agent in the country; the real worry was that the Henríquez brothers lacked domestic support.

Unfortunately for the Americans, the Dominican legislature refused to consider any other candidates for the presidency. On October 31, lawyers from the U.S. State Department and the navy reached the conclusion that the United States must either release the revenues to the Henríquez government or impose a formal occupation—with no revenue, the Dominican state was approaching total collapse. Faced with Dominican intransigence, and convinced the commitment would be low (and self-funded, via taxes imposed on the Dominican population), Wilson approved an occupation on November 26, 1916. "I am convinced it is the least of the evils in sight in this very perplexing situation." On November 29, Captain H. S. Knapp, U.S. Navy, began the process of taking over the government of the Dominican Republic, with himself as military governor.[36]

The American occupation of the Dominican Republic was in effect a military dictatorship. The Americans collected over 50,000 firearms, 200,000 rounds of ammunition, and 14,000 knives. The occupation government forbade Dominican newspapers from commenting on any of its acts. Phrases such as "freedom of thought" and "freedom of speech" were banned, as was the title "General" as applied to any Dominican. Knapp organized a new constabulary, the Guardia Nacional, based on the model of the Pennsylvania State Mounted Police. The quality of the Dominican recruits was not high. The guard's most able recruit, Rafael Leonidas Trujillo, was court-martialed in 1920 for holding a man for ransom and raping his teenage daughter; he was acquitted.[37]

The occupation government contracted several large foreign loans, allowing the American occupiers to expand the road and school system. Unfortunately, the replacement of Knapp with Rear Admiral Thomas Snowden as military governor in February 1919 revitalized anti-American sentiment. Snowden tried to mollify Dominican opinion by repealing censorship, but he undercut his own plan by replacing it with a decree that mandated jail time for seditious speeches or writings. Dominicans were not impressed that the occupation would no longer attempt to prevent them from protesting but would arrest them after the fact.

After a series of high-profile imprisonments of anti-American protestors brought the U.S. actions in the Dominican Republic under intense domestic criticism, the Wilson administration realized that an open-ended occupation was untenable.[38] (The approach of the 1920 election, in which Warren Harding campaigned *against* American involvement in Hispaniola and Nicaragua, helped to focus minds.) On November 29, 1920, the State Department submitted a plan to the secretary of the navy detailing a possible withdrawal "given the tranquility now existing in the Dominican Republic."[39] The plan, however, called for a withdrawal under a joint American-Dominican commission rather than the restoration of full sovereignty, and no prominent Dominican politicians could be found to support it. The occupation was handed off to the incoming Harding administration.

In conclusion, the Dominican customs receivership failed to produce the salubrious effects hoped for it. It did raise revenues in the short run, but it did not produce political stability. Nor did it stabilize Dominican finances in the long run, as instability begat pressures to use government revenues to buy off opponents and potential opponents. Eventually, the United States was forced into the Hobson's choice of taking over the government of the Dominican Republic or allowing the country to collapse. Woodrow Wilson, against his ideological predilections, chose the former. Wilson may not have sought conquest, but he certainly found it.

Nicaragua: Background to Intervention

> I have never been able to understand how compara-
> tively small American commercial interests backing
> the Revolution could control practically the whole
> American press and give such generally false views.
>
> *—Rear Admiral William Kimball, commander of the*
> *Nicaraguan Expeditionary Force*

The American experience in Nicaragua followed the Dominican example into failure. In fact, the Nicaraguan experience
was worse: the Nicaraguan customs receivership failed to increase revenues. (Nicaraguan customhouses had not been subject to regular attack before the receivership.) Pressed for revenues and beset by insurgents, the Nicaraguan state avoided
collapse because the Wilson administration found ways to sell
the U.S. Congress on the direct transfer of resources to Managua, something it manifestly failed to do in the Dominican
Republic. In addition, U.S. Marines stayed on for over a decade in support of the local government, and American officials
took over the management of its internal revenues. The United
States avoided the form of formal occupation but it did not
escape the substance.

Nicaragua had been a thorn in the side of American policy
in Central America since the 1893 rise to power of José Santos
Zelaya. A man of violent passions, Zelaya fervently believed
in Nicaraguan national greatness. In 1894, he established Nicaraguan control over the autonomous Mosquito Coast, historically a British protectorate centered on the Atlantic town of
Bluefields. Zelaya had regional ambitions, and in 1907 he supported Honduran exiles during their successful march on Tegu-
cigalpa while bloodily defeating a joint Honduran-Salvadoran
force at the battle of Namasigüe—only the intervention of U.S.
Marines prevented him from turning Honduras into Managua's puppet regime.[40]

Zelaya's domestic policies also antagonized the United States. In 1903, Zelaya began attacking private American interests. The first of these incidents came against the Massachusetts-based George Emery Company, owned by the eponymous George Emery. In 1893, the company received a mahogany lumber concession on the Atlantic coast, covering almost a fifth of Nicaragua's territory. The company paid $200,000 for the concession. (The payment was worth $4.7 million in 2011 dollars, using the GDP deflator—but measured as a proportionate share of America's GDP at the time, the concession cost was the 2011 equivalent of $196 million.)[41] In addition, the company paid an annual rent of $20,000 plus a per-log royalty. It ultimately employed 1,300 people and averaged $186,000 per year in profit between 1898 and 1906.[42] (The profits averaged $3.7 million per year in 2011 dollars.)[43] In 1906, Zelaya (truthfully) pointed out that Emery had failed to build fifty miles of promised railway and to reforest any of its logged-out properties. An arbitration panel held in Bluefields (run by two Americans, one appointed by Zelaya and the other by the company) fined Emery $12,000. The comparatively small fine displeased Zelaya, and in January 1907 he canceled the contact outright and took over the concession. The company cried expropriation, and the U.S. State Department protested.[44]

The second dispute was with La Luz y Los Angeles Mining Company. La Luz's 1903 contract gave its holding company a monopoly over prospecting across the concession area.[45] In 1907, Zelaya threatened to cancel the concession.[46] In 1908, he stepped up his bluster, with editorials in the (government-influenced) Managua press.[47] As the rhetoric escalated, in March 1909 the president of La Luz wrote to Secretary of State Philander Knox that he feared "unjust confiscation by the government of Nicaragua" and required "protection." He pointed out that La Luz was owned by important Pittsburgh interests.[48] Pittsburgh was Knox's hometown and political base. (Knox grew up in Brownsville, an industrial town on the

Monongahela River thirty-five miles south of Pittsburgh, and served as the junior senator from Pennsylvania between 1904 and 1909.)

La Luz's shareholders read like a who's who of Pennsylvania business: Thomas Riter, the primary shareholder, was the president of the Riter-Conley Manufacturing Company, which made blast furnaces and other heavy capital goods for U.S. Steel. (Riter-Conley was the largest steel construction firm in the United States.) The next two largest shareholders were the Fletcher brothers, Gilmore and Henry. Gilmore served as vice president of Riter-Conley, while Henry was a career diplomat. They were followed by William Rees (president of a Pittsburgh manufacturer of paddle wheelers), Durban Home (director of the Union National Bank), W. W. Blackburn (a vice president of Carnegie Steel), Robert Pitcairn (superintendent of the Pittsburgh Division of the Pennsylvania Railroad, director of two banks, and a personal friend of Andrew Carnegie), and Daniel Clemson (president of Carnegie Natural Gas and a director of Carnegie Steel).[49] These were all highly connected individuals, but the closest link was between the Fletcher family and Secretary Knox: Knox had worked for the Fletchers in Pittsburgh before joining government service.[50]

Zelaya showed little fear in going after American interests, but until 1909 he was careful to remain on the good side of the United Fruit Company, which he viewed as his protector against the U.S. government. Zelaya granted the Bluefields Steamship Company (51%-owned by United Fruit) a monopoly over the banana trade. In exchange, United Fruit paid $15,000 per year to the Nicaraguan government and another $10,000 to President Zelaya personally.[51] (In 2011 dollars Zelaya received $255,000 for his trouble. On the other hand, the world was much poorer around the turn of the twentieth century: after accounting for the growth of U.S. GDP, United Fruit was paying Zelaya the 2011 equivalent of $9.8 *million* per year.) In addition, United Fruit arranged a $1 million loan from the National State Bank of New Orleans.[52]

Zelaya's problem was that the steamship concession gave United Fruit a lock over roughly six hundred independent planters on the Atlantic coast. This situation made the planters unhappy with Zelaya's regime. This problem was compounded by ethnic differences: the Bluefields planters were either white American settlers or the black English-speaking descendants of migrants from the British West Indies.[53] The planters organized boycotts in 1901 and 1905; in 1903 they unsuccessfully tried to create an independent competing company. The Nicaraguan government responded by seizing and destroying the bananas headed for the independent shipper. Zelaya attempted to mollify the planters by allowing them to win a 1907 case against United Fruit before his own handpicked Supreme Court but then refused to enforce the decision.[54]

In 1909, Zelaya's balancing act collapsed. He raised export taxes on bananas and import duties on the goods the planters consumed. Protests prompted Zelaya to backtrack on the import duties, but in April the planters declared their intention to launch another boycott against United Fruit. The aim was to force the company to increase the price it paid for bananas. This time, Zelaya gave the planters his support.[55] Unfortunately, he tried to have it both ways. When the strikers attacked growers who continued to sell to United Fruit, Zelaya threatened to shoot the strikers and dispatched troops from the town of Rama to protect growers aligned with United Fruit. The soldiers, however, failed to arrive. United Fruit decided that Zelaya had double-crossed them, and appealed to the Taft administration. Taft dispatched a gunboat to Bluefields. At this point, Zelaya ordered the local governor to arrest hundreds of striking planters, under the rubric of heading off an American invasion.[56]

Zelaya had now managed to alienate all potential bases of support. The strike petered out but continued to generate dramatic incidents—such as the moment on May 17, 1909, when the pistol-packing wives of three imprisoned strikers boarded a Bluefields Steamship Company vessel loaded with bananas and destroyed the entire cargo. These incidents cost him the support of the local population. United Fruit, meanwhile, remained convinced that Zelaya had doubled-crossed it.[57] In October, the governor of Bluefields Province, Juan José Estrada, revolted against Zelaya. Estrada's financial backing came from Adolfo Díaz, an executive in the La Luz y Los Angeles Mining Company.[58] Díaz earned only $1,000 per year from the mining company ($25,200 in 2011 dollars) but somehow managed to loan Estrada *$600,000* for weapons and supplies.[59]

Estrada's revolt enjoyed the not-very-tacit support of the U.S. consul in Bluefields, Thomas Moffat.[60] On October 7, 1909, Moffat informed his superiors that the revolt would break out the next day and that the new government would desire U.S. recognition.[61] Zelaya's response, if not exactly swift (owing to poor communications between the Atlantic coast and Managua) was certainly brutal. Zelaya executed two American private contractors, Lee Leroy Cannon and Leonard Groce, captured attempting to mine the San Juan River.[62] (Both Americans lived in Bluefields Province; Cannon was a civil engineer and Groce a miner, the latter with a Nicaraguan wife and four children. They owned land in the area, and Cannon served on Estrada's staff.)[63]

The execution of the two Americans provoked a firestorm in the United States. President Taft ordered the formation of the Nicaraguan Expeditionary Force. On December 20, 1909, a regiment of U.S. Marines landed at Corinto, on the Pacific coast, less than a hundred miles from Managua.[64] American force levels quickly escalated to roughly 2,700. Zelaya, recognizing that he had been stalemated, fled on a Mexican warship stationed at Corinto, abetted by the Nicaraguan Expeditionary Force's commanding officer, Rear Admiral Kimball.[65] José Madriz assumed the presidency, but he stepped down on August 21, 1910 under American pressure. Juan José Estrada took over.

Nicaragua: Political Alignments behind Intervention

Intervention was easier when economic, strategic, and domestic political considerations pointed in the same direction. In the Nicaraguan case, the United States had no strategic reason to intervene—by 1907, the United States had successfully contained the Zelaya government. His neighbors certainly no longer believed Zelaya's regime to be a threat. When the U.S. government issued a "thinly veiled invitation to wage war against Nicaragua," the Costa Rican government demurred, as did Nicaragua's other neighbors. The Mexican government made it clear that it no longer considered Zelaya to be a destabilizing force.[66] That said, while the United States had little strategic reason to depose Zelaya in 1909, it also had little strategic reason to *refrain* from doing so. In April 1909 the Mexican government declared that it had no "practical interest" in Central America.[67] Mexico's neutrality removed the last strategic barrier to intervention.

American creditors had lent little to Nicaragua, because Zelaya preferred to take loans from European sources. In May 1909, Zelaya signed an agreement with a joint British-French group headed by the Ethelburga Syndicate of London for a £1.25 million loan to build a railroad to the Atlantic coast.[68] Secretary Knox asked the British and French governments to pressure the bankers into dropping the loan, but this resulted only in keeping the issue from being officially quoted on the Paris Bourse.[69] The U.S. objection was that Zelaya might use the money for the "purchase of munitions to maintain his tyranny and to enable him to attack neighboring states."[70] This was almost certainly the real reason—there is no evidence to support the idea that American bankers actively pushed to overthrow Zelaya in order to gain the dubious privilege of lending more to the Nicaraguan government.

Direct investors appear to have been the key drivers of the intervention. The primary evidence in support of this is the congressional testimony given by the U.S. consul in Bluefields, Thomas Moffat. Moffat explicitly told Congress, under oath, that the La Luz conflict was the reason for the intervention.[71] A telling series of exchanges between the State Department and company officials supports Moffat's testimony. On September 28, 1909, the company's president informed Knox that an agent, Captain Gardyne Stewart, would be traveling to Nicaragua to meet with President Zelaya "in the interest of our mining properties." Since "the owners of these properties and concessions" were "above all Pittsburgh interests" who had "upwards of a million dollars invested," he hoped that Knox could "give the Captain some of [his] valuable time in connection with the matter."[72] Knox did meet Stewart and broke off relations with Zelaya on December 1, after which Stewart thanked State "for its action in reference to the matter in question."[73]

American business interests also gave Estrada financial support, with the blessing of the State Department and in contravention of the Neutrality Act. State estimated that Estrada received at least $1 million from American interests.[74] Not only did the U.S. government refrain from enforcing the Neutrality Act against Estrada's supporters; it actively pressured the Honduran government to release a weapons-carrying ship.[75] Moffat reported that Estrada received at least 3,100 rifles and 300,000 rounds of ammunition from private U.S. sources.[76]

Did popular opinion act as a check on American intervention? The answer appears to be no: the execution of Cannon and Groce gave the companies in Nicaragua an opportunity to mobilize popular sentiment *against* the Nicaraguan government.[77] Rear Admiral William Kimball, unenthused with his role in leading the Expeditionary Force, wrote about the reaction to the murders: "I have never been able to understand how comparatively small American commercial interests backing the Revolution could control practically the whole American press and give such generally false views."[78]

Nicaragua: Failure of Intervention

The government of Nicaragua has also decided to engage an American citizen as collector general of customs. The work of the American financial adviser should accomplish a lasting good of inestimable benefit to the prosperity, commerce, and peace of the Republic.

—*President William Howard Taft*

The Taft administration believed that financial stability would lead to political stability. The administration's terms, therefore, included a customs receivership run by American officials, the establishment of a Nicaraguan central bank controlled by American bankers, and the appointment of an American adviser to bring Nicaragua onto the gold standard. On June 6, 1911, a loan treaty was signed in Washington and quickly ratified by the Nicaraguan National Assembly. The treaty, however, stalled in the U.S. Senate because of Democratic skepticism. Nevertheless, the American firm of Brown Brothers and Seligman proposed a short-term loan, contingent on the creation of an American-run customs collectorship. The Nicaraguan assembly agreed, and Clifford Ham became collector of customs. The convention allowed Ham to issue new customs regulations, but he could not unilaterally change tariff rates.[79] Taft, for his part, followed Roosevelt's 1905 precedent and authorized the receivership via executive order, sans treaty.

The Nicaraguan receivership was not a great success. Nicaraguan insurgents never used the customhouses as a source of revenue. Nor did the Nicaraguan government lack control of a key border with a hostile government, the way the Dominican Republic lacked control over the Haitian frontier. Real revenues rose during the first two years of the receivership, but to levels well within the recent past. Revenues then fell dramatically in 1914 and 1915, owing to the combination of the outbreak of World War 1 and a plague of locusts. (The locusts ruined the coffee crop in several counties, most notably Matagalpa.)[80] Nominal customs revenue in 1913 surpassed those of 1906, but only by 8.4%, and only in that year. Real revenue actually *fell* (see figure 4.1). The Nicaraguan government stabilized its total revenues by taking fiscal measures *outside* American control: it retained the state rum and tobacco monopolies against U.S. advice, raised stamp taxes, and imposed a property tax at a rate of $5 per $1,000 assessed value, above a $3,000 exemption.[81]

The receivership also failed in political terms. The United States' handpicked leader for Nicaragua, Juan José Estrada, turned out to be a paranoid drunk who quickly fled the country.

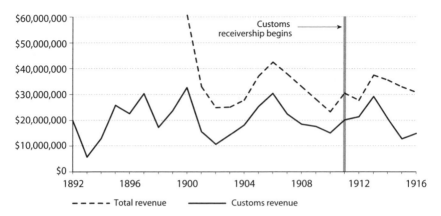

Figure 4.1. Nicaraguan fiscal revenues, 1892–1916, 2009 dollars

Source: The Statesman's Year-Book (various years); *Kimber's Record of Government Debts and Other Foreign Securities* (1922), pp. 645–46; *Latin-American Year Book for Investors and Merchants for 1918* , p. 455; and the *Memoria del Recaudor General de Aduanas por 18 Diciembre 1911 a 30 Junio 1913* (Washington, D.C.: GPO, 1913), pp. 44–46, 63, and 74.

Note: All values deflated using the U.S. GDP deflator.

His successor, Adolfo Díaz, proved to be a corporate nonentity unable to manage Nicaraguan national politics. The receivership created a problem of legitimacy for the Díaz government, thus adding to the political instability it was intended to avoid. An emergency goodwill visit by Secretary of State Knox to Managua in March of 1912 triggered anti-American protests, graffiti, and veiled insults from Nicaraguan legislators. Rumors flew of Knox's impending assassination, and the secretary quickly left the capital.[82] By the end of July of 1912, Díaz's own minister of war, General Luis Mena, was in open revolt. The American minister to Nicaragua, George Weitzel, wrote that U.S. investments were threatened by the unrest. Within a week, Taft authorized the use of U.S. Marines stationed in Nicaragua to support the government.[83] Mena surrendered at the end of September—his war-fighting abilities compromised by a severe attack of dysentery—and the United States authorized a "legation guard" of marines in Managua to serve as a rapid response force against threats to the Díaz regime.[84]

The revolt exacerbated the Nicaraguan fiscal deficit, and Díaz found himself taking out, in the words of the U.S. minister, "certain internal loans the conditions of which are improvident if not unconscionable." The money went to support the day-to-day operations of the government.[85] The impending replacement of William Taft with Woodrow Wilson put pressure on both the State Department and Díaz to find a quick solution to the fiscal problem. At first, they rushed through the Chamorro-Weitzel Treaty, which offered Nicaragua $3 million ($52.1 million in 2011 dollars) in return for the option to construct a transisthmian canal across Nicaragua (which would never be built) and basing rights for the U.S. Navy (which would never be used). Nicaragua approved the treaty on February 8, and State officials rushed to Washington, but the congressional session closed before the Senate could act.[86] (Getting the treaty to D.C. faster would have made no difference: the Democratic minority was strongly opposed.) On March 3, 1913, the day before Woodrow Wilson's inauguration, Brown Brothers and Seligman agreed to advance Nicaragua $150,000 and all customs receipts through June 30.[87]

Trapped in Nicaragua

The Nicaraguan situation at the beginning of 1913 looked like a countdown to disaster. The Díaz government was badly pressed for money. Nicaragua's arrangement with its American lenders was due to expire in June, but Democratic intransigence stalled the aid treaty in the Senate. In May, the State Department briefed Secretary of State Bryan on the previous administration's efforts in Nicaragua: "What Nicaragua needs and wants is peace. It seems doubtful whether she can secure it without some sort of support and cooperation on the part of the United States. . . . Perhaps the most marked instance of the so-called dollar diplomacy of the past administration was to secure these results to Nicaragua by means of the loan convention. The time has now arrived for the present administration to define its attitude towards that loan convention and towards the Nicaraguan questions in general."[88]

Bryan realized that the loan treaty of 1911 drafted under Taft was unviable. He instead decided to revise the treaty negotiated by Weitzel a few months earlier. The new treaty retained the Chamorro-Weitzel Treaty's essential feature: the United States would pay Nicaragua $3 million for the right-of-first-refusal on the construction of a transisthmian canal. Bryan's version added a ninety-nine-year lease on the Corn Islands off Nicaragua's Caribbean coast.[89] (The fact that the United States had no intention of using the lease was a feature of the agreement, not a bug, although the United States eventually built a lighthouse on Little Corn Island.) It also included a Platt-style amendment allowing for American military intervention. President Díaz welcomed the treaty "so that my countrymen may see Nicaragua's credit improved, her natural resources developed, and peace assured throughout the land."[90]

The problem was that the Platt-style amendment proved a bridge too far for the Senate Foreign Relations Committee. It balked at the prospect of open-ended involvement.[91] Unfortunately, Nicaragua's crisis was not going to wait on the Senate. Nearly bankrupt, Nicaragua negotiated a deal with Brown Brothers and Seligman in what would today be called privatization: $2 million in exchange for majority control of the Pacific Railroad and the National Bank.[92] Though Bryan mistrusted Brown Brothers and Seligman, he personally approved the contracts. In an attempt to avoid the dynamics of the empire trap, Bryan stated "this approval does not commit this Department to any further action, but is merely advisory." The creditors nonetheless interpreted State Department involvement as a guarantee, rather than a disavowal. The contracts were signed on October 8, 1913.[93]

The advance postponed but did not forestall more U.S. involvement. Most of the $2 million from Brown Brothers and Seligman went to Nicaragua's earlier obligations. By the beginning of 1914 Nicaragua was asking Brown Brothers and Seligman, through Bryan, for new loans.[94] The government financed itself through a combination of advances from President Díaz's own fortune, an emergency loan from the (now American-controlled) National Bank, and a November 1914 advance from Brown Brothers and Seligman.[95] Meanwhile, Bryan continued to push for the treaty he had negotiated as a means to aid Nicaragua. He removed the Platt provisions, and the Bryan-Chamorro Treaty was submitted to the U.S. Senate on August 5, 1914. Even then, the agreement languished for eighteen months until strong-armed through by President Wilson.[96]

The delay did not improve Nicaragua's finances. The onset of World War I cut off Nicaragua's European market. Brown Brothers and Seligman and the British bondholders agreed to temporarily suspend payments under promises that they would be compensated from the canal-treaty money. The problem was that the State Department also promised other foreign and U.S. claimants that *they* would be repaid from the treaty fund. The treaty passed the Senate in February 1916, but disputes froze $2.4 million of the $3 million.[97] Nicaragua was essentially broke, and the State Department pressed hard for Nicaragua to accept American supervision of its finances.

The new Nicaraguan president, Emiliano Chamorro (elected at the beginning of 1917) delayed acceptance of a financial adviser for months—at one point he threatened to take back control of the customhouses—but the outcome was not seriously in doubt. On October 20, 1917, Nicaragua signed a set of contracts with the United States and the bankers. The Nicaraguan budget would be limited to $95,000 per month, with overages of one-third more subject to the approval of a high commission made up of one Nicaraguan, one American, and an umpire chosen by the U.S. secretary of state. The treaty funds were divided among the British Ethelburga bondholders, Brown Brothers and Seligman, the National Bank of Nicaragua, and assorted claims, leaving $500,000 for the Nicaraguan government to pay back salaries.[98] The United States reappointed its former collector of

Figure 4.2. Nicaraguan government revenues, 1916–35, 2009 dollars
Source: The Statesman's Year-Book (various years); *Kimber's Record of Government Debts and Other Foreign Securities* (1922), pp. 645–46; *Latin-American Year Book for Investors and Merchants for 1918*, p. 455; *Latin-American Year Book for Investors and Merchants for 1920*, p. 532; and Knut Walter, *The Regime of Anastasio Somoza* (Chapel Hill: University of North Carolina Press, 1993), p. 37.

customs, Clifford Ham, as collector-general, now in charge of all Nicaraguan revenue institutions; his assistant, Irving Lindberg, who had come to Nicaragua in 1912 to reform its accounting system, became high commissioner. (Lindberg would remain at his post until 1952.)[99]

Nicaraguan finances improved through the remainder of Chamorro's and Wilson's terms in office.[100] (See figure 4.2.) The increase in collections, however, cannot be attributed to better management resulting from the creation of the office of high commissioner. Starting in 1919, the Nicaraguan government (admittedly at Lindberg's urging) began to impose a variety of new surtaxes, beginning with a 12% across-the-board hike in customs rates in 1919.[101] Moreover, tropical exports sustained a prolonged boom between 1921 and 1928. Rising tariff rates and internal taxes, combined with an export boom, unsurprisingly produced rising revenues.

In short, America was drawn into Nicaragua step-by-step and then found it impossible to withdraw despite the failure of intervention to produce the desired effects. U.S. economic interests feared expropriation by Zelaya and found ways to get the Taft administration to protect them. The Taft administration tried to solve what it believed to be Nicaragua's underlying problem through a combination of military and fiscal intervention. The latter, however, further bound Nicaraguan interests to the United States, both via the increasing involvement of American financiers and the unwillingness of the Wilson Administration to allow Nicaragua to descend into chaos on its watch. Woodrow Wilson's tenure saw the American government move deeper into Latin American affairs—even while preoccupied by the unfolding horrors on the battlefields of Flanders, and in spite of Wilson's ideological commitment to the self-determination of peoples. Neither presidential inclinations nor total war in Europe managed to dissolve, deflect, or distract the coalition of interests that powered the empire trap.

Taking Haiti

It is a very perilous thing to determine the foreign policy of a nation in the terms of material interest.
—*President Woodrow Wilson*

The U.S. presidential election of 1912 was a three-party race: Taft as the Republican incumbent; Theodore Roosevelt as the candidate of the newly created Progressive Party, split from the left wing of the Republicans; and New Jersey governor Woodrow Wilson as the candidate of the Democratic Party. A relative unknown, Wilson had leveraged his academic celebrity as a political scientist to win the governorship of New Jersey, and then won the Democratic nomination for the presidency on the forty-sixth ballot. Taft's intervention in Nicaragua was not a central campaign issue, but his pro-banking stance and ties to the "money trust" certainly were. Taft was repudiated at the polls, receiving 24% of the popular vote and winning only Utah and New Hampshire. Wilson won the election with 42% of the popular vote and a sweeping 435 electoral votes.

Wilson is remembered as one of the United States' most idealistic presidents. The term Wilsonian has come to describe a style of foreign policy that rejects realpolitik in favor of institutionalized cooperative internationalism, political democracy, and the self-determination of peoples. Consequently, his administration presents a stress test of the hypothesis that it was extremely difficult for elected American governments to refrain from intervening on behalf of their citizens' overseas economic interests.

Wilson did not want to run an empire, formal or informal. Outlining his Latin American policy in a famous speech in Mobile, Alabama, on October 27, 1913, Wilson stated, "It is a very perilous thing to determine the foreign policy of a nation in the terms of material interest. It not only is unfair to those with whom you are dealing, but it is degrading as regards your own actions. . . . Human rights, national integrity, and opportunity as against material interests—that, ladies and gentlemen, is the issue which we now have to face. I want to take this occasion to say that the United States will never again seek one additional foot of territory by conquest."[102]

The United States' prior commitments and its powerful overseas interests, however, made disengagement difficult and further entanglements easy. The Sisyphean labor of institutional reform—something Wilson managed to accomplish during his tenure as governor of New Jersey—proved to be too much when it came to dismantling the first American empire. In an irony of history, Wilson's high-mindedness would lead him to become the most interventionist American president of his era.

President Wilson's first actions appeared to foreshadow a withdrawal of the United States from other countries' affairs. He quickly disbanded the moribund international consortium for Chinese investment and currency stabilization, thinking it represented too much interference in internal Chinese affairs. He attempted to repair some of the diplomatic collateral damage caused by the Roosevelt and Taft administrations' machinations over the Panama Canal, repealing a provision in the Panama Canal Act of 1912 that granted preferential treatment to U.S. intercostal shipping. Wilson also negotiated an indemnity and official apology to the government of Colombia for Roosevelt's "taking" of Panama in 1904, although he failed to get the agreement through the Senate.

China and the Panama Canal Act were low-hanging fruit. The Chinese consortium was already essentially dead, while the Panama Canal Act was a clear violation of American treaty obligations and had already caused a serious diplomatic rift with Great Britain. Wilson's anti-imperial idealism would be put to its real test in the Western Hemisphere, starting in Haiti. There, the considerably greater American interests at stake would lead to a very different outcome.

The Taft administration wanted to use the tools of dollar diplomacy to stabilize Haiti. The political circumstances of independent Haiti, however, made the issuance of a controlled loan by the United States problematic. Haiti's political class looked to France, not the United States, while French and German commercial interests dominated the economy. In 1910, a loan of 65 million francs ($12.5 million, or $226 million in 2011 dollars) was issued by a consortium of French and German interests, in return for control of Haiti's National Bank. The U.S. State Department objected, calling it "plainly unconscionable" and unfair to the Haitian government, but dropped its complaint after the consortium agreed to include American banks.[103]

The trouble began when Haitian revolutionaries seized the customhouse at Cap Haitien in January 1914, while a different set of revolutionary forces under the Zamor brothers took control of the capital.[104] American investment in the island was *relatively* small—roughly $15 million, or $258 million in 2011 dollars. That said, the American economy was much smaller in 1914 than it was in 2011—relative to U.S. GDP, $15 million in 1914 was the equivalent of $6.3 billion in 2011. That was enough of an interest to generate substantial political pressures.

Strategic concerns over the possibility of German involvement gave business interests the "in" they needed to convince an anti-interventionist administration to protect their interests. Secretary Bryan came under pressure from Boaz Long (the head of the Division of Latin American Affairs) and Roger Farnham, the vice president of the Haitian National Bank (in which U.S. banks held a 40% stake). Long had deep ties to Wall Street and a personal friendship with an attorney for United Fruit—making him the perfect conduit for the business community to make its desires known to the new Democratic administration.[105] In May 1913, Long warned that the French had dispatched a gunboat to Haiti to protect their interests. More seriously, the next month Long told Bryan that the German government was trying to obtain a naval base at Mole St. Nicholas. Bryan's response was to try to negotiate Mole St. Nicholas's sale to the United States; that failed, but the Haitian government under President Michel Oreste agreed not to sell the harbor to any other power.[106] Bryan was therefore understandably concerned when Oreste's government fell to rebellion in January 1914, opening the possibility that a pro-German faction might come to power.

Roger Farnham "pushed the right buttons" when he telegrammed Bryan warning that French and German interests were behind the revolt and would dominate the new government.[107] Fighting continued throughout 1914. The Haitian congress confirmed Zamor in the presidency on February 8, but Bryan refused recognition until March. Bryan demanded that Zamor cede Mole St. Nicholas to the United States *and* give Washington control over the customhouses. Long advised Bryan to withhold recognition, but Bryan reversed course in March, in the hope that a conciliatory position would induce Zamor to agree to American terms. (Despite the Dominican and Nicaraguan experiences, Bryan still seemed to believe that a customs receivership would promote political stability.) Zamor rebuffed Bryan and upped the anti-American rhetoric. By July, the situation had grown so tense that Franklin Roosevelt, the assistant

secretary of the navy, ordered 750 marines based in Guantánamo to prepare for action in Haiti.[108]

The outbreak of war in Europe simplified the American position vis-à-vis the European powers, while causing the Haitian
economy—reliant on the export trade—to deteriorate even further. Had American concerns been strategic, no intervention in
Haiti should have been forthcoming: Germany dropped all attempts to obtain a base on Hispaniola after August 1914. In fact,
Germany went so far as to drop its largely pro forma objections
to an American customs receivership in Haiti. In the words of
historian Melvin Small, "The demand was forgotten after the
guns of August had sounded, for the Germans could ill afford to
alienate the number one neutral after August 4."[109] The problem
was that America's interests in Haiti were *not* all strategic.

The Haitian government collapsed over the course of 1915.
Joseph Davilmar Théodore overthrew the Zamor administration on November 7, 1914. Vilbrun Jean Guillaume Sam in
turn overthrew Théodore on March 4, 1915. In both cases, the
United States considered intervention, but the transition between governments was too rapid. On July 27, 1915, an uprising
in Port-au-Prince caught President Sam by surprise. Angry mobs
surrounded the presidential palace. Sam fled to the French legation, but not before ordering the execution of over a hundred
political prisoners, including former president Oreste Zamor.
On learning of the executions, the city's reaction was immediate
and violent. At 11:00 a.m. the next day, the chargé d'affaires
of the American legation telegraphed Washington one of the
most chilling notes in American diplomatic history: "At 10:30
mob invaded French Legation, took out President, killed and
dismembered him before Legation gates. Hysterical crowds pa-
rading streets with portions of his body on poles. *U.S.S. Washington* entering harbor."[110]

Wilson and his new secretary of state, Robert Lansing, were
appalled. Port-au-Prince was starving, its foreign population
terrified, and it seemed the broken pieces of the Haitian fiscal
apparatus merely served to fund a cycle of violent and preda-

tory governments. Wilson, after several days of consideration (and dire reports from Roger Farnham) decided to intervene in Haiti without a clear casus belli, writing to Lansing that "we do not have the legal authority to do what we apparently ought to do. . . . I suppose there is nothing for it but to take the bull by the horns and restore order."[111] Wilson's aims were humanitarian—but U.S. economic interests had given his administration a strong push.

The United States very quickly used its power to shape Haitian political outcomes. The most likely candidate to succeed Sam, Rosalvo Bobo, was viewed with suspicion by American authorities for his pro-German sentiments and his ties to insurgent forces now stationed in the city. The United States preferred the president of the Haitian Senate, Sudre Dartiguenave. The United States closely stage-managed the election by prohibiting all Haitians without a pass from the Haitian congress or the American military command from entering the building where the vote was taking place, and disarming those visitors who did. (Haitian legislators were normally allowed to keep their personal weapons.) Under those conditions, Dartiguenave won handily.[112] President-elect Dartiguenave soon felt the sharp limits to his power when, in discussions over a new treaty with the United States, he threatened to resign if the United States refused to consider his government's modifications to the text. The State Department informed him that it would happily establish a military government should he choose to renounce his office.[113] Dartiguenave signed the treaty.

Under the terms of the treaty of 1915, the United States would collect Haitian custom revenues, supervise Haiti's budget, manage Haiti's sanitation and establish public health programs, and organize an American-commanded constabulary—the Gendarmerie—on the Philippine model until enough Haitian officers became qualified.[114] Under the agreement, the United States continued to enforce the 1905 customs code. Any gain would be due to greater efficiency and less corruption, not a change in tariff rates. The treaty established American control in Haiti for ten years.

Haiti's new financial adviser, Addison Ruan, wanted to convince the French government to convert Haitian bonds held in France, in order to give Haiti more financial breathing space. In order to finance this settlement, the Haitian government would require a new and rather substantial loan issued from American banks. The State Department advised that these loans would best be made with an additional treaty extension in order to minimize perceived investor risk. With this in mind, on March 28, 1917, the Haitian government agreed to a protocol extending the life of the treaty from ten to twenty years. Ruan, however, was unable to negotiate a suitable price for the older bonds with the French government, while New York banks would only commit to a loan if the French agreed. Ruan's deal fell through, leaving Haiti with a longer treaty commitment but nothing to show for it.[115]

Did the U.S. occupation succeed in generating more revenue for the Haitian government? The data indicate that the United States was no more efficient in running the customs service than the Haitians had been previously. There are few good figures for the value of trade before the U.S. occupation (and such figures would be endogenous to customs collections), but revenues before occupation are available from two sources: *The Statesman's Year-Book* and a report prepared by the office of the American fiscal representative in 1935.[116] Both sources tell the same story: there was no discrete jump in revenue collection after the American takeover (see figure 4.3.) . Revenue gradually increased from its 1917 low but it never surpassed historic highs.

Nor did American fiscal intervention bring political stability. Both the United States and Haiti agreed that the treaty of 1915 was ill suited for the existing Haitian Constitution. The United States, Dartiguenave, and Dartiguenave's political opposition—increasingly anti-American in attitude—each favored a new constitution for their own reasons. The Constitution of 1918, however, was not a purely Haitian document, but one closely vetted by the State Department, the U.S. Navy, and the American Legation in Haiti. (Famously and untruthfully, Franklin Roosevelt claimed to have written the text while assistant secretary of the

Figure 4.3 Haitian customs revenue, 1901–34, millions of 2010 dollars

Source: *The Statesman's Year-Book* (various years) and Haiti, *Annual Report of the Fiscal Representative for the Fiscal Year October 1933–September 1934* (Port-au-Prince: Imprimerie de l'Etat, 1935), p. 120.

Notes: *The Statesman's Year-Book* did not report customs revenue per se, but it did report dollar and gourde revenues separately, noting that dollar revenues came mostly from trade taxes. Pre-1911 data from the fiscal representative represent total revenues, not customs revenue. Customs revenue amounted to 97% of total revenues in 1912–16, before the customs receivership came into effect. Nominal values deflated using the U.S. GDP deflator.

The fiscal representative reported revenues in gourdes, but at a fixed exchange rate of 5 to 1 with the U.S. dollar, rather than market exchange rates. The exact note to the datas read as follows: "Fluctuations in the value of the gourde prior to its stabilization May 2, 1919 have been calculated and are reflected in statistics of revenues before 1919–20." For the data between 1915 and 1919, which can be cross-checked against the reports of the customs receivership, the result was an exchange rate of 5 gourdes per dollar. (Between 1910 and 1915, a period of monetary instability in Haiti, the market rate of the gourde fluctuated between 3 and 7 per dollar. See O. Ernest Moore, "Monetary-Fiscal Policy and Economic Development in Haiti," *Public Finance*, vol. 9, no. 3 (1954), pp. 230–53.

navy.) The new Constitution allowed foreign ownership of Haitian land, which had been forbidden since the Haitian Revolution. The Constitution was approved by plebiscite on June 18, 1918, with the improbable margin of 98,225 to 768. American observers claimed apathy on the part of Haitian voters.[117]

The violent Caco revolts that followed the plebiscite were not triggered by the vote but by the U.S.-run Gendarmerie. Under the command of Major Smedley Butler, it enforced an archaic 1864 law requiring Haitian peasants who were unable to pay their taxes in cash to work in road gangs—the countryside being largely demonetized. The Americans formally abolished the corvée system on October 1, 1918, but continued to enforce it in districts away from the capital.[118] The Gendarmerie by itself was not enough to handle the resulting uprisings, which involved twenty thousand armed insurgents.

For two years, U.S. Marines and gendarmes conducted counterinsurgency operations (including aerial bombings) throughout rural Haiti. Port-au-Prince was attacked twice, in October 1919 and January 1920. The conflict had strong overtones of race war, the U.S. Marines being almost exclusively white and their opponents almost exclusively black; in one famous operation, the killing of Caco leader Charlemagne Péralte, the marines had to blacken their faces with burnt cork in order to pass through Péralte's guards.[119] Over two thousand Haitians were killed in the suppression of the Caco revolts, out of a contemporary population of two million. The United States remained in control of Haitian affairs until 1934. Wilson's intervention of 1915—"to do what we apparently ought to do"—had taken on a grim logic of its own.

Failure in Panama

American fiscal intervention proceeded in spite of its decidedly mixed record. Article 138 of the Panamanian Constitution mandated that $6 million of the proceeds from the Hay-Bunau-Varilla Treaty remain invested in New York real estate. When Panama attempted in 1911 to use the money to finance a railroad from Panama City to Chiriquí Province, the State Department announced that any diversion of the funds to other purposes would activate the American obligation to intervene under Article 136. American officials defended their actions by insisting that it was "notorious that Latin American officials are apt to be anything but cautious in entering financial obligations."[120]

Stereotypes aside, American worries about Panamanian prudence proved to be well founded. In 1914, the United States approved a $3 million loan from National City Bank to finance the construction of a railroad from the town of David, in Chiriquí Province, to Panama City. The $250,000 annuity from the United States for the Panama Canal secured the loan.[121] The next year, however, the National Assembly diverted one-third of the proceeds for an ill-defined series of "public works." The United States protested. In 1915 the Panamanian government issued a further $4.5 million in debt secured by the income from New York real estate.[122] Later that year, however, rumors surfaced that Panamanian president Belisario Porras had used $100,000 of the 1915 loan to meet the government's operating costs.[123] The next year American officials learned that the country had borrowed $750,000 from United Fruit, secured by half the revenue from the banana export tax.[124] The government's operating budget, in rough balance from 1904 to 1914, fell into a deficit of $2.2 million in 1916—fully 39% of expenditures.[125] In March 1917, the United States vetoed an attempt to repatriate the New York fund.[126] Finally, in 1918 the U.S. government learned that Panama had "balanced" its operating budget by redirecting the remaining proceeds from the 1914 loan.

As a result of the 1918 discovery, the State Department pressured Panama City into accepting an American "fiscal agent" who would have complete "control and charge of the national treasury." Addison Ruan, who had been the American financial adviser to Haiti and the disbursing officer for the American government in the Philippines, received the job.[127] Under Ruan's supervision, the Panamanian government ran generally balanced budgets—surpluses in 1919–20 covered deficits in 1921–22. In 1926, Panama negotiated a $2.6 million loan for further work on the Chiriquí Railroad and the construction of a wharf at Armuelles. The government secured the loan with revenue from export duties and the stamp tax.[128]

Table 4.1

Borrowing costs, adjusted for maturity

	Dec 1914	May 1915	Jun 1926	May 1928
United States	3.6%	3.6%	3.6%	3.5%
Colombia	6.0%	6.0%	6.5%	6.3%
Costa Rica	6.8%	7.6%	4.1%	3.7%
Cuba	4.7%	5.1%	4.9%	4.6%
Dominican Republic	na	na	5.6%	5.5%
El Salvador	6.1%	7.0%	7.5%	6.4%
Guatemala	8.4%	8.9%	8.3%	7.0%
Honduras	12.2%	26.7%	14.3%	10.5%
Nicaragua	7.7%	9.4%	6.9%	6.6%
Panama	5.2%	5.6%	6.3%	5.2%
Venezuela	5.5%	5.5%	3.6%	3.5%

Source: Maurer and Yu, *Financial Times*, and *Wall Street Journal*, various editions.

Note: Honduran and Panamanian debts were not publicly traded. Honduran interest rates based on short-term bank lending.

One would have expected American supervision to have produced a significant benefit for Panama. After all, the State Department closely watched Panamanian finances, and an American official directly signed off on budgets after 1918. Panamanian bonds did not trade openly on the secondary markets, but it is possible to calculate the maturity-adjusted interest rate that lenders charged the Panamanian government on its four major debt issues, and compare that to the yield on bonds issued by other Latin American sovereign borrowers.

The data show little sign of a beneficial "empire effect" for Panama, despite its constitutional relationship with the United States, the presence of the Panama Canal, and the installation of a fiscal agent (see table 4.1). In 1926—in the immediate wake of the 1925 use of three battalions of U.S. soldiers to quell riots in Panama City—Panama's borrowing costs were lower than those of most Central American countries but higher than the costs for Cuba, the Dominican Republic, Venezuela, and neighboring Costa Rica—and only slightly lower than those of Colombia.

Only in 1928, with the country having run a near-perfect streak of balanced budgets, was Panama able to borrow for less than the Dominican Republic.

Why did American intervention fail to reduce borrowing costs in Panama? The reason was Panamanian evasion of American financial control. The Panamanian government under Belisario Porras systematically refused to heed the fiscal agent's orders. In 1919, Porras obtained a loan of $150,000 from United Fruit using Panama's banana export revenue as collateral. Porras then passed a bill allowing the Panamanian treasury to cash drafts made by cabinet members, circumventing the fiscal agent entirely. When the American legation protested, Porras declared the fiscal agent's office unconstitutional, although Porras had signed it into law himself.[129] U.S. pressure quickly forced Porras to reverse that decision, but Panamanian officials continued to circumvent American wishes.[130] In late 1922, a frustrated Addison Ruan—the man who had organized *Haiti's* chaotic finances—resigned his position.[131] His replacement, Walter Warwick, in the words of the U.S. minister to Panama, "sat back and allowed the [Panamanian] government to do practically as it has seen fit, even to the extent of purchasing new, expensive automobiles for the use of the President and his cabinet, including one for the Fiscal Agent himself."[132] One must wonder where Warwick drove his new, expensive automobile in a country with so few paved roads.

The U.S. government ultimately admitted that the fiscal agent in Panama served as little more than an adviser. Government revenue rose steadily during the epoch of American control, but this corresponded with the recovery of commerce after the end of World War I and the full opening of the Panama Canal to commercial traffic in 1921 (see figure 4.4.). In 1924, a State Department official concluded that U.S. supervision accomplished little, adding, "I think it is about time we jacked Warwick up."[133] In early 1928, when the Panamanian government began planning a $16.2 million bond issue, Assistant Secretary of State Francis White stated that while the

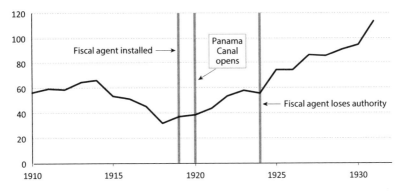

Figure 4.4 Panamanian government revenues, 1910–30, millions of 2011 dollars

Source: *The Statesman's Year-Book* (various years).

United States had "certain treaty obligations of a financial character with Cuba, Haiti, and the Dominican Republic, and also a special relationship with Nicaragua . . . such a relationship does not exist with Panama."[134]

America's African Outpost

Empire-trap dynamics also drew the United States deeper into the turbulent internal affairs of Liberia. The State Department found itself wielding the tools of intervention on the African coast: U.S.-backed controlled loans, customs receiverships, and American officials appointed to head state agencies. In Liberia the relationship was complicated by two other factors. First, Liberia's proximity to European colonial possessions in West Africa meant that European powers were willing and able to intervene should the United States fail to live up to its perceived duties as Liberia's protector. Second, Liberia's unique history meant that it held a particularly sensitive place in American racial politics. Those factors, however, pushed American administrations in the direction of more intervention.

The African nation of Liberia had been part of the United States' informal sphere since its colonization by African-

Americans in the 1820s. By 1900, Liberia was an independent nation controlled by the Americo-Liberian elite, its finances drained by the need to suppress internal revolts. As the Scramble for Africa intensified around the turn of the century, the European powers expressed impatience with Liberia's chronic instability. An attempt to professionalize the Liberian Frontier Force nearly led to disaster after its British commander, R. Mackay Cadell, staffed the force with Sierra Leonean colonial soldiers. Cadell then bullied the Monrovia City Council into appointing him chief of police, and he threatened mutiny when the national legislature asked him to step down.[135]

This not very subtle attempt to bring Liberia into the British sphere of influence caught the attention of the Taft administration. (It also helped to focus minds when the British consul general sent a note to the Liberian government reading, "[Liberia] must not lose a moment in setting herself seriously to work to put her house in order, or be prepared, at no distant date, to disappear from the catalogue of independent countries.")[136] The U.S. State Department advised Congress to agree to a loan and customs receivership and appoint American officers to train and command the Liberian Frontier Force.[137] The Taft administration, however, soon realized that a Congress that had balked at passing Honduran and Nicaraguan conventions was not going to approve a treaty with Liberia. Bypassing Congress, Taft brokered a deal for a $1.7 million loan between the government of Liberia and the North American Group, a consortium headed by the American firm of Kuhn Loeb. Most of the loan, $1.3 million, would be used to refinance Liberia's existing debt, and the State Department would nominate an American official to oversee Liberian customs. The customs receivership would pay service on Liberia's existing debt, after which the balance would be transferred to the country's treasury.[138]

To avoid European opposition, the United States brokered a settlement of Liberia's border disputes and allowed token British, French, and German representation in the North American Group. The boundary with Sierra Leone was settled by a swap of two provinces and a payment of £4,000 (worth $19,400 at the time, $353,000 in 2011 dollars).[139] Settling the boundaries with Guinea and Côte d'Ivoire was a bit easier—the French government accepted the Liberian claim in return for "the maintenance of absolute economic equality for all the powers in Liberia" and "the participation of France in the financial organization of the country," although no formal treaty was signed.[140]

Why did the United States want to preserve Liberia's independence? In this case, the interests were neither economic nor strategic. Rather, helping Liberia was a low-cost way to appease GOP-leaning black voters (and elites) without antagonizing white racists. Taft averred the political calculus on December 3, 1912: "It was also the duty of the American government to attempt to assure permanence to a country of much sentimental and perhaps future real interest to a large body of our citizens."[141] Democratic administrations supported Liberia from a similar rationale: racist white voters supported Liberia in the hope that African-Americans would choose to move there. During the race riots of 1919, a Wilson administration official wrote the following: "From the point of view of unrest among the negroes in the United States, it seems of the utmost importance to maintain undiminished our prestige in and control over the affairs of Liberia. The fact that these agitators can be confronted with the statement that if they are not satisfied with conditions in the United States, they can resort to a black man's land in Africa under republican form of government, will make in large measure for tranquility among the negroes in this country."[142]

The customs receivership came into being on November 26, 1912, headed by an American, Reed Paige Clark, with French, German, and British receivers under him.[143] The State Department first proposed Benjamin Davis, the U.S. military attaché to Liberia, as supreme commander the Liberian Frontier Force—he would later become the U.S. Army's first black general—but Davis withdrew his name from consideration. The United States then nominated Charles Young, the third black graduate of West Point.[144] Young accepted the job.

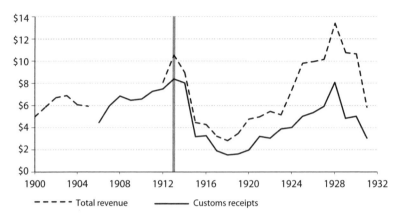

Figure 4.5 Liberian government revenues, 1900–31, millions of 2010 dollars
Source: The Statesman's Year-Book (various years).

The effects of the customs receivership in Liberia, as in Haiti and Nicaragua, can most charitably be described as disappointing (see figure 4.5.). The initiation of the receivership coincided with the outbreak of the First World War. Customs revenue plummeted along with the volume and value of trade—there was little that Mr. Clark could accomplish. Worse yet, the U.S.-recommended imposition of a hut tax on heretofore untaxed populations in the country's interior did little for Liberia's political stability.[145] Liberia faced rebellions among the coastal Kru populations in 1909–10, 1912–13, and 1915; the 1915 revolt saw Kru rebels, armed with British weapons, declare war on "Germany and Liberia" and call for annexation to the British Empire.[146] Facing internal rebellion and economic decline, the Liberian government suspended payments on its debts in July 1916. In the words of Liberian treasury secretary James Cooper, "It is evident that the government cannot continue the payments of interest and maintain itself."[147]

In theory, the United States could have continued interest payments and allowed Liberia to collapse: after all, it controlled the customs receivership. In practice, it understood that default was inevitable—James Cooper's analysis was entirely correct—but pressure from National City (and Liberia's position in American domestic politics) meant that it was impossible to just walk away. In early 1917, Secretary of State Lansing issued the Liberian government an ultimatum. "The government of the United States can no longer be subjected to criticism from other foreign powers as regards the loan agreement, and can no longer tolerate failure on the part of the Liberian government to institute and carry out necessary reforms. Unless the Liberian government proceeds without delay to act upon the advice and suggestions herewith expressed, this government will be forced, regretfully, to withdraw the friendly support that historic and other considerations have hitherto prompted it to extend." The suggestions included the reorganization of Liberia's governmental departments and tax system, and limits on legislative salaries. As a stopgap measure, in February 1917 the U.S. government brokered a deal with the Bank of British West Africa for a loan of $9,000 a month—the total sum not to exceed $100,000— for the day-to-day operation of the Liberian government.[148] Although the Liberian government managed to hold its borrowings from the Bank of British West Africa to $5,000 per month, austerity failed to stave off financial catastrophe. The American chargé d'affaires in Monrovia projected that the government's cash flow would turn negative in July 1918.[149]

The manager of the Bank of British West Africa, W. H. Ross-Bell, suggested to President Daniel Howard of Liberia that an "economic commission of enquiry" manage the country in order to solve "the financial problems of the Republic." The Liberian government interpreted this as another attempt to coerce Liberia into the British sphere of influence.[150] To prevent this outcome, Howard begged the U.S. State Department for a $5 million loan directly from the U.S. government, in return for American use of Liberia's spare labor force, its food supply, its two cables, and its two radio transmitters.[151] As the impending crisis moved closer, the Bank of British West Africa drew stricter terms for its support, drafting a twenty-five-year contract that would bypass Liberia's legislative and executive branches, in effect governing Liberia from the bank.[152] This development flabbergasted the Wilson administration, and the secretary of state's office wrote repeatedly to Treasury Secretary William McAdoo for approval of the Liberian line of credit. Treasury agreed to the loan in August 1918.[153]

Before Treasury could advance the money, the terms of the multinational customs receivership established in 1912 needed to be renegotiated—naturally excluding Germany. In 1919 talks held in Paris, France and Britain indicated their preference for greater American control in Liberia. What the Americans saw as a tentative plan for financial support and fiscal supervision the Europeans saw as a blueprint for an American protectorate over Liberia similar to the French protectorate over Morocco.[154] The United States eschewed the characterization, calling itself Liberia's "next friend," a legal term for an individual who acts on behalf of a person lacking the capacity for such action.[155] Dissatisfied with America's reluctance to take on explicit responsibility for Liberia, Britain proposed that the country be turned over to the United States as a League of Nations mandate.[156] Neither Washington nor Monrovia had any desire for that, leaving Britain and France with little choice but to accede to American desires. The two countries withdrew from the receivership in September 1919, leaving the United States as sole power.[157] The customs receivership continued, as ineffectual as before.

Conclusion

The American diagnosis of the cause of weak property rights in undeveloped nations turned out to be wrong on two counts. First, the simple act of putting Americans in control of government agencies did not automatically result in greater efficiency. In theory, an American manager had different incentives than a local citizen: the cost of engaging in corrupt behavior (or otherwise failing to perform) should be very high. It should also be more difficult for an American to hide corrupt behavior—after all, the American would need some way to transfer the ill-gotten gains to the United States. Moreover, ran the logic, the subordinates of a relatively uncorrupt American should have more fear for their positions should they steal or shirk. The American's local superiors, meanwhile, should find it harder to steal undetected.

Practice turned out to be quite different from theory. Corruption and bureaucratic inefficiency were not the primary challenges to collecting more revenue in the countries where America intervened. Rather, the problem was that those countries' economies generated little tax revenue while requiring relatively high levels of public spending. Only in the Dominican Republic did the mere act of placing customs under American management lead to dramatic revenue increases, but that was due to the fact that the U.S. presence caused Dominican insurgents to stop sacking the customhouses. In places where rebels did not regularly sack the customhouses, the Americans produced no change.

Second, increasing government revenue (where it occurred, as in the Dominican Republic and after a while—and with no credit to the Americans—Nicaragua) did not lead to increased political stability. Corrupt state institutions, particularly the army, meant that higher public spending did not lead to higher provision of public goods. Moreover, Dominican insurgents proved quite capable of financing themselves by means other than sacking customs facilities. Forced loans from the countryside, aid from Haiti, and funds siphoned from the government itself provided enough finances to destabilize the Dominican government. Eventually the state entirely collapsed, forcing the United States to choose between admitting failure or complete occupation.

That is not to say that the American strategy of placing countries into receivership was a complete failure. Domestic politicians in most of Latin America found the possibility of foreign control over their finances to very distasteful. American investors, in turn, believed that the threat of a fiscal receivership provided a powerful incentive to prevent politicians from threatening American property rights. (The receiverships, once in place, *ex ante* prioritized debt repayments—but the debt reschedulings under the Dominican Republic and Liberian receiverships show that generalization to be false *ex post*.) Inasmuch as a fiscal receivership was less damaging than bombardments or blockades, the American strategy provided a better means of sanctioning "irresponsible" governments. Military interventions still took place, of course, but they generally (there were exceptions) took place to prevent governments from collapsing into civil wars that would threaten American property rather than to punish otherwise stable governments. The problem with the strategy, as the Republican administrations that followed Wilson would discover, was that there was no easy way to unwind it.

Box 1

The Mexican Exception

Revolutionary Mexico was a partial exception to the logic of empire for a very simple reason: it was too big to invade. Mexico was in a state of civil war in 1914–17, and no government was in full control of the national territory. Under those conditions, with no organized government to sanction, the only way to protect American settlers, shopkeepers, and landowners was to occupy the entire country—a fiscal and military burden that no American government was prepared to bear. The United States could protect a subset of its investors, however, without employing military force. Oil and mining investments depended on access to the U.S. market for their value, and the same techniques that had worked against Porfirio Díaz could be used to force any revolutionary faction to refrain from confiscating or destroying the mines and oilfields.

President Woodrow Wilson had no doubts about the righteousness of American intervention in Mexico. He considered the military government established by General Victoriano Huerta in early 1913 to be illegitimate and refused to recognize it; Huerta, for his part, thought that Wilson was a hypocrite. The mutual hostility stemmed from the fact that the outgoing Taft administration authorized the coup that brought Huerta to power. The agreement to overthrow President Francisco Madero was signed inside the American embassy on February 18, 1913—ten days before Wilson's inauguration. Huerta's understanding of the American political system could be charitably described as incomplete. Huerta did not understand that the president-elect neither knew about nor approved of his predecessor's actions. Huerta therefore assumed that president-elect Wilson had no problem with his decision to arrest Madero, have him "shot while trying to escape" three days later, and then dissolve the Mexican Congress.

(continued)

(continued)

Huerta's actions horrified Wilson—and he was even more horrified to read about the U.S. ambassador's involvement in the coup in a March 4 story in the *New York World*. He immediately dispatched William Bayard Hale to find out what had actually happened. (Hale was a newspaper reporter and the author of Wilson's campaign biography.) On June 18, 1913, Hale reported that Ambassador Henry Lane Wilson (no relation to the president) had indeed approved the coup. "There was not a moment during [the coup] when it would not have been possible to end the distressing situation [and] put a stop to this unnecessary bloodshed by a stern warning from the American embassy to the traitorous army officers that the United States would countenance no methods but peaceful constitutional ones. . . . President Madero was not betrayed and arrested by his officers until it had been asserted that the American ambassador had no objection."[1] Ambassador Wilson denied Hale's allegations, but President Wilson nonetheless recalled him in July. President Wilson went on to demand that Huerta hold an "early and free election" from which Huerta would be barred. He then imposed an arms embargo. Huerta regarded these actions as a quite inexplicable betrayal.

It was in this supercharged atmosphere that a minor contretemps in Tampico in April 1914 escalated into a major diplomatic incident. The United States demanded a twenty-one-gun naval salute as an apology for the accidental arrest of a group of American sailors who had passed near a Mexican military installation. Huerta insisted on an equivalent salute to the Mexican flag, which American diplomats feared would be interpreted as a sign of recognition.[2] With the two sides at loggerheads, the arrival of the German steamship *Ypiranga* in Veracruz carrying a cargo of machine guns and ammunition provided the Wilson administration with a pretext to intervene. Wilson believed that the shock of military action would be enough to get Huerta—who was slowly losing the civil war started by his coup—to step down. As Mexico's largest port, a major source of tariff revenue,

BOX 1 | 138

and the historic gateway to Mexico City, Veracruz was an ideal site for military intervention. Wilson ordered the navy to take over the Veracruz customhouse and seize the *Ypiranga*'s cargo. Sailors and marines began landing on the morning of April 21, 1914. By April 24, the marines had secured the city. Seventeen Americans died in the operation, along with 126 Mexicans.[3]

Wilson's military triumph at Veracruz proved to be a political failure. Huerta appears to have been shocked by the American action, but he was not awed: both Huerta and the de facto head of his opponents, Venustiano Carranza, condemned the occupation. Mexican popular opinion moved sharply against the United States. Argentina, Brazil, and Chile proposed international mediation. Wilson, realizing his mistake, quickly agreed. The peace conference, held in the neutral location of Niagara Falls, Ontario, began on May 20, 1914, with representatives from both Huerta and Carranza. (William F. Buckley, Sr., served as counsel to the Huerta government.) Each party, however, had demands that infringed on the other's nonnegotiables—most notably, Huerta's resignation—and the conference rapidly deadlocked.

Huerta resigned a month after the conference, but not because the United States occupied Veracruz. Rather, he resigned because the combined forces of Venustiano Carranza and Francisco "Pancho" Villa defeated his military on the battlefield.[4] (The embargo on arms shipments was, of course, helpful to the rebels, but the United States did not need to physically occupy Veracruz to enforce it.) Huerta and his family wound up in a mansion in the tranquil Forest Hills neighborhood of Queens.[5] The winners of the counter-counterrevolution did not face as pleasant a fate. They quickly took to fighting among themselves in a no-holds-barred civil war, and the Veracruz occupation dragged on.

Ultimately, the occupation of Veracruz proved entirely counterproductive. In the war among the victors that followed Huerta's defeat, the Wilson administration favored Carranza's main opponent, Francisco Villa. The presence of American troops in Veracruz, however, ironically served to give *Carranza* a safe haven

(*continued*)

(continued)

in which to establish a temporary capital and regroup. Carranza went on to win the civil war, leaving Villa bitter at the United States for what he understandably viewed as a "betrayal." On March 14, 1916, Villa raided Columbus, New Mexico. Wilson responded in the only way that an American president possibly could under the circumstances: he invaded northern Mexico.

The intervention had the aim of capturing Pancho Villa. Unfortunately, it was not possible for the United States to send a division-size force into Mexico without engaging Carranza's army. In April, U.S. troops skirmished with Mexican forces outside Parral. Two months later, in July, U.S. forces engaged Mexican troops near Carrizal, Chihuahua. The Americans suffered sixteen deaths, and the Mexicans captured twenty-three cavalry soldiers. Once it looked as though the intervention ran the risk of starting a war with Carranza's government, the Wilson administration imposed restrictive rules of engagement designed to ensure that such battles would not be repeated. The American government then began to informally warn the Carranza regime of *all* military movements. With the military expedition effectively banned from engaging in military operation, the expedition singularly failed to achieve its goal: Villa was not captured by the time U.S. forces withdrew on February 7, 1917.

Too Big to Invade

The U.S. Army drew up several contingency plans to invade and occupy Mexico. In 1911, when disorder first broke out, the War College added meat to the bones of a sketchy 1904 plan. Plan A involved an advance from Texas, while the preferred Plan B called for 114,000 troops to invade from Texas while 137,000 operated from Veracruz. Plan B ruled out intervention between April and November, when the War College judged the disease environment in Veracruz to be too hostile to allow an invasion without untenable numbers of sick or dying soldiers.[6]

The scale of these projections was jaw-dropping at a time when the total active-duty strength of the U.S. Army came to 45,914, with only 116,124 additional soldiers in the active reserve and

BOX 1 | 140

National Guard (then generally called the"organized militia, although the term Ntional Guard was coming into currency).[7] As a result, the army approved a smaller plan involving a rapid advance on Mexico City, using only 115,000 troops. Later refinements in 1913 took the force requirement up to 130,000 troops (with an additional 16,800 to guard the U.S.-Mexico frontier), with plans to increase the combined size of the regular army and reserves (including the National Guard) to 248,753 in the event of hostilities.[8] Unlike a remarkably similar strategic concept rolled out for the invasion of Iraq ninety years later, in 1913 the leaner invasion option received serious pushback from civilian leaders, who protested that the military documents contained no provision for dealing with guerrilla resistance or occupying the country outside Veracruz and Mexico City. In response, the War College reworked the plan multiple times.

The final version of the war plan, published in July 1914, called for an invasion force of *352,985*.[9] In 1914, the U.S. Army consisted of 98,544 personnel on active duty. The 1914 invasion plan for Mexico called for increasing that number by 259,601, under the heroic assumption that existing National Guard troops were ready for combat—an assumption that proved false during the mobilization for World War I.[10] Even more optimistically, the plan assumed that the United States could expand the active reserve to 281,000 and activate *all* the new soldiers for combat duty outside the United States. Given the need to train and equip so many new soldiers, there would be at least a nine-month gap between giving the order and beginning the invasion.[11]

What would have been the fiscal cost of invading Mexico? It is possible to generate a minimum estimate from data in Senate war appropriations hearings, which projected the total cost of clothing, equipping, paying, provisioning, sheltering, and transporting an army with varying end-strengths of 122,000, 132,000, and 156,000 soldiers. (In most categories, unsurprisingly, the marginal cost was less than the average cost, but there were a few cases in which lumpy expenditures led to significantly rising

(continued)

(*continued*)

marginal costs.)[12] The marginal cost of raising, training, equipping, and transporting the additional forces would have come to $173 million in 1914. Under the more realistic assumption that National Guard forces would require the same training and provisioning as new recruits, the cost of raising the force required to invade Mexico would total $238 million—at a time when the *entire* defense budget of the United States came to $347 million. These estimates, moreover, do not include the costs of sustaining American forces in the field. Using data from World War I, the cost of keeping 352,985 troops in the field for six months would have been $125 million.[13] The total fiscal cost would have amounted to 1.3% of GDP—under the exceedingly unlikely assumption that the United States could have installed a friendly government and withdrawn its forces within six months of the start of combat operations. For every additional year of occupation, a lower-bound cost estimate was 2.6% of GDP.

In short, unlike the small (indeed almost negligible) fiscal cost of other American interventions between 1904 and 1934, invading Mexico would have involved a national effort on par with the Spanish-American War, at a time when the political support for such a venture was much lower than it had been in 1898. Moreover, the chances that such an intervention would precipitate a prolonged irregular conflict—at even greater fiscal and human cost—were quite large. American creditors, small investors, and landowners in Revolutionary Mexico, therefore, were on their own. The United States never managed to convince the Mexican government to recognize its pre-Revolutionary debts. Nor did it manage to obtain full compensation for American agricultural properties confiscated or damaged in the Revolution—Mexico would not begin paying the $53.5 million in claims against it until 1934.[14] (The settlement came to 1% of Mexico's GDP.)

PROTECTING AMERICAN PROPERTY
Mining and Oil

The nature of oil and mining investments in Mexico, however, made it possible to protect American property rights by means

BOX 1 | 142

other than invasion. Geography gave American companies and the State Department an easy-to-use set of tools. Revolutionary leaders soon learned that attempts to extort funds from foreign miners would lead to a boycott of Mexican exports, thus depriving the mines of any economic value. In theory, an American boycott could be avoided by refining the ore in Mexican-based smelters and exporting the refined metal to Europe (which had a higher value-to-weight ratio and could therefore be profitably shipped across the Atlantic), but that required the expertise to operate a smelter—expertise hard to acquire in war-torn Mexico.[15]

The first Mexican leader to learn this lesson was Victoriano Huerta, who attempted to extort funds from foreign miners in Durango, under pain of death. The American miners responded by shutting down their mines and leaving the state en masse.[16] The second Mexican leader to learn this lesson—over and over again—was Pancho Villa. Villa's forces controlled most of Mexico's major mining regions between 1913 and 1915. At first, Villa allied with American mine owners. In the words of an official of the American Smelting and Refining Company (Asarco): "We are on the most friendly terms with Villa and his men. . . . On several occasions they have gone out of their way to extend assistance to our company."[17] This is why, in the early years of the Revolution, U.S. mining interests lobbied the Wilson administration to support Villa.[18]

Try as he might, however, Villa could not jump-start the mining industry. For mines located away from the border regions, the fundamental problem was the lack of railway transport. Mexico was in the midst of a modern war, and that meant that troops and equipment had to be moved on the railroads. Railroads thus became strategic targets for demolition.[19] The result was that from 1913 until 1917 the railways were in ruin.[20] For mines located farther north, the problem was falling prices. The price of copper, which had been at 16.3 cents (U.S.) per pound in 1912, fell to 15.3 cents in 1913, and fell again to 13.6 cents

(continued)

(continued)

in 1914. Lead prices moved in a similar direction, from 4.5 cents per pound in 1912 to 3.9 cents in 1914.[21] The miners responded to low prices by cutting production and temporarily shuttering their highest-cost operations.

Some Villista officials believed that the mining companies could be forced to resume production. In May 1914, Tomás Urbina, the Villista governor of Durango, ordered foreign mining companies to resume work or face confiscation.[22] Two months later (July 1914) General Fidel Avila, governor-general of Chihuahua and Silvestre Terrazas, Villa's secretary of state, issued a decree giving companies one month to renew "mining, industrial, and other operations which might have been closed by war" and threatened confiscation "if they persist in the continued closure of their operations."[23] State and local leaders in fact seized some Mexican-owned mines.[24]

This strategy was doomed from the start. First, the Villistas had no way to smelt or chemically refine ore. The U.S.-owned American Smelting and Refining Company (Asarco) owned all the refining capacity in northern Mexico, and Asarco refused to process ore from confiscated mines.[25] Second, the Villistas could not take over the smelters, because they lacked the ability to run them. The Villistas tried on one occasion to fire up one of Asarco's smelters but quickly realized that they had no idea what they were doing.[26] Finally, attempts to ship unsmelted ore to the United States were blocked by the U.S. government, which worked with the mine owners to establish special offices to warn customs officials when "stolen" ore reached the border.[27] In short, Asarco and the U.S. Customs Service could effectively enforce the property rights of miners without the need to send in the marines—or, more likely in the case of northern Mexico, the army.

Villa wanted to extract more resources from the miners—the U.S. State Department simply blocked him from doing so. The Miners and Smelters Owner's Association (MSOA), founded in February 1915 by the largest (mostly American) mining

BOX 1 | 144

companies in Mexico, immediately set to work with the Villistas to hammer out a set of policies regarding taxation, labor rights, and the currency exchange rate. The Villistas were highly conciliatory on labor law (it would not be reformed), the exchange rate (it would be determined by the market), and the tax rate (it would be the same as under Díaz). The only concession that Villa extracted from the MSOA was that American mine owners agreed to pay a one-time, extraordinary war tax of 5% of revenues. Even this extraordinary tax was later reduced, when Villa declared (under pressure from the U.S. State Department) that it would not be collected "where impracticable."[28]

Villa simply could not find a way around the fact that running a smelter was not like running a cattle ranch; any ore he confiscated from mines was worthless because he could not export it to the United States, and the MSOA could send a cable to the State Department at the speed of electricity. In mid-March 1915, losing the war and desperate for revenue, Villa abandoned his alliance with the miners and decreed that mines that were not being worked would be subject to forfeiture. The MSOA and the State Department swung into action, and Villa backed down.[29] In July 1915, Villa needed funds to purchase 250,000 cartridges awaiting him in El Paso. Lacking the cash, his finance secretary demanded a loan of $300,000 dollars from the MSOA representative in Chihuahua. The miners refused. Villa responded by decreeing that all mining companies in Chihuahua had to resume operations at once and turn over their ore to his administration. The MSOA, predictably, cabled the State Department, which dispatched General Hugh Scott to see Villa. We do not know what Scott told Villa. We do know, however, that Villa dropped all his demands in exchange for a thousand tons of coal.[30]

By late 1916, Carranza's forces had essentially defeated Villa, and the Carrancistas soon ran headlong into the same forces that had constrained the Villistas. On September 14, 1916, Carranza decreed that idle mining properties would become subject to operation by the government or be thrown open for denouncement

(continued)

(*continued*)

by third parties.[31] The mining companies appealed to the State Department, and the State Department immediately protested. It also advised miners to file statements explaining why their mines were closed. On November 14, Carranza gave the miners an extension until February 14, 1917. The fact that Carranza had to make the threat twice (September 14, 1916, and again on November 14, 1916), and that he gave the companies until February 1917 to comply, indicates that he himself knew that he could not actually expropriate the miners without provoking an embargo that would deprive the mines of all value—something the mine owners certainly realized.[32] Not surprisingly, Carranza beat a strategic retreat: he did not rescind the law, but he never tried to enforce it either. The reports about conditions in Mexico published by the *Engineering and Mining Journal*, which tended to portray Carranza in the most negative light imaginable, do not mention a single case of confiscation under this law.[33]

Later events provide us with two tests of the proposition that the Carrancistas could not actually run a mine. The first occurred in early 1917 when the managers of the Chispas mine in Arizpe, Sonora, refused orders to raise wages, employ more men, and increase production. Carranza's government jailed the manager and seized the mine. The government soon found, however, that without the foreign managers it could not run the mine at a profit, and had to close down the operation. The government also found out that it could not effectively imprison the mine's manager, who escaped from jail and fled to Arizona. The second experiment occurred later that same year, in Coahuila, when, as a result of a labor dispute, the federal government decided to take over the state's coal mines and work them on its own account. The government quickly found out, however, that it could not unwater the mines and restart production without the cooperation of the mining companies' skilled staff, which was not forthcoming. The government therefore reversed its plans to confiscate the mines.[34]

Protecting the oil industry required a somewhat more proactive approach, since both crude oil and the products of Mexico's

BOX 1 | 146

(*continued*)

refineries could be economically shipped to Europe. In 1914, Secretary of State Bryan demanded that the oil region, centered on the port of Tampico, be declared a "neutral zone." For obvious reasons, no faction in the Revolution formally recognized the neutral zone's existence, but they all acted as if they did. The reason was that all factions understood that if they seized the oil fields they would enter an unwinnable conflict with the United States. The United States did consider seizing the oil fields for itself—Secretary of State Lansing, notably more bellicose than his predecessor Bryan, was a strong advocate of the idea—but the difficulty of capturing the fields before hostile resistance could destroy them annulled the plan.[35] What replaced it was the threat that should a hostile faction seize the oil fields, then the expropriating faction would enjoy the rents from the fields for precisely as long as it would take for an American expeditionary force to reach and retake them—with the fields in Mexican hands, the possibility of their destruction would no longer be an issue deterring U.S. intervention. This was not a risk that any Revolutionary faction particularly wanted to take. American petroleum companies might have their payrolls occasionally stolen by Mexican factions, and there was some bargaining over the tax rate, but the oil fields were not expropriated.[36]

Five
Banana Republicanism

> There is a distinct and binding obligation on the part
> of self-respecting governments to afford protection to
> the persons and property of their citizens, wherever
> they may be. The fundamental laws of justice are uni-
> versal in their application. These rights go with the
> citizen. Wherever he goes these duties of our govern-
> ment must follow him.
>
> —*President Calvin Coolidge, 1927*

Republican Warren Harding entered the White House
determined to escape the imperial entanglements that had en-
snared his predecessor. Harding's election by a 26-point margin
in 1920 was less an endorsement of the merits of the victor—a
relatively unknown senator from Ohio who beat a relatively unknown governor from Ohio—than a repudiation of the Wilson
years. His Democratic opponent, James Cox, won his only electoral votes in the "Solid South," a one-party fiefdom in which
the largest Republican constituency—African-Americans—was
denied the right to vote. Harding, campaigning on a return to
"normalcy," had little foreign policy knowledge and not a whole
lot more domestic experience. Wilson's imperialism in drag was
an easy target for Harding, who promised from the porch of
his Marion, Ohio, home that as president he would not "draft
a constitution for helpless neighbors in the West Indies and jam
it down their throats at the point of bayonets borne by United
States Marines."[1]

But Harding, like Wilson, found the empire trap nearly impossible to escape. The president's lack of a strong inner compass was certainly a contributing factor. Harding's image reflected his substance: a genial, nonideological man willing to support his friends and listen to his advisers. As a result, he had one of the most diverse cabinets of the twentieth century, in the sense that it combined corrupt cronies with some of the most high-powered professional know-how. Among Harding's appointees were Andrew Mellon, the billionaire Pittsburgh industrialist-banker, as secretary of the treasury; Herbert Hoover, the head of American relief efforts in postwar Europe, as secretary of commerce; and the former governor of New York, Supreme Court justice, and previous GOP nominee for president, Charles Evans Hughes, as secretary of state.

America's informal empire brought these strong personalities into opposition. On the interventionist side was Commerce secretary Herbert Hoover, who believed it was the United States' responsibility to actively oversee foreign investments on behalf of three principal groups: American direct investors, who wanted their business interests protected by the power of the U.S. government; American bankers, who wanted the benefits that American diplomacy could bring them; and the foreign governments themselves, who would (in Hoover's view) otherwise borrow imprudently. Mellon's Treasury, conversely, took a hands-off position. Private investors should be left to manage their own risks. Secretary of State Hughes split the difference. Over the objections of the Latin American Division, his State Department adopted a policy drafted by Arthur Young, the department's economic adviser.[2] This policy stated that State would vet foreign loans and large-scale investments, but only in an advisory capacity: after receiving data from the investors, the department would "give the matter consideration and, in the light of the information in its possession, endeavor to say whether objection to the loan in question does or does not exist. . . . It will not pass upon the merits of foreign loans as business propositions, nor assume any responsibility whatever in connection with loan transactions."[3]

After Harding died in 1923, midway through his first term, the substance of American foreign policy toward Latin America did not change, although it took on a more conventionally Republican pro-business rhetoric. Calvin "Silent Cal" Coolidge took over the presidency, and, after winning reelection in 1924, he replaced Hughes with Frank Kellogg, a self-taught international jurist and former senator from Minnesota. In contrast to Hughes's lofty, almost Olympian tone, rhetoric regarding Latin America under Coolidge and Kellogg was more pugnacious.[4] Secretary Kellogg was not above Red-baiting to bully Congress into intervention in Latin America. On little basis other than Trotsky's residence in Mexico, Kellogg testified before the Senate Foreign Relations Committee in 1927 that "the Bolshevist leaders . . . have set up as one of their fundamental tasks the destruction of what they term American imperialism as a necessary prerequisite to the successful development of the international revolutionary movement in the New World."[5] The specter of "Red Mexico" haunted Washington—and on more than one occasion the overheated rhetoric would box administrations into an interventionist stance.

The aggressive rhetoric masked a behind-the-scenes ambivalence. State worried that the United States' new status as the world's premier capital-exporting nation had made the empire trap more treacherous. There were too many opportunities for "dollar diplomacy" to lead to political entanglements. Despite repeated clarifications, many U.S. banks and foreign investors interpreted the department's "no objection" for loans and investment projects as a positive commitment by the U.S. government. It reached the point where Arthur Young, the official who had drafted the original policy, suggested that the department simply issue a confirmatory receipt for proposals instead.[6]

The imperial undertone of the intervention sphere was becoming harder to ignore. Despite its refusal to admit that it was in fact running an empire, the United States was already experiencing some of the classic problems of imperial governance.

American financial advisers were well compensated and set apart from the nations whose interests they theoretically served. For example, Collector-General Clifford Ham in Nicaragua earned a salary of $15,000 per annum—$366,000 in 2011 dollars (using the U.S. CPI). Contemporaries thought this a ludicrous level of compensation for "hardship": a State Department investigation found that Ham performed "comparatively little work" for his pay.[7] The United States sprinkled a few African-American officials throughout Haiti in an attempt to defuse racial tensions, but in Liberia the State Department approved advisory teams that were conspicuously all white.[8] (The officers sent to train the Liberian Frontier Force were the exception.) This cultural tone deafness, while small in itself, did little for U.S. efforts to promote stability within the intervention sphere.

American policy attracted some domestic opposition. Anti-imperialists convened high-profile Senate hearings in 1921 and 1922 on alleged atrocities by U.S. troops in Haiti and the Dominican Republic. The hearings could not avoid investigating—and lambasting—the policies that led to the occupations.[9] Internal resistance built up inside the State Department as well. At the tail end of Coolidge's term, Undersecretary of State J. Reuben Clark would write a commentary on the historical uses of the Monroe Doctrine in American diplomacy.[10] The two-hundred-page memorandum, mainly short case studies of the Monroe Doctrine in action, concluded: "It is not believed that this [Roosevelt] corollary is justified by the terms of the Monroe Doctrine, however much it may be justified by the application of the doctrine of self-preservation."[11]

The opposition had little effect. Congress remained divided. Internal State Department misgivings about the U.S. role in Latin America were, meanwhile, even less influential than Wilson's or Harding's anti-imperial campaign promises.[12] Even as the evidence piled up that American intervention had failed to improve the security of property rights in Latin America, the United States remained committed to its path. The United States had become the world's greatest capital-exporting nation by the

1920s, and American intervention shadowed American capital in countries plagued by political instability.

The key was that fiscal intervention was relatively cheap from a political point of view. The interventions of the 1920s rarely involved gunboats sailing into hostile ports—and when they went wrong, as in Hispaniola or Nicaragua, the problems took years to manifest themselves and in Hispaniola produced little drain on the American treasury. (The United States financed the occupations of Haiti and the Dominican Republic out of debt issued by the occupation governments in the name of the occupied countries.) Moreover, particular investors continued to vocally lobby for interventions even as their concrete benefit declined. With few countervailing pressures, the Republican administrations of the 1920s proved unable to resist. In Panama, Nicaragua, Haiti, Liberia, Bolivia, and Peru, "dollar diplomacy" was little more than a euphemism for the empire trap.

Wagging the Dog in Liberia

In the 1920s, Liberia caught the attention of American commercial interests. After failing to enter the Philippines, the Firestone Tire Company fixed on Liberia as a potential site for its own rubber plantations. Firestone, however, refused to invest without guarantees from the U.S. government that it would protect Firestone's property rights. The U.S. government was already under pressure from National City Bank to do something to get Liberia to resume payments on its debt. The result was an agreement that paid off the bankers, effectively signed over the governance of Liberia to the Firestone Tire Company, and obligated the United States as guarantor.

Early in the Harding administration, it looked as if Liberia would receive a $5 million loan ($54.5 million in 2011 dollars) from the U.S. government. Liberian president Charles King spent most of 1921 in the United States negotiating the loan agreement. The Liberian legislature approved it without amendment on January 23, 1922.[13] In the United States, the House of Representatives voted in favor on May 11, forwarding the resolution to the Senate.[14] Despite President Harding's endorsement—Secretary of State Hughes joked that aid to Liberia was the only policy agreed on by presidents Roosevelt, Taft, Wilson, and Harding—the resolution drew intense criticism on the Senate floor.[15]

William Borah (R-Idaho) raised the first objections with a legalistic antibanking argument, claiming that the loan's terms were designed for the wartime environment of 1917, which no longer applied, and would therefore give U.S. banks undue profits from previous Liberian claims.[16] Very quickly, however, the Senate debate took a strongly racial turn. The day after Borah made his statement, Senator Tom Watson (D-Georgia) mockingly suggested giving the money to African-Americans in the United States instead. "Five hundred dollars for every negro family in Liberia! Oh what a jubilation there would be if we made a present of $500 to every negro family in the District of Columbia."[17] As the debate dragged into November, Senator Pat Harrison (D-Mississippi) alleged that the loan would in fact funnel $650,000 to five African-Americans (whom he named) with ties to the Republican Party. Senator George Norris (R-Nebraska) joined the "criticism" (if it could be called that) with racial jokes about Liberians' fighting ability.[18] The final vote on November 27, 1922, ran 42 to 33 against, with 12 Republicans joined to a Democratic anti-loan phalanx. The resolution returned to the Senate Finance Committee without instructions, where it died.[19] In its postmortem, the *New York Times* suggested that rancor over the Dyer antilynching bill in the Senate poisoned the environment for passage of the Liberian loan resolution.[20] Whatever the case, American racism defeated any official American government loan to Liberia, and Harding's attempt to curry favor with black voters ended in failure. The American customs receivership in Liberia remained in place, however, and the State Department was still willing to advise American firms interested in investing.

Harvey Firestone saw opportunity in the failure of the official loan project. He could provide funds to the Liberian government on the same terms as the State Department, in return for which Liberia would lift its laws restricting foreign land ownership. Firestone, using the slogan "America must grow its own rubber," lobbied Congress for support. In March 1923, he managed to get Congress to appropriate $500,000 ($5.3 million in 2011 dollars) to conduct a survey of potential rubber-producing areas.[21]

The U.S. government survey mission arrived in Liberia in December 1923, where it examined the abandoned 2,000-acre Mount Barclay plantation.[22] The climate and geography appeared propitious, but two factors worried Firestone: the poor state of Liberia's transportation infrastructure and the constitutional ban on foreign ownership.[23] President King offered to lease a test plantation at Mount Barclay for $15,000 ($160,000 in 2011 dollars) per year. If the test proved successful, King promised to lease an additional 500,000 acres for $30,000 per year. After fifteen years, a 5% export tax on gross revenue would kick in.[24] In return, Liberia would contribute $300,000 to improve the harbor at Monrovia.[25] Considering the obstacles, Firestone rejected King's offer.[26]

The Liberian government's need for capital offered Firestone leverage in the subsequent negotiations. In crafting its political strategy, the Firestone Company received invaluable aid from the head of the customs receivership: Sidney De la Rue. A native of New Jersey, De la Rue had served as a civilian in the occupation government of the Dominican Republic before moving to Liberia in 1921.[27] De la Rue was *not* a State Department employee. Rather, he was an employee of the National City Bank of New York.[28] National City, of course, wanted to refinance its loans to Liberia, still in default.

In 1924, De la Rue traveled to the United States to meet with the Firestone Company and State Department officials. On July 1, 1924, De la Rue explained his political strategy to William Castle, the head of Liberian affairs at the State Department. The key was to win African-American support inside the United States. De la Rue suggested bringing Solomon Hood, the black American consul in Monrovia, back to the United States. At home, Hood could help lobby the "the Negro element." He also said that Firestone would agree to reserve jobs for black technicians, which would bring "all the radical press controlled by Du Bois on our side."[29] Later that month De la Rue met with Harvey Firestone. According to Roger Tredwell, a State Department official, De la Rue told Firestone, "The State Department would not approve of Firestone going into Liberia without a loan." Firestone "should not expect to have any control over the country or over the loan. It was explained that this must be a banker's loan and that the control would be exercised by an Adviser nominated by the government."[30]

Firestone was less than thrilled about the idea of negotiating with Liberia on behalf of National City Bank. He was willing to lend to Liberia, but only in return for some element of control over the Liberian government. On July 8, 1924, Firestone's general counsel, Amos Miller, met with Assistant Secretary of State Leland Harrison. Miller told Harrison that the company was prepared to loan $5 million to the Republic of Liberia, "through its fiscal agents, say the National City Bank of New York, provided that all the revenues of Liberia were assigned to the service of the loan, and provided further that the Liberian government should agree to the appointment by the President of the United States of Americans to collect and disburse all these revenues."[31]

When the assistant secretary asked why Firestone considered it necessary to take control of Liberia's entire revenue apparatus, Miller replied that the United States had failed to protect American investments in Mexico against political chaos, and moreover the Monroe Doctrine did not apply to Liberia. Harrison ultimately recommended the American appointment of "a financial commission for the government of Liberia, of a legal counselor and of . . . four senior officers of the Frontier Force."[32] On December 12, 1924, Secretary of State Hughes told Miller and

Firestone in a personal meeting that he agreed with Harrison's recommendations. He did, however, make it "clearly understood that there was no question of resort to force."[33]

When the Liberians balked at some of the terms, Firestone got the U.S. government to pressure them on his behalf. On April 30, 1925, he wrote President Coolidge: "I am having difficulty in securing signature of Liberian government to the rubber planting agreements which were approved by the State Department. . . . Knowing your interest in this rubber development I am taking liberty of advising you of the situation. Personal regards."[34] Soon thereafter, Secretary of State Frank Kellogg (who had replaced Hughes in March 1925) sent a message to the Liberians:

> "The Department appreciates the reluctance of the Liberian government to assume obligations toward private interests operating in Liberia identical with those which it might willingly assume toward the American government. . . . Obviously, however, it would be impossible to raise any loan in the United States on security which could be offered by Liberia unless there is to be the extensive development contemplated by the Firestone contracts. . . . Mr. Firestone has been already negotiating with rubber plantations in Dutch Borneo and . . . among the purposes of his journey to Washington was the discussion with the commissioner of rubber openings in the Philippine Islands. It would appear to the Department to be very unfortunate for Liberia should Mr. Firestone transfer his interests elsewhere."[35]

When Liberia continued to balk, Secretary Kellogg cabled Hood, the U.S. minister in Monrovia: "You will employ your best efforts to remove all possible misunderstanding . . . and to facilitate a prompt conclusion of the negotiations. To this end you may show and read this telegram to the Liberian authorities."[36] When the French seized the province of Zinta in 1925, the United States signaled that it would lend support against the surrounding European empires only if President King came to terms with Firestone.[37]

The final arrangement granted Firestone a ninety-nine-year lease on one million acres for $60,000 per year and a 1% tax on gross income.[38] Considering the domestic market for rubber in Liberia was nil, this was the equivalent of an export tax, but calling it a revenue tax allowed the King administration to portray the agreement as a nationalist victory. In return, Firestone arranged to lend $5 million to Liberia at a term of forty years and a nominal interest rate of 7%.[39] The U.S. government guaranteed the agreement. Not only did the agreement leave the customs receivership in place; it extended it by giving the U.S. government the right to appoint a "Financial Advisor to the President."[40] The so-called "Advisor" was given a line-item veto over all government spending. To add insult to injury, the adviser received a salary of $12,500 ($159,000 in 2011 dollars, using the U.S. CPI) *paid by the Liberian government*. Firestone itself received a veto over new borrowing by the Republic of Liberia.[41]

There was nothing particularly unjust about this arrangement per se—although the ability to veto legislative appropriations went beyond previous fiscal receiverships—but the Firestone Company wasn't quite done. Under the terms of the receivership, all customs revenue would be deposited in an account at the United States Trading Company Banking Department, which was a Firestone subsidiary. The United States Trading Company, in turn, charged a 1.5% commission on the *flow* of deposits into this account, and an additional 1% commission on the funds transferred to New York for debt repayment. In other words, thanks to the assistance of the U.S. government, the Firestone Company was able to impose a surtax on all Liberian government revenues.

Political Collapse in Nicaragua

Of the nations managed by the United States at the beginning of the Harding administration, Nicaragua seemed the most promising candidate for withdrawal. Under the generally buoyant economic climate of the early 1920s, Nicaraguan finances prospered. The 1920 Nicaraguan election suffered from severe irregularities—a State Department observer concluded that the lists were "enormously padded"—but the transfer of power from President Emiliano Chamorro to his uncle Diego went peacefully enough.[42] By 1923, the situation seemed sufficiently stable for the State Department to announce the contingent of U.S. Marines guarding the American legation would withdraw following the 1924 elections. As Secretary of State Hughes wrote to the American chargé d'affaires in Managua, "the success of the whole plan of withdrawal depends on the government coming into office . . . that it will be in such a strong position that when the Marines are then withdrawn there will be no occasion for political disturbances."[43] Conservative Carlos Solórzano duly won the October 1924 elections, in a fusion ticket with Juan Bautista Sacasa of the Liberal Party.

Unfortunately, Hughes's prediction that the new government would be strong enough to allow the withdrawal of the marines proved incorrect. Within a week of assuming the presidency, Solórzano was "genuinely alarmed by the prospect of losing the Marines," according to the American chargé d'affaires, who added that the general opinion in Managua was that "once the Marines have gone a revolution will be inevitable."[44] Solórzano requested that the United States postpone withdrawal until a Nicaraguan national force could be trained by U.S. instructors. Cannily, he emphasized the commercial consequences of military withdrawal: it would cause "uneasiness [to persist] in all the public businesses and activities and foreign capital in the country . . . the depression of the custom bonds and depreciation of the currency . . . the obligation of the government to create without delay a standing army . . . an organization which would divert for its maintenance considerable sums of money which could be better employed in the development of resources or in the upkeep of public administration."[45] Solórzano had obviously learned what concerned the United States.

The Coolidge administration was, however, loath to abandon its much-hyped declaration that America was withdrawing from Nicaragua. In order to speed departure, the United States agreed to support a newly formed National Guard in May 1925, "an institution foreign to all political influence." Once operational it would replace both the Nicaraguan Army and the country's multiple private militias. It would be trained by U.S. Army major Calvin Carter of Elgin, Texas.[46] The marines left Managua at the beginning of August.

On August 28, President Solórzano's brother-in-law, General Alfredo Rivas, sent a body of troops to the International Club in Managua, crashing a party being held there for the minister of public instruction and carrying off several prominent Liberals as prisoners. This all took place under the amazed eyes of many American guests. Rivas, in control of the local garrison, then negotiated with Solórzano at the president's home—with fifty armed men and two machine guns trained on the house. Solórzano, playing the only card he had available, requested that the United States send warships. The war vessels arrived within a week. Rivas backed down, and the ships withdrew.[47] It was evident to all parties that Solórzano's power, contrary to the hopes of Secretary of State Hughes, derived from the implied threat of American military might behind it.

At this point, Emiliano Chamorro decided to move openly against Solórzano. On October 25, 1925, Chamorro seized control of the Managua garrison and demanded to be appointed chief of the Nicaraguan Army. Solórzano quickly acquiesced, granting amnesty to all participating soldiers and even paying Chamorro's expenses. Chamorro, a former Nicaraguan ambassador to Washington, believed that the United States would not intervene as long as he maintained a fig leaf of constitutionality and avoided damaging American economic interests. Chamorro targeted the Liberal part of Solórzano's coalition, forcing Vice President Sacasa to leave the country. He then proceeded to unseat members of the ruling coalition from the Nicaraguan congress. The State Department was aware of Chamorro's strategy but did "not believe it wise to return Sacasa on a war vessel. That might create an embarrassing precedent."[48] Chamorro was elected to the Nicaraguan Senate on January 3, 1926, which designated him successor to the presidency on January 12. The Nicaraguan congress banished Vice President Sacasa from the country for a period of two years on January 13, and President Solórzano resigned on January 17. Chamorro became president—but to his apparent surprise, the United States refused to recognize his government, although the receivership did not withhold revenues.[49]

The political situation in Nicaragua soon degenerated into civil war. Liberal forces on the Atlantic coast seized $160,000 from the Nicaraguan National Bank in Bluefields—home to a substantial American colony—in order to fund an insurgency. In response, the United States sent warships and declared Bluefields a "neutral zone." Secretary of State Kellogg stated "Neither Liberal forces nor Chamorro forces should be hindered in their military operations except so far as may be necessary to assure protection to American lives and property." Unfortunately, Kellogg's previous rhetoric about "Red Mexico" came back to haunt him when Liberal forces began to purchase arms from the Calles government in Mexico City.[50]

In August 1926, Kellogg sent Chamorro an oblique threat to cut off all government revenues if he did not sit down and settle with the Liberals. "Anxious and desirous to avoid interference in the purely domestic affairs of Nicaragua, the Department of State cannot help but point out . . . actions on the part of those in control of the government of Nicaragua which . . . are tending to prevent the free operation of the Financial Plans of 1917 and 1920 [and] are being viewed with considerable anxiety by the United States Government."[51] Chamorro was "visibly moved" by Kellogg's implied threat, replying that "he had made up his mind to maintain his position against all Nicaraguans but would welcome intervention by American forces to whom he would cheerfully turn over government."[52]

In October 1926 the United States brokered a peace conference between the Conservative and Liberal factions aboard the USS *Denver*, stationed off the Pacific port of Corinto. Chamorro resigned to serve as a Nicaraguan minister-at-large in Europe. Former president Adolfo Díaz, a Conservative and Secretary of State Kellogg's preferred choice, became his designated successor. During the peace talks, however, former vice president Sacasa did not renounce his claims to the presidency. Kellogg was not about to let Sacasa's ambitions ruin his carefully crafted peace agreement: he instructed the State Department that should Sacasa establish a government in Nicaragua, "the Department could not consider him other than a revolutionist."[53]

Unfortunately, Kellogg's rhetorical excesses about "Bolshevist" Mexican influence in Nicaragua once again interfered with his ability to broker a peace. The banks refused to "lend money to wage a futile war against a Mexican-aided opponent."[54] At the end of 1926, without funds to prosecute the war, Díaz's cabinet informed the State Department that "the government was now absolutely [without] available funds to carry on military operations" and "would as necessity arose resort to all the measures and expedients employed by governments in desperate straits such as inflation of the currency, capital levies [i.e., expropriation] on Liberals first and then indiscriminately and ultimately suspension of payments on foreign debts."[55]

The realization that the Conservative government was on the verge of resorting to expropriation focused minds in Washington. On January 4, 1927, the United States landed marines from the USS *Galveston*.[56] Six days later, on January 10, President Coolidge announced to Congress that not only would he authorize arms sales to the Díaz government and " use the powers committed to me to insure the protection of all American interests in Nicaragua, whether they be endangered by internal strife or outside interference in the affairs of that Republic."[57]

Coolidge's forceful address to Congress emboldened Wall Street, and in March 1927 the Guaranty Trust Company and Seligman provided a $1 million loan to Nicaragua.[58] Unfortunately, Coolidge's threat also energized Liberal forces in Nicaragua, which adopted a new anti-American rhetoric. In order to restrict Liberal troop movements, the United States expanded its "neutral" zones along the coast, but Liberal forces were able to take advantage of the rugged Nicaraguan interior.[59]

In April 1927, the United States dispatched former secretary of war Henry Stimson on a peace mission to Nicaragua. Stimson quickly concluded that neither side was capable of winning the civil war without outside assistance, and that a modus vivendi could be reached. Both Liberal and Conservative factions agreed that U.S. supervision of the presidential elections of 1928 would be an acceptable condition for peace. Stimson himself believed that supervision, perhaps continued to subsequent elections, would be far more acceptable than the alternative of "naked military intervention."[60] In the small town of Tipitapa, Stimson met personally with General José María Moncada, the principal leader of the Liberal forces. Stimson convinced Moncada—using the carrot of peace and the stick of forced American disarmament—to agree to the election plan.[61] By the end of May (the start of the rainy season, which made campaigning near impossible) both sides had turned their weapons over to American military supervisors in return for cash, including over 11,000 rifles, 300 machine guns, and 500,000 cartridges. Sacasa terminated his claims to the presidency on May 20, 1927, although he refused to sign the agreement and left the country for Costa Rica. Another obscure Liberal military leader, Augusto César Sandino, also refused to disarm and lit out for the Honduras border.[62]

Surprisingly, Nicaragua's fiscal position had not been badly hurt by the war. The American chargé d'affaires believed that Nicaragua would repay the emergency 1927 Seligman loan by mid-1928 and that a further loan for war claims would be manageable.[63] Revenue was also needed to pay for the renovated

National Guard, which the Stimson plan envisioned as a non-partisan force replacing the Nicaraguan Army and police forces, trained and assisted by U.S. Navy and Marine Corps personnel.[64] Such a force would be expensive, but U.S. observers believed that Nicaragua had the wherewithal to fund it.[65]

The real problem was that, as Secretary of State Kellogg feared, many Nicaraguans had become radicalized by the war. They rejected American involvement in ideological terms. Almost immediately after the Stimson agreement, Sandino launched a guerrilla campaign against what he viewed as the complicit Nicaraguan government.[66] Ironically, Augusto Sandino, now the de facto military leader of the nationalists, had in fact learned his theories of social justice in Mexico *but not from the Mexican government*. Rather, he had become radicalized while working in Tampico as a laborer for a subsidiary of Standard Oil.[67]

Sandino's forces, never large, lost badly in direct battle with U.S. Marines but fought on more equal terms in small-scale hit-and-run operations.[68] The United States deliberately downplayed the ideological nature of Sandino's revolt. The United States, in fact, insisted that the Nicaraguan government refrain from acknowledging the insurgency at all. Instead, the State Department preferred to use the phrase "bandit activities."[69] Sandino, on the other hand, was explicitly ideological, specifically targeting U.S. troops and American-owned assets. He also courted publicity, especially in the North American press. Despite a Liberal victory in the 1928 election—supervised by the United States and widely regarded as honest—Sandino's insurgency and the American intervention continued to drag on. By the beginning of 1929 over three thousand marines were hunting Sandino's forces across rural Nicaragua.[70] The escalation alarmed many in the United States. In February 1929, the U.S. Senate voted to cut off further funding for marine operations in Nicaragua. In one of his last acts in office, however, Coolidge pressured members of the Senate to reverse their vote. The "small war" in Nicaragua continued into the Hoover administration.[71]

Trapped in Hispaniola

The Harding administration's efforts to extricate itself from its various military occupations were scarcely more successful on Hispaniola. The United States did manage to withdraw the occupation government from the Dominican Republic. Yet withdrawal in practice was a far cry from withdrawal in theory. Dominican nationals assumed nominal sovereignty, but the United States maintained a heavy hand in Dominican affairs: customs, internal revenue, and the Department of Public Works remained under U.S. control. Meanwhile, the U.S. occupation of Haiti dragged on, thanks in large part to the eager collaboration of Haiti's autocratic president, Louis Borno, who welcomed the American presence as a prop for his own regime.

On June 14, 1921, the United States presented its first withdrawal proposal for the Dominican Republic. Five conditions were applied to the proposed Treaty of Evacuation. First, the new government would ratify all legislative acts of the occupation, including loans taken out on the credit of the Dominican Republic. Second, the government would approve a final loan of $2.5 million, which was "the minimum loan required in order to complete the public works which are now in actual course of construction." Third, the customs receivership would remain in place. Fourth, the customs receivership would extend its authority "to the collection and disbursement of such portion of the internal revenues of the Republic as may prove to be necessary, should the customs revenue prove insufficient to meet the service of the foreign debt of the Republic." Fifth, the United States would continue to train—and if necessary command—the National Guard.[72] (The occupation authorities actually wanted the loan to be $10 million, since less would leave the main trunk roads across the island unpaved and uncompleted.[73] The State Department vetoed the idea, fearing that the bond issue would fail "in the face of our announced policy of withdrawing."[74])

Popular reaction in Santo Domingo was not positive: the U.S. minister described it as "a hot blast of protest."[75] The United

States responded by clarifying that it wanted to negotiate the treaty with the representatives of an elected congress.[76] In February 1922, facing a phalanx of opposition, the United States declared that unless an agreement could be hammered out, the occupation would continue until the highways were completed and a constabulary fully trained . . . or July 1, 1924, whichever came first.[77] The Dominicans refused—"We sustain our unswerving protest against the occupation of the Dominican Republic by the military forces of the United States"—and the United States duly withdrew its proposal.[78]

In essence, both sides called each other's bluff. A compromise was quickly reached, in which the United States agreed to permit the selection of a provisional president pending the final treaty, while the Dominicans agreed to the fiscal stipulations. The United States also agreed to withdraw its officers from inside the National Guard.[79] With the approval of High Commissioner Sumner Welles, Juan Bautista Vicini Burgos assumed the provisional presidency on October 21, 1922. Elections were held on March 15, 1924. Horacio Vásquez Lajara easily defeated Francisco Peynado, and on July 13 the United States returned sovereignty to Santo Domingo . . . except for customs, internal revenue, and the Department of Public Works. The National Guard was turned over to Dominican control, under the command of one Rafael Trujillo.

Neither political stability nor democracy survived the American withdrawal—after eight years of near-absolute control, the Americans had accomplished little in terms of lasting institutional change. What the Americans did accomplish, however, was the creation of a power center that could impose order without the need for American military support once political instability began to rear its head—that is, the National Guard.

The problems began when President Vásquez, in a move of dubious constitutionality, got the National Assembly to extend his term from four to six years. His primary rival, Federico Velásquez, reacted by organizing an insurgency. The insurgency failed to prove much of a threat to the newly organized National Guard, but Vásquez began losing political support.[80] In February 1930, Trujillo organized a coup. When reports of military uprisings in the provinces reached the presidential palace, Vásquez called in his military chief and asked, bluntly, "Am I still the President?" Trujillo responded that Vásquez was still president, and Trujillo was at his command—but he continued to replace Vásquez loyalists with his own men. Within a month, Vásquez was forced to resign.[81] Trujillo had been careful to wait until an election year to organize his putsch, and he maintained all the constitutional forms, insisting that Vásquez's resignation was voluntary. On March 19, 1930, two months before the elections, the State Department informed the U.S. minister, "The Department hopes that you will persuade Trujillo not to be [presidential] candidate, yet it realizes the great difficulty of bringing it about and should you not succeed and Trujillo be elected it is most important that you should not impair in any way your relations with him."[82] The scheduled elections took place on May 19, and Trujillo was elected president with 95% of the vote—the 223,851 votes for him exceeded the number of voters on the rolls.[83]

On the other side of Hispaniola, the United States continued its military occupation of Haiti. The Haitian government remained in place, subject to an effective American veto. Although U.S. Marines had suppressed most overt violence, anti-American sentiment ran high. In Port-au-Prince, it had become clear that Haitian president Dartiguenave, deeply unpopular with the Haitian public, had little interest in cooperating with the United States.[84] In the summer of 1920, Dartiguenave clashed with the U.S. financial adviser to Haiti, John Avery McIlhenny—of the McIlhenny Tabasco sauce family—over the reorganization of the National Bank of Haiti by National City Bank of New York and currency controls on the Haitian gourde. In response, McIlhenny suspended the Haitian cabinet's budget proceedings.[85] Dartiguenave remained obstinate, and so the American minister in Haiti suspended the Haitian cabinet's salaries, including that of the president, until a "change of attitude" was in evidence.[86] Despite the arrival in September of the USS *Minnesota* and Admiral Knapp to Port-au-Prince for negotiations, the Haitian government was not "accommodating."[87]

The State Department, aware that the limits of this tactic had been reached, in October ordered the American minister in Haiti to reinstate the salaries of Haitian cabinet officials over the minister's objections.[88] Dartiguenave hoped that the change in U.S. administrations would allow him more freedom of action. Instead, Secretary of State Hughes decided to use the Haitian electoral cycle against him. The new American high commissioner, Brigadier General John H. Russell, conspicuously refused to support the incumbent—issuing statements to the Haitian press that he "espouse[d] the cause of no candidate."[89] The Haitian Council of State instead elected Dartiguenave's minister of foreign affairs, lawyer Louis Borno, as president in April 1922.[90]

Commissioner Russell was at first doubtful about Borno's willingness to accept American financial arrangements. Borno, however, privately approached Russell about fast-tracking the required loan legislation through the Council of State.[91] The $40 million loan was then approved unanimously by the Council of State on June 26, 1922.[92] In the same manner, Borno quickly came to an agreement with National City Bank of New York regarding its management of the National Bank of Haiti—Borno's principal objection being that the bank maintain a *higher* reserve requirement at a time when City Bank despaired of legislating any reserve requirement at all.[93] Russell and Secretary of State Hughes were astounded.

Nevertheless, this ready compliance with American wishes came at a price for Haitian democracy. Borno, an admirer of Benito Mussolini, refused to allow legislative elections during his two terms of office and frequently arrested opposition journalists, preferring to govern autocratically through the Council of State.[94] American officials made few objections to Borno's dictatorship, other than his attempts to modify the Haitian Constitution for a longer term.[95] In fact, the United States thought so highly of Borno that the U.S. Navy moved its warships out of Haitian waters for several months at Borno's request to facilitate his reelection in 1926.[96]

Widening the Empire

If I could have my way, Peru would be practically American within ten or fifteen years.

—President Augusto Leguía

American financial supervision expanded to two unlikely countries during the 1920s: Peru and Bolivia. Neither was geographically close to the United States; nor did Washington think either particularly significant in strategic terms. What both had in common were leaders who believed that contracting out state functions to the United States would improve governance, attract foreign capital, accelerate economic growth—and help, of course, maintain them in power. The complicity of local leaders dovetailed with the desires of American companies to have the United States guarantee their property rights.

The process was smoothest in Peru. In 1912, at the behest of several American banks, the Taft administration began to support loans to the Peruvian government, with the aim to "give stability to our business interests" and "place in the hands of American capitalists the financial future of the Republic."[97] Little came of the policy until Augusto Leguía, Peru's president between 1919 and 1930, decided to deliberately integrate his country as deeply as possible into the informal American empire. Leguía followed the United States out of the League of Nations, supported the occupation of Nicaragua, hung a portrait of James Monroe in the presidential palace, and declared the Fourth of July a national holiday. He told the American embassy that he wanted "to put Peru into the hand of the United States . . . in the nature of a protectorate." Leguía even wrote, "My hope is to put an American in charge of every branch of our government's activities."[98]

Leguía proceeded to turn large parts of Peru's fiscal machinery over to the United States. (One might have thought that Leguía's enthusiasm would have cast some doubts on the market's apparent belief that a fiscal receivership was a *punishment*.) In May 1921, the Guaranty Trust Company of New York announced that it would lend to Leguía's government, but on the condition that Peru nominate an American appointed by the State Department to be head of the customs service. Leguía then asked Ambassador William Gonzales to have the United States appoint somebody to take the position *before* the loan was approved. Leguía told the ambassador that he did not want the transfer of authority to an American to appear connected to the loan.[99] He then gave the State Department carte blanche to decide the powers of the office.[100]

Leguía pestered the State Department through September, when Secretary of State Charles Evans Hughes finally announced that it would nominate William Cumberland, an economics professor from the University of Minnesota with extensive government experience. Hughes could not promise, however, that Cumberland would take the job until the Peruvian government specified his powers and compensation.[101] Leguía responded that Cumberland would have the power to reform the administration and collection of customs as he saw fit, as well as recommend changes in the tariff structure. He would be guaranteed a weekly meeting with the president, a seat on the board of the Peruvian central bank, and a salary of $16,000—$201,064 in 2011 dollars.[102] The final contract gave Cumberland the authority to "revise the present system of collecting the revenues and covering them into the public treasury . . . study the present system of import and export duties and suggest modifications thereof . . . propose the appointment, promotion, demotion, transfer or dismissal of employees in the customs service . . . [and] assure the lawful collection and safeguarding of the customs revenues by proper police protection." He would be "consulted in advance of administrative action or recommendations in regard to all financial policies . . . and shall become a director of any government financial fiscal agency which the Republic of Peru may establish." He also received the authority to hire four American citizens to serve respectively as auditor, customs inspector, statistician, and private secretary.[103]

Leguía appears to have hoped that the receivership would force the United States to support Peru in various territorial disputes with its neighbors. Such hopes went unfulfilled. The United States agreed to arbitrate Peru's disputes with Chile, Colombia, and Ecuador, but it acted as an evenhanded judge, not an advocate for Peru. The Colombian settlement was an especially bitter pill: the Salomón-Lozano Treaty of 1922 placed the border at the Putumayo River, favoring Colombia. Leguía procrastinated on sending the treaty to the Peruvian Congress; he finally did so in 1927 only under American pressure.[104] Leguía also believed that American fiscal control would lead to greater access to the U.S. market, but Washington refused, point-blank, to grant Peruvian sugar the same tariff preference granted to Cuban sugar.[105]

In addition, placing an American manager in charge of customs failed on its own terms: customs receipts barely surpassed their previous peak. Customs revenues did rise from their 1921–22 nadir (see figure 5.1), but it was a consequence of trade's recovery from the 1921 recession in the United States rather than any administrative magic. The failure of customs revenue to grow is even more striking in contrast with strong growth in the revenue streams *not* under American control. Cumberland was unable to reform the customs administration. As he later wrote, "Graft was rampant; very few people paid duties in accordance to what the tariffs called for—it was a matter of bargaining with Peruvian officials."[106] When Cumberland fired a corrupt official who had been caught taking bribes, the official challenged him to a duel.[107] (Academic politics was a vicious thing, then as now, but dueling was not standard operating procedure at the University of Minnesota.) Cumberland also proved impotent at controlling corruption at the central bank. A relative of Leguía, Eulogio Romero, "a most unscrupulous politician," became head of the bank. Romero concocted a

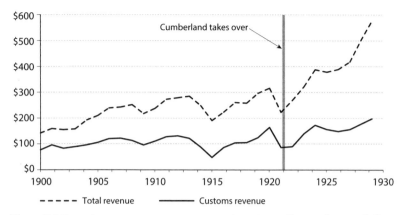

Figure 5.1 Peruvian government revenues, 1900–29, millions of 2009 dollars
Source: Oxford Latin American Studies Database.

scheme to illegally cut the silver content of the coinage. Cumberland discovered the scheme but could do nothing about it.[108] He was most horrified, in fact, by a voucher scheme used to pay schoolteachers. The teachers would exchange their vouchers for cash with their local congressmen, who took a 25% cut of the proceeds. "This was one of the major sources of graft in Peru and one of the principal motivations for men wanting to be a Senator or Representative. Each collected a substantial part of the salaries of the schoolteachers in his district." When Cumberland discovered the scheme, the Peruvian politicians involved responded by offering him a cut.[109]

Cumberland eventually couldn't take any more. Corruption and mismanagement, he found, extended to the highest level of Peruvian government. When he took over customs, he found spending levels running at roughly twice revenues in all the ministries, via "special credits" and other forms of evading financial controls. In Cumberland's words, "[Leguía] wrecked the finances of Peru just as thoroughly as if he had himself been a grafter."[110] He left in 1924, preferring to run *Haiti's* finances. The Guaranty Trust Company, not surprisingly, decided against granting a loan to Peru.

Leguía's embrace of the United States failed to increase customs revenue (relative to other revenues or the earlier trend), access to the U.S. market, or support for Peru's expansive territorial claims. Its primary benefit was to enlist the Coolidge administration as a booster for loans to Peru. When Guaranty Trust pulled out, the State Department brought in another bank, White-Weld. White-Weld signed a $7 million contract in October 1924, allowing Leguía to cover his chronic deficits. The Bureau of Foreign and Domestic Commerce began to issue bullish reports about Peru. When White-Weld's resources proved insufficient to meet Peru's financing needs, the U.S. government began to assure smaller banks that Peru was, in fact, creditworthy.[111]

Why did the U.S. government support such a feckless regime? Simply put, Jersey Standard owned significant (but politically sensitive) oil interests in the country, and there was little cost and some benefit to securing its investments. In 1922, a Canadian subsidiary of Standard Oil of New Jersey, the International Petroleum Company (IPC), purchased the rights to the La Brea and Pariñas oil fields on the northern coast. The problem was that IPC's claim was highly controversial and based on legal claims of arguable validity. The original claim came from a title for the La Brea hacienda issued by Simón Bolívar in 1826.[112] The land had been granted to José Antonio de la Quintana in payment for loans made to Bolívar's revolutionary movement, and contained a "pitch mine." In 1873, Peru passed an oil and mining law that provided for the issuance of separate mining claims. An 1877 law required that all existing titles be submitted for validation, but La Brea's owner failed to do so. A British citizen, Herbert Tweddle, then bought the title in 1888. He asked the government to clarify its status. The Peruvians ruled that it was private property but left the boundaries of the claim vague. In 1890, Tweddle leased it to the London and Pacific Petroleum Company.[113] The claim was apparently the only one in the country that combined surface and subsurface rights.[114] In 1914, the British subleased the property to IPC. IPC invested $19 million; by 1921 it was yielding 7,741 barrels per day.[115]

Once IPC started producing oil, the vagueness of the original claim became a pressing issue. In 1916 the Peruvian government claimed that the area of land was much larger than had been thought, and therefore the British owners—and, indirectly, IPC—would be liable for much higher taxes.[116] The company's estimated bill rose from £30 per year to £120,000. The IPC sent a delegation to negotiate, but the Peruvians refused to talk. The company, therefore, in 1918 cut back production and shut down its refinery. Since Peruvian oil was aimed at the domestic market, this immediately created a sense of crisis. The Peruvian government had few levers that it could use to force IPC to produce, since its Peruvian refinery was small and most of the crude was shipped to California for refining. The government could not force the company to refine crude oil in California and ship it back to Peru.[117] Were it to expropriate, it would need to market the crude and buy refined products on the world market, a daunting task.

What Peru could do, however, was threaten to transfer the concession to another international company. Despite his public declarations of fealty to Washington, Leguía skillfully played off British and American interests. He promised Royal Dutch Shell an exclusive right to prospect, fully understanding that the U.S. ambassador would protest.[118] Jersey Standard suggested submitting the dispute to an ad hoc arbitration panel consisting of jurors from Canada, Peru, and Switzerland. Leguía demanded $1 million before he would agree to allow the arbitration to proceed. The IPC agreed, and the arbitration went forward. The arbiters decided in favor of the government: the owners of the claim would pay £120,000 through 1972.[119] In issuing its decision, however, the panel implicitly also recognized the British company's ownership of the subsoil rights, which it immediately sold to IPC. IPC then invested $60 million in its operations, bringing production up to 29,600 barrels per day by 1929 and 41,300 at its 1936 peak.[120]

Jersey Standard realized that its position in Peru was relatively precarious. The legal basis for the company's concession

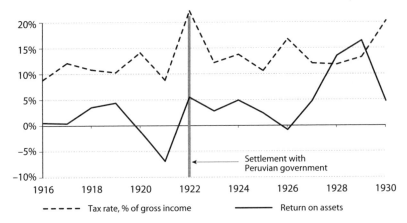

Figure 5.2 Tax rates on IPC and its returns on assets (after tax), 1916–30

Source: Rosemary Thorp and Geoffrey Bertram, *Peru, 1890–1977: Growth and Policy in an Open Economy* (New York: Columbia University Press, 1978), pp. 104–6. Thorp and Bertram combined income figures denominated in Peruvian soles with tax payments denominated in U.S. dollars.

Note: The 1922 spike in tax payments is due to the $1 million special payment IPC made to the Peruvian government as part of the 1922 settlement.

was contestable. Moreover, it depended upon President Leguía's support for the company's tax exemptions and the rates fixed by the 1922 agreement (see figure 5.2). In fact, the company's relatively low tax rates were widely seen as a quid pro quo for IPC's help in attempting to arrange loans for the Peruvian government. The U.S. government therefore agreed to help Jersey Standard by lending its support to Peru's quest for foreign funding.[121]

It should be noted that two other American companies were deeply vested in Peru (although it is not clear that they directly lobbied the U.S. government on Leguía's behalf): the Cerro de Pasco Corporation and W. R. Grace. Cerro de Pasco was founded in 1902 by a Turkish-American named James Ben Ali Haggin and boasted J. P. Morgan, a member of the Vanderbilt family, William Randolph Hearst's mother, and Ogden Mills's grandfather among its principals. By 1916, Cerro de Pasco's investment in Peru (including a railroad to serve the mine) had reached $30 million ($429 million in 2009 dollars).[122] By 1929 the book value of its investments had reached $50 million ($517 million in 2009 dollars), rivaling Jersey Standard's investment of $68.5 million. W. R. Grace controlled shipping between the United States and Peru and owned interests in textile factories (where it controlled 90% of Peru's output), sugar plantations and mills (18% of Peruvian production), and electricity generation and transmission.[123] W. R. Grace, in fact, was the largest single commercial enterprise in the country.

The Permanent Fiscal Commission in Bolivia

Bolivia is a case where American fiscal intervention produced higher revenues—because the Americans pushed through an initial round of tax hikes on the tin industry, not because the new American managers reduced corruption. The tax hikes then triggered a round of conflicts between American creditors and American tin miners. The tin miners won those conflicts, capping the ability of the U.S. administrators of Bolivia's fisc to raise revenue. Ultimately, then, the fiscal intervention failed: by 1928, the American administration of Bolivian finances began to believe that default was inevitable.

Extensive graft prompted the American fiscal intervention in Bolivia. State Department officials reported that the finance minister "personally retained"—that is, stole—20% of all taxes collected in-country.[124] The Bolivian head of customs estimated that 25% of customs revenue disappeared between collection and delivery to the central government.[125] With the backing of the Harding administration, American bankers persuaded the Bolivian government to agree to a 1922 loan contract for $33 million ($361 million in 2011 dollars) that mandated that Bolivia place much of its revenue under the control of an organization called the Comisión Fiscal Permanente (CFP).[126] Three officials constituted the CFP: one appointed by the Bolivian government and two by New York banks. Under the contract, the CFP gained the power to administer parts of the tax system and, within limits, alter tax rates.[127]

When the Bolivian government showed some reluctance to sign, Secretary of State Hughes weighed in directly. He wrote the American minister in La Paz: "Representatives of Equitable Trust have informed the Department that . . . the President of Bolivia has declined for the present to grant the power of attorney [to the Bolivian minister in Washington to sign the bonds]. . . . Orally and informally bring the bankers' views in the matter to the attention of the President of Bolivia."[128] When that proved insufficient, Hughes stepped up the pressure. "You will say," he told the minister, "that this government, speaking as a sincere well-wisher of Bolivia, recommends most earnestly and strongly that he carry out immediately the terms of the contract, and that the collapse of Bolivia's credit would appear to be the only alternative. Impress upon him the fact that should the bankers not be in a position to deliver the definitive bonds . . . serious losses would follow to a very numerous body of American investors who purchased them confiding in the good faith and integrity of the Bolivian government. . . . It might even be impossible for Bolivia to contract other foreign loans."[129]

Under pressure from the United States (and needing the money) Bolivia ultimately signed the agreement. On November 30, 1923, the CFP replaced the mining profits tax with a 9% tax on gross mining revenues.[130] The switch to a revenue tax was intended to be revenue-neutral, but the Bolivian Congress (under CFP prodding) also raised taxes on the transfer of mineral properties and the sales and profit tax on commerce and industry. This was followed by increases in the mining export tax.[131] In 1927–28, on the recommendation of a visiting American commission led by economist Edwin Kemmerer, the Bolivian Congress reversed the increases on export taxes, lowering them by a quarter, but compensated for that with a 35% hike in import tariffs.[132] Effective tax rates almost doubled from 6.5% of mining export revenues in 1920–23 to 12.8% in 1924–28.[133] (See figure 5.3.)

The CFP followed up the implementation of the new code with aggressive enforcement. It immediately began annual audits

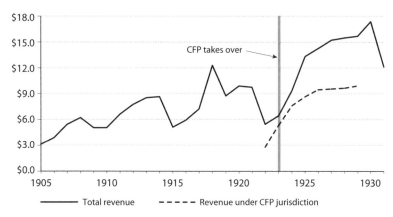

Figure 5.3 Bolivian government revenue, 1905–31, millions of 2009 dollars
Source: Comisión Fiscal Permanente, *Sexta Memoria presentada al Ministerio de Hacienda, 1928–29* (La Paz, I929), pp. 3 and table 3; pre-1920 data from Oxford Latin American Studies Database. All figures deflated by using the U.S. GDP deflator.

of the major mining companies. Between 1923 and 1926, annual mining tax revenues rose from $557,000 to $2.0 million in nominal terms.[134] The State Department claimed that the CFP raised revenue by 20% by removing opportunities for corruption, but provided no substantiation.

Did CFP enforcement efforts raise significant revenue compared to the tax hikes? About one-third of the revenue increase (32.8%) came from the incorporation of Patiño Mines and Enterprises Consolidated, which generated transfer tax revenues. An additional 17.8% came from the switch to a gross revenue tax on mining. Finally, 18.2% of the rise was due to increases in export taxes.[135] In short, at least two-thirds of the revenue increases were due to windfall revenues or tax increases.

We can also observe how much the CFP collected from corporate audits. Between 1923 and 1930 the CFP audited the books of the country's largest commercial firms (in practice, the mining industry). It claimed 9.7 million bolivianos in back taxes, of which it collected 5.2 million ($18.2 million in 2009 dollars).[136] These revenues totaled only 2.4% of the total revenues collected by the CFP in 1923–30. In addition, it appears that the revenue under CFP jurisdiction was headed upward *before* the commissioners actually took control of the fiscal apparatus (see figure 5.3). This is consistent with the fact that Bolivia was beginning a long tin-driven commodity boom. It is not consistent with the hypothesis that outsourcing management to American officials begat an administrative revolution that increased revenue by reducing corruption.

Limits to Fiscal Reform in Bolivia

The CFP ran into strong opposition from the mining companies. The companies protested the tax increases, and they formed the Asociación de Industriales Mineros de Bolivia to lobby against further levies. In 1924 the largest of the tin-mining companies, Patiño Mines and Enterprises Consolidated, offered to underwrite a loan to the government of £600,000 ($2.9 million, or $31 million in 2011 dollars) at 8% to complete the Sucre-Potosí railroad. In return, the government had to promise no new taxes on tin production or export.[137] The miners also directly lobbied the State Department and the New York bankers who ran the CFP. The Asociación wrote Equitable Trust in ungrammatical shorthand:

> Failure to pass law with its contingent clause fixing taxation for five years will leave road open to higher taxation on mining industry which latter happening would automatically compel members of this association to consider with all seriousness united action in shutting down their mines . . . if because of your opposition or intervention of S[tate] D[epartment] W[ashington] loan should fail and railway not built great proportion of responsibility therefore will be laid to United States and broadcasted throughout country thus lowering prestige United States this country . . . we hope you will comprehend that failure of the

Patiño loan contains the greater danger of damaging credit of Bolivia and lowering quotation of its bonds in your market with the further danger of damaging the prestige of the United States here depending upon the action pursued by yourselves and the State Department in Washington.[138]

The lobbying worked. In December 1924, the Bolivian Congress authorized the Patiño loan; the bonds were floated in London in 1925. In return, the CFP froze tax rates and eased up slightly on collection. By 1930, the CFP had collected $1.8 million in arrears, but accounting operations found $3.4 million in unpaid taxes over the same period.[139]

Why did the CFP agree to benefit the tin companies at the expense of the bondholders? Simply put, American investors owned a large share of the Bolivian tin industry. In 1926, Patiño Enterprises controlled 42% of Bolivian production—and thus 11% of world output—making it the largest tin-mining company in the world. Patiño had been founded by a Bolivian store clerk in Oruro named Simón Patiño. As a clerk, Patiño had granted a store credit of $250 to a prospector using the prospector's claim as security. When the prospector failed to pay, the store fired Patiño, who was left with the deeds to the prospector's claim.[140] Those deeds turned out to be for the phenomenally productive Llallagua and Uncia tin properties. Patiño and his wife worked the claims themselves until he could take out a loan from a British commercial house, which granted relatively easy terms in return for the right to market the output.[141] In 1922, Patiño sold a $1.5 million stake ($15.9 million in 2009 dollars) in the Llallagua mine to the National Lead Company of Philadelphia. Two years later, he reincorporated Patiño Mines and Enterprises Consolidated in Delaware. National Lead took 4% of the new company, whose stock now had a par value of $30 million.[142] Patiño himself moved to Paris with his family. In December 1926, the company sold 200,000 out of 1.5 million shares at $25 in New York, with Lehman as the underwriter.

By then shareholders living in the United States owned 17% of Patiño Enterprises.[143]

The Guggenheim family of New York controlled the second-largest tin company in the country, Caracoles. Caracoles produced 16% of Bolivia's tin output in 1925. In 1922, Simon Guggenheim bought several existing properties in Quimsa Cruz, between La Paz and Oruro, for $16 million. The properties were in very mountainous terrain, requiring the company to build an aerial tramway from the sorting station at 15,300 feet altitude to the concentrating mill at 12,500 feet.[144] Americans also owned several smaller properties, including Fabulosa Mines Consolidated, the Bolivia Tin Corporation, the Berenguela Tin Mines, Ltd., and the tiny Compañía General de Minas in La Paz Province.[145]

Once tin prices began to fall in 1927, there was no way to square the circle between the interests of the tin companies and the bondholders. The deal with the tin companies took tax hikes on Bolivia's major industry off the table. Attempts to reduce evasion ran into strong opposition. In 1927, the CFP estimated that the tax authorities were losing 15% of their income from evasion. It recommended a few simple reforms, such as requiring alcohol manufacturers to open their books to the government. The Bolivian Congress refused to approve any of the recommendations. Moreover, corruption in other parts of the government made the CFP's job more difficult. In 1926, for example, the State Department reported that the finance minister tried to bully the commission in order "to wrest back taxes from the mining companies upon which [he] received a percentage."[146]

The Bolivian government made two additional attempts at revenue reform. First, in April 1928, it incorporated the Corporación Recaudadora Nacional (CRN). The CRN was a private, for-profit company charged with collecting domestic excise taxes for the government. The CRN managed to increase domestic excise tax receipts—in 1929, alcohol tax receipts jumped by a factor of 2.7. The CRN also made short-term loans to the government at 6% a year, and its coffers served as collateral against which the government could take out additional long-term loans from domestic bankers. The CRN was a successful fiscal reform—but it should be noted that it was a *Bolivian* reform, organized by "local bankers and businessmen."[147]

The second—rather less successful—measure consisted of the 1927 "Kemmerer mission." Edwin Kemmerer was a Princeton economist who had since 1923 carried out financial reforms in a broad series of countries, including Colombia, Chile, Ecuador, Guatemala, and Peru, with the general approval of the State Department. (Kemmerer had also implemented monetary reforms in the American possessions of the Philippines and Puerto Rico, and ran advisory missions in China, Germany, Poland, and Turkey.)[148] Kemmerer missions were seen as a "good housekeeping seal of approval" in the United States, a necessary but not sufficient precursor to accessing credit in New York. With a budget deficit looming, Bolivian president Hernando Siles hoped that the mission would make it easier for him to float foreign loans even with the disapproval of the CFP.[149] The American ambassador to Bolivia pledged to support Kemmerer's mission "in any way possible."[150] Kemmerer recommended a cut in export taxes, which he believed to be above the revenue-maximizing level.[151] He also recommended the establishment of a personal income tax, customs reorganization, and the creation of an "Office of the Comptroller General," which would complement the CFP and be staffed by an American.[152] It is not clear what Kemmerer's mission accomplished in concrete terms: Bolivia enacted none of the proposed reforms. On the other hand, the prospect that Bolivia might enact them persuaded Wall Street to advance money *despite* the CFP's disapproval. Without any reform on Bolivia's part, Dillon, Read & Co. of New York arranged a $14 million loan before the mission was even complete. A second loan followed in 1928 for $23 million ($152 and $247 million in 2011 dollars).[153] It seems that Wall Street continued to prefer to make loans to nations that had been intervened in, not because the interventions produced greater revenue but because they believed that the receiverships would prioritize repayment of new capital.

The Failure of Dollar Diplomacy

The individual stories of this and the previous chapter, taken together, represent a litany of failure. The United States believed that poor revenue collection was the root of unstable property rights, but proved unable to increase revenues in the countries it intervened. A skeptical reader, however, might object that the stories of individual fiscal intervention uses those same countries before the intervention as the counterfactual. Perhaps revenues would have decreased (or decreased even more) in the *absence* of American officials?

In order to test the hypothesis that revenue would have fallen without American intervention it was necessary to control for revenue trends in other Latin American countries and general economic conditions. This entailed collecting fiscal data for 12 Latin American nations that were never subject to fiscal intervention, in addition to the eight receiverships. It also entailed collecting data on export and import prices for those countries, as a proxy for economic conditions. A country undergoing an export boom, for example, would be expected to have higher fiscal revenues than one which was not.

When the receiverships are put into comparative perspective, American interventions perform even *worse* than indicated by the specific examples. The regression in Table 5.1 uses a fixed-effects specification to determine the effect of fiscal intervention on the natural log of revenues, adjusting for terms of trade, export prices, World War I, and changes in the revenues earned by *other* Latin American countries. The first four specifications use customs revenue as a dependent variable; the second four use total revenue. In all specifications, the result is the same: revenue in countries enjoying American fiscal supervision is lower than countries that manage their own fiscal systems.

The fiscal receiverships did little to lower the cost of capital enjoyed by the intervened nations relative to their neighbors.

Table 5.1
Revenue regressions, Latin America, 1900–1931

Dependent variable: natural log customs revenue in (1) to (4); total revenue in (5) to (8)

	(1)	(2)	(3)	(4)	(5)	(6)	(7)	(8)
Receivership	−2.56**	−2.56**	−2.08**	−1.38**	−2.01**	−2.01**	−1.45**	−1.15**
	(0.74)	(0.74)	(0.53)	(0.42)	(0.66)	(0.66)	(0.43)	(0.39)
World War I		0.61	1.38	1.72*		1.12**	1.23**	1.95**
		(0.92)	(0.79)	(0.74)		(0.39)	(0.38)	(0.39)
Terms of trade			−0.005				0.000	
			(0.005)				(0.004)	
Export prices				0.011*				0.011*
				(0.005)				(0.004)
Constant	9.63**	9.63**	9.45**	9.71**	9.26**	9.26**	9.26**	10.12**
	(0.84)	(0.84	(0.86)	(0.69)	(0.44)	(0.44)	(0.64)	(0.48)
Country fixed effects	yes	yes	yes	yes	yes	yes	yes	yes
Time fixed effects	yes	yes	yes	yes	yes	yes	yes	yes
Number of observations	366	366	337	337	525	525	493	494

Note: Robust standard errors clustered by country in columns (5) through (8).
Coefficients that are significantly different from zero are denoted as * 5% and ** 1%.

In fact, when a fiscal receivership was announced, the yields on sovereign debt issued by *other* Latin American countries jumped an average of 50 basis points.[154] Rather than provide reassurance that Uncle Sam stood ready to fix fiscal problems in Latin America, the fiscal receiverships appeared to remind investors what a risky place Latin America really was.

The average spread between the maturity-adjusted yields on sovereign debt issued by the Southern Cone countries of Argentina, Brazil, and Chile (which were not going to enter an American fiscal receivership under any conceivable circumstances) and debt issued by the countries inside the American sphere in the circum-Caribbean and Andes steadily widened after 1925, growing practically monotonically from 22 basis points in January 1925 to 175 points by the October 1929. This spread remained lower than the 300 basis points it averaged before the 1904 declaration of the Roosevelt Corollary, but the deterioration was marked.

Conclusion

The first informal American empire started within the circum-Caribbean region with a series of interventions on behalf of American creditors and investors. This began the empire's vertical expansion: in order to guarantee that states would refrain from expropriation and default, the United States promised to help them reform their fiscal systems. The catch was once American officials were on the ground managing core state functions, it became impossible to withdraw when the countries fell into political instability. In Haiti and the Dominican Republic, the United States installed American occupation governments. In Nicaragua, the United States never officially displaced the local government, but in practice this was a distinction without a difference.

The empire also spread horizontally (see figure 5.4). Once the United States pledged to protect investors in the circum-Caribbean, investors in other countries began to demand that the U.S. government also protect *their* interests. The binding limit to the spread of this policy was the ability of the United States to project and exercise power. In Liberia, the United States trained, equipped, and commanded a proxy force, commanded by Americans, to put down the Kru revolts. Even in a place as distant as Bolivia, the United States could effectively wield a stranglehold over the country's commerce given Bolivia's traditional hostility to Chile and Paraguay, its lack of transport links with Argentina and Brazil, and the absence of other

Hawaii

Puerto Rico

Liberia

■■■ U.S. territory (Philippines and Guam not on map)   ▓▓▓ Informal intervention sphere

■■■ Formal protectorate   ▒▒▒ Mexico

■■■ Fiscal receivership

Figure 5.4 The first American empire, circa 1929

plausible sources of foreign capital. By the end of the period, few Latin American countries were too far away for the United States to credibly threaten economic sanctions (at low domestic cost) should they act against the interests of American investors. Nevertheless, because of their large size, relative military power, and links with Europe, Argentina and Brazil remained generally outside the American ambit.

The limits to the spread of the informal empire suggest a corollary of their own: American imperial power stopped when the costs to the overall national interest rose so high that parochial economic interests could not mobilize sufficient domestic support to overcome opposition. The converse explains why preferential trade tariffs were not on the table in the 1920s (except for Cuba's existing privileges) despite the benefits they would have conferred on American investors overseas. Lowering tariffs would have incurred the wrath of domestic industry interest groups. No administration could have overcome the resulting opposition at an acceptable political cost. Woodrow Wilson was barely able to repeal the clause of the Panama Canal Act that granted preferential treatment to American shipping, despite the fact that it violated treaty agreements with Great Britain.

The correlation of political forces was such that no administration, whatever its intentions, was capable of escaping the empire trap. The Wilson and Harding administrations both came to power explicitly promising to get the United States out of the business of using the power of the state to protect American overseas economic interests. Instead, they presided over a deepening of the extent of intervention inside the sphere Roosevelt had established *and* a widening of its ambit to include Liberia and the Andean nations. The fact that direct American efforts to reform the institutions of foreign countries had been a failure did little to stop the expansion. The political cost of intervention to the United States as a whole—military and otherwise—was simply too small compared to the benefits to individual bondholders.

The idea of an American empire attracted no ideological support; no one wrote poetry or drama about the U.S. Marines in Santo Domingo or the customs administrators in Nicaragua. People like William Cumberland and Calvin Carter did not become national heroes or have public schools named after them. Nevertheless, as long as the cost was low enough, it was impossible to muster the political support to unwind America's commitment to defend its citizens' property rights where it had the power to do so. That is not to say that Americans could rely on a blank check from their government, or that investors got their way in every dispute. It is to say that the coalition between the owners of foreign bonds and the owners of foreign direct investments was sufficiently strong—and the cost of intervention to the wider public sufficiently low—that the best intentions of Republican and Democratic administrations were not enough to extricate America from the informal empire it had created for itself.

six

Escaping by Accident

It ought not to be the policy of the United States to intervene by force to secure or maintain contracts between our citizens and foreign states or their citizens.

—*President Herbert Hoover*

The Great Depression was a breakpoint between two eras, a sharp discontinuity between the global boom of the 1920s and the palsied, stunted economies of the 1930s. The Depression was also a time of rapid political transition. In many countries, political opportunists used the Depression to pursue nationalist, militaristic, and even genocidal goals. Hitler, Stalin, Mussolini, and other demagogues skillfully played on Depression-era fears and anxieties to maximize their own power and garner support for the use of force—against their own populations as well as foreign ones.

In the United States, however, the Depression reorganized politics in such a way as to *reduce* militarism and interventionism. Protracted economic stagnation allowed the government to escape the pattern it had created for itself over the past generation—the empire trap—by fragmenting the political coalition that had sustained interventionism over the previous quarter century. First, it split the interests of bondholders and direct investors. Second, it greatly weakened the domestic political power of bondholders and financiers. Third, it strengthened domestic producers who began pushing for higher protection against foreign competition, which in turn lowered the value of American-owned overseas direct investments.

The chain of events that led the United States to withdraw from its financial protectorates began abroad. In prosperous times, a debtor nation in the American sphere of influence could usually manage to keep up with debt payments while also keeping taxes low with sufficient public spending to provide sufficient public goods. Depression-era scarcity, however, confronted these nations with a hard choice. They could maintain payments on their sovereign debt—but at the cost of austerity that undermined political stability. Alternatively, they could maintain public spending but default on their debts, at the cost of potential American retaliation.

The holders of sovereign debt and the owners of direct investments no longer wanted the same outcomes. Financiers wanted governments to do everything possible to continue servicing their debt. They considered it acceptable—even desirable—to raise tariffs and excises, alter concession terms, suspend tax exemptions, and slash spending. Owners of direct investments, on the other hand, found none of these actions agreeable. Higher taxes and tariffs had a direct impact on the value of their investments. Lower public spending generated political instability, which threatened their property rights.

The Depression ensured that the direct investors would win the resulting political battles. The reason was that (unlike the lesser depression that began in 2007) the Great Depression prompted a sustained political reaction against the banks. In the wake of scandals (and the disappearance of most of the wealth that the financiers claimed to have created) it would have been difficult at best for creditors to wield the influence over foreign policy that they had enjoyed before 1929.

The Depression, however, wasn't a clear win for American foreign direct investors. Scarcity roused the behemoth of domestic industry. In flush times, when there was enough demand to go around, domestic producers had better things to do than raise barriers against their U.S.-owned overseas competitors.

There was protectionism, but it was *relatively* restrained. As consumption dropped, however, domestic producers grimly set about leveraging their political capital in order to eliminate their competitors. American interests abroad didn't stand a chance. The lowered value of foreign investments, in turn, reduced the power of their owners to lobby Washington to protect them from host governments, creating a vicious—or virtuous—cycle of decreased political influence.

In this way, the political logic of the Depression upset the previous pecking order of commercial interests. With the American domestic lobbies that had promoted the empire trap at odds, Hoover and Roosevelt began to dismantle America's informal empire. Hoover administration officials signed off on the Bolivian, Dominican, Panamanian, Peruvian, and Salvadoran defaults, and Hoover famously signed the Smoot-Hawley Act, which raised duties on the products produced by American-owned investments abroad. The political shifts had some consequences that can only be called unusual: Franklin Roosevelt went so far as to *overthrow* the Cuban government when its refusal to default on its foreign debt threatened the security of American direct investments on the island.

Herbert Hoover and America's Informal Empire

Herbert Hoover did not intend to dismantle America's informal empire. In fact, as commerce secretary, he proposed that a public corporation be created to assess the viability of all Latin American loans. Hoover also tried to get the Coolidge administration to take up the cause of "currency reform"—meaning fixed exchange rates against the U.S. dollar—in the belief that flexible exchange rates discouraged American trade and investment.[1]

During his tenure as secretary of state, Hoover's cabinet colleague, Charles Evans Hughes, reaffirmed the doctrine that the United States had the right to intervene abroad when American property came under threat. As the head of the U.S. delegation to the Sixth International Conference of American States, held in Havana in early 1928, Hughes declared, "A government is fully justified in taking action—I would call it interposition of a temporary character—for the purpose of protecting the lives and property of its nationals." Hughes attempted to soften his statement by adding, "I would say that it does not constitute an intervention." Needless to say, the Latin American delegations were not particularly pleased with Hughes's declaration—with the notable exception of Cuba.[2]

President-elect Hoover made a grand gesture toward respecting Latin American sovereignty when he set off on a symbolic "goodwill tour" in November 1928, shortly after his election. Paying for additional expenses out of pocket, Hoover deadheaded on the American battleship USS *Maryland*, visiting Honduras, El Salvador, Nicaragua, Costa Rica, Ecuador, Peru, and Chile, where he crossed the Andes to Argentina. From Argentina he boarded the USS *Utah* and visited Uruguay and Brazil on his return. A recurrent theme in the twenty-five addresses the president-elect made during his travels was the U.S. desire to be a "good neighbor" to Latin America—a phrase more often associated with his successor.

Local reactions to Hoover's visits could best be characterized as mixed. Factional intrigue nearly wrecked his visit to Nicaragua, where, despite the obviously unsettled circumstances, Hoover pledged to withdraw American troops. In Peru and Brazil, on the other hand, Hoover's visit sparked acclaim and civic celebration.[3]

Until 1931, however, Hoover's actions were rather less magnanimous than his words. His administration threatened the Dominican Republic on three separate occasions, and he failed to withdraw from Haiti after the Haitian legislature unanimously rejected his proposed settlement. Hoover managed to withdraw from Nicaragua, but only by turning over authority to Anastasio Somoza, who later proved one of the more brutal and kleptocratic leaders in Latin America.[4] He did resist the temptation to intervene when unrest flared up in Costa Rica and Panama, but neither situation posed a serious threat to American interests.

There was, however, some ambivalence in Washington about U.S. policy in Latin America, although the discussion was less critical than is generally believed. In December 1928, Undersecretary of State Reuben Clark produced a long report on the Monroe Doctrine for president-elect Hoover. Many historians came to believe that the Clark Memorandum repudiated intervention.[5] In fact, it did nothing of the sort. In oddly legalistic language, Clark's report held that the Monroe Doctrine did not apply to, well, almost everything: civil wars, wars between Latin American states, wars between a parent country and a former colony (except in the case of an attempted "reannexation by Spain"), or wars between European and Latin American countries.[6] The only goal of the Monroe Doctrine, in Clark's view, was to prevent the "permanent occupation" of Latin American territory by extra-hemispheric powers.[7] Clark went so far as to argue that the Monroe Doctrine did not "relieve Latin American states of their responsibilities as independent sovereignties," and European states could still intervene in the event that Latin governments failed to protect their nationals or property.[8] Moreover, Clark argued that the United States had the same right:

> The [Monroe] declaration does not apply to purely inter-American relations. Nor does the declaration purport to lay down any principles that are to govern the interrelationship of the states of this Western Hemisphere as among themselves. . . . Such arrangements as the United States has made, for example, with Cuba, Santo Domingo, Haiti, and Nicaragua, are not within the Doctrine as it was announced by Monroe. They may be accounted for as the expression of a national policy which, like the Doctrine itself, originates in the necessities of security or self-preservation.

The so-called "Roosevelt corollary" was to the effect, as generally understood, that in case of financial or other difficulties in weak Latin American countries, the United States should attempt an adjustment thereof lest European governments should intervene, and intervening should occupy territory—an act which would be contrary to the principles of the Monroe Doctrine. . . . As has already been indicated above, it is not believed that this corollary is justified by the terms of the Monroe Doctrine, however much it may be justified by the application of the doctrine of self-preservation.[9]

The First Defaults

Our investments and trade relations are such that it is almost impossible to conceive of any conflict anywhere on earth which would not affect us injuriously.
—*President Calvin Coolidge, 1928*

With so little domestic opposition, why did Hoover wind up dismantling the United States' economic protectorates in Latin America? The answer was that the Great Depression forced his hand. The first domino to fall was Bolivia. Bolivia's geographic position ensured that it would never be fully under American protection. Unlike the rest of Latin America (save Paraguay) Bolivia was conspicuously absent from the Army War College's roster of contingency plans.[10] Only the country's lack of transport links with Argentina, Brazil, and Chile provided the United States with potential leverage.

Bolivia was, however, under American financial supervision, via the Comisión Fiscal Permanente (CFP).[11] In 1928, Bolivia contracted new loans over CFP opposition.[12] Edwin Kemmerer, who led an American advisory mission to Bolivia, told the State

Department that he did not believe that Bolivia would be able to repay its debts; in fact, "he doubted whether the country would eventually survive as a nation." The Commerce Department recommended that the United States reject the loans.[13] The State official charged with reviewing policy toward Bolivia added his voice to the chorus. He wrote that new issues only "assured [the bankers] a substantial profit and their clients, purchasers of prior issues . . . a breathing spell from an inevitable default."[14] Other officials, however, worried about the impact in Bolivia should the loans fall through. The reason was the money was needed to maintain government employment. The State Department decided to avoid vetoing the loans. It did, however, warn the bankers that the United States considered them to be taking their own risks.[15] It is questionable whether the doubts and disavowal were believed, however, and the loans went through.

When Bolivian government revenue fell as expected in 1930 (see figure 6.1), U.S. analysts believed that the only ways to avoid default would be to (a) badly damage the mining industry via "confiscatory" taxes, or (b) risk the stability of the government via draconian spending cuts. As a result, the State Department declared default to be "unavoidable." The CFP concurred, also claiming that tax rates had reached their practical maximum.[16]

In June 1930, Bolivian president Siles resigned under pressure from the military. The military then forcibly removed his cabinet from office. The new regime tried to maintain payments on the foreign debt, but falling revenues put it in a bind. The government therefore requested refunding loans from a consortium of U.S. banks. The mining industry, fearing higher taxes, declared its opposition. The American bankers asked the State Department to participate in their debt discussions. The Hoover administration sided with the miners against refunding and rebuffed the request.[17] With that decision, in January 1931, the U.S.-controlled CFP signed off on a moratorium on debt payments, and Bolivia became the first Latin American nation to default.

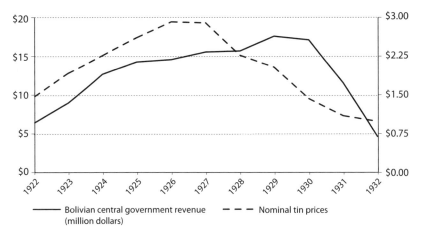

Figure 6.1 Bolivian central government revenue (left axis) and tin prices (right axis), 1922–32

Source: Figures for 1900–1986 are from Ocampo and Parra, "Los Términos de Intercambio de los Productos Básicos en el Siglo XX," *Revista de la CEPAL* 79 (2003), pp. 7–35, with data from the World Bank. Government revenues from tables 3 and 11, Mario Napoleón Pacheco, "The Foundation of the Central Bank of Bolivia (1929–1932)," *Revista de Humanidades y Ciencias Sociales* (Santa Cruz de la Sierra), vol. 12, nos. 1–2 (June/December 2006), pp. 133–184.

The Default Wave

Bolivia kicked off a wave of default throughout Latin America. The next domino to fall was Peru, in March 1931.[18] As in Bolivia, the Depression caused Peru's revenues and economy to collapse, precipitating the Leguía government's downfall. Colonel Luis Sánchez Cerro ousted Leguía in August 1930. Sánchez served as president until his assassination in April 1933, save for a brief hiatus in late 1931 when he temporarily stepped down to run in a special presidential election.

The country faced a grim economic situation. Exports and tax revenues fell in dollar terms.[19] (See figure 6.2.) The State Department worried that the downturn was strengthening the opposition Alianza Popular Revolucionaria Americana (APRA), led by Victor Haya de la Torre. APRA favored nationalizing American investments.[20] Washington was not reassured when, speaking to

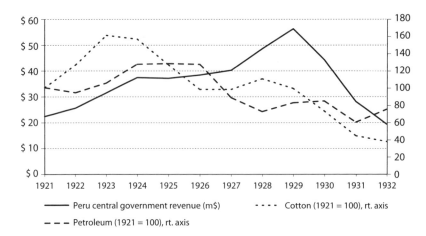

Figure 6.2 Peruvian central government revenue and oil and cotton prices, 1921–32

Source: Index of cotton market prices from Ocampo and Parra, "Los Términos de Intercambio de los Productos Básicos en el Siglo XX," *Revista de la CEPAL*, vol. 79 (2003), pp. 7–35, with data from the World Bank. Government revenue from Oxford Index of Petroleum Market Prices (1970 = 100): Figures for 1920–70 from Baptista, *Bases Cuantitativas de la Economía Venezolana, 1830–1989* (1989). (The Venezuelan basket price is used as a proxy for Peruvian oil prices.) Government revenue from the Oxford Latin American Studies Database.

the United States ambassador, Haya de la Torre described APRA as "a pure fascist rather than a communist organization."[21]

The Hoover administration badly wanted Sánchez to remain in power. Sánchez therefore reluctantly agreed to host an economic reform mission led by Edwin Kemmerer, the goal being to attract more loans to prop up his government. The Hoover administration recognized that Sánchez accepted Kemmerer's visit very reluctantly. "I am sure that if there were any way out, other than inviting more Yankee financial assistance," wrote an American official in Lima, "the present Peruvian government would have found it."[22] The American embassy tried to bolster Sánchez's political position by ignoring entreaties from the bankers to link recognition of his government to a resolution of the country's debt issues.[23]

As in Bolivia, Washington's coolness toward the bankers was helped by the fact that the interests of direct investors in Peru diverged from the interests of creditors. The depreciating sol decreased Peru's ability to pay, which creditors hated, but increased the competitiveness of Peru's primary product exports, which direct investors loved. Moreover, much of Peru's government spending went to infrastructure, particularly export-oriented railroads, which were primarily built by American construction companies. These companies had no more desire to see government spending cut than did Sánchez.[24]

Kemmerer's final report proposed that Peru should default on its *domestic* debt and American bankers should help the country with a short-term loan. The Peruvian government rejected these suggestions. In fact, it did the precise opposite. On May 29, 1931, the Peruvian government suspended *foreign* debt payments while it "studied" Kemmerer's recommendations. The government then issued more domestic debt, which it tried to force resident American companies to purchase, warning "that if they do not subscribe he [President Sánchez] cannot guarantee that communism will not break out and cannot guarantee that the government can preserve law and order."[25] That did not go over well with the American companies, who refused to purchase the new issues. The next month the Peruvian government suspended *all* debt payments. The U.S. government, on Kemmerer's personal advice, decided to "go slow and let matters ride" given the disastrous shape of the Peruvian treasury and the threats against American mining and agricultural companies.[26]

American officials signed off on—indeed, vocally supported—the first two Latin American defaults, but the United States had rather less control over the next three countries to suspend payments. Brazil and Chile were outside the American orbit. In Ecuador, it was true that an American official, William Roddy, had run the country's customs service between 1925 and 1930. Ecuador, however, was *already* in default on some of its foreign

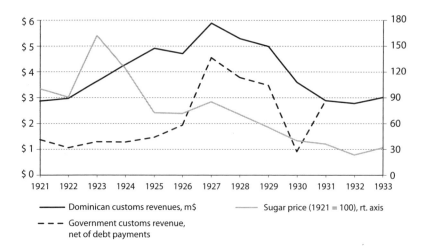

Figure 6.3 Dominican customs revenue and sugar prices, 1921–33

Source: Government revenues from annual reports of the Dominican Customs Receivership (various years). Index of sugar market prices from Ocampo and Parra, "Los Términos de Intercambio de los Productos Básicos en el Siglo XX," *Revista de la CEPAL*, vol. 79 (2003), pp. 7–35, with data from the World Bank.

debt and had been for some time. Moreover, the Coolidge and Hoover administrations refused to recognize the military junta that deposed the elected government in 1925, despite the appointment of an American to head the customs service. Under those circumstances, few were surprised when the Ecuadorean government suspended convertibility and defaulted on its remaining debts.

The United States, however, did have control over the sixth country to default: the Dominican Republic. The republic faced a trifecta of economic woes. First, collapsing sugar prices eviscerated government revenues (see figure 6.3). Second, in March 1930 amortization began on a 1926 loan taken out by the American occupation authorities. Annual loan service jumped from $1.1 million to $2.9 million.[27] Third, on September 3, 1930, Hurricane San Zenón made landfall. A U.S. Weather Service report estimated four thousand dead and $50 million ($555 million in 2011 dollars) in property damage.[28] The triple crisis threatened Trujillo's government, according to a 1930 report from the Brookings Institution.[29] The U.S.-run Dominican customs receivership was a bit more understated, but in its own way just as dire: "65.24% or practically two-thirds of the entire customs revenue [went to debt service]. The foregoing, on account of the notable reduction in volume of collections, left a comparatively small amount for the government after deduction of cost of operation. In fact, the total was $848,870.76, *the lowest amount the government has received in a single year, with the exception of 1921*" (italics added).[30]

In order to ameliorate the impending fiscal catastrophe, President Trujillo tried to raise revenue by leasing Samaná Bay to the U.S. Navy. Although a naval commission reported that Samaná "possessed superior advantages over any other position as a main base for the defense of the Caribbean," the Hoover administration had no intention of increasing the United States' military presence. He rejected Trujillo's offer.[31]

Under the circumstances, the U.S. government decided that the Dominican Republic had little choice but to default. William Pullium, the head of the customs receivership, recommended a "moratorium." Pullium had run the Dominican receivership since 1907, and he was probably more familiar with the country's finances than anyone else on the planet. Nevertheless, the American ambassador to Santo Domingo, Charles Boyd Curtis (not to be confused with the vice president of the same last name), disagreed with Pullium's recommendation. Curtis feared that default would damage the Dominican Republic's credit rating.[32] Facing conflicting recommendations from his men in Santo Domingo, Herbert Hoover, in his own words, "asked Mr. Eliot Wadsworth, of Boston, to go to Santo Domingo on a special mission for the Government. After consultation with the Santo Domingan [sic] government we thought it desirable to send someone to discuss the whole question of Santo Domingan treaties, with view to development of some financial assistance to Santo Domingo in their reconstruction."[33] Wadsworth recommended a two-year moratorium, combined with new loans for hurricane relief.[34]

An unexpected obstacle emerged in the form of Rafael Trujillo. Trujillo *rejected* default. Rather, he proposed $30 million in new private loans, plus an additional $5 million from the U.S. government.[35] Trujillo's proposal was, of course, a fantasy. Undersecretary of State Joseph Cotton rejected it in January 1931 on the grounds that the future debt service would require "too great a proportion of the government's income."[36] Secretary of State Stimson had confidence in Trujillo's ability to prevent "vultures" and "politicos" from stealing the money—for reasons that are less than clear—but he also opposed an increase the Dominican Republic's debt burden.[37]

Trujillo was not so easily deterred: he negotiated a $5 million, thirty-year loan with the J. G. White Company, a construction and engineering firm, at an effective interest rate of 6.1%.[38] Secretary Stimson was skeptical, believing the interest rate was too good to be true.[39] Stimson asked the Dominican minister to the United States, Rafael Brache, if it was a "straight loan proposal" or required that public works contracts be steered to J. G. White. Brache told Stimson that it was a straight loan, although J. G. White "naturally hoped that they would be given preference on all public works to be undertaken in the future" at "cost plus 12%." Stimson then told Brache that the U.S. government had been "very much chagrined to hear some months ago, in connection with another loan in another country, that a commission had been paid by the bankers to an intermediary—in this case, to a relative of a high officer of the government." Brache reassured the secretary of state that nothing untoward was involved.[40]

Stimson was not convinced by Brache's assurances that the loan was on the up-and-up. On February 12, the United States refused to grant the $5 million loan a priority lien on the customs revenues. The project died.[41] The banking firm of Lee, Higginson and Company then offered to lend the Dominican Republic $5 million, but only if the United States guaranteed the debt. This was *more* protection than enjoyed by the existing Dominican debt issues. Stimson again refused.[42]

Creditors now believed that the Dominican Republic would have to default. "[Sinking fund] payments now aggregate $1,851,667 annually," wrote Lee, Higginson and Company. "As the total revenues of the Dominican government for 1931 are tentatively estimated at $8,300,000, it appears that the sinking funds alone absorb about 22% of the government's income. This is a tremendous drain on the government's current resources, and unless there is an immediate return to prosperity . . . and no such return of prosperity seems to be in immediate prospect, we feel that no marked improvement in the position of the Dominican treasury can be expected."[43]

U.S. opposition left the Dominican government with no option. On August 25, 1931, Trujillo sent a two-year moratorium proposal to President Hoover, "to request Your Excellency's approval of the plan of the Dominican government as an emergency measure."[44] Hoover cabled approval on September 5. Hoover's wording is amusingly mealymouthed, as if he did not want to admit that he was allowing *el Generalísimo* to break a contractual obligation that the United States had enforced for a quarter century:

> Great and good friend: I take great pleasure in acknowledging the receipt of Your Excellency's important communication under date of August 25, 1931, outlining the efforts which the Dominican government has successfully made to maintain its financial credit through the prompt payment of the service on its foreign debt, despite the burdens imposed upon it by the present world depression and by the disastrous hurricane which visited Santo Domingo in September of 1930.
>
> Your Excellency also set forth in that letter the impossibility of maintaining an adequate public administration in the Dominican Republic and at the same time of satisfying the amortization payments on its debt, and requested the cooperation of the government of the United States in obtaining some solution for the financial problem.

The present financial problem confronting Your Excellency's government will have the sympathetic and prompt consideration of my government.[45]

The State Department requested and received some minor revisions to the plan. On October 22 the revised plan passed both houses of the Dominican legislature.[46] It suspended all amortization payments for two years. Revenues above and beyond those needed for interest on the 1922 loan would go into an "Emergency Fund" administered by an American citizen. The Emergency Fund would pay, in order: interest on the 1926 loan, the operating expenses of the U.S.-run customs service and Emergency Fund, government salaries, monies owed to the Red Cross on account of the hurricane, remaining current expenses, salary arrears—government salaries had been unpaid for several months leading to October—and finally principal.[47] When U.S. creditors complained, the State Department responded that the United States had received advance notice of the Dominican government's intention to default and agreed with the decision.[48]

Trujillo himself appears to have regarded the entire operation as a bit of political Kabuki designed to distract the bondholders from the fact that the United States had, in essence, hung them out to dry.[49] In fact, Washington had two good reasons not to simply *order* the Dominican Republic to default. First, it was politically costly for the Hoover administration to renege on the U.S. government's twenty-five-year-old promise to protect American creditors. The Dominican regime may have run out of options—other than allowing the country to collapse—but it was better for Hoover that it seem as though *Trujillo* was taking the initiative. Stimson could then take a "tone of grudging acquiescence in a regrettable turn of events," even as he reminded the bankers that the collapse of the Dominican state would be bad for their interests.[50] Second, the appearance of a Dominican initiative allowed Hoover to maintain the image of a "Good Neighbor." Instead of ordering its Dominican satrap to carry out a policy made in Washington, the United States could pretend to be watching a sovereign state carry out its own economic policy.[51]

More Dominoes Fall

America's other formal and informal economic protectorates quickly followed the Dominican Republic into default. The American fiscal agent approved default on three-quarters of Panama's foreign loans in January 1932. Colombia defaulted in February. Costa Rica began to issue bonds to cover the interest on its debt in November 1932; it defaulted on those bonds in 1935. The United States declined to impose a customs receivership, in contravention of the loan agreements. El Salvador defaulted in January 1933, and Guatemala stopped making amortization payments on its outstanding debts in February. In all these cases, U.S. agents stood ready to take over the fiscal administration in the event of default; in none did the United States take action.

The United States signed off on most of these defaults owing to fears of political instability. El Salvador provides an example: save for the need to increase the military budget in order to put down a putatively communist revolt, the country's ability to pay was never in question (see figure 6.4). In addition, the Salvadoran default marked the moment when the United States *officially* abandoned its promotion of "constitutional government" in favor of strongman regimes that could preserve internal order. The rise to power of men like Sánchez and Trujillo elsewhere in America's informal empire had already placed the U.S. commitment to constitutional democracy in doubt, but it was the Salvadoran experience that finally killed it.

Americans owned $29 million in direct investments in El Salvador in 1929 ($310 million in 2011 dollars). This was a large but not overwhelming amount: as a proportion of U.S. GDP, it was the 2011 equivalent of $4.2 billion. The largest

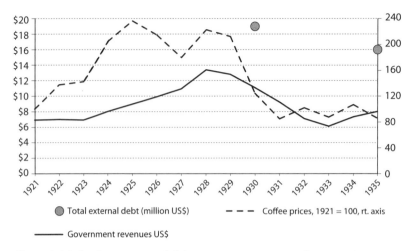

Figure 6.4 Salvadoran external debt, customs revenue, and sugar prices, 1921–35

Source: Oxford Latin American Studies Database.

investment was the United Fruit railway line that crossed the country from the Guatemalan border to the port of La Unión.[52] In addition, the Salvadoran government owed $21 million to American creditors. An American agent supervised revenue collection. The American, however, did not have full control: under the 1926 agreement that would come only in the event of default.[53]

As the Depression settled in, President Pío Romero Bosque unexpectedly began to *open* the Salvadoran political process. The American minister, Warren Robbins, believed this to be a substantial error. In June 1929, Robbins reported that President Romero "disapproved of the custom of succession," in which Salvadoran presidents effectively appointed their successors, and that Romero planned on holding free elections in 1931.[54] Robbins worried that this decision could trigger unrest. (Romero, conversely, appears to have believed that free elections were the best way to prevent instability.)[55] The first reports of political violence aimed at the landed elite reached Washington in March 1930. More seriously, from Washington's point of view, the

Communist Party organized a series of mass demonstrations on May Day.[56] President Romero nonetheless maintained his determination to hold free elections in 1931, although he did detain 1,200 political activists in the run-up to the vote.[57] Turnout was very high: 86% of the adult male population voted on January 11, 1931. Arturo Araujo, who had a reputation as a radical despite being a prominent landowner, won 47%.[58] His platform included a compensated land reform, minimum wage laws, and the legalization of rural labor unions.

President Araujo soon found himself trapped between wealthy landowners hostile to his intended reforms and the rising expectations of his poor constituency. The oligarchy of the "Fourteen Families" (actually there were more than fourteen) refused to allow any of their supporters to take jobs under his administration. The election for the Salvadoran legislature occurred two days after the presidential poll; conservative representatives took control and blocked Araujo's land and tax reform bills. A series of rural strikes broke out in April 1931 and had to be repressed by the military. Agustín Farabundo Martí—one of the founders of the Communist Party of Central America and an active participant in the Soviet-backed Socorro Rojo Internacional alternative to the Red Cross—declared a hunger strike.[59] Martí's arrest prompted further demonstrations. Later in April, the military fired upon protestors in the rural town of Sonsonate and the following day killed more peasants during a demonstration against the Sonsonate massacre in Zaragoza.

The Depression worsened the unrest. The price of coffee, El Salvador's primary export crop, fell by half in 1931. Real GDP in El Salvador fell 11% in 1931, while nominal GDP collapsed by an astonishing 37%. Emergency tax increases held the fall in nominal government revenues to 29% ($21 million to $15 million). On July 11, the legislature approved a $1 million loan from American banks. The loan vote, however, prompted a student demonstration the next day, which clashed with the military and forced Araujo to declare a state of siege. On October 7, the government banned gold exports, losing the remainder of its elite supporters.[60] American officials in San Salvador were less than sympathetic, blaming the unrest on the idea that Araujo "led many farmers and laborers to think that the millennium was likely."[61]

As government revenues fell, the Araujo administration fell behind in paying the military, thereby sealing Araujo's political fate.[62] The military deposed him on December 2, 1931. General Maximiliano "El Brujo" Hernández Martínez took control. The coup put the United States in a difficult position. On the one hand, Martínez prevented Communist candidates from taking office when they won the January 1932 municipal elections and promised the American minister that the government would pay its debts.[63] On the other hand, the United States had pledged to refuse recognition to unconstitutional governments in Latin America. In 1923, for example, the United States called a conference among all five Central American states (sans Panama) in order to sign a general peace treaty. Article 2 of the resulting General Treaty of Peace and Amity read as follows:

> The governments of the contracting parties will not recognize any other government which may come into power in any of the five republics through a coup d'état or a revolution against a recognized government, so long as the freely elected representatives of the people thereof have not constitutionally reorganized the country.[64]

The United States did not sign the treaty, but as a party to the negotiations, the Harding administration promised to uphold its stipulations.[65] When a right-wing coup ousted the Ecuadorean government in 1925, President Coolidge refused recognition, the Republican Party proudly accepting the mantle of democracy promotion in Latin America.

President Hoover upheld the tradition set by his predecessors, and refused to recognize the Martínez regime. Secretary of

State Stimson angrily chastised the American minister, Charles Curtis, for failing to inform the coup planners that the United States would not support them. Stimson was particularly angered by Curtis's insistence that the coup was constitutional, a position Stimson considered specious.[66] Hoover sent a special representative, Jefferson Caffrey, to try to persuade Martínez to step aside. Martínez refused, and Caffrey wrote Stimson that "unfortunately the better elements here are now supporting General Martínez, because he offers for the moment a stable government." Caffrey returned to Washington on January 8, 1932.[67]

El Salvador erupted into chaos days after Caffrey's departure. On January 10, 1932, a group of "Communists" attacked government offices in Ahuachapán. Thirty people died in the fighting. The Ahuachapán attack was followed on January 19 by the arrest of several army NCOs for suspicion of "communistic activities." The same day, "several hundred Communists including students well-armed and with dynamite bombs" attacked a cavalry barracks.[68] On January 22 organized peasant groups seized control of several towns. The next day, the American chargé d'affaires, Frank McCafferty, wrote, "If the [State] Department can help in any way it might prevent the threatened establishment of a communistic state here accompanied by much bloodshed. I and the principal Americans here believe that there is really serious danger to American and foreign lives and property."[69]

Now facing a generalized (and apparently Communist) insurgency, the Salvadoran government requested $250,000 from the American embassy ($2.8 million in 2011 dollars) to pay for military supplies and salaries. President Hoover refused to provide the cash directly, but the administration interceded with Manufacturer's Chatham Bank to advance the funds.[70] The United States also dispatched from Panama three warships carrying a battalion of Marines; two destroyers from the Royal Canadian Navy joined them.[71]

The Salvadoran government put down the rebellion in the most brutal fashion. On January 25, the *New York Times* reported 600 dead.[72] Four days later, the Salvadoran government reported that "4,800 Bolshevists have been accounted for."[73] Over the next month, the Martínez regime killed around 30,000 people, roughly 2% of El Salvador's population. In one vivid description, "Roadways and drainage ditches were littered with bodies, gnawed at by buzzards and pigs. Hotels were raided; individuals with blond hair were dragged out and killed as suspected Russians. Men were tied thumb to thumb, then executed, tumbling into mass graves they had first been forced to dig."[74]

Faced with what it believed to be the spectre of an openly Communist state in the Americas the United States abandoned both its promotion of democracy in El Salvador and the last vestiges of its commitment to financial stability. On January 29, 1932, Martínez notified the American chargé d'affaires that he wished to abolish the office of the American fiscal agent and suspend service on the foreign debt. The chargé reported favorably on the proposal. "The danger is by no means past. The continual maintenance of order during the next few months seems [to] depend largely on the ability of the authorities to obtain sufficient funds to pay the armed forces," he wrote. "At the present time the revenues from all sources except the customs are negligible. Therefore, the government has issued a decree providing for the temporary collection from January 25 of 100% of the import and export revenues directly by the government," leaving nothing for debt service. "The decree states that it has been absolutely necessary to take this measure because the serious communist movement threatens the very life of the state, emphasizes its temporary nature and reiterates the government's intention of complying with contracted obligations as soon as circumstances permit."[75]

With American acquiescence in hand, El Salvador discontinued payments on all of its foreign debts and went into technical default on February 27.[76] The 1926 loan agreement called for the U.S. government to step in and establish a fiscal receivership in the event of default, which the United States now categorically refused to do.[77] In fact, not only did the United States refrain from punishing Martínez; it arranged for a new $400,000 loan to purchase ammunition. The American legation reported that the loan was actually "for the purpose of maintaining himself [Martínez] in office," but from Washington's point of view, faced with the specter of a Communist victory, keeping Martínez in office was better than the alternative.[78]

The Hoover administration was not yet ready to completely abandon democracy promotion. Once the immediate crisis passed, it therefore attempted to ease Martínez out of office with promises of new loans to a civilian government from private or U.S. government sources. The offer appeared attractive. Martínez told the American legation in San Salvador that he would step down from the presidency and become secretary of war.[79]

Martínez lied. On June 8, 1932, he announced that he intended to remain in office until 1935. The American chargé d'affaires reported that the reason for Martínez's decision was that he had become convinced that the Depression meant that no new foreign loans would be forthcoming regardless of his decision.[80] The Guatemalan government told the American representative that "Martínez has put something over on the United States" and suggested that "an economic boycott would bring Martínez to heel in short order."[81] The other Central American governments, however, did not agree with the Guatemalan position.[82] Secretary of State Stimson considered recalling the American legation from San Salvador but decided that the risk of destabilization was too high.[83]

The recognition issue continued after the election of Franklin Delano Roosevelt. On December 5, 1932, El Salvador announced a program of debt restructuring with a private bondholders' protective committee, chaired by the American banker J. Lawrence Gilson. Under this program, El Salvador would resume full interest payments on its A and B series of preferred debt—having missed two coupons—and pay interest on the remaining C series bonds, half in cash and half in new debt yielding a 4% nominal coupon starting in 1935.[84] On June 28, 1933, El Salvador became the first Latin American country to resume interest payments.[85]

The American diplomat Sumner Welles then presented a plan under which Nicaragua, Guatemala, and Honduras would continue to respect the 1923 General Treaty between themselves (in which they pledged not to recognize any government that came to power through a coup d'état), while nevertheless recognizing the Salvadoran government. Roosevelt gave the plan a thumbs-up. On January 24, 1934, the Central American governments recognized Martínez, and the United States followed two days later.[86] With that, democracy promotion within the American sphere of influence was dead. Save for a brief flicker during the Carter administration, it would not revive in any serious way until the 1990s.

Cuba in the American Empire

Cuba provides the canonical case of how the Depression broke open the fault lines in the first American empire, destroying the political coalitions that sustained interventionism. These conflicts of interest combined to produce the ultimate absurdity: overthrowing the government of Cuba because it insisted on repaying its foreign loans.

The Depression weakened Cuba's preferential access to the U.S. market. The United States employed a three-tiered tariff system for sugar imports. Sugar from the insular possessions of Hawaii, Puerto Rico, and the Philippines paid no tariffs. Countries under the American informal empire received the full tariff on their sugar, which was set prohibitively high.[87] The third tier consisted of Cuba. Cuba faced a tariff, but a preferential one. This policy guaranteed that very little sugar would come from outside the American customs area. Over time, American investors in Cuba captured the returns from preferential access to the U.S. market.

As commodity price declines set in during the 1920s, the *domestic* political cost of providing benefits to the mostly American owners of Cuban sugar plantations and mills rose ever higher. The Hoover administration proved unable to resist pressures to increase tariffs on Cuban sugar. In fact, it proved almost utterly uninterested in resisting them. Higher tariffs, in turn, gravely wounded an already ailing Cuban economy. The ailing Cuban economy, in turn, split the alliance between the American holders of Cuban government debt and the American owners of Cuban sugar mills. With government revenue falling, creditors wanted the debt paid by any means necessary. Direct investors, conversely, wanted Cuban taxes to remain low and Cuban public services to remain high. This circle could not be squared.

In an ironic twist, the split between bondholders and direct investors did not allow the United States to forgo intervention. The Cuban government, for its own reasons, decided that no matter how hard the Cuban economy was squeezed, it was going to repay. As salaries went unpaid and antigovernment violence ratcheted up—including unrest among sugar workers—Cuba's insistence on paying debts increasingly looked to be a cause of instability. The Roosevelt administration was therefore forced to choose between protecting bondholders and protecting American sugar interests. The end result was the deliciously confusing sight of the government of one sovereign state covertly conspiring to overthrow the government of another because the latter refused to default on its debts to the citizens of the former.

American Beets versus Cuban Cane

That the United States is fundamentally interested in Latin America requires no reiteration. In the upbuilding of our relations there is nothing more important than our common interest in trade. The mutual objects must be to increase the standard of living of all

our peoples. . . . [The] more we can amplify this inter-
change of goods, the more we can contribute to our
joint advance in civilization and the more our inter-
commerce expands, the more certain is the development of our long established friendships.

—*Commerce Secretary Herbert Hoover, March 1921*

The dominant product of the Cuban economy in the early
twentieth century was sugar. As Alan Dye and Richard Sicotte
have pointed out, this had important consequences for the
relationship between the two nations. The First World War
prompted a boom in sugar prices (see figure 6.5). The boom
ended in a precipitous bust, and the resulting bankruptcies
caused much of the Cuban sugar industry to fall into North
American hands. American- and Canadian-owned operations
controlled 38% of Cuba's sugar capacity in 1914; by 1924,
they controlled 65%.[88]

Cuban raw sugar fed refineries in a few northeastern states,
which also happened to be the home of most of the corporate
and individual American owners of Cuban sugar lands. In 1903,
when the reciprocity treaty giving Cuba preferential access was
first negotiated, U.S. sugar production was concentrated in
only six states. Florida and Louisiana grew cane sugar. An additional eleven states grew beet sugar, but California, Colorado,
Michigan, and Utah accounted for 87% of beet production.[89]
As a result, the pro-Cuban and anti-Cuban sugar lobbies were
relatively evenly matched. The sugar interests were powerful
enough to keep Cuba from receiving tariff-free access but not
powerful enough to shut it out completely.

The First World War, however, changed the geography of
beet sugar. In order to convince beet sugar growers to expand
production during the war, the U.S. government had to provide
assurances that the sugar tariff would not be reduced in the
future.[90] The policy succeeded quite well: by 1920, no fewer
than *twenty-one* states were producing beet sugar. Domestic

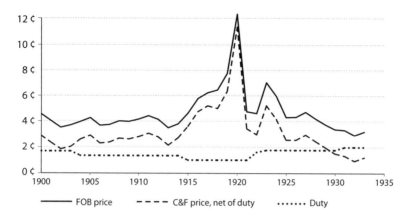

Figure 6.5 Nominal Cuban sugar prices (cents per lb.) annual averages, 1900–1933

Source: Alan Dye and Richard Sicotte, "The Political Economy of Exporting Economic Instability: The US Sugar Tariff and the Cuban Revolution of 1933," Barnard College Working Paper Series #99-05, November 1998, p. 40.

beet sugar had an additional advantage in that it went directly to consumers in a single production stage: there was no need to ship it to the Northeast to be refined.[91]

Politically, therefore, by the mid-1920s beet sugar producers had gained an advantage in congressional debates over the refiners of Cuban sugar and the owners of Cuban sugar lands.[92] The combination of Republican victories in the 1920 election and the recession of 1921 made tariff increases inevitable. In 1921, the Emergency Tariff Act took the tariff on Cuban sugar up to 1.3 cents per pound.[93] A bill passed the House that would make the emergency permanent and take the tariff on Cuban sugar up to 1.6 cents.[94]

What the Cuban sugar interests couldn't win in the legislature, however, they hoped to gain in the executive. The sugar interests were major donors to the Republican Party, and Secretary of Commerce Herbert Hoover came under pressure from the "Cuba lobby" to keep tariffs low.[95] In conjunction with Senator Reed Smoot (R-Utah), he proposed a compromise: in return for holding the tariff at 1.4 cents, Cuban producers would "voluntarily" restrict sales to the United States.[96] Hoover's proposal did not spring fully formed from his forehead. Rather, the idea was based on a Cuban precedent. Between February 11 and December 21, 1921, the Cuban government operated the Cuba Sugar Finance Commission.[97] President Menocal created the commission in order to "take in their charge the sale and shipment of the 1920–21 crop," in order to maintain prices.[98]

The experience of the Sugar Finance Commission, however, had not been a happy one. First, the commission charged a commission of 0.5 cents per pound, which came to 17% of the average free-on-board price of sugar in Cuban ports. Second, the creation of the commission paralyzed credit markets, as it became impossible to know how long sugar would be stored before the government would issue export permits. Finally, the commission was a failure on its own terms, since it failed to stem the price decline. In fact, the commission almost completely withdrew Cuban sugar from the market between late May and early August 1921, to little effect.[99] The Harding administration tried to prevent Cuba from abolishing the commission, because "if the Commission were disbanded and the sugar now held in Cuba thrown on the market great losses for these banking interests [lenders to Cuban mills] would result."[100] Nonetheless, by November 1921, the commission's failure was apparent. National City Bank informed the State Department that it no longer supported the activities of the Sugar Finance Commission, and it soon became moribund.[101]

Given its bad experience with the Sugar Finance Commission, it should not be surprising that the Cuban government rejected the Hoover-Smoot initiative. In response, Smoot "ripped into" the bankers and eastern refiners, accusing them of fomenting a "Wall Street Plot" to destroy the beet sugar industry.[102] The final version of the Fordney-McCumber Tariff Act raised tariffs on Cuban sugar to 1.6 cents in 1922 and 1.76 cents in 1923.[103] High sugar prices relieved the pressure on Cuba in 1923 and

1924, but the record Cuban crop of 1925 sent prices falling to a postwar low. By the end of 1925, unsold stocks of Cuban sugar had doubled to 1.8 million tons. A contemporary observer wrote that "sugar producers of the world were stunned with surprise."[104]

The Cuban economy contracted with the fall in sugar prices and sales. President Gerardo Machado pled with the American government to cut the tariff.[105] In a strange case of ostrich-like behavior, the State Department—realizing that there was no chance of congressional approval but not wanting to disappoint the Cubans—ordered Ambassador Crowder not to reply to Machado.[106] The Cuban ambassador to the United States, Orestes Ferrara, then raised the matter directly with Secretary of State Frank Kellogg.[107] Kellogg bluntly told Ferrara that the Senate would never approve a cut in the tariff. When Ferrara continued to press the issue, Kellogg curtly informed him that Ferrara's analysis was based on the erroneous assumption that the current tariff benefited the United States and hurt Cuba.[108] As a narrow point of economic theory, Kellogg's assertion was of course correct: the tariff damaged the overall economies of *both* nations. As a point of practical politics, however, the tariff greatly benefited the domestic beet sugar industry, and from the point of view of politicians inside the United States, that is what mattered.

With no help from American trade policy, President Machado tried to reintroduce crop limitation to boost the prices of Cuban sugar. In 1926, he mandated that Cuban producers cut their production 10%. The strategy created two problems. The first was that while Cuba was a major producer, it was simply not large enough to raise prices with a 10% production cut. The second was that Cuban crop restriction provided American beet sugar producers with rhetorical ammunition to lobby for even more protection. American beet lobbyists accused Cuba of trying to "eliminate the domestic sugar industry." This accusation made no economic sense, but it provided the beet sugar lobby a threat that they could take to the Cuban government in order to demand—paradoxically—even further crop restrictions. In 1927, the Cuban government tried to negotiate an agreement with the island's major sugar exporters to further curb production. Unfortunately, sugar prices continued to decline. Internal opposition to the production limits rose sharply, and Machado abandoned them on December 27, 1928.[109]

The Smoot-Hawley Act and Its Discontents

In his 1928 presidential campaign, Herbert Hoover pledged to increase agricultural tariffs. Upon taking office in March 1929, President Hoover called for tariff reform. Senator Smoot chaired the Senate Finance Committee. Unsurprisingly, the resulting Tariff Act of 1930—the infamous "Smoot-Hawley" Act—raised the duty on Cuban sugar from 1.76 cents to 2.0 cents per pound.

Senator Smoot encountered strong opposition in his attempt to raise the tariff on Cuban imports. Two groups mobilized to defend Cuban interests in the halls of Congress. The first was a coalition of the American Chamber of Commerce of Cuba and the United States Sugar Association.[110] The second was an alliance of the American Bottlers of Carbonated Beverages, the Hershey Foods Corporation, and an association of sugar brokers led by H. H. Pike.[111] The first coalition represented the American owners of Cuban sugar producers, while the second one represented intermediate consumers of Cuban sugar. Hershey Foods cut across both groups: the company was not only a consumer of sugar but also owned sixty-five thousand acres of Cuban sugar land and employed twelve thousand people on the island.[112]

The two Cuba lobbies put on a full-court press to protect their investments. They raised $95,000, the equivalent of $1.0 million in 2011 dollars, to lobby Congress and President Hoover. (In terms of national income, the coalition raised the 2011 equivalent of $15 million.) With this money, the Cuba lobbies hired Edwin Shattuck, a New York lawyer with close personal ties to Hoover. In the words of Herbert Lakin, the president of the Cuba Company and a major principal in the U.S. Sugar Association, "By great and good fortune I find that Shattuck is perhaps Hoover's closest legal friend. He is the personal attorney for Hoover and all his family. I think I have persuaded him to undertake a confidential mission first to convince Hoover, and secondly to work on the committees and members of Congress, on behalf of Cuba."[113] In addition, Shattuck had served with Hoover on the Sugar Equalization Board, the American Relief administration, and the European Children's Fund.

In his capacity as a lobbyist, Shattuck met with President Hoover in Miami after Hoover's return from his 1928 goodwill tour of Latin America. Hoover assured Shattuck that whatever resulted from the new tariff bill under consideration would not "embarrass" him.[114] In discussions, Shattuck tried to convince Hoover and Senator Smoot to support a plan that would evict the Philippine Islands from the American tariff wall. Unfortunately for Shattuck, devoted opposition from Secretary of State Henry Stimson, who had just finished his term as governor-general of the Philippines, put paid to that idea.[115]

Two congressional representatives were particularly important in leading the fight against the tariff hike on Cuban sugar. Representative Ruth Pratt (R–New York) served as the public face against the tariff hike. Pratt was the first woman to serve in Congress from the state of New York. She was also a Republican, serving the Seventeenth Congressional District on Manhattan's Upper East Side, then the wealthiest district in the state.[116] The head of the Cuban lobby's publicity bureau gave Representative Pratt information for her floor speeches.[117] On the other side of the aisle, the Cuba lobby planned to hire Cordell Hull (D-Tennessee) as a lobbyist if he left Congress. When Hull decided not to retire, he became the de facto leader of the behind-the-scenes effort against the tariff.[118]

On May 7, 1929, the House Ways and Means Committee reported to the floor a tariff bill that included a tariff on Cuban sugar of 2.4 cents. Hull believed that the sugar tariff hike was unpopular and would fail in the House if his faction could force a separate floor vote. For this, however, the Cuban lobby required a strong wedge issue. On May 21, Pratt assailed the beet sugar industry for its terrible labor conditions. Brandishing a letter from the president of the American Federation of Labor, she proclaimed, "This testimony is final on the matter of the employment of women and children and Mexican labor in the beet fields. My reason for standing against an increase in the tariff on sugar is the obvious impossibility of an expansion of the sugar industry in this country to a point where it can even begin to supply our needs. The domestic industry is not only bound by its labor problems; it is limited by our climate."[119]

Unfortunately for the Cuba lobby—and by extension, the Cuban economy—the Republican leadership in the House outmaneuvered the sugar tariff opponents. On May 25, 1929, the *New York Times* reported that "the Republican steamroller, well-oiled and in high gear, ran over the Democratic minority in the House of Representatives. . . . By a vote of 234 to 138, the House, in accordance with the dictates of the Republican caucus held [on May 24] adopted a rule . . . under which all amendments to the bill, except those approved by the Republican majority of the Ways and Means Committee, would be scrapped without debate or consideration of any character."[120] Party discipline among the Republicans was so high that Representative Pratt voted *for* the gag rule, despite her opposition to the sugar tariff.[121] Pratt's decision led to the following odd exchange between her and Representative John Nance Garner (D-Texas), the minority leader:

> GARNER: When you go back to your constituency and you have not offered an amendment striking out that clause on sugar, I want you to tell them you deliberately took away from yourself the right to offer such an amendment because the exigencies of your party appealed more to you than patriotism to your country.

PRATT: New York is the one state that understands that perfectly.

GARNER: Then I understand you to say that in New York it is already understood that party allegiance is worth more than your patriotism.[122]

The House bill then went to the Senate. On January 16, 1930, Senator Pat Harrison (D-Mississippi) pushed through an amendment from the floor that overturned the 2.4 cents tariff provision with a 50 to 40 vote. A group of Cuban automobile dealers and the island's Metro-Goldwyn-Mayer film distributor cabled their congratulations to the sugar lobby.[123] They spoke too soon. As chair of the Senate Finance Committee, Smoot countered Harrison's amendment with a second amendment that raised the tariff to a "compromise" 2.0 cents rate. Smoot then used his control over the committee agenda to block a second attempt to hold the rate at 1.76 cents.[124] Given the House vote and Smoot's well-known preference for a high tariff, this would have ensured an adoption of the 2.4 cents rate when the House and Senate bills were merged in conference. In a procedural tactic, however, opponents of the bill managed to peel off sufficient Republicans in the House to refuse to give the conference committee control over the sugar tariff. As a result, the conference committee accepted the 2.0 cents rate. The eleventh-hour Democratic maneuver prevented the rate from rising to 2.4 cents but could not prevent the rise to 2.0 cents.[125] President Herbert Hoover signed the Tariff Act on June 17, 1930.

Despite a concerted lobbying effort, high-level contacts up to the president himself, mass public expenditures, and a strong legislative strategy, the American advocates for Cuban sugar failed to preserve Cuba's access to the American market. At best, they managed to prevent a bad outcome from becoming much worse. The Tariff Act of 1930 marked the triumph of domestic producers over the owners of foreign investments.

Keynesianism on One Island

The U.S. government was not blind to the troubles of the Cuban economy. It had no interest in taking on the domestic sugar interests for the benefit of Cuba, but it could sign off on Cuban attempts to resuscitate its economy in a crude proto-Keynesian way, since the United States controlled Cuban finances. The legal justification for its control was Article 2 of the Platt Amendment: "[The Cuban] government shall not assume or contract any public debt, to pay the interest upon which, and to make reasonable sinking fund provision for the ultimate discharge of which, the ordinary revenues of the island, after defraying the current expenses of government shall be inadequate."

The United States interpreted this article broadly to mean that Washington retained a veto over any borrowing by the Cuban government. Neither Washington nor Havana, however, wanted to delegitimize the Cuban state by requiring its president to ask the resident ambassador for permission every time it wanted to take out a debt. Rather, a subtle convention emerged in which American banks would, after completing negotiations with Cuba, ask the State Department for its opinion. The State Department in Washington would then ask the American ambassador in Havana his opinion of the proposed loan. The Secretary of State would then pass along its opinion, with the implicit understanding that disapproval would obviate the contract.[126]

In practice, the United States allowed loans it might otherwise have rejected, provided the monies would go to projects that maintained Cuban employment. In late 1926, for example, President Gerardo Machado requested a $10 million loan ($108 million in 2011 dollars) from Chase National Bank in order to accelerate a public works program started in 1925. Following the convention, Chase asked if the State Department had any objections to the loan—which President Machado claimed was not really a loan but rather an "advance" against future tax revenues. The State Department responded that it could not parse

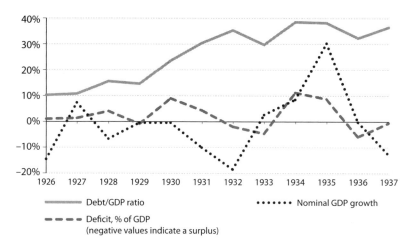

Figure 6.6 Cuban government debt, net borrowing, and nominal GDP growth, 1926–37

Source: Global Financial Database and *Foreign Relations of the United States*.

the difference between an advance and a loan but nonetheless had no reason to object.[127] In June 1927 the Cuban government requested $9 million ($98 million in 2011 dollars) from J. P. Morgan, in order to finance accounts payable related to public works projects. The loan was not small: it would boost the total Cuban budget deficit for the year to $19 million, around 3% of Cuba's GDP (see figure 6.6). Secretary Kellogg worried about the deteriorating state of Cuban finances, but with unemployment rising on the island he had no desire to force Havana to cut back.[128]

Despite the *relative* fiscal profligacy, Cuba's economy continued to shrink. President Machado responded by borrowing more to avoid austerity. The United States reluctantly continued to accommodate Machado. On March 31, 1928, he began to negotiate for a $20 million credit line ($214 million in 2011 dollars) with Chase National Bank. Two weeks later, he upped the request to $25 million. A week after that, it was up to $32 million. By the beginning of May, the Cuban government was in negotiations for $50 million.[129] The American chargé d'affaires in Cuba, Charles Boyd Curtis, was annoyed by the fact that Machado did not consult with the American embassy as the size of the loan spiraled upward. "I am, however, considerably surprised that he should have permitted that step to have been taken at all when one considers his repeated assurances that no further financing would be undertaken." Curtis went on to warn Washington that "government revenues are falling off seriously and give promise of declining further before improving. With a continuation of the economic crisis a deficit of considerable size looms."[130]

The United States ultimately approved the loan, despite knowledge that Cuba was lying about its uses and intended to use it to meet current expenditures. Secretary of State Kellogg instructed Curtis to "discuss" the loan with the Cuban government. He also told Curtis to remind the Cuban government that American banks would ask the State Department its opinion. "It is not desired that you base your remarks on the Platt Amendment or the Treaty of 1903, but there should be no appearance of avoiding discussion thereof."[131] When asked a second time, the Machado administration clarified that the loan was for the completion of the Central Highway project, a twenty-two-foot wide paved road running 707 miles between Pinar del Río in the west and Santiago in the east.[132] The American embassy, however, knew full well that Machado was lying: the Cuban Congress had already passed legislation to allow the loan proceeds to be used to meet current expenditures. Nevertheless, fearing the consequences of sudden cuts in public spending, the State Department gave Chase National the go-ahead on June 20, 1928.[133]

Hoover took office in March 1929. In February 1930, Chase National purchased fifteen-year Cuban bonds with a face value of $40 million at 95% of par and an effective interest rate of 5.8%. The Cuban government deposited an additional $40 million in unissued bonds at the bank to be used as security on a $20 million credit line.[134] Cuba exhausted the credit line by August 1930. The Cuban government then entered negotiations with the two prime contractors on the Central Highway project (Warren Brothers and the Compañía Cubana de Contratistas) to issue $19 million in five-year bearer bonds, also at 5.8%.[135] Total government borrowing in 1930 came to $77 million ($853 million in 2011 dollars), a whopping 13% of Cuba's GDP. Washington, fearing the impact on employment of cutting spending, approved the loans.[136]

Political Instability and Government Debts

The State Department continued to approve the loans to Cuba for fear that further economic contraction would destabilize the island. In 1931, Cuba's ambassador to the United States bluntly told the State Department, "The root of the whole matter is economic. Cuba has gone from great riches to poverty. It is not the fact of being poor that has affected the people so much as the change from affluence to poverty."[137]

In November 1928, after securing passage of a set of constitutional reforms, President Machado won reelection. In fact, Machado, notionally a member of the Liberal Party, won the nomination of all three political parties. The American embassy believed that he had used government funds to bribe the leaders of the Conservatives and the Cuban People's Party.[138] The center-left opposition, led by Carlos Mendieta, regrouped under the rubric of the "Nationalist Union," only to find themselves harassed by police and excluded from 1928 ballot.[139]

Rural and urban violence increased in the run-up to the 1930 congressional elections.[140] President Machado characterized the outbreaks as "the logical concomitant of Cuba's economic depression."[141] When police broke up a demonstration at the University of Havana, gunfire wounded three students and one policeman.[142] One of the wounded students died the next day.[143] In response, Machado pushed through a congressional vote temporarily suspending all constitutional guarantees.[144] He also used the police to close opposition newspapers.[145] Nearly all newspapers suspended publication.[146] In May, several police officers and civilians were killed in an attempt to break up a Nationalist Union meeting in Artemisa.[147]

In the wake of escalating violence, opposition leaders asked the United States to invoke the Platt Amendment.[148] The United States refused. In a press conference, Secretary of State Stimson stated, "American forces have never landed in Cuba when there was any regime to maintain. The only times we have gone in to Cuba was when there was no government."[149] Cuba's November congressional election came off with, in the words of a former State Department official, "no more violence than was customary."[150]

Disorder worsened after the elections. In December 1930, President Machado closed the university, high schools, and normal schools. They remained closed for the rest of his time in power.[151] In January the entire university student directorate was arrested, including several female students. The American embassy reported "hardly a night passes without the explosion of one or more small bombs," with political meetings disrupted by tear gas and "stink bombs."[152] Ambassador Guggenheim warned President Machado that "nearly everyone was opposed to the government except those being paid by it." Guggenheim advised the president that he should reconcile with the opposition, lest his regime go the way of the recently deposed Peruvian government. The president agreed, and in return asked Guggenheim for help in postponing a $20 million payment due Chase Bank.[153] A week later the president introduced a bill allowing him to indefinitely suspend constitutional guarantees.[154]

The litany of bombings and violence grew worse, and the number of political prisoners in Cuban jails spiraled upward. A bomb was placed in the Presidential Palace on February 23, 1931.[155] By April, Secretary Stimson had become worried by the number of people Machado had placed in detention.[156] Stimson's attempts to broker a political settlement failed. Machado agreed to step down in 1933 instead of 1935 but refused to call new elections. He also refused to shorten congressional terms. When Guggenheim pressed him, Machado threatened to resign *without designating a successor.* As both men knew, this was a recipe for throwing Cuba into chaos. Guggenheim wrote that he suspected Machado was unwilling to step down until he had been able to "recoup the large sum which he had allegedly paid Zayas [the previous president] for the presidency."[157]

In August 1931, the Cuban opposition launched an organized rebellion. Troops fought rebels in Havana, Matanzas, Pinar del Río, and Santa Clara, with most of the fighting in Santa Clara.[158] The revolt collapsed within a week, but reprisals continued. Not all reprisals were carried out by the police: by the end of 1931 Machado had granted 489 pardons to his supporters, 400 of them for violent offenses.[159] Bombs continued to explode in the capital.[160]

Violence worsened in 1932. On January 1, bombings resumed with an attack on the Tobacco Selectors' Union in Santa Clara.[161] A wave of bombings then hit Havana, mostly organized by two groups: the ABC and the Organización Celular Radical Revolucionaria. (The name of the ABC derived from its cell structure: an "A" cell and a "B" cell and so forth.)[162] Both organizations espoused remarkably moderate political platforms, even by the standards of the time—they called for consumer protection, progressive taxation, nationalized utilities, protective labor legislation, and in the case of the ABC, a *narrowing* of the franchise to exclude illiterates—but their tactics consisted of bomb attacks against government offices and officials.[163] On January 12, twelve separate bombs exploded in Havana. On January 25, the police discovered a dynamite-laden automobile packed full with glass and nails.[164] That same month, the ABC mined a house on Flores Street. An anonymous tip sent two policemen to the house, who were killed when they triggered the bombs by using the phone.[165] On February 19, a bomb thrown onto a bus injured three passengers.[166] Nine days later, one man was shot and one woman died in a bomb attack during primary elections; two more bombs exploded in Santiago with no injuries.[167] On April 19, following another wave of bomb attacks, the police raided the home of Antonio Chivas, an engineering professor at the University of Havana, where they discovered "an infernal machine which was in reality an automobile made into a monster bomb." According to the police report, some "youths planned to abandon the car close to police headquarters so that when the handbrake was released to remove the car from the streets, the circuit would be closed, exploding the huge [350-pound] TNT charge, thus wrecking the headquarters building and killing the majority of police reserves quartered there."[168]

On May 20, another bombing campaign began in Havana, and mail bombs sent to police officers became a regular occurrence.[169] Several were killed in coordinated attacks.[170] On May 31, three bombs exploded at Havana's foremost private schools.[171] On June 9, a bomb exploded at a concert in Santa Clara, killing two and wounding twelve.[172] The next day, a bomb was discovered minutes before President Machado was scheduled to drive past it.[173] Hundreds of arrests followed.[174] Bombings increased in July. That month an opposition leader, Esteban Delgado, died in a gun battle with the police. (Delgado's driver had been gunned down the day before.) Two days later, a bomb planted in a house that was being searched killed one policeman and wounded four. The trigger had been disguised as a book left on a table.[175] The Cuban government posted extra guards around the American embassy.[176] On July 10, gunmen pulled up next to a car carrying Miguel Calvo, the head of the Cuban security services, and killed everyone in the car with shotguns.[177] On September 28, the ABC killed the president of the Senate, Clemente Vazquez Bello, on the heels of a bomb attack that killed two policemen.[178] The ABC then attempted to bomb Bello's funeral, wiring the cemetery with three hundred pounds of dynamite in twenty-three separate mines. The plot failed because a gardener discovered the explosives.[179] Machado reacted with another wave of violent repression.[180] Gunmen then killed two opposition members of Congress, and their siblings died in what the American embassy believed to be reprisals.[181] In October, Machado floated a plan that would mandate the death penalty for illegal possession of guns or explosives.[182]

By the end of 1932, the State Department had lost faith in Machado's ability to restore order. The American diplomatic staff in Havana, moreover, was finding it difficult to maintain its neutrality in Cuban internal affairs. Secretary Stimson sternly warned Guggenheim that he alone would express public disapproval of President Machado. In a tight-lipped letter, he chastised Guggenheim for getting too close to the opposition:

> I feel that any indication, such as you suggest, of lack of sympathy with President Machado . . . would be tantamount to taking sides on a purely internal political question. . . . In view of the foregoing I trust that you will refrain from taking any attitude or position with respect to Cuban internal political questions. . . . Your dispatch under reference terminates with the following sentence regarding your recommended change of policy: "This would at least tend to relieve our government from responsibility for the inevitable consequences of Machado's persistence in his present course." The Department cannot acquiesce in the view that the continuance of its policy of non-interference in Cuba's internal affairs involves our government in any responsibility for the policies of the Cuban executive.[183]

The difficulty, from the State Department's point of view, was that Machado retained the support of American bankers. Stimson told Guggenheim in a personal meeting why the United States had to refrain from criticizing or weakening Machado: "The bankers, who had [*sic*] a big stake in Cuba, are working hard on a scheme which they hope will work out satisfactorily."[184] The scheme in question was a renegotiation of the debt, in which Cuba would suspend amortization but continue to pay interest.[185]

Machado had three reasons to avoid default. The first, of course, was the worry that default might cut off Cuba's access to foreign capital markets. The second was the fear of American intervention, although this should have been (but apparently was not) reduced in light of the American approval of defaults elsewhere.[186] The third reason, however, was the key: Cuba's lenders provided Machado and his supporters with *personal* incentives to continue the government's debt payments. Chase Bank granted Machado personal loans worth $130,000 ($2.15 million in 2011 dollars), "with little prospect of immediate payment" in the words of a later Senate investigatory committee. Chase also made loans to enterprises owned by the Cuban president: it gave $45,000 ($745,000 in 2011 dollars) to a construction company and $89,000 ($1.48 million in 2011 dollars) to a shoe factory. In addition, Chase hired Machado's son-in-law, José Emilio Obregón, even though, as Chase officials themselves wrote, "As we know, from any business standpoint he is perfectly useless."[187] Although Obregón was perfectly useless to Chase's business, he nevertheless received a starting salary of $12,000 (which rapidly rose to $19,000, for a rise from $202,000 to $319,000 in 2011 dollars) and an additional $500,000 commission ($8.5 million in 2011 dollars) for his role in securing the 1928 public works loan.[188] In addition, Cuban families close to Machado were invested in the Cuban public debt. The State Department reported that at least $1.5 million of the Cuban public works bonds ($26.3 million in 2011 dollars) was held by "individuals close to the President," with an additional $5.5 million ($96.8 million in 2011 dollars) belonging to the Compañía Cubana de Contratistas, "in which those chiefly interested are Augustus Alvárez and Rodolfo Arrelano, both of them intimately connected with the President."[189]

Default for Stability

The United States finally withdrew its support for Machado when it became convinced that his policies would lead to the collapse of the Cuban state. In one of the supreme ironies of the first American empire, Machado's policies were neither radical nor, in the conventional sense, irresponsible. After all, Cuba was paying its debts. The problem was that paying its debts meant shutting down the school system, allowing government salaries to go unpaid, and raising taxes to confiscatory levels. Those actions prompted the sugar lobby to turn on Machado. Once it did so, the U.S. government followed. In a previous decade, the banks that owned Cuban debt might have pushed back successfully—but in the context of the early 1930s, they lacked the influence.

The State Department realized that a debt renegotiation would be in the U.S. interest as early as mid-1931.[190] Machado, however, remained dead set against any action that might undermine the value of Cuban debt. He therefore continued to service the debt, even when his efforts became unpopular. In December 1931, for example, Machado asked the banks to keep the scheduled $2.25 million debt payment a secret, because the government had missed several paychecks and he feared the public outcry.[191] The next month, in January 1932, the American ambassador reported, "Default on the public debt cannot be postponed much longer."[192]

Ambassador Guggenheim was wrong in his prediction about Cuban default. Machado took increasingly "heroic" measures to continue payments. In March, he authorized the coinage of silver with a face value of $6 million at a cost of $2 million—the seigniorage went to debt payments.[193] In December the Machado administration cobbled together a combination of new loans and tax hikes. Chase National agreed to advance $1.65 million and allow the government to postpone principal payments on 30% to 40% of the public works debt.[194] In addition, the three largest oil companies operating in Cuba agreed to advance $1.84 million ($26.4 million in 2011 dollars) against their 1933 tax payments.[195] Cuba, in turn, imposed a 1 cent per pound excise tax on refined sugar at a time when sugar (net of U.S. tariffs) traded at 0.9 cents in New York. In other words, Machado was willing to impose a tax on sugar *over* 100% of its market price. Considering that the American sugar market was competitive, it was unlikely that the growers would be able to pass along much of the burden to consumers. Not surprisingly, the tax ignited a furious response from the sugar growers.[196] Once again, Ambassador Guggenheim wrote Washington in favor of default, bluntly stating that it would be better than the plan proposed by the bankers and the oil companies.[197]

Machado's government also cut expenses—but in a haphazard and politically explosive manner. In December 1931, it postponed government paychecks for several weeks. In June 1932 it again began to fall behind on wages, paying only the judiciary, high officials, and military.[198] In September 1932 it stopped paying the judiciary. In January 1933 it stopped paying the heads of executive departments. By May, salary arrears had reached $19 million, out of a total government budget for the year of $40 million.[199]

The newly appointed U.S. ambassador to Cuba, Sumner Welles, recommended that Cuba declare a moratorium on all principal payments in light of the onerous tax burden on American enterprises on the island. The State Department agreed in principle, mentioning specifically the "dangers inherent in the situation growing out of the alarming salary arrears to Cuban government personnel." The incoming Roosevelt administration also agreed with this assessment, but it was not yet ready to order the Cuban government to default on American bankers. "[The administration] cannot take the initiative with the bankers in suggesting a suspension of payments," wrote Acting Secretary of State Cordell Hull in June 1933.[200] The problem, from Roosevelt's point of view, was not the bankers' political power at home. The Great Depression had already greatly reduced their influence. Rather, the problem lay in *Cuban* politics. Ambassador Guggenheim summed it up succinctly: "Any effort by our government to induce the bankers to relieve the financial strain on the Machado administration will be generally condemned as United States support of the unpopular Machado administration."[201]

Machado, of course, faced his own catch-22: he could not default on the debt without alienating his political base, but he could not continue to pay the debt without eviscerating the Cuban state. In March 1933, he tried to relieve the burden of new taxes by declaring a two-year suspension of all *private* debt payments by railroad companies, sugar mills, and farms. He also capped interest on urban mortgages at 5%.[202] This move, not surprisingly, did little for either Cuba's economy or Machado's popularity.

Machado's determination to pay the foreign debt—much like Nicolae Ceauçescu's in a later era—provoked increasing opposition. By March 1933, Ambassador Guggenheim reported a "wide campaign of responsible criticism against further payments on principal of foreign debt."[203] Machado refused to budge. "President Machado himself will not take the initiative in the matter," wrote Ambassador Welles two months later. "He feels that the strongest support which he has in his present position is the support given him by the American banking groups and he has further the conviction, which nothing will shake, that any default of obligations by his administration will make more likely the possibility of American intervention."[204]

Machado's conviction was in fact the *opposite* of the American position. The United States preferred default. Two American ambassadors from two different administrations told Machado he was mistaken, to no avail. Nor was Machado swayed by Washington's support for defaults in South America and in the Dominican Republic. Even when American *bankers* offered Machado a two-year holiday on principal payments on the $20 million public works credit (something the U.S. government considered inadequate) he refused.[205]

The United States therefore made the decision to remove Machado. A general strike on August 4, 1933, provided the pretext. Government employees walked out, stores closed, and Welles worried that "there will be a state of near starvation within the next 24 hours." Welles went to Machado, warning him that unless he appointed an impartial secretary of state to run the government, followed by the reinstatement of the office of vice president and Machado's own resignation, Cuba would fall into anarchy.[206] The general strike turned violent on August 7, when the police fired on demonstrators. On August 8, Machado declared that he would not be "pushed out by the United States."[207] Later that day, he personally told Welles that he would "prefer armed intervention to the acceptance of any such proposal." Welles thought Machado "was in a state of mental disturbance bordering on hysteria."[208]

On August 9, Machado's time ran out. In a meeting in Washington, President Roosevelt gently suggested to the Cuban ambassador that Machado step down "to prove to the world his high purpose in this crisis" and perform "a noble act" suitable for "a great man, a great leader, and a great patriot." Roosevelt even offered to provide unspecified political cover so that Machado would not lose face. Roosevelt also implied the United States would withdraw recognition of the Machado government if he did not step down, as "recommended by the representatives of all the Cuban political parties." Moreover, although Roosevelt said that he had "no desire to intervene," he ominously added that he felt a "duty to do what we could so that there should be no starvation and chaos among the Cuban people."[209]

The following day, the Mexican foreign minister, José María Puig, confided to the U.S. ambassador in Mexico City that while Mexico could not countenance a unilateral American intervention, even with the support of the Cuban population, it would support a move against Cuba if it was taken "in cooperation with other countries on this continent." Puig backed up his private statements with public support for the United States when the Japanese ambassador to Mexico accused the United States of doing in Cuba what it "condemned Japan for doing in Manchuria."[210]

With presidential approval and Mexican support in hand, Ambassador Welles held meetings with the leaders of Cuba's three major parties and the military. Welles' meeting was followed by a mutiny by the First Artillery Battalion and proliferating rumors of a coup. Machado then anticlimactically stepped down on August 13, 1933. Carlos Manuel de Céspedes took over as provisional president. Machado left by plane for the Bahamas. He would die in 1939 in the traditional land of Cuban exile: Miami.

With Machado gone, the United States immediately implemented a plan for orchestrating a Cuban default. Bureaucratic conflicts between State and Treasury led to a less smooth roll-out than Ambassador Welles hoped, but it nonetheless worked. On August 20, Welles reiterated his support for a moratorium on debt payments, covering "both sinking fund and interest charges." He then suggested that the United States immediately lend Cuba the cash it needed to meet current expenses.[211] Dean Acheson, the new undersecretary of the treasury, was sympathetic to the moratorium, but he worried that Article 1, Section 9, Clause 7 of the U.S. Constitution prevented the department from issuing Treasury bills or notes on behalf of a foreign government without congressional authorization. As a workaround, however, Acheson ordered the Philadelphia Mint to speed up the coinage of Cuban silver, and he sent Adolf Berle, the special counsel to the Reconstruction Finance Corporation (RFC), to Havana to establish a commission to work out an orderly default.[212]

As expected, Berle's commission concluded that Cuba needed to prioritize general expenses and salary arrears ahead of debt payments. "We do not believe that the ordinary budget now in force can be decreased; on the contrary, government salaries should be partially restored. They have been cut below the danger point now. [Paying back salaries] is necessary for the stability of the government. It would have the advantage of giving some slight impetus to economic activity within the island." Nor did Berle believe that Cuba could increase government revenues. "Tax rates," he wrote, "have reached if not yet passed the point of diminishing returns." The commission proposed a conditional default on all debt payments as long as general expenses and back salaries were unmet. It also suggested a legal way for the United States to aid Cuba without the need for congressional approval: the minting of $14 million ($201 million in 2011 dollars) in silver coin, financed by a $4 million loan from the RFC to the seller of the raw silver.[213]

One More Coup

The new government will have large public support. The communistic element will, of course, make every effort to stir up trouble for it.

—*Jefferson Caffery, personal representative of the president in Cuba, 1934*

The Cuban saga was not quite over. Two days before the Berle commission published its report, Sergeant Fulgencio Batista led a mutiny of noncommissioned officers. The proximate cause of the mutiny was a [false] rumor that the government intended to cut enlisted pay from $22 a month to $13.[214] (This was the equivalent of a cut from $375 to $221 a month in 2011 dollars, although this calculation does not account for the fact that the cost of living was lower in Cuba than on the mainland.) Radical student leaders quickly arrived at the mutineers' headquarters. The mutineers agreed to support the students and declared a new government on September 4 under a five-man executive commission composed of Ramón Grau, Porfirio Franca, Guillermo Portela, Jose Irizarri, and Sergio Carbó.[215] Five days later, Grau assumed the presidency.[216] Recalcitrant Cuban Army officers held out in the National Hotel in Havana—home to much of Havana's American community, including Ambassador Welles. On October 2, 1933, Grau's soldiers stormed the hotel and captured or killed the holdouts.[217]

Grau's regime rapidly lost support after the hotel attack. Ambassador Welles used his offices to coordinate Grau's opponents and assure them of American support. By September 11, 1933, all the parties that had formed part of the original power-sharing deal declared their opposition to the Grau government, including both the ABC and Organización Celular Radical Revolucionaria.[218] By October 7, Grau had lost Batista's support: the sergeant-turned-general told Welles that he "realized now fully that the present regime was a complete failure."[219]

Welles believed the Grau administration to be under "ultra-radical control," and reported "that Communistic elements are having an unfortunate influence."[220] This view was reinforced by seizures of sugar properties by striking workers, including two American-owned mills, and decrees intervening directly in the management of the American-owned Cuban Electric and Cuban Telephone companies.[221] The United States took the interference in the utilities in stride, but responded strongly to Grau's failure to protect American property: hurricane relief funds ceased and Cuban silver coins that had already been minted sat in Philadelphia under embargo.[222]

Terrorism soon reemerged after the imposition of sanctions, including bombings and assassinations in Havana. The most dramatic incident occurred on November 8, 1933, when anti-Grau troops from Camp Columbia "flying stolen fighter planes, swooped low over the city of Havana, spraying 50-caliber machine gun bullets into the streets, across the roof tops, and into the streets again."[223]

Once again, the Roosevelt administration came under pressure to intervene. The U.S. Chamber of Commerce and Standard Oil asked for intervention. Bethlehem Steel requested protection for the iron mines at Daiquiri. United Fruit asked that U.S. Marines be sent to its plantations near Antilla, on the coast;

President Roosevelt dispatched a destroyer.[224] He then ordered twenty-nine naval vessels to proceed to Cuba and Key West. The Marine Corps put its air squadrons on alert, with pilots at Quantico, Virginia, ordered to be packed and ready to fly to Cuba "on a moment's notice." Five marine battalions were activated and prepared for deployment at Quantico, Virginia, and Port Everglades in Fort Lauderdale, Florida.[225]

Fortunately, President Roosevelt did not need to pull the trigger. The U.S. embassy forwarded reports to Batista that the United Kingdom might recognize Grau. Batista then contacted Carlos Mendieta, the head of the opposition Nationalist Union, and asked him if he would support a coup. Mendieta agreed, but only if Batista could guarantee American support. Jefferson Caffery, President Roosevelt's personal representative in Cuba, readily gave that support.[226] Roosevelt refused to give Batista an official guarantee that the United States would recognize a new government, but Batista considered Caffery's word sufficient. The Cuban Army ousted Grau on January 15, 1934.[227] Carlos Hevia became provisional president. Within days he turned that office over to Mendieta. On January 19, Caffery reported that the new government met the Roosevelt administration's requirements, and on January 23, 1934, the United States extended "formal and cordial recognition."[228] Within four months, the two countries signed an agreement formally abrogating the Platt Amendment.

The Depression and the Withdrawal from Formal Empire

The same Depression-induced logic of withdrawal held for America's formal empire. As with Cuba, the driving forces were domestic lobbies roused by economic scarcity. In the case of the Philippines, however, it was the entry of foreign persons rather than foreign products that provoked resistance. Philippine independence was the price of ending Filipino immigration.

The Democratic Party supported Philippine independence since the 1900 presidential election, but it had never followed through. In large part, this was because there was no serious constituency for independence in the Philippines itself. Major Filipino leaders claimed to support independence in public, but what they wanted in private discussions with American officials was in fact *autonomy*.

Most Filipino leaders appeared to be essentially satisfied with the status quo established by the Philippine Autonomy Act of 1916, save for a brief episode in the 1920s when the confrontational Leonard Wood attempted to actually *exercise* the powers reserved to the governor-general. (In fact, the first draft of the Autonomy Act had been written by the Philippines' non-voting representative in the U.S. Congress, Manuel Quezon.)[229] When Filipino leaders made specific demands on Washington, they were for the formalization of some sort of final status that would give the Philippines de jure as well as de facto domestic autonomy, while retaining the islands' commercial, defense, and judicial links with the United States. No Filipino leader wanted to see an unelected foreigner exercising executive power the way Governor-General Wood had done, but neither did any wish to lose the benefits of association with the United States. Manuel Quezon, who became leader of the Philippine Senate in the 1920s and 1930s, quietly tabled independence bills. In 1927, Quezon explicitly told Secretary Kellogg, "We will take dominion status," if only the Americans would codify the islands' autonomy.[230] Not even the sheer obnoxiousness of Leonard Wood could upset the imperial applecart; his successors were more respectful of Filipino sensibilities.

The onset of the Great Depression did what Leonard Wood could not; it broke the political balance maintaining the Philippines' links with the United States. Simply put, the political cost to *American* politicians of retaining the Philippines rose precipitously as the domestic economy declined. The first danger sign appeared in an unlikely place: Watsonville, California.

Unlike the residents of Hawaii (who became American citizens under the Hawaiian Organic Act of 1900) or the residents of Puerto Rico (who became American citizens under the Jones Act of 1917), Filipinos had an intermediate status in the United States. The Philippine Organic Act of 1902 created a special category of "citizens of the Philippine Islands . . . entitled to the protection of the United States." (Their status was loosely akin to that of the modern-day inhabitants of American Samoa, who are nationals of the United States but not American citizens.) There were no legal restrictions on Philippine migration to the United States.

Few Filipinos migrated to the United States until 1908, when Japan agreed to limit Japanese emigration to the United States. This so-called Gentlemen's Agreement had a loophole: it did not apply to the Territory of Hawaii, to which Japanese continued to migrate.[231] Nevertheless, Hawaiian plantations, which were heavily dependent on Japanese labor, feared that the Japanese loophole would soon close. They therefore began to actively recruit Filipinos. Their fear proved accurate in 1917, when anti-Asian hysteria prompted Congress to pass the Asiatic Barred Zone Act, which prohibited *all* migration from the Asian mainland and "persons who are natives of islands not possessed by the United States adjacent to the continent of Asia."[232] The Japanese were thus excluded even from Hawaii. Filipinos, of course, were natives of islands possessed by the United States. Filipino migration to Hawaii accelerated, and many of those migrants moved on to the United States, particularly California (see figure 6.7). By 1930, California was home to slightly over thirty thousand Filipinos.[233]

The number of Filipinos in California was small, but unemployment caused by the Depression provoked a wave of violence aimed against them. On January 20, 1930, after a series of small incidents in the Central Valley, mobs of white people in the coastal town of Watsonville descended upon Filipino shops and homes, killing one Filipino immigrant, Fermin Tobera, and wounding several others. Within a week, the anti-Filipino rioting

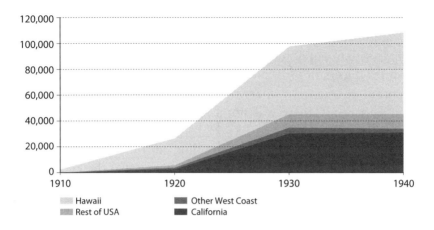

Figure 6.7 Filipino residents of the United States, 1910–40
Source: U.S. Census Bureau.

spread to Stockton—where nativists dynamited a Filipino community center—San Jose, and Los Angeles. In Watsonville itself, a second mob estimated by law enforcement at roughly seven hundred people began indiscriminately attacking Filipinos in the streets, killing several and forcing the police to round up most of the Filipinos in the town "for their own protection."[234] The California legislature then voted in support of granting the Philippines immediate independence—not out of political idealism, but in order to include the Philippines in the Asiatic Barred Zone. Soon thereafter, the American Federation of Labor and the Congress of Industrial Organizations added their voices to the call for Philippine independence, not because of a principled stance in favor of decolonization, but so that Filipino labor would not compete against American union members.[235]

Sugar producers and the dairy industry also jumped into the surge of anti-Filipino sentiment to push for immediate decolonization. The beet sugar industry had obvious reasons to want to expel the Philippines from the American customs area. The opportunity partnered the beet sugar industry with the formidable lobbying machine constructed by the Cuban sugar lobby—Philippine independence being perhaps the one policy position on which the two groups could agree. The sugar interests were soon joined by a coalition of Midwestern dairy farmers—under the less-than-euphonious "Tariff Defense Committee of American Producers of Oils and Fats"—who worried about the competition to domestic margarine posed by Philippine coconut oil. As a result, there was not a lot of pushback in 1930 when Republican congressmen like Harold Knutson (R-Minnesota) broke with the GOP's long-standing anti-independence platform. "It is generally agreed," said Knutson, "that the Philippine Islands today constitute the greatest single menace to our dairy industry."[236]

There was little domestic opposition to Philippine independence. No "Philippine lobby" ever emerged to match the Cuba lobby. The reason, of course, was that the opponents of annexation had written restrictions on the ability of American citizens to invest in the Philippine Islands into the Philippine Organic Act of 1902. The restrictions prevented the emergence of groups with a vested interest in the retention of the Philippines. In other words, the restrictions kept the empire trap from closing in America's easternmost possession. Of course, the Democratic anti-imperialists could not completely prevent the creation of economic links between the "incorporated" United States and its "unincorporated" Pacific possession. The 1909 and 1912 Tariff Acts brought the Philippines into the American customs area. Nonetheless, the investment restrictions ensured that it would be mostly *Filipino* landowners and entrepreneurs who benefited from access to the American market, not residents of the United States. (The Philippine Autonomy Act of 1916 gave the newly created Philippine legislature the power to extend Philippine citizenship to resident American citizens. No legislation was written to enable this, however, and rather few Americans pressed the issue once the courts ruled that they would be subjected to double income taxation if they did.)

It took three decades, but the Democratic anti-imperialist strategy paid off once Californian race riots put the issue of Philippine independence back on the table. After the 1930 election, Congress passed several independence bills. President Hoover vetoed all of them, at the private urging of Manuel Roxas and Sergio Osmeña, two of the Philippines' most important political leaders. In his memoirs, Hoover expressed some dismay at the difference between Roxas and Osmeña's public pro-independence statements and their private opposition.[237] The Philippine leaders, conversely, saw no contradiction in their stance, since from their point of view previous Republican administrations had been mysteriously unwilling to make an offer that they could accept—for example, full executive autonomy combined with perpetual commercial and defense links.

Congress passed the Hare-Hawes-Cutting Act in December 1932, during President Hoover's final months in office. Hoover, as he had done to all previous legislation mandating Philippine independence, vetoed it. Congress overturned Hoover's veto on January 17, 1933. This time the *Philippine* Senate rejected the bill, but the new, overwhelmingly Democratic Congress under the incoming Democratic president was not to be deterred. The bill was slightly revised to eliminate the retention of non-naval bases in the Philippines. With this cosmetic change, Congress passed a new bill, the Tydings-McDuffie Philippine Independence Act of 1934. The Philippine legislature had little choice but to accept.

The Philippine Independence Act imposed an immigration quota of *fifty* visas per year and phased out free trade in stages between 1940 and 1946. In 1935, the United States would impose quotas on the Philippines of 850,000 long tons of sugar, 200,000 tons of coconut oil, and 3 million pounds of cordage. Even this proved insufficient for the domestic farm lobby, which lived in mortal fear of the threat of cheap margarine. The Revenue Act of 1934 added a 3 cents tax on every pound of coconut oil coming into the United State from the Philippines. (Although the exigencies of American constitutional law required that the tax revenues go to the Philippine treasury, this was hardly enough to compensate the Philippines for its lost access to American markets.)[238] In the middle of the Great Depression, and in the midst of an escalating arms race in the Pacific, the newly formed Commonwealth of the Philippines was economically on its own.

It is worth noting that President Manuel Quezon of the Philippines attempted to forestall full independence. In 1938, the U.S. high commissioner, Paul McNutt, began to publicly advocate that the two nations retain permanent trade and defense links. Quezon stated that McNutt's logic was "inassailable." In the absence of an official U.S. proposal, however, Quezon kept his bargaining options open, contradictorily stating that he could not agree to U.S. control over "foreign affairs, tariff, immigration, currency and public debt" while simultaneously declaring that he was open to "any economic relationship . . . based on mutual advantages to the two countries." He also declared that he would be willing to submit "indefinite postponement" of independence to a plebiscite.[239] Unsurprisingly, the U.S. Congress refused to take up Quezon's offer. After raising a few more trial balloons to no response from Washington, Quezon finally shut the door on "dominion status" on December 9, 1939, when he declared, "I prefer a government run like hell by Filipinos to a government run like heaven by the Americans."

Conclusion

Just as Wilson and Harding preferred to dismantle America's informal empire, Herbert Hoover—a mining engineer who made his pre-presidential fortune extracting precious metals and minerals from China and Australia—was more inclined to promote it. Presidential preferences, however, meant little in the face of global economic changes. The Great Depression set in less than a year after Hoover's inauguration, fundamentally altering the political conditions that had drawn the United States into its economic protectorates. The politics of scarcity revealed a distinct hierarchy among American economic interests: in times of limited resources, domestic producers trumped American producers exploiting foreign resources and facilities, who in turn trumped the holders of foreign debt.

In the absence of a united coalition lobbying for action, the U.S. government relinquished a number of its overseas commitments. In Bolivia, the United States ignored the desires of bankers because the austerity measures needed to maintain debt payments would have disadvantaged American-owned mining companies. A similar chain of events followed in Peru, Ecuador, and El Salvador. The Americans needed to *appear* sympathetic to creditors injured by the Dominican default, but there, too, the United States ultimately sided with direct investors rather than financiers.

The Depression also eroded the formal parts of the American empire. Domestic sugar producers lost patience for preferential tariffs on Cuban sugar, and they successfully lobbied for the Smoot-Hawley Act to raise those duties. The domestic forces that raised barriers to the entry of foreign products also successfully raised barriers to the entry of foreign persons. Unemployment and anti-Asian hysteria in California led to hostility against Filipino immigrants. Bowing to pressure from organized labor (joined by sugar and dairy interests), the United States mandated Philippine independence. None of these interests cared much in the abstract about ending imperial (or quasi-imperial) rule in Cuba or the Philippines—it was simply a by-product of their protectionist goals.

A curious sequence of events in Cuba, however, made it clear that American overseas interests were not rendered entirely powerless. As the Cuban economy declined, the United States heeded the plaints of investors who feared that President Machado's economic policies—which mainly involved maintaining the government's ability to borrow at all costs—would lead to the complete collapse of the Cuban state. Under pressure from Bethlehem Steel, United Fruit, and the U.S. Chamber of Commerce, the United States lent its support to regime change in Cuba not once but *twice* in 1933–34.

The Cuban episode illustrated the fact that the United States' escape from the empire trap was only partial. Neither Hoover nor Roosevelt disengaged the United States from the defense of its citizens' economic interests abroad. The Roosevelt administration may have overthrown a government because it refused to default on its debt to American creditors, but it did so precisely *because* doing so created "chaos," which threatened the investments of prominent American citizens. After Machado's successor fell to a left-wing coup, the Roosevelt administration came very close to invading the island—only the success of an American-abetted countercoup short-circuited military intervention. In short, while the Depression allowed the United States to escape the empire trap in part, the pressures that had originally caused the trap still existed—and would resume once global economic conditions improved.

seven
Falling Back In

Every observing person must by this time thoroughly understand that under the Roosevelt Administration the United States government is as much opposed as any other government to interference with the freedom, the sovereignty, or other internal affairs or processes of the governments of other nations.

—*Secretary of State Cordell Hull, December 22, 1933*

Though it was Herbert Hoover who coined the phrase "good neighbor" to describe the United States' ideal relationship with Latin America, the Good Neighbor policy ultimately became associated with his successor, Franklin Roosevelt. In his inaugural address, Roosevelt strove to distance himself from Hoover's more ambiguous public statements about America's informal empire: "In the field of world policy I would dedicate this nation to the policy of the good neighbor, the neighbor who resolutely respects himself and, because he does so, respects the rights of others, the neighbor who respects his obligations and respects the sanctity of his agreements in and with a world of neighbors."[1]

Roosevelt's words are typically taken as an earnest reconsideration of U.S. relations with Latin America. "The Good Neighbor policy was a policy; it was not simply rhetoric," historian Bryce Wood has written. Behind the policy was a genuine reorganization of priorities. In Wood's words, the Good Neighbor policy meant that the United States "curbed its finance capital" and downgraded the protection of American overseas private investments.[2] The high point is typically located in Roosevelt's temperate reaction to the 1938 dispute between the foreign oil companies and the Mexican government. Washington, concerned with the high politics of building coalitions to contain the rise of the Axis powers, decided to conciliate Mexico. Bryce Wood again: "The solution of the . . . oil disputes with the United States, which were negotiated by equals and not determined by arbitral tribunals, were good examples of 'the mild-mannered methods' of the Good Neighbor policy. . . . Diplomats of this period did not differentiate between nonintervention and noninterference; both were regarded as prohibited."[3]

The only problem with the standard narrative is that it does not fit the facts. The Roosevelt administration took a hard line with the Mexican government over the expropriation. Roosevelt employed sanctions, and the Mexican government eventually paid compensation worth more than the companies' market value. Rather than representing the epitome of the Good Neighbor policy, the Mexican oil expropriation represented its end. American-owned overseas interests rediscovered their ability to steer policy in Washington, and the United States fell right back into the empire trap.

The empire trap that emerged in the late 1930s differed in three important ways from its pre-Depression predecessor. First, the United States abandoned direct attempts to reform foreign institutions. The reason, simply put, was that the tactics of dollar diplomacy—customs receiverships, fiscal advisers, and government-backed private loans—had not worked. The Depression-era defaults put the last nail in their coffin. The fiscal receivership in the Dominican Republic would limp along into the 1940s, but outside the occupations in Germany, Korea, and Japan the United States would not again attempt to place Americans inside the governmental structures of foreign nations until 2003.[4] Even in South Vietnam, U.S. officials would not be an official part of the local government's chain of command—something that frustrated Ambassador Henry Cabot Lodge to no end.

Second, private creditors were no longer a factor. Because Roosevelt had to deal with the owners of the defaulted debt from the pre-1929 era, his administration created institutions designed to insulate the government from the (politically weakened) bondholders. Once these institutions had served their purpose vis-à-vis the pre-1929 debt, Roosevelt's successors faced no serious pressure from bondholders for the simple reason that the Depression had destroyed the private market for sovereign debt. There were no substantial creditors to foreign sovereigns to clamor for protection. The sovereign debt market would not revive until the great wave of syndicated bank debt in the 1970s, and a market for sovereign bonds wouldn't be re-created until the 1990s. The empire trap of the 1930s and beyond concerned direct investors.

Third, new technologies of foreign intervention replaced the old techniques. These developments occurred in two forms: foreign aid and covert action. During the 1930s, U.S. state-to-state lending became routine, but after 1945 the United States began to grant large-scale aid as part of its Cold War strategy. Once intergovernmental loans and grants became routine, the United States could influence foreign governments by credibly threatening to cut them off. Similarly, covert action had been used before 1945, but it took the Second World War to create an entire agency of government dedicated to it.

The end result was that the United States found itself back in the business of protecting the property rights of Americans overseas before the end of Roosevelt's second term. Of course, U.S. foreign policy had many other concerns besides the protection of American investments. That said, as an empirical matter, the Roosevelt, Truman, and Eisenhower administrations never failed to protect American interests when they were threatened by Third World governments. The only exceptions were in the

Eastern European countries that fell under the sway of the Red Army.[5] Investors found ways to persuade U.S. administrations to support them against foreign governments. Administrations varied, of course, in how much they needed to be pushed (Roosevelt quite a bit, Eisenhower rather less), but when push came to shove, they acted, and acted successfully. This "second American empire," inasmuch as the peculiar mix of aid, sanctions, and covert action used to protect American property rights could be called an empire, worked from the point of view of American investors.

The Economic Policy of Good Neighborliness

The first step in the Good Neighbor policy was relatively cost-less for the Roosevelt administration. On December 26, 1933, at the Seventh Pan-American Conference in Montevideo, the United States signed the Convention on the Rights and Duties of States. As written, the convention was a strong statement of the equal rights of states. Article 8 proclaimed, "No state has the right to intervene in the internal or external affairs of another." Article 9 stated, "The jurisdiction of states within the limits of national territory applies to all the inhabitants. Nationals and foreigners are under the same protection of the law and the national authorities and the foreigners may not claim rights other or more extensive than those of the nationals."

The United States was, however, one of three signatories that appended reservations to the convention. Upon his arrival in Montevideo, Cordell Hull privately told the U.S. delegation, "There are a number of situations that justify a state in intervening in the affairs of another state." Hull also, however, realized that "the demand for unanimous affirmative vote was very vociferous and more or less wild and unreasonable."[6] Neither Hull nor Roosevelt was willing to wreck the conference or anger the Latin American delegations over what was, in essence, a declaration of intent with little practical force. Hull limited himself to adding a somewhat cryptic reservation to the convention, which implied that he did not interpret its wording in quite the same way as the other delegates.

> I think it unfortunate that during the brief period of this Conference there is apparently not time within which to prepare interpretations and definitions of these fundamental terms that are embraced in the report. Such definitions and interpretations would enable every government to proceed in a uniform way without any difference of opinion or of interpretations.

Although Hull assured the other delegates that they need not fear intervention on the part of the Roosevelt administration, he also pledged the United States to "the doctrines and policies which it has pursued since March 4 which are embodied in the different addresses of President Roosevelt since that time and in the recent peace address of myself on the 15th day of December before this Conference and in the law of nations as generally recognized and accepted."[7] Hull did not want to spoil the party, but neither did he wish to tie his hands.

Staying Out of Debt Enforcement

Once the Montevideo convention was signed, President Roosevelt's second order of business was to ensure that the U.S. government would not be drawn into negotiations over the rescheduling of defaulted Latin American debt. The solution was to give a public imprimatur to a private body: the Foreign Bondholders Protective Council (FBPC). Roosevelt created the organization by executive order in October 1933. The FBPC was chartered as a Maryland nonprofit corporation, with a board of fifteen appointed by the president.[8] The theory was that negotiations between a debtor and a unified block of creditors would produce a better outcome for everyone involved. The creditors would gain more negotiating power, since they could (in theory) coordinate credit boycotts and other punishments. The debtors, meanwhile, would be freed of the "holdout" problem, in which key creditors refused to restructure their loans, knowing that they might be able to get a better deal if enough *other* creditors agreed to restructure first.

The ostensible reason for the FBPC, however, was *not* the real reason. The real reason was to protect the Roosevelt administration from any political pressure the bondholders could muster. Herbert Feis, the State Department economic adviser, stated so explicitly: "The Department of State would not be committed to any action in regard to any situation. In fact, it was hoped that the existence of the council would perhaps lessen the necessity under which the Department of State might have to take cognizance of default situations."[9]

As a means of protecting bondholders, the FBPC was a failure. Its president and vice president, J. Reuben Clark and Francis White, invariably took an unproductively hard line. "A believer in the sanctity of contracts, Clark's approach consisted of arguing why debtors should adhere to the letter of their loan contracts, which left little room for negotiation."[10] In December 1935, Clark went so far as to publicly blast debtor countries for such "extravagances" as schools, hospitals, and jails. He went on to call the practice of debtors buying up their own debt "immoral." In 1936, the FBPC's annual report announced that it would now officially resist *any* restructuring: no interest rate cuts, no alteration in terms, no haircuts on principal. The organization claimed that any debtors who kept up their interest payments would be able to refund their debts at lower rates on the market.[11] Of course, this hard line did nothing to resolve the problems of countries in default. Moreover, it was deucedly odd for an organization created to facilitate renegotiation to refuse to renegotiate. The FBPC took credit for the decisions by the Brazilian and Dominican governments to resume debt service, but that was the limit of its success, and it was not at all clear that the organization made any difference in either case. In negotiations with Cuba in 1936–37, the FBPC managed to antagonize *both* Chase Bank and the State Department.[12]

As a means of circumventing investor pressure on the U.S. government, however, the FBPC was a full success. The State Department routinely referred inquiries directly to the FBPC's offices. The Depression had gotten the U.S. government out of the business of defending the creditor rights of American bondholders, and FBPC served the purpose of helping the government to stay out of that business. The failure of sovereign debt markets to revive only made it easier to resist the entreaties of the remaining creditors. The U.S. government's disinvolvement was not total, of course. The Roosevelt administration actively helped renegotiate Cuba's debts in 1937–38. In addition, with the establishment of the Export-Import Bank the U.S. government began to make direct loans to foreign governments. In general, however, the FBPC kept Washington out of the debt enforcement business. A key feature of the first American empire was no more.

Ending the Protectorates

Roosevelt understood that the Good Neighbor policy would never be viewed as credible unless the United States could regularize its relationship with its formal protectorates in Panama and Cuba. Both countries owed their independence to American intervention, and both countries' constitutions gave the United States extraordinary rights that were popularly resented. In Cuba, the second and third clauses of the Platt Amendment, appended to the end of the Cuban Constitution of 1902, read as follows:

> II. That said government [Cuba] shall not assume or contract any public debt, to pay the interest upon which, and to make reasonable sinking fund provision for the ultimate discharge of which, the ordinary revenues of the island, after defraying the current expenses of government shall be inadequate.

III. That the government of Cuba consents that the United States may exercise the right to intervene for the preservation of Cuban independence, the maintenance of a government adequate for the protection of life, property, and individual liberty, and for discharging the obligations with respect to Cuba imposed by the treaty of Paris on the United States, now to be assumed and undertaken by the government of Cuba.

In Panama, Article 136 of the Constitution of 1904 was equally sweeping:

The government of the United States of America may intervene, in any part of the Republic of Panama, in order to re-establish public tranquility and constitutional order in the event that they have been disturbed, providing that said nation shall assume or have assumed by treaty the obligation of guaranteeing the independence and sovereignty of this Republic.

Discussions began first over Panama. President Arnulfo Arias met Roosevelt in Washington in October of 1933. One of the biggest bones of contention between the two countries was a Panama Canal Zone agency known as the "Commissary." The Commissary held a monopoly over imports of consumer goods into the zone and the sale of provisions and services to transiting vessels. It also controlled the docks on both sides of the canal and received subsidized rates on the Panama Railroad. At the meeting, Roosevelt personally pledged that he would curb the Commissary's excesses and maintain the value (in gold) of the Panama canal annuity. The subsequent devaluation of the U.S. dollar in January 1934 violated that pledge and deeply embarrassed the American president. Secretary of State Cordell Hull suggested that the need to renegotiate Panama's annuity could form the basis for a new treaty. Negotiations began in April 1934.[13]

The toughest part of the talks often appeared to be between Washington and the administration of the Panama Canal Zone, rather than between Washington and the Panamanian government. The Canal Zone's governor, for example, insisted that the United States take over the town of New Cristóbal (which bordered the Atlantic side of the Zone) in the face of Panamanian protests. The legal authority for this derived from Article 2 of the treaty establishing the Canal Zone, which read:

> The Republic of Panama further grants to the United States in perpetuity the use, occupation and control of any other lands and waters outside of the zone above described which may be necessary and convenient for the construction, maintenance, operation, sanitation and protection of the said Canal.

The Roosevelt administration supported the Panamanians in the dispute over New Cristóbal despite protests that American women in New Cristóbal were "subjected to the grossest indecencies and physical handlings by hoodlums."[14] When it leaked that the proposed treaty (which coincided with the end of Prohibition) would impose American excise taxes on beer, the local army commander had to warn that such taxes "might result in unfortunate incidents." The chief labor union in the zone, meanwhile, protested that any agreement would require Americans "to contribute to the welfare of a foreign nation to whom they are not in any sense obligated." Roosevelt himself had to cram through a compromise that left low-alcohol beer and light wines untaxed but required the zone to purchase supplies of all stronger drink from Panama. "Liquor is luxury," wrote the president, "and I see no reason for the government to supply it in the Zone as though it were a food necessity."[15]

American officials in the Canal Zone feared—and rightly so—that their privileged position would be considerably diminished by the new agreement. The Canal Zone's general counsel, Frank

Wang, worried that Roosevelt had accepted the principle that the United States did not have sovereignty within the zone. For his part, Canal Zone governor Julian Schley resented the implication in the treaty drafts that there was "a partnership between the United States and Panama in the pecuniary profits from the Canal."[16] Schley, for his part, managed to pressure Washington into rejecting a Panamanian proposal to grant Panama a share of the canal's gross revenues in lieu of a fixed annuity. President Roosevelt, in turn, cut Schley out of the talks as much as possible: during his visit to Panama in October 1935, he instructed the American legation to keep all treaty amendments private and refused to communicate with Schley about the "informal" talks.[17]

Though the United States retained a number of rights and privileges relating to the canal, they were overshadowed by those it relinquished. The treaty was signed on March 2, 1936. The nominal value of the canal annuity rose from $250,000 to $430,000. Panamanian merchants gained the right to sell goods directly to passing ships and bid on supply contracts within the zone.[18] The treaty permitted the Panamanian government to begin construction on the Trans-Isthmian Highway between Panama City and Colón, which the Canal Zone administration had previously vetoed. Finally, the treaty revoked the U.S. right to intervene, although Article 136 remained part of the Panamanian Constitution until 1941.[19]

The treaty with Panama had been hard; tying up loose ends with Cuba would prove harder. A new Treaty of Relations on May 29, 1934, formally abrogated the Platt Amendment.[20] Since the Cubans had never officially recognized the Platt Amendment as anything more than an "appendix" to their constitution, that ended the U.S. symbolic right to intervene. The task of ending the American protectorate in Cuba, however, could not be addressed by symbolic action alone. Roosevelt had faced a tough enough battle in regularizing U.S. relations with Panama, where the only interest group was the residents of the Canal Zone. In the Cuban case, the sugar industry needed to be brought on board. The American owners of Cuban properties wanted greater access to the American market. Without greater access, the Cuban economy would continue to stagnate—worsening the political instability on the island and leading to a repeat of the uncomfortable events of 1933. Domestic sugar producers, on the other hand, wanted continued protection, or at least some sort of guarantee that Cuba's ability to produce nearly unlimited amounts of low-cost sugar would not cause prices to collapse.

The effects of the 1929 Smoot-Hawley Act on the Cuban sugar industry were worse than feared. An internal memorandum of the U.S. Trade Commission dated April 6, 1933, stated: "The tariff on sugar has not been effective either as a price protection to domestic producers, or as an encouragement to expansion in production, but has primarily served on the one hand to destroy the Cuban industry, and on the other hand to bring about continuous and very rapid expansion in Puerto Rico and the Philippines." (By April 1933 sugar prices were 20% lower than three years earlier.) Five days later, Trade Commission chairman Robert O'Brien explained to the president, "The situation in Cuba . . . is such that the higher the American tariff may be the lower are the costs of producing sugar in Cuba. . . . The result is that the price is gone down to a point which is disastrous both for American and for Cuban producers. It is evident that no increase of the American tariff can relieve the resulting situation in this country or in Cuba."[21]

Why did Smoot-Hawley fail to protect American mainland sugar? First, Cuban wages (and other domestic costs) were extremely flexible downward. When the Depression began, in 1929, Cuban nominal wages were on par with those in the southern United States. Inasmuch as Smoot-Hawley drove down the nominal price of Cuban sugar, it also drove down the nominal value of Cuban wages. Nominal daily wages during the sugar harvest fell from $1.80 in 1929 to $1.09 in 1933.[22] (Collapsing prices meant that real wages dropped "only" 20% over the same period.) Other costs also declined: raw cane costs in Cuba dropped by half in 1930–32, and the total production cost of raw sugar fell 15%.[23] Cuba remained the lowest-cost sugar supplier to the U.S. market despite the tariff. Cuba, therefore, retained more of its cost advantage than mainland producers had hoped—albeit at the price of widespread hardship on the island. Second, whatever benefits Smoot-Hawley did generate went to Hawaii, the Philippine Islands, and Puerto Rico. All three areas produced sugar at a higher cost than Cuba, but at less cost than most domestic producers.

In theory, Congress had the power to apply tariffs to Puerto Rican and Philippine exports to the continental United States. In practice, doing so was politically impossible. Puerto Rico was entirely populated by American citizens, who would emigrate en masse if the island's economy collapsed.[24] In addition, Puerto Rican sugar plantations and mills were owned by mainland investors and vertically integrated into mainland refining operations: unlike their Cuban equivalents, they sold little production on the open market.[25] Deliberately impoverishing American citizens and breaking up vertically integrated U.S. operations to aid Cuba would be politically problematic, to say the least.

Puerto Rico in fact enjoyed particularly effective congressional representation in the persons of Santiago Iglesias Pantín and Vito Marcantonio. As "resident commissioner," Iglesias did not have a vote on the House floor, but he did have a full vote in committee. Elected in 1933 on a somewhat counterintuitive pro-statehood Republican-Socialist fusion ticket, he obtained seats on the Agriculture and Insular Affairs committees, which had oversight over any bills affecting the Puerto Rican sugar industry. Moreover, Iglesias had a long-standing relationship with the Roosevelt family, and he was highly connected with the American Federation of Labor.[26] In addition, New York's growing Puerto Rican population meant that Representative Vito Marcantonio of East Harlem (R–New York) became known as the "Congressman from Puerto Rico."[27] Marcantonio had the support of much of the rest of New York's congressional delegation, since the big sugar firms were headquartered in Manhattan and many jobs in the northern suburbs and Brooklyn depended on Puerto Rican sugar. (The National Sugar Refining Company's plant on Buena Vista Avenue in Yonkers, New York, which processed the company's Puerto Rican production, is still in operation under different owners.)[28]

The Philippine Islands, meanwhile, were still an American possession in 1934. Imposing tariffs on the Philippines would have been easy in terms of domestic politics. The problem was that allowing the Philippine economy to collapse *before* formal independence could have provoked unrest, which American forces would then have needed to contain. Roosevelt was determined to avoid that result. Two other factors made it impossible to exclude the Philippines. First, the Philippine legislature needed to approve separation: it was unlikely that it would do so unless it retained access to the American market for at least some period of time. Second, a study by R. I. Nowell of the Federal Farm Board concluded that "a tariff on Philippine sugar would have a negligible effect on sugar prices in the United States but would represent welcomed protection for the Cubans."[29]

Roosevelt, then, faced a multipronged problem. He needed to help rescue the Cuban economy in order to reduce instability on the island and protect the value of American investments. He also needed to satisfy the domestic sugar interests. And he needed to avoid selling out the Philippines and Puerto Rico. The solution was to impose quotas on Cuban sugar while cutting the tariff. That would aid Cuba while easing fears that expanded Cuban production would drive other producers out of the market.

Determining the optimal size of the quota, however, was not easy. In the summer of 1933, the sugar producers tried to hash out a *voluntary* quota system under the Agricultural Adjustment Act of 1933. The sugar producers came up with a system that would give the mainland and Puerto Rico quotas well above current production. Hawaii would receive a quota equal to 97% of current production. The burden of adjustment would fall on Cuba and the Philippines. Cuba would receive a quota

Table 7.1

Quotas under the U.S. Sugar Act of 1934, thousands of tons

		1934	1935	1936	1937	1938	1939	1940
Mainland beet	Final adjusted quota	1,556	1,550	1,342	1,417	1,584	1,567	1,550
sugar	Actual deliveries	1,562	1,478	1,364	1,245	1,448	1,809	1,550
Mainland cane	Final adjusted quota	261	260	392	472	429	425	420
sugar	Actual deliveries	268	319	409	491	449	587	406
Hawaii	Final adjusted quota	916	926	1,033	984	922	948	938
	Actual deliveries	948	927	1,033	985	906	966	941
Puerto Rico	Final adjusted quota	803	788	909	897	816	807	798
	Actual deliveries	807	793	907	896	815	1,126	798
Philippines	Final adjusted quota	1,015	899	1,001	998	991	1,041	982
	Actual deliveries	1,088	917	985	991	981	980	981
Cuba	Final adjusted quota	1,902	1,822	2,103	2,149	1,954	1,932	1,749
	Actual deliveries	1,866	1,830	2,102	2,155	1,941	1,930	1,750
Full-duty foreign	Final adjusted quota	17	17	26	27	27	27	27
	Actual deliveries	17	25	29	115	81	27	24
Total consumption	Final adjusted quota	6,470	6,262	6,806	6,944	6,723	6,747	6,464
	Actual deliveries	6,556	6,289	6,829	6,878	6,621	7,425	6,450

Source: Alan Dye and Richard Sicotte, "The Origins and Development of the U.S. Sugar Program, 1934–59," paper prepared for the 14th International Economic History Conference, 2006, p. 3.

of 1.7 million tons. A State Department official called Cuba's proposed quota a "residual quota, being what remained after the demands of all other sugar groups had been satisfied."

President Roosevelt rejected the "voluntary" plan.[30] The resulting Sugar Act of 1934 brought sugar under the Agricultural Adjustment Act but made the domestic beet sugar quota effectively nonbinding.[31] Cuba received a quota of 1.9 million tons (see table 7.1). In March 1934, the president used his executive authority under existing legislation to cut the tariff on Cuban sugar to 1.5 cents (down from 2.0 cents). A little over two months later, on May 29, 1934, the United States and Cuba signed a treaty that brought rates down to 0.9 cents.

The new arrangement was far from perfect, but it succeeded in its two main goals. First, it stabilized the Cuban economy (and the value of U.S. sugar investments) at minimal domestic cost. The nominal value of Cuban sugar exports to the United

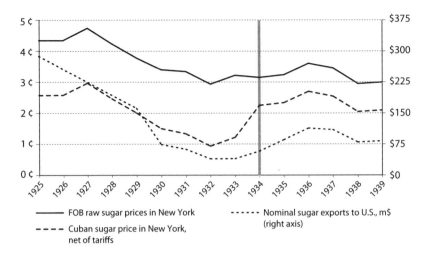

Figure 7.1 Nominal sugar prices (cents per lb.) and the value of Cuban exports, 1925–39

Source: Calculated from data in Alan Dye and Richard Sicotte, "The Interwar Turning Point in U.S.-Cuban Trade Relations: A View through Sugar-Company Stock Prices," paper for "The Origins and Development of Financial Markets and Institutions" conference, April 28–29, 2006, p. 41; Dye and Sicotte, "The Origins and Development of the U.S. Sugar Program, 1934–59," paper prepared for the 14th International Economic History Conference, 2006, p. 37; and *Historical Statistics of the United States, Millennial Edition*, series Da1433–1435.

States jumped in 1934 and 1935 (see figure 7.1). Second, it limited the damage that Cuban sugar could inflict on the American sugar industry. Finally, it allowed the United States to abrogate its formal protectorate over Cuba without seeming to extract a quid pro quo, thus preserving the form of the Good Neighbor policy. It failed, however, to resuscitate the Cuban economy. Cuban wages never recovered relative to the United States.

Reciprocal Trade Agreements

The last element of Roosevelt's approach involved opening the U.S. market to Latin American exports from outside the U.S. customs area. The legislative cornerstone of the strategy was the Reciprocal Trade Agreements Act of 1934. The act empowered the president to enter into mutual tariff reductions with foreign countries, subject only to the limitation that "no proclamation shall be made increasing or decreasing by more than 50 per centum any existing rate of duty."[32] The passage of some sort of liberalizing trade bill was a foregone conclusion after the 1932 elections: lower tariffs had been a Democratic plank for some time.[33] On March 20, 1934, the House approved the reciprocal trade bill on a party-line vote, with 96% of Democrats in favor and 98% of Republicans against. The Senate vote was almost as partisan: 93% of Democrats in favor and 85% of Republicans opposed.[34]

The new trade policy was a partial success. Roosevelt managed to secure agreements with many of the countries that formed part of the former American intervention sphere: Cuba (1934), Honduras (1935), Colombia (1936), Guatemala (1936), Costa Rica (1936), and El Salvador (1937). The trade agreements clearly improved the tone of relations with the countries that signed them. The Colombian foreign minister, for example, effusively praised the "new criterion in the diplomatic sphere, and commercial relations based on liberal principles which consecrate the operation of the most favored nation clause."[35] On the other hand, the United States was unable to sign agreements with the countries that had been in its outer sphere (Ecuador, Peru, and Bolivia) or outside its sphere altogether (Argentina, Brazil, Chile, and Uruguay) despite intensive efforts.

The Bolivian Oil Nationalization

The Good Neighbor policy faced its first serious challenge in Bolivia. In 1937, the Bolivian government nationalized properties belonging to Standard Oil of New Jersey (aka Jersey Standard). The putative reason was unpaid taxes. Jersey Standard's 1922 concession stated that the land tax would jump from 2.5 centavos per hectare to 10 centavos after production started, and then rise to 50 centavos over seven years. The government and Jersey Standard immediately began to argue over whether the contract's definition of "production" meant that the higher rate would kick in when oil was struck or when commercial sales began. In 1928, the parties agreed that the higher rates would start in 1930, but in 1931 the government of President Daniel Salamanca rescinded the agreement and demanded back taxes through 1924—a total of 1.4 million bolivianos, or $447,284 at current exchange rates. The dispute went into the black hole of the Bolivian legal system and remained there, during which Jersey Standard continued to pay current imposts but refused to meet the demand for back taxes.

By 1937, Jersey Standard was marking time with its Bolivian operation. The company had invested in Bolivia with the aim of exporting oil to Argentina. In 1925, however, Argentina denied permission to run a pipeline from Bolivia. In 1927, it imposed prohibitive tariffs on oil imports. In 1931, Jersey Standard capped the Bermejo well and began shipping equipment back to the United States.[36] The next year, it stopped drilling new wells.[37] Production rose during the Chaco War (1932–36), owing to demand from the Bolivian military, but only by more intensive working of existing fields.

Jersey Standard's marginal operation became, in essence, a victim of Bolivian internal instability and external rivalry. In 1932, the Bolivian Army attacked Paraguayan forces in the disputed Chaco region. Public opinion commonly held the war to be about oil, since the region was (incorrectly) viewed to be rich in petroleum deposits. Jersey Standard's fields were actually located in Tarija and Santa Cruz. Paraguayan forces didn't reach them until 1935, and were unable to hold the area after General Germán Busch's successful counteroffensive.[38]

During the war Jersey Standard made a number of missteps that alienated Bolivian public opinion. First, in 1933 the government asked Standard to increase production of aviation fuel at its refinery. Standard agreed, but at a price it set and only if the government bought all ancillary products from the refinery *that it did not need* for the war effort . . . also at prices set by the company. The military responded by temporarily taking over the refinery but soon decided that the middle of a war was a bad time to try to figure out how to produce aviation fuel. Jersey Standard got its way.[39] The Bolivian government then requested a $5 million loan from the company to finance the war effort—which Jersey Standard refused.[40] (The loan would have come to $68.3 million in 2011 dollars.)

Right after the war ended in 1936, Colonel David Toro came to power with the avowed aim "to implant state socialism with the aid of the parties of the left." Jersey Standard offered to sell its properties for $3 million.[41] This was not charity on Jersey Standard's part: at a conservative 5% discount rate, a value of $3 million implied an average profit margin of 52% of revenues. Considering Jersey Standard's *internal* complaining about the unprofitability of its Bolivian venture, it is highly unlikely that it was anywhere near that profitable—or worth anywhere near $3 million. In fact, it was far from clear that Jersey Standard's properties in Bolivia had *any* market value. No investments had been made since 1932, and production was low and declining.

Toro agreed to the offer but did not sign a deal—and on March 13, 1937, he reversed himself and confiscated Jersey Standard. Toro decided to expropriate for two reasons, one domestic and one foreign. The domestic reason was his rivalry with the hero of the Chaco War, Germán Busch. Busch was rather more radical than Toro—Toro feared that he would be overthrown unless he moved to put meat on the bones of Bolivia's "military socialism."[42] (Busch overthrew Toro anyway on July 13, 1937.)[43] Toro in fact began preparing the expropriation in December 1936, in order to ensure that the Bolivian government could run the properties once it took them over.[44] The foreign reason for the expropriation was that the Argentine government told the Bolivian foreign minister, Enrique Finot, that Buenos Aires would guarantee Bolivia's security against Paraguay *on the condition* that the oil fields be confiscated and turned over to Yacimientos Petrolíferos Fiscales Argentinos (YPF), the Argentine state-owned oil company. YPF, in turn, would give Bolivia a 14% royalty on production (in addition to the land tax) instead of the 11% paid by Jersey Standard.[45] Ironically, the official reason the Bolivian government gave for the nationalization was Jersey Standard's unregistered sale of oil to Argentina in 1926–27.[46]

Bolivia did not hand the properties over to Argentina, but it did lay the groundwork for exporting to that country. The Bolivian government formed its own oil company—Yacimientos Petrolíferos Fiscales Bolivianos (YPFB)—which then signed barter agreements with Argentina and Brazil to export excess production. In April 1937, La Paz announced the Yacuiba–Santa Cruz railway project to link the Bolivian fields with Argentina.[47]

The U.S. government had few tools with which to pressure Bolivia. Military intervention was as logistically infeasible in 1937 as it had been in 1931; the United States lacked even *plans* to intervene. Nor could the Americans feasibly prevent Bolivia from exporting to Argentina. Paraguay acceded to a U.S. request to embargo Bolivian oil (and Peru might have proved amenable to U.S. suasion), but the Argentine government bluntly refused a "polite request" from the U.S. embassy.[48] In February 1938, Assistant Secretary of State Sumner Welles advised the Bolivian government to go to arbitration. His explanation to Bolivian officials was that "the only way in which public opinion in this country was going to support the 'Good Neighbor' policy as a permanent part of our foreign policy would be for the policy to be recognized throughout the continent as a completely reciprocal policy and not one of a purely unilateral character."[49]

Both the Bolivian government *and* Jersey Standard, however, resisted arbitration. Bolivia argued that its action was fully legal under local law. Jersey Standard argued that going to arbitration to ask for compensation would mean recognizing the validity of Bolivia's right to confiscate its assets. Moreover, it was far from clear that Standard wanted compensation. Rather, in the words of John Muccio, the American chargé d'affaires, "The Standard Oil Company prefers to accept financial loss than to allow these countries to get the impression that it can be forcibly expulsed."[50] The end result was that the U.S. government took little action in 1937 or 1938. Welles, in fact, had to pressure *Jersey Standard* to file suit in Bolivian courts.[51] Unsurprisingly, the Bolivian Supreme Court rejected the claim a year later.

The Mexican Oil Expropriation

It was a second expropriation, in Mexico, that provoked the United States to act on behalf of American-owned private property. Mexico expropriated the foreign oil companies in 1938, a year after Bolivia. The Mexican expropriation, however, was neither encouraged by nor an imitation of the Bolivian action. Rather, it was the unfortunate result of a series of miscalculations on the part of the oil companies and Mexican labor unions.

The Mexican oil industry was not doing well by the late 1930s. Three traded companies—Mexican Eagle, Mexican Petroleum (a subsidiary of Jersey Standard), and Penn-Mex—produced almost all their oil in Mexico. A fourth, Mexican Seaboard, produced 62% of its oil in Mexico until the late 1930s.[52] Together, these companies produced 78% of all oil in Mexico in 1937. Their share prices had been in decline since the 1920s (see table 7.2). Mexican Eagle shares fell 89% (in real terms) between 1920 and 1930. Share prices briefly rallied when the company's Poza Rica fields came on line in 1933 but soon began to decline once again. With some vertiginous ups and downs, Mexican Seaboard shares collapsed by half in 1922 and then lost almost all their remaining value between 1925 and 1931 before recovering somewhat. The recovery, however, coincided with a monotonic decline in Mexico's share of the company's production from 57% in 1931 to 20% in 1936 and 1937—in other words, the market rewarded Mexican Seaboard's ability to transform itself from a Mexican oil company into a Californian oil company.[53] Penn-Mex shares slid in value because of a 1932 decision by its owner, the South Penn Oil Company, to

Table 7.2

Real share price index of Mexican oil companies, adjusted for splits, 1921 = 100

	Mexican Eagle	Mexican Petrolem	Penn-Mex	Mexican Seaboard	Standard Oil of N.J.	Sinclair Consolidated	Texas Company
1912		87			82		86
1913		54			71		99
1914	59	66			79		104
1915	42	132	525		106	217	180
1916	37	358	408		79	301	146
1917	43	213	297		69	117	62
1918	47	105	266		70	145	73
1919	80	126	271		71	138	86
1920	103	82	133		55	63	60
1921	100	100	100	100	100	100	100
1922	70	250	85	47	89	101	92
1923	34		224	42	38	119	84
1924	32	159	115	43	20	77	87
1925	37	188	89	41	22	73	82
1926	36		92	23	21	84	114
1927	31	214	177	189	23	195	136
1928	30	267	164	15	30	96	136
1929		205		5	36	64	113
1930	11	146	99	3	27	32	66
1931	10	98	68	2	18	19	28
1932	10	72	43	7	22	19	38
1933	19	79	20	11	34	37	66
1934	12	72	8	9	30	26	54
1935	7	89	11	13	35	31	75
1936	7		9	16	46	51	137
1937	7		7	7	29	26	94
1938	8		1	8	35	27	119

Source: 1924 and 1925 Mexican Petroleum from *Moody's*; it is the annual average. 1921 Mexican Seaboard from Moody's. Mexican Eagle data from Alberto de la Fuente, "El desplazamiento de México como productor de petróleo en los años veinte," B.A. thesis (ITAM: Mexico City, 1998), p. 98, *Moody's*, and the *Times of London*. Mexican Eagle share prices were converted to dollars at the market exchange rate and deflated using the U.S. producer price index. 1915–35 Penn-Mex from the *Wall Street Journal* and *Moody's* thereafter. Other data are from the *Wall Street Journal* and Wharton Research Data Services, http: //wrds-web.wharton.upenn.edu.

liquidate most of the enterprise. South Penn (which owned 55% of Penn-Mex) arranged to swap the company's existing stock, with a par value of $25, for new shares with a par value of $1. It then authorized Penn-Mex's directors to "pay dividends out of any available funds . . . regardless of whether or not the excess was created through net earnings."[54] The directors immediately paid a special dividend of $5.18. Four days later, South Penn sold its remaining stake in the company to Sinclair Consolidated for $1 per share immediately plus an additional $18.75 to be paid out over an unspecified period of time.[55]

Mexican Petroleum's share price was rescued from oblivion through negotiations by Jersey Standard and Standard Oil of Indiana (later Amoco) over the latter's overseas assets. Indiana Standard owned 97.3% of the Pan-American Petroleum and Transport Company, which in turn owned 96% of Mexican Petroleum. Mexican Petroleum (which was separately traded) made up 21% of Pan-American's assets by market value, the rest of which were located in Venezuela and the Dutch Antilles. (Pan-American refined Venezuelan crude in Aruba.) In April 1932, with the U.S. Congress debating oil import tariffs, Indiana agreed to sell Pan-American to Jersey Standard. Jersey Standard possessed a distribution network in South America and Europe, and thus could more easily divert Latin American production to those markets than could Indiana Standard. Jersey Standard wanted only the Venezuelan assets, but Indiana Standard refused to sell Pan-American's properties separately.[56] The deal closed at the end of 1932, and Jersey Standard acquired Indiana Standard's stake in Pan-American. In 1935, Jersey Standard decided to buy up the remainder of "Mexican Pete" at par and delist the stock.[57]

Data from the companies' published financial statements bear out the verdict of the stock market (see table 7.3). Mexican Eagle's return on assets declined from 9% in 1921 to nil by 1928 and remained low until the Poza Rica discoveries boosted it back to 7%. Mexican Petroleum steadily lost money over the 1930s.

Table 7.3
Returns on assets, Mexican oil companies

	Weighted average	Mexican Eagle	Mexican Petroleum	Sinclair Pierce	California Standard	Imperio	Mexican Seaboard	Stanford	Penn-Mex	Agwi	Consolidated
1921	11%	9%	12%				34%		2%		
1922	15%	8%	22%				53%		-7%		
1923	6%	2%	9%				5%		6%		
1924	3%	2%	3%				33%		5%		
1925	11%	2%	16%				22%				
1926	12%	2%	18%				16%				
1927	6%	2%	8%				4%				
1928	5%	0%	8%				0%				
1929	7%	7%	7%				2%				
1930	4%	5%	3%				7%		4%		
1931	0%	-1%	0%				10%		0%		
1932	-4%	2%	-9%				7%		0%		
1933	-2%	5%	-7%				10%				
1934	3%	7%	-2%	3%	3%	16%	8%	1%	5%	29%	4%
1935	4%	7%	0%	1%	6%	25%	7%	13%	2%	18%	2%
1936	3%	8%	-1%	-5%	0%	18%	7%	11%	1%	22%	-3%
1937	5%	9%	-1%				8%				

Source: Annual reports of Mexican Eagle, Pan-American Foreign, Standard Oil of New Jersey, and Mexican Petroleum; Moody's for Mexican Seaboard and Penn-Mex, *Mexico's Oil* for the other companies, and Mexican Petroleum in 1934–36. Author's estimate for 1937 using production and price data from Standard Oil of New Jersey.

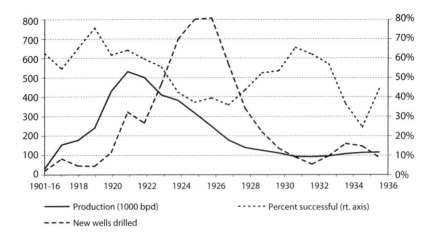

Figure 7.2 Mexican crude oil production, new wells drilled, and success rate, 1901–36

Source: Stephen Haber, Noel Maurer, and Armando Razo, "When the Law Does Not Matter," *Journal of Economic History* (March 2003).

Note: 1901–16 is an annual average.

Did Mexican policy contribute to the oil companies' parlous financial state? The answer appears to be no. First, the oil companies continued to prospect for oil during the 1920s and 1930s (see figure 7.2) Production peaked in 1921, five years before exploration began to decline. When the companies found oil, as in Poza Rica in 1930, they invested.

Second, the tax burden on the industry fell consistently after 1921. It is true that *gross* receipts from petroleum taxes as a percentage of the value of crude oil production rose from a low of 15% in 1925 to more than 30% by 1931. By the 1930s, however, production charges, export duties, royalties, and income taxes made up less than a third of government oil revenue. The remainder came from oil import duties and excises on domestic sales of refined products. The burden of import duties, obviously, did not fall on oil producers. Gasoline excise taxes might have fallen on crude producers but for the fact that the United States imposed no tariffs on oil or gasoline imports until 1932.

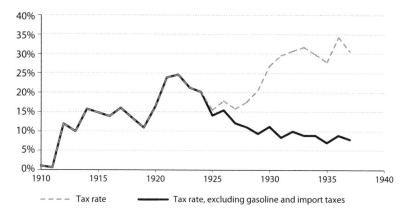

Figure 7.3 Mexican taxes (including royalties) as percent of the gross value of crude oil production, 1910–37

Source: Stephen Haber, Noel Maurer, and Armando Razo, "When the Law Does Not Matter," *Journal of Economic History* (March 2003), p. 10; Luz María Uhthoff, "Fiscalidad y Petróleo, 1912–1938," paper presented at the Segundo Congreso de Historia Económica, Asociación Mexicana de Historia Económica, October 2004; and Wendell Gordon, *Expropriation of Foreign-Owned Property in Mexico* (Washington, D.C.: American Council on Public Affairs, 1941), p. 80.

If a foreign-owned Mexican refinery could not pass along the burden of excise taxes to consumers, it would export instead. In fact, most of Mexico's production of refined products was exported. The maximum burden of Mexican refined product taxes on producers was therefore equal to the cost of transporting refined products to the United States, which a congressional report estimated to be 28 cents ($3.90 in 2011 dollars) per barrel in 1931.[58] The tax burden on the companies fell almost monotonically after 1922 (see figure 7.3).

Government action did reduce the value of the Mexican oil companies—but the government in question was not Mexico's. Mexican production competed with output from producers in Texas, California, and Oklahoma—which together produced 84% of American output—and smaller fields in Kansas (4%), Arkansas (3%), Louisiana (2%), Wyoming (2%), and Pennsylvania (1%). In all, nineteen states produced oil in commercial quantities by 1930.[59] As the Depression set in, protectionist pressures built. In 1930, Congress reported that refineries using imported oil earned a profit of 26 cents per barrel while refineries using domestic oil earned only 11 cents. Despite the opening of the Panama Canal, which made it feasible for the first time to export Californian oil to the East Coast, Mexican and Venezuelan oil was still often cheaper in eastern markets. The independent producers and refiners therefore claimed that the "Big Four" oil companies used their access to foreign oil as a club to "coerce the independents and to break American markets." Moreover, they presented evidence that the Big Four did not fully pass along lower crude oil prices to consumers. In 1931, the governors of Oklahoma, Texas, Kansas, and New Mexico urged President Hoover to impose "voluntary" import quotas on the oil companies. Jersey Standard, Standard Oil of Indiana, Gulf Oil, and Sinclair agreed to reductions of a quarter, and Shell cut imports by half. The voluntary quota did not satisfy the protectionists.

The U.S. Congress passed a bill imposing tariffs on imported oil on June 6, 1932. The rates were 21 cents per barrel on crude oil, $1.05 per barrel on gasoline, and $1.68 per barrel on lubricants.[60] Hoover, of course, gladly signed the bill. The result was a doubling of the gap between the export price of Mexican crude and the New York price for oil of the same grade. Unlike Cuban sugar producers, however, the oil companies in Mexico exported relatively little of their crude to the United States. (The companies mostly refined their product in Mexico and exported to Europe.) The tariff, therefore, had little direct effect on their bottom lines. Rather, it raised the differential between the U.S. oil price and the Mexican oil price. Since the ability to export surplus production to the American market effectively kept a lid on the ability of the Mexican government to directly tax crude production in the home market, the U.S. policy had the perverse effect of giving Mexico City more leeway in taxing the industry while having little effect on the U.S. market.

The Labor Disputes

The parlous state of oil company finances was on collision course with the increasing militancy of the oil unions. Strikes hit the Mexican Eagle refineries in Tampico in Minatitlán in April 1915, followed by a second set in 1916 and 1917. In May 1917 the labor unrest spread to Pierce's operations in Tampico and Mexican Petroleum's refinery in Mata Redonda.[61] The government of the state of Tamaulipas stepped in and settled the Pierce strike, mandating a 25% wage increase.[62] In June, Mexican Petroleum conceded the same benefits.[63] Mexican Eagle gave in to a 1924 strike, conceding an eight-hour work-day and the first collective bargaining agreement in the history of the Mexican industry.[64] Other companies signed similar contracts.[65] The strikes were violent: a Mexican government report stated, "Most workers do not agree with the [labor] movement and on various occasions told us that if most of them didn't return to work, it was from fear of becoming victims of the violence committed against the persons of some other workers."[66]

Follow-up strikes met a more determined response from the companies, *with the support of the Mexican government*. Mexican Petroleum, for example, conceded a collective bargaining agreement with the Huasteca union after a 1925 strike. When workers from a competing union killed a Huasteca member in 1925, the union declared a second strike. With government support, management fired the striking workers. It then rehired only a third of them.[67] Mexican Eagle ended a refinery strike that same year by paying $123,000 to the leadership of the national Confederación Regional de Obreros Mexicanos, who in turn convinced the government to declare the strike illegal.[68] Nevertheless, overall wage rates rose from 6 cents (U.S.) per hour in 1913 to 16 cents per hour in 1934.[69] (In 2011 dollars, this was the equivalent of a rise from $1.40 per hour to $2.68 per hour, although that calculation does not take into account changes in the relative cost of living in Mexico or the overall lower cost of living in that country relative to the contemporary United States.)

The final wave of labor disputes began at Mexican Eagle in 1934. The company's union wanted a larger share of the returns from the new Poza Rica fields. The Mexican president, Abelardo Rodríguez, stepped in to mediate a settlement.[70] In the wake of the settlement, the various oil unions united into the Sindicato de Trabajadores Petroleros de la República Mexicana (STPRM).[71] A new set of strikes hit Mexican Petroleum in January 1935. According to U.S. government observers, the company preferred to close its facilities "rather than compromise with the workers."[72] The Federal Labor Board (Junta Federal de Conciliación y Arbitraje) declared the strikes legal, but the Mexican Supreme Court reversed the decision and ordered the workers back to their posts.

The imposed labor peace did not last. On November 3, 1936, the STPRM demanded a $2.3 million wage hike, eighteen paid holidays, twenty to sixty days paid vacation, health insurance, twenty-five days of severance pay for each year of service in the case of voluntary separation, and ninety days of severance in the case of involuntary separation. The union leaders were not naïve—they understood that the companies would react to increases in labor costs by reducing their workforces. The union leaders also understood that most Mexican oil fields were in decline and the Poza Rica finds were unlikely to generate enough new jobs to compensate for layoffs elsewhere. The STPRM therefore also demanded control over all hiring and firing decisions, leaving only 110 positions across the entire *industry* under management control. Union negotiators requested a response by November 17, 1936.[73]

The oil companies rejected the deadline. "The union draft contains over 250 clauses, covers 165 pages of legal-size script of which almost 40 embrace the wage schedule and took several months to formulate, and yet the companies were to 'discuss' and 'approve' the document in the peremptory period of

10 days," said company representatives. The companies also refused to give up control over hiring and firing. "Owing to the present restricted number of supervisory positions, the industry is already suffering the consequences of lack of control and discipline."[74]

The problem was that the STPRM rank and file wanted job security even more than they wanted higher wages. The one benefit that the companies could not concede under any circumstances was also the one benefit that the union considered nonnegotiable.[75] Talks dragged on until May. On May 28, 1937, the unions called a strike.[76] President Cárdenas personally intervened to head it off. In August, Cárdenas again intervened to avert a second strike.

In an attempt to bring labor peace, President Cárdenas then appointed a special commission to look into the companies' finances. On August 14, 1937, the commission reported that the companies could afford a settlement of $7.3 million—in other words, everything the union was demanding (see table 7.4). A wildcat strike immediately broke out at Poza Rica.[77] Cárdenas ordered it stopped.[78] A second wildcat hit Mexican Eagle in September. An exasperated Cárdenas accused the workers of helping "capitalist interests" by turning the country against the labor movement.[79] The strike ended when the company agreed to pay the workers 75% of lost wages and gave the union leadership an additional $6,944.[80] (The payment to the leadership was worth $103,744 in 2011 dollars, using the CPI.)

On December 18, 1937, the Federal Labor Board published its initial award. The award granted the union its full $7.3 million. The companies would be allowed to reduce the number of personnel, as long as they made their reductions in order of seniority and paid severance worth three months' pay plus ten additional days' wages for every six months of service.[81] The companies could fire workers for cause, but only after an investigation by a newly created National Mixed Commission of the Oil Industry. The companies, of course, appealed. On

Table 7.4

1936 demands of Mexican oil workers' union, annual costs, dollars

	Government estimate	Company estimate
Wage increases	$2,265,492	$3,438,506
Overtime	$333,431	$993,148
Holidays	$92,496	$311,434
Vacations	$334,139	$428,145
Savings funds	$636,077	$902,370
Medical service	$277,778	$463,512
Housing benefits	$901,217	$1,115,105
Other	$2,474,024	$3,097,312
TOTAL	$7,314,654	$10,749,533

Source: Wendell Gordon, *Expropriation of Foreign-Owned Property in Mexico* (Washington, D.C.: American Council on Public Affairs, 1941), p. 112.

March 2, 1938, the Federal Labor Board denied the appeal. The Supreme Court upheld the decision the next day.

Mexican Petroleum reacted by closing twenty-three wells, moving oil stored in the fields to the port of Tampico (presumably for quick export), shutting down the Mata Redonda refinery, and sending a letter to every employee stating that it would be unable to comply with the board's order.[82] The STPRM called for a national strike. The March 7 deadline fixed by the Federal Labor Board came and went. On March 14, the Labor Board warned that it needed a response from the companies by the following day. On March 15, the companies reported that they could not comply. The Federal Labor Board responded by suspending all contracts.[83] With their pay contracts suspended and a strike deadline looming, workers began to seize loading terminals and shut down pipelines.[84] The oil industry began to shut down.

President Cárdenas faced the imminent collapse of Mexico's most important industry. By 1938, Mexico depended on petroleum for energy. As early as 1925, 63 percent of Mexico's thermal energy consumption derived from petroleum (as opposed to coal).[85] Mexican railroads had mostly switched to oil burners—by 1932 the railroads used 73 percent of all the fuel oil consumed in Mexico. Moreover, a road-building spree made trucking ever more important: the number of cargo trucks on Mexico's roads jumped from 7,999 in 1925 to 33,746 by 1937. Finally, oil provided a small but significant part of Mexico City's electrical supply: the eighty-megawatt Nonoalco plant consumed 2,000 barrels of fuel oil a day.[86] If the oil industry shut down, so would the Mexican economy.

Cárdenas could not allow that to happen. On March 18, 1938, he nationalized the companies. "Under such conditions, it is urgent that the public authorities take adequate measures to prevent grave domestic disturbances due to the paralysis of transportation and industry, which would make it impossible to satisfy collective needs and supply the consumer goods needed by our population centers."[87] The companies' properties were placed under the control of a state-owned oil company called Petróleos de México, or Pemex. The oil workers went back to work, and Mexican avoided economic disaster.

Could the companies have afforded the settlement? Table 7.5 presents two estimates of the annual burden of the wage settlement: one using data from the Federal Labor Board and one from oil company accounts. According to company figures (taken from annual reports for Mexican Eagle, Mexican Petroleum, and Penn-Mex, and figures compiled by the Mexican government for the remainder), the oil companies earned $3.7 million in 1936. Eliminating depreciation and depletion expenditures implies a net cash flow of $7.0 million, *less* than the official estimate of the settlement. The first row in the table shows the government's estimate of the cost of the labor settlement as a percentage of profits and cash flow; the second row repeats the exercise using company estimates.

The Mexican government accused the companies of transfer pricing, and estimated their profits at $15.4 million (see table 7.6).

Table 7.5
Burden of the 1937 Mexican oil industry labor settlement

	Percent of cash flow	Percent of profits
Federal Labor Board	39%	47%
Oil company accounts	153%	288%

Source: See text.

Mexican Eagle accounted for most of the difference between the companies' reported profits and the Mexican government's estimate. Mexican Eagle was profitable by any measure. The lowest estimate of the burden on Mexican Eagle would have been 31% (using the government's figures) and the highest 102% (using the company's). Even the low figure, however, would have been a substantial hit to the company's bottom line, and the high figure would have put the company into the red. For the other companies, the burden would have been higher.

The companies had three additional reasons to go to the mat over the union demands. First, they did not want to lose the ability to hire and fire at will. If the union prevailed on this issue, it would gain greater leverage to make future demands, and management's ability to cut costs would be greatly reduced (or even eliminated). Second, the companies had not expected the Mexican government to nationalize. After Cárdenas issued his decree (in response to the threatened shutdown of the industry), they expected the government to place their properties into some sort of temporary receivership. President Cárdenas, however, decided against receivership because he feared the consequences of "interminable legal proceedings."[88]

Finally, many of the companies had profitable assets—but also militant workforces—in the West Indies, Venezuela, and California. They wanted to maintain a reputation of refusing to give in to labor demands. Jersey Standard, in particular, was losing money on its Mexican properties but had hugely profitable operations in Venezuela, where it faced very real labor

Table 7.6

Mexican oil company profits, 1936, millions of dollars

	Profits		Cash flow	
	Gov't estimate	Company estimate	Gov't estimate	Company estimate
Mexican Eagle	$11.9	$3.9	$13.2	$5.2
Mexican Petroleum	$1.9	($0.8)	$2.7	($0.0)
Pierce-Sinclair	$0.6	($0.2)	$1.1	$0.3
California Standard	$0.1	($0.0)	$0.5	$0.4
Agwi	$0.2	$0.1	$0.2	$0.1
Penn-Mex	$0.0	$0.1	$0.0	$0.1
Stanford	$0.1	$0.1	$0.2	$0.2
Richmond	$0.0	$0.0	$0.0	$0.0
Imperial	$0.1	$0.1	$0.1	$0.1
Cía. de Gas y Combustible	$0.3	$0.3	$0.3	$0.3
Sábalo	$0.1	$0.1	$0.1	$0.1

Source: *Mexico's Oil: A Compilation of Official Documents in the Conflict of Economic Order in the Petroleum Industry, with an Introduction Summarizing Its Causes and Consequences* (Mexico City: Government of Mexico, 1940), pp. 293–95, 317–19, 331–33, 347–49, 365–67, 381–84, 390–92, and 433; *Moody's Manual of Investments*, various.

threats. After twenty-seven years of rule, Venezuelan President Juan Vicente Gómez died on December 17, 1935. After his death, riots wracked the Maracaibo oil zone. The violence became so bad that foreign oil executives and their families were forced to flee aboard oil tankers. Gómez's successor, Eléazar López Contreras, calmed the crisis via the "February Program," which promised wage hikes and improvements in working conditions for the oil workers. He then passed the Labor Act, which allowed collective bargaining and mandated profit-sharing, and introduced a new constitution that allowed for export taxes. On December 11, 1936, a forty-three-day strike hit the oil zone, cutting production 39% before President López intervened to end it.[89] The López administration then sued the *companies*, accusing them of owing unpaid royalties and taxes.[90] In June 1937, López altered the buoy tax on ships transiting Lake Maracaibo from one calculated on tonnage to one based on the value of the crude they carried, in effect raising its burden.[91] In a January 1938 meeting with American officials, a Venezuelan representative stated, "[The] government had no desire to tangle with the companies and become involved in a protracted fight [but] if the companies did not appear more responsive, the government will have no other recourse."[92] The government also announced its attention to revoke the companies' exemption from import tariffs.[93] When the companies protested, the government reopened the lawsuits. In April 1938—scarcely two weeks after President Cárdenas ordered the expropriation of the Mexican industry—the Supreme Court of Venezuela ordered the Mene Grande Company to pay $4 million in back taxes.[94]

In short, the oil companies in Mexico made rational gambles. They gambled low-value assets against the probability that the union or the government would refuse to back down. For them, it was a good bet. First, the assets they gambled with were relatively low value. Second, the union demands were unaffordable. Third, they had not expected the government to nationalize. Finally, several of the companies had a reputation to maintain in other jurisdictions.

The unions and government also behaved rationally. The primary union interest was not a wage increase. Rather, it was job security. Union members rejected any attempt by the leadership to trade job security for higher wages.[95] Similarly, the Mexican government's goal was not higher revenue (or even a symbolic nationalist victory) but the need to keep the oil-burning domestic economy running. Combine that with the need to maintain the *existing* stream of tax revenues generated by the oil industry, and it is clear that once the unions took steps to shut down the industry, the government had little choice but to act. Nationalization was the easiest way to ensure that the industry would remain open—the political benefit was merely icing on the cake.

The Oil Companies Respond

President Franklin Roosevelt had little regard for the oil companies. The Good Neighbor policy eschewed intervention, and Roosevelt was ideologically sympathetic to labor and state control over natural resources. The oil companies, however, had a number of tools at their disposal to involve the American administration and rearm the empire trap. After several years of disuse, however, its hinges were rusty, and there would be a few failed attempts before the oil companies succeeded in moving the United States to action.

The first move was to mobilize public opinion. The U.S. ambassador to Mexico, Josephus Daniels, complained that the companies quickly "started to build propaganda fires under the government to compel a return of the properties."[96] Jersey Standard, in particular, financed a large-scale publicity campaign. It distributed a wide array of free publications, from short press releases to full-length books. Editorial cartoons distributed by Standard portrayed the expropriation as a direct assault on American interests.[97] The *New York Times* reproduced Jersey Standard press releases almost verbatim. The paper's editorial page consistently called for "punitive" action against Mexico.[98] Moreover, the companies' propaganda highlighted "terrorist" incidents aimed at Americans and called for U.S. tourists to stay away.[99] The companies also resorted to selective leaking, in an attempt to tie the American government's hands. For example, on March 28, 1938, Secretary of State Cordell Hull delivered a private note to the Mexican government requesting "fair, assured and effective compensation." To Hull's dismay, the key phrase appeared in the next day's papers, where Hull's demand was described as "forceful."[100]

The propaganda campaign had little success. Unverified reports indicated that Mexico's tourism receipts dropped by 33% in 1938.[101] Harder data showed a 21% drop in the number of tourist visas issued by the Mexican government. The problem

Figure 7.4 Tourist entries to Mexico, 1929–46
Source: Instituto Nacional de Estadística y Geografía.

was that 1937 was a particularly good year for Mexican tourism: the number of entries in 1938 was still higher than it had
been in 1936 and rapidly resumed its upward trend (see figure
7.4). Moreover, the U.S. recession that began in May 1937 did
not end until June 1938, and the drop in tourist entries was as
likely due to poor economic conditions as to the efforts of the
oil companies.

The American public did not take much notice of events in
Mexico. In December 1938, Gallup asked the following question: "Which (1938) news story do you consider most interesting?" The answers included the invasion of Czechoslovakia
(23%), Nazi persecution of Jews (12%); Republican gains in
Congress (10%), Corrigan's flight (7%), the Fair Labor Standards Act (6%), the New England hurricane (5%), the recession (5%), the New York Yankees World Series sweep of the
Cubs in four games (5%), the Japanese invasion of China (4%),
and labor unrest (4%). The oil expropriation did not make the
cut.[102] This is not to say that Mexico's action enjoyed public
support in the United States. It is to say that public outrage
was insufficiently large to force the Roosevelt administration
to take action.

The oil companies then tried to boycott Mexico's oil exports. Only the United Kingdom gave official support. (It could afford to do so because, by 1938, Mexico provided only 2.1% of British oil imports, down from 10.1% in 1935.)[103] Courts outside the United Kingdom blocked attempts to extend the boycott. A U.S. federal district court dismissed a case accusing the Eastern States Petroleum Company of importing $1.7 million worth of oil claimed by Mexican Eagle. Belgian and Dutch courts decided similarly. In France, Mexican Eagle won a lower court decision, but an appellate court overturned it and forced *Mexican Eagle* to pay damages to distributors who had been unable to take possession of their oil. A state judge in Alabama went so far as to order sheriffs to prevent Mexican Eagle from taking possession of expropriated tankers.[104] The legal basis behind these decisions was Mexico's sovereign immunity.

The fundamental problem with the boycott was not that it lacked government support—although that didn't help—but that it was ultimately self-defeating. With domestic demand for fuel skyrocketing, Pemex made up for lost export revenues by selling more to the domestic market.[105] Before 1938, Mexico simultaneously exported and imported refined oil products. (Such a pattern was not at all unusual in the 1930s and is not at all unusual in the 2010s.) By 1940, however, the Mexican industry had reoriented itself around the domestic market. Sales recovered to 1936 levels because of a rise in domestic sales from around 75 million pesos to 150 million pesos.[106] (See figure 7.5.) Real revenues didn't surpass their 1937 peak until 1947, but the Mexican oil industry survived the boycott.[107]

Rousing the Americans

Private attempts to coerce the Mexican government having failed, the oil companies devised a political strategy to drag the U.S. government into the dispute. Doing so was an uphill battle. Not only had many of the Good Neighbor–era policy

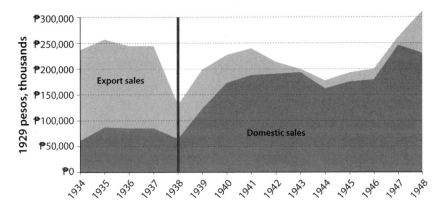

Figure 7.5 Domestic and export sales of Mexican petroleum products, 1934–48

Source: Export sales from J. Richard Powell, *The Mexican Petroleum Industry, 1938–50* (Berkeley: University of California Press, 1956), p. 118. Domestic sales, 1934–36, from *Mexico's Oil: A Compilation of Official Documents in the Conflict of Economic Order in the Petroleum Industry, with an Introduction Summarizing Its Causes and Consequences* (Mexico City: Government of Mexico, 1940), pp. 293–95, 317–19, 331–33, 347–49, 365–67, 381–84, 390–92, and 433. Domestic sales, 1938–48, from Powell, *The Mexican Petroleum Industry*, appendix table 17.

changes blunted the political influence of private interests in American foreign policy, but also there was a strong current in Washington against confronting Mexico. The most hostile official (from the companies' point of view) was Interior Secretary Harold Ickes. "If bad feelings should result in Central and South America as a result of the oil situation that exists just now with Mexico," wrote Ickes, "it would be more expensive for us than the cost of all the oil in Mexico."[108] Moreover, Ickes feared that sanctions could cause the Mexican government to collapse, which would be far worse for American interests than the loss of some oil fields.[109] Josephus Daniels, the U.S. ambassador to Mexico, shared Ickes's hostility toward the companies.[110] Ickes and Daniels were joined by Treasury Secretary Henry Morgenthau. Morgenthau worried that economic instability in Mexico might push the Mexican government into allying with the Axis or turning toward communism.[111]

Secretary of State Cordell Hull provided the oil companies the opening that they needed. Hull was no fan of the oil industry, but he did want to get a reciprocal trade agreement from the Mexican government. He was angry about a Mexican decision to increase tariffs, and he was easily persuaded of "the need to punish Mexico economically to gain its respect for American business before closer economic ties with the country could be achieved."[112] The oil companies therefore lobbied the secretary of state to craft a plan that would unite a divided executive branch around sanctions.[113]

The plan hinged on exploiting political divisions over the Silver Purchase Act of 1934. The Silver Purchase Act committed the Treasury to buying a fixed quantity of silver every year until silver stocks reached 25% of its total specie reserves or the price reached $1.29 an ounce. This was an enormous boon for Mexico, which became the United States' third-greatest silver supplier after Hong Kong and China. The demand for Mexican silver increased employment in the mining sector and provided tax revenue. In 1936, the Mexican government earned 24% of its revenue from silver, twice what it earned from oil.[114] By focusing on silver rather than oil, he United States could hit Mexico where it hurt.

Moreover, the Silver Purchase Act was far from universally popular. Morgenthau was ambivalent about the act. It allowed the Treasury to build up specie reserves that it could use to counteract Federal Reserve policy, but the concurrent Gold Stabilization Act of 1934 provided ample resources for that purpose. The Silver Purchase Act, in this view, was just a waste of money.[115] There was also opposition to U.S. purchases of Mexican silver in Congress, most notably from Senator Key Pittman (D-Nevada), who had authored the original bill but was unhappy with the extent to which it was used to buy silver from overseas rather than domestic producers—most of which were located in his home state.

Hull focused his energies on these two pressure points: Congress and Morgenthau. As his opening salvo, Hull sent a note to

Mexico on March 26, 1938, denouncing expropriation without compensation. In Congress, Hull's allies introduced bills threatening to take the initiative on sanctions away from the White House—thus maintaining pressure on the executive to act. In January 1939, Samuel McReynolds (D-Tennessee), the chairman of the House Foreign Affairs Committee, introduced a bill calling for an end to the silver purchases that subsidized Mexico's economy.[116] (Hull had served in Congress with McReynolds, and both had been judges back in Tennessee.)[117] Other congressmen, notably Martin Kennedy (D–New York) and Hamilton Fish (R–New York) also introduced anti-Mexico resolutions. Hull ensured that the bills would not pass, since they would interfere with the negotiations between the Mexican government and the oil companies, but they served as a useful cudgel against opposition to sanctioning Mexico inside the Roosevelt administration.[118]

Hull also convinced Morgenthau that the oil expropriation was a convenient excuse to suspend the Silver Purchase Act.[119] (In this, Hull had the support of Treasury economist Harry Dexter White.) Because halting purchases would lower the price of silver and devalue years of accumulated reserves, Morgenthau carefully designed the policy to make it appear as though his hand was being forced by events in Mexico. First, the State Department announced the suspension, not the Treasury. (State and Treasury played a deliberate game of buck-passing, depending on the audience: State announced the suspension to domestic audiences, while pinning responsibility on Morgenthau in a letter to President Cárdenas.) Second, Morgenthau well knew that suspending silver purchases would do little to harm Mexico unless the United States also cut the official support price, since Mexico could sell silver on the open market at the U.S.-supported price. He also knew, however, that other countries would immediately start dumping their silver stockpiles in the world market once the rumors of the new policy got out, in the fear that the United States would try to punish Mexico by lowering the price. Of course, if enough countries started to dump their silver reserves, the United States would be forced to lower the silver price or see taxpayers' money flow away to foreign central banks. Leaking the possibility of a support-price cut, then, could create a situation where Morgenthau would *have* to cut the support price.[120] Spain fulfilled Morgenthau's prediction when its ambassador to the United States announced the sale of 56 million ounces of silver. Feigning indignation, Morgenthau called that "the last straw" and lowered the silver price from 45 cents to 43 cents an ounce.[121]

Morgenthau's plan had an additional legislative component designed to win President Roosevelt's support. At the time of the Mexican oil expropriation, the Fair Labor Standards Act was bottled up in a House committee. Once released and passed on the House floor, it would then go to a conference committee where it would face hostile Democratic senators from the silver-producing state of Nevada. Once Morgenthau cut the support price for silver—ostensibly to sanction Mexico—Roosevelt could hold out a promise to reinstitute price supports for *domestic* silver as a way to keep recalcitrant Nevadan legislators inside the New Deal coalition.[122] Morgenthau was hesitant to explicitly commit Roosevelt to the strategy, so he sent a letter to the president while he was on vacation in Warm Springs, New York, stating simply that Morgenthau would interpret a lack of communication from Roosevelt as consent.[123]

Final Settlement

The silver sanctions got Mexico to the table, but what Hull failed to anticipate was that the *oil companies* wanted to delay resolution as long as possible to cause Mexico as much pain as possible. After all, they knew that their Mexican properties were worth little. They wanted to set a precedent that would discourage other countries from attempting to alter oil concessions. This was not an abstract fear. Spain nationalized Jersey Standard's properties in 1927. (The U.S. companies received full compensation in 1928.)[124] In 1931, Uruguay established a state-owned oil-refining and retailing company that drove down the private share of the market from 100% in 1931 to 50.2% by 1937.[125] In 1932, Chile threatened expropriation, the advent of which was headed off only by a well-timed military coup.[126] In March 1937, as we have seen, the Bolivian government nationalized Jersey Standard's concessions, and the Argentine junta was openly hostile to foreign oil companies.[127] In 1939, Chile under President Pedro Aguirre again proposed nationalization, but the Chilean Congress demurred.[128] None of these areas were particularly important, but the companies felt they needed to draw a line before nationalization threatened something lucrative—such as, as we have also seen, their assets in Venezuela.

The result was a long and drawn-out drama, the end result of which was known by all the parties in advance. The oil companies demanded a long-term contract to operate the expropriated properties, after which they would turn them over to the Mexican government. They also insisted on compensation for lost revenues and wanted the agreement enshrined in a treaty with the United States.[129] Needless to say, the Mexican government did not find this acceptable.[130] President Cárdenas proposed compensation for the properties as they were valued in 1938. Alternatively, he suggested the formation of multiple oil consortia, in which the companies would have a financial interest equal to their interest in the expropriated properties, but over which Mexico would exercise control by appointing a majority of the directors.[131] (The initial draft of Cárdenas's second proposal seemed to offer the companies double compensation: payment for property *and* a financial stake in the new consortia.) The Mexicans also wanted a short contract, because they feared that new technologies would reduce oil consumption in the future.[132]

Roosevelt attempted to break the logjam by suggesting that the oil companies accept Cárdenas's proposal on a temporary basis with boards split between the companies and the government, but both sides demurred.[133] The United States then tried to suggest that the companies use the 1929 General Treaty of Inter-American Arbitration to settle their claims. The companies refused, since the treaty provided for state-to-state arbitration, and not investor-state arbitration; the companies would therefore be reliant on the Roosevelt administration to select the arbiters and represent the companies' interests.[134]

In 1940, Sinclair Oil broke with the other companies. It accepted an offer of $8 million in cash compensation plus 20 million barrels sold at a 25 cents per barrel discount off market prices.[135] Negotiations with the other companies continued to drag. By the middle of 1941, the Roosevelt administration had run out of patience and effectively imposed a settlement.[136] Under an agreement made with Mexico on November 19, 1941, the two governments appointed a two-person committee consisting of Morris Cook and Manuel Zevada, both trained engineers. The two spent five months researching, and presented their outline of a final settlement on April 17, 1942. The Mexican government immediately credited $9 million to the United States. The two governments approved the payment schedule for the rest of the compensation, including interest, in September 1943. The lion's share of the settlement was paid by 1947; Mexico made additional small interest payments through 1953.[137] Ultimately, the compensation payments exceeded the agreed-upon amount by almost $6 million in nominal terms.[138]

Did the American companies receive fair compensation? It is possible to compute the price Jersey Standard paid to acquire Mexican Petroleum in 1932.[139] Jersey Standard purchased Pan-American for $47.9 million in cash and 1,778,973 Jersey Standard shares. Pan-American owned 97% of Mexican Petroleum, which was traded separately on the NYSE. At market value, Mexican Petroleum made up 21% of Pan-American.[140] Jersey Standard's shares were valued at $26.13 at the time of the deal: both the cash and shares were delivered in four annual payments. The discounted 1932 value of the deal (using the interest rate on corporate debt) came to 21% × 97.3% × 96% × ($44.3 million in cash + $43.0 million in shares) = $17.5 million.[141]

Adjusted for inflation, that figure was $17.9 million in 1938 dollars. Adding in the value of the outstanding shares bought at par in 1935 raises the total price that Jersey Standard paid for its Mexican assets to $19.2 million (see table 7.7). By that standard, the Mexican government fairly compensated Jersey Standard. It should be noted that the settlement allowed Jersey Standard to retain most of Mexican Petroleum's liquid assets and the company's tanker fleet.

It is unlikely that Jersey Standard's Mexican assets were worth more in 1938 than in 1932. First, Mexican Petroleum paid no dividends after 1932. Second, it lost money every year, save a brief moment of breakeven in 1935. It is possible that Jersey Standard used transfer pricing to extract value, but that begs the question of why the company would transfer income from a jurisdiction with no corporate income taxes to one with a 19% rate on all corporate income above $25,000.[142] Third, the fields controlled by the American companies (most of which were owned by Mexican Petroleum) were in decline and continued to decline after 1938, unlike the Poza Rica fields (see figure 7.6).

Did the Mexican government compensate Mexican Eagle fairly? There are reasons to believe that it might not have. First, the British government, unlike the American one, had no levers to use against Mexico once the oil boycott failed. Moreover, London could not credibly promise to end the boycott that it had started, because of fears that ending it to conciliate Mexico would anger its allies in Venezuela and Iran. The British ambassador to Caracas reported that the government there would be "most disturbed if they had any reason to believe that [Britain] might resume oil buying in Mexico to the detriment of Venezuela."[143] London feared that an angry Venezuela might be tempted to try "squeezing us over the condition on which we purchase their oil."[144] Britain also worried about Iran, enough to make extra royalty payments of $6.6 million in 1939 and $17.7 million in 1940 and 1941 in order to compensate Tehran for a decision to maximize tanker use by restricting its ex-

Table 7.7

Value of Mexico's final settlement with foreign oil firms, dollars

Company	Nominal compensation	1938 net present value	Market value
Mexican Eagle	$132,769,721	$43,552,824	$12,233,340
Jersey Standard	$23,138,947	$19,371,222	$19,188,049
Sinclair	$9,643,827	$8,602,638	
Socal	$4,515,602	$3,780,325	
Sábalo	$1,129,381	$945,483	
Conoco	$792,807	$663,714	
Seaboard	$613,171	$513,328	

Source: In addition to the sources mentioned in the text, see U.S. Department of State. "Compensation for Petroleum Properties Expropriated in Mexico." *The Department of State Bulletin*, Vol. 6, April 18, 1942, p. 351, Tables 5 and 10.

Note: Compensation was valued by converting all payments into 1938 dollars using the U.S. GDP deflator and discounting them back to 1938 using the 3.2% rate at which the U.S. government lent to Mexico in 1943. (This rate was approximately equal to a 3.1% rate on 10-year corporate bonds in the United States.) The second column assumes that the additional payments were divided among the receiving corporations in proportion to their share of the original deal.

ports to markets west of Suez.[145] The situation was a problem for London: after all, if the United Kingdom could not credibly offer to lift the sanctions, then Mexico had no reason to offer compensation. Foreign Secretary Anthony Eden was not happy—"I do not like giving the Shah and Venezuela a veto on our relations with anybody."[146]

Second, Mexican Eagle's Poza Rica oil fields were most emphatically not in decline at the time of nationalization (see figure 7.6). They were expected to produce significant income in the future. Mexican Eagle risked losing a substantial option value on those properties.

Third, in 1938, the U.S. government had few reasons to care about protecting British investors in Mexico—in fact, rather the opposite. In 1941, the United States weakened Britain's bargaining position by explicitly requesting that the United Kingdom reestablish relations with Mexico. Eden decided not to ask for anything from the Americans in return. The reason was that

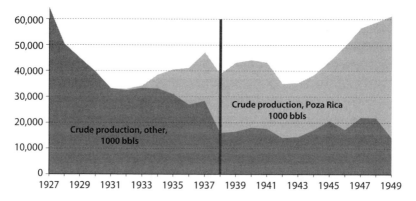

Figure 7.6 Mexican oil production by field, 1927–49
  Source: J. Richard Powell, *The Mexican Petroleum Industry, 1938–50* (Berkeley: University of California Press, 1956), p. 56.

Eden wanted to secure future American cooperation against Hitler. The United States, he believed, would be more amenable if Whitehall refrained from bargaining over Mexico.[147] The United Kingdom therefore reopened relations with Mexico on October 21, 1941. Charles Bateman, the new British minister to Mexico City, privately wrote that Eden had made a grave mistake, since it would now be impossible (he believed) for the Mexican government to make a better offer to a British company than it had made to American ones.[148]

Bateman turned out to be wrong—with American support, Mexican Eagle secured compensation from Mexico far in excess of the market value of its assets. Paradoxically, the decline in Britain's position during World War II *strengthened* the country's bargaining position against Mexico. In 1938, the United States had no desire to help the business interests of a potential rival. Nor did the United States have strategic reasons to help London, which did not need Mexican oil. By 1946, on the other hand, the United Kingdom had been transformed from a potential U.S. rival to an important junior partner facing substantial balance of payments problems. Under the new circumstances, Washington reacted differently to British requests for help. The United States had leverage over Mexico stemming from Mexico's need for official U.S. capital: in 1943, Mexico negotiated a $10 million loan from the U.S. Export-Import Bank for the construction of a new refinery at Azcapotzalco and production facilities at Poza Rica. In 1946, it began discussions over new credits, worth potentially $150 million. When London asked Washington to refrain from extending any loans to Pemex pending a settlement, the United States tacitly agreed.[149] The United States then signaled Antonio Bermúdez, who would later become the general director of Pemex, that a rapid settlement of outstanding British claims was the only way to receive the credit.[150] The Mexican government responded: talks between Mexico and the United Kingdom began in January 1947.

The British representative, Professor Vincent Illing, opened with a demand of $257 million. Antonio Bermúdez countered with an offer of $42.9 million. The two sides settled for $81.5 million. Payments began in 1948, and with interest totaled $132.8 million through 1962. Mexican accounts portrayed the settlement as a great nationalist triumph. Historians have generally agreed with that assessment. For example, Lorenzo Meyer wrote, "The way in which El Águila [Mexican Eagle] was compensated meant, among other things, that Mexico did not pay the full value of the oil deposits claimed as its own by the company. In fact, by compensating only a third of total property value . . . the last vestiges of the Calles-Morrow agreement were destroyed and the original spirit of Paragraph 4 of Article 27 of the 1917 Constitution at last came into effect."[151]

Sadly for the nationalist view, the available data indicate that the British (thanks to the Americans) ran away with the store. The ex ante 1938 net present value of the payments came to an astronomical $82.6 million. The postwar inflation in the United States drove the 1938 net present value of the deal down to a still rather high $43.6 million (see table 7.7). Mexican Eagle's market capitalization in 1936, right before the outbreak of labor unrest, was only *$12.2 million*. The book value of the company's assets in 1937 came to only $16.5 million. Considering that the settlement came to almost five times the former amount, it would be hard to argue that the company was *undercompensated* for its properties.

Resolving the Bolivian Impasse

The U.S. response to the Mexican expropriation had the additional side effect of prompting the State Department to intervene on behalf of Jersey Standard in its ongoing dispute with Bolivia. After all, once the Roosevelt administration had made the decision to back the oil companies in Mexico, it become difficult to do otherwise in Bolivia. Moreover, in 1939 the United States had a tool that it had lacked two years earlier: state-to-state loans from the U.S. Export-Import (Exim) Bank.

The Exim Bank had been created by Roosevelt in 1934 under the National Industrial Recovery Act. Its original purpose, clear from the name, was to help finance foreign trade. (The Depression had destroyed trade credit along with other sorts of credit.) The Exim Bank was not originally intended for use in commercial relations with the financially unstable nations to the south. In fact, its original policy was to avoid loans to states or state-owned entities, especially if those states were in default on their debts to private American creditors.

In 1937, however, a Treasury official named Herbert Feis ran into unexpected resistance from American direct investors when he rejected loans to countries that were in default on their private foreign debts. Feis rejected loans to Peru, Ecuador, the state-owned Central Railways of Brazil, and the Chilean State Railways because he believed that those countries were not trying to resolve their outstanding debt issues. In an earlier time, Feis's position would have been uncontroversial. In 1937, however, Feis's decisions annoyed major industrial companies, such as Westinghouse, at a time when American financiers retained little political power. Feis had to back down over the Chilean deal almost immediately.[152] In March 1938, Sumner Welles intervened to approve the loan to Brazil's railway company.[153] In June, the engineering firm of J. G. White approached Exim to discount $5 million in 4% notes issued to it by the Haitian government. Morgenthau and Harry Dexter White supported the rediscount, arguing that Haiti was cruising toward another default, and might abandon the dollar and restrict imports if Exim refused. Welles worried that the loan might raise cries of "imperialism," but he ultimately changed his mind, going so far as to insist that the credit be tied to U.S. exports.[154] Soon thereafter, Exim began to lend directly to Latin American governments.

In Bolivia, the government desperately wanted Exim credit. Its leaders also desperately wanted to stay in office. They feared that any appearance of caving in to Jersey Standard might lead to their overthrow by more radical elements.[155] This fear was far from groundless. President Germán Busch committed suicide on August 23, 1939, and his successor, Carlos Quintanilla, handed power over to Enrique Peñaranda after an obviously rigged election. Peñaranda faced opposition from Busch's socialist base of support.

The United States denied Bolivia access to official credit unless it compensated Jersey Standard. In September, the heads of the Exim Bank and the RFC told the U.S. Senate that it would refuse loans to "a country that is confiscating our property."[156] On December 26, 1939, the Bolivian government formally requested an American development loan. The State Department responded with a list of potential projects, but included a somewhat long-winded caveat:

> In view of the fact that satisfactory achievement of this economic cooperation in all respects must depend upon assurance that the undertakings will rest on a secure basis, and in order to secure the necessary support and cooperation of American private interests, it is believed to be essential before American financial assistance is given that a settlement will have been reached of the unfortunate

controversy that has arisen in regard to the cancellation of concessions of American oil properties in Bolivia. If the plans for economic cooperation are to be fruitful, it is believed that this difficulty must be gotten out of the path.[157]

President Peñaranda could not persuade the Bolivian Congress to give him the authority to negotiate with Jersey Standard, but the foreign minister privately told American officials that he was willing to talk. The rub was that Jersey Standard no longer *wanted* to talk to Bolivia. "It might indicate that confiscations by a foreign government are merely private matters between the government and its victim, although such confiscations materially impair the interests of all American citizens in the confiscating country and in others."[158] Jersey Standard wanted the U.S. government to negotiate on its behalf. In keeping with this position, the company agreed to allow a negotiating board to propose—or better yet, impose—a settlement.[159]

Finally, at the beginning of 1942, with the Bolivian Congress out of session, Bolivia desperate to receive American loans, and the U.S. government impatient to secure Bolivian support in World War II, the Peñaranda administration proposed $1 million in compensation for Jersey Standard. On January 27, the Bolivians upped their offer to $1.7 million. Jersey Standard accepted, and the State Department communicated that American aid was contingent on the Bolivian Congress's approval of the offer. Said approval came in April, and Jersey Standard received a check for $1,729,375. In return, Bolivia received $25 million in various development loans from the United States.[160] In a sense, Washington provided the cash to compensate Jersey Standard, but it should be noted that Bolivia repaid its loans from the U.S. government in full and on time.

Did Jersey Standard receive fair compensation? The book value of the company's investment was roughly $17 million, but that is not a good estimate of value. Jersey Standard stopped exploring in 1932 and concentrated on developing its existing

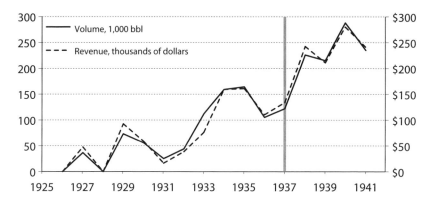

Figure 7.7 Bolivian oil production (thousands of barrels, left axis) and gross revenues (millions of 2011 dollars, right axis), 1926–41
Source: Statistics Norway and *Comercio exterior de Bolivia* (various years).

fields. It is likely that the market value of the company's investment was significantly less than its book value. We do not have market prices against which we can benchmark the compensation. We do know, however, that between 1927 and 1936, Jersey Standard's operation in Bolivia generated gross revenues around $760,000 (see figure 7.7). At a discount rate of 10%, the company would need to have been enjoying margins above 68% to justify a price of $1.7 million. Margins that high are not consistent with Jersey Standard's reluctance to invest.

Additional evidence that Jersey Standard's Bolivian properties were not profitable comes from the industry's postnationalization experience. The new state-owned company, Yacimientos Petrolíferos Fiscales Bolivianos (YPFB), retained most of Jersey Standard's technical employees. YPFB expanded production by more intensively working Jersey Standard's properties; the company drilled only five exploratory wells between 1939 and 1949.[161] Finance was not an issue: $8.5 million of Bolivia's $25 million 1942 U.S. loan package went to the construction of a small refinery at Cochabamba and a crude pipeline to link the refinery to the Camiri oil field.[162] In order to ensure a market for its production, YPFB signed barter agreements with Brazil and

Argentina. The Brazilian agreement forced YPFB to buy pipeline equipment from Brazilian suppliers, and its revenues from Brazilian sales could only be used to purchase Brazilian goods. The same stipulations applied to the Argentine agreement.[163] As disadvantageous as the agreements were, however, Jersey Standard would not have accessed either market at all.

Despite higher production, new markets, and plentiful capital, YPFB in its first decade earned most of its profits from the duty-free importation of petroleum products. It lost money on the domestic production of oil.[164] Government revenues rose post-nationalization, but they did not come from YPFB. In fact, the government does not appear to have received the 11% royalty that it was supposed to receive from YPFB.[165]

In short, the evidence indicates that Jersey Standard received fair compensation, courtesy of the Roosevelt administration. With the oil expropriations in Mexico and Bolivia, American-owned foreign producers rediscovered their political clout, and the empire trap was back in operation.

The Empire Trap Strikes Back

America's informal empire of the late 1930s and beyond was a mixture of old and new. On the one hand, the political pressures that drove the U.S. government—the demands of American-owned overseas interests threatened by local political or financial instability—were virtually unchanged despite a decade-long pause. The mechanisms, however, were considerably changed, enough to warrant a distinction between a first and second American empire. For one thing, the coalition of bondholders and direct investors that powered the empire trap during its first iteration was wholly absent during its second. With the demise of the private market in foreign debt came the near-total collapse in the existing bondholders' political clout. There were still Americans who held sovereign loans made years and decades ago, but their ability to lobby Washington was tiny. For another, the dollar diplomacy that was so prominently a feature of America's pre-Depression relations with Latin America and Liberia—the receiverships, the fiscal advisers, the government-backed private loans—disappeared completely.

The second American empire was a different beast. It relied on institutions such as the Export-Import Bank, the promise of whose loans was wielded to such effect in Bolivia in the early 1940s. The growing anxiety over the spread of communism also radically changed the politics of intervention, while the increasing reliance on covert action after World War II opened up a whole new set of possibilities.

The interventions of the early 1950s display this mix of old and new. An intervention in Bolivia demonstrates the extent of the continuity in America's informal empire across the first-second divide: to ensure compensation in an expropriation dispute, the Eisenhower administration in 1951–52 exercised the same leverage that Roosevelt had used more than a decade earlier. And though the global spread of communism radically changed the calculus of intervention, it was less of a *driver* than the received wisdom suggests: during the early years of the Cold War, the Department of State was not so preoccupied by the Sino-Soviet threat that it ignored the demands of American interests abroad, at least in Latin America. Meanwhile, the increasing deployment of covert action changed the face of U.S. intervention across Latin America and beyond.

Bolivia Redux

Political instability in Bolivia touched off a classic crisis that would not have been out of place half a century earlier. In May 1951, the Bolivian Movimiento Nacional Revolucionario (MNR) won a plurality of votes for its presidential candidate, Víctor Paz Estenssoro, then in exile in Argentina. The Constitution, however, required a candidate to win an outright majority to take office. A military junta subsequently took control. On

April 9, 1952, the MNR struck back, overthrowing the junta and destroying the Bolivian military as an effective fighting force in a matter of days. President Paz Estenssoro, at the urging of his leftist minister of mines and petroleum, Juan Lechín Oquendo, nationalized the Aramayo, Hochschild, and Patiño tin companies on October 31.[166] The signing of the decree symbolically took place in Catavi, where a government massacre of striking Patiño mine workers in 1942 had catalyzed the rise of the MNR. Bolivia offered compensation of $21.75 million ($157 million in 2011 dollars), with $7.5 million to Patiño, $9.25 million to Hochschild, $0.5 million to Aramayo, and the remainder to their subsidiaries. The companies, meanwhile, claimed their properties were worth $60 million.[167]

Secretary of State Dean Acheson paid close attention to the Bolivian Revolution. Bolivia controlled the Western Hemisphere's largest supply of tin, a strategic resource. Additionally, Acheson feared nationalization not "out of sympathy for the Patiño and Hochschild interests," who were "in large part responsible for their present predicament," but because of "the unsettling effect which any confiscatory action would have on private investment in Latin America, including U.S.-owned copper companies in Chile and petroleum interests in Venezuela."[168] In addition, the companies themselves actively lobbied the Eisenhower administration. Hochschild and Aramayo retained former Senator Millard Tydings (D-Maryland) to express their position to the State Department.[169] Tydings told Acheson that some form of "apportionment of ores" would be acceptable compensation.[170]

The State Department was only concerned about compensating *American* investors. It was not concerned with foreign interests, unless those interests were in countries of strategic importance to the United States (such as the United Kingdom). In the Bolivian case, State's Deputy Legal Adviser Jack Tate counseled that "the United States obligation to secure just compensation was limited to American citizens affected by the nationalization decree."[171] Deputy Assistant Secretary of State Thomas Mann recommended that "an exchange of notes be arranged wherein the Bolivian government agrees to submit the settlement of prompt, adequate and effective compensation for *bona fide U.S. stockholders* in nationalized Bolivian companies to a joint arbitration committee."[172] Secretary of State Acheson and Bolivian ambassador Andrade agreed with Mann. The agreement would be enforced by the automatic withholding of revenues from Bolivian tin sales to the United States.[173]

The rapid decline of world tin prices in 1953 caused the Paz Estenssoro government to panic. Facing fiscal and economic collapse, it accused the Eisenhower administration of "economic imperialism" and trying to destabilize Bolivia. Quick diplomacy on the part of the Eisenhower administration and "free and easy" communications between La Paz and Washington averted a crisis.[174] With active involvement by the State Department, on June 13, 1953, the Bolivian government reached a "Definitive Agreement on Retentions" with the mining companies, in which the companies would retain a portion of the proceeds from tin exports, provided the price remained above 80 cents a pound. When the price was between 80 cents and 90 cents, Bolivia would pay 1.0% of gross revenues. When the price was between 90 cents and $1.06, that proportion would rise to 2.5%. For a price between $1.06 and $1.215, the rate would be 5%, and then increase a further 1% for every 6 cents above $1.215.[175] This formula was remarkably close to the Tydings proposal.[176]

Was Eisenhower's apparent leniency toward Bolivia the last stand of the Good Neighbor policy, as Bryce Wood suggests?[177] The evidence suggests not. In fact, the Eisenhower administration employed the same sort of carrot-and-stick strategy as had Roosevelt and Truman with Mexico. First, the United States had market power over Bolivian tin, and made it clear that it was willing to use it. Bolivian concentrate could only be processed in Britain, at a Patiño-controlled facility, or in the United States at a Texas City tin smelter operated by the Reconstruction Finance Corporation. The RFC clearly stated that it would not purchase Bolivian tin without a clear settlement of the question of legal ownership.[178] The State Department supported the

RFC.[179] Second, the Exim Bank was in the process of making developmental loans to the Bolivian government. These could be turned off if the United States believed that Bolivia was obstructing a settlement—just as they had been in Mexico. The revolutionary Bolivian government knew this. During the negotiations, the Bolivian government went out of its way to emphasize it would use the Exim Bank loans exclusively "to increase [tin] production."[180]

It is true that the United States made considerable emergency grants to Bolivia. The collapse in world tin prices left Bolivia without enough foreign exchange to meet its food import needs. The CIA believed this would cause "economic chaos" in Bolivia.[181] The State Department was even more pessimistic: it believed that Bolivia faced "actual starvation."[182] The Eisenhower administration considered aiding Bolivia by ordering the RFC to purchase Bolivian tin at long-term contract prices rather than at collapsing spot prices, but congressional opposition caused Eisenhower to hold off on that idea. (The GOP disliked the RFC in general, which was losing millions of dollars a year on its Texas City tin smelter.) Instead, the United States extended a balance-of-payments loan. The U.S. government realized Bolivia would find the loan extremely difficult to repay. Therefore, at the urging of Secretary of State John Foster Dulles, the Eisenhower administration in September 1953 allotted Bolivia $9 million ($63 million in 2011 dollars) in grants through the Mutual Security Act of 1951.[183] Total aid in fiscal 1954 came to $15.8 million ($109 million in 2011 dollars), all in grants, up from $1.3 million the year before.[184]

While the United States certainly viewed its grants to Bolivia as humanitarian aid, they were also understood by both sides as a quid pro quo for following American financial and anticommunist policies. In fact, the Eisenhower administration used the hostile U.S. domestic reception to its aid policy as additional leverage against the Bolivian government. Assistant Secretary of State for Inter-American Affairs John Cabot told the Bolivian ambassador that the administration "had to be mindful of this criticism, and we should be less capable of helping Bolivia in proportion as any actions of the Bolivian government might give rise to an increase in such criticism."[185] After another extension of aid to Bolivia, Cabot's successor, Henry Holland, met personally with President Paz Estenssoro in La Paz. Holland "asked him if he felt that his government could adopt fiscal revisions suggested by the IBRD [International Bank for Reconstruction and Development] or the Exim Bank and designed to increase Bolivia's borrowing capacity. He assured me that he would try to follow any suggestions. I asked him if he felt confident of his ability to control the Communist problem in Bolivia. He said that he did."[186]

Ultimately, Truman and Eisenhower used the same combination of carrots and sticks in Bolivia that Roosevelt had used in Mexico. Even if the United States failed to establish effective compensation from the Bolivian government for *all* shareholders[187]—the MNR felt little affection for the Patiño or Hochschild families—the total amount of *American* investment in the expropriated companies was small.[188] This made proper American compensation an acceptable goalpost for both parties during negotiations. In fact, Bolivian negotiators up to and including President Paz Estenssoro himself quickly agreed to give American investors precedence in compensation even *before* the expropriation decree was signed.[189] The Cold War context had little changed the dynamics of American empire.

Covert Action and Communism

One of the major distinguishing characteristics of the second American empire was its reliance on covert action. Such operations are typically associated with the fight against communism, but they were also deployed in the protection of American property. In fact, there is evidence that communism was not a cause but an excuse for interventions on behalf of private investors.

Covert action was one of a number of new technologies that enabled the United States to fulfill the role of the world's first global superpower. These included the better-known advances in scientific technology, such as radar or the atomic bomb, but advances in *organizational* technologies were equally important. For example, American advances in logistics developed for the invasion of Western Europe and the western Pacific fed directly into the success of the Berlin Airlift in 1948–49 that broke the Soviet blockade of the city. This is not to say that covert action—defined as an operation, such as the subversion of a hostile government, designed to enable the responsible government to plausibly deny involvement—was invented in the 1940s.[190] The U.S. government's actions in Cuba in 1933–34 were straight out of what later became the CIA playbook, to say nothing of Secret Service operations dating back to the Revolutionary War. But prior to World War II, the United States had no centralized intelligence service, relying instead largely on scattered reports collected by the State Department, the FBI, the armed forces, and other groups on an ad hoc basis. The personnel who carried out the operations were also scattered among various agencies, primarily the diplomatic corps. These earlier efforts, moreover, were halting and uncoordinated compared with the techniques that the United States developed to use against the Germans in their occupied territories.

The agency that played the greatest role in U.S. relations with Latin America (and other parts of what became called the "Third World") was the Central Intelligence Agency (CIA), which started life as the World War II–era Office of Strategic Services (OSS). After the United States entered the war in 1941, the OSS quickly became the United States' chief covert arm against the Axis. The OSS conducted wide-ranging anti-Japanese operations in mainland Asia and significant clandestine intelligence operations in occupied Europe, including Germany itself. By the end of the war, the OSS had become the leading agency for covert paramilitary operations and played a key role in the collection of secret intelligence. Though President Truman formally disbanded the OSS less than two months after the Japanese sur-render in August 1945, its covert operational and intelligence divisions formed the core of a new, cabinet-level agency: the CIA. This agency was charged by the National Security Council in 1948 with conducting not only espionage and counterespio-nage activities but also covert operations, defined as:

> All activities (except as noted herein) which are conducted or sponsored by this Government against hostile foreign states or groups or in support of friendly foreign states or groups but which are so planned and executed that any U.S. Government responsibility for them is not evident to unauthorized persons and that *if uncovered the U.S. Government can plausibly disclaim any responsibility for them* [italics added]. Specifically, such operations shall include any covert activities related to: propaganda, economic warfare; preventive direct action, including sabotage, anti-sabotage, demolition and evacuation measures; subversion against hostile states, including assistance to underground resistance movements, guerrillas and refugee liberation groups, and support of indigenous anti-communist ele-ments in threatened countries of the free world.[191]

President Truman first used the CIA's capacity for covert oper-ations in Italy, where the CIA funneled $10 million ($78 million in 2011 dollars) in captured funds to the Christian Democrats during the 1948 general elections.[192] "We had bags of money that we delivered to selected politicians, to defray their political expenses, their campaign expenses, for posters, for pamphlets," recounted F. Mark Wyatt, the CIA official in charge of the op-eration.[193] The purpose was to limit the electoral success of the Communist-led Popular Front, which Truman feared might, if brought into the government, seize control of the Italian gov-ernment and take it into the Communist bloc.[194] This was no idle fear: the Communists had done exactly that in Czechoslovakia in February 1948, where they held 38% of the parliamentary seats. In Italy, the Communists held 19% of Parliament before the election (to the Christian Democrats' 37%), and they seemed primed to gain more. It is impossible to know if the CIA campaign was the key in holding off the Communist electoral threat—the United States also made it quite clear that Italy would not receive any Marshall Plan aid (or the territory of Trieste) if the Communists won—but the operation was considered a success when the Christian Democrats won 55% of the seats and the Communists were held to 33%.[195]

The Italian operation was almost entirely strategic in motivation, but soon enough the U.S. government found itself employing covert action to protect private interests. On March 15, 1951, the Iranian parliament unanimously voted to nationalize the Anglo-Iranian Oil Company. Britain responded by blockading the port of Abadan, Iran's major oil export hub. Despite the resulting collapse in Iranian oil revenue, the nationalization made Prime Minister Mossadegh immensely popular at home. Britain therefore turned to the United States for help. President Truman, however, strongly opposed "the use of force or the threat of the use of force" against Iran. Truman judged that Britain was in a better position than it had been during the dark days of 1942.[196] Moreover, no American-owned assets were involved.

The incoming Eisenhower administration, however, was not as reticent as Truman to aid its junior partner in the Cold War. The U.K. government realized that part of U.S. reluctance to intervene in Iran stemmed from its unwillingness to step into another country's investment disputes. British intelligence officials, therefore, pulled no stops in trying to convince their American counterparts that Mossadegh was too weak to stave off Communist influence.[197] The Americans were an easy sell, for entirely understandable and legitimate reasons: the United States had just held off genuine Soviet threats in Berlin, Greece, Turkey, and Italy; and it was engaged in a hot war against Communist expansion in Korea. In 1946 the United States had come close to war with the Soviet Union over Stalin's refusal to withdraw troops from northern Iran. The Soviets had gone so far as to establish two puppet governments before withdrawing under pressure. With this sort of recent track record, the U.S. government was understandably inclined to believe that paranoia in pursuit of anticommunism was no vice.

The Eisenhower administration lacked the economic tools to lever Iranian policy the way it had managed the outcome in Bolivia. It consequently turned to its covert arm. The CIA under its new director, Allen Dulles—the brother of Eisenhower's secretary of state—came to believe that Iran represented "the building up of a situation where a Communist takeover" was becoming "more and more of a possibility."[198] The State Department and the CIA convinced a reluctant Eisenhower that the United States could not "make a successful deal with Mossadegh . . . it might not be worth the paper it was written on, and the example might have very grave effects on United States oil concessions in other parts of the world."[199] Once Eisenhower agreed to the broad-brush outlines of covert action, he let his advisers hash out its details. On June 25, 1953, Eisenhower's staff approved the plan to overthrow the Iranian government, codenamed Operation Ajax.[200] Ajax involved the judicious application of bribe money to military officers, members of the Iranian parliament, and paid demonstrators to create a strong antigovernment atmosphere in the capital, in which military elements could depose Mossadegh. The plan probably would not have worked in a country with strong political institutions. Iran, however, did not have strong political institutions. The coup began on August 15, 1953. On August 19, after a fierce gun battle, Mossadegh was captured in the steel-lined bedroom of his Tehran house.[201]

The Eisenhower administration also used its covert arm to resolve an investment dispute in Guatemala. On June 17, 1952, President Jacobo Árbenz and the Guatemalan National Assembly passed the Agrarian Reform Act. This law designated uncultivated land, rented land, and land not directly cultivated for its owner as available for redistribution. The Guatemalan government would compensate the owners for such lands at their de-clared tax value with twenty-five-year bonds offering 3% inter-est.[202] Under the Reform Act, the United Fruit Company stood to lose a minimum of 450,000 acres—over 700 square miles, 1.6% of Guatemala's land area.[203] United Fruit argued before the Guatemalan agrarian commissions that the book values of their property were far too low, and that Guatemalan bonds would be heavily discounted if cashed soon after issue.[204] (The latter argument had the advantage of being true: ten-year U.S. federal bonds yielded only 2.96% at the time.) United Fruit also protested that the law prevented disputes from going through the Guatemalan civil court system. Rather, the law mandated that such disputes could be appealed only through the Guatema-lan Department of Agriculture, with the Guatemalan president as the final authority. Finally, United Fruit complained that even if the law were reformed to allow appeals to the civil courts, the Árbenz administration had staffed the Supreme Court with pro-expropriation judges.[205]

All of United Fruit's objections were legitimate, but the com-pany presented its case to the Eisenhower administration as one of Communist subversion. This was not a particularly difficult case to make. Árbenz had in fact secretly asked the (outlawed) Communist Party leadership in 1951 for their input into the draft of the agrarian reform law.[206] Then, in December 1952, Árbenz legalized the Guatemalan branch of the Communist Party under the name of the Guatemalan Labor Party.[207] The name change derived from Árbenz's concern that the CIA had drawn up a contingency plan during the Truman administration—which was generally reluctant to intervene—to overthrow or even as-sassinate him because of his Communist connections. That plan in fact existed. Truman chose to mothball it because Secretary of State Dean Acheson believed that should it be discovered, the damage to U.S. credibility would outweigh the benefits from ousting Árbenz.[208] Acheson's successor in the Eisenhower ad-ministration, John Foster Dulles, had few such doubts. Dulles had worked for United Fruit as a lawyer during the Depression, and his brother Allen was a former board member of United Fruit—and the head of the Central Intelligence Agency.[209]

United Fruit did not place all its hopes on sympathetic administration officials—it also roused U.S. public opinion. It hired the public relations guru Edward Bernays to create a propaganda campaign against Communist subversion in Guatemala. Bernays, a longtime friend of the United Fruit Company, took up the task wholeheartedly. Soon, pro–United Fruit or anti-Árbenz articles started appearing in the *New York Times*, the *New York Herald-Tribune*, the *Atlantic Monthly*, *Time*, and *Newsweek*. In Bernays's proudest success, *The Nation*, the most widely read left-liberal weekly in the United States, ran anti-Árbenz articles.[210] United Fruit used Bernays's campaign to build a base of voters to pressure their representatives in Washington, who in turn pressured Eisenhower.

In the face of growing public, private, congressional, and executive branch concerns about Communist infiltration in Guatemala, the National Security Council authorized covert action against Árbenz on August 12, 1953—three days before the CIA launched its Iranian coup attempt. On December 9, CIA director Allen Dulles approved the plan to overthrow Árbenz—the infelicitously named Operation PBSUCCESS—allocating $3 million to the project. In March 1954, Operation PBSUCCESS graduated its first class of Guatemalan saboteurs; in April, its first paramilitary leaders; and in May, its first communication specialists. On June 15, the operation's sabotage teams infiltrated Guatemala, while a small exile force assembled in Honduras. On June 18, at 8:20 p.m., Colonel Carlos Castillo Armas and his force crossed the Honduran border. The CIA provided air support, including strafing and bombing runs against Guatemalan positions. Árbenz surrendered on June 27, 1954, after nine days of fighting.[211]

A skeptical reader might question whether investor disputes really played a significant role in the Eisenhower administration's overthrow of the Iranian and Guatemalan governments. After all, Eisenhower was elected on an anticommunist platform, and the standard story of American international relations high-lights the very real fear of the expansion of Soviet power as the overwhelming foreign policy concern of the period. Worries about Communist subversion by itself might have caused the United States to intervene in Iran and Guatemala, regardless of pressure from investors.

Stock price movements suggest otherwise. Arindrajit Dube, Ethan Kaplan, and Suresh Naidu estimated the effect of *secret* U.S. coup authorizations on the stock price of expropriated companies.[212] The stock values of both United Fruit and the Anglo-Iranian Oil Company showed a cumulative abnormal return (e.g., price rise) of 2.4 to 2.6% over the three days fol-lowing the secret coup authorizations. The secret authorizations, in fact, engendered *greater* gains than the coups themselves. Clearly, investors in the expropriated companies were plugged in to the highest levels of the decision-making process. A purely anti-Soviet strategy would have left the nationalizations in place (or ignored compensation): after all, the United States was will-ing to ally itself with plenty of nominally socialist governments in Europe, and it ignored the interests of non-American inves-tors in Bolivia.

Ironically, the expectations of Anglo-Iranian investors were not met. The United States was now the primary stakeholder in the Iranian political situation. As such, the U.S. government was going to act on behalf of American interests. Unlike the 1946 situation in Mexico, where the Truman administration pressured Mexico into compensating (indeed *over*compensating) British-owned Mexican Eagle, American firms in Iran in 1953 stood to gain from British losses. The Iranian regime and the U.S. gov-ernment proposed that an international consortium take over the Iranian concessions. Both governments also agreed that the share for British companies should not exceed 50%, and that Anglo-Iranian itself should be limited to a minority interest.[213] Such an outcome had not been imaginable in Mexico eight years earlier: the Mexican government was vulnerable to American economic pressure, but it was not an American client. All sides knew that that Mexico was not going to return the properties to the British, let alone transfer them to American owners.

In September 1953, President Eisenhower appointed Herbert Hoover, Jr., to oversee the negotiations creating the new oil consortium through the State Department.[214] At a meeting of the National Security Council, Hoover called the result "perhaps the largest commercial deal ever put together."[215] The Justice Department, under pressure from the State Department, the Department of Defense, the Joint Chiefs of Staff, and President Eisenhower himself, created an antitrust exemption so that multiple American companies could participate in the reorganized "National" Iranian Oil Company.[216]

Anglo-Iranian still believed that it could obtain compensation from the Americans. It demanded $1.27 billion from the consortium and 110 million tons of free oil from the Iranian government ($1.27 billion in 1954 came to $8.8 billion in 2011 dollars; 110 million tons of oil was worth $2.3 billion at the time, or $15.8 billion in 2011 dollars). The U.S. government objected.[217] The non-British companies then offered $1 billion to Anglo-Iranian for its share in the consortium. Secretary of State Dulles warned the British that the offer was "one billion dollars more than [they] have now—which is nothing."[218] The British Foreign Office, for its part, realized that $2.3 billion from the Iranian government was a nonstarter. It suggested lowering Iranian compensation to Anglo-Iranian to $280 million.[219] The U.S. State Department thought even that was too high, instead proposing a settlement of $5 *million*.[220] On July 28, 1954, Iran agreed to pay Anglo-Iranian $28 million for its distribution facilities and $42 million for "the damage done to AIOC's business between 1951 and 1954." In addition, Anglo-Iranian received a tax break worth $56 million. The settlement also specified that Anglo-Iranian would pay $140 million to Iran under the terms of the 1949 Supplemental Oil Agreement. (Anglo-Iranian had earlier dismissed the agreement.) The net was that Anglo-Iranian ended up *paying* Iran $14 million as a result of the settlement.[221]

The final agreements were signed in Tehran on September 2, 1954, and in London and New York on September 20—the foreign signatories did not want to risk making the agreement subject to Iranian law by signing it in Iran.[222] At the conclusion of the deal, Anglo-Iranian held only 40% of the shares in the new consortium. Five American companies—Jersey Standard, Socony-Vacuum, Texas, SoCal, and Gulf—held another 40%. The Compagnie Française de Pétroles held 6%, and Royal Dutch Shell took the remaining 14%. (The end result did not bring the share of British companies above 50%, since Royal Dutch Shell had 60% Dutch ownership.)[223] The Iranian government received 50% of the net profits, but it was not allowed to audit the consortium's books and had no say in management.[224] The Eisenhower administration, armed with the tools of covert action, completed the slide back into the empire trap that had begun toward the tail end of Franklin Roosevelt's second term.

Conclusion

The Mexican oil expropriation of 1938 is often viewed as the harbinger of two defining characteristics of the modern age. The first is the end of empire. In this view, the United States chose not to employ all elements of its national power in defense of its economic interests. Rather, it respected the rights of a fellow sovereign nation to control its own economic policies. What could have been decided by force or sanctions was instead worked out through negotiations inside the ambit of international law. The second is resource nationalism. Mexico took over not only the rights to its subsoil resources; it established the first of the great national oil companies that would come to dominate the world's energy scene. Moreover, the country seized control of a large-scale source of rents that it could use to develop the country—and in turn ushered in an era of weakened property rights across what would become known as the Third World.

As with most historical memories, the above has a core of truth. The Roosevelt administration was in fact hesitant to intervene against Mexico. The Mexican government did in fact establish the first of the great national oil companies. But beyond that, the actual historical record diverges substantially from the accepted view. The U.S. government ultimately intervened to defend the property rights of American (and allied) companies. The Mexican government, in turn, compensated the companies for their properties at more than their market value. The nationalization itself was the product of an out-of-control labor dispute, rather than a grand plan, and the companies were not particularly profitable. Neither the Mexican government nor the oil workers benefited much from the nationalization. Once the United States had brought its economic power to bear against Mexico, there was little reason for it to avoid using the same tools against Bolivia. In the Bolivian case, Washington relied more on low-cost carrots—bilateral official credits that Bolivia would be *very* reticent to default upon—rather than sticks, but the end result was the same. American power ensured that American (and allied) investors received compensation for their nationalized investments greater than their fair market value or their value as a going concern.

None of this is to say that the Good Neighbor policy was merely a veil—quite the opposite, in fact. The Roosevelt administration went out of its way to tie up the remaining loose ends of empire and to institutionalize U.S.-Latin American (and U.S.-Philippine) relations on a new, more equitable footing. It ended the protectorates over Cuba and Panama. It completed the withdrawal of American troops from Haiti. It partially succeeded in ending unfair commercial discrimination against Panama. It opened American markets to Honduras, Colombia, Guatemala, Costa Rica, and El Salvador. It granted political independence to the Philippines. In short, with a few small exceptions, it effectively wound up the first American empire.

But it did not eliminate the empire trap itself. Many of the new policies, procedures, and institutions of the Good Neighbor policy were made possible by Depression-era changes in the domestic influence of overseas interest groups. Depression austerity split the coalition of bondholders and direct investors that had powered the pre-Depression empire trap. Moreover, financially squeezed American domestic producers mobilized against long-standing special provisions for U.S. protectorates. The politics of scarcity declawed the empire trap, and as that scarcity eased it was only a matter of time before American overseas interests would find new ways to flex their political muscle.

Despite the accomplishments of the Good Neighbor era, and despite Roosevelt's deep-seated aversion to intervention and coercion, business interests succeeded in lobbying the executive branch to protect their interests when push came to shove. The oil companies were not left to the mercy of the decisions of the Mexican government. The United States mobilized state power to protect the property rights of its citizens overseas. The Mexican expropriation of 1938 was not the harbinger of a new age. Rather, it was a sign of the United States slipping back into an old one.

America's victory in the Second World War, and the development of an entire agency of government dedicated to covert action, would create a de facto second American empire, even without the benefit of an official "Roosevelt Corollary"–like declaration. In Western Europe and Japan, this would be an "empire by invitation," dedicated to stopping Soviet expansion and (mostly) respectful of national sovereignty. Elsewhere, however, private interests rapidly learned that they could mobilize this new global America to protect their private interests, just as they had before the war. The American preoccupation with containing communism changed the rules of the game but did not overrule the concerns of overseas investors. At times, as in Bolivia, Iran and Guatemala, Cold War politics could even provide a pretext for private interests to demand intervention. After a brief escape, the empire trap was once again closing.

eight
The Empire Trap and the Cold War

Foreign investments will always be welcome and secure here.

—*Fidel Castro, 1958*

After 1945, the United States once again found itself dragged into fights over the property rights of American citizens outside its territory. Despite revolutionary changes in the strategic environment, the pattern changed little from the one established during the Roosevelt administration. Foreign governments would nationalize or threaten to nationalize American investments. The American government would respond with sanctions or threats of sanctions, the possibility of covert action hovering in the background. After a delay—with one major exception in Cuba—the sanctioned country would reverse the nationalization or provide more-than-adequate compensation.

In the context of the Cold War, however, the foreign policy costs of these fights rose substantially. Brinkmanship with a Soviet ally or client state had the potential to turn an investor-state dispute into a full-fledged superpower confrontation. Less dramatically, but just as seriously, conflicts with an expropriating state ran the risk of driving that state into the Soviet sphere. The Soviets stood ready to provide aid, markets, and technical assistance—which made U.S. success less likely and the cost of failure more serious. Even success could prove Pyrrhic, playing into Communist propaganda and costing the West political support in places far removed from the investment dispute in question.

Unfortunately for American leaders, the increase in the potential strategic cost of intervention did not lead to any mitigating decrease in the domestic political costs of *refraining* from intervention. American direct investors abroad were still wealthy and powerful individuals with peerless connections in Washington. Congress could be counted on to call for action. If anything, Congress resented expropriation even *more* during the Cold War. Expropriations could now be linked to the spread of communism. Communism had always been a useful rhetorical cudgel, as the 1920s fuss over "Red Mexico" demonstrated, but now it was a real threat linked to two military giants armed with nuclear weapons. In addition, with the expansion of foreign aid, the notion of a government accepting American handouts with one hand and confiscating American property with the other was simply intolerable. In 1962, over presidential objections, Congress successfully passed the Hickenlooper Amendment to the Foreign Aid Act *requiring* the executive to withhold all aid to governments that expropriated American property. U.S. administrations generally succeeded in avoiding the formal invocation of the Hickenlooper law, but only by the de facto expedient of slashing aid whenever battles erupted over the possible expropriation of American property without adequate compensation. The dangers of intervention so apparent to the State Department were far less obvious in corporate boardrooms and heartland living rooms.

The Consequences of the Second Mr. Castro

The aftermath of the Cuban Revolution illustrates the clash between the domestic and foreign politics of expropriation during the Cold War. American sanctions may have played a role in driving Castro into the Soviet bloc—at least, so thought many highly placed policymakers—but domestic anger at Castro's actions rose to heights unseen during previous crises in Nicaragua, Venezuela, Mexico, Bolivia, and Guatemala.

Few in Washington had any inkling that Cuban political instability in the 1950s would alter the calculus of intervention abroad for the next quarter century. The Truman administration shrugged when Fulgencio Batista, the former president of Cuba, reassumed power after a coup in the spring of 1952. The incoming Eisenhower administration paid no more attention. After all, the previous Cuban government had been less than a paragon of democracy. American investment still flowed safely into Cuba, and Cuban exports still flowed safely to the United States.

Under the radar, however, an idealistic young lawyer named Fidel Castro began his campaign to overthrow Batista. His first action did not end well: an inept attack on the Moncada army barracks on July 26, 1953, resulted in a fifteen-year prison term. Batista was not particularly worried by the young lawyer and released Castro after less than two years. Castro soon tried again to overthrow the government, and he failed just as miserably. Operating in Mexico, Castro's agent purchased a yacht, the *Granma*, from a spelling-challenged American who had named it in honor of his grandmother. Castro and his Argentine colleague, Ernesto "Che" Guevara, accompanied by eighty armed supporters, attempted a landing on Cuba's southeastern coast on December 2, 1956. Castro's group was reported wiped out by Cuban government forces. Castro himself, however, escaped and went on to garner increasing attention from the American press. On February 24, 1957, the *New York Times* published a front-page story complete with dramatic photo of the bearded young rebel holding a rifle.[1] His movement quickly grew, and by 1958 Fulgencio Batista's regime was on the defensive.

The Eisenhower administration remained unworried about the prospect of a Castro government. On December 14, 1958, U.S. ambassador Earl Smith met with Cuban Foreign Minister

Gonzalo Güell to inform him that "the United States will no longer support the present government of Cuba." In a longer meeting with Güell and Batista on the evening of December 17, Smith emphasized that the United States would not intercede on Batista's behalf. Batista was furious, claiming the United States was now "mediating on behalf of the Castros."[2] Fear of Communists within Castro's movement, however, prevented the United States from throwing its unambiguous support to the rebels. At a meeting of the National Security Council on December 23, 1958, CIA director Allen Dulles gave his agency's appraisal of Castro: "The Communists appear to have penetrated the Castro movement, despite some effort by Fidel to keep them out." In the words of Vice President Nixon, it would be undesirable to "take a chance on the Communist domination of Cuba."[3]

Hours before dawn on January 1, 1959, Fulgencio Batista fled Cuba for the Dominican Republic. Fidel Castro declared victory in Santiago and marched victoriously into Havana on January 8. Eisenhower recalled Ambassador Smith—who could not speak Spanish—and replaced him with Philip Bonsall, a career diplomat with extensive Latin American experience.[4] On February 7, 1959, the new government declared the Fundamental Law, which had the effect of continuing Batista's 1950 suspension of the Constitution of 1940. Article 24 of the Fundamental Law protected private property, albeit with a loophole for "collaborators":

> The confiscation of goods is prohibited, although it is authorized for the property of the tyrant deposed on December 31, 1958 and his collaborators, natural or judicial persons responsible for the crimes committed against the national economy or public treasury, and those who were or have been illicitly enriched by the use of public power. No other natural or corporate persons may be deprived of their property unless with proper judicial authority, for reasons of public utility or social interest, and always with the previous payment of the corresponding indemnization in cash.[5]

Initially, Washington believed that it could work with Castro, despite a trickle of defections of high-level Cuban officials fearing a Communist takeover. Castro went to the United States in April 1959 with the express purpose of seeking credits from the World Bank—an objective that did not smack of Communist orthodoxy.[6] After meeting Castro personally in Washington, Vice President Nixon wrote, "My own appraisal of him as a man is somewhat mixed. The one fact we can be sure of is that he has those indefinable qualities which make him a leader of men. . . . He is either incredibly naive about Communism or under Communist discipline—my guess is the former. . . . because he has the power to lead to which I have referred, we have no choice but at least to try to orient him in the right direction."[7]

On May 17, 1959, the Cuban government announced its long-awaited (or long-feared) land reform policy. The Agrarian Reform Act limited individual landholdings to 995 acres, but allowed sugar and cattle holdings up to 100 *cabellarías*, or 3,300 acres, slightly more than five square miles.[8] No non-Cubans would be allowed to purchase rural property in the future. Corporations could own land, but all shareholders had to be Cuban citizens. No shareholder in a corporation that grew sugarcane could own shares in a corporation that processed sugarcane. This provision cost sugar processors about 2 million acres.[9] The act provided for compensation, but only at the value of 1958 tax assessments. Since Cuba lacked sufficient dollars to compensate investors in cash, it offered nontransferable twenty-year bonds with an interest rate capped at 4.5%, 12 basis points above the rate on ten-year U.S. government securities.[10]

The initial U.S. reaction was quite moderate. On June 11, the State Department sent Castro an official note, in which it stated its support for "the objectives which the government of Cuba is presumed to be seeking" but asked for the "payment of prompt, adequate, and effective compensation" in accordance with the Fundamental Law of 1959. The American dispute centered on the use of peso-denominated bonds to compensate the investors, rather than cash, although State was open to compensation in "long-term bonds that would be marketable and would be payable in dollars."[11]

Investor pressure soon forced the Eisenhower administration off the fence in regard to Cuba. The first major expropriations began in late June of 1959, in Camagüey Province. American investors panicked. One of the loudest voices was Robert Kleberg, the proprietor of the one-thousand-square-mile King Ranch in south Texas. Kleberg had extensive holdings in Cuba, including a $3 million ranch in Camagüey. Kleberg used his Texas connections to complain about the expropriations to Senate majority leader Lyndon Johnson—whose first political job in Washington had been as administrative assistant to Richard Kleberg, the "cowboy congressman"—and Secretary of the Treasury Robert Anderson, a Texan oil executive.[12] In addition, Assistant Secretary of State for Inter-American Affairs Roy Rubottom and Assistant Secretary of State for Economic Affairs Thomas Mann were both from Texas and "sympathetic to King Ranch complaints."[13]

Kleberg obtained a meeting with Secretary of State Christian Herter on June 24, 1959, where they discussed the "Communist inspired" land reform. Kleberg had a solution: "If Cuba were deprived of its [sugar] quota privilege," he argued, "the sugar industry would promptly suffer an abrupt decline, causing widespread further unemployment. The large numbers of people thus forced out of work would begin to go hungry. They would then readily perceive the catastrophic nature of Castro's program, and that would mean the end of Castro politically."[14] The next day, Kleberg met for an hour with President Eisenhower "on the grounds that he could tell the President (and no one else) certain things." These certain things included a call for the immediate suspension of the Cuban sugar quota and the seizure of all Cuban assets in the United States. Eisenhower "had not thought it necessary to comment to Bob" about how he would respond to the Cuban government's actions.[15]

Few American investors in Cuba had Kleberg's access, but in aggregate they formed a formidable lobbying group. Sugar interests had little trouble convincing Senator George Smathers

(D-Florida) to bring before the Senate the possibility of cutting Cuba's sugar quota.[16] On September 24, 1959, a high-powered group of American sugar executives met with a similar group of high-ranking State Department officials in a meeting chaired by Roy Rubottom and attended by Ambassador Bonsall. The executives did not want the sugar quota cut if the Cuban situation remained salvageable. Rather, they preferred to have the U.S. government ask Castro for a sugarcane exemption to the Agrarian Reform Act. "Other lands present no real problem— they are not a serious matter." The sugar *refiners*, however, preferred a harder line, since they could use domestic beet sugar for American consumption should the United States "punish Cuba through the sugar quota." As William Oliver, the president of the American Sugar Refining Company, told the State Department, "There are no secrets in the sugar business."[17]

As the sugar harvest neared, Cuban counterrevolutionaries based in Florida started targeting Cuban sugar mills from the air. The first attacks began in mid-October 1959. The outraged Cuban foreign minister, Rail Roa, stated that if the raids were not a deliberate provocation on the part of the U.S. government, they were at best an act of malign negligence: "The Cuban people know, from bitter experience, that if the government of the United States sets in motion its formidable system of vigilance and defense it is almost impossible to conspire in its territory, traffic in arms, leave its ports illegally, or take off in airplanes without proper papers."[18] The attacks involved white phosphorus bombs and strafing runs, including one on the outskirts of Havana on October 21, 1959, and they continued well into 1960.[19] The attacks appear to have hardened the Cuban line on the sugar properties. On January 11, 1960, for example, Ambassador Bonsall delivered a formal protest to the Cuban government regarding its decision to pay expropriated American companies in peso bonds rather than cash.[20] This was immediately followed by a series of air raids that dropped incendiaries on Cuban sugar mills. The Cuban government took the raids as a threat and ignored Bonsall's note.[21]

Castro made some minor moves against other American companies in 1959, but they attracted little attention. In the summer, his government cut electricity rates 30%, which the American and Foreign Power Company stated cost its Cuban subsidiary $13 million over the year. In November, a new law placed a 60% royalty on the oil companies and mandated they drill their concessions on threat of forfeiture.[22] The U.S. response to both issues was mild compared with the Sturm und Drang over the sugar industry. Oil production in Cuba was low and declining, having fallen from 1,715 barrels per day in 1956 to 1,100 in 1958 before plunging to 552 in 1959.[23] The confiscation of concessions of dubious value was not going to mobilize the oil companies into actions that could backfire against their profitable refinery operations. As for the power company, there was a long history in Latin America of imposing price controls on foreign utilities, dating all the way back to Porfirio Díaz in 1893. American and Foreign Power was already looking for a buyer for its Cuban assets. The problem was the sugar industry.

The ongoing air attacks by Florida-based counterrevolutionaries created an opportunity for the Soviet Union. On February 4, 1960, First Deputy Anastas Mikoyan traveled to Havana and negotiated a deal to purchase 425,000 tons of sugar in 1960 and 1 million tons per year over the subsequent four years at a fixed price of 3 cents per pound.[24] In economic terms, the arrangement was extraordinarily bad for the Cubans. The U.S. price for Cuban sugar was 5.4 cents per pound. Moreover, the Soviets agreed to pay only 20% in cash; 70% would be paid with raw materials at world market prices, and the remaining 10% with Soviet manufactured goods.[25] Nevertheless, as a political measure, the deal appeared to be extraordinarily popular in Cuba. Crowds chanted for Mikoyan to send "guns and planes too." CIA director Dulles tried to find a bright side. He failed, stating only that the "provision of MIGs to Cuba by the USSR would be a development favorable to the United States, since it would unmask Soviet intentions."[26]

Castro's agreement with the Soviet Union galvanized Washington. The Senate Committee on Foreign Relations immediately held closed-door hearings with Ambassador Bonsall.[27] In open hearings, Thomas Mann testified that the United States "faced two dilemmas" with the sugar quota as an instrument of state. Extending the sugar quota to Cuba "smacks of appeasement and encouragement. . . . On the other hand, I think that we have to be equally aware of the dangers of the other extreme. . . . if by our own acts and words and deeds we convict ourselves of intervention in the internal affairs of Cuba, I think we make it easier for Castro . . . to wrap the flag of nationalism around him. It would strengthen him in Cuba, and if isn't done very expertly and very carefully it will rally support throughout the whole hemisphere to Castro."[28]

Within the State Department, officials believed that sacrificing American economic interests on the island would be an acceptable price to keep Cuba out of Soviet hands. The mood within the Bureau of Inter-American Affairs was, in the words of Henry Ramsey, a member of the Policy Planning Staff, "one of defeatism." He went on to write, "I think all of us must approach Cuba with great humility. We have never in our national history experienced anything quite like it in magnitudes of anti-U.S. venom, claims for expropriation, or Soviet threats to the hemisphere. . . . I think our point of departure must be that keeping Cuba out of the Sino-Soviet orbit, and returning it to the Inter-American system, is more important than the salvaging of the U.S. investment in Cuba to the complete satisfaction of the U.S. business community. This is a bitter pill to swallow."[29]

The State Department repeatedly warned Eisenhower that economic retaliation against Cuba would have disastrous political effects. In July 1959, Harry Turkel, the director of the State Department's Office of Inter-American Regional Economic Affairs, outlined the likely results. Describing the tactic as a "sledge hammer," he wrote, "Cutting the sugar quota is the ultimate weapon in relations with Cuba. . . . It will rally nearly all Cubans behind Castro. . . . The step is probably irreversible," since other allied countries would demand their share of the Cuban quota, and once granted it would be impossible to then cut them off. There was only one case under which Turkel recommended its use: *after* the Soviet Union took an action "supporting Castro which we consider intolerable."[30]

Ambassador Bonsall agreed that cutting the sugar quota would be catastrophic. In September 1959, he warned Assistant Secretary Rubottom that "even to contemplate in our legislative the possibility that our executive might cut the Cuban U.S. quota for punitive or retaliatory reasons connected with domestic Cuban legislation would, in my judgment, prove disastrous not only to our relations with Cuba but also to our relations with other Latin American countries."[31] William Wieland, the director of the Office of Caribbean and Mexican Affairs, sent Rubottom a similar warning in December. "The political effects of a quota cut would be: (a) to create hatred of the United States in Cuba and elsewhere in the hemisphere; (b) to increase sympathy for Castro, thereby probably prolonging the tenure of his regime; (c) to give what would be, with perhaps some justification, clear evidence of a policy of economic coercion of a country 90 miles from our shores; and (d) to create for ourselves the eventual problem of trying to pull up Cuba's weakened economy after Castro has gone."[32]

The CIA did not believe that Cuba had yet allied itself with the Soviet Union. A National Intelligence Estimate dated March 22, 1960, bluntly stated, "We believe that Fidel Castro and his government are not now demonstrably under the domination or control of the international Communist movement." The estimate went on to state, equally bluntly, that the CIA did not believe that Castro's regime was vulnerable to falling under such domination. According to the report, damage to America's strategic interests was being caused by the U.S. *reaction* to Castro's policies, not Castro's actions themselves.[33]

The CIA's warnings were not heeded. Secretary of the Treasury Robert Anderson proposed weakening the Cuban economy by cutting off American oil exports to the island, but by late April 1960 Cuba had undercut the plan by receiving tankers of Soviet oil.[34] The Banco Nacional de Cuba notified the refineries that they would be required to accept the Soviet crude oil as payment from the Cuban government for past debts. The Banco Nacional also informed them that it would no longer convert pesos into U.S. dollars.[35] On May 31, 1960, representatives of Cuba's three major oil refineries—Esso, Texaco, and Royal Dutch Shell—met with Assistant Secretary of State Mann and Secretary of the Treasury Anderson. A former oil industry executive himself, Anderson said, "It would be in accordance with this government's policy toward Cuba if the companies decided to reject the Cuban demand," although he added that "they themselves would have to make this decision." The State Department then suggested ways to provide diplomatic cover.[36] After the meeting, Esso, Texaco, and Shell instructed their managers in Cuba to refuse Soviet oil.[37] Castro, predictably, was furious, and called the oil companies' refusal "a concrete act of aggression." On June 28, 1960, he signed Decree 188 mandating that Texaco's plant in Santiago refine Soviet crude. Texaco refused, at which point the Instituto Cubano de Petróleo took over the refinery. The same drama played out again a few days later at Esso and Shell.[38]

Washington reacted swiftly to Castro's takeover of the refineries. On June 29, 1960, the House advanced the White House's proposed amendment to the Sugar Act of 1948 to the floor.[39] The legislation gave the executive branch control of the Cuban sugar quota: "The President shall determine notwithstanding any other provisions of title II, the quota for Cuba for the balance of calendar year 1960 and for the three-month period ending March 31, 1961, in such amount or amounts as he shall find from time to time to be in the national interest." The bill passed the House on June 30 by the astounding margin of 396 to 0.[40] The Senate passed the bill by an equally astounding vote of 84 to 0 on July 2.[41] President Eisenhower signed the bill on July 6, 1960, and reduced the Cuban quota by 700,000 short tons from its original 1960 quota of 3,119,655, essentially eliminating the entry of Cuban sugar for the remainder of the year.[42]

The Eisenhower administration went on to purge the State Department of its chief Cuba dissenters. Assistant Secretary Rubottom was appointed ambassador to Argentina in August 1960 and was not reappointed to any diplomatic post afterward. Ambassador Bonsall was recalled to Washington in October. Bonsall was afterward appointed ambassador to Morocco, a posting far removed from his Latin American expertise. Most troublingly, Wieland became the subject of a homophobic witch hunt in Congress and the news media as a result of his role in the "loss" of Cuba.[43]

Back in Cuba, Castro was livid at the sugar quota cut, bitterly ranting the next day to a small rally of Cuban workers about Yankee economic aggression.[44] He then signed Law 851, which authorized (but did not mandate) the expropriation all American property in Cuba. Law 851 allowed for compensation paid for by thirty-year bonds paying 2% interest and financed from an account funded by 25% of sugar revenue from sales to the United States above an annual level of 3 million tons and a price of 5.75 cents per ton, which happened to be the U.S. domestic sugar price at the time.[45] Needless to say, the law would not raise much compensation even if the United States removed the sanctions, considering that the pre-sanction quota was only 3.119 million tons. On July 8, the *New York Times* editorialized, "The question whether the exact method used by the Eisenhower Administration—cutting the sugar quota—was the right one will only be answered by time. The choice of retaliatory action was limited; the pressure to take action was overwhelming. The die is cast and there is no question that the United States, Cuba, and Latin America are entering a new era."[46]

The new era began the very next day. From the first, the Soviet-Cuban alliance emphasized the possibility of an attack on American soil. On July 9, 1960, Nikita Khrushchev spoke on the Cuban situation before the unlikely forum of the Russian Federative Soviet Republic's Teacher's Congress. He thundered to the audience—which included, symbolically, his own childhood teacher—that as a result of the American "economic blockade," Cuba would now be under the umbrella of Soviet rocketry. "It should be borne in mind that the United States is now not at such an inaccessible distance from the Soviet Union as formerly. . . . Soviet artillerymen can support the Cuban people with their rocket fire, should the aggressive forces in the Pentagon dare to start intervention against Cuba. And the Pentagon would be well advised not to forget that, as has been shown by the latest tests, we have rockets which land accurately in a pre-determined square target 13,000 kilometers away. This, if you wish, is a warning to those who might like to solve international problems by force and not by reason."[47] The next day, Ernesto "Che" Guevara proclaimed before a crowd of 100,000 Cuban workers in front of the Presidential Palace in Havana: "Cuba is now, in addition, a proud Caribbean island defended by the missiles of the greatest military power in history."[48]

Khrushchev's warning to the United States was a bluff. The Soviet Union had *no* operational intercontinental ballistic missiles capable of reaching the United States. The first deployable Soviet ICBM, the R-16 (also known as the SS-7 Saddler), would not become fully operational until late 1961. The Cubans, however, did not know this. Cuba had willingly and irrevocably entered the Soviet defensive sphere.

With a (perceived) Soviet security blanket in place, the way was open to expropriate the remaining American properties on the island. In August 1960, Castro nationalized thirty-six sugar mills, the oil refineries (already occupied by Cuban officials), and the electric and phone companies. In September, he took over three American-owned banks. On October 13, 1960, he nationalized nineteen more American companies, including the local subsidiaries of Procter & Gamble, DuPont, and Swift. The United States responded on October 20 with an embargo on exports to Cuba, save medicine and a few food products. Cuba, in a tit-for-tat process, nationalized 166 U.S.-owned hotels, insurance companies, and other enterprises, including the Nicaro

Nickel plant and subsidiaries of Woolworth, Sears Roebuck, International Harvester, and Coca-Cola. The process reached its conclusion in December, when President Eisenhower reduced Cuba's sugar quota to zero. Diplomatic relations ended in January 1961.[49]

Relations deteriorated still further with the ill-fated Bay of Pigs invasion, a supposedly covert operation planned by the CIA to land a small force of Cuban exiles in support of a general insurrection against Castro. Although the initiative began under Eisenhower, its implementation fell to his successor, John Kennedy. This was not an inheritance Kennedy welcomed. As he told his aides on the eve of the Bay of Pigs, in a direct comparison with the Soviet invasion of Hungary in 1956: "I'm not going to risk an American Hungary. And that's what it could be, a fucking slaughter."[50] As a result, he pared back the initial plans to support the invasion with air cover from the U.S. Air Force and supplies brought in by the navy. The mission was marked throughout by incompetent execution. The "secret" invasion was practically public knowledge. On January 11, 1961, the *New York Times* ran a story on the training of the anti-Castro force on its front page, including a *map* of its staging base in Guatemala and its likely destination in Cuba.[51] The Soviet Union, meanwhile, knew the date of the operation.[52] Cuban forces crushed the incursion within three days of the initial landing on April 17, 1961.

The U.S. weakness in Cuba led Khrushchev to stage intermediate-range missiles on the island in 1962. This led directly to the Cuban missile crisis, possibly the closest the two superpowers ever came to war. Cuba had expropriated at least $524 million and probably well over $1 billion dollars of property from the United States, according to State Department estimates in 1964—the equivalent of $3.1–$6.0 billion in 2011 dollars.[53] This amount, while large, does not compare to the amount that would have been lost by the destruction of even one American city as a result of a nuclear war.[54] No rational executive would make that trade-off.

From the point of view of many in Washington, Cuba entered the Soviet bloc as a consequence of American retaliation over expropriation disputes. Arguments continued over whether the United States pushed Castro into Soviet hands or whether he jumped—but uncertainty over the issue made the U.S. government very conscious of the risk that overzealous protection of American private property could push a neutral government into the Soviet bloc. The Cuban situation became an experience that no U.S. administration wanted to repeat.

Brazil, the Empire Trap, and the Hickenlooper Amendment

[Congressional action was] needed to counter the reckless abandon that seemed to be prevailing in certain countries relating to the expropriation of American property.

—*Senator Hubert Humphrey, 1963*

Though none of the expropriation conflicts of the 1960s and '70s resulted in an outcome as dire as the Cuban debacle, the United States found itself dragged into a number of strategically risky fights over the nationalization of American property. The domestic political costs of an executive failure to act continued to rise. The theft of American property abroad raised patriotic hackles as never before, and in 1962 Congress passed a measure—the Hickenlooper Amendment to the Foreign Aid Act—that mandated aid cutoffs against expropriating governments. By dint of good fortune and hard work the State Department (with some help from the CIA) managed to navigate the expropriation conflicts of the 1960s without further strategic losses—but only just.

The train of events leading to the Hickenlooper Amendment began on February 16, 1962, when the government of the Brazilian state of Rio Grande do Sul (RGS) expropriated the Companhia Telefonica Nacional (CTN), a subsidiary of International Telephone and Telegraph (ITT). The dispute was not new. In 1953, the state government refused to renew ITT's concession owing to its poor service. Requests for new telephones took up to four years to be fulfilled, and that waiting list of 25,000 far exceeded its 19,000 customers.[55] ITT countered that the CTN operated in the red and required a rate increase in order to improve service. The dispute dragged on until 1959, when ITT's new president, Harold Geneen, offered to invest $40 million in exchange for rate hikes. RGS's new governor, Leonel Brizola, countered with a proposal to convert CTN into a joint venture, the state and ITT each holding 25% of the shares. ITT agreed to examine the offer.[56] The story followed a pattern that had been common in Latin America (indeed, the world) since the turn of the twentieth century, and attracted little attention until the two parties failed to reach agreement.

RGS and ITT delegated valuation of CTN to a three-judge panel, one chosen by ITT. ITT claimed a value between $6 million and $8 million. (In 2011 dollars, $36 to $48 million.)[57] The panel returned a valuation of $7.3 million.[58] It is not clear whether ITT or Brizola rejected the panel's valuation, but discussions collapsed. Brizola placed Cr$149,748,000 ($400,000 at contemporary exchange rates) into an escrow account—the panel's valuation of ITT's holdings minus such categories as lands donated to the company for right-of-way and "profits illegally exported"—and seized the company's facilities.[59] It is unlikely that ITT cared much about a single, small, money-losing subsidiary. ITT did, on the other hand, care very much about its investments in other Latin American countries. The expropriation of its Cuban operations had shocked management, and with Chile providing a full 12% of the company's earnings, it was worried that the Brazilian example might spread across the Andes.[60]

The Brazilian government in 1962 was almost tailor-made to arouse anticommunist sentiment in the United States. The relatively new president, the left-leaning João "Jango" Goulart, had a radical image, despite being a wealthy landowner. More-over, Goulart was visiting the People's Republic of China when President Quadros resigned to bring him to office. Worse yet, he appointed a Communist to be his public face as press sec-retary.[61] In September 1961, the CIA concluded that Goulart, "wittingly or unwittingly, is paving the way for effective Com-munist infiltration designed as a prelude to an eventual take-over."[62] Governor Brizola, meanwhile, had already seized sev-eral power plants owned by the American and Foreign Power Company (Amforp) in 1959.[63] Amforp had entered Brazil in 1927. By 1959, like the CTN, the company was losing money.[64] The company's management wanted out, and the easiest exit was to sell to the local government. In Argentina and Mexico, the company managed to negotiate such deals. In Brazil, Am-forp was in talks with the federal government when Governor Brizola expropriated its assets.[65] Amforp remained confident that it could strike a deal with Goulart, and the company did not try to enlist Washington's help. Nevertheless, there were more than enough ominous parallels to Cuba for anyone who went looking for them.[66]

Brizola's unexpected expropriation of ITT put the Kennedy administration in an uncomfortable position. Brizola's move came six weeks before a Washington meeting between Presi-dent Kennedy and Goulart on April 3, 1962.[67] ITT deliberately fanned the flames of public opinion. The day after Brizola's an-nouncement, Geneen sent telegrams to Secretary of State Rusk and the White House decrying the situation in Brazil.[68] That same day, an article appeared on the front page of the *New York Times*, headlined "Brazilians Seize U.S. Phone System." The piece quoted Geneen at length.[69] In response to the *Times* story, outraged businessmen flooded the State Department with let-ters, telegrams, and phone calls, to the point that Secretary Rusk felt the need to bring it up when briefing Lincoln Gordon, the new ambassador to Brazil.[70] Gordon, a Harvard professor and native New Yorker, had no particular sympathy for U.S. mul-tinationals, but he received instructions to provide his "fullest possible support to the effort to obtain 'prompt and adequate' compensation, utilizing in this regard full weight and influence USG [United States government]."[71]

The Kennedy administration wanted to keep the negotiations quiet, but Congress got into the act. Congress had already attempted to mandate sanctions in the wake of the Cuban Revolution. In July 1959, Senators Olin Johnston (D–South Carolina) and Styles Bridges (R–New Hampshire) introduced an amendment to the Mutual Security Act that would require the suspension of all foreign aid in the event of expropriation.[72] Not surprisingly, the State Department objected. Senator J. William Fulbright (D-Arkansas) led the opposition, arguing that the bill would damage relations with otherwise friendly countries: "Instead of being deterred, certain countries would only be irritated."[73] The amendment went down 44 to 39.[74] Senator Bridges submitted another amendment, which this time allowed the president discretion in denying aid. The amendment passed 59 to 32.[75]

Events in Brazil changed the congressional calculus—not least because of ITT's skilled lobbying. On March 1, 1962, Senator Russell Long (D-Louisiana) thundered, "We should not continue generous U.S. foreign aid at the same time that the aid's recipients are seizing, virtually without compensation, valuable property of those U.S. taxpayers who are paying for that very aid."[76] ITT approached Senator Bourke Hickenlooper (R-Iowa), a man of impeccable anticommunist credentials, and asked him for help.[77] Hickenlooper obliged, introducing an amendment to the Foreign Assistance Act of 1962 that *retroactively* ordered the president to cut off foreign aid in the event of expropriation.[78] Support crossed party and ideological lines. Liberal senators Mike Mansfield (D-Montana) and Hubert Humphrey (D-Minnesota) both supported the legislation, Humphrey later explaining it as "needed to counter the reckless abandon that seemed to be prevailing in certain countries relating to the expropriation of American property."[79]

ITT continued to lobby. On May 9, at the Commodore Hotel in New York City, Harold Geneen addressed ITT's shareholders about the expropriation problem. Geneen advised investors "not to retire from Latin America or other foreign areas in panic." Instead, he urged them to "persuade our government that its Alliance for Progress should not grant aid to countries that expropriate private United States investments without fair and prompt compensation." The shareholders, the *New York Times* reported, applauded Geneen in an otherwise "quiet and orderly" meeting.[80]

Were these empty words on the part of corporate America? Despite the lobbying industry's professional veil of secrecy, there is confirmation of the corporate efforts in favor of the Hickenlooper Amendment. George Pavlik, then a legislative assistant to Senator Hickenlooper, recounted in a telephone interview that ITT, Texaco, Standard Oil of New Jersey, United Fruit, and "several copper companies" all actively lobbied for the amendment.[81]

The Kennedy administration opposed the amendment. On March 7, 1962, President Kennedy told reporters, "I can think of nothing more unwise than to attempt to pass a resolution at this time which puts us in a position where we sanction a national government for the behavior of one of its state governments."[82] The State Department sent experts to testify against the amendment, including Secretary of State Dean Rusk. In Hickenlooper's words, "The State Department raised all sorts of objections. They wrote memorandums; they appeared before the Committee; they said, in effect, 'We will protect American rights. Please do not write any such laws. Some of the countries will take offense at us and will not take our money.' The Committee held a hearing, and considerable influence was brought to bear by administration sources to soften the amendment."[83]

Why didn't President Kennedy threaten a veto? The answer is threefold. First, a veto threat would have been empty. Foreign aid was still popular in 1962, but there was enough opposition to make it extremely difficult to pass an alternative bill.[84] Second, the Kennedy administration opposed Hickenlooper but had no desire to find itself backed into the corner of appearing to turn a blind eye to foreign expropriation. Third, Kennedy and the State Department believed that they would be able to circumvent or subvert the amendment if national security truly required it.

On June 5, 1962, the Senate committee on the Foreign Assistance Act unanimously approved the addition of the Hickenlooper Amendment.[85] The amendment then passed on the floor of the Senate by acclamation.[86] With somewhat more debate, the key provisions passed in the House of Representatives by a vote of 153–120.[87] President Kennedy signed the Foreign Assistance Act, including the Hickenlooper Amendment, on August 1, 1962.

Hickenlooper in Action

The Hickenlooper Amendment was only officially applied twice: once against Ceylon (now Sri Lanka) and again, nearly thirty years later, against Ethiopia. There were few strategic costs to sanctioning Ethiopia in 1979. In 1979, the nation's Communist government was in the process of joining the Soviet bloc. Fear of driving a country into Soviet hands made the United States leery of sanctions, but once a country had jumped into the Soviet orbit, there was little reason not to throw the book at them. (See Box 2.)

The Ceylonese situation in 1962 was different: the United States had significant strategic interests at stake. The Dominion of Ceylon gained independence from Great Britain in 1948. The island nation's government seesawed between the right-leaning United Nationalist Party (UNP) and the left-leaning Sri Lanka Freedom Party (SLFP). In 1960, SLFP candidate Sirimavo Bandaranaike became Ceylon's—and the world's—first female prime minister following the assassination of her husband by a Buddhist monk the year before. Bandaranaike's personal policy preferences were socialist, and Ceylon had a severe balance of payments problem. This created an opening for the Soviet Union. In June 1960, Moscow offered to sell gasoline, kerosene, and fuel oil to Ceylon at discounts of 10% to 20% off the world price. Moscow would in turn accept payment in Ceylonese rubber and tea.[88] The Bandaranaike government drove a hard bargain. In January 1961, Ceylon cheerfully agreed to the Soviet deal for petroleum at 25% below the U.K. price, on six months credit, paid for in Ceylonese rupees.[89]

The Ceylonese government planned to create a state oil company to go with the Ceylonese-Soviet oil agreement.[90] The reasoning was simple: Ceylon worried that the Anglo-American oil distribution companies would refuse to market Soviet oil that undercut their own product. The legislation gave the government the authority to nationalize service stations and other oil company assets. The domestic debate broke on party lines: former UNP prime minister Dudley Senanayake claimed the legislation would discourage foreign investment, to which SLFP trade minister T. B. Ilangaratne riposted that foreign capital had shown no interest in Ceylon since 1948.[91] The American chargé d'affaires and the British high commissioner protested the legislation.[92]

The new law passed on May 5, 1961, and the Ceylonese government asked Caltex (a joint venture of Texaco and SoCal), Esso Standard Eastern, and Shell to sell discounted Soviet products. They refused. The government then nationalized the gas stations on April 27, 1962.[93] The expropriation involved 108 stations, which the oil companies claimed were worth $3.5 million ($20.8 million in 2011 dollars). The Ceylonese government offered $1.2 million.[94] The facilities amounted to only about a fifth of the companies' properties in Ceylon.[95] With only a few assets in play, the oil companies were willing to gamble, much as they had been in Mexico in 1938. From their point of view, Ceylon was a good place to draw the line, because they could afford to lose.[96]

The U.S. government did not immediately press the issue, since the Ceylonese legislation included a provision for compensation tribunals. After three months, however, no tribunals had been appointed. U.S. ambassador Frances Willis sent a note to Finance Minister Felix Dias Bandaranaike—the prime minister's nephew—reminding him that the Hickenlooper Amendment, if applied, would cut off U.S. foreign aid. The prime minister replied directly to Willis, stating "the best form of foreign aid the U.S. can give to small countries is to abstain from interfering in their affairs."[97] On August 1, 1962, the Hickenlooper clock started ticking. In the hope of avoiding a confrontation, the U.S. embassy in Colombo reminded the Ceylonese government *thirty-five* times about the Hickenlooper Amendment.[98] On January 11, 1963, the State Department officially informed Ceylon that it would cut off all aid on February 1 if the government did not take steps to compensate the oil companies.[99]

When the clock ran out on February 1, the Kennedy administration tried to refrain from cutting off aid, but it came under irresistible pressure from the oil companies. Secretary of State Rusk told President Kennedy, "It was made clear by Esso and Caltex executives and lawyers when we decided on February 1 [1963] to delay suspension that the oil companies were unhappy with our decision and would have preferred to see an example made of Ceylon at that time. The crucial February 6 meeting failed to produce the evidence of 'appropriate steps' being taken which we need to forestall the suspension of aid. . . . Before we actually carried out the suspension, we spoke to the presidents of the two companies and they said they saw no objection to our action."[100] On February 7, 1963, the United States immediately terminated its Agency for International Development (USAID) mission. The canceled programs included $1.55 million in grants and a $3.2 million loan.[101] (The United States continued its Food for Peace program in Ceylon, which was not included in the Foreign Assistance Act, and thus not subject to the Hickenlooper Amendment.)[102]

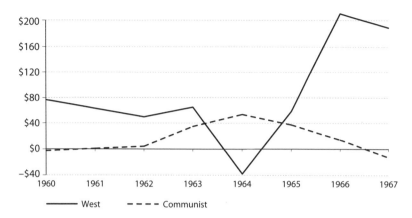

Figure 8.1 Official loans and grants to Ceylon from Western and Communist sources, net annual flow, 1960–67, millions of 2009 dollars

Source: Richard Stuart Olson, "Expropriation and International Economic Coercion: Ceylon and the 'West,' 1961–65," *The Journal of Developing Areas*, vol. 11, no. 2 (January 1977), pp. 205–26: 212 and 214.

The impact of the sanctions was multiplied by the fact that the World Bank and the United Kingdom followed the American lead. The World Bank had authorized $15 million in credits in 1961, some of which were still being disbursed in 1963; after that, no new inflows were forthcoming. The president of the World Bank, George Woods, made the connection clear in Tokyo when he announced that the bank would deny credits to governments that "belabor foreign countries."[103] Similarly, official inflows from other Western nations (primarily the U.K. and West Germany) fell off. Total net official flows to the Dominion of Ceylon turned *negative*, as credits came due and were not renewed (see figure 8.1). In December 1963, the oil companies suspended all exports to Ceylon. The Ceylonese government retaliated by seizing the companies' remaining assets on January 1, 1964. In February, Colombo asked the companies to lift the embargo, but they refused.[104]

The aid cutoff produced the adverse side effect feared by the State Department as Communist countries stepped in to fill the gap with short-term loans to the Ceylonese government (see figure 8.1). The Soviets also provided emergency shipments of refined goods, although tanker shortages made adjustment difficult. The democratic SLDP was not about to take Ceylon into the Soviet bloc (and the U.S. State Department knew that), but the increase in Soviet aid made for worrying moments in Washington.

Colombo ultimately folded. The Ceylonese economy was vulnerable to capital flight. Ceylon's official reserves had been falling since 1956. They fell 12% in 1963 and 31% in 1964, at which point they were enough to cover only forty-five days of imports.[105] Moreover, Bandaranaike was politically vulnerable. The economy was deteriorating, and she had triggered a campaign of civil disobedience among the Tamil population by her decision to replace English with Sinhala as the country's official language. The Bandaranaike government began to walk back its rhetoric on April 19, 1964. The trade minister complained that "Ceylon was losing aid because of the delay in settling the claims for compensation."[106] The opposition UNP promised that it would settle the dispute "within 24 hours." Bandaranaike's campaign portrayed the 1965 general election as a choice between socialism and capitalism, but the voters chose capitalism on March 22, 1965. It took the UNP only 120 hours to sign a preliminary agreement with the oil companies. Shell received $7 million, and Esso and Caltex each received $2.3 million.[107]

Economic Empire against Political Hegemony

If we cut off all assistance, Sukarno will probably turn to the Russians.
—*Lyndon Johnson, 1964*

After Ceylon, American administrations managed to avoid the de jure invocation of the Hickenlooper Amendment—but only by its de facto implementation. U.S. presidents resisted Hickenlooper in order to preserve executive privilege. The problem was that they could not resist the underlying political pressure that had led Congress to pass the amendment in the first place. The result was a series of aid cutoffs (or threatened cutoffs) without the formal invocation of U.S. law. When cutting aid proved insufficient, other sanctions followed. No matter the potential strategic costs, the United States found itself again and again playing from the same script.

From the point of view of American investors, the Ceylonese episode appeared a success. The United States had employed sanctions to convince a government far outside its traditional sphere of influence to respect the property rights of American companies. In Washington, however, it was viewed as a failure. In a May 23, 1963, memorandum to President Kennedy, Secretary of State Dean Rusk wrote that the use of sanctions "did not accomplish its desired objective since the prospect of the suspension of U.S. assistance constituted insufficient leverage on the part of the government of Ceylon." (Rusk was incorrect in the sense that sanctions brought the Ceylonese to the table, but the episode's resolution took two more years.) In addition, "friendly elements in the government of Ceylon were weakened and the extreme left parties benefited noticeably." The specter of Cuba clearly haunted Rusk. It was unclear "whether the adverse political effects in Ceylon of aid suspension will be counterbalanced or outweighed by the deterrent effect that the suspension may have upon other nations contemplating expropriations of American private interests."[108] Sanctions created an opening for the Soviet Union on the cheap.[109] There was one bright spot, Rusk noted: sanctions were a domestic winner. "American businessmen and Congressmen have widely applauded our action," Rusk wrote. "Failure to suspend under the circumstances would have had adverse repercussions on the Hill and elsewhere."[110]

The next crisis occurred in Indonesia, where in 1963 the Sukarno government demanded a renegotiation of oil concessions belonging to Caltex Pacific (a joint venture between Texaco and SoCal), Stanvac Indonesia (a joint venture between Jersey Standard and Mobil), and the local subsidiary of Royal Dutch

Shell. Unlike the earlier Ceylon imbroglio, the Indonesian dispute involved substantial amounts. The American ventures in Indonesia enjoyed gross export revenues around $186 million, or $1.1 billion in 2011 dollars. The entire industry generated an after-tax cash flow of $70 million per year, $49 million of which went to U.S. firms ($288 million in 2011 dollars).[111] Under the Dutch colonial government, oil companies faced a 4% tax on gross revenues, a 20% tax on oil profits, and an additional graduated income tax up to a top rate of 20%.[112] As a practical matter, the system resulted in an overall tax rate around 50% of the companies' net income.[113] The colonial-era concessions, however, were slated to expire in 1968.[114] In 1963, the now-independent Republic of Indonesia changed the tax system to a flat rate of 52% on net income, combined with a demand from President Sukarno that the companies turn over their refining and distribution facilities. They responded that they were willing to accept a rise in the tax rate to 60% (*more than* Sukarno's proposal) but did not want to abandon refining and distribution.[115]

The Kennedy administration intervened in order to head off congressional action. The *New York Times* reported that "[Congress] has served doubly as an asset to the oil industry."[116] In May, the administration sent an envoy to Indonesia to warn the government not to take unilateral action against U.S. companies. The negotiators told reporters that their job was "to convince Mr. Sukarno that if Jakarta makes it impossible for American oil companies to operate in Indonesia, resentment in the United States may bring an end to American aid."[117] Kennedy's intervention produced an acceptable compromise. The government got 60% of the profits and a minimum income stream of 20% of the companies' gross revenues. The companies agreed to sell their distribution assets within fifteen years at 60% of acquisition cost, including depreciation on a twenty-year schedule.[118]

That might have been the end of the problem had the Sukarno government not proceeded to go on a nationalization spree in 1964. The State Department was called into disputes with

Goodyear Tire and Rubber (which owned two rubber estates and a tire plant), International Flavors and Fragrances, the Motion Picture Export Association of America, National Carbon Company (today Union Carbide), the National Cash Register Company, Singer Sewing Machine, and the U.S. Rubber Company (now Uniroyal), which owned fifty-four thousand acres.[119] U.S. companies reported to the State Department that the value of the investments at stake exceeded $500 million.[120] Told of the Hickenlooper Amendment's existence, the Indonesian industrial minister retorted simply, "If it were true and it contains a threat, then Indonesia is prepared to face it."[121]

President Lyndon Johnson had no desire to invoke Hickenlooper against Sukarno. At a January 1964 meeting in the White House, Rusk warned the president that an aid cutoff would be counterproductive. Not only would Sukarno likely nationalize all American properties as a result, but also "in the case of a showdown he might ask help from China and even Russia. . . . We want to keep the United States in a position to influence Sukarno, but we must keep our good relations with Congress and not allow congressmen to think we are disregarding the legal requirement they imposed upon us when the foreign assistance act was amended." Undersecretary of State Averell Harriman bluntly stated that an aid cutoff could end with Beijing in effective control of the oil.[122] After a failed meeting between Robert Kennedy and Indonesian representatives in Tokyo, Johnson called a group of congressmen to the White House, where he explained, "If we cut off all assistance, Sukarno will probably turn to the Russians."[123]

If ever there was a case for treading lightly in defense of American property rights, Indonesia was it. The country was far outside the U.S. traditional sphere of influence. Military intervention was a nonstarter—far from seeking a war, the United States feared that it might get dragged into one in Malaysia in order to defend against Sukarno's undeclared assault on that country.[124] Covert action to overthrow the government in Jakarta was a possibility, but such action had just failed spectacularly in Cuba, a small Western country with which the United States had been intimately linked for six decades.

Congress, however, was unwilling to hear that case as Sukarno nationalized more American assets. Senator Birch Bayh (D-Indiana) argued for Hickenlooper's activation. "It is absolutely imperative for the Senate to determine that when our foreign dollars are spent, they are spent for the cause of perpetuating freedom, and not spent as they have been spent in the past years in Indonesia." Other representatives were less circumspect. William Broomfield (R-Michigan) accused the White House of "mollycoddling this minor-league Hitler." Harold Ryan (D-Michigan) took the alarmist rhetoric even further, informing President Johnson that on a visit to the Wolverine State, Sukarno had made the "astonishing request that our Detroit Police Department supply him with women for immoral purposes."[125]

President Johnson avoided the formal invocation of the Hickenlooper Amendment, but in March 1964 he buckled and slashed Indonesian aid to its lowest level in a decade (see figure 8.2). Rusk, Harriman, and Ambassador Howard Jones all advised against the move, but Lyndon Johnson, domestic politician extraordinaire, felt that congressional and public opinion left him no other choice.[126]

Subsequent events validated those who had worried that cutting support to Sukarno would drive him into the Communist camp. Sukarno allowed Communist Party members to attack American libraries, met personally with a North Korean delegation, and obtained a Soviet commitment to supply MiG-21 jet fighters. In August 1964, he denounced American meddling and Johnson's support for Malaysian independence. He ended with the announcement that he would be infiltrating an additional thirty thousand troops into Malaysia. Francis Galbraith, who was filling in for Ambassador Jones, reported that "despite [the speech's] many blatant contradictions, errors of fact and ridiculous statements, one thing stands out: Sukarno declares Indonesia in the camp of the Asian communist countries and opposed to the United States—opposed not only on the issues

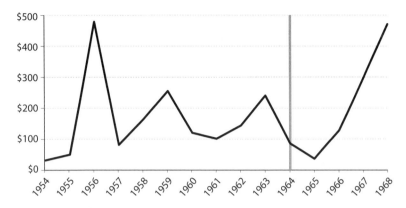

Figure 8.2 Official loans and grants to Indonesia, net annual flow, 1955–68, millions of 2009 dollars

Source: USAID *Greenbook*.

of the day like Vietnam and Malaysia, but fundamentally opposed to our thought, our influence, and our leadership. . . . It would be fatuous to pretend that the speech is other principally than a declaration of enmity towards us."[127] The CIA agreed, reporting to the president that Sukarno was "well on his way to becoming a captive of the Communists."[128] On March 2, 1965, the CIA reported that the government had decided to "seize all Western business interests . . . in particular the Stanvac and Caltex oil companies."[129] By September 1965, the CIA could write a National Intelligence Estimate titled "Prospects for and Strategic Implications of a Communist Takeover in Indonesia." The report concluded, "If Sukarno lives, it is probable that in two or three years the Indonesian state will be sufficiently controlled by the Communists to be termed a Communist state."[130] It went on to state, "Sukarno's Indonesia already acts in important aspects like a Communist state."[131] Sukarno had now, in the eyes of both the State Department and the CIA, begun to move over to the other side in the Cold War.

As things turned out, Sukarno never moved Indonesia any further toward communism. He fell to a coup in October 1965. His fall began with a coup attempt that rapidly led to fighting among factions in the armed forces, during which several top Indonesian generals were assassinated and General Nasution, chief of staff of the armed forces, barely escaped with his life. The fighting became widespread as General Suharto gained control of the army in Jakarta and, blaming *Communists* for the attempted coup, launched an anticommunist purge that escalated to a reign of terror and the massacre of at least 500,000 Indonesians.

The available evidence indicates that the initial coup was not orchestrated by the Johnson administration. That said, the United States had made it clear to the Indonesian military that it would support a coup against Sukarno and had advance warnings that one was in the works. On March 3, 1964, Rusk told the U.S. embassy in Jakarta, "The Department believes we should now try to build up pressures on Sukarno from Indonesian military sources." He followed with a set of instructions to reach out to military leaders, as long as the Indonesian government could be kept in the dark.[132] Ambassador Howard Jones met with the Indonesian chief of staff, General Nasution, and dropped blunt hints about American desires. "I asked him directly whether some military leaders welcomed the disintegration of the economy on the theory that the PKI [Communist Party] would make a bid for power and the military could then crack down on the PKI." Jones also reported that "at no time did he [Nasution] pick up obvious hints of U.S. support."[133] On January 21, 1965, the U.S. ambassador wrote that the military possessed "specific plans for a takeover."[134] The United States then moved to supply the Indonesian Army with equipment for "internal communications."[135]

The United States may not have planned the coup, but it certainly threw its support behind the prevailing faction once the fighting started. U.S. officials immediately gave word to the military that it had American support. According to an aide of General Nasution, "This was just what was needed by way of assurances that we [the army] weren't going to be hit from all angles as we moved to straighten things out."[136] In November, the United States "made clear that embassy and USG generally sympathetic with and admiring of what Army doing."[137] On December 1, 1965, representatives of General Suharto (the primary leader by that point) visited the embassy and told U.S. officials that "the right horse was now winning and the U.S. should bet heavily on it."[138] U.S. officials then provided radios to the army, in order to help them coordinate their efforts. The United States also provided large quantities of rice and other aid to the army, including a $10 million covert aid package.[139] It also provided 50 million rupiah to Suharto's anticommunist campaign.[140] (At black market rates, 50 million rupiah in December 1965 was on the order of $10 million, or $56.9 million in 2011 dollars.) The United States also appears to have sent the names of suspected Communists to the Indonesian military.[141]

Suharto soon established himself in de facto control, although Sukarno remained the official head of state until 1967. The new government returned all the expropriated American properties to their original owners.[142] It also turned Indonesia into a reliable ally of the United States. The coup came at a fortuitous time, allowing the United States to avoid the worst potential strategic consequences of its hard line on investments, but the event showed how far domestic pressures could drive the United States toward strategic disaster in its willingness to defend the property rights of its citizens.

Virtual Hickenlooper

Whenever the aid weapon was available, the United States did not hesitate to wield it during disputes involving natural resource investments or the outright expropriation of other American-owned assets. Between 1963 and 1979 the United States faced investment disputes with nine different Latin American nations. In every case, the UnitedStates cut aid by a substantial amount (see figure 8.3). Of all the cases in which the United States cut aid, the Venezuelan dispute (discussed in detail in the next

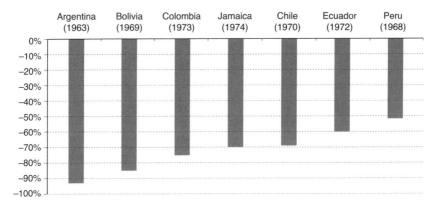

Figure 8.3 Percentage change in aid following expropriation
Source: USAID *Greenbook*.

chapter) was the only one in which the fall had been planned before the expropriation event. In Guyana, the U.S. government explicitly threatened to cut aid, but did not need to follow through on its threats.

The pattern was slightly different in other regions. In Asia, there were very few contested investment disputes during this period. In fact, there were very few expropriations at all outside of India and Pakistan—and in those countries, expropriations of American property consisted overwhelmingly of insurance companies and other service firms, all of whom expressed satisfaction to the State Department about their treatment. Outside Indonesia, the only natural resource investment dispute concerning American firms occurred in the Philippines in 1977; the Marcos administration soon reversed the action under U.S. pressure.[143] Middle Eastern nations did nationalize American oil operations in the 1970s (something discussed in the next chapter) but American aid was not important for those nations against the scope of their oil revenues.

In Africa, the Latin American pattern held generally, but there were exceptions when the expropriations involved very small interests or had the approval of the French government. In Guinea, a 1961 dispute involved a 1957 bauxite mining project with a *Canadian* company (but which enjoyed substantial American ownership) that had not yet become operational. According to the Canadian company (Alcan), "In August [1961] it became clear that appropriate long-term financing could not be obtained for such a large-scale project and the Government of Guinea was so informed. In consequence, the Government of Guinea has taken over all of the Company's assets in the country on the grounds that compensation was owing for the Company's failure to proceed with the project as foreseen in the long-term convention entered into in 1958."[144] As of the time of the cancelation, Alcan's subsidiary had constructed only a pier at Dougoufissa and 55 kilometers of railroad bed. In 1963, the Guinean government signed a contract with Halco Mining (a subsidiary of California-based Harvey Aluminum) to develop the deposits. Halco and Alcan then entered negotiations to settle claims under the earlier concession.[145] The Liberian dispute was similar to the Guinean one, in that it involved the cancellation of unused exploration rights: little American capital had been invested. The Kenyan dispute involved overlapping boundaries for a ruby mine. The dispute went through Kenyan courts, but the owner engaged the State Department in 1976 when he disagreed with the compensation offered—by then it was rather late (and the investment rather small) for the United States to use its muscle against a small African ally.[146] The Togolese and Mauritanian disputes involved minority shares held by American companies—38% in a Togolese phosphate mine and only 3% in a Mauritanian iron-mining consortium. In both cases, the French government held the largest stake in the enterprise: when it chose to support the nationalizations it became very difficult for the United States to oppose them.[147]

Declassified CIA documents provide a rough-and-ready indicator of the strategic importance of expropriation disputes, at least through 1972. There is no relationship between the number of CIA references to an expropriation dispute and subsequent fall in U.S. aid. If an American company was involved and the dispute involved natural resource production (i.e., oil, mining or agriculture) then the U.S. government would go to bat for its investors. The only exceptions were small minority investments or situations where the dispute was resolved quickly to the satisfaction of the American company.

Conclusion

The logic of the empire trap did not go away with the advent of the Cold War. What changed was the strategic risk of intervention (diplomatic, covert, economic, or otherwise) on behalf of American overseas investors. Those risks were not much apparent during the Eisenhower administration, but as the Soviets and Chinese became more active in the "Third World," the strategic dilemma became impossible to avoid. Ham-handed or unsuccessful actions now ran the risk of driving a foreign government into the hands of the other side in the Cold War. Such risks were not theoretical, as the Cuban case demonstrated to many observers. The United States came perilously close to losing Indonesia, a fate only avoided by abetting and later condoning the massacre of almost half a million people in a coup that more resembled a horribly one-sided civil war. The problem for American governments was that the political pressures pushing for intervention did not fall commensurately with the rise in strategic risk. If anything, the threat of communism gave investors *more* leverage over the policymakers in Washington. And investors, as the next chapter will show, continued to support the American-enforced property rights regime because it *worked* for them, much better than many have realized. There were large, headline-grabbing expropriations, but again and again the U.S. government ensured successfully that U.S. investors were made whole. In the face of such success (and with Cuba as the only—much disputed!—failure), no one had much incentive to escape the trap.

Box 2

Ethiopia and Nicaragua

The Carter and Reagan administrations saw expropriation disputes mixed up with Cold War politics in two cases: Ethiopia and Nicaragua. On the surface, both cases appear to be classic Cold War empire trap dilemmas like Cuba and Indonesia. On closer view, however, neither case truly resembles those earlier parallels. In Ethiopia, the Derg resolved early on to attack American property and integrate itself into the Soviet bloc. Once that became clear, the Carter administration faced none of the uncertainty that had bedeviled Eisenhower, Kennedy, and Johnson—there was no reason not to sanction Ethiopia to the maximum extent possible. In Nicaragua, the situation was the converse. The Sandinistas were socialist but resolved not to antagonize the United States. They therefore gave American property special treatment until it became clear to them that the United States opposed their regime regardless, at which point they lost their incentives to cooperate.

The Derg took power in Ethiopia on September 12, 1974, after deposing Emperor Haile Selassie. The next year, it nationalized most private enterprise. Roughly twenty American businesses were swept up in the nationalizations, the largest of which—a subsidiary of the Kalamazoo Spice Extraction Company—was valued at $11 million, or $41 million in 2011 dollars.[1] The Derg disavowed compensation. President Carter came under severe congressional pressure regarding claims against Ethiopia.[2] In 1976, Ethiopia further antagonized the United States by doing something unprecedented: it defaulted on its government-to-government military credits.[3] As a result, Congress passed the Brooke-Alexander Amendment, which cut *all* assistance to countries in default on official loans for more than one year.[4] Brooke-Alexander, unlike Hickenlooper, gave the president leeway in deciding whether or not to invoke it.

In 1977, however, the Ethiopian government managed to remove any reason the Carter administration might have had to exercise forbearance *by openly switching sides in the Cold War.*

(*continued*)

(*continued*)

In April, Ethiopia canceled the U.S.-Ethiopia mutual defense agreement. In July, Somalia invaded across the border and Ethiopia requested Soviet assistance. Large numbers of Cuban combat troops began arriving on Soviet transport planes.[5] By February 1978 the Cuban presence numbered seventeen thousand soldiers. The Soviet satellite of South Yemen provided an additional two thousand troops, and East German and Soviet "advisers" built roads and manned artillery units. In addition, the Soviet Union supplied the Ethiopian armed forces with eighty aircraft, six hundred tanks, and three hundred armored personnel carriers. The last straw, from the Carter administration's point of view, came in November 1978 when the "Provisional Military Government of Socialist Ethiopia" signed a Treaty of Friendship and Cooperation with the USSR.[6] At that point there was no longer any strategic reason to withhold sanctions—even had the Carter administration wanted to do so. In January 1979, Brooke-Alexander went into effect. In March, the United States blocked an African Development Bank loan to Ethiopia. Finally, in May, Hickenlooper kicked in, although by then its impact was moot.[7]

The second episode came in Nicaragua after the Sandinistas deposed Somoza in the Nicaraguan Revolution of 1979. The Sandinistas displayed remarkable forbearance with regard to American property. When they nationalized the insurance industry in October, American firms were deliberately exempted, although they were banned from issuing new policies. In November 1979, the Sandinistas nationalized the mining industry, including the U.S.-owned Neptune Mining Company (an Asarco subsidiary) and the Rosario Mining Company—but they were careful to offer compensation based on the "going concern" standard rather than book value. Rosario rejected the Sandinistas' first offer, on the grounds that the government had confiscated inventory along with the mines. It took four years of tough negotiations, but in 1983 the Sandinistas agreed to Rosario's terms, paying $4.5 million for the company's gold and silver inventory and $4.3 million in foregone interest. The Sandinistas also nationalized agricultural holdings belonging to Standard Fruit (now the Dole

Food Company). Standard reached an agreement with Nicaragua in January 1981. Under that agreement, for five years all high-quality bananas would be sold to Standard Fruit at a discount, during which Standard Fruit would receive $13 million in compensation for its properties. Officials in Managua also promised to halt all "anti-Standard Fruit rhetoric" in return for which Standard would supervise packing and banana planting. (It was not clear why the Nicaraguan government thought that Standard was making a concession by continuing to supervise the packing and planting of its product.) In October 1982, Standard Fruit decided that it would abandon Nicaragua and apply for a $3 million claim against the Overseas Private Investment Company (OPIC), a U.S. government agency that provided expropriation and war insurance.[8] General Mills also pressed OPIC claims, but these were not for expropriation—the Sandinistas exempted its properties from their socialization campaigns. Rather, General Mills' claims involved the Sandinista government's decision to ration foreign exchange and war damage to its properties incurred during the Revolution of 1979.[9]

The only American claim to be unresolved during the period was the nationalization of PMA of Nicaragua, a holding company of the American textile firm Leigh Fiber Inc. of Boston. That nationalization, however, occurred in 1984, by which point the Reagan administration was trying to overthrow the Sandinistas by force of arms for reasons unrelated to American property claims. (Several more claims against Nicaragua later entered arbitration or U.S. courts, but those were by Nicaraguans who moved to the United States after the Sandinistas came to power.) The Nicaraguan situation, then, was the converse of Ethiopia. In Ethiopia the Carter administration likely would have sanctioned regardless but lost any incentive to tread gently once that country jumped into Soviet arms. In Nicaragua the socialist *Sandinistas* tried to avoid antagonizing the powerful United States, but once Washington decided that it wanted to overthrow them for strategic reasons, Managua lost any incentive to give U.S. property special treatment.

nine

The Success of the Empire Trap

Once is happenstance. Twice is coincidence. The third
time it's enemy action.

—*Ian Fleming, 1959*

From the investors' point of view, the post-1945 second
American empire worked very well. Between 1945 and the Iranian Revolution of 1979, American investors failed to recoup
the value of their investments in only four disputes over natural
resource investments that did not involve the Soviet Union: Bolivia in 1952 and 1969, Ecuador in 1972, and Kuwait in 1975.
In Bolivia, the reason for the losses was not that the Bolivian
government resisted American pressure, but that the American
investors asked for and received what turned out to be a bad
deal ex post. Libya, Iraq, and Syria also failed to provide full
compensation to U.S. investors in nationalization disputes—but
all were openly aligned with the Soviet Union.

State Department records indicate that the majority of investment disputes outside hard-rock natural resources (including oil
and gas) were settled to the mutual satisfaction of both parties.
The problem is that, unlike the hard-rock mineral sector, the
value of utilities, banks, and insurance firms cannot be inde-
pendently verified. Without a clear way to confirm the value of
the investment it is possible that the companies merely settled
for what they could get. (Of course, it is hard to understand
why American companies would lie to the State Department

about the adequacy of compensation.) This chapter, therefore, focuses on mineral investments, except for the few cases (such as Peru's nationalizations in 1968-70) where independent valuations of non–natural resource investments could be assessed against compensation.

How well did America's sanction regime work at defending American property rights against foreign governments? Table 9.1 accounts all the hard-rock natural resource investment disputes (including oil and gas) in which American companies requested official U.S. government support. The data indicate that U.S. support was an overwhelming success for investments in hard-rock natural resources, especially in Latin America. In all but three cases, the U.S. companies involved in the disputes received fair market value. A similar pattern played out in Africa, where only Mauritania failed to offer full compensation.

This chapter proceeds as follows. First, it discusses the partial exceptions in the Middle East, where the oil companies were compensated via higher oil prices—prices that they could not have legally obtained without the nationalization of their assets. (In Latin America, the Ecuadorean oil nationalization parallels the Middle Eastern experience.) Second, it will examine the inadequately compensated Bolivian nationalizations in 1952 and 1969. Exceptions only prove rules, of course, when they turn out upon examination to not actually be exceptions. That is the case in both Bolivian episodes. The U.S. government intervened on behalf of its companies, threatened sanctions, and strong-armed La Paz into providing the compensation that the companies wanted. In both cases, however, unexpected events (in the first case, a decline in tin prices; in the second, an acceleration of American inflation) caused the Americans to receive less in compensation than initially expected. The chapter then examines in detail the iconic expropriation episodes in Peru in 1968 and Venezuela in 1976. American power came under pressure during the late 1960s and 1970s—militarily from the loss in Vietnam, economically from the collapse of the Bretton Woods monetary system—but as the denouements in Peru and Venezuela

Table 9.1

Latin American and Sub-Saharan African natural resource investment disputes reported to the State Department, 1946–80*

Country	Year	Fair value?	Method	Company or individual
Latin America				
Antigua	1975	Yes	Market	West Indies Oil Co. (100% Natomas Oil)
Argentina[1]	1963	Yes	See note 1	Argentine Cities Service Development Co.
Argentina[1]	1963	Yes	See note 1	Argentinian Southeastern Drilling Co.
Argentina[1]	1963	Yes	See note 1	Continental Oil Co. of Argentina
Argentina[1]	1963	Yes	See note 1	Esso Argentina (Jersey Standard)
Argentina[1]	1963	Yes	See note 1	Marathon Petroleum Argentina Ltd.
Argentina[1]	1963	Yes	See note 1	Pan American Internat'l Oil Co. (Indiana Standard)
Argentina[1]	1963	Yes	See note 1	Shell Production Co. (U.K.)
Argentina[1]	1963	Yes	See note 1	Tennessee Argentina S.A.
Argentina[1]	1963	Yes	See note 1	Transworld Drilling Co.
Argentina[1]	1963	Yes	See note 1	Union Oil Co. of California
Bolivia	1952	No	See text	Tin mines, including Patiño interests
Bolivia	1969	No	See text	Bolivian Gulf Oil Co.
Bolivia	1971	Yes	OPIC	International Metals Processing Corp.
Bolivia	1971	Yes	OPIC	Mina Matilde Corp. (U.S. Steel and Philipp Bros.)
Chile	1971	Yes	Market	Anaconda, Kennecott, and Cerro
Chile	1971	Yes	Market	ARMCO Chile S.A. (70% Armco Steel)
Chile	1971	Yes	Market	Bethlehem-Chile Iron Mines Co.
Chile	1971	Yes	Market	Cia de Cobre Chuquicamata, née Chile Exploration Co. (49% Anaconda)
Chile[2]	1971	Yes	OPIC/Market	Cía. Minera Andina (70% Cerro)
Chile[3]	1971	Yes	OPIC/Market	Cía. Minera Exótica (75% Anaconda)
Chile[4]	1971	Yes	OPIC/Market	Cia. De Cobre El Salvador S.A., née Andes Copper Co. (49%Anaconda)
Chile[4]	1971	Yes	Market	Cia de Cobre Chuquicamata, née Chile Exploration Co. (49% Anaconda)
Chile	1971	Yes	Market	Cobre Cerrillos (>50% Phelps Dodge)
Chile[5]	1971	Yes	OPIC/Market	Soc. Minera El Teniente (49% Kennecott)
Chile	1971	Yes	Market	Sociedad Quimica y Minera de Chile S.A. (Soquimich) (49% Anglo Lautaro Nitrate)
Chile	1972	Yes	Returned	Petroquimica Dow S.A. (70% Dow)
Colombia	1973	Yes	Market	Frontino Gold Mining, Ltd. (100% IMC)
Colombia	1973	Yes	Returned	Cia. Minera Choco Pacifico (100% International Mining Corp.), Pato Consolidated Gold Dredging, Ltd.(100% of 65% IMC), Frontino Gold Mines

continued

Table 9.1 (*continued*)

Country	Year	Fair value?	Method	Company or individual
Latin America				
Costa Rica	1973	Yes	Company statement	Refinadora Costarricense de Petroleo, S.A. (Allied Chemical)
Ecuador[6]	1972	Yes	See note 6	ADA consortium (23.75% equity funding, 23.31% Bell Oil and Gas, 17.89% Ada Oil, 5.0% Phillips, 15.83% OKC, 11.05% American Ultramar, 3.17% General Exploration)
Ecuador[6]	1973	No	See note 6	Minas y Petroleos (57% Amerada Hess, 32% Aminoil)
Ecuador	1974	Yes	Market	Texaco-Gulf consortium (100%)
Ecuador	1976	na	Concession expired	Esso-Andina
Ecuador	1976	Yes	Market	Gulf Oil Co. (now Chevron)
Guyana[7]	1971	Yes	Market	Demara Bauxite, aka Demba (100% Alcan)
Guyana	1976	No data		West Indies Oil Co. (100% Natomas Oil)
Jamaica	1974	See text	Tax hike	Alcan (45%)
Jamaica	1974	See text	Tax hike	Alcoa (100%)
Jamaica	1974	See text	Tax hike	Alpart (100% Reynolds, Anaconda, Kaiser)
Jamaica	1974	See text	Tax hike	Kaiser (100%)
Jamaica[8]	1974	See text	Tax hike	Revere Copper and Brass (100%)
Jamaica	1974	See text	Tax hike	Reynolds Aluminum (100%)
Jamaica	1975	Yes	Returned	Esso West Indies (100% Exxon)
Mexico	1961	Yes	Market	Asarco and Industrias Peñoles
Mexico	1967	Yes	NPV	Cia Azufrera Mexicana and Cia Explotadora del Istmo
Mexico	1969	na	Bankruptcy	Cia de Azufre Veracruz S.A. (CAVSA)
Nicaragua	1979	No	NPV	Neptune Mining Co. (ASARCO)
Nicaragua	1979	No	NPV	Rosario Mining Co.
Peru	1966	Yes	NPV	Marcona Mining Co.
Peru	1968	Yes	Market	Cerro de Pasco
Peru	1968	Yes	Market	Esso Standard (100%)
Peru	1968	Yes	Market	IPC (99% Jersey Standard)
Peru	1969	Yes	Market	International Petroleum Company
Peru	1970	Yes	Market	Asarco, Andes de Peru (Anaconda), and Cerro de Pasco
Peru	1972	Yes	Market	Conchan (100% Standard Oil of California)
Peru	1973	Yes	Market	Cerro de Pasco (100% Cerro Corp.)

continued

Table 9.1 (*continued*)

Country	Year	Fair value?	Method	Company or individual
Latin America				
Venezuela[9]	1976	na	See note [9]	CODSA (100%)
Venezuela	1976	Yes	See text	Amoco (100%)
Venezuela	1976	Yes	See text	Atlantic Richfield (100%)
Venezuela	1976	Yes	See text	Chevron Oil Co. (100% Socal)
Venezuela	1976	Yes	See text	Continental Petroleum Co. (100%)
Venezuela	1976	Yes	See text	Creole Petroleum (100% Exxon)
Venezuela	1976	Yes	See text	Mene Grande Oil (>50% Gulf)
Venezuela	1976	Yes	See text	Mobil Oil of Venezuela (100% Mobil)
Venezuela	1976	Yes	See text	Occidental Petroleum (100%)
Venezuela	1976	Yes	See text	Philips Petroleum Co. (100% Mobil)
Venezuela	1976	Yes	See text	Sinclair Oil Co. (100%)
Venezuela	1976	Yes	See text	Sun Oil Co. (100%)
Venezuela	1976	Yes	See text	Superior Oil Co. (100%)
Venezuela	1976	Yes	See text	Texaco Maracaibo (100% Texaco)
Venezuela	1976	Yes	See text	Texas Petroleum Co. (100% Texaco)
Sub-Saharan Africa				
Ghana[10]	1972	Yes	Market	British Aluminum (49% Reynolds)
Ghana[11]	1972	No data	No data	African Manganese Co. Ltd. (100% Union Carbide)
Guinea[12]	1961	na	See note 12	Bauxites de Midi (Bamidi, subsidiary of Canadian Alcan)
Kenya[13]	1974	na	See note 13	Ngana (Miller) Ruby Mine (49% John Saul, individual)
Liberia[13]	1971	na	See note 13	Liberia Mining Co. (60% Republic Steel)
Liberia	1972	Yes	Returned	Liberian American Swedish Minerals Co. Joint Venture (LAMCO) (25% Bethlehem Steel)
Mauritania[14]	1974	No	Market	Société des Mines de Fer de Mauritanie (Miferma) (3% International Minerals and Chemical Corp.)
Nigeria	1973	Yes	Market	Gulf (100%)
Nigeria	1973	Yes	Market	Mobil (100%)
Nigeria	1973	Yes	Market	Caltex (Texaco/Chevron) (100%)
Togo	1974	No data		Compagnie Togolaise de Mines du Benin (37.5% W. R. Grace)
Zambia	1969	Yes	Market	Zambian Anglo-American (Zamanglo)
Zambia	1970	Yes	Market	Roan Selection Trust Ltd.

Notes to Table 9.1

Sources: U.S. Senate, Committee on Foreign Relations, Appendix no. 8 to Report on S. 2996: Letter from the Department of State to Senator J. W. Fulbright Concerning Expropriation of U.S. Private Investments, with Attachment "Major Instances of Expropriation of Property Belonging to U.S. Nationals Since World War II," 87th Congress, 2nd session, Report no. 1535, May 7, 1962; Ellen Collier, "Expropriation of American-Owned Property by Foreign Governments in the Twentieth Century," Committee on Foreign Affairs of the U.S. House of Representatives, 88th Congress, 1st session, July 19, 1963; U.S. Department of State, Bureau of Intelligence and Research (henceforth BIR), "Nationalization, Expropriation, and Other Takings of United States and Certain Foreign Property Since 1960," Research Study RECS-14, November 30, 1971; BIR, "Disputes Involving U.S. Foreign Direct Investment: July 1, 1971, through July 31, 1973," Research Study RECS-6, February 28, 1974; BIR, "Disputes Involving U.S. Foreign Direct Investment: August 1, 1973, through January 31, 1975," Research Study RS-240, March 20, 1975; BIR, "Disputes Involving U.S. Foreign Direct Investment: February 1, 1975, through February 28, 1977," INR Report no. 855, September 19, 1977; and BIR, "Disputes Involving U.S. Private Foreign Direct Investment: March 1, 1977, through February 29, 1980," Report no. 1441, August 18, 1980; BIR, "Disputes Involving U.S. Private Direct Foreign Investment: March 1, 1980, through September 30, 1982," Report 555-AR, February 15, 1983; BIR, "Disputes Involving U.S. Private Direct Foreign Investment: October 1, 1982, through December 31, 1984," Report 1023-AR, March 6,1985; and BIR, "Disputes Involving U.S. Private Foreign Direct Investment: January 1, 1985, through May 1, 1987," IRR no. 102, July 6, 1987.

Notes: "Market" means that the real value of compensation (in net present value terms at the time of the expropriation) was greater than or equal to the market value of the assets. When the subsidiary was publicly traded, its market value was used. When the subsidiary was part of a larger entity, the cash flows were evaluated using the value of the cash flows generated by the subsidiary. "NPV" means that the net present value of compensation was measured against the net present value of cash flows generated by the subsidiary, using the 10-year rate on high-quality corporate bonds at the time of expropriation. "OPIC" means OPIC insurance paid; "OPIC/Market" means that the company received compensation from the expropriating country as well as OPIC. Results for the Middle East and North Africa are discussed in the text.

* The only major natural resource expropriations in noncommunist Asia reported to the State Department occurred in Indonesia in 1964–65 (which are extensively discussed in the text), Burma in 1965 (Burma Mines, Ltd., a 65% U.S.-owned company for which adequate compensation was not forthcoming), and the Philippines (where the Marcos government canceled the Maranaw Timber Company's concession in 1977, a decision that was later reversed).

[1] In some cases, such as Argentina and Chile (or Indonesia), compensation arrived after the U.S.-approved overthrow of a government. In Argentina, President Arturo Frondizi signed a series of "service contracts" (structured like modern production-sharing agreements) with American oil companies. In March 1962, the military overthrew Frondizi (in a coup that did not have U.S. approval). In 1963, elections brought Arturo Illia to the presidency. Illia canceled all the contracts with U.S. companies. As a result, the Kennedy administration slashed economic and military aid, and the IMF and World Bank denied the country credits. After a few years of confrontation, a U.S.-supported coup overthrew Illia in June 1966. In 1967 the new government under General Juan Carlos Onganía settled the dispute. Companies that had found oil were compensated for the value of their initial investment, plus 15% annually on the value of that investment prior to the contract's annulment. Payment came in the form of dollar-denominated bonds bearing interest rates between 6.5% and 6.75% for terms ranging from 9 to 24 years. (The Conoco-Marathon joint venture failed to find oil and in turn requested no compensation.) See Nicolás Gadano, "Urgency and Betrayal: Three Attempts to Foster Private Investment in Argentina's Oil Industry," in William Hogan and Federico Sturzenegger, eds., *The Natural Resources Trap* (Cambridge, Mass: MIT Press, 2010), pp. 369–95, especially p. 375. The terms of the annulment agreements with Tennessee Gas, Esso, and Shell are translated in *International Legal Materials*, vol. 5 (1966), p. 103; vol. 6 (1967), p. 1; and vol. 6 (1967), p. 19, respectively. See also *Virginia Journal of International Law*, vol. 15 (1974–75), p. 308.

Notes to Table 9.1

[2] OPIC guaranteed Cerro Corporation's loans to the Compañía Minera Andina.

[3] The Exótica was a new operation started as a joint venture with the Chilean government in 1964.

[4] Anaconda's investment in El Salvador enjoyed $51.4 million in coverage against political risk from USAID. The Chuquicamata investment enjoyed coverage of $184.0 million ($164 million and $588 million respectively in 2011 dollars). USAID's successor organization in providing risk insurance, OPIC, attempted to deny coverage. An arbitration panel held for Anaconda. In addition to the OPIC payouts, the Pinochet government paid Anaconda $253 million in compensation ($808 million in 2011 dollars). See *Reports of Overseas Private Investment Corporation Determinations* (Oxford: Oxford University Press, 2011), pp. 357 and 364, and Paul Sigmund, *Multinationals in Latin America* (Madison: University of Wisconsin Press, 1980), p. 171.

[5] In 1967, Kennecott sold 51% of its interest in the mine to the Chilean government for $80 million ($429 million in 2011 dollars). Kennecott then loaned an additional $81.6 million to the venture through a subsidiary, the Braden Copper Company. OPIC insured these loans. The Allende government nationalized the remainder of Kennecott's interest, for which the subsequent Pinochet regime paid $68 million in compensation. See Paul Sigmund, *The Overthrow of Allende and the Politics of Chile, 1964–1976* (Pittsburgh: University of Pittsburgh Press, 1977), p. 261.

[6] The Ecuadorean government overcompensated the companies for the value of their investments using 1972 oil prices. It did not, however, compensate them for what they would have earned following the run-up in oil prices over the course of 1973. In this, they followed the precedent set by other OPEC nations, save Kuwait. See text for more discussion of the Kuwaiti case.

[7] The Guyanese nationalization was unexpected and contentious. The Demerara Bauxite Company (Demba) was 100% owned by Alcan, a Canadian company. The U.S. government became involved for two reasons. First, 55% of Alcan shares were held by U.S. residents. Second, the United States wanted to ensure that Alcan received at least a decent settlement, in order to set a precedent for American investments in Guyana and Jamaica. The U.S. government was dissatisfied at the Canadian lack of reaction, although we now know that Canada readied military contingency plans should the Jamaicans attempt a similar surprise nationalization without compensation of Alcan's facilities there. The Nixon administration sent former Supreme Court justice and U.N. ambassador Arthur Goldberg to argue on behalf of Alcan. Under pressure (and facing the threat of severe cuts in foreign aid) Guyana agreed to pay $53.8 million in compensation, on assets with a book value of $50 million, according to Alcan documents. (The value declared for tax purposes was $46 million.) According to Alcan documents, the Guyana subsidiary generated a free cash flow of $3.6 million in 1970. In that same year, Alcan's share price traded at a multiple of only 10.1 against its overall cash flows. Data on payments, prices, and profits from United Nations Centre on Transnational Corporations, *Transnational Corporations* in the *Bauxite/Aluminum Industry* (New York: United Nations, 1981), pp. 70 and 80; U.S. Bureau of Mines, *Minerals Yearbook Metals, Minerals, and Fuels 1970*, vol. (Washington, D.C.: GPO, 1972), pp. 215–16; and *Demerara Bauxite Company, Where Did the Money Go? The Demba Record in Guyana* (Georgetown: Demerara Bauxite Company, 1970). See also Isaiah Litvak and Christopher Maule, "Forced Divestment in the Caribbean," *International Journal*, vol. 32, no. 3, Image and Reality (Summer 1977), pp. 501–32; David Reece, *"Special Trust and Confidence": Envoy Essays in Canadian Diplomacy* (Ottawa: Carleton University Press, 1997), p. 253n4; and Yves Engler, "The Black Book on Canadian Foreign Policy," *Canadian Dimension* (May 6, 2009), http: //canadiandimension.com/articles/2292/, accessed August 11, 2012.

[8] Revere shut down operations in 1975, after the imposition of the bauxite levy. Revere claimed that the levy violated its 1967 concession, which prohibited tax hikes. Revere had, however, been losing $12 million per year before the levy. OPIC denied its expropriation claim.

[9] The company decided not to appeal the cancelation of a gold and diamond mining concession.

[10] The British-Aluminum Company's (BAC) bauxite operations in Ghana were operating at a loss. The Ghanaian government took a controlling stake in the enterprise to prevent them from being shut down. The takeover was authorized under Mining Operations (Government Participation) Decree, 1972 (NRCD 132). The Ghanaian government then announced its intention to acquire a 55% stake in BAC: 25% free of charge and the remainder paid for from future dividends. Reynolds reported the expropriation to the State Department but did not ask for assistance. See Thomas Akabzaa and Abdulal Darlmanl, "Impact of Mining Sector Investment in Ghana," SAPRI Draft Report, January 20, 2011, pp. 10–11, and J. Y. Abogaye, "Public-Private Partnership in the Management of Ghana's Mineral Resources: A Historical Perspective," Presentation for the Mining Forum, Yaoundé, Cameroon, May 27–28, 2009, p. 11.

[11] The government assumed control over the Nsuta mine in a negotiated settlement with Union Carbide. According to the U.S. Bureau of Mines, the mine had only a "short life left" at the time of nationalization. U.S. Bureau of Mines, *Minerals Yearbook Area Reports: International 1974*, vol. 3 (Washington, D.C.: GPO, 1974), p. 398.

[12] The Guinean government granted Alcan a concession to develop the Boke bauxite mines in 1957. According to Alcan, "In August [1961] it became clear that appropriate long-term financing could not be obtained for such a large-scale project and the Government of Guinea was so informed. In consequence, the Government of Guinea has taken over all of the Company's assets in the country on the grounds that compensation was owing for the Company's failure to proceed with the project as foreseen in the long-term convention entered into in 1958." As of the time of the cancelation, Alcan's subsidiary had constructed only a pier at Dougoufissa and 55 kilometers of railroad bed. In 1963, the Guinean government signed a contract with Halco Mining (a subsidiary of California-based Harvey Aluminum) to develop the Boke deposits. Halco and Alcan then began negotiations to settle claims under the earlier concession. See World Bank, "Engineering Loan for Boke Infrastructure Project, Republic of Guinea," Projects Department Report no. TO-506c, March 14, 1966, p. 1; and Aluminum Limited, *Annual Report for the Year 1961* (Montreal: Alcan, 1962), p. 8, http://digital.library.mcgill.ca/hrcorpreports/pdfs/A/Aluminum_Ltd_1961.pdf, accessed August 15, 2012.

[13] The Kenyan dispute was a disagreement about overlapping boundaries for a ruby mine. The Liberian dispute concerned unused exploration rights. The Kenyan dispute went through local courts, but Saul engaged the State Department in 1976 when he disagreed with the compensation offered. In February 1978, Saul received a cash payment and a share of future profits from a joint venture. The Liberian dispute was never resolved.

[14] The Mauritanian government granted compensation of $90 million: $40 million was to be paid by April 1976, with the remainder in five annual payments through 1981. Between 1968 and 1972, Miferma (an iron-mining enterprise) earned an estimated $15.8 million per year. In 1968 and 1969, the two years for which data are available, it paid dividends averaging $4.0 million. The $90 million in compensation rapidly lost value owing to inflation. International Minerals and Chemical Corporation, however, earned only $118,518 per year in dividends from its 3% stake in the enterprise. Moreover, the French government owned 24% of Miferma—when it chose not to contest the settlement, it became extremely difficult for the United States to oppose it. In short, the combination of the tiny American stake and French acquiescence in the Mauritanian nationalization led to a marginally unfavorable settlement. Calculated from data in Pierre Bonte, "Multinational Corporations and National Development: Miferma and Mauretania," *Review of African Political Economy*, vol. 2, no. 2 (1975), pp. 89–109 (pp. 100–101 in particular), and U.S. Bureau of Mines, *Minerals Yearbook Area Reports: International 1971*, vol. 1 (Washington, D.C.: GPO, 1971), p. 590.

show, the ability of the second American empire to defend the property rights of American investors continued unabated.

The Oil Nations of the Middle East

In the early 1970s, the Middle East was a partial exception to the standard pattern of expropriation events in two ways. First, Soviet allies (Libya, Iraq, and Syria) succeeded in taking American assets without adequate compensation. Soviet support provided these governments three benefits. First the Soviets explicitly provided an alternative market for raw materials. The Soviet bloc did not need Libyan, Iraqi, or Syrian oil, but the Soviets could import oil in order to support their Middle Eastern allies, paying for it in hard currency earned by their own oil exports. In addition, Soviet aid could replace American assistance. Since open Soviet allies were likely to have their U.S. aid cut regardless of their attitude toward American property, moving against U.S. assets was relatively costless. Covert action was certainly possible against Soviet allies, but as the Bay of Pigs had shown, it was far from easy. In addition, covert action worked best in conjunction with powerful allies inside the targeted country, particularly the military. Such a strategy was difficult to pull off inside the de facto military dictatorships of the Middle East.

Second, when America's Arab allies demanded "participation" (equity stakes) in U.S. oil companies in 1971 and 1972, they compensated the companies in the form of windfall profits and favorable marketing arrangements in addition to direct payments. (The modal formula for direct compensation was twice net book value, adjusted for inflation.)[1] In all cases but one, the combination of direct payments plus oil sold back to the companies at a discount was enough to make up for the loss of the cash flows associated with participation (and later full nationalization)—at least as they were valued before the big oil price increase of late 1973 and 1974. OPEC governments, not unreasonably, argued that the price increases were a *result* of their decision to seize control of upstream operations, and therefore not something for which the oil companies should be compensated. The real annual earnings from American-owned oil investments (in 2011 dollars, including dividends and interest payments from subsidiaries) went up with oil prices from $5.6 billion in 1970 to $8.3 billion in 1971 and $10.4 billion in 1972. After a brief dip to $7.0 billion in 1973 (due to the Arab oil embargo) their earnings skyrocketed to *$31.2 billion* in 1974. Participation brought that number down to an average $4.4 billion for the rest of the 1970s—only 20% lower than the $5.5 billion average of the late 1960s.[2] Cash compensation filled the gap; the net result was that with the exception of Gulf Oil's operations in Kuwait, the oil companies suffered no losses from the nationalizations.

The CIA worried about the potential loss of foreign oil profits for the United States but believed that *access* to oil would not be a problem.[3] That belief was sorely tested during the brief Arab oil embargo of 1973–74 (the United States contemplated military action), but the embargo was not repeated. Nor was the embargo dependent on state ownership of the oil companies: Arab governments could have just as easily shut down the export operations of private companies.

Kuwait was different: it drove a harder deal than other U.S.-allied or neutral Arab governments. Gulf Oil owned half the Kuwait Oil Company (British Petroleum owned the other half), which produced 3.1 million barrels per day in 1972. Gulf Oil expected to receive $300 million for its stake, plus some amount of discounted oil.[4] It actually received $81.25 million.[5] In 1975, Gulf Oil capitalized the net present value of future deliveries of discounted oil at $275.4 million, for total compensation of $357.8 million.[6]

Was Gulf Oil fairly compensated? Probably not—but it is not clear. In 1972, the company earned $92 million from the "eastern hemisphere." Not all this income came from the Kuwait

Oil Company, however: Gulf Oil also possessed significant operations in Iran, Nigeria, and Angola. If we assume that *all* of Gulf's Eastern Hemisphere earnings came from Kuwait, then its stake in the Kuwait Oil Company was worth $1,085 million in 1972, using Gulf Oil's overall 1972 price-earnings (P/E) ratio of 11.8. By that standard, Kuwait did not fully compensate Gulf Oil, even after discounting the post-1973 price increases.

The calculation is not so clear-cut, however. The Kuwaitis argued that Gulf Oil's windfall earnings in 1973 and 1974 should be considered part of its compensation. Gulf Oil ceased reporting its earnings from Eastern Hemisphere oil in 1973, but its earnings from foreign oil production jumped from $150 million in 1972 to $560 million in 1973 and $594 million in 1974. In 1975, following the nationalization, earnings from foreign oil production dropped back to $213 million. It is possible to use data on royalty rates, tax rates, and historical costs (including amortization) to estimate how much the Kuwait Oil Company's earnings per barrel rose with oil prices, assuming that costs rose in line with U.S. inflation.[7] Under that assumption, earnings per barrel rose from 25 cents in 1972 to 42 cents in 1973 and $1.55 in 1974. Windfall profits commensurately rose to $51 million in 1973 and $69 million in 1974, even after taking into account the fact that participation drove down Gulf Oil's share of Kuwaiti output in both years.[8] Adding those windfall profits would value Gulf Oil's total compensation around $579 million—53% of its 1972 valuation.

A bigger problem in valuing Gulf Oil's investment in Kuwait is that the market began to heavily discount the value of oil companies during the early 1970s, despite the run-up in prices. Gulf Oil (which received 44% of its earnings from American operations before the 1975 nationalization) saw its P/E ratio collapse from 11.8 in 1972 to only 3.6 in 1974. At the price that Gulf Oil's earning streams commanded in 1974, its investment in the Kuwait Oil Company was worth $341 million—slightly *less* than the $358 million that it received in compensation.[9] Most of the decline in the price of oil shares was *not* due to foreign expropriation risk. Rather, the fears were about federal price controls and the threat of windfall taxation—that is, *domestic* policy changes, not foreign expropriation. (The price-earnings ratios of all oil companies, including exclusively domestic ones, declined by similar amounts.) Cash flows from oil production sold cheaply in the 1970s, for reasons made in Washington, not overseas. By 1979, 77% of Gulf Oil's upstream earnings came from North America—but its P/E ratio rose to only 4.3.[10] At a P/E ratio of 4.3, Gulf Oil's lost Kuwaiti cash flows were worth $431 million.

It is not clear what action the U.S. government could have taken to get a better deal for Gulf Oil. Aid flows from the United States were not relevant for the Middle East oil powers. The United States had already pulled out its diplomatic stops and other forms of pressure: the major American oil producers in other countries credited "some USG [U.S. government] help" in negotiating their compensation agreements.[11] Covert action was not a useful tool against a Gulf monarchy. Military action was a possibility, but the United States had already considered and rejected such action during the 1973–74 oil boycott. First, the U.S. military was in a parlous state following the defeat in Vietnam. Second, there was a very high risk of war with a Soviet ally, if not the USSR itself: a contemporary U.K. document about American operational plans read, "The greatest risk of such confrontation in the Gulf would probably arise in Kuwait, where the Iraqis, with Soviet backing, might be tempted to intervene."[12] The United States, therefore, rejected intervention *unless* the embargo continued for a long period.[13] (In fact, the embargo ended in March 1974.) Those factors were all still in place when Kuwait nationalized in 1975, with far less possible gain for the United States—especially when it was unclear that Gulf Oil had received a bad deal and eminently clear that the other Arab Gulf governments had protected the interests of American companies.

The Andean Exception?

In the United States' long-standing sphere in the Western Hemisphere, American investors received less than an upper-bound estimate of the market value of their assets in only three cases, one in Ecuador and two in Bolivia.[14] The Ecuadorean case involved an undeveloped offshore concession obtained by means that were at the very least questionable; moreover, when the Ecuadorean government canceled the concession, it followed Cipriano Castro's 1902 precedent and ensured that *other* American companies would benefit. The standard politics of the empire trap were thereby forestalled. In Bolivia, in both cases, the American companies received the settlement they desired, but unforeseen macroeconomic events (in one case, a dramatic decline in tin prices; in the other an unexpected acceleration in American inflation) led them to collect less compensation than they had anticipated. We will consider all three cases below.

In Ecuador in 1968, President Otto Arosemena granted forty-year offshore exploration concessions to six Ecuadorean citizens led by an American geologist, Joseph Wolfe. The Ecuadoreans then sold their rights to a consortium of American companies.[15] The consortium, known as ADA, discovered reserves of natural gas but made no effort at development. The deal attracted a great deal of negative attention within Ecuador, and when the military overthrew Arosemena in 1972, one of the new government's first actions was to revoke the concession. The government then began judicial proceedings and ultimately sentenced the former industry minister, Pico Mantilla, to five years in prison. Joseph Wolfe also received nine years, but both Wolfe and Mantilla had left the country. The tribunal censured Arosemena, although it refrained from sentencing the former president. The government then granted a new concession to Northwest Pipeline Corporation of Salt Lake City.[16] The dispute with ADA dragged on, but the ethical murkiness of the situation— and the fact that the Ecuadorean generals had set up the situation as a conflict between *two* different American interests—

meant that the U.S. government refrained from involvement. (In this the generals replicated the strategy that Cipriano Castro had employed in Venezuela seven decades earlier.)

In 1952, the Bolivian government expropriated the tin industry. (See chapter 7 for a detailed account of the episode.) Patiño Mining was incorporated in the United States, and American residents owned approximately a quarter of the company's shares. The compensation arrangement closely resembled the one proposed by the companies' chief lobbyist in the United States: former Senator Millard Tydings (D-Maryland). At prevailing tin prices, the companies received 5% of the *gross* revenues from the newly nationalized industry. If prices fell below $1.06, that share fell to 2.5%.[17]

Unfortunately for Patiño shareholders, the revenue-linked compensation scheme that they wanted turned out to be a bad deal. Tin prices fell 21% in 1953, from $1.21 per pound to 96 cents.[18] They would not recover to the $1.06 threshold until 1961. Worse yet, Bolivian output declined with prices: from a 1953 peak of 35,384 tons, output fell to 18,014 tons by 1958 before recovering. Patiño received only $4.4 million by 1961, as opposed to the $13.9 million ($1.5 million per year) that it would have received had output and prices remained steady. In 1962, the company and the Bolivian government agreed to discontinue the agreement with an additional payment of $4.2 million.[19] The total compensation of $9.7 million was not enough to compensate shareholders for the company's pre-expropriation peak market value of $14.8 million in April 1952, when the Bolivian revolutionary government came to power.[20] In present value terms, the compensation was worth only $8.0 million in 1952, using the ten-year rate on U.S. government bonds. Obviously, that discount rate is too low for a variable stream linked to tin prices. Using the inverse of Patiño's P/E ratio for 1951 (12.7%) as the discount rate, the net present value of compensation came to only $4.7 million.

A similar story played out in Bolivia in 1969. On October 17, 1969, the Bolivian government expropriated the assets of

Gulf Oil (now Chevron). The net present value of compensation came to less than the market value of the assets, and as in 1952 the reason was an unforeseen exogenous economic shock—this time an unexpected acceleration in American inflation, which reduced the real value of compensation.

The Gulf Oil nationalization had many roots, not least of which was President Alfredo Ovando's political vulnerability from the left. Gulf Oil presented an attractive target because of Bolivia's particularly generous fiscal regime. The Bolivian oil code allowed the provinces to collect an 11% royalty on oil production. The central government charged an income tax of 30% but allowed the company to deduct a depletion allowance worth 27% of the gross value of production.[21] In Bolivia, unlike most of the United States, oil reserves belonged to the state. Critics, therefore, angrily criticized the very existence of the depletion allowance—why was a company allowed to amortize an asset that it did not own? Nationalists also protested Gulf Oil's competitive challenge to state-owned YPFB, including an alleged proposal to build a petrochemical complex in Brazil that would have used Bolivian natural gas.[22]

The dispute played out in essentially the same manner as the 1952 tin nationalization. Henry Kissinger instructed the U.S. ambassador to issue a démarche to La Paz and called the expropriation "a potential Hickenlooper problem."[23] President Ovando hired a French company, Geopetrole, to audit Gulf's books and determine a valuation.[24] The Nixon administration did not invoke Hickenlooper but suspended aid nonetheless: "Immediately after the nationalization, we adopted a policy of refraining from new commitments and starts on U.S. assistance programs."[25] Aid commitments fell from $33 million in 1969 ($162 million in 2011 dollars) to $5 million in 1970 ($23 million in 2011 dollars). Credits from multilateral lending institutions declined from $48 million ($236 million in 2011 dollars) to $2.8 million ($13 million).[26] The U.S. embassy hinted that stronger sanctions would be in store if Bolivia did not provide adequate compensation:

This is the test whether a government which launched itself as extremist, leftist, and possibly even Castroist can be nurtured back to moderation, induced to pay for what it took. . . . If this or a successor regime shows little or no inclination to move toward moderation, fails to make progress on a Gulf settlement (perhaps moving on to other nationalizations), and, indeed, construes our willingness to assist as license to follow heedlessly the design of close-minded nationalism, we face a different situation requiring a different posture. In such a circumstance, we would have little alternative but to batten the hatches and drastically reduce program, staff, and visibility.[27]

On September 10, 1970, after Geopetrole valued Gulf Oil's operations at $101.1 million ($471 million in 2011 dollars), President Ovando issued a decree to pay that much in compensation—minus a 22% special tax that cut compensation to $78.6 million.[28] A lawyer who consulted with the Bolivian government stated that the reason for the tax was a desire by the Bolivian government to claim U.S. taxes that Gulf Oil would otherwise pay on the settlement: the foreign tax credit meant that Gulf would pay no U.S. taxes, but Bolivia would save $22.5 million.[29] The Bolivian government later added an additional $16.4 million to the compensation, putatively as payment for debts owed a Gulf Oil subsidiary, making total compensation $95 million.[30]

It possible to estimate Gulf Oil's cash flow by dividing its income tax payments by 0.3 (the income tax rate), adding back the depletion allowance, and subtracting royalties, income tax payments, and estimated capital expenditures (see table 9.2). Multiplying those cash flows by Gulf Oil's price-earnings ratio in 1969 (9.9) gives a value for its Bolivian subsidiary of between $83.4 million and $117.7 million.

The above estimates of the value of Gulf Oil's Bolivian operations are almost certainly too high. First, they are based on the negotiated oil price used to calculate royalties. In 1969, that

Table 9.2

Gulf Oil in Bolivia, selected figures

| | Barrels per day | | Millions of U.S. dollars | | | | | U.S. cents |
	National oil production	Gulf Oil production	Gulf Oil revenue	Royalty payments	Income tax payments	Estimated cash flow (low)	Estimated cash flow (high)	Lifting cost per barrel
1962	7,975	223	$0.11	$0.01	$0.00			
1963	9,318	248	$0.13	$0.01	$0.00			
1964	8,753	54	$0.03	$0.00	$0.00			
1965	9,197	—	$0.00	$0.00	$0.00			
1966	16,671	7,904	$5.17	$0.57	$0.00			
1967	39,800	32,260	$22.14	$2.44	$0.70	$3.61	$7.11	28.9¢
1968	40,959	32,415	$23.73	$2.61	$3.32	$10.15	$13.65	30.8¢
1969	40,436	32,199	$22.49	$2.47	$2.60	$8.63	$12.13	47.0¢

Source: Gulf Oil production from IMF, *Recent Economic Developments*, July 11, 1975, p. 36. Central government royalty rates from George Ingram, *Expropriation of U.S. Property in South America: Nationalization of Oil and Copper Companies in Peru, Bolivia, and Chile* (New York: Praeger Publishers, 1974), pp. 163 and 167. Royalty payments to provincial governments from Instituto Nacional de Estadistica, *Bolivia: Impuesto Nacional y Regalías Departamentales Pagados por Y.P.F.B.* Income tax payments from IMF, *Bolivia – Request for Stand-by Arrangement* (December 18, 1968), p. 4; and IMF, *Bolivia—Recent Economic Performance* (October 16, 1970), p. 32.

Note: 1969 figures have been adjusted to take into account that Gulf Oil was nationalized on October 17. High estimates of cash flow assume capital expenditures of $500,000 per year (the lowest on record); low estimates assume $4 million. The calculation of lifting costs per barrel for 1967 is unreliable.

price was $2.00 per barrel. The actual average export price of Bolivian crude that year, however, was $1.64.[31] Moreover, the cost of transporting crude to the export terminal in Arica, Chile, ran about 25 cents per barrel.[32] Adjusting for this difference reduces the company's value to something between $65.0 and $99.0 million.[33]

Bolivia's compensation, therefore, came to 96% of the high estimate of the company's value. The problem was that compensation did not arrive until 1973, when the Bolivian government began to transfer 25% of its oil export earnings to Gulf Oil. The payments lasted until 1976. Between 1970 and 1976, U.S. inflation (using the GDP deflator) averaged 6.5% per year. Converting payments into 1970 dollars and then discounting using the 1970 ten-year rate on federal bonds (8.4%) gives a 1970 net present value of only $60.2 million. It is possible that were Bolivia Gulf Oil a separate company in 1970, its value would have been less than $60.2 million—but that is not likely.

¡Peru, Sí!

The Peruvian expropriations of American oil and mining interests (along with a host of other investments) are often taken to be an example of successful expropriation. Careful examination of the data, however, tells a different story: the Nixon administration proved perfectly capable of extracting sufficient compensation to make the companies whole. Peru (unlike Kuwait and Bolivia) was not an exception. In fact, the Peruvian story is almost perfectly representative of the way expropriation battles played out against notional American allies.

In 1968, a military coup brought a left-wing government to power in Lima. That government proceeded to nationalize American investments. In a counterfactual world without the Soviet Union, the U.S. government would not have hesitated to impose severe sanctions. The world of 1968 did, however, contain a hostile Soviet Union, and the new Peruvian government (while avowedly anticommunist) made it clear to the Nixon administration that it would not hesitate to turn to the Soviets for aid. (In the clearest possible signal, the Peruvian junta purchased arms from Moscow.)

The Peruvian economy of the 1960s relied heavily on primary products—mining, cotton, fishing, and petroleum—with most of these commodities produced or marketed by U.S.-owned companies. One particular company, however, stood out in the minds of Peruvian policymakers: the International Petroleum Company (IPC).[34] As the Peruvian economy expanded, more and more of IPC's production went to the domestic market, where the price of gasoline was fixed. In 1957, IPC proposed to renegotiate a concession from the business-friendly administration of Manuel Prado. IPC would give up its private property rights in return for a long-term concession and higher gasoline prices. Prado agreed, raising gasoline prices on July 25, 1959. The price hike immediately mobilized an ideologically diverse opposition, uniting leftists, centrists, conservatives, and, most tellingly, the Peruvian military. The deal failed. In 1962, the military staged a coup when the general elections indicated that a right-left coalition would install former Peruvian president Manuel Odría in office. The military allowed elections in 1963, in which the centrist candidate Fernando Belaúnde received more than a third of the vote, leading to a Belaúnde presidency and an opposition Congress.[35]

The delicate political situation, therefore, led to a ratchet effect in Peruvian politics, with each faction competing to put forward more nationalist proposals regarding IPC. Divided government, however, prevented the policies from being enacted. After his election, Belaúnde proposed that IPC return the oil fields to Peru, in exchange for a twenty-five-year concession. With no quid pro quo on retail prices, IPC refused. Belaúnde then sent the Peruvian Congress a proposal to change IPC's property and tax status. Congress refused to pass Belaúnde's gradualist proposal, instead passing its own legislation annulling the terms of IPC's 1922 concession.[36] Belaúnde, in turn, refused to implement the legislation.

By the end of 1964, the Johnson administration began to worry that IPC would be nationalized as a way to break the domestic political impasse. Assistant Secretary of State Thomas Mann attempted to dissuade Belaúnde against this course of action by stalling economic aid to Peru. "The idea was to put on a freeze, talk about red tape and bureaucracy, and they'd soon get the message," explained one anonymous U.S. official.[37] Unfortunately, the Peruvian government did not get the message. Aid dropped by more than half in 1965, but it was not cut off, and the variation was well within previous swings (see figure 9.1). President Belaúnde was honestly shocked when National Security Adviser Walt Rostow personally offered him a quid pro quo in 1966: a resumption of aid to Peru in return for

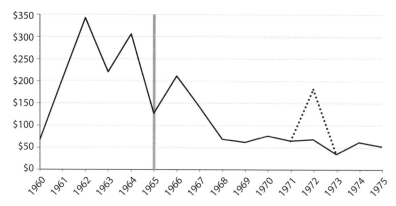

Figure 9.1 U.S. assistance to Peru, 1960–75, millions of 2009 dollars
Source: USAID Greenbook.
Note: The 1972 spike in aid shown by the dashed line consisted entirely of emergency spending of $113 million for humanitarian relief after an earthquake and severe flooding in Lima.

the nonexpropriation of IPC.[38] This had the effect of convincing Peruvian leaders that the United States was attempting to strong-arm them on IPC, which of course it was. It was not the Johnson administration's finest hour.

IPC itself realized its position in Peru was increasingly shaky. Three days before Belaúnde's State of the Nation address on July 28, 1968, IPC told Belaúnde that it was willing to hand over the La Brea y Pariñas oil fields to the Peruvian state oil company in return for marketing and refining concessions and the right to participate in new exploration elsewhere in Peru. This willingness may have been prompted by recent oil discoveries in the Amazonian regions of Ecuador: trading a mature and increasingly unprofitable field to Peru in exchange for the possibility of new fields in the Peruvian Amazon seemed like a rational exchange. IPC's terms were in fact *more* generous for Peru than the terms Belaúnde offered IPC in 1963. After a series of all-night negotiating sessions in the Presidential Palace, Belaúnde and IPC came to an agreement—the Act of Talara—and the Peruvian government formally took possession of the La Brea y Pariñas fields on August 13, 1968.[39]

Politically the Act of Talara turned out to be a disaster for Belaúnde. It quickly became a focus for domestic political resentment. Carlos Loret de Mola, the head of the Peruvian state oil company, resigned on September 7, 1968. Three days later he appeared on national television to announce that the official copy of the Act of Talara was missing a final page (the eleventh) on which he had penned an addendum to the contract stating that IPC would compensate Peru a favorable minimum price per barrel in U.S. dollars.[40] The resulting split within Belaúnde's party seemed to guarantee the election of the leftist Víctor Raúl Haya de la Torre, whom the Peruvian Army despised. On October 3, a military coup led by the chief of the Peruvian Armed Forces Joint Command, General Juan Velasco Alvarado, deposed Belaúnde. Six days later, on October 9, the coup leaders renounced the Act of Talara and occupied IPC's principal refinery, in addition to the La Brea y Pariñas fields.

The Revolutionary Government of the Armed Forces under President Juan Velasco expropriated the remaining properties of IPC in Peru, including the Esso gas stations located throughout the country. The takeover went smoothly, since most of IPC's personnel were already Peruvian and IPC's focus had been on the Peruvian domestic market.[41] The Revolutionary Government refused to pay compensation. Moreover, in February 1969 the Revolutionary Government adopted a proposal of the senior lawyer of the Lima bar, Alberto Ruiz Eldredge, called *revindicación*, which required restitution from IPC for the value of the extracted petroleum.[42] This totaled $690 million ($3.4 billion in 2011 dollars)—calculated as the total output of the La Brea y Pariñas fields from 1924 to 1968 at East Texas prices, minus production and shipping costs.[43] For its part, IPC claimed a valuation of its holdings of $200 million. On February 6, President Velasco assured the world, "The case of the International Petroleum Company is unique. It is a singular case."[44] Less than two weeks later, Peru signed a trade pact with the Soviets.[45]

In a somewhat less contentious transfer of power, Richard Milhous Nixon was elected the thirty-seventh president of the

United States on November 5, 1968. Nixon chose former attorney general and longtime legal adviser William Rogers as his secretary of state, and Henry Kissinger as his national security adviser. This was part of Nixon's strategy to rein in and diminish the influence of the State Department, which he deeply distrusted. Nixon instead preferred to use multiple competing agencies as extensions of his executive power, using Rogers to keep the State Department in line, while relying on Kissinger for foreign policy and domestic advice. As a result, Kissinger would come to occupy a prime minister–like position within the Nixon White House, while Nixon was insulated from the traditional pressures exerted by the cabinet.

Peru was not Nixon's chief foreign policy concern in 1969. (This should not be surprising, considering that the Vietnam War was still in full swing.) Peru was not even Nixon's chief foreign policy concern in Latin America. Kissinger considered the new military government in Peru—despite its ominous name—to be anticommunist.[46] The CIA agreed that Velasco posed no threat. In March 1969, it reported, "Peru's recent moves to establish diplomatic and economic relations with the USSR and other European Communist countries, which were begun last year under President Belaúnde, probably are more a show of independence from the U.S. than a serious intention to develop a firm and close relationship. . . . [Velasco's] personal entourage is composed of men whose views cover the political spectrum from extreme right to extreme left. . . . There is no evidence so far that the advice or support of the Peruvian Communist parties has been important to Velasco." The CIA went on to report that despite their nationalist and left-wing economic views, "The officers now in the regime . . . have uniformly anti-Communist backgrounds."[47]

The clock of the Hickenlooper Amendment (and related anti-expropriation legislation) however, mandated that the United States would have to cut off the remaining flow of aid to Peru and (more importantly) all imports of Peruvian sugar by April 9, 1969. Both State and the CIA worried about the strategic repercussions of such a move. Within days of Nixon's inauguration, the State Department advised Kissinger, "Suspension of aid and the sugar quota will have a serious adverse impact on the Peruvian economy, probably lead to reprisals against other U.S. investments, alienate the Peruvian people and stimulate an actively hostile policy toward the U.S., perhaps push Peru further toward economic and diplomatic relations with the Soviet bloc, and damage U.S.-Peruvian relations for a long time to come— all with repercussions harmful to our interests elsewhere in the hemisphere."[48] The CIA, meanwhile, feared that sanctions might cause the Peruvian government to collapse. "It seems likely that as economic strains mounted, the regime and the populace would become increasingly frustrated and emotional. With Velasco in power, the regime could become more radical and begin attacking entrenched Peruvian economic interests, with the result that a revolutionary situation could emerge."[49]

The problem for the State Department and National Security Council was that Richard Nixon was not willing to ignore the expropriation of American assets. At a press conference on March 4, 1969, Nixon explained to reporters the administration's position on Peru: "Now, if they do not take appropriate steps to provide for that [expropriation] payment, then under the law—the Hickenlooper amendment, as you know—we will have to take appropriate action with regard to the sugar quota, and also with regard to the aid programs. I hope that is not necessary; because that would have a domino effect, if I can be permitted to use what is supposed to be an outworn term—a domino effect all over Latin America."[50]

The National Security Council examined a set of immediate "hard-line" and "soft-line" options regarding Peru, ranging from an extremely strict set of economic sanctions in the hardest to virtually nothing in the softest. (With the United States fighting in Vietnam and barely able to maintain sufficient forces in West Germany and South Korea, military action was a nonstarter. Kissinger meanwhile disapproved of covert action against an anticommunist government.) In the opinion of the council's analysts, "Selection of this [softest] option would imply a judgment that adverse effects from invoking these sanctions would inflict unacceptable damage to our long-range hemispheric foreign policy interests. *The decision would clearly reject the future use of Hickenlooper-type devices for protecting U.S. investment abroad, at least in Latin America*" (emphasis added).[51]

Nixon sent John Irwin II as a special envoy to Peru in mid-March. Irwin had a great deal of experience in Latin American affairs, having served as the deputy assistant secretary of defense for international security affairs under Eisenhower and, more recently, as the U.S. representative for Panama Canal negotiations in the Johnson administration. Irwin suggested to the Peruvians that they use international arbitration to resolve the IPC dispute. Arbitration would give the United States a "fig leaf" for inaction, calm U.S. domestic pressures to impose stronger sanctions or otherwise intervene, and allow the Peruvians to present a case that Irwin believed to be strong. The Peruvians rejected this approach, since it violated the Calvo Doctrine. The Peruvians in turn suggested that IPC use Peruvian administrative channels to appeal the $690 million judgment. After several meetings with Velasco himself, Irwin returned to the United States on April 3, six days before the Hickenlooper deadline, pessimistic that the situation could be resolved.[52]

Nixon waited until the last days of the Hickenlooper deadline to come to a decision. On April 5, the Saturday morning before the deadline, Kissinger phoned Nixon at the president's compound in Key Biscayne, Florida, to discuss the Peruvian situation. Kissinger informed Nixon that his advisers agreed on the usefulness of extending the deadline, but "we've got to have some excuse unless we just say that the negotiations . . . which have been going on for two weeks, and we'll give them another 30 days as a sign of leaning backwards." Nixon disagreed. "No, that won't do. I don't think that will do. My inclination is to give them more time than that. Have in mind the purpose is not to negotiate, but purpose is to fight. Line up the troops and go after them every which way we can. Maybe it will take three months." "Don't move it to his [Velasco's] timetable, that's for sure," said the president. Kissinger agreed, commenting, "IPC has been a lousy company, but that isn't the issue now." Nixon replied, "No, it sure isn't." Nixon postponed the imposition of sanctions until August 6, using IPC's tentative acceptance of the Peruvian terms for administrative appeal as the fig leaf.[53] Nixon thus extended the Hickenlooper deadline not because he "blinked" but in order to confront Velasco at a time of Nixon's choosing.

Nixon delayed in part because IPC's owners did not want sanctions prematurely imposed—Jersey Standard explicitly told the State Department that it *preferred* a long deferral, believing that "internal pressures will build and force moderation if sufficient time is allowed."[54] The only parties who wanted immediate sanctions were members of Congress. Jack Edwards (R-Alabama), for example, had entered the House during Goldwater's 1964 sweep of the Deep South. Edwards believed in the "knuckle" theory of geopolitics: "Neither Peru nor any other country is going to stop harassing the United States so long as we knuckle under to every outrage perpetuated on us, calling it a new and greater triumph. Let us use some commonsense in our dealings with other countries, for once."[55] Nixon made sure to keep Edwards in the loop so that he could "cool off congressional critics of deferral."[56] The president did not want legislators to mistake a tactical delay for capitulation.

On April 6, Irwin met with Nixon in Key Biscayne for an hour after the Nixon family attended Easter church services.[57] Irwin then returned to Peru to inform Velasco that IPC would accept the minister of finance's appeal process, rather than international arbitration, as the venue in which it would argue against the $690 million the Revolutionary Government demanded that IPC should pay for the value of oil it had extracted from Peruvian oil fields. On Monday, Secretary of State Rogers announced at a press conference that the appeal process and negotiations satisfied the Hickenlooper Amendment's requirement of "appropriate steps" toward compensation.[58]

By July 22, Nixon had agreed to a set of policies drafted by the National Security Council with regard to IPC. First, the United States would "continue to maintain non-overt economic pressures on Peru to provide a framework for settlement and constructive change." In practice, this translated into an unofficial suspension of international development lending to Peru. Second, the United States would "defer applying the Hickenlooper Amendment so long as any plausible basis to do so can be found." Third, Washington would "actively seek a basis for such deferral even beyond the end of the administrative appeal process."[59] The August 6 deadline of the Peruvian administrative appeal passed without incident. Two weeks later, the Peruvian government expropriated the last of IPC's assets. IPC continued to appeal through the Peruvian courts and to the Peruvian cabinet, even though further judicial appeals were unlikely to work: Velasco would replace all but two members of the Peruvian Supreme Court in December 1969, as well as create an executive council that could suspend or remove any judge. The United States exerted "non-overt" economic pressure on Peru to resolve the dispute, in the form of pressuring the World Bank and the Inter-American Development Bank to withhold or delay loans to Peru, while postponing bilateral aid projects to Peru.[60]

The Peruvian Settlements

It took some time, but Nixon's strategy ultimately made whole the American companies damaged by the Revolutionary Military Government. It is possible that if Velasco had stopped with IPC, then Peru might have been able to avoid paying compensation. President Velasco, however, did not stop with IPC. In August 1969—six months after it announced that IPC owed Peru $690 million—he nationalized the sugar industry. Most Peruvian sugar lands were domestically held, but W. R. Grace and Company held a substantial stake. In 1970, Peru opened negotiations with the Cerro Corporation over the sale of its copper assets. By 1973, it was clear to all observers Velasco intended to nationalize the copper mines, which he did in January 1974. All these investments enjoyed USAID insurance against capital controls; the United States did not, however, have an agreement with Peru that would have allowed USAID to offer expropriation insurance.[61]

In early 1973, Nixon bypassed the State Department in sending a negotiating team to Peru. He tapped James Greene, the senior vice president of Manufacturers Hanover Trust, to head negotiations. Greene had been responsible for negotiating large loans to the Peruvian government, and he knew both the Spanish language and the key players in the Peruvian government. Greene arrived in Lima on February 19, 1973, without the knowledge of the local U.S. embassy.[62] Greene had canvassed U.S. companies to collect their minimum acceptable compensation levels (see table 9.3). In some cases, those levels were significantly below the companies' claim before the Peruvian government. Cerro Corporation, for example, initially claimed that its investments were worth $175 million. In July 1972, it offered to sell its operations to the Peruvian government for $30 million in cash, $49 million in sales revenue over the next five years, a $96 million claim on profits over the next seven, and a management fee of $3.9 million for fifteen years.[63] At the 1972 ten-year rate on corporate bonds (7.2%), the net present value of this demand was $178 million.[64] When Greene inquired, however, Cerro reported that it would accept as little as $65 million.

How did Cerro Corporation arrive at $65 million? Cerro demanded and received market value plus a small premium for its assets. In 1971, Peru generated 40% of the company's net mining income: 40% of Cerro's market capitalization came to $58 million. (In 1972, Peru generated 45% of the net income: an equivalent calculation would have yielded $57 million.) Cerro's stock price was depressed, but so were the share prices of all the major copper companies, most of which had no exposure to Peru and relatively less to Chile (see figure 9.2).

Table 9.3

Peruvian expropriation settlements, thousands of current dollars

	Date of loss	Company claim	November 1973 minimum settlement	Share in lump sum	Individual payments	TOTAL
Brown and Root	1 Feb 1970	$1,234		$100		$100
Cargill Peruana, S.A.	7 May 1973	$4,724	$1,300	$1,300	$48	$1,348
Cerro Corp.	1 Jan 1974	$175,000	$65,000	$10,000	$58,000	$68,000
IPC: La Brea and Pariñas fields, Talara complex, 50% Lobitos refinery, Lima concession, marketing assets	9 Nov 1968 & 14 Feb 1969	$85,000	$20,000	$22,000		$22,000
General Mills	7 May 1973	$2,574	$1,100	$1,200		$1,200
Gold Kit S.A.	7 May 1973	$3,037	$1,800	$600	$2,242	$2,842
H. B. Zachry Co.	1 Feb 1979	$3,000	$1,000	$1,200		$1,200
International Proteins Co.	7 May 1973	$11,279	$8,600	$8,900		$8,900
Morrison-Knudsen	1 Feb 1970	$6,991	$2,000	$2,000		$2,000
Socal-Chevron in Conchan refinery	16 Jun 1972	$3,000	$2,000	$2,000		$2,000
Star-Kist	17 May 1973	$15,000	$7,175	$7,300	$1,318	$8,618
W. R. Grace and Co.	14 Feb 1974	$60,185	$20,000	$19,200	$2,805	$22,005
TOTAL		$371,024	$129,975	$75,800	$64,413	$140,213

Source: Victor Arnold and John Hamilton, "The Greene Settlement: A Study of the Resolution of Investment Disputes in Peru," Texas International Law Journal, vol. 13, no. 2 (Spring 1978), pp. 286–87.

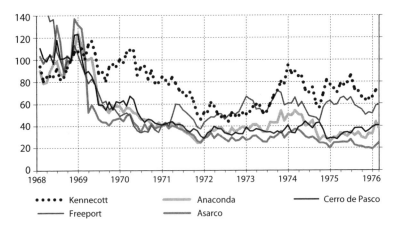

Figure 9.2 Indexed share prices for major copper companies, 1968–76 (October 31, 1968 = 100)

Source: New York Stock Exchange.

The ultimate settlement consisted of $76 million transferred by Peru to the U.S. government, which then doled it out to the claimants, and $64 million in payments made directly to the expropriated companies. Most of the companies received close to the reservation compensation that they reported to the U.S. government. IPC received what it claimed for its share in the Lobitos refinery, its unexplored concessions, and its retail distribution assets. The Peruvian government expressed public anger that the United States transferred $22 million to IPC, but it is hard to believe that the Peruvians were unaware that the U.S. government intended to transfer a portion of the settlement to IPC's owners.

Did IPC receive adequate compensation? In nominal terms, the company's average annual profit over the decade preceding the nationalization was $1.9 million. Given the riskiness of oil companies (small independent American oil companies had P/E ratios less than 5 in the early 1970s), $22 million appears more than fair. The problem is that such a calculation does not account for inflation. U.S. inflation was low in the 1960s, but it was not zero—in the decade between 1958 and 1967, the U.S.

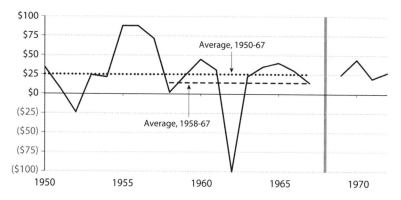

Figure 9.3 IPC annual earnings, 1950–72 (PetroPerú for 1969–72), millions of 2009 dollars

Source: IPC earnings calculated from data in Rosemary Thorp and Geoffrey Bertram, *Peru, 1890–1977: Growth and Policy in an Open Economy* (New York: Columbia University Press, 1978), p. 278. Depreciation and amortization estimated by the author, using a 9-year average for nonrefining investments and a 10-year average for refineries. PetroPerú earnings from "Economia politica de la privitización," *Revista de la Facultad de Ciencias Económicas de la UNMSM*, vol. 2, no. 2 (December 1996), pp. 13–50.

GDP deflator rose 24%. Moreover, compensation did not arrive until 1974, by which point American prices had risen a further 39%. Once inflation is taken into account, IPC's compensation came to 4.5 times its average annual earnings over the preceding ten years (see figure 9.3). This figure still exceeded the market value of a risky oil venture at the time—and it would be hard to argue, *ex ante* or *ex post*, that the company's Peruvian investments were not very high risk.

In short, the Nixon administration managed to extract a favorable settlement in the IPC dispute. It wielded a very credible threat of sanctions against Peru, since Peru needed support from the World Bank and International Monetary Fund (IMF) to keep its economy ticking. Congressional anger at the expropriations was strong; all sides knew that if the settlement did not satisfy the companies, sanctions would crush the Peruvian economy.

The CIA continued to play a role in investment disputes through the early 1970s. With Nixon increasingly insulated from the traditional methods of investor pressure on the executive branch—the State Department and congressional lobbyists—investors sought nontraditional channels. In the case of Chile, this channel was the Central Intelligence Agency.

CIA interference in Chilean politics was nothing new. In the 1964 Chilean presidential election, the CIA spent $3 million to ensure that Salvador Allende would lose, providing over half the Christian Democratic Party's campaign costs, and additionally producing twenty radio spots and an hour of television programming a day to saturate the Chilean media market with CIA propaganda efforts. These actions, however, were funded by the U.S. government. The CIA at that time *rejected* an offer of $1.5 million from a group of American businessmen in Chile to fund antigovernment activities.[65]

How did the CIA come to be more receptive to influence through nontraditional channels? In the case of Harold Geneen's ITT—whose operations in Chile were considerably more valuable than the unprofitable Brazil subsidiary whose expropriation led to the Hickenlooper Amendment several years earlier—there were three phases. John McCone, the CIA director who oversaw the agency's involvement in the 1964 Chilean elections, became a director of the board of ITT shortly after resigning from the CIA in 1965. In June 1970, the ITT board of directors discussed the possible consequences of an Allende victory. Afterward, McCone, who still acted as a consultant for the CIA, spoke several times with CIA director Jesse Helms about Chile. Intermediates carefully arranged a personal meeting between Geneen and William Broe, the chief of the CIA's Western Hemisphere Division, in the lobby of the Sheraton-Carlton Hotel in Washington, D.C., in the late evening of July 16, 1970. At this meeting, Geneen offered to fund anti-Allende efforts in Chile for the CIA. Broe declined, but offered to explain how ITT could channel its funds on its own to anti-Allende candidates, which ITT did. Allende was nonetheless elected on September 4, 1969.[66]

In the second phase, during the ITT board meeting immediately following Allende's election, Geneen privately told McCone that he was willing to spend $1 million to assist any U.S. plan to stop Allende. On September 11 and 12, McCone met with Kissinger and Helms to discuss Geneen's offer. McCone would later testify he received no reply. (This offer was also transmitted by more traditional lobbying techniques to Kissinger's staff, to the State Department, and, oddly enough, to the attorney general.) At the same time, Nixon was separately considering using the CIA to plan a coup d'état against Allende. On September 15, Nixon informed CIA director Helms of his decision.[67]

In the third phase, the CIA asked for ITT's help. On September 29, Broe met with ITT vice president Ned Garrity in New York to outline a dramatic plan for creating economic chaos in Chile in order to cause the Chilean Congress to vote against confirming Allende as president. Garrity cabled Geneen, then in Brussels, regarding the plan, including his doubts. Geneen spoke with McCone regarding its viability, both of them regretfully deciding it "would not fly." Broe contacted ITT several times again in the first week of October, sounding a more pessimistic note each time. On October 20, ITT's preferred candidate, Alessandri, withdrew from the election, and on October 24, the Chilean Congress confirmed Allende as the new Chilean president, 153 to 35.[68] At this point, ITT switched to a strategy of direct engagement with Chilean leaders, and its documented contacts with the CIA diminished—although the Allende government showed little sign of agreeing to ITT's demands, even under intense economic pressure from the United States.

Were these nontraditional channels of influence effective? It is certainly true that on September 11, 1973, the government of Chile under Salvador Allende was overthrown in a military coup with U.S. backing. It is also true that ITT attempted to influence the CIA—and, by extension, executive branch policy—twice through monetary aid, which was twice rejected. The executive branch then attempted to influence ITT to help cause economic chaos in Chile; ITT in turn rejected the executive branch's plan. The testimony delivered by ITT executives during Senate hearings suggests that ITT's attempts to influence U.S. foreign policy through its agencies slowed as ITT dealt with the Allende government more directly. Absence of evidence, however, is not evidence of absence, especially in the covert world.

If U.S. investor companies had a channel to the private-investment policy decisions of the executive branch, the price of their stock should quickly reflect this information. On the other hand, if no channel existed, one would expect no effect on the price of their stock. Dube, Kaplan, and Naidu found that putatively "secret" National Security Council meetings on the Chilean situation generated an average abnormal return of 1.45% over four days, rising to 3.04% over thirteen days for companies facing expropriation by the Allende government—even after documented contacts with the agency stopped.[69] It should come as no surprise that the Pinochet regime that overthrew Allende returned most of the expropriated properties and paid compensation in excess of pre-Allende market value for the ones that it did not, primarily copper mines.

The Venezuelan Exception?

The decision by President Carlos Andrés Pérez of Venezuela to nationalize the U.S.-owned oil companies in 1975 was remarkably uncontentious. Why did the Venezuelan decision to take American property attract so little political attention in the United States? The Ford administration could have taken a much more active stance against the takeover. In fact, the Ford administration did take an active role in obtaining compensation for American investors in Peruvian iron mines that were nationalized in the same year.[70] What made Venezuela different?

The answer, quite simply, is that the United States did not need to reach into its still formidable arsenal of coercive tools, because the Venezuelan government agreed to fairly compensate the oil companies from the beginning. In fact, many of the oil companies preferred nationalization to the alternatives. The reason is that under the Oil Act of 1943 all Venezuelan oil concessions were scheduled to expire in 1983.[71] The companies were not, therefore, negotiating over their right to enjoy income from their property; rather, they were negotiating over the returns that they would earn for an eight-year period between 1975 and 1983.

Compensation came in four ways. First, the companies received a lump-sum payment for their assets: $1.02 billion in nominal terms, or $3.25 billion in 2011 dollars.[72] Second, the companies received a fee per barrel for all oil produced that ranged from 16 cents to 19 cents (51 cents to 61 cents in 2011 dollars). Third, the companies received annual technology-licensing payments of 700 million bolívares, or $163 million ($520 million in 2011 dollars). Finally, the companies received marketing contracts to sell Venezuelan oil in international markets. Since Venezuelan oil was particularly heavy, it could only be refined in specialized facilities, most of which were located in the United States.[73]

Unsurprisingly, given these terms, per barrel revenues for the major oil companies that had been operating in Venezuela did not decline after nationalization (see figure 9.4). According to Osmel Manzano and Francisco Monaldi, "Former multinational oil executives interviewed argue that nationalization was at that point almost promoted by the oil multinationals. Their goal was to obtain lucrative distribution agreements that they thought would be more stable."[74] Those executives succeeded in their goals. In effect, Venezuela designed a nonexpropriation expropriation that guaranteed the oil companies their income for as long as their concessions would have lasted.

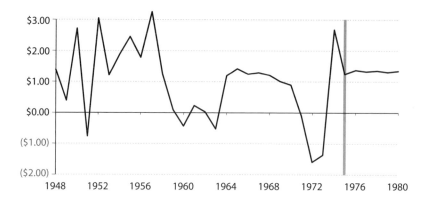

Figure 9.4 Operating income per barrel, private oil companies in Venezuela, 1948–80, 2009 dollars

Source: Data from Osmel Manzano and Francisco Monaldi, "The Political Economy of Oil Contract Renegotiation in Venezuela," in William Hogan and Federico Sturzenegger, eds., *The Natural Resources Trap: Private Investment Without Public Commitment* (Cambridge, Mass: MIT Press, 2010) , pp. 409-66, and George Philip, *Oil and Politics in Latin America: Nationalist Movements and State Companies* (Cambridge: Cambridge University Press, 1982), p. 475.

Note: Postnationalization revenues include the expropriation payments, calculated as the value of the compensation ($3.15 billion) multiplied by the short-term interest rate on ordinary funds. By this measure, the value of the expropriation payments came to approximately 19% of postnationalization revenue. The declines in profitability during the early 1960s and early 1970s had different causes. The early 1960s decline was due to the overvaluation of the bolívar; when it was devalued in 1964, operating costs fell and profits rebounded. The fall in the early 1970s was due mostly to increases in taxes.

The Second American Empire

The United States continued to defend—successfully—the property rights of its citizens whose property was outside the country. For a variety of idiosyncratic reasons, governments across the Third World chose to nationalize or partially nationalize foreign investments during the 1970s. In almost every case, the U.S. government had no strategic reason to oppose those nationalizations. Direct equity participation or ownership gave foreign governments no greater control over the actions of American companies than such governments already enjoyed. (Libya, for example, was quite capable of ordering American oil companies to cut output well before its government took equity stakes.)[75] It is true, as Stephen Krasner pointed out in *Defending the National Interest*, that where natural resources were concerned, the interests of foreign governments might not be the same as the interests of the United States. Foreign governments generally preferred higher prices, which was not in the interest of American consumers. But higher prices *were* in the interest of American raw materials producers. Inasmuch as foreign governments could collude to raise prices without fear of federal antitrust authorities, nationalization or participation was in the interest of American companies as long as they could retain some minimum interest in the marketing of the commodity. The profits earned from the Middle East by U.S. oil companies *after* nationalization demonstrate the point.

In cutting aid and threatening economic sanctions, postwar American governments followed the precedent set by Franklin Roosevelt. Some countries, however, were immune to these sanctions. If a country was openly allied with the Soviet Union, then it could resist most forms of American pressure. In addition small, rich oil producers such as Kuwait were relatively immune—as were African countries within the French sphere of influence, such as Mauritania. These exceptions, however, were few and far between, and even Kuwait offered compensation above a reasonable lower bound of the value of the expropriated firms.

The U.S. government defended American property rights even when strategic logic pointed in the other direction. This meant that U.S. policy toward Cuba helped drive Fidel Castro into the arms of the Soviet Union. U.S. policy toward Indonesia did the same with Sukarno and Communist China. Threats of economic sanctions also risked losing Ceylon and Peru, and the use of covert action threatened blowback all over the planet. Nevertheless, the United States continued to reach into its investor protection tool kit everywhere the Soviet bloc did not hold sway. It refrained from doing so only in cases, such as Venezuela, where it did not need to.

The world did not stand still during the Cold War, however. A series of mostly unplanned legal and institutional changes created a new technology that private investors could use to protect their property rights—*without* the need to lobby the U.S. government. These new institutions changed the logic of intervention in a way that obviated the empire trap. The next chapter explores these changes.

ten

Escaping by Design?

As the executive head of the nation, the President is made the only legitimate organ of the general government, to open and carry on correspondence or negotiations with foreign nations, in matters concerning the interests of the country or of its citizens. It is to him, also, the citizens abroad must look for protection of person and of property.

—*Justice Samuel Nelson, writing in*
Durand v. Hollins, 1860

The world of investor protection changed radically between 1945 and 1990. The changes were slow, incremental, and mostly unplanned. Their cumulative effect, however, was revolutionary. Before 1945, the only substantive recourse available to an American company caught in an investment dispute with a foreign government was to call on the coercive power of the U.S. executive branch. American courts were useless; sovereign immunity reigned supreme. The executive might threaten, sanction, or overthrow foreign governments, but U.S. courts would not enforce judgments against them. International tribunals existed but required the U.S. government to espouse the claims of its citizens and depended on executive action for enforcement.

By the 1990s, American investors had access to an array of mechanisms to protect their property rights that did *not* depend on executive discretion. Private investors could now take foreign governments to arbitration without the intervention of their home government. Those decisions were enforceable in domestic courts, not just of the United States, but of *any* country that signed the New York or Washington conventions. With the necessary legal infrastructure in place—which took two treaties, a federal law, and a Supreme Court decision—investors could potentially enforce their property rights without recourse to the State Department at all. A second set of reforms provided expropriation insurance to American companies. These programs began under the rubric of foreign aid, but the system was eventually regularized and placed under the Overseas Private Investment Corporation (OPIC). In the 1980s, the World Bank began to offer similar insurance and a private market eventually joined the government providers.

The system did not spring into place suddenly with the end of the Cold War. Arbitration treaties dated back to the Taft administration. The New York Convention of 1958 committed its signatories to the enforcement of cross-border commercial arbitrations. The 1965 Washington Convention established the International Centre for Settlement of Investment Disputes, providing a set of procedures by which investors could directly take sovereign states to arbitration. The González Amendment of 1971 and Trade Act of 1974 added teeth to the American commitment to arbitration. OPIC came into existence in 1971. The final prong of the system appeared under President Ford: the Foreign Sovereign Immunities Act of 1976 exempted the "commercial activities" of foreign states from sovereign immunity; U.S. investors could now file lawsuits against foreign governments in U.S. courts. Finally, in 1992 the Supreme Court ruled in *Argentine Republic v. Weltover* that the issuance of sovereign debt was a "commercial" function. The new tools combined with an effort by the Reagan administration to push foreign countries into signing "bilateral investment treaties" to create an entirely new world for foreign investors from the one they had faced previously. The empire trap was not so much escaped as superseded.

Guns, Lawyers, and Money

Before 1965, no standard legal remedy existed for a foreign company to bring suit against a national government. By definition, a sovereign state had no higher jurisdiction than itself. In nations that followed the Calvo Doctrine—primarily in Latin America—foreign investors lacked even diplomatic recourse in an expropriation dispute. Under Calvo, disputes between foreign investors and states had to follow the same judicial procedures as domestic disputes. Calvo himself was aware that this presented difficulties with regard to foreign investment, but he believed that foreign nationals should not have *greater* rights against a government than its own citizens.[1]

In practice, of course, the Calvo Doctrine meant little as far as American investors were concerned. American investors often included arbitration clauses in loan and concession contracts because they provided the U.S. government with an excuse to intervene if things went wrong. The Porter Convention of 1907 (part of the Hague Peace Conference) read: "The Contracting Powers agree not to have recourse to armed force for the recovery of contract debts claimed from the Government of one country by the Government of another country as being due to its nationals. *This undertaking is, however, not applicable when the debtor State refuses or neglects to reply to an offer of arbitration, or, after accepting the offer, prevents any compromise from being agreed on, or, after the arbitration, fails to submit to the award*" (italics added).[2] Investors and the U.S. government interpreted this as an excuse to impose sanctions (or use force) if a country refused arbitration. (Ironically, the recourse clause was never used; as previous chapters have shown, the United States found other means to intervene.)

Arbitration as it was practiced was not between foreign investors and the host state but between sovereign states, in which one acted as the representative of private interests against the other. The reason for this was simple: a contract between a foreign investor and a state was not—and still is not—an instrument of international law. With no enforcement, arbitration therefore could be ignored by the host state as an infringement on its national sovereignty, regardless of the contract. The limitations meant that as a tool, arbitration was little used and less effective.

Early Investor Arbitrations

Two major disputes between investors and states went to arbitration before 1965: *Lena Goldfields Limited v. USSR* and *Radio Corporation of America v. China*. Both actively involved the investors' home government. Lena Goldfields was a British company that obtained a gold-mining concession in Russia in 1908. In 1925, Moscow authorized a new concession, a quid pro quo for dropping Lena Goldfields's previous claims against the Soviet government. The new concession included an arbitration clause.[3] In December 1929, the OGPU—the precursor of the KGB—raided Lena Goldfields's offices. Its Moscow manager, a British national, was sentenced to hard labor, and the British ambassador had to directly intervene in order to secure his release. The board of Lena Goldfields decided to request arbitration under terms of its concession. Unsurprisingly, the United Kingdom agreed to espouse the claim. More surprisingly, the Soviet Union agreed. The British and Soviet governments put together a panel of British, German, and Soviet arbiters.

The Soviet Union did not behave in good faith. During the proceedings, Moscow conducted show trials of four employees of Lena Goldfields; their ultimate fate is unknown. The Soviets also claimed that Lena Goldfields had abandoned their concession. Finally, the Soviet arbiter and the Soviet Union withdrew from the proceedings midway. This left the British and German arbiters to decide in favor of Lena Goldfields to the sum of £13 million (roughly $800 million in 2011 dollars). In the decades following, it fell to the British government to attempt collection. It was not successful.[4]

The second case, *Radio Corporation of America v. China*, was more akin to modern investor-versus-state arbitration—but only in part.[5] The Radio Corporation of America (RCA) was founded in 1919 as a public corporation at the behest of the U.S. government in order to give U.S. electrical manufacturers incentives to develop wireless communications. The government (particularly the U.S. Navy) then pushed RCA to obtain a radio concession in China. RCA was reluctant, since its other Asian concessions operated at a loss. The problem for the United States was that all traffic between China and the United States, including official communications, had to go through British cables or German radio. RCA agreed to the navy's request and completed its transmitter in 1928.[6]

In 1932, another American firm, the Mackay Radio and Telegraph Company, signed a competing agreement with China to establish radio traffic between China and the United States. Mackay began transmitting in 1933. RCA believed that this represented a breach of contract between RCA and the Chinese government and held China liable for all of Mackay's profits and transmissions. The situation put the United States in a bind. In the face of escalating tensions in the Pacific, it was strategically vital that the United States maintain independent communications links with China. (The Japanese military viewed the Mackay transmitter with suspicion, as "it might be used to Japan's disadvantage in case of war.")[7] The United States also did not want to push China into a position that would complicate other aspects of U.S.-Chinese relations. Finally, the dispute involved a violation of the rights of one American company in order to benefit another American company. For the United States, the best solution was arbitration. The arbiter, Dr. J. A. van Hamel, the director of the Legal Section of the League of Nations, proposed to hold the tribunal at the Permanent Court of Arbitration in The Hague, not as a dispute "between states" under the Hague Convention but as a personal request with the permission of the League secretary-general.[8] The panel decided in favor of China in *Radio Corporation of America v. China*, finding that it did not break its contract with RCA.

These early, irregular cases are very far from clear-cut examples of investor-versus-state arbitration, although later jurists would cite them as precedents. When it was in the national interest of the *investor's* home government—and when special contract provisions so allowed—unique tribunals could be created. Without enforcement mechanisms, however, these tribunals were not very useful. (Lena Goldfields ultimately made out well because the *British* government ended up footing the bill for the company's settlement.) Sovereign debt contracts sometimes contained arbitration provisions, but in 1957 the jurist Georges Delaume dismissed these as "sham provisions."[9] The Permanent Court of Arbitration fell into stasis.[10] The International Court of Justice, established by the U.N. Charter, was a bit more active but its jurisdiction was limited to disputes between states. It accepted disputes involving foreign private entities when their home government espoused the claim.

The International Chamber of Commerce (ICC) in Paris handled disputes between private parties and states but it avoided expropriation cases. The ICC first arbitrated a case between a state and a private party in December 1922, when a private firm asked it to arbitrate a dispute with a Balkan state over an unpaid grain shipment during World War I. Between 1945 and 1965, the ICC arbitrated disputes between the Cuban government and a French auto importer, a Czech company and a state-owned French mining company, the Greek Health Ministry and a Danish manufacturer of lab equipment, the Indian government and a Swiss bank over infrastructure finance, a Bolivian state-owned bank and a German capital goods firm, and the city of Frankfurt and a Swedish manufacturer of prefabricated houses. In only one case did a losing state refuse to accept the ICC's decision.[11] The ICC arbitrations had two things in common. First, recourse to the ICC was in the original contract. Second, they were all arm's-length contractual disputes. The case that came closest to the sort of investment dispute that could drag sovereign states into conflict was the case between the Hyderabad Relief and Rehabilitation Trust and its Swiss financiers—but tiny Switzerland was highly unlikely to be sucked into an empire trap regarding the faraway and gigantic Republic of India.

In addition, there were a series of ad hoc arbitrations involving the interpretation of oil concessions in the Middle East, including Abu Dhabi, Qatar, Saudi Arabia, and Iran. As David Yackee has pointed out, in several of these cases the arbiters asserted their authority over governmental arguments that "questions affecting the exercise of the sovereign rights of a State are, by their very nature, incapable of being 'the subject matter of arbitration.' "[12] None of the Middle Eastern cases, however, involved expropriation. The Abu Dhabi case determined that an onshore concession did not cover the continental shelf; the Qatari case decided that the concession was enforceable under Islamic law; the Saudi case decided that the Aramco concession prohibited the Saudi government from granting Aristotle Onassis's shipping company a "right of priority" over moving Saudi oil; and the Iranian case asked whether a small Canadian oil company had complied with its agreement to invest $18 million in petroleum exploration and production in return for a 25% profit share.[13]

Avoiding the Empire Trap: The Origin of ICSID

Dissatisfaction with this state of affairs became general in the postwar period. In 1953, the ICC recognized its limits and proposed at the Lisbon conference a stronger system of recognition and enforcement to replace the toothless interwar conventions. The United Nations took over the ICC's proposal and, with modifications, passed it in 1958 as the Convention on the Recognition and Enforcement of Foreign Arbitral Awards, more commonly known as the New York Convention. Under the New York Convention, an arbitration award issued in any state could now be enforced by the courts of any other signatory state. The New York Convention, however, applied only to the enforcement of arbitration between private investors of different nationalities. It was not intended to apply to the enforcement of awards against sovereign states.[14]

In the late 1950s, the Organisation for European Economic Co-operation, which in 1961 was superseded by the trans-European Organisation for Economic Co-operation and Development (OECD), tried to create a multilateral convention to set common standards on the treatment of foreign property. This became the OECD's Draft Convention on the Protection of Foreign Property of 1962.[15] The convention failed to pass, however, because the OECD's less-developed economies—Greece, Turkey, and Portugal—objected. In the late 1950s, less-developed nations had generally refused to accept norms of foreign property protection. Even capitalist NATO members rejected them, let alone the newly independent states emerging from the wreckage of the European empires.

Accordingly, investor-versus-state disputes threatened to spiral into international incidents. After Cuba, Ceylon, and Indonesia, a North African dispute erupted and once again took on Cold War significance—even though no American properties were involved. In 1964, Tunisia nationalized 500,000 hectares of French agricultural properties. France responded by pulling $20 million in annual aid, derailing a further $22 million in private loans, and canceling the country's preferential access to the European Economic Community.[16] (There were also veiled military threats, at a time when France was heavily involved in sub-Saharan Africa.) The Johnson administration worried that the French action could have the effect of driving Tunisia into the hands of the Soviet bloc, giving the USSR a naval base in the Mediterranean. It therefore stepped into the gap, replacing French transfers with increased American aid. Johnson was fortunate that the former French Empire was not popular in the United States.[17]

The immediate impetus for the formation of a reliable and standardized system of arbitration for investor-versus-state disputes, however, was not Tunisia—once again, it was Cuba. In September 1961, the American president of the World Bank, Eugene Black, made the initial proposal for what would become the International Centre for Settlement of Investment Disputes (ICSID). Black spoke at the annual meeting of the World Bank's board of governors, held that year in the Hofburg Palace in Vienna: "Our experience has confirmed my belief that a very useful contribution would be made by some sort of special forum for the conciliation or arbitration of these [investor-state] disputes. I therefore intend to explore with other institutions and with our member governments whether something might not be done to promote the establishment of machinery of this kind."[18] The bank itself would formulate a convention on investment disputes and broker it to national governments. This was an unusual role, although Black had recently overseen the successful Indus Waters Treaty between India and Pakistan through the World Bank.[19]

The primary architect of the ICSID Convention, Aron Broches, the general counsel for the World Bank, realized that any convention on investor-versus-state disputes would have to concentrate on procedural issues rather than the substantive law of foreign investment.[20] The standards of investor protection were therefore kept to a minimum. To ensure the convention had as wide a consensus as possible, the World Bank scheduled four consultative meetings in Addis Ababa, Santiago de Chile, Geneva, and Bangkok, to hear legal experts from eighty-six countries.[21] Even in Latin America, where the Calvo Doctrine held sway, the legal reaction to the draft was "doubtful" but not unfavorable.[22] At the World Bank's annual meeting in Tokyo in September 1964, the board of governors resolved to finalize the draft and submit it to national governments.

The meeting produced a document known as the Washington Convention, officially titled the Convention on the Settlement of Investment Disputes between States and Nationals of Other States. The Washington Convention did not set up an international institution per se—that would have been a bridge too far for most of the states that Black (and the Johnson administration) wanted to bring on board. Rather, the convention set up a series of procedures under which a foreign investor could bring a state to arbitration over an investment dispute. Once a dispute went to arbitration, the Washington Convention prevented either party from unilaterally withdrawing. ICSID's secretary-general—an appointee of the World Bank—had a "gatekeeper" function, in that he or she could disqualify a dispute.

The convention allowed the parties to a dispute to decide to handle their arbitrations however they would like—but if they could not agree, it laid down a series of default rules. Tribunals would consist of three judges, one appointed by each party and the third by agreement. If no agreement was forthcoming, the secretary-general would appoint the arbiters. The arbitration could take place wherever the parties wanted, but without agreement it would take place in Washington, D.C.[23] All signatories would enforce awards—in fact, they would be legally required to treat awards as if they were final judgments issued by domestic courts.[24] The one loophole was in Article 55: "Nothing in Article 54 shall be construed as derogating from the law in force in any contracting State relating to immunity of that State or of any foreign State from execution."[25]

The twists and turns of the ratification process indicate that few, if any, of the parties involved foresaw ICSID's ability to protect states from intervention on the part of stronger nations. For one thing, a group of members from nineteen Latin American nations (plus the Philippines) dissented from the majority, stating that the convention was "contrary to the accepted legal principles of our countries." This would become known as "El no de Tokio."[26] Ironically, but not coincidentally, the Latin American nations (again with the Philippines) were also the countries most vulnerable to U.S. pressure. Their governments feared that any chink in the armor of the Calvo Doctrine would enable more U.S. intervention, not less. It would be very difficult domestically for them to justify junking long-standing doctrines that denied the United States *any* right to intervene in their countries—even if those doctrines had proved valueless in the crunch. In other words, the nations with the most to gain from the Washington Convention were the ones who rejected it.

A second irony came from the United States, where the Washington Convention had an easy ratification process. Both those who supported retaliation in the case of expropriation of American property and those who opposed it believed that the new arbitration procedures would further their aims. Liberals believed that the convention would reduce pressures on the U.S. government to go to bat for American investors whenever they ran into trouble with a foreign government. Conservatives believed that the organization would further protect American property rights overseas, without compromising the sovereignty of the United States. The Senate held hearings before the Committee on Foreign Relations in the spring of 1966. Senator Wayne Morse (D-Oregon) was enthusiastic that the convention would defuse international tension over investment disputes.[27] Senator George Aiken (R-Vermont) was more hard-nosed about the practicalities. Aiken asked Undersecretary of the Treasury Joseph Barr specifically about the Hickenlooper Amendment: "Wouldn't this [ICSID] permit the case to get into court for arbitration and, perhaps, get around our requirement that aid be suspended in that country?"[28] Barr responded in the affirmative, pointing out that arbitration would be in fact an "appropriate step" under the Hickenlooper Amendment. Aiken, believing that the Washington Convention would protect American property, did not object. The U.S. Senate ratified the convention on May 16, 1966, by a vote of 72 to 0, including Senator Bourke Hickenlooper (R-Iowa), even though all involved knew—*because they had been told so during the debates*—that the convention's proponents believed that it would insulate the U.S. government from investor pressure and provide an excuse to postpone Hickenlooper sanctions.[29]

The U.S. domestic legislation to enable the Washington Convention passed equally smoothly. On May 21, 1966, the secretary of the treasury submitted to the House and Senate the Convention on the Settlement of Investment Disputes Act. This legislation would enter the award obligations of the ICSID Convention into domestic law. Senate hearings on the act were perfunctory, and it passed by acclamation on July 19, 1966.[30] The House, however, brought up its concerns in discussions regarding this legislation. Representative Donald Fraser (D-Minnesota) asked the State Department's deputy legal adviser, Andreas Lowenfeld, specifically about U.S. oil companies in Peru. "Is that the kind of dispute that would be amenable to this procedure? This involved a threatened executive action rather than a judicial question, I gather."[31] (The answer was affirmative.) Representative Albert Johnson (R-Pennsylvania) openly wondered if *Cuba* could be brought into the ICSID Convention, perhaps by the Red Cross: "I just bring this up in the hope that Mr. Castro will hear of what we are talking about this morning and that he will finally 'get financial religion' and come forth to pay the unfortunate investors in America whose investments have been confiscated by Cuba."[32] The disputes in Ceylon and Indonesia also occupied the minds of the committee—Representative H. R. Gross (R-Iowa) was one of several who mentioned them, although Gross went on to conclude the hearings by badgering the general counsel of the Treasury Department about the British spelling of "Centre."[33] The act passed the House by acclamation on August 1, 1966.[34]

The Washington Convention went into effect one month after the twentieth country deposited its ratification. On August 23, 1965, Nigeria became the first nation to ratify; on September 14, 1966, Broches's home country of the Netherlands made the twentieth. Fifteen of the center's founding twenty nations were African, including Tunisia and Mauretania. The convention went into force on October 14, 1966.

The new nations of Africa signed up relatively quickly (see figure 10.1). Remarkably, the motives of the United States aligned with those of the postcolonial governments of Africa. The African governments wanted to reassure foreign investors that their financial interests would be protected while retaining the right to expropriate when in the national interest (or the

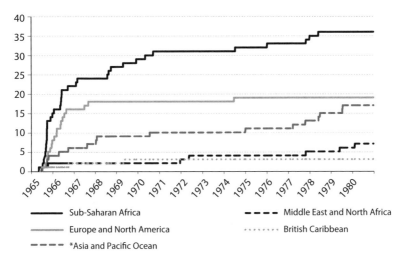

40
35
30
25
20
15
10
5
0

1965 1966 1967 1968 1969 1970 1971 1972 1973 1974 1975 1976 1977 1978 1979 1980

——— Sub-Saharan Africa   – – – Middle East and North Africa
▬▬▬ Europe and North America   ········· British Caribbean
– – – *Asia and Pacific Ocean

Figure 10.1 Numbers of ICSID member nations, by region, 1965–81
   Source: International Centre for Settlement of Investment Disputes.

political interest of the particular group in power). The United States wanted to reduce the political costs of investment disputes between aggrieved American investors and friendly African governments. Fighting Soviet influence in Africa was difficult enough; there was no need to repeat the U.S. experience in Latin America. Both the Africans and the Americans, meanwhile, wanted to see the remnants of the European empires wrapped up with minimal fuss. By providing a set of procedures for handling investor-versus-state disputes, implicitly backed by the authority (and resources) of the World Bank, ICSID provided a way for a European government *that wanted to take it* to gracefully back away from the need to protect colonial-era investments against the desires of the newly independent governments.

The Origins of the Bilateral Investment Treaty

The bilateral investment treaty (BIT) was another institution that the United States repurposed as a legal alternative to intervention. A BIT spelled out exactly which investments and classes of investments would have recourse to ICSID or other forms of international arbitration without the need for a specific clause in a concession. In addition, it spelled out exactly what would and what would not be considered expropriation. "Fiscal stability clauses," for example, specified allowable tax changes. BITs were not a requirement for a private investor to have recourse to ICSID—a concession contract could be sufficient if it contained a provision allowing for arbitration—but as time passed they proved to be a valuable buttress to the newly standardized practice of investor-versus-state arbitration.

As it happened, the first BITs had nothing whatsoever to do with the United States. In fact, the first three dozen or so bilateral investment treaties were promoted by countries that had virtually no capacity to sanction governments that appropriated their nationals' assets (see table 10.1). West Germany signed the first BIT with Pakistan in November 25, 1959, and it barely had an independent foreign policy of any sort. It would not become a major source of foreign aid until the 1970s. Between NATO restrictions and the limitations of West Germany's own Basic Law, the German government could not, under any circumstances, protect its investors outside its borders without upsetting the entire postwar world order. German investors, however, wanted to invest abroad—but they also wanted protection. The Federal Republic therefore pursued a diplomatic solution. It was the least Bonn could do, given that without enforcement, a bilateral investment treaty was not worth much more than the paper upon which it was written; but it was also the most Bonn could do, given the constraints on West Germany. The West German government, it should be noted, was also a pioneer in introducing government-provided expropriation insurance in 1959, around the same time as it began to sign bilateral investment treaties.[35]

Other small countries with little or no intervention capacity followed the same logic: if a country lacked the ability to sanction foreign nations, it could at least make a bid for the moral

Table 10.1
Chronological list of bilateral investment treaties, 1959–65

Investor	Host Country	Year	Investor	Host Country	Year
West Germany	Pakistan	1959	Switzerland	Liberia	1963
West Germany	Dominican Republic	1959	Switzerland	Cameroon	1963
West Germany	Malaysia	1960	West Germany	Sri Lanka	1963
West Germany	Greece	1961	West Germany	Tunisia	1963
Switzerland	Tunisia	1961	West Germany	Sudan	1963
West Germany	Togo	1961	Italy	Guinea	1964
West Germany	Thailand	1961	Switzerland	Togo	1964
West Germany	Liberia	1961	West Germany	Senegal	1964
West Germany	Morocco	1961	West Germany	Niger	1964
Switzerland	Niger	1962	Switzerland	Madagascar	1964
Switzerland	Côte d'Ivoire	1962	Belgium	Tunisia	1964
Switzerland	Guinea	1962	West Germany	South Korea	1964
West Germany	Cameroon	1962	Switzerland	Tanzania	1965
Switzerland	Congo	1962	Switzerland	Malta	1965
Switzerland	Senegal	1962	West Germany	Sierra Leone	1965
West Germany	Guinea	1962	Switzerland	Costa Rica	1965
West Germany	Turkey	1962	West Germany	Ecuador	1965
West Germany	Madagascar	1962	Netherlands	Cameroon	1965
Switzerland	Rwanda	1963	Netherlands	Côte d'Ivoire	1965
Netherlands	Tunisia	1963	Sweden	Côte d'Ivoire	1965

Source: Zachary Elkins, Andrew Guzman, and Beth Simmons, "Competing for Capital: The Diffusion of Bilateral Investment Treaties, 1960–2000," *International Organization*, vol. 60 (Fall 2006), pp. 811–46: 816.

suasion of an investment treaty. Switzerland signed its first BIT with Tunisia in 1961, the Netherlands signed its first also with Tunisia in 1963, Belgium with Tunisia yet again in 1964, and Sweden with Côte d'Ivoire in 1965.[36] The treaties tended to be between unlikely investment pairs that lacked historical connection—Switzerland and Rwanda had few historical links, for example—which also meant that they had few long-standing informal ties that could give investors some degree of certainty against governmental opportunism.

The European treaties provided a template for Washington. The United States initially resisted BITs, believing them unnecessary.

Memorandums on their use floated around the State Department during the Carter administration, but it was not until Ronald Reagan entered the White House that the United States decided to make use of the institution. Shortly after his inauguration, President Reagan approved an interagency program between the State Department and the Office of the United States Trade Representative, with input from the Departments of Commerce and the Treasury, to pursue the development of a template for a standard U.S. bilateral investment treaty. In less than a year, the drafters revised the boilerplate "Friendship, Commerce, and Navigation" treaties used by the United States along the lines of a European-style BIT. There was, however, one difference between U.S. BITs and their European predecessors. European BITs generally allowed the receiving country to restrict the repatriation of profits and impose entry and performance requirements; U.S. BITs generally did not.[37] The United States signed its first BIT on September 29, 1982, with Egypt.[38] Panama followed shortly thereafter.[39] (See table 10.2.)

The Reagan administration conceived of the BITs as a way to reaffirm investor protection in states that *already* protected U.S. investment. Giving U.S. investors in those states automatic access to ICSID was an added bonus. As a result, the United States made few concessions during negotiations. In the words of Kenneth Vandevelde, the official charged with negotiating BITs at State's Office of the Legal Adviser, "If partner was unwilling to accept the substance of the agreement as proposed, then in the United States' view it did not have the policy towards foreign investment that the BIT was intended to reflect, and negotiation . . . would therefore be undesirable."[40] The BITs also codified compensation for expropriation as "the fair market value of the property as of the date of expropriation, including interest from the date of expropriation to the date of payment." When market values were not available, the discounted cash flow method was used, or the investment was compared with comparable ones for which market values existed.[41]

Table 10.2

United States bilateral investment treaties, 1982–2012

Investor	Host Country	Year	Investor	Host Country	Year
Egypt	29 Sep 82	27 Jun 92	Belarus	15 Jan 94	Not ratified
Panama	27 Oct 82	30 May 91	Jamaica	4 Feb 94	7 Mar 97
Senegal	6 Dec 83	25 Oct 90	Georgia	7 Mar 94	17 Aug 97
Haiti	13 Dec 83	Not ratified	Estonia	19 Apr 94	27 Jun 92
Zaire (later DRC)	3 Aug 84	28 Jul 89	Trinidad	26 Sep 94	26 Dec 96
Morocco	22 Jul 85	29 May 91	Mongolia	6 Oct 94	1 Jan 97
Cameroon	26 Feb 86	6 Apr 89	Uzbekistan	16 Dec 94	Not ratified
Bangladesh	12 Mar 86	25 Jul 89	Albania	11 Jan 95	4 Jan 98
Grenada	2 May 86	3 Mar 89	Latvia	13 Jan 95	26 Dec 96
Poland	21 Mar 90	6 Aug 94	Honduras	1 Jul 95	11 Jul 01
Tunisia	15 May 90	7 Feb 93	Nicaragua	1 Jul 95	Not ratified
Ukraine	4 Mar 91	16 Nov 96	Croatia	13 Jul 96	20 Jun 01
Czech Republic	22 Oct 91	20 Jun 01	Jordan	2 Jul 97	12 Jun 03
Slovakia	22 Oct 91	19 Dec 92	Azerbaijan	1 Aug 97	2 Aug 01
Argentina	14 Nov 91	20 Oct 94	Lithuania	14 Jan 98	22 Nov 01
Sri Lanka	20 Nov 91	1 May 93	Bolivia	17 Apr 98	6 Jun 01
Kazakhstan	19 May 92	12 Jan 94	Mozambique	1 Dec 98	3 Mar 05
Romania	28 May 92	15 Jan 94	El Salvador	10 Mar 99	Not ratified
Russia	17 Jun 92	Not ratified	Bahrain	29 Sep 99	30 May 01
Armenia	23 Sep 92	29 Mar 96	Pakistan	28 Sep 04	Not ratified
Bulgaria	23 Sep 92	2 Jun 94	Uruguay	4 Nov 05	1 Nov 06
Kyrgyzstan	19 Jan 93	12 Jan 94	Rwanda	19 Feb 08	1 Jan 12
Moldova	21Apr 93	25 Nov 94	Congo	12 Jan 90	13 Aug 94
Ecuador	27 Aug 93	11 May 97	(Brazzaville)		

Source: U.S. Department of Commerce, Trade Compliance Center, http://tcc.export.gov/Trade_Agreements/Bilateral_Investment_Treaties/index.asp, accessed August 20, 2012.

(Not coincidentally, those are the three methods used to evaluate compensation payments in this book.) Moreover, BITs prevented American investors from asking the U.S. government for support once an ICSID arbitral decision had been made.[42]

Why did the Carter administration propose and the Reagan administration push forward the BITs? According to Kenneth Vandevelde, the first goal was to "reaffirm that the protection of United States foreign investment remained an important element of United States foreign policy."[43] The second goal, in conjunction with ICSID, was that by "providing the investor with a legal remedy that did not depend upon espousal [by the U.S. government], these BIT provisions depoliticized investment disputes. That is, they placed investment protection in the realm of law rather than politics."[44]

Money for Nothing:
The Origins of Investment Guarantees

The investment guarantee program did not begin as a way to protect American companies from expropriation. Rather, it began as a way to protect American companies against European capital controls. The United States wanted to promote Western European recovery after the war. It therefore wanted to encourage American investment, but it also wanted to allow European governments the option of imposing temporary capital controls whenever the need to maintain economic stability required it. Such controls, however, interfered with the ability of American companies to freely repatriate their profits. The 1948 legislation that enabled the Marshall Plan therefore included provisions for the Investment Guaranty Program (IGP), under which the U.S. government agreed to cover the risk that Western European nations would impose capital controls. In the event, the IGP would compensate investors in fifteen European nations until such time as controls were lifted.

As Europe recovered, the Truman and Eisenhower administrations expanded the IGP's geographic remit. The Mutual Security Act of 1951 allowed the program to be expanded to underdeveloped "areas."[45] Participation in the program required Senate approval of a reciprocal agreement with the government of the country in question. The Senate approved participation for Taiwan, Greece, the Philippines, Turkey, and Yugoslavia in 1952; the State Department negotiated agreements with Colombia, Ethiopia, and Israel.[46] By 1955, participation in the program had expanded to Bolivia, Ecuador, Haiti, Honduras, Paki-

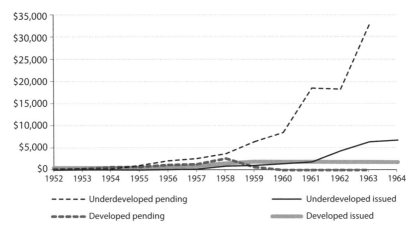

Figure 10.2 Investment guarantees issued and pending, 1952–64, millions of 2009 dollars

Source: Calculated from data in United States, *Mutual Security Program, Non-Regional Programs*, fiscal years 1957, 1958, and 1959; and Marina von Neumann Whitman, *Government Risk-Sharing in Foreign Investment* (Princeton, N.J.: Princeton University Press, 1965), pp. 94–95.

Note: The figures include expropriation, convertibility, and war insurance. Separate figures for each category are only available for 1955, 1956, and 1957.

stan, Paraguay, and Thailand, although actual commitments were small.[47] Investors were not yet particularly interested in expropriation insurance.

Interest in expropriation insurance peaked in two waves.[48] The first major wave of applications came in 1956, when interest suddenly tripled (see figure 10.2). The wave was driven by the Suez debacle, after which American investors in European colonial territories began to doubt the longevity of the remaining European empires. Insurance applications for projects in French West Africa constituted *all* the increase in pending investment guarantees for underdeveloped countries in 1956.[49] (Under U.K. policy, British dependent territories were not eligible for the program until they achieved full independence.) Applications then steadily increased through 1960, coming mainly from Iran, Turkey, and various African countries.

The second wave arrived in 1961—coinciding with the failure of the Bay of Pigs and Castro's subsequent alignment with the Soviet bloc. Applications again skyrocketed, this time from Latin America. The rise in demand should not be surprising. USAID charged only 0.5% per year of the value of the investment.[50] In fact, insurance was even cheaper: in any given year an investor could reduce the amount covered without affecting the ability to raise coverage back to the initially authorized level.[51] Moreover, Congress defined expropriation very broadly:

> Any abrogation, repudiation, or impairment by a foreign government of its own contract with an investor, where such abrogation, repudiation, or impairment is not caused by the investor's own fault or misconduct, and materially adversely affects the continued operation of the project.[52]

By 1963 further agreements had been ratified with Afghanistan, Costa Rica, El Salvador, Guatemala, India, Iran, Jamaica, Jordan, Liberia, Malaya, Nicaragua, Nigeria, Panama, Peru, Sierra Leone, South Korea, South Vietnam, Tunisia, and Venezuela.[53] (Brazil joined in 1965, and the United States began to guarantee investments in Argentina without a properly ratified agreement in 1963.)[54] The program moved around from agency to agency, starting with the Export-Import Bank, then moving to the Mutual Security Agency, the International Cooperation Agency, and the Foreign Operations Administration of the State Department, before settling with USAID in 1962.[55]

The program failed to meet the demand. Authorizations lagged applications, and the backlog continued to grow. After a brief burst of activity, approvals slowed dramatically when the program was transferred to USAID. In theory, guarantees were available to any American-owned company that invested in a new project in an area with an agreement with the United States.[56] (Guarantees were limited to undeveloped countries after 1962.) The problem was that USAID had broad leeway in determining which projects were eligible. In the words of a contemporary observer, writing in 1964: "AID, unfortunately, has not seen fit to apprise the investment community of the considerations that actually motivate its decisions."[57] Another wrote, "The vague criteria now available do not offer adequate basis for predicting the disposition of [an] application."[58]

The main factor slowing the application of investment guarantees appears to have been the fact that the program was run out of USAID, a State Department agency with conflicting mandates. First, the Foreign Assistance Act of 1961 mandated that guarantees would only go to investments that "furthered the development of the economic resources and productive capacities of less developed friendly countries and areas." USAID appears to have taken that mandate quite seriously, slowing the approval process. Second, there was no small amount of nervousness on the part of State Department officials that an American investor with a government guarantee might "conduct himself in such a way as to become unpopular with the local government or the people."[59] This created an institutional reluctance to grant any but the safest guarantees. Finally, USAID required that the host government specifically and explicitly approve any investment receiving a guarantee.[60] Many foreign governments (especially in Latin America) were reluctant to make such declarations, since the law mandated that should a guarantee be exercised, the U.S. government would take possession of the investment and enter into arbitration with the host government. Defying a state-versus-state arbitration with the United States at the peak of its power was not a step that any Latin American government wanted to take lightly. They understandably tightly scrutinized all investment projects under the program, further slowing the issuance of new guarantees.

Seeking Profit, Not Adventurism:
The Overseas Private Investment Corporation

It would be Richard Nixon, fresh from the expropriation crisis in Peru, who would regularize the provision of investment guarantees. On May 28, 1969, President Nixon proposed to Congress a "fresh approach" to the question of foreign aid. First and foremost was "the establishment of the Overseas Private Investment Corporation [OPIC]." This government-owned corporation was to bring a "businesslike management" to the United States' system of insurance and guaranties for overseas investment, using the insurance industry's expertise to sell political risk insurance. Nixon noted to Congress that OPIC was "expected to break even or to show a small profit."[61]

Nixon's proposal was not a reaction to the Peruvian crisis, though it was timed to take advantage of it. A Republican plan for a corporation to handle investment risk insurance outside USAID had been in the works since the Johnson administration, spearheaded by Senator Jacob Javits (R–New York). Javits criticized the USAID program not because he was opposed to foreign aid or political risk insurance—rather, he believed both to be "indispensable to the public policy of the United States"— but because he was dissatisfied with the program's inconsistent administration and slow growth. Under Javits's sponsorship, the Foreign Assistance Act of 1966 created an International Private Investment Advisory Council within USAID, which convened a panel of business leaders for their suggestions.[62] In 1968, Javits called for a federally charted corporation to "mobilize and facilitate the use of U.S. private capital and skills in less-developed friendly countries and areas." Javits's amendment was rejected, 12 votes in favor versus 65 against.[63] At the same time, however, USAID's Investment Council published an advisory report, which coincided with Javits's proposal. The head of Nixon's transition team, future chairman of the Federal Reserve Board Arthur Burns, included the council's proposal among the "early action" recommendations presented to

Nixon before his inauguration. Nixon reviewed the matter in February 1969.[64]

The amendment that created OPIC in fact nearly died in the Senate Foreign Relations Committee, where Senator J. William Fulbright (D-Arkansas) blocked it from inclusion in the Foreign Assistance Act of 1969.[65] Javits, aided by support from inside the National Security Council, set out to line up enough votes from both parties to pass the bill as a floor amendment. As Javits's special assistant for economic affairs later recounted, "The influence of a committed and influential Senator in securing the Congressional passage of legislation which he considers 'his baby' cannot be overemphasized."[66] On December 12, 1969, Javits brought the amendment to the floor, where bipartisan approval overcame bipartisan opposition, 53 to 34 (Fulbright voted no).[67] President Nixon signed the Foreign Assistance Act containing Javits's amendment on December 31, 1969.[68] OPIC began operation on January 19, 1971.[69]

OPIC raised concerns that it might lead to *more* intervention rather than less. On September 4, 1973, a week before the Chilean coup against Salvador Allende, a Congressional Research Service report concluded that "a major foreign policy consideration of OPIC involvement in investment disputes is the chance of direct government-to-government conflict over subrogated assets. To date this has not happened. However, OPIC currently holds assets of four companies expropriated by the Government of Chile, the Sudan, and Haiti. Those rights could be pursued at any time. If either or both the ITT and Anaconda claims are arbitrated in favor of the companies, OPIC says it will 'vigorously pursue' its subrogation rights in Chile. Such action could lead to new political problems between the United States and the government of Chile."[70]

In the wake of the coup against Allende, OPIC appeared to Senator Frank Church (D-Idaho) to create its own form of the empire trap. The United States, as the underwriter of expropriation insurance, would naturally want to act in such a way as to not pay off expropriation claims—and it could do so by overthrowing a government that expropriated American companies and installing one more compliant to American investor wishes. Similar worries had come up during the initial debates over expanding the Mutual Security Act to cover war damages, when Senator Walter George (D-Georgia) openly worried that companies losing money abroad would organize insurrections simply to collect the guarantee.[71] Senator George's worries, however, were different from Church's. George worried that companies might abuse government insurance programs for their profit; Church worried that the U.S. government might abuse such programs for its *own* profit.

Senator Church's reasoning was only partially correct. It assumed that the executive branch would choose to use its own profit motive as its proximate cause to intervene in a foreign country. What Church overlooked, however, was that it was now the executive branch's *choice* to do so. OPIC insulated the president from the lobbying of investors abroad by assuming their political risk. The executive branch could then decide for reasons of state, not reasons of domestic business, how to respond to the expropriating country. Very few American presidents have viewed the United States government as a for-profit venture—and compared with the federal budget, the sums at risk were chump change. In short, as Charles Lipson astutely pointed out, OPIC was "effectively shielded from any larger foreign policy goals" *by design.*[72]

Sanctions and the González Amendments

By the end of Nixon's first term, the mechanisms by which the U.S. government would eventually escape the empire trap were mostly in place. The arbitration procedures contained in the Washington Convention provided a way to postpone imposing Hickenlooper sanctions. OPIC provided a way to insure American companies against expropriation—and a backdoor route to state-to-state arbitration of the type Nixon effectively employed in Peru. What was needed, however, was an enforcement mechanism. Institutions deliberately designed to delay action were all well and good, but they needed to be credible if they were to succeed at their political purpose.

The first solution to the enforcement problem came from an unlikely source: a liberal Democratic member of Congress from San Antonio named Henry González. Born in Texas in 1916 to parents who had fled the destructiveness of the Mexican Revolution, González worked his way through college and law school before being drafted to serve as a military censor during World War II. Upon his return to civilian life, he became a probation officer, a reformist member of the San Antonio City Council, and in 1956 a state senator—where he and State Senator Abraham Kazen held marathon filibusters to kill bills aimed at circumventing *Brown v. Board of Education.* In 1961, he became the first Mexican-American congressional representative from the state of Texas. In Congress, González retained his reputation as an outspoken liberal. In 1963, Representative Ed Foreman (R-Texas) called González a "pinko" on the House floor, provoking a confrontation that almost ended in both men being ejected. (In 1986, at the age of seventy and still serving in the House, González punched a man in the face in a San Antonio diner for calling him a "Communist.") Nor did González have any love for oil companies: in fact, he ran for governor in 1958 on the platform of imposing a pipeline tax.

While González might have been very liberal, he was still a Texan, and he received no satisfaction from seeing foreign governments seize American property without what he considered due process. The Senate version of the bills authorizing the expansion of the Inter-American Development Bank, the Asian Development Bank, and International Development Association made no reference to expropriation.[73] Predictably, given its Latin American focus, the Inter-American Bank bill came under fire by pro-Hickenlooper senators of both parties. Harry Byrd (D-Virginia) complained, "There is nothing in the act that would restrict the directors of that Bank from making loans to

Chile, though Chile has just expropriated American property and refused to pay the owners of the property that they have taken."[74] Bill Brock (R-Tennessee) cried, "I saw Brazil expropriate the telephone company in 1963, if I remember correctly. I remember the action of the Peruvian government and, even more recently, the actions of Chile. I simply cannot understand why the State Department or this government itself continues to allow the United States to be made a patsy, in effect, by those who have no regard for international law in the application of their government processes."[75] Nevertheless, the three bills passed the Senate handily: the Inter-American Bank bill by 49 to 31;[76] the Asian Bank bill on a voice vote;[77] and the International Development Association bill by 49 to 34.[78]

As the chair of the House Subcommittee on International Finance, González inserted Hickenlooper-like language into all three 1971 multilateral development banking bills. The González amendments mandated that the United States vote against loans from *any* multilateral institution for any country that nationalized or expropriated an American company, unless "the Secretary of the Treasury determines that (A) an arrangement for prompt, adequate, and effective compensation has been made, (B) the parties have submitted the dispute to arbitration under the rules of the Convention for the Settlement of Investment Disputes, or (C) good faith negotiations are in progress aimed at providing prompt, adequate, and effective compensation under the applicable principles of international law."[79]

The González amendments differed from the Hickenlooper Amendment in four important respects. First, the Treasury Department, not the president, determined whether negotiations were sufficient to avoid enforcement. This was apparently González's attempt to placate the interests of the Treasury Department—and private companies that trusted Treasury officials more than they trusted State.[80] (In fact, some people involved in the legislative process later claimed the Treasury Department drafted the amendments for González.)[81] Second, the

González amendments mandated "prompt, adequate, and effective compensation" softening (at least rhetorically) the Hickenlooper Amendment's draconian "speedy compensation . . . in convertible foreign exchange, equivalent to the full value thereof." Third, the González amendments were *immediately* punitive. Unlike the Hickenlooper Amendment, the González amendments had no language regarding "appropriate steps" and no six-month grace period of the sort that President Nixon had so skillfully used as a "fig leaf" in Peru. The subcommittee had several motives for this addition. González wanted "a *clear* policy on U.S. expropriations" (emphasis added).[82] He believed a strong policy on expropriation would enable the United States to make its voice heard more clearly within the multilateral agencies.[83] A Republican on the committee, on the other hand, had a much more straightforward point of view that led to the same conclusion: "The Hickenlooper didn't mean anything and the Commies had taken over and were getting to be a problem in Chile. So we decided to write a few words."[84]

Fourth and finally, the González amendments specified that ICSID arbitration could delay implementation. This excluded most Latin American nations, for the only Western Hemisphere countries other than the United States that as of 1972 had agreed to ICSID were the Republic of Trinidad and Tobago, Jamaica, and Guyana (the latter two engaged in disputes with North American companies over bauxite mines). The González amendments thus ensured that a violator of an ICSID judgment among those nations risked losing all its access to multilateral aid and credit.

Henry González fully intended that his namesake amendments would give ICSID teeth. "I would like to emphasize that the expropriation amendment will provide much encouragement for the use of the International Centre for the Settlement of Investment Disputes, which is set up in the World Bank for the exact purpose of arbitrating differences involving international investments."[85] González shepherded the three amended bills through the House all on the same day: the Inter-American

Bank bill by 285 to 102;[86] the Asian Bank bill by 255 to 132;[87] and the International Development Association bill by 208 to 165.[88] (The falling votes in favor of the acts appear to reflect aid fatigue on the part of legislators.)

González's optimism about ICSID's usefulness was not warranted by the organization's track record at the time. Despite Broches's elegant design, the center adjudicated only a handful of cases by 1980. As Broches was well aware, even the best-designed institution required an enforcement mechanism. Charles Kindleberger believed "the [World] Bank had laid an egg in this field." Now that ICSID had become part of American law, however, with clear penalties that could be enforced internationally, ICSID gained an enforcement mechanism, albeit one still dependent on executive action.

The Last Hurrah of Imperial Investor Protection

Expropriation went into temporary decline during the 1980s. The principal reason for this was, ironically enough, the reemergence of private capital flows and the resulting debt crisis. In the 1960s, annual lending to Latin American governments almost tripled, from $115 million to $313 million. The run-up in oil prices further increased lending, as oil-producing countries "recycled" their immense oil income by depositing it in Western banks. Those banks, in turn, lent the funds at low interest rates: the inflation-adjusted interest rate on U.S.-dollar-denominated commercial bank loans to Latin American countries averaged only 0.3% during the 1974–78 period, and it actually turned negative in 1979 as inflation in the United States accelerated.[89] As early as 1978, foreign banks began to declare that smaller countries, like Bolivia, could not possibly service any more debt, but in most cases lending continued.[90]

The debt bubble might have deflated calmly had it not been for two events: the jump in oil prices following the Iranian Revolution in 1979, and Paul Volcker's decision to kill U.S. inflation in 1982. The former increased the Latin American demand for funds: oil-importing nations borrowed to cover their import bills, while oil-producing nations borrowed to finance increases in their oil output. The latter suddenly increased the burden of servicing the region's foreign debts, most of which were made at variable interest rates.[91]

The result was widespread default and rescheduling of debts—but also economic collapse. As in the 1930s, governments defaulted on their debts because they could not maintain payments while also maintaining a functioning state. The problem was that Latin American countries still required access to foreign financing to forestall further economic collapse. In 1982, when Mexico kicked off the big wave of defaults (Bolivia's 1980 rescheduling caused few ripples), the U.S. government responded by providing funds to the affected countries— particularly Mexico—in all sorts of ad hoc ways. (For example, the Reagan administration used the Strategic Petroleum Reserve to buy oil now that Mexico would provide later.)[92] The result was that the U.S. government and IMF gained remarkable leverage over economic policy. Governments were reluctant to antagonize the hand that fed them.

The exception was Peru. In 1985, Alan García's newly elected government decided that it could not afford to continue paying the monies that it owed the IMF. It also in that year expropriated offshore oil fields belonging to Belco Petroleum, a subsidiary of Enron. Belco's contract had expired on August 29, and the company and the government failed to agree over tax rates or a commitment to expand exploration in return for additional acreage.[93] As a result, García canceled the concession and took control of the fields. Peru stopped payments on its IMF debt in September 1985, the month after the expropriation. The IMF cut the country off from all lending from that organization in August 1986.[94]

Enron chose not to ask for U.S. support, because it had taken out an insurance policy from AIG against political risk. AIG, along with Lloyd's of London, "noting OPIC's profitable history," began offering such insurance during the 1980s, albeit for only short periods compared with OPIC.[95] Private political risk insurance was significantly more expensive and less comprehensive than OPIC insurance, but OPIC operated only in countries that signed investment agreements with the United States. By 1986 these included Belize, Brazil, Cameroon, Chile, Costa Rica, the Dominican Republic, Ecuador, Egypt, El Salvador, Grenada, Guatemala, Guyana, Haiti, Honduras, India, Indonesia, Jamaica, Jordan, Kenya, Liberia, Malaysia, Malta, Nepal, Nigeria, Pakistan, the Philippines, Saint Kitts and Nevis, Saudi Arabia, Somalia, South Korea, Sudan, Taiwan, Thailand, Tunisia, Turkey, Uruguay, Zaire, and Zambia—but not Peru.[96]

The AIG policy covered Enron for expropriation losses up to the lesser of 90% of the loss or $200 million. AIG tried to contest the Belco policy, but in December 1988 an arbitration panel ruled in Enron's favor. It found the losses amounted to $161 million, and ordered AIG to pay $144.9 million, plus interest.[97] Compensation appears to have been based on the value of the operation as a going concern: Belco operations earned $19.1 million in 1985.[98] The New York State Supreme Court upheld the decision in January 1990.[99] Once it was clear that AIG was on the hook to Belco, it appealed to the Bush administration to use its authority under the Trade Act of 1974 to pressure Peru into paying. The Trade Act of 1974 enabled the president to remove the preferential tariff rates granted to poor countries under the Generalized System of Preferences (GSP) should they expropriate American investments without compensation. The Office of the United States Trade Representative had until April 1990 to decide on AIG's petition.[100]

The sanctions never needed to be imposed. The Constitution of Peru prevented García from running for reelection in 1990. On April 8, 1990, the two candidates who emerged from the first round of the presidential election were the conservative Alberto Fujimori and the equally conservative (at least on economic issues) Mario Vargas Llosa. Both candidates intended to return to economic orthodoxy and regain access to IMF support, which meant settling outstanding expropriation claims. Almost immediately after winning the second round of the election in June, President Fujimori entered negotiations with AIG. The company ultimately received $184.8 million in compensation, plus interest to compensate it for the delay.[101]

The Return of Creditors and the Role of Official Lenders

As Stephen Kobrin predicted in 1984 and Michael Minor confirmed ten years later, the debt crisis caused expropriation to decline dramatically during the 1980s.[102] During the crisis, international lending institutions possessed unprecedented leverage, which they used to discourage expropriation. In fact, they went the other way: privatization became a touchstone of most IMF structural adjustment programs. Moreover, the 1980s was a time of low commodity prices: as the García administration discovered in Peru, there were few rents available to grab. Peru was an exception because it had already antagonized the United States and the multilateral lending institution by its hard-line approach to sovereign debt. The García government therefore believed that it had little to lose from taking an equally aggressive stance against the offshore oil companies. In this, however, it was wrong: the country needed IMF support, and therefore had little choice but to pay fair value for the expropriated assets.

In general, American debt policy proved *more* creditor-friendly in the 1980s than it had been in the 1930s. In the 1980s, U.S. policy put great pressure on Latin American countries to maintain payments. Ultimate recovery rates and net transfers from debtor nations to creditors were much larger than in the 1930s.[103] The Brady Plan resulted in a relatively orderly write-down of Latin American (and other less-developed countries') foreign bank debt, which was replaced by securitized bonds with the principal held in escrow by the U.S. Treasury. Brady deals restructured $202.8 billion of debt for eighteen countries.

The result was $63.7 billion of debt relief and the re-creation of an active secondary market in bonds issued by developing-country governments.

The reason for the U.S. government's more active role in the 1980s was simple: in 1931, when Washington began to sign off on Latin American defaults, U.S. banks had already mostly failed—the additional impact of Latin American defaults would be minimal. That was not true in 1982. The U.S. government feared a systemic bank collapse in the United States should there be large-scale defaults and repudiations by Latin American governments. As a result, the United States took a more proactive line. That said, what the U.S. policy did not do was abandon the interests of foreign direct investors. In fact, the United States—through the IMF—used its new leverage to pry open foreign sectors to U.S. direct investment.

Toward the very end of the debt crisis the multilateral lending agencies became more directly involved with investor protection when the World Bank established the Multilateral Investment Guarantee Agency (MIGA). Created in 1985 and implemented in 1988, MIGA was an insurance scheme designed along the lines of OPIC. The idea (backed by the Reagan administration) was to build on the success of OPIC and other national political risk insurance schemes in depoliticizing investment disputes. In the words of World Bank president Tom Clausen, a Reagan appointee: "MIGA will be placed in a unique position to facilitate an amicable settlement and to make sure matters are discussed on the basis of legal and economic criteria only. In other words, as in the case of ICSID, MIGA should contribute significantly to the depoliticization of investment disputes."[104] As with OPIC, MIGA charged investors a fee in return for insurance of up to 90% of the value of a claim. Claims, once paid by MIGA, would then be subrogated to the World Bank, which would attempt to collect from the expropriating country.[105]

MIGA had some interesting features. First, host states were ultimately expected to subscribe to 40% of the institution's capital, in effect having them post a bond against future expropriation or renegotiation. Second, under some circumstances residents of the host country could apply for MIGA insurance if the capital they used to finance the investment was repatriated from abroad.[106] Finally, because MIGA was neither a foreign corporation nor a foreign government, but rather an international organization, it was hoped that disputes involving it could get around the reluctance of some Latin American governments to submit investment disputes to international arbitration.[107] The founders also hoped that MIGA would do a better job of ensuring that initial concessions and contracts were fair toward the host country, and thus MIGA would both help avoid disputes and retain more moral authority should they occur.[108]

The Domestic Legal Underpinnings

By the mid-1970s, there existed two of the underpinnings of a new "technology" that would allow foreign investors to obtain compensation for expropriation (or de facto expropriation) without the need to harness the power of their home governments. The first was the ability of foreign investors to directly take foreign states to international arbitration tribunals. The second was the creation of professionally run political risk insurance programs. The González amendments provided an enforcement mechanism for ICSID, but one that still depended on U.S. executive discretion. The true third leg for a new system would be the ability to use American and European courts to enforce ICSID judgments against foreign governments. In theory, the New York and Washington conventions enjoined courts to enforce arbitration decisions as if they were the decisions of local courts. In practice, the doctrine of absolute sovereign immunity limited that ability.

Under absolute sovereign immunity, states could not be sued in the courts of another sovereign state. Absolute sovereign immunity became a problem after the Second World War as governments and government-owned companies increasingly engaged in cross-border commercial activities. Private firms complained that sovereign immunity put them at a disadvantage when dealing with state-owned competitors. After all, did Air France or British Steel enjoy absolute immunity when doing business in Germany? Belgium and Italy were the first countries to deny sovereign immunity in such cases. Switzerland, France, Austria, and Greece soon followed.[109]

The United States partially joined the bandwagon in 1952. In what became known as the "Tate Letter," the acting legal adviser for the secretary of state, Jack Tate, declared that absolutely sovereign immunity was no longer the official position of the State Department. The Tate Letter stated that the department now held that states were not immune "with respect to claims arising out of activities of the kind that may be carried on by private persons." The reason for the switch was that "the widespread and increasing practice on the part of governments of engaging in commercial activities makes necessary a practice which will enable persons doing business with them to have their rights determined in the courts." In addition, "the granting of sovereign immunity to foreign governments in the courts of the United States is most inconsistent with the action of the government of the United States in subjecting itself to suit *in* these same courts *in* both contract and tort."[110] In other words, the State Department considered it odd that foreign governments enjoyed legal privileges that the federal government did not.

Unfortunately, the State Department interpreted the Tate Letter in a confusing and contradictory manner, usually allowing political considerations to guide its decisions.[111] Moreover, as the Tate Letter itself noted, "It is realized that a shift in policy by the executive cannot control the courts."[112] The result was a mass of confusing and contradictory decisions, compounded by the fact that different countries interpreted restricted immunity quite differently. The resulting uncertainty led the Council of Europe to begin in 1963 to negotiate a convention to codify "restricted immunity"; that is, the circumstances under which sovereign immunity did not apply. The negotiations took nine years, ending with the 1972 European Convention on State Immunity.[113] Austria, Belgium, Cyprus, and the Netherlands ratified almost immediately.[114] Other countries did not ratify, but by 1976 all the countries of Western Europe (save the United Kingdom) had de facto adopted restricted sovereign immunity.[115] The United Kingdom adopted restricted sovereign immunity with the State Immunity Act of 1978, and by 1990 Australia, Canada, Pakistan, Singapore, South Africa and Switzerland had either adopted the European Convention or passed laws embodying its precepts.

The United States did not ratify the convention, but Congress passed the Foreign Sovereign Immunity Act (FSIA) in 1976, which wrote most of the European Convention's stipulations into American law. The FSIA waived sovereign immunity in nine situations: (1) voluntary waiver; (2) commercial activity; (3) expropriation; (4) property in the United States; (5) tort injury occurring in the United States; (6) arbitration; (7) torture, extrajudicial killing, sabotage, or kidnapping; (8) enforcement of a maritime lien; and (9) foreclosure of a maritime mortgage.[116] The FSIA (along with legislation in the United Kingdom and Belgium) expressly granted sovereign immunity to central bank reserves.[117]

The FSIA did not mention sovereign debt, but U.S. courts eventually brought it under the purview of the law. Allied Bank became the first creditor to use the FSIA to sue a sovereign in 1982, when Costa Rica defaulted on the debt it owed a thirty-nine-bank consortium to which Allied belonged. Allied received a favorable ruling in 1985, but the U.S. government pressured the bank into settling on the same terms as the other thirty-eight creditors.[118] The next year, in 1986, Argentina's central bank defaulted on a series of special dollar-denominated bonds that it had issued in 1982 to refinance existing debts. Two Panamanian corporations and a Swiss bank sued in New York. In 1992, the U.S. Supreme Court ruled in their favor in *Weltover v. Republic of Argentina*: sovereign bond issues in the United States qualified as commercial activities, and sovereign immunity did not automatically apply.[119] As a means of forcing defaulted sovereigns to make good on their debt, the inclusion of sovereign debt failed because courts proved reluctant to attach assets. As a way of strengthening the regime around expropriation, however, by introducing the threat of interference with the issuance of new debt should a country ignore an arbitration judgment, it succeeded.

Arbitration in Action

The debt-crisis-driven 1980s hiatus in expropriation faded in the 1990s and conclusively ended in the first decade of the twenty-first century. By then, however, the new technology of investor-versus-state arbitration had been firmly established. In the past, a foreign investor facing a violation of its perceived property rights had two options: cooperate with the local government or ask its home government for support. Now there was a third option: use the mechanisms of arbitration. As expropriation returned with the waning of the 1980s economic crisis, arbitration proved a very attractive option.

The most radical shift was an exponential increase in the number of investor-versus-state disputes (see figure 10.3). Before 1996, investors registered just 35 claims before ICSID. The low level of use was not a signal of failure; rather, it indicated that few of the states that had signed on to the system violated the contractual or treaty-based property rights of foreign investors. During the ten years from 1996 to 2005, however, the number of ICSID cases rose to 166. As of early 2011, the number of pending cases passed 200. In part, the caseload rose because Latin American nations reversed the "no de Tokio" during the 1980s and 1990s, agreeing to ICSID arbitration as part of the implicit quid pro quo under which the United States helped them restructure their debts and opened its markets to their exports under reciprocal free trade agreements. The United States began to make investor protection a requirement for aid starting

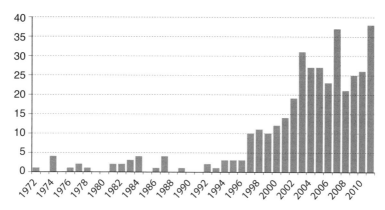

Figure 10.3 Annual ICSID cases filed, 1972–2011
Source: International Centre for Settlement of Investment Disputes.

with the Caribbean Basin Initiative in 1983; that continued as the United States began to sign free trade agreements that contained investment protection clauses.

How did investor-versus-state arbitrations proceed in practice? Foreign investors could take a government to arbitration under the terms of a bilateral investment treaty (BIT), clauses in the investment contract, or domestic law. Each party selected one arbiter. If the two parties failed to agree on the identity of the third arbiter, then the secretary-general of ICSID would choose the third.[120] (Concession contracts sometimes specified non-ICSID forums, such as the International Chamber of Commerce, but the general rules were similar.) The tribunal, once constituted, accepted arguments from both parties and rendered a decision. If it found for the government, then the process would end. If it found for the claimant, the tribunal decided the amount of compensation. The general aim—as with the U.S. government in its interventions on behalf of its citizens—was to leave the claimant in the same economic position that it would have had absent the dispute. When market values were available, arbiters took them into account. More commonly tribunals attempted to calculate the net present value of future cash flows in order to value compensation. Arguments involved the appropriate time to value the investment and an appropriate discount rate. Tribunals had no explicit requirement to follow precedents.[121]

Should the tribunal find for the claimant, ICSID allowed governments to attempt to annul the decision. Annulments, it should be stressed, were *not* appeals. Article 52 of the Washington Convention laid out the only grounds for annulment: (1) improper selection of the tribunal; (2) manifest overstepping of its powers; (3) corruption; (4) violation of a fundamental procedural rule; or (5) failure to explain the reasoning behind the award. The Secretary-General was responsible for the decision whether to appoint a panel to decide on annulment.

The arbitration process was generally slower than the use of American power that had preceded it. In general, arbitrations lasted three to four years between the filing of a request for arbitration and the decision on the final award.[122] Some BITs, in addition, required a year or more of negotiation or the use of local courts *before* a panel could even be constituted. Arbitrations also tended to be rather expensive. ExxonMobil and Venezuela, for example, spent $24.9 million and $18.5 million in legal expenses, plus $2.7 million for the cost of the tribunal.[123] It was standard, however, for judgments to accrue interest retroactively to the beginning of the dispute, in order to compensate victorious claimants for delay.

If a government refused to pay, claimants went to national courts to collect. Embassies, consulates, military assets, and central bank reserves, however, were not subject to attachment. In 2007 claimants against Argentina attempted to attach the presidential jet when it landed in the United States; a U.S. court dismissed that case, since the jet was registered to the Argentine Air Force.[124] In 2011, the Argentine embassy in France briefly had to pay its employees in cash after a judge attached its accounts on behalf of investors, but the Court of Cassation rapidly overturned that decision, since embassies were protected even under restricted sovereign immunity.[125]

Other government assets were vulnerable to legal action. In extremis, national courts could grant worldwide freezing orders (also known as "Mareva injunctions") that would prevent the government from removing, spending, or dissipating expropriated assets (including inventory). Claimants could also go after the assets of state-owned corporations. In 2003 the Paris Court of Appeals allowed the attachment of assets belonging to the Congolese and Cameroonian national oil companies, even though they were not directly involved in the disputes.[126] Courts in the United States and United Kingdom allowed similar moves against state-owned companies in cases against Cuba and Nigeria.[127] In effect, national courts could be used to coordinate boycotts. The first type was a boycott of the assets seized by the expropriating government, inasmuch as the production of those assets was marketed in countries that had signed the ICSID convention. The second, broader boycott was against all the commercial activities of companies or organizations owned by the expropriating government. (U.S. courts held that companies needed to be at least 51% state-owned in order to be the target of legal action.) There was some doubt as to whether ICSID judgments would be enforceable in the People's Republic of China: China was a signatory to the Washington Convention, but its courts still hewed to the idea of absolute sovereign immunity, although courts in Hong Kong did not.[128] By 2012, however, there had been no reported attempts of a country trying to avoid ICSID judgments by exporting raw material or finished goods to China.

Legal action could reduce the value of expropriation for expropriating governments even when the assets did not produce for export. In 2012, the Argentine government expropriated 51% of the YPF oil company, which had been 57% owned by Spain's Repsol. Before the expropriation, the Argentine government had floated plans to invest $20.3 billion dollars in new oil and gas investments in the Vaca Muerta fields. Eleven different companies—Chevron, ConocoPhillips, Ecopetrol,

EOG, ExxonMobil, Shell, Sinopec, Statoil, Talisman, Vale do Río Doce, and Venoco—discussed drilling more than twelve thousand wells. ConocoPhillips and Talisman had been expected to jointly put in about $4.3 billion.[129] Once the nationalization occurred, however, most plans to invest in the Vaca Muerta asset evaporated. Even Gazprom appeared reluctant to invest.[130]

The reason the oil companies were reluctant to enter Argentina after the YPF episode was *not* the poor reputation of the Argentine government. In previous expropriation episodes—including Venezuela in 1900, Mexico in 1938, Libya in 1971, and Peru in 1986—oil companies had no compunction about investing in countries that had just expropriated competitors' assets. Rather, what dissuaded Repsol's competitors from entering Argentina in 2012 was that Repsol had access to legal tools that would have been ineffective before 1976. Repsol's first move was to file a lawsuit against the Argentine government in the U.S. District Court in Manhattan.[131] The lawsuit itself was not intended to gain compensation from the Argentine government. Rather, it was intended to warn other oil companies that they would enter a legal minefield should they do business with any of the expropriated assets. For any oil company that did business inside the United States—and they all did, even the state-owned Chinese giants—this was a serious threat. The threat, it should be noted, was *not* implicit: Repsol sent letters to the other major international oil companies, including ExxonMobil, Chevron, ConocoPhillips, and Shell, bluntly stating that it would defend its claim: Repsol would sue if any of them invested in YPF or YPF assets or otherwise took actions "prejudicing Repsol's ability to fully defend and recover its rights."[132] "It wasn't a threat so much as a statement," said Juan José Aranguren, the president of Shell Argentina, about the letter. "I do not believe that any company will deal with the Argentine government or the nationalized assets without some sort of guarantee."[133]

Repsol's "statements" were not idle. When Chevron announced a memorandum of understanding with the now nationalized YPF to invest in the Vaca Muerta fields, Repsol sued in a Spanish court on November 20, 2012, asking for a cease-and-desist order under Spain's competition law.[134] On December 4, Repsol followed up with a second lawsuit against Chevron in New York.[135] (Chevron also faced legal difficulties in Argentina over an environmental lawsuit in Ecuador.)[136] Should Chevron ultimately decide to go into business with YPF (assuming, of course, that it escaped cease-and-desist orders from the courts in Madrid and New York) it would be making a deliberate decision to accept a large contingent future liability should Argentina lose the ICSID arbitration and refuse to pay.

The arbitration regime affected the behavior of the United States. When in 2007 the government of the Bolivarian Republic of Venezuela announced that it intended to effectively take over four heavy-oil projects in the Orinoco River basin—as well as expropriate Verizon's stake in the country's largest telecom company and AES's ownership of Electricidad de Caracas—the Bush administration limited itself to an anodyne announcement that it expected "fair and quick compensation." Despite repeated provocations by the Venezuelan government, including a threat to expel the U.S. ambassador, the United States stuck to that line. No sanctions were implied or threatened. Nor did the affected companies lobby Congress or try to mobilize political pressure.[137] (The closest was a quixotic and abortive campaign to remove the iconic Citgo sign from the Boston skyline.) The United States was certainly supportive of the 2002 coup attempt against Hugo Chávez's government after the fact, but the coup attempt predated Chávez's attacks on foreign properties and was wholly made in Caracas.[138] The difference between George W. Bush's reaction to expropriation and the reaction of U.S. governments as recently as Ronald Reagan—let alone Richard Nixon—was striking.

ExxonMobil and ConocoPhillips (along with Verizon and AES) pursued their claims against Venezuela through arbitrations at the International Chamber of Commerce and ICSID. The ICC arbitrations were undertaken on the basis of the "association agreements" that the oil companies had signed with Venezuela's state-owned Petróleos de Venezuela (PDVSA), while the ICSID proceedings occurred under the rubric of the Netherlands-Venezuela bilateral investment treaty. The Bolivarian Republic paid the judgment against it in the ICC hearing. (As of 2013, the ICSID proceedings were still underway.) That judgment came to $906.7 million, and was substantially less than what many analysts expected. The reason the judgment was lower than expected, however, was not that the tribunal was biased toward Venezuela or that it worried that the Venezuelan government would refuse to pay. (PDVSA owns Citgo, which has billions of dollars of assets in the United States.) Rather, the reason for the low judgment was that PDVSA's negotiators had written into the original contract a ceiling on the price of oil that arbiters could use to calculate the value of the cash flows generated by ExxonMobil's investment. The key clause was Article 15 of the association agreement:

> . . . after the first period of six consecutive months during which the price of Brent crude oil is in excess of the threshold price [$27 in inflation-adjusted 1996 dollars], Lagoven CN [PDSVA's subsidiary in the Cerro Negro venture] will not be required to compensate any foreign party for any discriminatory action(s) with respect to any fiscal year in which the average price of Brent crude oil is in excess of the threshold price, and such foreign party received net cash flow commensurate, after taking into account the effect of the discriminatory action(s), with a reference price for the production produced by the parties that bears at least a reasonable relationship, adjusted for quality and transportation differences, to the threshold cash flow for such fiscal year.

In other words, the well-designed (from Venezuela's point of view) contract stipulated that the highest possible oil price that could be used to value damages in the event of expropriation was $27 per barrel in 1996 dollars, $37.50 at the time of the expropriation. Moreover, the contract allowed the price to be further marked down to adjust "for quality and transportation differences." When Brent traded at $37.50, Venezuela's Mesa crude traded at $32, and that was the price the arbiters had to use, rather than the $72 that the Mesa blend fetched in the market in 2007.[139] In short, Venezuela did well in arbitration because of clever contract design and not because it refused to pay.

In general, expropriating governments have done *relatively* well at arbitration proceedings. Susan Franck evaluated the universe of investment treaty arbitration cases (that is, investor-versus-state arbitrations brought under the rubric of a BIT) and found that governments won 58% of cases. Investors won 38%, and the remainder were settled. She also found, not surprisingly, a large gap between the average claim and the average amount awarded by arbitration panels: between 1990 and 2006 the average claim was for $343.4 million (the median was $59.0 million), whereas the average award came to only $10.4 million. The highest claim came to $9.4 billion, but the highest award was only $269.8 million. Energy cases made up 29% of the caseload and mining an additional 6%, the remainder being mostly in public services.[140] Firms in mining and energy did rather better than other firms. Using a sample of cases from 1990 to 2011, energy and mining companies received awards in 80% of their arbitral cases, including a recent award of $1.8 billion for Occidental Petroleum against the Ecuadorean government.[141]

As a practical matter, few countries defaulted on arbitration judgments, although there was evidence to suggest that collecting awards required some action in national courts.[142] The Russian Federation refused to pay Franz Sedelmayer, a German national, a $2.4 million judgment in 1998 after it seized a villa on which Sedelmayer had a twenty-five-year lease.[143] Sedelmayer was unable to attach overflight fees paid by Russia to Germany, but he did take possession of real estate in Cologne owned by the Russian security services—real estate that produced rental revenue of $348,000 per year.[144] (It is worth noting that the largest and most famous recent expropriation case in Russia, the forced sale of half of Shell's 55% stake in the $22 billion Sakhalin Island project to Gazprom, did not go to arbitration.)[145] Recently, Kyrgyzstan, Thailand, and Zimbabwe all delayed payments; after legal action, the Kyrgyz and Thai governments paid. (German courts seized a Thai airplane in 2011.) Despite loud and angry rhetoric, even the Bolivarian Republic of Venezuela has paid its ICSID judgments—not least because PDVSA owns billions of dollars worth of refineries and gas stations in the United States via its Citgo subsidiary. As of November 2011, only three states (the Argentine Republic, the Russian Federation, and Zimbabwe) had outstanding payment issues.[146] (We will return to the challenge Argentina poses to the survival of the arbitral system in the next chapter.)

Conclusion

In 1940, the only defense an American investor had against a hostile action by a foreign government was to ask the United States for assistance. The U.S. government had several arrows in its quiver: diplomatic espousal, state-to-state arbitration, trade sanctions, the denial of aid, the denial of official credit, and covert action. What these arrows all had in common was that they required action by the executive branch to take effect. When the executive was reluctant, U.S. investors could and did pressure Congress to mandate executive action or otherwise turn up the heat on the president, but at the end of the day it was the president that had to act. Should an American investor attempt to use American courts to enforce its property rights overseas, its attempts would be dismissed—as Mexican Eagle discovered when an Alabama judge refused to allow it to take back tankers seized by the Mexican government.

By 1990, a series of institutional changes had made it possible for American companies to defend their overseas property without calling on the State Department or the CIA. The changes took two forms. The first set of changes provided expropriation insurance (also known as investment guarantees) to compensate investors for their losses. Political risk insurance effectively repurposed a series of ad hoc programs administered by USAID and originally intended to promote U.S. investment in the war-ravaged nations of Western Europe by insuring them against those countries' capital controls or the possibility of war with the Soviet Union. Again, it was a short step from insurance against capital controls or Communist invasion to insurance against expropriation.

The second set of changes gave private companies the ability to take foreign states to arbitration without the involvement of their home government. Here the goal was explicitly to "depoliticize" investment disputes. Depoliticization meant that governments no longer needed to "espouse" (to use the legal term) the claims of their nationals. Investor-versus-state disputes, therefore, no longer created diplomatic incidents. Companies could choose arbitration over espousal—simply put, the new system gave managers an option that they previously lacked. In other words, the new institutions created the possibility of a mostly unplanned escape from the empire trap. Arbitration, however, required an enforcement mechanism. In fact, so did OPIC, if it was to be able to collect subrogated claims without creating diplomatic incidents, as Senator Church had feared. The third set of changes, therefore, ended the long-standing doctrine of absolute sovereign immunity. U.S. courts—as well as the courts of foreign countries—could now be used to enforce arbitration judgments against foreign governments.

Expropriation went into eclipse during the 1980s because a debt crisis increased the need of foreign governments, particularly in Latin America, for foreign capital. Once the crisis passed, expropriation returned to the scene. This time, though, the response of the U.S. government was completely different than in the past. The two reforms of judicialization and insurance—or, more cynically, lawyers and money—helped to protect the U.S. government against the demands of American overseas investors almost as much as they worked to protect American overseas investors against foreign governments.

eleven

The Empire Trap in the
Twenty-first Century

This book has sought to explain patterns of U.S. government intervention on behalf of its citizens' overseas property rights over the course of the twentieth century. The point of departure was the following paradox: although U.S. governments throughout the century categorically rejected interventionism designed to favor or protect Americans, time and again they found themselves compelled to interfere in the affairs of foreign nations on behalf of private American interests.

The mechanism of the empire trap explains U.S. administrations' apparent inability to avoid overseas entanglements, even when presidential preferences and the national interest pointed toward nonintervention. The political clout of private interests meant that the domestic political costs of refusing to intervene were often far higher and more immediate than the costs of intervening. Calls to punish kleptocratic foreign governments that preyed on the property of Americans stirred patriotic sentiment, especially after the onset of the Cold War. Moreover, once committed to the protection of American interests—either by attempting to engineer political and financial stability, sanctioning expropriating governments, or installing sympathetic regimes—U.S. administrations found it very difficult to walk away from those commitments. Despite the relative insignificance of their investments compared with the size of the domestic economy, the proprietors of American interests overseas were, historically, very difficult to ignore.

Intervention took place in two distinct phases across the century. The United States began protecting its citizens' overseas property rights as soon as it gained the capacity to do so. Theodore Roosevelt created an informal intervention sphere across most of Latin America outside the Southern Cone. Pressure to uphold existing commitments continued to draw future administrations into further entanglements until the Great Depression. The Depression broke up the political coalition that had sustained foreign intervention on behalf of American property rights. Franklin Roosevelt took advantage of the situation to undertake a number of institutional measures—beginning the withdrawal of American sovereignty from the Philippines, ending the protectorates over Cuba and Panama, and signing reciprocal trade agreements with Latin American countries—that put an end to the first American empire. But not even Franklin Roosevelt could eliminate the political pressures that powered the empire trap, which reemerged in full force as soon as global economic conditions improved.

After the Second World War, the United States emerged as one of two superpowers, practically unchallenged outside the Soviet sphere. In Western Europe, America's dominance took the form of an "empire by invitation," dedicated to stopping Soviet expansion. Elsewhere, however, private interests rapidly learned that they could mobilize this new, globally powerful America to protect their private interests, just as they had before the war. The United States continued to defend American property overseas, adding new tools: covert action, the withdrawal of trade preferences, and the denial of financial assistance. The "uninvited" portion of the second American empire was not unlimited in scope, but it now ranged across all of Latin America, much of insular Asia, and parts of Africa and the Middle East. Ex post, the system worked well, at least for investors in natural resources. Ex ante, however, the system was highly uncertain, forcing American companies to design new political strategies designed to mobilize the U.S. government with every new expropriation or investment dispute.

Imperial intervention on behalf of U.S. investors didn't so much decline as be superseded. New institutions slowly emerged, chiefly investor-versus-state arbitration and political risk insurance. These institutions provided overseas investment managers with a third option between cooperation with the expropriating state and confrontation backed by the United States. Arbitration was slow (by design), and companies with claims against foreign governments did not always win (by design), but the system provided the United States executive with an ability to gracefully exit from the sorts of continual confrontations that had preoccupied it from the days of William McKinley to the administration of Jimmy Carter. There was no grand design—although some of the designers of parts of the system hoped it would "depoliticize" investment disputes—but the system provided investors with a less uncertain means of resolving their claims.

The Argentine Challenge to Investor-versus-State Arbitration

The system of investor-versus-state arbitration, however, came with two hidden flaws. The first was that its enforcement mechanisms depended on the presence of some sort of "hostage" outside the boundaries of the nation being sued. That did not mean that the system had no means of enforcement. In fact, the system was shaped such that many assets could be seized in the event of nonpayment: (1) income streams from the expropriated assets themselves; (2) commercial assets, activities, or income streams earned by overseas entities owned and controlled by the expropriating state; and, under limited circumstances, (3) sovereign debt issued by the expropriating state in foreign jurisdictions. The problem was that not every investment dispute involved a country that possessed these vulnerabilities.

The second flaw was that the legitimacy of the system of investor-versus-state arbitration came under threat from the nature of many post-2001 expropriation cases. The problem was not that the public in Europe and the United States supported the right of foreign governments to expropriate their co-nationals' property. Public opinion polls in Spain showed that 77% of the public considered the 2012 Argentine expropriation of Spanish-owned YPF "unjustified," and 60% supported "reprisals" against Argentina.[1] A second poll found that 58.5% supported taking Argentina to arbitration; 54.1% *also* supported trade sanctions.[2] No opinion polls were conducted in the United States when Venezuela nationalized American oil investments in 2007, but there was little evidence that U.S. popular opinion supported Hugo Chávez. There was certainly no evidence that American public opinion opposed the oil companies' use of investor-versus-state arbitration to obtain compensation.

The rub is that not every foreign property dispute is as clear-cut (from a political point of view) as the expropriation of natural resource investments. Many are contract disputes over foreign-owned public utilities. Public policy changes that would be completely legal inside the United States (e.g., changes in rate controls or service requirements) are effectively banned under most bilateral investment treaties and many concession contracts. The result is the spectacle of U.S. and European companies suing foreign governments for compensation (and winning!) for government actions that would be utterly unremarkable at home.

These suits weaken the legitimacy of the investor-versus-state arbitration system. Before the advent of such arbitration, it was extremely difficult to get the U.S. government to respond to adverse price regulation of transport or power utilities. Such regulation dates back before the First World War: both the Mexican and Brazilian government heavily regulated foreign railroads and power utilities; in the Mexican case to the point of bankruptcy.[3] The U.S. government, however, did not respond. The reason was quite simple: attempts to persuade or pressure American administrations into acting against other governments for doing exactly what the U.S. federal and various state governments were doing at home mobilized political resistance—the beneficiaries of U.S. domestic regulation protested any attempt to delegitimize similar regulation abroad, fearing it would become a thin edge of the wedge issue at home. (Actions against the foreign expropriation of natural resource investments engendered, as we have seen, no such domestic counterpressures.) Administrations and Congress occasionally worried about "creeping expropriation," but the United States acted only in cases when governments engaged in the outright uncompensated nationalization of electric utilities, as in Brazil in 1963. Such political limits, however, do not apply to the new system.

Argentina presents the clearest example of the problem with investor-versus-state arbitration. Under Carlos Menem in the early 1990s, the Argentine government privatized a host of public services, ranging from water supply to telecommunications to ports. In 1998, Argentina fell into recession: GDP dropped 8.7% over the next three years, and unemployment ballooned from 12.1% to 18.1%. At the end of 2001, after three grinding years of recession, the wheels came off the bus when a collapsing economy forced the government to break the peso's one-to-one link to the dollar. The economy contracted a further 10.9% in 2002, and the peso lost two-thirds of its value against the dollar. The Argentine government responded with "pesification," in which dollar-linked rate contracts were converted to pesos at a one-to-one rate and then frozen. In the face of 1.2 million job losses and a sudden two-thirds loss of purchasing power (in dollar terms) by most of the population, it was entirely reasonable to freeze utility rates (including domestic natural gas prices). Sticking to the letter of the contracts would have required nominal rates to *triple* in the middle of a depression.

The rate freezes were understandable under the circumstances, but they opened the country to a wave of ICSID arbitration. Of Argentina's forty-six post-2001 arbitration cases, thirty-two were a direct result of the 2001 devaluation. Moreover, holders of Argentine bonds tried to broaden ICSID's remit by suing Argentina in that forum for defaulting on its sovereign debt. If those three cases are added, then thirty-five out the country's forty-six cases (76%) stemmed from the depression-scale economic crisis and resulting devaluation. In fact, the number of cases attributable to the crisis is even higher, since four of the remaining eleven cases were canceled procurement or construction contracts: for example, a canceled contract with Unisys to modernize the judiciary's IT systems and an abandoned project with Impregilo S.p.A. to build a highway (see table 11.1). Louis Wells compellingly likened the foreign companies pressing claims against Argentina to a housepainter who sued a home owner for payment even though the house burned down before the work could be completed. "Governments facing a collapsing economic house have not generally been relieved of any of their contractual obligations to foreign direct investors when cases have gone to arbitration."[4]

The Argentine government responded with a defense that challenged the very legitimacy of the system. In an argument harking back to the Calvo Doctrine, the Argentines denied the right of a bilateral investment treaty to supersede the Constitution, insisting that claimants must first exhaust all local remedies before turning to international tribunals. Even more directly, the Argentine government denied that "public services" belonged under ICSID's remit at all. "To admit ICSID's jurisdiction in this realm would be to grant it, and the corporations it protects, the right to determine public policy."[5] In no case has the Argentine government yet paid a post-2001 ICSID claim.

The irony behind the Argentine government's hard-line stance is that it actually did not do all that badly in arbitration. Of its post-2001 cases, thirty-three had been decided by August 2012. Argentina won eight, or 24%. Of those eight, it won five in arbitration. Two were annulled, and one (the case against BG Group) was overturned by a U.S. district court. It lost nine (27%), but annulment hearings were still pending for five of those nine. If those five are placed into the not-yet-decided category, then Argentina's percentage of wins goes to 32% against a loss percentage of 16%, with 52% settled out of court. According

Table 11.1

Arbitration cases against Argentina filed since 2001

	Date filed	Date decided OR discontinued	Annulment decided	Outcome for government	Amount*	Industry
CIT Group	27 Feb 04	12 May 09		Won	zero	Leasing
Impregilo S.p.A.	15 Oct 08	21 Jun 11		Won	zero	Highway construction
Metalpar and Buen Aire	7 Apr 03	6 Jun 08		Won	zero	Motor vehicles
TSA Spectrum	8 Apr 05	19 Dec 08		Won	zero	Telecoms
Wintershall A.G.	15 Jul 04	8 Dec 08		Won	zero	Gas and oil production
BG Group	25 Apr 03	24 Dec 07		Overturned	$185.3	Gas distribution
Enron and Ponderosa Assets	11 Apr 01	22 May 07	30 Jul 10	Annulled	$106.2	Gas transportation
Sempra Energy	6 Dec 02	28 Sep 07	29 Jun 10	Annulled	$128.2	Gas distribution
AES Corp.	19 Dec 02	23 Jan 06		Settled	na	Electricity distribution
Aguas Cordobesas, Suez, and Sociedad Gen'l de Aguas de Barcelona	17 Jul 03	24 Jan 07		Settled	na	Water
BP America	27 Feb 04	20 Aug 08		Settled	na	Hydrocarbon concession
Camuzzi International	23 Apr 03	25 Jan 07		Settled	na	Electricity distribution
Camuzzi International	27 Feb 03	21 Jun 07		Settled	na	Gas distribution
CGE Argentina	4 Feb 05	28 Jul 09		Settled	na	Electricity distribution
Electricidad Argentina and EDF	12 Aug 03	5 Feb		Settled	na	Electricity distribution
Enersis	22 Jul 03	28 Mar 06		Settled	na	Electricity distribution
France Telecom	26 Aug 04	30 Mar 06		Settled	na	Telecoms
Gas Natural SDG	29 May 03	11 Nov 05		Settled	na	Gas distribution
Pan-American Energy (BP)	6 Jun 03	20 Aug 08		Settled	na	Hydrocarbon concession
Pioneer Natural Resources	5 Jun 03	23 Jun 05		Settled	na	Hydrocarbon concession

(continued)

Table 11.1

Arbitration cases against Argentina filed since 2001

	Date filed	Date decided OR discontinued	Annulment decided	Outcome for government	Amount*	Industry
RGA Reinsurance Co.	11 Nov 04	14 Sep 06		Settled	na	Financial reinsurance
Saur International	27 Jan 04	7 Apr 06		Settled	na	Water and sewer
Telefónica	21 Jul 03	2 Oct 09		Settled	na	Telecoms
Unisys Corp.	15 Oct 03	26 Oct 04		Settled but unpaid	$8.0	Information services
Azurix	23 Oct 01	14 Jul 06	1 Sep 09	Lost	$165.2	Water and sewer
CMS Gas	24 Aug 01	12 May 05	25 Sep 07	Lost	$133.2	Gas distribution
Continental Casualty	22 May 03	5 Sep 08	16 Sep 11	Lost	$2.8	Insurance
Impregilo S.p.A.	25 Jul 07	25 Jul 07	21 Jun 11	Lost	$21.3	Water
EDF, Saur and León	12 Aug 03	11 Jun 12	Pending	Lost	$136.1	Electricity distribution
El Paso Energy International	12 Jun 03	31 Oct 11	Pending	Lost	$43.0	Hydrocarbon concession
LG&E Energy	31 Jan 02	25 Jul 07	Pending	Lost	$57.4	Gas distribution
National Grid plc	25 Apr 03	3 Nov 08	Pending	Lost	$53.6	Electricity transmission
Siemens	17 Jul 02	6 Feb 07	Pending	Lost	$237.8	Information services
Asset Recovery. Trust S.A	23 Jun 05			Pending	tbd	Collection contract
AWG Group Ltd.	17 Jul 03			Pending	tbd	Water and sewer
Azurix (Mendoza)	8 Dec 03			Pending	tbd	Water and sewer
DaimlerChrysler Services A.G.	14 Jan 05			Pending	tbd	Leasing
Giordano Alpi and others	28 Jul 08			Pending	tbd	Bondholders
Abaclat	7 Feb 07			Pending	tbd	Bondholders
Giovanni Alemanni and others	27 Mar 07			Pending	tbd	Bondholders
Hochtief Aktiengesellschaft	18 Dec 07			Pending	tbd	Highway construction
Mobil Argentina	5 Aug 04			Pending	tbd	Gas production

(continued)

Table 11.1

Arbitration cases against Argentina filed since 2001 (*continued*)

	Date filed	Date decided OR discontinued	Annulment decided	Outcome for government	Amount*	Industry
Suez, Sociedad General de Aguas de Barcelona S.A., and Interagua Servicios Integrales de Agua S.A.	17 Jul 03			Pending	tbd	Water
Suez, Sociedad General de Aguas de Barcelona S.A., and Vivendi Universal S.A.	17 Jul 03			Pending	tbd	Water
Total S.A. production Urbaser S.A. and Consorcio de Aguas Bilbao Biskaia, Bilbao	22 Jan 04			Pending	tbd	Gas
Biskaia Ur Partzuergoa	1 Oct 07			Pending	tbd	Water

Source: Noel Maurer and Gustavo Herrero, "YPF—the Argentine Oil Nationalization of 2012," Harvard Business School case no. 713-029, June 30, 2012, p. 18.

* na = not available; tbd = to be decided. Award amounts, in millions of current dollars, do *not* include interest.

to research by Susan Franck (pre-2007), governments won 58% of ICSID cases, investors won 38%, and the remainder were settled.[6] By that standard, Argentina did well.

The terms of investor-versus-Argentina settlements were not officially made public, but enough known to make some generalizations. First, they were mostly in public services: five (31%) were in electricity, three (20%) in natural gas production and distribution, two (13%) in water and sewer systems and an additional two (13%) in telecoms. The final one was the Unisys contract mentioned previously. The settlement with AES involved electricity rates: the company owned several power plants, and dropped its suit once the Argentine federal Congress and the Buenos Aires provincial legislature ratified new rate agreements. Pan-American Energy (a subsidiary of BP) sued at ICSID over the pesification of domestic hydrocarbon contracts and the imposition of an oil-export tax. It dropped its claim after Chubut province agreed to renegotiate its exploration and development concession by enough to compensate it for the federal freeze on prices.[7]

Argentina could take a hard line because it had few assets or income streams which foreign courts could attach. Unlike Venezuela or Ecuador, the Argentine state owned no large export-oriented companies. Its central bank reserves were protected even under restricted sovereign immunity.[8] In France, a court temporarily attached Argentine bank accounts, forcing the Argentine embassy in Paris to make payments in cash withdrawn from its ambassador's personal account, but that decision was rapidly overturned.[9] In the United States, a federal judge ruled that airplanes belonging to Aerolíneas Argentinas could not be attached even though the airline was state-owned, because it had passed into state hands as a result of bankruptcy.[10] Argentina would, of course, have a hard time accessing foreign capital markets, but as of mid-2013 it had not needed to do so on a large scale.

Argentina's apparent immunity from judicial actions caused in turn the United States and the European Union to bring state sanctions back into investment disputes. In September 2011, in response to Argentina's refusal to pay compensation in the Azurix and CMS Gas cases, President Barack Obama announced that Argentina "has not acted in good faith in enforcing arbitral awards in favor of U.S. owned companies."[11] The Obama administration then began to vote against all credits for Argentina, beginning with a $230 million loan from the Inter-American Development Bank, until it paid Azurix and Blue Ridge.[12] In April 2012, President Obama used his authority under the Trade Act of 1974 to suspend Argentina's duty-free allowances under the GSP program. The action hit $477 million in Argentine exports, costing exporters (chiefly of cheese, candy, and leather goods) $17 million per year.[13]

Argentina's successful defiance of the international investment regime over its post-crisis cases prompted moral hazard. Justice and common sense was on Argentina's side in the contract disputes of 2001–2. That was nowhere near as true in the oil expropriation of 2012, when Argentina seized 51% of the YPF oil company from Repsol, its Spanish owner. It was certainly true that Repsol paid itself extraordinarily high dividends: between 1999 and 2011, the payout ratio was equivalent to 98.1% of net income, reaching a total of $16.9 billion, of which Repsol collected $15.0 billion. The company's indebtedness throughout the period grew 275%. Disinvestment affected production: YPF experienced a 42.5% drop in oil production and a 31% drop in gas, a significantly worse performance compared with its competitors: the company's market share fell from 40% to 34% in oil and from 32% to 23% in gas.[14] Axel Kicillof, Argentina's economy minister, not unfairly characterized Repsol's policy as treating YPF as a "dairy cow that they were going to milk until dead."[15]

It was also true, however, that Argentine policy bore much of the responsibility for Repsol's disinvestment and falling oil output. Argentina imposed export taxes that capped the effective export price of oil at $42 per barrel. The effect was to prevent exports and drive a wedge between the Argentine oil price and the international price—in 2011, YPF sold its crude domestically for $56 per barrel, half the world price.[16] In addition, government policy openly abetted YPF's high dividend payments. With the blessing of former president Néstor Kirchner, Repsol sold a 25% stake in YPF to the Eskenazi family of Argentina. As part of that deal, YPF promised to distribute 90% of net profits in dividends to the shareholders for a period of ten years starting in 2008.[17]

YPF was a classic expropriation dispute of the type that ICSID was supposed to depoliticize—the problem for investors was that YPF was selling mostly to the domestic market. That meant that it would not be easy to seize YPF's income streams should Argentina refuse to pay a future arbitration judgment. The Spanish government therefore imposed a ban on imports of Argentine biodiesel. The move bloodied the nose of an important Argentine industry: in 2011, Argentina sold $990.6 million of biofuel to Spanish consumers.[18] (Spain also zeroed out aid to Argentina worth approximately €4 million in 2011, but the cut was part of the country's general austerity and applied to all foreign aid recipients.)[19] The European parliament supported Spain, passing a resolution calling for sanctions.[20] In theory, the European Union could sanction against Argentina's annual exports of $10.4 billion; in practice, the European Commission lacked the legal authority to take such a step. On May 25, however, the European Union filed a suit at the World Trade Organization. The suit did not directly involve the nationalization—rather, it protested Argentina's import licensing regime—but observers believed that the nationalization played a key role in the decision to bring suit.[21]

In other words, the way in which the Argentine government capitalized on the flaws in the arbitration system did not bring back the Calvo Doctrine. Rather, it brought back the 1970s, when investment disputes were politicized and powerful nations used their diplomatic and economic muscle to defend the property rights of their citizens. Because of its many-headed constitutional structure and vague lines of authority, the European Union found it harder to play the game than the United States, but Repsol nevertheless mobilized the Spanish and European governments (inasmuch as the European Union could be called a government) to sanction Argentina on its behalf. The return of sanctions represented a weakening of the international system that had been slowly built up since 1965. If more countries followed Argentina, then the system could collapse.

The Latin American Backlash

Argentina's travails had the worrying effect of catalyzing opposition to the entire system of investor-versus-state arbitration. The backlash took two forms. The first was a small but growing mobilization of nongovernmental organizations and activist groups. In October 2011, a coalition of activist groups called ICSID an "an architecture of impunity for transnational corporations . . . [that] undermines the sovereignty and constitutions of both developed and developing countries, democratic governance and peoples' interests."[22] Norway's government responded to domestic pressure by introducing a new template for investment treaties that reigned in the protections that the system currently offers.[23] Australia soon followed. When Bolivia withdrew from ICSID, more than eight hundred citizen groups from fifty-nine different countries wrote the president of the World Bank in support.[24]

The second form of backlash was the withdrawal of several Latin American countries from the system. Bolivia and Ecuador pulled out in 2007 and 2009 respectively.[25] On January 24, 2012, Venezuela announced that it would follow.[26] President Rafael Correa of Ecuador stated that ICSID "signifies colonialism, slavery with respect to transnationals, with respect to Washington, with respect to the World Bank."[27] Ecuador's president was being a bit self-serving—his government's largest arbitration was a classic investment dispute against Occidental Petroleum—but the critics raised points that go to the very heart of the system's legitimacy.[28] Only foreign investors can bring suit under the current regime—host nations cannot challenge foreign investors for failing to comply with their end of a concession agreement. In addition, the system is highly secretive, and there is a striking lack of diversity among the arbiters: most hail from the United States or the United Kingdom.[29]

In the short run, the consequences of the pullouts will be small. Current Ecuadorean and Venezuelan cases before ICSID will not be affected. Moreover, bilateral investment treaties will remain in effect, even if the parties have to use ad hoc arbitrations instead of ICSID. The Venezuela government has stated that it will not pay any ICSID rulings in the future, but such a threat is empty given that Venezuela is a major oil exporter and owns billions of dollars of commercial assets in the United States in the form of Citgo.

In the long run, however, the consequences of large-scale withdrawals would be considerable. It is true that OPIC and its counterpart at the World Bank, the Multilateral Investment Guarantee Agency (MIGA), still exist, while private insurers have joined the public institutions as purveyors of political risk insurance.[30] The problem is that the volume of political risk insurance would have to be much greater than at present to provide the same level of protection provided by investor-versus-state arbitration. The private market for political risk insurance is nearing its limit.[31] Investors therefore, will have few options other than recourse to their home governments. The strategic costs of intervention of behalf of private investors are rather lower today than they were during the Cold War: without hostile rival superpower blocs, the likelihood of creating another Cuba is vanishingly small. If this book has shown anything, it is that democratic governments find it very difficult to ignore calls to protect their citizens' property overseas.

Back to the Future?

What would the world look like if the current institutions governing investor-state relations disappeared? The past offers guidance . . . but there are contemporary examples. One that is often mentioned is the People's Republic of China. China is a member of ICSID, of course, so its behavior is not a clean test. Nonetheless, it is telling that China has confronted few expropriation disputes in the countries receiving its investment—despite the fact that it is unclear that ICSID rulings are enforceable in Chinese courts.[32] Qianru Song and Rodrigo Wagner have suggested that the reason is because China stands willing to punish, and punish massively, countries that expropriate their property. They use China's extralegal response to a trade dispute as an example: "When Argentina imposed barriers to trade in manufacturing, especially from China, China responded in a few weeks, stopping purchases of Argentine soybean oil and creating important losses for the industry; which for almost two years had trouble reallocating its exports somewhere else."[33] Song and Wagner found that Chinese investment in nontradables (exactly the type of investment least protected by the current investor-versus-state arbitration system) is greater in countries that are more vulnerable to Chinese trade sanctions, which is consistent with their hypothesis. That said, in the absence of an investment dispute against which the Chinese respond with overwhelming sanctions, it is hard to conclusively demonstrate that Chinese investments are more politicized than those of other nations—it is difficult to spot the dog that does not bark.

Brazil's economic relations with its neighbors provide a better example of what the relationship between politics and foreign investment might look like should the current investment regime fall apart. Brazil is not a member of ICSID and signs few BITs (while ratifying none), yet its companies invest across South America. In recent years, the Brazilian government has taken a remarkably hands-on approach toward Brazilian investment in nearby countries. In July 2009, Brazil signed a generous settlement with Paraguay regarding revenues from the Itaipú Dam, shared between the two countries. The reason was not Paraguayan pressure but a Brazilian desire to shore up its southern neighbor: giving it a greater share of the dam revenues was easier than voting a foreign aid program. Carlos Mateo Balmelli, the Itaipú-Paraguay dam director, explained "It is not convenient for Brazil to have a poor and powerless neighbor."[34] Brazilian president Dilma Rouseff's special foreign policy adviser, Marco Aurelio, reaffirmed in April 2, 2011, "Supporting neighboring countries is something which does not have a price for Brazil and that is why we accepted increasing the annual payment to Paraguay from 120 million to 360 million dollars annually."[35]

Two months after agreeing to give the Paraguayans a bigger share of the dam's production, in November 2009, Brazil staged Operation Laçador. Operation Laçador involved an eight-thousand-soldier exercise aimed at "liberating" the Itaipú Dam during a war between Paraguay and Brazil.[36] The explicit goal was to send "a strong message to Paraguay."[37] The head of Brazil's Southern Command, General José Elito Carvalho Siquiera, told Brazilian newspapers: "The time for hiding things is over. Today we have to demonstrate that we are a leader, and it is important that our neighbors understand this. We cannot continue to avoid exercising and demonstrating that we are strong, that we are present, and we have the capacity to confront any threat."[38] The Paraguayan minister of foreign affairs, Leila Rachid, privately told American diplomats that "Amorim [the Brazilian foreign minister] is pushing an agenda designed to minimize U.S. influence in South America and assert Brazilian dominance, a course she strongly opposes because it translates into unfettered Brazilian control of Paraguay's destiny."[39] Rachid was upset not only about the dam but also about active Brazilian interference on behalf of 350,000 Brazilian settlers in Paraguay.

Brazil's flirtation with the empire trap was clearer in neighboring Bolivia. When Bolivian president Evo Morales nationalized Brazilian-owned natural gas assets on May 1, 2006, Brazilian president Luis "Lula" Da Silva's first impulse was to conciliate. The Brazilian president, in the words of U.S. diplomats, "issued a stunningly bland public statement . . . recognizing Bolivia's sovereignty to act as it did but reaffirming that Brazil would act to protect the interests of . . . Petrobras."[40] The government's conciliation brought Lula a great deal of grief at home, especially after Bolivia sent troops into the gas fields. American diplomats noted that "Lula and his foreign policy team could not look worse at this moment. The image of Bolivian soldiers moving into Petrobras installations is vivid and offensive for Brazilians of all classes, and will appear to many as a massive rebuke to the Lula administration's theology of a Brazilian-led new era of 'regional integration.' Indeed, in the Brazilian press and popular imagination, Lula is increasingly seen as outmaneuvered, manipulated and flimflammed by his 'hermanos,' Chávez and Morales."[41] Public outrage, stoked by Petrobras, continued at a high pitch. "The largest newsmagazine [pilloried] President Lula's chief foreign policy advisors for their handling of the Bolivian episode, labeling them at one point, 'Sheep in Sheep's Clothing.' "[42]

The Brazilian government then reversed course and threatened retaliation. Brazilian negotiators rebuffed Morales's demands for a price increase and refused to accept the loss of managerial control. Brazil then threatened to stop paying for Bolivia's gas exports. "This is a poker game," said Marcel Biato, Lula's deputy foreign affairs adviser.[43] Eventually, Bolivia walked back the nationalization: the final settlement amounted to little more than a tax increase from 50% of gross revenues to something between 67 and 75%, depending on gas prices.[44] A great nationalist expropriation turned into a modest tax hike.

The story played out again in 2007 and 2008. In 2007, Bolivia nationalized Petrobras's refining assets. The Brazilian government angrily stood firm and extracted $112 million in compensation.[45] The same year, explicit Brazilian pressure forced Evo Morales to rewrite a land reform law to effectively exempt fifteen thousand Brazilian settlers in the frontier zone.[46] In 2008, when natural gas revenues again became an issue, Brazilian foreign minister Celso Amorim responded with a threat, this time that his government was prepared to "open direct contacts with [Bolivia's] eastern governors if necessary."[47] The Brazilian defense minister than repeated the statement. At the time, Bolivia's eastern governors were openly threatening to secede from Bolivia; the implication did not need to spelled out.

The clearest example of the empire trap at work came from Ecuador. Problems at the San Francisco hydroelectric dam led the Ecuadorian government to cancel its $243 million contract with Odebrecht, a Brazilian construction company. President Rafael Correa of Ecuador sent troops to seize the San Francisco dam along with an irrigation project, a hydropower plant, a highway, and an airport Odebrecht was building. Odebrecht officials fled to the Brazilian embassy for protection.[48] As a result, Brazil recalled its ambassador. Foreign Minister Celso Amorim said, "There are no plans for the ambassador's return to Quito."[49] The Brazilians then threatened to cancel all development loans and credits. The Ecuadorian government backed down, and Brazil's ambassador returned in January 2009.[50] In a second investment dispute, Ecuador made sure to conciliate the Brazilians. In 2010, Petrobras rejected a contractual change from the Ecuadorean government that transformed its production-sharing agreements into a service contract offering a flat per barrel fee. In 2008, when these changes were mooted, Petrobras wrote in its annual report that the contract shift would reduce the recovery value of their assets by $174.3 million.[51] The changes in the Ecuadorean contracts reduced Petrobras's revenue (at 2008 prices) by $25.0 million per year.[52] In 2012, Ecuador agreed to compensate Petrobras $217 million.[53]

Despite President Lula's ideological predilection, the Brazilian government found itself involved in disputes with three nearby countries over investments. In Bolivia and Ecuador, the Brazilian government actively intervened in disputes between Brazilian companies and foreign governments. The Bolivian and Paraguayan cases held special potential for trouble, considering the large and growing Brazilian populations in both countries and the multiplicity of interests that Brasilia has beyond the protection of foreign direct investment. Brazil's travails over the last decade provide a cautionary tale of what might happen if the international institutions underpinning investor-versus-state arbitration are allowed to collapse. Major regional powers like China and India can easily play the game of empire.

There are risks in allowing the current system governing investor-versus-state disputes to lose its legitimacy, but a sustained rise in the riskiness of foreign investment—at least in extractive industries—is not among them. Should the international institutions that protect investors lose their enforcement mechanisms or otherwise become ineffective, then investors from large countries will still be significantly protected against predation or opportunism on the part of smaller foreign governments. That protection, however, will come from investors' ability to influence or manipulate the foreign policy of their home nation—in other words, the empire trap. The history of the first and second American empires indicates that it is not the international investor who is at risk from the loss of the institutions that protect foreign investment, but the independence of national foreign policy.

NOTES

Abbreviations

AG. Archivo General de la Nación, Mexico City
FRU. Foreign Relations of the United States
GPO U.S. Government Printing Office
NA. National Archives, Washington, D.C.

Chapter 1: Introduction

1. John Crook, "U.S. Response to Venezuelan Nationalizations," *American Journal of International Law*, vol. 101, no. 3 (July 2007), pp. 645–47.

2. Soviet allies include Baathist Syria and Iraq and Libya under Qaddafi—although it is not clear that Qaddafi actually caused American oil investors in his country to lose income.

3. There were two other cases, both in Bolivia, where the United States strong-armed the Bolivian government into granting variable compensation arrangements *as desired by the investors*, but which turned out to be bad for the former owners because of unforeseen macroeconomic events.

4. Fair compensation is defined as either the market value of the earnings from the investment or the net present value of the cash flows using the prevailing rate on U.S. corporate bonds. It is unfortunately near-impossible with available data to estimate the fair market value of utilities, banks, and insurance firms. Most such disputes were resolved to the satisfaction of the companies involved, which suggests that they got a good or at least an acceptable deal, but the hypothesis that they were settling for less than fair value cannot be eliminated.

5. This pattern of brief intervention, of course, changed once the Cold War ended. If there was a third American empire developing after 1989, however, it died stillborn in the sands of Iraq and Afghanistan.

6. México, Secretaria de Relaciones Exteriores, *Memoria de 1938–1939*, vol. 1, pp. 83, 93–94, 114–19, 135–39, 148.

7. Robert H. Bates, Avner Greif, Margaret Levi, Jean-Laurent Rosenthal, and Barry R. Weingast, *Analytic Narratives* (Princeton, N.J.: Princeton University Press, 1998).

8. Jessica Einhorn, *Expropriation Politics* (Lexington, Mass: Lexington Books, 1974); George Ingram, *Expropriation of U.S. Property in South America: Nationalization of Oil and Copper Companies in Peru, Bolivia, and Chile* (New York: Praeger Publishers, 1974); Paul Sigmund, *Multinationals in Latin America: The Politics of Nationalization* (Madison: University of Wisconsin Press, 1980); Sidney Weintraub, *Economic Coercion and U.S. Foreign Policy: Implications of Case Studies from the Johnson Administration* (Boulder, Colo: Westview Press, 1982).

9. Stephen D. Krasner, *Defending the National Interest: Raw Materials Investments and U.S. Foreign Policy* (Princeton, N.J.: Princeton University Press, 1978), pp. 38–40.

10. Krasner, *National Interest*, pp. 79–82.

11. Krasner, *National Interest*, pp. 82–88.

12. Krasner, *National Interest*, pp. 337–42.

13. Charles Lipson, *Standing Guard: Protecting Foreign Capital in the Nineteenth and Twentieth Centuries* (Berkeley: University of California Press, 1985), p. 262.

14. Lipson, *Standing Guard*, p. 251.

15. Lipson, *Standing Guard*, p. 143.

16. Lipson, *Standing Guard*, p. 251.

17. Jeffry Frieden, "The Economics of Intervention: American Overseas Investments and Relations with Underdeveloped Areas, 1890–1950," *Comparative Studies in Society and History*, vol. 31, no. 1 (1989), pp. 55–80: 80.

18. Frieden, "Intervention."

19. Michael Tomz, *Reputation and International Cooperation: Sovereign Debt across Three Centuries* (Princeton, N.J.: Princeton University Press, 2007).

20. Michael Tomz and Mark Wright, "Sovereign Theft: Theory and Evidence about Sovereign Default and Expropriation," in William Hogan and Federico Sturzenegger, eds., *The Natural Resources Trap: Private Investment without Public Commitment* (Cambridge, Mass: MIT Press, 2010), pp. 69–110.

21. Available at http://www.chartercities.org/concept, accessed August 29, 2012.

22. The Spanish text of the constitutional amendments can be found at http://nacerenhonduras.com/2011/01/el-decreto-de-ciudad-modelo-regiones.html, accessed August 29, 2012.

23. See "Update on Honduran Progress" at http://chartercities.org/resources, accessed August 29, 2012.

24. "Estatuto Constitucional de las Regiones Especiales de Desarollo," *La Gaceta Oficial no. 32,601*, August 23, 2011, Sección A, "Acuerdos y Leyes," pp. A3–A12.

Chapter 2: Avoiding the Trap

1. The United States made a few small attempts at formal expansion after 1898 for strategic reasons: successfully in American Samoa (1900), the Virgin Islands (1917), and Micronesia (1945); unsuccessfully in Trinidad and Bermuda (1931); and temporarily in the Panama Canal Zone (1903–79) and Okinawa (1945–72). The United States gave up sovereignty over parts of Micronesia in 1986 and 1994, but the Northern Marianas remained an American commonwealth, and the U.S. government retained special privileges (including the right to seize land for defense purposes and control over foreign treaties) in the rest of the former Trust Territory of the Pacific Islands via the "Compacts of Free Association" signed with the successor states. In return, the three successor states retained access to some U.S. government services (such as the National Weather Service) and free labor migration.

2. See Albert Hogan, *Pacific Blockade* (Oxford: Clarendon Press, 1908).

3. In the event, this assumption turned out to be incorrect.

4. In Puerto Rico, where the population was considered majority white *and* which attracted relatively little investment interest from the mainland, Congress failed to impose impediments to American capital. Congress did, however, keep Puerto Rico outside the American tariff wall until 1912. The text of the Foraker Act of 1900, which provided civil government to the island, can be found at http://www-rohan.sdsu.edu/dept/polsciwb/brianl/docs/1900ForakerAct.pdf, accessed February 27, 2012. It is quite possible, even probable, that had it not been for the fact that the Philippines were annexed at the same time, Congress would have extended the Constitution to the island.

5. The pattern was stylized, and it did not always hold. Very few Americans lived in the Mexican Cession when it was annexed in 1848, for example; the government moved in advance of its people. Conversely, mass

American settlement in Alberta did not lead that province to switch allegiance from London to Washington.

6. Sumner La Croix and Christopher Grandy, "The Political Instability of Reciprocal Trade and the Overthrow of the Hawaiian Kingdom," *Journal of Economic History*, vol. 57, no. 1 (March 1997), pp. 161–89: 174.

7. King Kamehameha III offered to cede his country to the United States, but the United States refused in order to avoid antagonizing France.

8. La Croix and Grandy, "Hawaiian Kingdom," p. 168.

9. La Croix and Grandy, "Hawaiian Kingdom," p. 172.

10. Hawaiian Islands and Alatau Atkinson, *Report of the General Superintendent of the Census, 1896* (Honolulu: Hawaiian Star Press, 1897), pp. 21 and 51.

11. Hawaiian Islands and Atkinson, *Report*, pp. 21 and 51.

12. Hawaiian Islands and Atkinson, *Report*, pp. 34 and 38. The total population was 109,020.

13. LaCroix and Grandy, "Hawaiian Kingdom," p. 173, and Hawaiian Islands and Atkinson, *Report*, p. 34. The census divided the Hawaiian population into Hawaiians and "half-Hawaiians," numbering 31,019 and 8,485 respectively.

14. For a taste of the debate over the proper racial status of the Portuguese, see Lorrin Thurston, "A Hand-Book on the Annexation of Hawaii" (University of Manchester, John Rylands University Library, 1897), p. 32.

15. LaCroix and Grandy, "Hawaiian Kingdom," p. 179.

16. President Grover Cleveland's message of December 18, 1893. Cited in U.S. Congress, *Hawaiian Islands:Report of the Committee on Foreign Relations, United States Senate, with Accompanying Testimony, and Executive Documents Transmitted to Congress from January 1, 1883 to March 10, 1894* (Washington, D.C.: GPO, 1894), p. 1253.

17. Grover Cleveland, "1893 State of the Union Address," http://www.usa-presidents.info/union/cleveland-5.html, accessed February 27, 2012.

18. David Pletcher, *The Diplomacy of Involvement: American Economic Expansion across the Pacific* (Columbia: University of Missouri Press, 2001), pp. 271–72.

19. George Frisbie Hoar and John Bellows, *Autobiography of Seventy Years*, vol. 2 (New York: C. Scribner's Sons, 1903), pp. 305–67.

20. The exact status of the Hawaiian Islands would not be fully clarified until the Organic Act of 1900.

21. "I ask the Congress to authorize and empower the President to take measures to secure a full and final termination of hostilities between the government of Spain and the people of Cuba, and to secure in the island

the establishment of a stable government, capable of maintaining order and observing its international obligations, insuring peace and tranquility and the security of its citizens as well as our own." Julius Muller, ed., *Presidential Messages and State Papers*,vol. 8 (New York: Review of Reviews Company, 1917), pp. 2967–69.

22. Miller, *Presidential Messages and State Papers,* vol. 8, pp. 2967–69.

23. *The Abridgment Containing the Annual Message of the President of the United States to the Two Houses of Congress with the Reports of the Heads of Departments,* vol. 2 (Washington, D.C.: GPO, 1899), p. 904.

24. See George Dewey, *Autobiography of George Dewey* (New York: Charles Scribner's Sons, 1913), p. 299, and George Loud, "The Battle of Manila Bay—The Destruction of the Spanish Fleet as Told by Eye-Witnesses, Part I, Col. George Loud's Narrative of the Battle of Manila Bay," *The Century,* vol. 56, no. 4 (August 1898), pp. 611–18.

25. Paul A. Kramer, *The Blood of Government: Race, Empire, the United States, & the Philippines* (Chapel Hill: University of North Carolina Press, 2006), p. 94.

26. Dominic Tierney, *How We Fight: Crusades, Quagmires, and the American Way of War* (New York: Little, Brown, and Company, 2010), p. 98.

27. Tierney, *How We Fight,* p. 104.

28. Kramer, *Blood of Government,* p. 110.

29. John McGrath, "Boots on the Ground: Troop Density in Contingency Operations," Global War on Terrorism Occasional Paper 16 (Fort Leavenworth, Kans.: Combat Studies Institute Press, 2006), p. 9.

30. Because the Philippine War lasted 28 months, as opposed to the 102 months of the Iraq War, the total proportion of Americans who served in the Philippines was much lower. The 126,000 people who served in the Philippines over the entire course of combat operations amounted to 0.2% of the U.S. population, compared with the roughly 0.6% of the U.S. population who served at least one tour of duty in Iraq between March 20, 2003, and the official end of combat operations on August 31, 2010.

31. Iraq casualty rates per 100,000 ran at 718 in 2003, 650 in 2004, 588 in 2005, 583 in 2006, and 610 in 2007. They then dropped precipitously to 199 in 2008, 135 in 2009, and 121 in 2010. Calculated from data in Amy Belasco, "Troop Levels in the Afghan and Iraq Wars, FY2001–FY2012: Cost and Other Potential Issues," Congressional Research Service report, July 2, 2009, and the Brookings-Saban Iraq Index, http://www.brookings.edu/saban/iraq-index.aspx, accessed March 4, 2011. Philippine data from

John Tierney, *Chasing Ghosts: Unconventional Warfare in American History* (Washington, DC: Potomac Books, 2006), pp. 110–14.

32. For more detail, see John Gates, "Philippine Guerrillas," *Pacific Historical Review*, vol. 46 (February 1977), pp. 51–64. Iyengar and Monten find a similar result for the Iraqi insurgency: see Radha Iyengar and Jonathan Monten, "Is There an 'Emboldenment' Effect? Evidence from the Insurgency in Iraq" NBER Working Paper No. 13838 (March 2008).

33. *Report of the Taft Philippine Commission* (Washington, D.C.: GPO, 1901), pp. 5–7. In 1900, public lands made up an estimated 93% of the Philippine Islands' total area. Ibid, p. 33.

34. Alan Dye and Richard Sicotte, "The Political Economy of Exporting Economic Instability: The U.S. Sugar Tariff and the Cuban Revolution of 1933," Barnard College Working Paper Series #99-05, p. 18.

35. Glenn May, *Social Engineering in the Philippines: The Aims, Execution and Impact of American Colonial Policy, 1900–13* (Westport, Conn.: Greenwood Press, 1980), p. 151.

36. Henry Teller of Colorado became a Silver Republican in 1896, and formally switched his party affiliation to Democratic at the end of the 55th Congress in March 1901. Strangely, he nonetheless continued as chairman of the Committee on Private Land Claims, even though the GOP held the majority. Teller opposed allowing American private investment to freely enter the Philippines.

37. May, *Social Engineering*, p. 151.

38. "Philippine Problem before the Senate: Senator Hoar Talks for an Investigating Committee," *New York Times*, January 15, 1902, p. 3.

39. "Told of 'Water Cure' Given to Filipinos: Witnesses Went into Details before Senate Committee on the Philippines," *New York Times*, April 15, 1902; "Saw the 'Water Cure' Given," *New York Times*, April 18, 1902, p. 3; "Testified on 'Water Cure,'" *New York Times*, April 22, 1902, p. 2; "The Water Cure Described: Discharged Soldier Tells Senate Committee How and Why the Torture Was Inflicted," *New York Times*, May 4, 1902; "One 'Water Cure' Victim Witness Tells of the Case before Senate Committee," *New York Times*, May 11, 1902, p. 5; "'Water Cure' and Wine: Witness before the Senate Philippine Committee Says One Is No Worse Than the Other," *New York Times*, May 16, 1902, p. 3; "Cruelty in Philippines: Corp. O'Brien Makes Accusation against Army Officers," *New York Times*, May 20, 1902, p. 3; "The Concentration Camps: Assistant Adjutant General Wagner Describes One—Filipinos Were Surprisingly Contented, He Says," *New York Times*, May 30, 1902, p. 3; "Says a Village Was Burned: Assistant Adjt. Gen. Wagner, USA., Continues His

Testimony before the Senate Philippines Committee," *New York Times*, June 1, 1902, p. 5; "Tell of 'Water Cure' Cases: Witnesses Give Further Testimony before the Senate Committee on the Philippines Regarding Filipinos' Treatment," *New York Times*, June 13, 1902, p. 3.

40. "The Philippine Inquiry Senate Minority Want Major Gardener Summoned from Manila," *New York Times*, May 1, 1902, p. 3, and "Philippine Bill Discussion: In the Senate It Revolved around the Resolution Calling for Major Gardener," *New York Times*, May 4, 1902, p. 13.

41. The fusion ticket combined the Democratic, Republican, and Silver Republican parties.

42. "Philippine Question Up in the Senate: Mr. Beveridge Criticises the Minority's Attacks on the Army," *New York Times*, May 7, 1902, p. 3.

43. *Cong. Rec.*, 57th Congress, 1st session, May 31, 1902, p. 6145.

44. *Cong. Rec.*, 57th Congress, 1st session, May 23, 1902, p. 5862.

45. *Cong. Rec.*, 57th Congress, 1st session, 1902, p. 2076.

46. *Cong. Rec.*, 57th Congress, 1st session, June 24, 1902, p. 7344.

47. *Cong. Rec.*, 57th Congress, 1st session, June 20, 1902, p. 7132.

48. *Cong. Rec.*, 57th Congress, 1st session, June 30, 1902, pp. 7699–7700.

49. *Cong. Rec.*, 57th Congress, 1st session, February 22, 1902, p. 2076.

50. *Cong. Rec.*, 57th Congress, 1st session, April 23, 1902, p. 4571.

51. *Cong. Rec.*, 57th Congress, 1st session, February 24, 1902, p. 2113.

52. *Cong. Rec.*, 57th Congress, 1st session, May 23, 1902, p. 5860.

53. *Cong. Rec.*, 57th Congress, 1st session, April 4, 1902, p. 3681.

54. *Cong. Rec.*, 57th Congress, 1st session, May 13, 1902, p. 5354.

55. May, *Social Engineering*, p. 154.

56. Cited in May, *Social Engineering*, p. 152.

57. Cited in May, *Social Engineering*, p. 152.

58. Text of the Philippine Organic Act of 1902, http://www.chanrobles .com/philippinebillof1902.htm, accessed March 4, 2011.

59. May, *Social Engineering*, pp. 158–59.

60. Susan Carter, ed., *Historical Statistics of the United States*, Millennial Edition (New York: Cambridge University Press, 2006), table Ef93–99. Value calculated by multiplying output in tons by the export price to the United States.

61. Catherine Porter, *Crisis in the Philippines* (New York: Knopf, 1942), p. 28.

62. Charles Maclean, "Right Foot Forward," *Whisky Magazine* (March 1999).

63. Frank Golay, *Face of Empire: United States–Philippine Relations, 1898–1946* (Manila: Ateneo de Manila University Press, 1998), p. 266.

64. Golay, *Face of Empire*, p. 244.

65. Cited in Golay, *Face of Empire*, p. 267.

66. Golay, *Face of Empire*, p. 267.

67. Golay, *Face of Empire*, p. 267.

68. Cited in Golay, *Face of Empire*, p. 267.

69. Cited in Golay, *Face of Empire*, p. 267.

70. Golay, *Face of Empire*, p. 268.

71. Golay, *Face of Empire*, p. 268.

72. U.S. Tariff Commission, *Philippine Trade Report* no. 118 (1937), p. 191.

73. Samuel Tan, *A History of the Philippines* (Quezon City: University of the Philippines Press, 2009), p. 70.

74. U.S. Deptartment of Commerce, *American Direct Investments in Foreign Countries* (Washington, D.C.: GPO, 1930), p. 28.

75. "Return of the King," *Time*, March 8, 1948.

76. http://avalon.law.yale.edu/19th_century/sp1898.asp, accessed February 25, 2012.

77. Louis Pérez, "Cuba between Empires, 1898–1899," *Pacific Historical Review*, vol. 48, no. 4 (November 1979), pp. 473–500: 474.

78. Juan Santamarina, "The Cuba Company and the Expansion of American Business in Cuba, 1898–1915," *The Business History Review*, vol. 74, no. 1 (Spring 2000), pp. 41–83: 45.

79. The text of the amendment as it was appended to the Cuban Constitution is reproduced in Albert Norton, *Norton's Complete Hand-Book of Havana and Cuba* (New York: Rand, McNally & Company, 1900), p. 280.

80. Joseph Foraker, *Notes of a Busy Life*, vol. 2 (Cincinnati: Stewart & Kidd Company, 1917), p. 44.

81. Foraker, *Notes*, p. 46.

82. *Meetings of the Directors of the Cuba Company: From Incorporation to 1913*, 1–15, Cuba Company Records, Special Collections, University of Maryland at College Park Libraries, series 1, box A.

83. Santamarina, "Cuba Company," p. 52.

84. Santamarina, "Cuba Company," p. 55.

85. Santamarina, "Cuba Company," pp. 56–57.

86. U.S. War Department, Division of Insular Affairs, *Translation of the Proposed Constitution for Cuba, the Official Acceptance of the Platt Amendment, and the Electoral Law* (Washington, D.C.: GPO, 1901), pp. 23–24.

Chapter 3: Setting the Trap

1. The text of the treaty can be found in "San Domingo's Annexation to the United States," *New York Times*, January 13, 1870.

2. The bonds had a nominal coupon of 6% and were sold at 83.5% of face value, for an effective rate of 7.2%.

3. Before decimalization in 1971, there were 240 pence to the pound.

4. The bonds had a nominal coupon of 6% and were offered at 77% of face value, for an effective rate of 7.8%.

5. John Moore, *Case of the United States Before the Commission of Arbitration under the provisions of the Protocol of January 13, 1903, between the United States of America and the Dominican Republic for the settlement of the claims of the San Domingo Improvement Company* (February 12, 1904), pp. 4–7.

6. Moore, *Case*, p. 7.

7. Heureaux had ruled as a dictator since 1882; Dominican courts were far from independent.

8. Moore, *Case*, pp. 12–13.

9. Moore, *Case*, pp. 12–13.

10. For the details of the confrontation and the U.S. role, see U.S. Department of State, Office of the Historian, *FRUS*, 1895, part 1, pp. 235–43 and 397–402.

11. Moore, *Case*, p. 17.

12. Moore, *Case*, p. 19.

13. Moore, *Case*, p. 18.

14. "A Brief History of U.S. Navy Cruisers: Part I—The Early Years (1900–1905)," http://www.navy.mil/navydata/ships/cruisers/history/cghist2.html, accessed December 27, 2010.

15. William Wynne, *State Insolvency and Foreign Bondholders: Selected Case Histories of Governmental Foreign Bond Defaults and Debt Readjustments* (New Haven: Yale University Press, 1951), pp. 225–26.

16. Moore, *Case*, p. 28.

17. Wynne, *Insolvency*, pp. 228–29.

18. Wynne, *Insolvency*, p. 234.

19. Wynne, *Insolvency*, p. 230.

20. Moore, *Case*, p. 33.

21. Suárez worried that the insurgency threatened the company's cane crop, which he estimated to be worth $250,000. Cited in J. Fred Rippy, "The Initiation of the Customs Receivership in the Dominican Republic,"

Hispanic American Historical Review, vol. 17, no. 4 (November 1937), pp. 419–57: 421.

22. Richard Grimmett, "Instances of Use of United States Armed Forces Abroad, 1798–2001," Congressional Research Service report, February 5, 2002, p. 12.

23. Cited in Rippy, "Initiation," pp. 420–23.

24. Rippy, "Initiation," pp. 431–32.

25. *Bradstreet's*, February 27, 1904, p. 1.

26. Rippy, "Initiation," p. 419.

27. Dawson to Hay, September 12, 1904, *FRUS*, 1904, p. 280.

28. Dawson to Hay, September 12, 1904.

29. Rippy, "Initiation," pp. 420–23.

30. Jacob Hollander, *Report on the Debt of Santo Domingo*, 59th Congress, 1st session, Senate Executive Document (Washington, D.C.: GPO, 1905), p. 48.

31. Dawson to Hay, September 27, 1904, *FRUS*, 1904, p. 280.

32. Dawson to Hay, October 6, 1904, *FRUS*, 1904.

33. Dana Gardner Munro, *Intervention and Dollar Diplomacy in the Caribbean, 1900–1921* (Princeton, N.J.: Princeton University Press, 1964), pp. 93–94. Powell to Hay, 16 and 18 April 1904, and Powell to P. Castillo, 17 and 19 April 1904, in Dispatches from U.S Ministers to the Dominican Republic, M93, roll 11, NA; Hay to Powell, 4 May 1904, in Diplomatic Instructions of the Department of State, M77, roll 98, Record Group 59, NA.

34. Dillingham to Secretary of Navy, 19 April 1904, Santo Domingo Correspondence Group, entry 305, pp. 1–2, Record Group 45, NA.

35. *Papers Relating to the Foreign Relations of the United States*, Part I (Washington, D.C.: GPO, 1909), p. 595; David MacMichael, "The United States and the Dominican Republic, 1871-1940: A Cycle in Caribbean Diplomacy" (Ph.D. dissertation, University of Oregon, 1964), p. 164; Hollander, *Debt of Santo Domingo*, p. 127.

36. Dillingham to Secretary of Navy, 18 April 1904, Confidential Ciphers Received, entry 40, p. 137, Record Group 45, NA.

37. Roosevelt to Charles W. Eliot, in Morison, *Letters of Theodore Roosevelt*, vol. 4 (Cambridge, Mass.: Harvard University Press, 1954), p. 770.

38. "We Are Well Disposed to All—Roosevelt," *New York Times*, May 12, 1904, p. 6.

39. Rippy, "Initiation," p. 419.

40. Ahmed, Alfaro, and Maurer, "Gunboats," p. 9.

41. Wynne, *Insolvency*, p. 238.

42. Moore, *Case*, p. 111.

43. Cited in Cyrus Veeser, "Inventing Dollar Diplomacy: The Gilded-Age Origins of the Roosevelt Corollary to the Monroe Doctrine," *Diplomatic History*, vol. 27, no. 3 (June 2003), p. 307.

44. Carlos Morales to Emilio Joubert, November 22, 1904, in tomo 11, Presidencia de la República, Archivo General de la Nación, Santo Domingo, Dominican Republic.

45. Dawson to Hay, October 6, 1904.

46. Munro, *Intervention*, p. 98.

47. Munro, *Intervention*, p. 101.

48. *FRUS*, 1905, pp. 334–42.

49. W. Stull Holt, *Treaties Defeated by the Senate: A Study of the Struggle between President and Senate over the Conduct of Foreign Relations* (Union, N.J.: Lawbook Exchange, 2000), p. 218.

50. *FRUS*, 1905, p. 358.

51. *FRUS*, 1905, p. 366.

52. Theodore Roosevelt, *An Autobiography* (New York: Charles Scriber's Sons, 1926), p. 524.

53. Office of the General Receiver of Dominican Customs, "Final report of the transactions of the Dominican customs receivership under the 'modus vivendi', covering the twenty-eight months April 1, 1905, to July 31, 1907" (Washington, D.C.: Bureau of Insular Affairs, 1907), p. 7.

54. General Receiver, "Report," p. 11.

55. *FRUS*, 1907, vol. 1, p. 337.

56. General Receiver, "Report," p. 11.

57. Using the U.S. Consumer Price Index.

58. Calculated from data in Moore, *Case*, pp. 88 and 92. Data from the 1902–3 fiscal year.

59. Frank Moya Pons, *History of the Caribbean: Plantations, Trade, and War in the Atlantic World* (Princeton, N.J.: Markus Wiener Publishers, 2007), p. 301.

60. *FRUS*, 1907, vol. 1, p. 338.

61. *FRUS*, 1907, vol. 1, p. 339.

62. *FRUS*, 1907, vol. 1, p. 342.

63. Cited in Veeser, "Gilded-Age," p. 321.

64. Veeser, "Gilded-Age," p. 322.

65. Herbert Pierce, Acting Secretary of State, to Hugh O'Beirne, June 27, 1905, *FRUS*, 1905, pp. 377–78.

66. Veeser, "Gilded-Age," p. 324.

67. Cited in Emily Rosenberg, *Financial Missionaries to the World: The Politics and Culture of Dollar Diplomacy, 1900–30* (Durham, N.C.: Duke University Press, 2003), p. 45.

68. Rosenberg, *Missionaries*, p. 46.

69. Wynne, *Insolvency*, p. 261.

70. See Kris James Mitchener and Marc Weidenmier, "Empire, Public Goods, and the Roosevelt Corollary," *Journal of Economic History*, vol. 65 (September 2005), pp. 658–92.

71. "South American Bonds up Over 100 Per Cent," *New York Times*, April 5, 1905.

72. For an excellent treatment of the causes and consequences of the Barings crisis, see Kris Mitchener and Marc Weidenmier, "The Baring Crisis and the Great Latin American Meltdown of the 1890s," *Journal of Economic History*, vol. 68 (June 2008), 462–500.

73. Frank Colby and Allen Churchill, eds., *The New International Year Book: A Compendium of the World's Progress* (New York: Dodd, Mead and Company, 1913), p. 51.

74. Robert Scheina, *Latin America's Wars: The Age of the Professional Soldier, 1900–2001* (Washington, DC: Brassey's, 2003), p. 38.

75. Colby and Churchill, *Year Book*, p. 145.

76. For data on relative fleet sizes during this period, including discussion of the logistical problems and technological limitations faced by the various navies, see Robert Gardiner, ed., *Conway's All the World's Fighting Ships, 1906–1921* (London: Naval Institute Press, 1985).

77. Sidney Ballou, *Comparisons of Naval Strength* (Washington, D.C.: Navy League of the United States, 1916), table II.

78. Nancy Mitchell, *The Danger of Dreams: German and American Imperialism in Latin America* (Chapel Hill: University. of North Carolina Press, 1999), pp. 126–32.

79. Mitchell, *Imperialism*, p. 153.

80. See Lars Schoultz, *That Infernal Little Cuban Republic* (Chapel Hill: University of North Carolina Press, 2009), pp. 25–28.

81. The result is statistically significant at the 95% level.

82. J. N. Larned, Donald Smith, Charles Seymour, Augustus Hunt Shearer, and Daniel Knowlton, *The New Larned History for Ready Reference, Reading and Research* (Springfield, Mass: C. A. Nichols Pub. Co, 1922), p. 1502.

83. Brian McBeth, *Gunboats, Corruption, and Claims: Foreign Intervention in Venezuela* (Westport, Conn.: Greenwood Press, 2001), pp. 31–35.

84. McBeth, *Gunboats*, 31–35.

85. Richard Rothwell, ed., *The Mineral Industry*, vol. 9 (New York: Scientific Publishing Co., 1901), p. 49.

86. Most of Hamilton's stake in the company ended up in Guzmán's hands. McBeth, *Gunboats*, p. 42.

87. McBeth, *Gunboats*, pp. 43–44.

88. Calculated from data in McBeth, *Gunboats*, p. 47, and Department of the Interior, United States Geological Survey, *Mineral Resources of the United States* (Washington, D.C.: GPO, 1902), pp. 637 and 640. For comparison, labor costs in the asphalt fields came to 4.9% of the company's export revenues in 1900. (Calculated from data in Rothwell, *The Mineral Industry*, pp. 49–50.)

89. McBeth, *Gunboats*, p. 46.

90. McBeth, *Gunboats*, p. 47.

91. McBeth, *Gunboats*, p. 48.

92. William Calhoun, "Wrongs to American Citizens in Venezuela," Senate document no. 413, 60th Congress, 1st session, September 1907, p. 310.

93. William Sullivan, "The Rise of Despotism in Venezuela: Cipriano Castro, 1899–1908," Ph.D. dissertation, University of New Mexico, 1974, p. 487.

94. McBeth, *Gunboats*, pp. 54–58.

95. McBeth, *Gunboats*, p. 92.

96. Calculated from data in Jackson Ralston, "Venezuelan Arbitrations of 1903," document no. 316, 58th Congress, 2nd session (Washington, D.C.: GPO, 1904), pp. 260, 291, 490, 510, 641, 871, 888, 916, 942, 954, and N. Veloz Goiticoa, ed., *Venezuela: Geographical Sketch, Natural Resources, Laws, Economic Conditions, Actual Development, Prospects of Future Growth* (Washington, D.C.: GPO, 1904), p. 426.

97. *Mexican Year Book*, 1908 (London: McCorquodale & Co. Ltd., 1908), pp. 510–11; *Engineering and Mining Journal*, June 13, 1908, pp. 1210, 1214.

98. *Engineering and Mining Journal*, January 5, 1907; *Engineering and Mining Journal*, March 13, 1909; *Engineering and Mining Journal*, October 2, 1909. Zinc output figures indicate that in 1911 Mexico's zinc output was only 7% of its 1907 level.

99. That delegation included Federal Deputy José Luis Requena and Senator Ramón Alcaraz. *Engineering and Mining Journal*, June 20, 1908, p. 1267; *Engineering and Mining Journal*, October 23, 1909.

100. *Engineering and Mining Journal*, August 1, 1908, p. 252.

101. *Engineering and Mining Journal*, October 24, 1908, p. 833.

102. *Engineering and Mining Journal*, November 21, 1908, p. 1025.

103. *Engineering and Mining Journal*, October 23, 1909.

104. *Mexican Yearbook*, 1909–10, pp. 520–21; *Engineering and Mining Journal*, June 13, 1908, p. 1214.

105. *Mexican Yearbook*, 1909–10, pp. 520–21; *Engineering and Mining Journal*, February 19, 1910, pp. 416–19.

Chapter 4: The Trap Closes

1. Jack Lane, *Armed Progressive: General Leonard Wood* (Lincoln: University of Nebraska Press, 2009), p. 104. In a separate letter to President McKinley, Wood specified a rate of 6%.

2. Mitchener and Weidenmier, "Roosevelt Corollary."

3. *FRUS*, 1905, p. 379.

4. Otto Schoenrich, *Santo Domingo: A Country with a Future* (MacMillan: New York, 1918), p. 49.

5. *FRUS*, 1905, p. 408.

6. Schoenrich, *Santo Domingo*, p. 49.

7. Dawson to Secretary of State, February 2, 1906, *FRUS*, 1906, pp. 552–53.

8. Dawson to Secretary of State, May 10, 1906, *FRUS*, 1906, pp. 562.

9. Schoenrich, *Santo Domingo*, p. 50.

10. Welles, cited in Whitney Perkins, *Constraint of Empire: The United States and Caribbean Interventions* (Westport, Conn.: Greenwood Press, 1981), p. 46.

11. Munro, *Intervention*, pp. 260–61.

12. Russell to Secretary of State, April 15, 1912, *FRUS*, 1912 p. 346.

13. Russell to Secretary of State, September 16, 1912, *FRUS*, 1912, p. 366.

14. Russell to Secretary of State, August 3, 1912, *FRUS*, 1912, p. 363.

15. Russell and the Special Commissioners to the Secretary of State, November 13, 1912, *FRUS*, 1912, p. 375.

16. Russell and the Special Commissioners to the Secretary of State, November 13, 1912, *FRUS*, 1912, pp. 375–76.

17. Munro, *Intervention*, pp. 262–64.

18. Perkins, *Empire*, p. 47.

19. Munro, *Intervention*, pp. 262–64.

20. Munro, *Intervention*, pp. 265–67.

21. *FRUS,* 1913, pp. 421–22.

22. *FRUS,* 1913, p. 427.

23. Munro, *Intervention*, pp. 277–81.

24. *FRUS,* 1913, pp. 449–53; Munro, *Intervention*, pp. 281–82.

25. Munro, *Intervention*, pp. 283–91.

26. Munro, *Intervention*, pp. 283–91.

27. Munro, *Intervention*, pp. 292–93.

28. Munro, *Intervention*, pp. 292–93.

29. Munro, *Intervention*, pp. 293–95.

30. Munro, *Intervention*, pp. 295–302.

31. Munro, *Intervention*, pp. 302–4.

32. Munro, *Intervention*, pp. 295–302.

33. *FRUS,* 1916, pp. 221–27.

34. Lester Langley, *The Banana Wars: United States Intervention in the Caribbean, 1898–1934* (Lexington: University Press of Kentucky, 1983), pp. 137–41.

35. Munro, *Intervention*, pp. 307–14.

36. Munro, *Intervention*, pp. 307–14; Wilson's quote, *FRUS,* 1916, p. 242.

37. Munro, *Intervention*, pp. 314–25; Langley, *Banana Wars*, pp. 144–49.

38. Munro, *Intervention*, pp. 314–25; Langley, *Banana Wars*, pp. 144–49.

39. *FRUS,* 1920, vol. 2, pp. 136–38.

40. Langley, *Banana Wars*, pp. 52–53.

41. Calculated using the online tools at http://www.measuringworth .com/uscompare/relativevalue.php, accessed March 21, 2012.

42. The company's manager, Sam Spellman, presented these figure to Congress in 1914. Michael Gismondi and Jeremy Mouat, "Merchants, Mining and Concessions on Nicaragua's Mosquito Coast: Reassessing the American Presence, 1895–1912" *Journal of Latin American Studies*, vol. 34, no. 4 (November 2002), p. 859.

43. Using U.S. GDP deflator.

44. Gismondi and Mouat, "Merchants," p. 859.

45. Gismondi and Mouat, "Merchants," pp. 859–60.

46. Merry to Secretary of State Root, 19 December 1907, Record Group 84, NA. See also Kinzer, *Overthrow: America's Century of Regime Change from Hawaii to Iraq* (New York: Times Books/Henry Holt, 2006), p. 64.

47. Clancy to Assistant Secretary of State, 12 September 1908, M862, microfilm roll 283, NA. See also Kinzer, *Overthrow*, p. 64.

48. Salisbury (President, U.S. and Nicaragua Company) to Secretary Knox, 22 March 1909, M862, microfilm roll 283, NA.

49. Gismondi and Mouat, "Merchants," pp. 878–79.

50. Mark Strecker, *Smedley D. Butler, USMC: A Biography* (Jefferson, N.C.: McFarland & Co, 2011), p. 43. See also Gismondi and Mouat, "Merchants," p. 863, n. 74.

51. Benjamin Harrison, "The United States and the 1909 Nicaraguan Revolution," *Caribbean Quarterly*, vol. 41, no. 3 (1995), p. 54.

52. Thomas O'Brien, *The Revolutionary Mission: American Enterprise in Latin America, 1900–1945* (New York: Cambridge University Press, 1996), p. 63.

53. Otto Schoenrich to William Bryan, Washington D.C., January 4, 1915, 417.00/200, Record Group 59, NA. United Fruit, it should be noted, produced about a quarter of the area's production on its own lands.

54. O'Brien, *Mission*, p. 62.

55. Henry Gregory to Secretary of State, Bluefields, 30 April 1909, case 19745/8, roll 1066, M-862, and case 19475/61–74, roll 1066, M-862, Numerical and Minor Files of the Department of State, NA.

56. O'Brien, *Mission*, p. 64.

57. O'Brien, *Mission*, pp. 64–65.

58. Gismondi and Mouat, "Merchants."

59. Lawrence Lenz, *Power and Policy: America's First Steps to Superpower, 1889–1922* (New York: Algora Pub., 2008), pp. 177–79.

60. Langley, *Banana Wars*, pp. 56–57.

61. Scott Nearing and Joseph Freeman, *Dollar Diplomacy; A Study in American Imperialism* (New York: B.W. Huebsch and the Viking Press, 1925), p. 152.

62. *FRUS*, 1909, pp. 446–57.

63. "Zelaya Broke Faith to Kill Americans," *New York Times*, November 23, 1909, and Jorge Eduardo Arellano, "La ejecución de los estadounidenses Cannon y Groce," *El Nuevo Diario*, November 28, 2009.

64. United States, *Annual Report of the Secretary of the Navy: 1910* (Washington, D.C.: GPO, 1910), p. 803. The initial landing force consisted of 700 Marines.

65. Langley, *Banana Wars*, p. 59.

66. Richard Salisbury, *Anti-Imperialism and International Competition in Central America, 1920–1929* (Wilmington, Del: SR Books, 1989), p. 10.

67. Jürgen Buchenau, "Counter-Intervention against Uncle Sam: Mexico's Support for Nicaraguan Nationalism, 1903–1910," *The Americas*, vol. 50, no. 2 (October 1993), pp. 207–32: 221.

68. Adjusted for purchasing power, the £1.25 million loan came to $147 million in 2010 dollars. That number, however, fails to capture the contemporary magnitude of the loan: after accounting for U.S. economic growth, the loan was the 2010 equivalent of $2.7 *billion*. Calculated using the on-line tools at http://www.measuringworth.com/calculators/exchange/result_exchange.php and http://www.measuringworth.com/calculators/compare/index.php, accessed March 22, 2012.

69. Munro, *Intervention*, p. 169.

70. Richard Salisbury, "Great Britain, the United States, and the 1909–1910 Nicaraguan Crisis," *The Americas*, vol. 53, no. 3 (January 1997), pp. 379–94: 383–84.

71. United States, *Foreign Loans: Hearings before the Subcommittee of the Committee on Foreign Relations, United States Senate, Sixty-Ninth Congress, Second Session, Pursuant to S. Con. Res. 15 Relative to Engaging the Responsibility of the Government in Financial Arrangements between Its Citizens and Sovereign Foreign Governments, January 25, 26, 27, and February 16, 1927* (Washington, D.C.: GPO, 1927), p. 42.

72. William Rees to Secretary of State Knox, 14 September 1909, M862, roll 283, NA.

73. Gardyne Stewart to Wilson, 7 December 1909, M862, roll 283, NA.

74. Harrison, "Nicaraguan Revolution," p. 55.

75. Harrison, "Nicaraguan Revolution," p. 55.

76. Thomas Moffat to Assistant Secretary of State, 27 November 1909, SD 6369/365, NA.

77. *FRUS*, 1909, pp. 446–57. For examples of the U.S. press outrage, see Kinzer, *Overthrow*, p. 65.

78. Quoted in Gismondi and Mouat, "Merchants," p. 869.

79. Munro, *Intervention*, pp. 192–99.

80. Henry Stimson, *Henry Stimson's American Policy in Nicaragua: The Lasting Legacy* (Princeton, N.J.: Markus Wiener Press, 1991), p. 159.

81. A. F. Lindberg, "Nicaragua: The Central American Republic with a Future," *The Bankers Magazine*, vol. 100 (1920), p. 261. United States Bureau of Manufactures, *Special Agents Series*, nos. 110–18 (Washington, D.C.: GPO, 1916), p. 144.

82. Langley, *Banana Wars*, pp. 61–63; Rosenberg, *Missionaries*, p. 77.

83. *FRUS*, 1912, pp. 1028–33.

84. Langley, *Banana Wars*, pp. 68–70.

85. *FRUS*, 1912, p. 1102.

86. Munro, *Intervention*, pp. 212–13.

87. *FRUS*, 1913, p. 1039.

88. *FRUS,* 1913, pp. 1040–42.

89. The United States renounced its formal rights over the islands in 1970.

90. *FRUS,* 1914, p. 953.

91. Munro, *Intervention,* pp. 390–91.

92. *FRUS,* 1913, pp. 1052–56.

93. *FRUS,* 1913, pp. 1057–58.

94. *FRUS,* 1914, pp. 944–45.

95. Munro, *Intervention,* pp. 399–400; *FRUS,* 1914, pp. 952–53.

96. Munro, *Intervention,* pp. 400–402; *FRUS,* 1914, p. 966.

97. Munro, *Intervention,* pp. 405–6.

98. Munro, *Intervention,* pp. 414–16.

99. "Irving Lindberg, Nicaraguan Aide," *New York Times,* April 9, 1957, p. 33.

100. Munro, *Intervention,* pp. 416–17.

101. *Latin-American Year Book for Investors and Merchants for 1920* (New York: Criterion, 1921), p. 532.

102. Woodrow Wilson, Address before the Southern Commercial Congress in Mobile, Alabama, October 27, 1913, http://www.presidency.ucsb.edu/ws/index.php?pid=65373.

103. Hans Schmidt, *The United States Occupation of Haiti: 1915–1934* (New Brunswick, N.J.: Rutgers University Press, 1995}, pp. 38–39.

104. Munro, *Intervention,* p. 333.

105. Edward Kaplan, *U.S. Imperialism in Latin America: Bryan's Challenges and Contributions, 1900–20* (Westport, Conn.: Greenwood Press, 1998), p. 44.

106. Kaplan, *Imperialism,* pp. 57–58.

107. Kaplan, *Imperialism,* p. 58.

108. Kaplan, *Imperialism,* pp. 59–60.

109. Melvin Small, "The United States and the German 'Threat' to the Hemisphere, 1905–1914," *The Americas,* vol. 28, no. 3 (January 1972), pp. 252–70: 260.

110. *FRUS,* 1915, p. 475.

111. Munro, *Intervention,* p. 353.

112. Munro, *Intervention,* pp. 354–56.

113. Munro, *Intervention,* pp. 357–58.

114. Munro, *Intervention,* p. 364.

115. Munro, *Intervention,* pp. 367–68.

116. Haiti, *Annual Report of the Fiscal Representative for the Fiscal Year October 1933–September 1934* (Port-au-Prince: Imprimerie de l'Etat, 1935), p. 120.

117. Munro, *Intervention*, pp. 368–71.

118. Langley, *Banana Wars*, pp. 153–55.

119. Langley, *Banana Wars*, pp. 155–57.

120. John Major, *Prize Possession: The United States and the Panama Canal, 1903–1979* (Cambridge: Cambridge University Press, 1993), pp. 129–30.

121. Calculated from data in "Newspaper Specials," *Wall Street Journal*, December 3, 1914.

122. Calculated from data in "Newspaper Specials," *Wall Street Journal*, December 3, 1914.

123. Major, *Prize Possession*, p. 132.

124. Major, *Prize Possession*, p. 133.

125. Calculated from data in *International Historical Statistics: The Americas, 1750–2005* (Houndmills, Basingstoke: Palgrave Macmillan, 2007), pp. 699 and 721.

126. Major, *Prize Possession*, p. 137.

127. Major, *Prize Possession*, pp. 139–40.

128. Calculated from data in "Republic of Panama Loan," *Wall Street Journal*, June 15, 1926.

129. Major, *Prize Possession*, pp. 144–45.

130. "Panama Reappoints American as Agent: Choice of Fiscal Officer Thought Significant," *New York Times*, April 1, 1921.

131. Addison Ruan to Secretary of State, Dec. 18, 1922, State Department, 1910–45, 819.51A/24, NA.

132. Minister John South to Secretary of State, Apr. 11, 1924, State Department, 1910–49, 819.154/115, NA.

133. Major, *Prize Possession*, p. 146.

134. Assistant Secretary of State White to Lawrence Bennett of Murray, Aldrich, and Roberts, May 28, 1929, State Department, 819.51/615, NA. Loan details from from the *Wall Street Journal*, May 25, 1928.

135. Frederick Starr, *Liberia: Description, History, Problems* (Chicago: 1913), pp. 121–27.

136. Starr, *Liberia*, p. 277.

137. Rosenberg, *Missionaries*, pp. 69–70.

138. Starr, *Liberia*, p. 206.

139. *FRUS*, 1911, pp. 338–42.

140. Pichon to the American ambassador to France, December 5, 1910, *FRUS* 1911, p. 344.

141. *Message of the President of the United States on Our Foreign Relations* (Washington, D.C.: GPO, 1912), p. 22.

142. Emily Rosenberg, "The Invisible Protectorate: The United States, Liberia, and the Evolution of Neocolonialism, 1909–40," *Diplomatic History*, vol. 9, no. 3 (July 1985), pp. 191–214: 198.

143. *FRUS*, 1911, pp. 342–47; *FRUS*, 1911, pp. 692–94; Rosenberg, *Missionaries*, p. 75.

144. *FRUS*, 1912, pp. 662–64; Claude A. Clegg, "'A Splendid Type of Colored American': Charles Young and the Reorganization of the Liberian Frontier Force," *The International Journal of African Historical Studies*, vol. 29, no. 1 (1996), pp. 47–70: 51.

145. Carl Burrowes, *Power and Press Freedom in Liberia, 1830–1970* (Trenton, N.J.: Africa World Press, 2004), p. 114.

146. Andrew Roberts and Roland Anthony Oliver, eds., *The Cambridge History of Africa*, vol. 8 (Cambridge: Cambridge University Press, 1986), p. 457.

147. *FRUS*, 1916, pp. 458–61.

148. *FRUS*, 1917, pp. 877–90.

149. *FRUS*, 1918, pp. 505–13.

150. *FRUS*, 1918, pp. 505–13.

151. *FRUS*, 1918, pp. 514–16.

152. *FRUS*, 1918, pp. 522–24.

153. *FRUS*, 1918, pp. 533–36.

154. *FRUS*, 1919, vol. 2, pp. 471–73.

155. *FRUS*, 1919, vol. 2, pp. 466–67.

156. *FRUS*, 1919, vol. 2, pp. 476–77.

157. *FRUS*, 1919, vol. 2, pp. 482–84.

Box 1: The Mexican Exception

1. Cited in Mark Benbow, "All the Brains I Can Borrow: Woodrow Wilson and Intelligence Gathering in Mexico, 1913–15," *Studies in Intelligence*, vol. 51, no. 4 (December 11, 2007). https://www.cia.gov/library/center-for-the-study-of-intelligence/csi-publications/csi-studies/studies/vol51no4/intelligence-in-another-era.html, accessed March 6, 2011.

2. Langley, *Banana Wars*, pp. 82–84.

3. Langley, *Banana Wars*, pp. 86–95.

4. Langley, *Banana Wars*, pp. 104–5.

5. Forest Hills later became famous for producing the Ramones, comedian Danny Hoch, and the fictional Peter Parker. "Huerta's Big Family Arrives from Spain; Former Dictator's Wife, Children, Tutors, and Servants

Comprise Party of Thirty; Had More Than 100 Trunks; Senora Huerta Feared Immigration Officials Might Detain Her—Go to Forest Hills Today," *New York Times*, May 14, 1915.

6. Steven Ross, *American War Plans, 1890–1939* (London: Frank Cass, 2005), pp. 68–69.

7. Ross, *War Plans*, pp. 68–69.

8. Ross, *War Plans*, pp. 70–71.

9. Ross, *War Plans*, pp. 73–74.

10. *Annual Reports of the Secretary of War* and First Deficiency Appropriation Bill, 1919, Hearing before Subcommittee of House Committee on Appropriations, 65th Congress, 2nd session (Washington, D.C.: GPO, 1918), pp. 275, 324, 345, 1087–89, 1244–45.

11. Ross, *War Plans*, pp. 73–74.

12. *Annual Reports of the Secretary of War* and War Department Appropriations Bill, 1923, pp. 706–63.

13. *Annual Reports of the Secretary of War* and First Deficiency Appropriation Bill, 1919, pp. 275, 324, 345, 1087–89, 1244–45.

14. The United States did not reach a final agreement with Mexico over agricultural claims until 1938. See John Sloan, "United States Policy Responses to the Mexican Revolution: A Partial Application of the Bureaucratic Politics Model," *Journal of Latin American Studies*, vol. 10, no. 2 (1978), pp. 283–308: 301 and 305.

15. Stephen Haber, Noel Maurer, and Armando Razo, *The Politics of Property Rights: Political Instability, Credible Commitments, and Economic Growth in Mexico, 1876–1929* (Cambridge: Cambridge University Press, 2003), pp. 254–62.

16. *Engineering and Mining Journal*, October 18, 1913, p. 763.

17. William Meyers, "Pancho Villa and the Multinationals: United States Mining Interests in Villista Mexico, 1913–1915," *Journal of Latin American Studies*, vol. 23, no. 2 (1991), p. 346.

18. Meyers, "Pancho Villa,"p. 347.

19. *Engineering and Mining Journal*, February 15, 1913, p. 394; *Engineering and Mining Journal*, November 15, 1913, p. 916.

20. *Engineering and Mining Journal*, January 8, 1916, p. 95.

21. Haber, Maurer, and Razo, *Property Rights*, p. 257.

22. Meyers, "Pancho Villa," p. 349.

23. Meyers, "Pancho Villa," pp. 350–51.

24. Meyers, "Pancho Villa,", p. 349.

25. Meyers, "Pancho Villa," p. 350.

26. This experiment took place in September 1915, when the Villistas were losing the war against Obregón and were desperate for any source of

revenue. Meyers, "Pancho Villa," p. 358; *Engineering and Mining Journal*, January 8, 1916, p. 116.

27. Meyers, "Pancho Villa," p. 351.

28. Meyers, "Pancho Villa," pp. 355–56.

29. *Engineering and Mining Journal*, April 10, 1915, pp. 668–69; Meyers "Pancho Villa," p. 356.

30. Meyers, "Pancho Villa," pp. 357–58.

31. The decree specified that any mine that had been idle for two consecutive months, or idle at various times for a total of three months in one year, could be denounced or confiscated and worked by the government. *Engineering and Mining Journal*, October 14, 1916, p. 729; *Engineering and Mining Journal*, March 3, 1923, p. 403; Martin Bernstein, *The Mexican Mining Industry, 1890–1950* (Albany: SUNY Press, 1964), pp. 112–13.

32. *Engineering and Mining Journal*, May 19, 1917, p. 909.

33. See, for example, *Engineering and Mining Journal*, January 11, 1919, pp. 112–13; Bernstein reaches a similar conclusion: "It appears that no property was declared forfeit under the law of 9/16/1916." Bernstein, *Mexican Mining*, p. 114.

34. *Engineering and Mining Journal*, November 27, 1920, p. 1056.

35. Haber, Maurer, and Razo, *Property Rights*, pp. 200–201.

36. Haber, Maurer, and Razo, *Property Rights*, pp. 254–62.

Chapter 5: Banana Republicanism

1. "Favors Body with 'Teeth,' " *New York Times*, August 29, 1920, p. 1.

2. Rosenberg, *Missionaries*, pp. 106–7.

3. *FRUS*, 1922, vol. 1, pp. 557–58.

4. Calvin Coolidge, Address at the Dinner of the United Press at New York City, April 25, 1927, http://www.presidency.ucsb.edu/ws/index .php?pid=419.

5. Frank Kellogg, "Bolshevik Aims and Policies in Mexico and Latin America," memorandum submitted to the U.S. Senate Foreign Relations Committee, January 12, 1927.

6. Rosenberg, *Missionaries*, p. 247.

7. Rosenberg, *Missionaries*, p. 225.

8. Rosenberg, *Missionaries*, p. 226.

9. United States, *Inquiry into Occupation and Administration of Haiti and Santo Domingo: Hearings before a Select Committee on Haiti and*

Santo Domingo, United States Senate, Sixty-seventh Congress, First–Second Session, vols. 1 and 2 (Washington, D.C.: GPO, 1922).

10. Robert Ferrell, "Repudiation of a Repudiation," *Journal of American History*, vol. 51, no. 4 (March 1965), pp. 669–73.

11. J. Reuben Clark, *Memorandum on the Monroe Doctrine* (Washington, D.C.: GPO, 1930), pp. xxiii–xxiv.

12. In fact, Clark was quite careful to hedge his conclusions: "But, recalling that the Doctrine is based upon the recognized right of self-preservation, it follows (it is submitted) that by the specification of a few matters in the Doctrine, the United States has not surrendered its right to deal, as it may be compelled, and under the rules and principles of international law, with the many others which are unspecified as these may arise, which others might, indeed, have been included in the declaration with as much propriety, legally, as those which were mentioned. By naming either one act or a series of acts which challenges our self-preservation, we do not estop ourselves from naming others as they may arise; otherwise the mention of one such act would foreclose all others. The custom of nations shows that invoking the right as to one menace does not foreclose a power from invoking it as to others." Clark, *Memorandum*, p. xxi.

13. Rosenberg, "Invisible Protectorate," pp. 191–214: 200; *FRUS, 1922*, vol. 2, p. 611.

14. *FRUS, 1922*, vol. 2, p. 617.

15. *FRUS, 1922*, vol. 2, p. 617; "Harding For Liberia Loan," *New York Times*, September 2, 1922, p. 4.

16. "Borah Makes Fight on Liberian Loan," *New York Times*, September 12, 1922, p. 32.

17. "Senators Wrangle over Liberia Loan," *New York Times*, September 13, 1922, p. 41.

18. "Loan to Liberia Opposed In Senate," *New York Times*, November 25, 1922, p. 23.

19. *FRUS, 1922*, vol. 2, pp. 632–33; "Senate Rejects Loan for Liberia," *New York Times*, November 28, 1922, p. 23.

20. "The Liberian Loan," *New York Times*, November 29, 1922, p. 13.

21. Harvey Firestone to Secretary of State, 10 December 1924, *FRUS, 1925*, vol. 2, p. 384.

22. Van der Kraaij, *The Open Door Policy of Liberia—An Economic History of Modern Liberia* (Bremen: Uebersee Museum, 1983), p. 47.

23. Harold Nelson, *Liberia: A Country Study* (Washington, D.C.: GPO, 1984), pp. 41–42.

24. Van der Kraaij, *Open Door*, p. 47.

25. The draft agreements can be found in *FRUS*, 1925, pp. 369–79.

26. Van der Kraaij, *Open Door*, p. 47.

27. Frank Chalk, "The Anatomy of an Investment: Firestone's 1927 Loan to Liberia," *Canadian Journal of African Studies/Revue Canadienne des Études Africaines*, vol. 1, no. 1 (March 1967), pp. 12–32: 18.

28. William Castle to Richardson, 5 March 1926, Record Group 59, 882.617 F 51/149, NA.

29. Chalk, "1927 Loan," p. 20.

30. Chalk, "1927 Loan," p. 21.

31. Memorandum by the Assist. Sec. of State (Harrison), 12 Dec. 1924, *FRUS*, 1925, vol. 2, pp. 385–87.

32. Memorandum by the Assist. Sec. of State (Harrison), 8 July 1924, *FRUS*, 1925, vol. 2, p. 380–82.

33. Memorandum by the Assist. Sec. of State (Harrison), 12 Dec. 1924, *FRUS*, 1925, vol. 2, pp. 385–87.

34. Telegram from Havery Firestone to President Coolidge, 30 April 1925, *FRUS*, 1925, vol. 2, p. 426.

35. Secretary of State to the Minister in Liberia (Hood), 22 May 1925, *FRUS*, 1925, vol. 2, pp. 432–33.

36. Secretary of State to the Minister in Liberia (Hood), 26 June 1925, *FRUS*, 1925, vol. 2, pp. 446–47.

37. Van der Kraaij, *Open Door*, p. 48.

38. Nelson, *Liberia*, p. 42.

39. Van der Kraaij, *Open Door*, p. 49.

40. Nelson, *Liberia*, p. 42.

41. Van der Kraaij, *Open Door*, pp. 49–50.

42. Ternot MacRenato, *Somoza: Seizure of Power, 1926–39* (La Jolla: University of California Press, 1991), p. 68.

43. *FRUS*, 1923, vol. 2, pp. 607–12.

44. *FRUS*, 1925, vol. 2, p. 619.

45. *FRUS*, 1925, vol. 2, p. 621.

46. *FRUS*, 1925, vol. 2, pp. 629–34.

47. *FRUS*, 1925, vol. 2, pp. 636–38; Langley, *Banana Wars*, pp. 178–79.

48. *FRUS*, 1925, vol. 2, pp. 639–46.

49. *FRUS*, 1926, vol. 2, pp. 780–85.

50. *FRUS*, 1926, vol. 2, pp. 786–87; Langley, *Banana Wars*, p. 180.

51. *FRUS*, 1926, vol. 2, pp. 788–90.

52. *FRUS*, 1926, vol. 2, pp. 788–90.

53. *FRUS*, 1926, vol. 2, pp. 795–806.

54. *FRUS*, 1926, vol. 2, pp. 813–14.

55. *FRUS*, 1927, vol. 3, pp. 285–88.

56. *FRUS*, 1927, vol. 3, pp. 287.

57. *FRUS*, 1927, vol. 3, pp. 288–98.

58. *FRUS*, 1927, vol. 3, pp. 429–33.

59. Langley, *Banana Wars*, p. 184.

60. *FRUS*, 1927, vol. 3, pp. 319–25.

61. *FRUS*, 1927, vol. 3, pp. 337–42.

62. *FRUS*, 1927, vol. 3, pp. 337–50.

63. *FRUS*, 1927, vol. 3, pp. 410–12.

64. *FRUS*, 1927, vol. 3, pp. 433–39.

65. *FRUS*, 1928, vol. 3, pp. 546–50, 557–59.

66. *FRUS*, 1927, vol. 3, pp. 439–40.

67. Neill Macaulay, *The Sandino Affair* (Durham, N.C.: Duke University Press, 1985), p. 51.

68. Langley, *Banana Wars*, pp. 189–93.

69. *FRUS*, 1928, vol. 3, p. 561.

70. Langley, *Banana Wars*, pp. 193–97.

71. Rosenberg, *Missionaries*, pp. 237.

72. *FRUS*, 1921, pp. 836–37.

73. *FRUS*, 1921, p. 863.

74. *FRUS*, 1921, p. 868.

75. *FRUS*, 1921, p. 838.

76. *FRUS*, 1921, p. 839.

77. *FRUS*, 1922, vol. 2, p. 15.

78. *FRUS*, 1922, vol. 2, pp. 17–18.

79. *FRUS*, 1922, vol. 2, pp. 46–47.

80. Emelio Betances, *State and Society in the Dominican Republic* (Boulder, Colo.: Westview Press, 1995), p. 96.

81. Betances, *State and Society*, p. 97.

82. Cited in Michael Hall, *Sugar and Power in the Dominican Republic* (Westport, Conn.: Greenwood Press, 2000), p. 44.

83. Hall, *Sugar and Power*, p. 44.

84. Schmidt, *Occupation*, pp. 129–31.

85. *FRUS*, 1920, vol. 2, pp. 762–67.

86. *FRUS*, 1920, vol. 2, pp. 770–71, 800.

87. *FRUS*, 1920, vol. 2, pp. 800–806, 808.

88. *FRUS*, 1920, vol. 2, pp. 810–11.

89. *FRUS*, 1922, vol. 2, pp. 468–70.

90. *FRUS*, 1922, vol. 2, pp. 468–70.

91. *FRUS*, 1922, vol. 2, pp. 492–93.

92. *FRUS,* 1922, vol. 2, pp. 499–502.

93. *FRUS,* 1922, vol. 2, pp. 532–34.

94. Schmidt, *Occupation,* pp. 194–96; see also Borno's remarkable objection to elections in *FRUS,* 1925, vol. 2, pp. 294–98.

95. *FRUS,* 1927, vol. 3, pp. 48–77.

96. *FRUS,* 1926, vol. 2, p. 396.

97. Cited in Paul Drake, *The Money Doctor in the Andes: The Kemmerer Missions, 1923–1933* (Durham, N.C.: Duke University Press, 1989), p. 214.

98. Drake, *Money Doctor,* p. 217.

99. Ambassador Gonzales to Secretary of State, June 7, 1921, *FRUS,* 1921, vol. 2, p. 656.

100. Ambassador Gonzales to Secretary of State, June 7, 1921, *FRUS,* 1921, vol. 2, p. 656, and Gonzales to Secretary of State, May 16, 1921, Record Group 59, 823.51/179, NA.

101. Secretary of State to Gonzales, September 7, 1921, *FRUS,* 1921, vol. 2, p. 657.

102. Ambassador Gonzales to Secretary of State, September 20, 1921, *FRUS,* 1921, vol. 2, pp. 657–58.

103. Contract between the Republic of Peru and William Cumberland, October 31, 1921, *FRUS,* 1921, vol. 2, pp. 659–62.

104. David Mares, *Violent Peace: Militarized Interstate Bargaining in Latin America* (New York: Columbia University Press, 2001), p. 71, and Rex Hudson, "The Eleven-Year Rule, 1919–30," in *Peru: A Country Study* (Washington, D.C.: GPO, 1992), http://memory.loc.gov/frd/cs/petoc.html, accessed January 9, 2011.

105. Chargé Boal to Secretary of State, October 5, 1927, *FRUS,* 1927, vol. 2, pp. 597–98. The U.S. favoring of Colombia should not be viewed as surprising: Colombia's economic relationship was more important than Peru's, even if the United States never took formal control of Colombian governmental institutions. U.S. administrations were particularly "fearful of the possibility of having American [petroleum] properties nationalized," something a Colombian government unsuccessfully attempted in 1919. See Joseph Tulchin, *The Aftermath of War: World War I and U.S. Policy towards Latin America* (New York: NYU Press, 1971), pp. 140–43.

106. William Wilson Cumberland, *The Reminiscences of William Wilson Cumberland: Result of Interviews Conducted by Wendell H. Link, April–May, 1951* (New York: Oral History Research Office, Columbia University, 1972), p. 125.

107. Cumberland, *Reminiscences,* p. 135.

108. Cumberland, *Reminiscences*, p. 127.

109. Cumberland, *Reminiscences*, p. 135.

110. Cumberland, *Reminiscences*, p. 132.

111. Barbara Stallings, *Banker to the Third World: U.S. Portfolio Investment in Latin America, 1900–1986* (Berkeley: University of California Press, 1987), p. 258.

112. Frances Hogan, "The Hickenlooper Amendments: Peru's Seizure of International Petroleum Company as a Test Case," *Boston College Law Review*, vol. 11, no. 77 (1969), p. 78.

113. Margaret Champion, *Peru and the Peruvians in the Twentieth Century: Politics and Prospects* (New York: Vantage Press, 2006), p. 263.

114. Hogan, "Hickenlooper," p. 78.

115. Jonathan Brown, "Jersey Standard and Latin American Oil Production," in John Wirth, ed., *The Oil Business in Latin America: The Early Years* (Washington, D.C.: Beard Books, 2001), pp. 16–17.

116. Champion, *Peru*, p. 264.

117. *Proceedings of the Second Pan American Scientific Congress: Washington, U.S.A., Monday, December 27, 1915 to Saturday, January 8, 1916*, vol. 8 (Washington, D.C.: GPO, 1917), p. 198.

118. Mira Wilkins, "Multinational Oil Companies in South America in the 1920s: Argentina, Bolivia, Brazil, Chile, Colombia, Ecuador, and Peru," *The Business History Review*, vol. 48, no. 3, Multinational Enterprise (Autumn 1974), pp. 414–46: 437–38.

119. Brown, "Jersey Standard," p. 18 and 20.

120. Brown, "Jersey Standard," p. 21, and Champion, *Peru*, p. 264.

121. See Lawrence Clayton, *Peru and the United States: The Condor and the Eagle* (Athens: University of Georgia Press, 1999), p. 93, and Rory Miller, "Small Business in the Peruvian Oil Industry: Lobitos Oilfields Limited before 1934," *The Business History Review*, vol. 56, no. 3 (Autumn 1982), pp. 400–423: 415–16. The 1922 agreement fixed export taxes at 3.5 soles per ton at a time when the sol traded at roughly 39 cents U.S. In 1927, the Peruvian government violated the agreement by switching export taxes to dollars.

122. Clayton, *Peru*, pp. 86–87.

123. Ingram, *Expropriation*, p. 27.

124. Manuel Contreras, "Debt, Taxes, and War: The Political Economy of Bolivia, c. 1920–1935," *Journal of Latin American Studies*, vol. 22, no. 2 (May 1990), pp. 265–87: 274.

125. Gallo, Carmenza, *Taxes and State Power: Political Instability in Bolivia, 1900–1950* (Philadelphia: Temple University Press, 1991), p. 100.

126. Only $29 million in bonds were actually issued; the remaining $4 million for a railroad between Sucre and Potosí was left pending until Bolivia balanced its current budget. Contreras, "Debt," p. 269.

127. Contreras, "Debt," p. 274.

128. Sec. of State to the Minister in Bolivia (Cottrell), April 3, 1923, *FRUS,* 1923, vol. 2, pp. 442–43.

129. Sec. of State to the Minister in Bolivia (Cottrell), April 9, 1923, *FRUS,* 1923, vol. 2, pp. 443–44.

130. See data in Margaret Marsh, *The Bankers in Bolivia: A Study in American Foreign Investment* (New York: Vanguard Press, 1928), p. 209.

131. Contreras, "Debt," p. 275.

132. Contreras, "Debt," p. 275.

133. Contreras, "Debt," p. 269.

134. $b1.8 million and $b6.0 million, respectively, at current exchange rates.

135. Contreras, "Debt," p. 278.

136. Comisión Fiscal Permanente, *Tercera Memoria* (La Paz, 1928), pp. 33–39, 104; *Septima Memoria* (La Paz, 1930), p. 46 (hereafter, CFP report, 1930).

137. Cited in Contreras, "Debt," pp. 271–72.

138. Cited in Contreras, "Debt," pp. 271–72.

139. $b5.2 million and $b9.7 million at current exchange rates. Contreras, "Debt," pp. 269 and 272.

140. "Patiño Tin Stock on Market Today," *New York Times,* December 22, 1926, p. 28.

141. Mahmood Ali Ayub and Hideo Hashimoto, *The Economics of Tin Mining in Bolivia* (Washington D.C.: World Bank, 1985), p. 11.

142. Marsh, *Bankers,* p. 46–47 and 210.

143. "Patiño Tin Stock," p. 28.

144. Marsh, *Bankers,* p. 48. On a cash flow basis, Caracoles lost money through the 1920s.

145. Marsh, *Bankers,* p. 49. Berenguela's British owners sold to American investors for £130,000.

146. Cited in Contreras, "Debt," p. 274.

147. Contreras, "Debt," p. 276.

148. Drake, *Money Doctor,* p. 2.

149. Drake, *Money Doctor,* p. 188.

150. Drake, *Money Doctor,* p. 190.

151. Drake, *Money Doctor,* p. 205.

152. Drake, *Money Doctor,* pp. 200–201.

153. Drake, *Money Doctor*, p. 202.

154. Author's calculations, based on monthly sovereign debt bond prices from the New York and London stock exchanges.

Chapter 6: Escaping by Accident

1. William Walker, "Crucible for Peace: Herbert Hoover, Modernization, and Economic Growth in Latin America," *Diplomatic History*, vol. 30, no. 1 (January 2006), pp. 87–117: 98.

2. C. Neale Ronning, "Intervention, International Law, and the Inter-American System," *Journal of Inter-American Studies*, vol. 3, no. 2 (April 1961), pp. 249–71: 252–53.

3. Alexander DeConde, *Herbert Hoover's Latin-American Policy* (New York: Octagon Books, 1970), pp. 13–24.

4. William Leuchtenburg, *Herbert Hoover* (New York: Macmillan, 2009), pp. 120–21.

5. Gordon Connell-Smith, "Latin America in the Foreign Relations of the United States," *Journal of Latin American Studies*, vol. 8, no. 1 (May 1976), pp. 137–50: 141.

6. Clark, *Memorandum*, pp. 186–98 and 216–19.

7. Clark, *Memorandum,* p. 202.

8. Clark, *Memorandum*, pp. 199–201.

9. Clark, *Memorandum*, pp. xix and xxiii–xxv.

10. "For each South American country, the basic purpose of [Intervention Plan] Purple was to seize an important strategic area, generally the capital, and 'hold it pending the outcome of a naval blockade.' Because of the long distances from the United States and the size of most South American countries, there was no provision for occupation or for establishing long-term U.S.-controlled native constabularies as had been the case in the 'Color' plans for Mexico, Central America, and the Caribbean." John Child, "From 'Color' to 'Rainbow': U.S. Strategic Planning for Latin America, 1919–1945," *Journal of Interamerican Studies and World Affairs*, vol. 21, no. 2 (May 1979), pp. 233–59: 244.

11. A 1922 loan for $33 million ($350 million in 2009 dollars) mandated that Bolivia place its finances under the control of the Comisión Fiscal Permanente (CFP). Only $29 million in bonds were actually issued; the remaining $4 million for a railroad between Sucre and Potosí was left pending until Bolivia balanced its current budget. Contreras, "Debt," pp. 265–87: 269.

12. Dillon, Read & Co. of New York arranged a $14 million loan in 1927 and a second one a year later for $23 million ($147 and $239 million in 2009 dollars). Drake, *Money Doctor*, p. 202.

13. Drake, *Money Doctor*, pp. 202–3.

14. Cited in Contreras, "Debt," p. 273.

15. Drake, *Money Doctor*, p. 204.

16. CFP report, 1930, p. 2. (See previous chapter, note 136.)

17. Drake, *Money Doctor*, p. 208.

18. Cited in Drake, *Money Doctor*, p. 214.

19. While the sol lost nearly half its dollar value between the middle of 1930 and March 1931.

20. Drake, *Money Doctor*, p. 228.

21. Cited in Drake, *Money Doctor*, p. 223.

22. Cited in Drake, *Money Doctor*, p. 222.

23. Drake, *Money Doctor*, p. 226.

24. Drake, *Money Doctor*, p. 241.

25. Cited in Drake, *Money Doctor*, p. 241.

26. Drake, *Money Doctor*, p. 242.

27. Charge d'affaires Thomas Stafford to Stimson, September 14, 1931, 839.51/3487, Record Group 59, NA.

28. F. Eugene Hartwell, "The Santo Domingo Hurricane of September 1 to 5, 1930," *Monthly Weather Review* (September 1930), pp. 362–63.

29. Eric Roorda, *The Dictator Next Door: The Good Neighbor Policy and the Trujillo Regime in the Dominican Republic, 1930–45* (Durham, N.C.: Duke University Press, 1998), p. 67.

30. Dominican Customs Receivership, *Report of the 24th Fiscal Period* (Washington, D.C.: GPO, 1931), p. 2.

31. Roorda, *Dictator*, p. 53.

32. Roorda, *Dictator*, p. 68.

33. Herbert Hoover, News Conference, September 23, 1930, http://www.presidency.ucsb.edu/ws/index.php?pid=22356, accessed August 9, 2010.

34. *Wadsworth Report*, October 13, 1930, 839.51 Economic Mission/13, Record Group 59, NA.

35. Dominican economic mission to President Hoover, December 31, 1930, 839.51 Economic Mission/5, Record Group 59, NA.

36. Memorandum of the Assistant Secretary of State, *FRUS*, 1931, vol. 2, p. 84.

37. Roorda, *Dictator*, p. 69.

38. The coupon rate would be 5.5% at 90% of par. Memorandum of the Assistant Sec. of State, *FRUS,* 1931, vol. 2, p. 86.

39. Memorandum of the Assistant Secretary of State, *FRUS,* 1931, vol. 2, pp. 86–87.

40. Memorandum of the Assistant Secretary of State, *FRUS,* 1931, vol. 2, pp. 86–87.

41. Memorandum of conversation, Rafael Brache with Secretary of State, February 12, 1931, *FRUS,* 1931, vol. 2, pp. 88–90.

42. Lee, Higginson and Company to the Assistant Secretary of State, July 23, 1931 *FRUS,* 1931, vol. 2, p. 108.

43. Lee, Higginson and Company to the Assistant Secretary of State, June 20, 1931, *FRUS,* 1931, vol. 2, pp. 104–6.

44. President of the Dominican Republic to President Hoover, August 25, 1931, *FRUS,* 1931, vol. 2, p. 114.

45. President Hoover to the President of the Dominican Republic, September 5, 1931, *FRUS,* 1931, vol. 2, pp. 117–18.

46. Schoenfield to Secretary of State, October 24, 1931, *FRUS,* 1931, vol. 2, p. 132.

47. Dominican Minister to Secretary of State, October 20, 1931, *FRUS,* 1931, vol. 2, pp. 124–30.

48. Lee, Higginson and Company to Secretary of State, November 9, 1931, and Secretary of State to Lee, Higginson and Company, November 10, 1931, *FRUS,* 1931, vol. 2, pp. 134–35.

49. Schoenfeld to Bundy, November 14, 1931, 839.51/3607, Record Group 59, NA.

50. Roorda, *Dictator,* p. 70.

51. Roorda, *Dictator,* p. 69.

52. U.S. Department of Commerce, *U.S. Business Investments in Foreign Countries* (Washington, D.C.: GPO, 1960), p. 92.

53. In the event of default, the American fiscal agent would nominate two people to take over the customs services. The Salvadorean government would then ratify one of them after running the decision "through the office of the Secretary of State of the United States . . . any disagreement, question or difference of any nature whatever" would be referred to the binding authority of the U.S. Chief Justice. Juan Francisco Paredes to Charles Evans Hughes, Oct. 20, 1921, 816.51/176, Record Group 59, NA.

54. Robbins to Stimson, June 7, 1929, 816.00/748, Record Group 59, NA.

55. Robbins to Stimson, 4 October 1929, 816.00/754, Record Group 59, NA.

56. Schott to Stimson, 30 March 1930, 816.00B/11, Record Group 59, NA.

57. David Schmitz, *Thank God They're on Our Side: The United States and Right-Wing Dictatorships, 1921–65* (Chapel Hill: University of North Carolina Press, 1999), p. 63.

58. Calculated from data in Schmitz, *Thank God*, p. 63, and Dirección General de Estadística y Censos, *Censo de Población de El Salvador 1930*, p. 8, http://www.ccp.ucr.ac.cr/bvp/censos/El_Salvador/1930/index.htm, accessed July 4, 2010.

59. The author's maternal grandfather served in the Socorro Rojo during the 1930s.

60. Jeffery Paige, *Coffee and Power: Revolution and the Rise of Democracy in Central America* (Cambridge, Mass: Harvard University Press, 1998), p. 112.

61. Robbins to Stimson, March 27, 1931, 816.00/801, Record Group 59, NA.

62. Curtis to Secretary of State, December 5, 1931, *FRUS*, 1931, vol. 2, p. 177.

63. The general was known by his maternal last name in El Salvador.

64. "General Treaty of Peace and Amity," *The American Journal of International Law*, vol. 17, no. 2, Supplement: Official Documents (April 1923), pp. 117–22.

65. See Chandler Anderson, "Our Policy of Non-Recognition in Central America," *American Journal of International Law*, vol. 25, no. 2 (April 1931), pp. 298–301.

66. Secretary of State to Curtis, December 7, 1931, *FRUS*, 1931, vol. 2, p. 187.

67. Schmitz, *Thank God*, pp. 66.

68. McCafferty to Secretary of State, January 20, 1932, *FRUS*, 1932, vol. 5, p. 613.

69. McCafferty to Secretary of State, January 23, 1932, *FRUS*, 1932, vol. 5, p. 614–15.

70. McCafferty to Secretary of State, January 23, 1932, *FRUS*, 1932, vol. 5, p. 614–15.

71. "115 Marines on Three Warships," *New York Times*, January 25, 1932, p. 10.

72. "600 Dead Reported in Salvador Revolt," *New York Times*, January 26, 1932, p. 1.

73. "El Salvador Reds Routed," *New York Times*, January 30, 1932, p. 8.

74. Raymond Bonner, cited in Schmitz, *Thank God*, p. 67.

75. McCafferty to Secretary of State, January 29, 1932, pp. 619–20.

76. "Reports Salvador Able to Pay Debts," *New York Times*, Mar 20, 1932; p. 9.

77. "Doubts Contract on Salvador Loan," *New York Times*; Aug 16, 1932, p. 25.

78. McCafferty to Secretary of State, *FRUS*, 1932, vol. 5, p. 603.

79. Schmitz, *Thank God*, p. 71.

80. McCafferty to Secretary of State, *FRUS*, 1932, vol. 5, p. 603.

81. Donald to Secretary of State, June 18, 1932, *FRUS*, 1932, vol. 5, p. 604.

82. Eberhardt to Sec. of State, *FRUS*, 1932, vol. 5, p. 604; Higgins to Sec. of State, p. 604; Hanna to Sec. of State, p. 605; and Finley to Sec. of State, p. 605.

83. Schmitz, *Thank God*, p. 71.

84. "El Salvador Plan Offers Adjustment," *Wall Street Journal*, December 5, 1932, p. 9, and "Salvador Bond Interest," *Wall Street Journal*, June 17, 1933, p. 8.

85. "First Nation to Resume," *Wall Street Journal*, June 28, 1933, p. 6.

86. Schmitz, *Thank God*, p. 72.

87. This led to such oddities as the American-owned and American-protected Dominican sugar industry exporting most of its production to the United Kingdom.

88. Alan Dye and Richard Sicotte, "The Interwar Turning Point in U.S.-Cuban Trade Relations: A View through Sugar-Company Stock Prices," paper for "The Origins and Development of Financial Markets and Institutions" conference, April 28–29, 2006, p. 5.

89. Alan Dye and Richard Sicotte, "The Political Economy of Exporting Economic Instability: The U.S. Sugar Tariff and the Cuban Revolution of 1933," Barnard College Working Paper Series #99-05, p. 18.

90. Richard Sicotte and Alan Dye, "The Origins and Development of the U.S. Sugar Program, 1934–59," paper prepared for the 14th International Economic History Conference, 2006, p. 5.

91. Dye and Sicotte, "Interwar," pp. 7–8.

92. Dye and Sicotte, "Interwar," pp. 7–8.

93. Alan Dye and Richard Sicotte, "U.S.-Cuban Trade Cooperation and Its Unraveling," *Business and Economic History*, vol. 28, no. 2 (Winter 1999), p. 24.

94. H. O. Neville, "Looking Backward over the Past Year in Cuba's Sugar Industry," *Cuba Review*, vol. 21, no. 4 (March 1923), pp. 18–19.

95. "The U.S. Department of Commerce in Cuba," *Cuba Review*, vol. 21, no. 2 (January 1923), pp. 17.

96. Dye and Sicotte, "Interwar," p. 12.

97. "Cuba Cane Sugar Corporation, Seventh Annual Report, for the Fiscal Year Ended September 30, 1922," *The Cuba Review*, vol. 21, no. 2 (January 1923), p. 19.

98. "The Sugar Industry," *Cuba Review*, vol. 20, no. 2 (January 1922), p. 31.

99. H.O. Neville, "Some Sugar History," *Cuba Review*, vol. 20, no. 4 (March 1922), pp. 11–14. Data on the fob price of Cuban sugar calculated from data on p. 14 of the article.

100. Secretary of State to Cable, September 17, 1921, *FRUS*, 1921, vol. 1, p. 803.

101. Crowder to Secretary of State, December 21, *FRUS*, 1921, vol. 1, p. 805.

102. Dye and Sicotte, "Interwar," p. 12.

103. Dye and Sicotte, "Cooperation," p. 24.

104. Dye and Sicotte, "Interwar," p. 13.

105. Crowder to Secretary of State, April 8, 1926, referencing a letter dated October 30, 1925, *FRUS*, 1926, vol. 2, pp. 10–11.

106. Secretary of State to Crowder, April 30, 1926, *FRUS*, 1926, vol. 2, p. 12.

107. Cespedes to Secretary of State, May 5, 1926, *FRUS*, 1926, vol. 2, pp. 12–16, and Ferrara to Secretary of State, April 11, 1927, *FRUS*, 1927, pp. 503–4.

108. Memorandum of the Secretary of State of a conversation with the Cuban Ambassador, December 2, 1927, *FRUS*, 1927, vol. 2, pp. 506–8; Ferrara to Secretary of State, December 15, 1927, *FRUS*, 1927, vol. 2, pp. 508–16; and Dana Munro, *The United States and the Caribbean Republics, 1921–1933* (Princeton, N.J.: Princeton University Press, 1974), pp. 343–44.

109. Dye and Sicotte, "Interwar," pp. 13–14.

110. Robert Smith, *The United States and Cuba: Business and Diplomacy, 1917–1960* (Bookman Associates: New York, 1960), p. 54.

111. Hugh Thomas, *Cuba, or, the Pursuit of Freedom* (New York: Da Capo Press, 1998), p. 561.

112. In fact, Hershey built a henequen plant and peanut oil mill in addition to sugar mills, sugar refineries, railroad systems, and the entire town

of Central Hershey, Cuba, located about 40 miles east of Havana. Christina Hostetter, "Sugar Allies: How Hershey and Coca-Cola used Government Contracts and Sugar Exemptions to Elude Sugar Rationing Regulations," Ph.D. dissertation, University of Maryland, College Park, 2004, pp. 3–4. Central Hershey is now officially called Camilo Cienfuegos, but the populace and signage within the town still use the old name.

113. Lakin to Crowder, January 29, 1929, Senate, Subcommittee of the Committee on the Judiciary, *Hearings, The Lobby Investigation, Part 4*, 71st Congress, 1st session, 1930 p. 1671.

114. Lakin to Crowder, February 1, 1929, Lakin to Aballi, February 27, 1929, and Lakin to Tarafa, February 1, 1929, Senate, Subcommittee of the Committee on the Judiciary, *Hearings, The Lobby Investigation, Part 4*, pp. 1552, 1566, and 1540–41.

115. Smith, *United States and Cuba*, p. 58.

116. Gerrymandering has caused the 17th District to migrate north and west from Manhattan's Upper East Side, where it was located when Pratt was first elected in 1928. The district currently starts in the North Bronx (including the Bronx neighborhoods of Kingsbridge and Riverdale, the entire city of Mount Vernon, and the southern half of Yonkers), then runs north in a thinly populated strip along the Hudson River, then jumps west over the river to include the blue-collar towns around Spring Valley in southern Rockland County along the New Jersey border. Not only has the district moved its geographic boundaries, but it's also moved socially far from its WASP silk-stocking roots. Its population is about 34% African-American, 22% Latino (predominantly of second- and third-generation Puerto Rican descent), and 14% Jewish. One-fifth of the labor force works for the government, mostly in local police and fire departments. See the American Community Survey, *2003 Population and Housing Profile: Congressional District 17, New York*, www.census.gov, and David Paul, "Jewish Population Survey of Congressional Districts: 2000 and 2006," *Mandell L. Berman Institute and North American Jewish Data Bank*, mimeo, June 2009.

117. Smith, *United States and Cuba*, p. 61.

118. Lakin to Shattuck, February 7, 1929, Senate, Subcommittee of the Committee on the Judiciary. *Hearings, The Lobby Investigation, Part 4*, p. 1685.

119. "Conferees in Clash on Debenture Plan," *New York Times*, May 21, 1929, p. 1.

120. "House Adopts Rule to Rush Tariff Bill; Democrats Cry 'Gag,' " *New York Times*, May 25, 1929, p. 1.

121. "House Adopts Rule," p. 1.

122. "House Adopts Rule," p. 1.

123. Smith, *United States and Cuba*, p. 66.

124. Alan Dye and Richard Sicotte, ""The Institutional Determinants of the Hawley-Smoot Tariff," *Barnard Working Paper Series #02* (April 2001), pp. 27–28.

125. Dye and Sicotte, "Hawley-Smoot," p. 29.

126. In 1930, President Machado and Ambassador Guggenheim explicitly discussed this procedure in a private conversation. Guggenheim to Acting Secretary of State, January 29, 1930, *FRUS*, 1930, vol. 2, pp. 686–88.

127. Kellogg to Crowder, December 11, 1926, 837.154/59, Record Group 59, NA.

128. Kellogg to Ferrara, June 25, 1927, *FRUS*, 1927, vol. 2, pp. 530–31.

129. Memorandum by the Acting Economic Advisor, May 3, 1928, *FRUS*, 1928, vol. 2, p. 643–46.

130. Curtis to Secretary of State, May 3, 1928, *FRUS*, 1928, vol. 2, p. 643.

131. Secretary of State to Curtis, May 5, 1928, *FRUS*, 1928, vol. 2, p. 647.

132. Edwin Foscue, "The Central Highway of Cuba," *Economic Geography*, vol. 9, no. 4 (October 1933), pp. 406–12.

133. Secretary of State to the Chase National Bank, *FRUS*, 1928, vol. 2, pp. 652–53.

134. Guggenheim to Secretary of State, October 23, 1930, *FRUS*, 1930, vol. 2, pp. 691–92.

135. Guggenheim to Secretary of State, October 23, 1930, *FRUS*, 1930, vol. 2, pp. 692–95.

136. Guggenheim to Secretary of State, June 15, 1931, *FRUS*, 1933, vol. 5, pp. 546–48.

137. Memorandum by the Assistant Secretary of State, April 10, 1931, *FRUS*, 1931, vol. 2, p. 51.

138. Curtis to Secretary of State, October 29, 1928, 839.00/2714, Record Group 59, NA.

139. Munro, *Caribbean Republics*, p. 349.

140. Munro, *Caribbean Republics*, p. 360.

141. Reed to Secretary of State, September 23, 1930, *FRUS*, 1930, vol. 2, pp. 657–59.

142. Reed to Secretary of State, September 30, 1930 and October 3, 1930, *FRUS*, 1930, vol. 2, pp. 660–61 and 666.

143. Munro, *Caribbean Republics*, p. 359.

144. Reed to Secretary of State, September 30, 1930 and October 3, 1930, *FRUS, 1930,* vol. 2, pp. 660–61 and 666.

145. Reed to Secretary of State, September 23, 1930, *FRUS, 1930,* vol. 2, pp. 657–59.

146. Munro, *Caribbean Republics,* p. 359.

147. Guggenheim to Secretary of State, July 25, 1932, *FRUS, 1932,* vol. 5, p. 553.

148. Guggenheim to Secretary of State, October 23, 1930, *FRUS, 1930,* vol. 2, pp. 667–68.

149. Memorandum of conference by the Secretary of State with the press, October 2, 1930, *FRUS, 1930,* vol. 2, pp. 662–65.

150. Munro, *Caribbean Republics,* p. 359.

151. Commission on Cuban Affairs, *Problems of the New Cuba* (New York: Foreign Policy Association, 1935), p. 10.

152. Guggenheim to Secretary of State, January 8, 1931, *FRUS, 1931,* vol. 2, pp. 41–42.

153. Guggenheim to Secretary of State, January 20, 1931, *FRUS, 1931,* vol. 2, pp. 44–46.

154. Guggenheim to Secretary of State, January 27, 1931, *FRUS, 1931,* vol. 2, pp. 46.

155. Guggenheim to Secretary of State, April 8, 1931, *FRUS, 1931,* vol. 2, pp. 50.

156. Memorandum by the Assistant Secretary of State, April 10, 1931, *FRUS, 1931,* vol. 2, p. 51.

157. Enclosure to the dispatch of May 29, 1931, 837.00/3075 Record Group 59, NA.

158. Guggenheim to Acting Secretary of State, August 12, 1931, *FRUS, 1931,* vol. 2, p. 69.

159. Harry Guggenheim, *The United States and Cuba: A Study in International Relations* (New York: Macmillan Co., 1934), p. 165.

160. Guggenheim to Secretary of State, December 24, 1931, *FRUS, 1931,* vol. 2, p. 80.

161. "Cuban Bombings Resumed," *New York Times,* January 2, 1932, p. 2.

162. Mike Davis, *Buda's Wagon: A Brief History of the Car Bomb* (Brooklyn: Verso, 2007), p. 16.

163. Jules Benjamin, "The Machadato and Cuban Nationalism, 1928–32," *Hispanic American Historical Review,* vol. 55, no. 1 (February 1975), pp. 66–91: 79–80.

164. Munro, *Caribbean Republics,* p. 368.

165. Thomas, *Cuba*, p. 595.

166. "3 Hurt by Bomb in Havana," *New York Times*, February 20, 1932, p. 9.

167. "Two Dead in Cuba in Bitter Election," *New York Times*, February 29, 1932, p. 36, and "Many Hurt in Disorders," *New York Times*, February 29, 1932, p. 36.

168. Davis, *Buda's Wagon*, p. 17.

169. "Cuba Seizes Chiefs of 1931 Rebellion," *New York Times*, May 24, 1932, p. 9.

170. Thomas, *Cuba*, p. 595, and "Other Officers Get Bombs," *New York Times*, May 23, 1932, p. 5.

171. "Three Bombs Explode at Havana Schools: Beginning of New Terroristic Campaign," *New York Times*, June 1, 1932, p. 4.

172. "Bomb Kills Two in Cuba," *New York Times*, June 9, 1932, p. 5.

173. "Secret Police Head Is Slain in Havana," *New York Times*, July 10, 1932, p. 1.

174. "Cuba Starts Drive on Foes of Regime: Hundreds Are Seized or Sought on Charges," *New York Times*, June 15, 1932, p. 4.

175. Guggenheim to Secretary of State, July 25, 1932, *FRUS*, 1932, vol. 5, pp. 553–54.

176. "Cuba Guards Our Embassy against Bombing by Reds," *New York Times*, August 1, 1932, p. 15.

177. "Secret Police Head," p. 1.

178. "Bomb Blast in Cuba Kills Two Officials," *New York Times*, September 7, 1932, p. 10.

179. "Cuba Thwarts Plot to Murder Leaders," *New York Times*, September 29, 1932, p. 8.

180. Fritz Berggren, "Machado: An Historical Reinterpretation," Ph.D. dissertation (University of Miami, 2001), p. 103.

181. Reed to Secretary of State, September 29, 1932, *FRUS*, 1932, vol. 5, p. 557.

182. "Cubans Plan Death for Arms Owners," *New York Times*, October 20, 1932, p. 6.

183. Secretary of State to Guggenheim, April 26, 1932, *FRUS*, 1932, vol. 5, pp. 543–47.

184. Memorandum: Conversation between Harry Guggenheim and Secretary Stimson, November 13, 1931, 837.00/3207, NA. See also Perkins, *Empire*, p. 96.

185. Memorandum, conversation between Shepard Morgan and L. S. Rosenthall (both of Chase Bank) and the Assistant Secretary of State, November 6, 1931, 837.51/1484, NA.

186. Welles to Secretary of State, May 22, 1933, *FRUS*, 1933, vol. 5, pp. 570–71.

187. James Bruce to Joseph Rovensky, February 23, 1931, reproduced in Senate Committee on Banking and Currency, *Hearings on Stock Exchange Practices*, 73rd Congress, 2nd session, 1933 and 1934, part 5, pp. 2631–33.

188. "Fee of Half Million Paid on Cuba Loan," *New York Times*, January 28, 1932, p. 13.

189. Welles to Secretary of State, May 25, 1933, *FRUS*, 1933, vol. 5, pp. 571–72.

190. Memorandum: "Republic of Cuba-Debt Situation," by Adam Geiger (Chase Bank), October 27, 1931, in Senate, *Stock Exchange Practices*, part 5, pp. 2674–78. Memorandum, conversation between Shepard Morgan and L. S. Rosenthall (both of Chase Bank) and the Assistant Secretary of State, November 6, 1931, 837.51/1484, NA.

191. "L. S. Rosenthall to Shepard Morgan," December 12, 1931, in Senate, *Stock Exchange Practices*, part 6, 2774–75.

192. Guggenheim to Secretary of State, January 25, 1932, *FRUS*, 1932, vol. 5, p. 536.

193. L. S. Rosenthall to Adam Geiger, March 22, 1932, in Senate, *Stock Exchange Practices*, part 6, p. 2777. See also Welles to Secretary of State, May 22, 1933, *FRUS*, 1933, vol. 5, pp. 570–71.

194. Guggenheim to Secretary of State, December 3, 1932 and December 19, 1932, *FRUS*, 1933, vol. 5, pp. 561–63.

195. The tax payments were principally customs duties on petroleum imports; Cuba produced no oil itself. Shell lent $200,000, Sinclair $500,000 (including $100,000 to cover current tax liabilities), and Jersey Standard $750,000 (with $200,000 going to pay off the company's current liabilities). Guggenheim to Secretary of State, November 29, 1932, *FRUS*, 1933, vol. 5, pp. 559–60. See also Guggenheim to Secretary of State, December 19, 1932, *FRUS*, 1933, vol. 5, p. 563.

196. Guggenheim to Secretary of State, December 19, 1932, *FRUS*, 1933, vol. 5, p. 563.

197. Guggenheim to Secretary of State, November 29, 1932, *FRUS*, 1933, vol. 5, pp. 559–61.

198. "Cuba Faces Ordeal of Cutting Budget," *New York Times*, September 25, 1932, p. 5.

199. Welles to Secretary of State, May 22, 1933, *FRUS*, 1933, vol. 5, pp. 570–71.

200. Acting Secretary of State to Welles, June 2, 1933, *FRUS*, 1933, vol. 5, p. 573.

201. Guggenheim to Secretary of State, March 15, 1933, *FRUS*, 1933, vol. 5, p. 565.

202. Guggenheim to Secretary of State, March 23, 1933, *FRUS*, 1933, vol. 5, p. 566.

203. Guggenheim to Secretary of State, March 15, 1933, *FRUS*, 1933, vol. 5, p. 565.

204. Welles to Secretary of State, May 22, 1933, *FRUS*, 1933, vol. 5, pp. 570–71.

205. Welles to Secretary of State, June 9, 1933, *FRUS*, 1933, vol. 5, p. 574.

206. Welles to Secretary of State, August 7, 1933, *FRUS*, 1933, vol. 5, pp. 336–37.

207. Memorandum by the Undersecretary of State (Phillips), August 8, 1933, *FRUS*, 1933, vol. 5, p. 339.

208. Welles to Secretary of State, August 7, 1933, *FRUS*, 1933, vol. 5, pp. 340.

209. Secretary of State to Welles, August 9, 1933, *FRUS*, 1933, vol. 5, pp. 347–48.

210. Daniels to Secretary of State, August 10, 1933, *FRUS*, 1933, vol. 5, pp. 350.

211. Welles to Secretary of State, August 20, 1933, *FRUS*, 1933, vol. 5, pp. 578–79.

212. Undersecretary of the Treasury (Acheson) to Assis. Secretary of State (Caffrey), August 26, 1933, *FRUS*, 1933, vol. 5, pp. 582–83.

213. Preliminary Report on Cuban Finances, September 5, 1933, *FRUS*, 1933, vol. 5, pp. 583–88.

214. Welles to Secretary of State, October 16, 1933, *FRUS*, 1933, vol. 5, p. 488.

215. Louis Pérez, "Army Politics, Diplomacy and the Collapse of the Cuban Officer Corps: The 'Sergeants' Revolt' of 1933," *Journal of Latin American Studies*, vol. 6, no. 1 (May 1974), pp. 59–76: 66.

216. Perkins, *Empire*, p. 176.

217. Welles to Secretary of State, September 8, 1933, *FRUS*, 1933, vol. 5, p. 407. Pérez, "Army Politics," p. 75.

218. Welles to Secretary of State, September 11, 1933, *FRUS*, 1933, vol. 5, pp. 419–20 and 422.

219. Welles to Secretary of State, October 7, 1933, *FRUS*, 1933, vol. 5, p. 477.

220. Pérez, "Army Politics," p. 69, and Memorandum by the Assis. Sec. of State (Caffrey), September 8, 1933, *FRUS*, 1933, vol. 5, pp. 408–9.

221. Welles to Secretary of State, December 7, 1933 and December 8, 1933, *FRUS*, 1933, vol. 5, pp. 533–36.

222. Jules Benjamin, "The New Deal, Cuba, and the Rise of a Global Foreign Economic Policy," *Business History Review* (Spring 1977), pp. 57–78: 73.

223. Edmund Chester, *A Sergeant Named Batista* (New York: Henry Holt and Company, 1954), chap. 15.

224. Smith, *United States and Cuba*, p. 151.

225. See Pérez, "Army Politics," p. 73; Memorandum of Telephone Conversations between the Secretary of State and the Ambassador in Cuba on September 5, 1933 and between the Assistant Secretary of State (Caffery) and the Ambassador in Cuba, *FRUS*, 1933, vol. 5, pp. 385–87); "Marines Prepare Air Unit for Cuba," *New York Times*, September 8, 1933, p. 3; and "Intervention Is Put Off; Officials Hope Display of Naval Force Will Calm Island," *New York Times*, September 8, 1933, p. 1.

226. Jefferson Caffery to the Acting Secretary of State, January 14, 1934, *FRUS*, 1934, vol. 5, p. 98.

227. Acting Secretary of State to Jefferson Caffery, January 14, 1934, *FRUS*, 1934, vol. 5, p. 100.

228. Smith, *United States and Cuba*, p. 156.

229. Peter Stanley, *A Nation in the Making: The Philippines and the United States, 1913–1921* (Cambridge, Mass.: Harvard University Press, 1974), pp. 214–15.

230. Stanley Karnow, *In Our Image: America's Empire in the Philippines* (New York: Random House, 1989), p. 252.

231. For details, see Kiyo Sue Inui, "The Gentlemen's Agreement: How It Has Functioned," *Annals of the American Academy of Political and Social Science*, vol. 122, *The Far East* (November 1925), pp. 188–98.

232. 1917 Immigration Act (39 Stat. 874), February 5, 1917, sec. 3.

233. 1930 U.S. Census.

234. Kevin Starr, *Golden Dreams: California in an Age of Abundance, 1950–1963* (New York: Oxford University Press, 2009), pp. 450–51, and "Racial Hate Once Flared on Central Coast," *Gilroy Pinnacle*, October 27, 2006.

235. There were no similar calls to expel Puerto Rico. Puerto Ricans were American citizens, and the Fourteenth Amendment prohibited Congress from involuntarily stripping Americans of their citizenship. Moreover, the AFL had a strong presence in Puerto Rico, and a former AFL organizer, Santiago Iglesias, represented the island in the U.S. Congress.

Finally, Puerto Rican migration was almost exclusively concentrated in New York City (in fact, it was almost exclusively concentrated in the overwhelmingly Italian neighborhood of East Harlem), where it attracted little opposition. When East Harlem's congressional representative, Vito Marcantonio, introduced a bill for Puerto Rican independence, the bill mandated *perpetual* free immigration and permanent inclusion in the American customs area.

236. *Cong. Rec.*, 71st Congress, 2nd session, December 14, 1929, p. 690.

237. Herbert Hoover, *The Memoirs of Herbert Hoover: The Cabinet and the Presidency, 1920–1933* (New York: Macmillan, 1952), p. 361.

238. American law in fact prohibited the Philippine government from using the proceeds of the remitted coconut oil tax for defense purposes, even as the Independence Act required the Philippines to build up its own defense force in preparation for decolonization. See Garel Grunder and William Livezey, *The Philippines and the United States* (Norman: University of Oklahoma Press, 1951), pp. 237–38. General Douglas MacArthur (a personal friend of Manuel Quezon) traveled to the islands in 1935 to supervise the creation of a defense force that numbered 130,000 (including reservists) by the end of 1941.

239. See "Quezon Abandons Independence Cry," *New York Times*, March 16, 1938, p. 10, and "Quezon to Consider Status of Dominion," *New York Times*, March 17, 1938, p. 4.

Chapter 7: Falling Back In

1. Franklin Delano Roosevelt, First Inaugural Address, Washington, D.C., March 4, 1933.

2. Bryce Wood, *The Dismantling of the Good Neighbor Policy* (Austin: University of Texas Press, 1985), pp. 344 and 360.

3. Wood, *Good Neighbor*, pp. xi–xii.

4. In 1995, in the aftermath of the Bosnian War, NATO installed a High Representative to exercise executive power in Bosnia and Herzegovina. The High Representative was not an American, however, and he was chosen by a Peace Implementation Council with representatives from Canada, France, Germany, Italy, Russia, Japan, the United Kingdom, the United States, two separate European Union bodies, and the Organization of Islamic Cooperation.

5. A pedantic reader will note that Eastern Europe was not considered part of the Third World as the term was originally conceived. Rather, it was in the Second World, which consisted of the Communist countries.

6. Cited in Lars Schoultz, *Beneath the United States: A History of U.S. Policy towards Latin America* (Cambridge, Mass.: Harvard University Press, 1998), p. 304.

7. The entire text of the Montevideo Convention, including Hull's reservations, can be found at http://www.cfr.org/sovereignty/montevideo-convention-rights-duties-states/p15897, accessed September 30, 2012.

8. The FBPC was modeled on the British Corporation of Foreign Bondholders. See Michael Adamson, "The Failure of the Foreign Bondholders Protective Council Experiment, 1934–40," *Business History Review* (Autumn 2002).

9. Feis to Secretary of State, March 15, 1933, *FRUS*, 1933, vol. 1, p. 934.

10. Adamson, "Failure," p. 493.

11. FBCP, *Annual Report for 1936* (New York, 1937), pp. 6–11.

12. Adamson, "Failure," pp. 496–506.

13. John Major, "F.D.R. and Panama," *Historical Journal*, vol. 28, no. 2. (June 1985), pp. 357–77, 359–60.

14. Major, *Prize Possession*, p. 232.

15. Major, *Prize Possession*, p. 234.

16. Major, *Prize Possession*, pp. 235–36.

17. Major, *Prize Possession*, pp. 236–37.

18. Bonded warehouses stored goods for which no duties had been paid. Their presence allowed shippers to transfer goods inside the Zone, or engage in additional work to prepare goods for their final destination.

19. The United States implemented the Hull-Alfaro Treaty slowly and halfheartedly. In 1937, for example, Congress finally agreed to let the Panama Railroad sell its properties in Colón to the Panamanian government, but only in return for the annexation of New Cristóbal to the Canal Zone. Treaty ratification had to wait until 1939. When Panama asked for restrictions on the subsidized sale of U.S. consumer goods to Canal Zone employees, the United States rejected out of hand "the amazing proposition that the cost of living of all militaty and Canal Zone personnel be increased for the benefit of the Republic of Panama." In December 1939, the United States went further and prohibited the importation of Panamanian meat, eggs, butter, cheese, and potatoes. Finally, Roosevelt in late 1939 signed—under protest—a bill reserving high-paid Canal jobs for American citizens.

20. Article I of the Treaty of Relations between the United States and Cuba abrogates the 1903 Treaty of Relations. Article II ratifies the actions of the U.S. occupation government in 1898–1902. Article III continues the U.S. lease on Guantánamo. Article IV allows each signatory to close its ports to commerce from the other in the event of an outbreak of contagious disease. Article V states that the treaty shall be ratified by both countries according to their respective constitutions.

21. Sicotte and Dye, "Origins and Development" pp. 4 and 6.

22. Calculated from data in Jeffrey Williamson, "Real Wages, Inequality, and Globalization in Latin America before 1940," *Revista de Historia Economica*, vol. 17, special number (1999), pp. 101–42.

23. Sicotte and Dye, "Origins and Development," pp. 4 and 6.

24. The Jones-Shafroth Act of 1917 explicitly did not eliminate the category of Puerto Rican citizen, which Congress had created under the Puerto Rico Organic Act of 1900. Rather, section 5 of the act *extended* American citizenship to all Puerto Rican citizens unless they actively chose to reject it. Puerto Ricans who chose to reject U.S. citizenship were allowed to do so by taking an explicit oath reading: "I, __, being duly sworn, hereby declare my intention not to become a citizen of the United States as provided in the Act of Congress conferring United States citizenship upon citizens of Porto Rico and certain natives permanently residing in said island." The text of the Jones-Shafroth Act can be found in "An Act to Provide a Civil Government for Porto Rico and for other Purposes," *The American Journal of International Law*, vol. 11, no. 2, Supplement: Official Documents (April 1917), pp. 66–93.

25. César Ayala, *American Sugar Kingdom: The Plantation Economy of the Spanish Caribbean, 1898–1934* (Chapel Hill: University of North Carolina Press, 1999), pp. 117–18.

26. Cited in William Whittaker, "The Santiago Iglesias Case, 1901–1902: Origins of American Trade Union Involvement in Puerto Rico," *The Americas*, vol. 24, no. 4 (April 1968), pp. 378–93.

27. See Gerald Meyer, *Vito Marcantonio: Radical Politician, 1902–1954* (Albany, N.Y.: SUNY Press, 1989), p. 145. After losing reelection to James Lanzetta in 1936, Marcantonio switched his allegiance from the Republicans to the American Labor Party. He went on to regain his seat in 1938. Lanzetta, in a sign of the close ties between New York and Puerto Rico, went on to work as a lobbyist for the Puerto Rican government in Washington, D.C. Marcantonio's seat in East Harlem passed back to the Democrats in 1950, and he was succeeded by James Donovan, Alfred Santangelo, Adam Clayton Powell, Jr., and Charlie Rangel.

28. The plant now belongs to the American Sugar Refining Company and no longer processes Puerto Rican sugar. Puerto Rico, in fact, no longer produces sugar in any appreciable quantity. Wages have risen too high.

29. R. I. Nowell, "Probable Effects of a Duty on Philippine Sugar," *Journal of Farm Economics*, vol. 14, no. 4 (October 1932), pp. 599–604: 604.

30. Sicotte and Dye, "Sugar Program," pp. 7–8.

31. Sicotte and Dye, "Sugar Program," pp. 7–8.

32. Abraham Berglund, "The Reciprocal Trade Agreements Act of 1934," *The American Economic Review*, vol. 25, no. 3 (September 1935), pp. 411–25: 416.

33. Douglas Irwin, "From Smoot-Hawley to Reciprocal Trade Agreements: Changing the Course of U.S. Trade Policy in the 1930s," in Michael Bordo, Claudia Goldin, and Eugene White, eds., *The Defining Moment: The Great Depression and the American Economy in the Twentieth Century*, a National Bureau of Economic Research Project Report (Chicago: University of Chicago Press, 1998), pp. 325–52: 338.

34. Irwin, "Trade Policy," p. 340.

35. Cited in Peter Smith, *Talons of the Eagle: Dynamics of U.S.-Latin American Relations* (New York: Oxford University Press, 2000), p. 73.

36. George Philip, *Oil and Politics in Latin America: Nationalist Movements and State Companies* (Cambridge: Cambridge University Press, 1982), p. 194.

37. Ingram, *Expropriation*, p. 112.

38. Herbert Klein, *A Concise History of Bolivia* (Cambridge: Cambridge University Press, 2003), pp. 175 and 182.

39. Philip, *Oil and Politics*, p. 195.

40. John Finan, "Foreign Relations in the 1930s," in Harold Eugene Davis, John Finan, and Frederic Peck, eds., *Latin American Diplomatic History: An Introduction* (Baton Rouge: Lousiana State University Press, 1977), pp. 191–221: 207.

41. Cited in Philip, *Oil and Politics*, p. 196.

42. Herbert Klein, "David Toro and the Establishment of 'Military Socialism' in Bolivia," *Hispanic American Historical Review*, vol. 45, no. 1 (February 1965), pp. 25–52: 49.

43. Herbert Klein, "German Busch and the Era of 'Military Socialism' in Bolivia," *Hispanic American Historical Review*, vol. 47, no. 2 (May 1967), pp. 166–84: 168.

44. Philip, *Oil and Politics*, p. 196.

45. Muccio to Secretary of State, January 14, 1937, *FRUS, 1937*, vol. 5, p. 276.

46. Executive resolution of March 13, 1937, Cancelling concession of the Standard Oil Company of Bolivia and confiscating its property, *FRUS,* 1937, vol. 5, pp. 277–78.

47. Philip, *Oil and Politics,* p. 197.

48. Ingram, *Expropriation,* p. 118.

49. Cited in Smith, *Talons,* p. 75.

50. Cited in Ingram, *Expropriation,* p. 118.

51. Smith, *Talons,* p. 76.

52. *Moody's Manual of Investments,* 1938, pp. 792–94.

53. *Moody's Manual of Investments,* various issues.

54. "Penn Mex Cash Aids South Penn," *Wall Street Journal,* October 3, 1932, p. 5.

55. "Consolidated Oil in Deal in Mexico," *New York Times,* October 5, 1932, and "Acquires Penn Mex Fuel," *Wall Street Journal,* October 6, 1932, p. 2. The smaller company paid dividends of 50 cents in 1932; 75 cents in 1933, 1934, and 1935; 50 cents in 1936; and 30 cents in 1937. *Moody's Manual of Investments,* various issues.

56. "S.O. N.J. Acquiring Foreign Properties," *Wall Street Journal,* April 20, 1932.

57. "Mexican Petroleum and Utah Copper to Leave Exchange," *Wall Street Journal,* July 12, 1935.

58. Data from U.S. House of Representatives, "Production Costs of Crude Petroleum and of Refined Petroleum Products," House Document no. 195, 72nd Congress, 1st session (Washington, D.C.: GPO, 1932), p. 49.

59. *Mineral Resources of the United States,* 1929.

60. Brian McBeth, "Venezuela's Nascent Oil Industry and the 1932 U.S. Tariff on Crude Oil Imports, 1927–1935." *Revista de Historia Económica,* vol. 27, no. 3 (2009): 427–62.

61. Jonathan Brown, "Ciclos de sindicalización en las compañías extranjeras," working paper (University of Texas, 2004), p. 39.

62. Warren to H. C. Pierce, May 8, 1917, 812.504/97, Record Group 59, NA.

63. McHenry to Secretary of State, June 17, 1917, 812.504/110, Record Group 59, NA.

64. Dawson to Secretary of State, April 20, 1924, 850.4, Record Group 84, Tampico post records, NA.

65. Dawson to Secretary of State, April 20, 1924, 850.4, Record Group 84, Tampico post records, NA.

66. H. R. Márquez, "Memorandum al C. Presidente," October 27, 1924, Fondo Obregón-Calles, 407-T-13, anexo II, AGN.

67. Araujo to Jefe, May 13, 1925, AGN Depto. de Trabajo, box 725, file 2; and Bay to Secretary of State, May 26, 1925, 850.4, Record Group 84, Tampico post records, NA.

68. "Conflicto: La Compañía Petrolera El Águila y sus empleados, 1925–26," AGN Depto. de Trabajo, box 772, file 1.

69. J. Rennow to Luis Rodríguez, December 15, 1934, AGN Fondo Lázaro Cárdenas, box 432, file 1.

70. J. Rennow to Luis Rodríguez, December 15, 1934, AGN Fondo Lázaro Cárdenas, box 432, file 1.

71. "Extractos," August 4, 1935–September 3, 1935, AGN Fondo Lázaro Cárdenas, box 437.1/37.

72. R. Henry Norweb to Secretary of State, June 29, 1934, 812.45/212, Record Group 59, NA.

73. "Proyecto aprobado en la primera Gran Convención Extraordinaria del Sindicato de Trabajadores Petroleros de la República Mexicana," AGN, Archivo Histórico de Hacienda, C1857-117.

74. Brown, "Labor and State in the Mexican Oil Expropriation." Texas Papers on Mexico 90-10 (University of Texas, Austin, 1990), p. 19.

75. In early 1938, the companies basically capitulated, offering a $6.5 million wage hike as long as they could retain control over staffing. The unions realized that the implication of a settlement on those terms would be large-scale layoffs. Brown, "Labor and State," pp. 26–27.

76. Government of Mexico, *Mexico's Oil: A Compilation of Official Documents in the Conflict of Economic Order in the Petroleum Industry, with an Introduction Summarizing its Causes and Consequences* (México, DF: Gobierno de México, 1940), p. 707.

77. James Steward to Secretary of State, August 17, 1937, 812.00-Tamaulipas/307, Record Group 59, NA.

78. Pierre de Boal to Secretary of State, August 10, 1937, 812.45/495, Record Group 59, NA.

79. Brown, "Labor and State," p. 26.

80. Jack Neal to Secretary of State, September 30, 1937, 812.00-Tamaulipas/320, Record Group 59, NA.

81. Government of Mexico, *Mexico's Oil,* pp. 746–47.

82. Brown, "Labor and State," p. 24.

83. Gordon, *Expropriation,* p. 117.

84. Brown, "Labor and State," p. 27.

85. Calculated from data in Mauricio Folchi y María del Mar Rubio, "El consumo de energía fósil y la especificidad de la transición energética en América Latina, 1900–1930," *III Simposio Latinoamericano y Caribeño de Historia Ambiental, Carmona (Sevilla)* (4–6 de abril de 2006), Cuadro 2, p. 27.

86. Luz María Uhthoff López, "La industria del petróleo en México, 1911–1938: del auge exportador al abastecimiento del mercado interno. Una aproximación a su estudio," *América Latina en la historia económica*, no. 33 (Ene/Jun 2010), pp. 7–30: 17–18, 20, 22.

87. Cárdenas, *Decreto*. Author's translation.

88. Wendell Gordon, *The Expropriation of Foreign-Owned Property in Mexico* (Washington, DC: American Council on Public Affairs, 1941), p. 120.

89. Kelvin Singh, "Oil Politics in Venezuela During the López Contreras Administration (1936–1941)," *Journal of Latin American Studies*, vol. 21, no. 1 (1989), pp. 89–104: 95.

90. Department of State Memorandum, 2 June 1937, 831.6363/976, Record Group 59, NA.

91. Department of State Memorandum, 2 June 1937, 831.6363/976, Record Group 59, NA.

92. Department of State Memorandum of Conversation, January 24, 1938, 831.6363/1011, Record Group 59, NA.

93. Department of State Memorandum, 4 October 1938, 863.6, Record Group 59, NA.

94. Nicholson/Secretary of State, April 11, 1938, 831.6363/1028, Record Group 59, NA.

95. Brown, "Labor and State," pp. 27–28.

96. Josephus Daniels, *Shirt-Sleeve Diplomat* (Chapel Hill: University of North Carolina Press, 1947), p. 231.

97. Robert Huesca, "The Mexican Oil Expropriation and the Ensuing Propaganda War," Texas Papers on Latin America, No. 88-04 (University of Texas, Austin, 1988), p. 3.

98. Huesca, "Propaganda War," p. 15.

99. Lorenzo Meyer, *Mexico and the United States in the Oil Controversy, 1917–42* (Austin: University of Texas Press, 1977), p. 204.

100. Huesca, "Propaganda War," p. 21.

101. Meyer, *Mexico*, p. 204.

102. Huesca, "Propaganda War," p. 23.

103. Brian McBeth, *British Oil Policy, 1919-1939* (London: Frank Cass, 1985), p. 127.

104. México, Secretaria de Relaciones Exteriores, *Memoria*, pp. 83, 93–94, 114–19, 135–39, 148.

105. Jack Powell, *The Mexican Petroleum Industry, 1938-1950* (Berkeley: University of California Press, 1956), p. 116.

106. Export sales from from Powell, *Petroleum*, p. 118. Domestic sales, 1934–36, from Government of Mexico, *Mexico's Oil*, pp. 293–95, 317–19, 331–33, 347–49, 365–67, 381–84, 390–92, and 433. Domestic sales, 1938–48, from Powell, *Petroleum*, appendix table 17.

107. Powell, *Petroleum*, p. 116.

108. Harold Ickes, *The Secret Diary of Harold Ickes, Vol. 2* (New York: Simon & Shuster, 1954), p. 352.

109. Ickes, *Secret Diary*, p. 521.

110. Daniels to Roosevelt, August 31, 1938, in the Josephus Daniels Papers #203, Southern Historical Collection, Wilson Library, University of North Carolina at Chapel Hill.

111. Catherine Jayne, *Oil, War, and Anglo-American Relations* (Westport, Conn.: Greenwood Press, 2001), p. 48.

112. Jayne, *Oil*, p. 44.

113. Huesca, "Propaganda War," p. 24.

114. Nominal Mexican government income from silver seigniorage of $30.5 million from Jayne, *Oil*, p. 48. Total government income calculated from figures in Luz María Uhthoff, "Fiscalidad y Petróleo, 1912–1938." Working Paper, Universidad Autónoma Metropolitana-Iztapalapa, 2004, table 5.

115. Morgenthau's most famous statement about the power the Gold Stabilization Act gave him went as follows: "The way the Federal Reserve Board is set up now they can suggest but have very little power to enforce their will. . . . The Treasury's power has been the Stabilization Fund plus the many other funds that I have at my disposal and this power has kept the open market committee in line and afraid of me." Blum, *Diaries*, p. 352.

116. Samuel McReynolds, *Senate Resolution 72*, 76th Congress, 1st session, February 1, 1939.

117. Jayne, *Oil*, p 109.

118. Frank Kluckhohn, "House Rules Out Inquiry on Mexico," *New York Times*, February 8, 1939.

119. The Silver Purchase Act committed the Treasury to buying a fixed quantity of silver every year until silver stocks reached 25% of its total specie reserves or the silver price reached $1.29 an ounce. (In 1936, the U.S. began to purchase silver directly from the Mexican government.)

Morgenthau was initially ambivalent about the Silver Purchase Act, because it allowed the Treasury to build up specie reserves that it could use to counteract Federal Reserve policy, but the concurrent Gold Stabilization Act of 1934 provided ample resources for this purpose. Conversation with Taylor and Lochhead, March 28, 1938, Morgenthau Diary #117, *Presidential Diaries of Henry Morgenthau, Jr. 1938–1945*, Lamont Library, Harvard University. Morgenthau's most famous statement about the power the Gold Stabilization Act gave him went as follows: "The way the Federal Reserve Board is set up now they can suggest but have very little power to enforce their will . . . The Treasury's power has been the Stabilization Fund plus the many other funds that I have at my disposal and this power has kept the open market committee in line and afraid of me." John Blum, *From the Morgenthau Diaries: Years of Crisis, 1928-1938* (Boston: Houghton Mifflin, 1959), p. 352.

120. Conversation with Taylor and Lochhead, March 28, 1938, Morgenthau Diary #117, Presidential Diaries of Henry Morgenthau, Jr. 1938–1945, Lamont Library, Harvard University.

121. Conversation with Taylor and Lochhead, March 28, 1938, Morgenthau Diary #117.

122. Morgenthau believed that Senator Key Pittman, the author of the Silver Purchase Act of 1934, cared only about the domestic industry. Conversation with Taylor and Lochhead, March 28, 1938, Morgenthau Diary #117.

123. Jayne, *Oil*, p. 49.

124. The Spanish government nationalized mainly refining and distribution assets, since Spain and its small African territories produced little crude. Bucheli, "Multinational Corporations, Business Groups, and Economic Nationalism: Standard Oil (New Jersey), Royal Dutch-Shell, and Energy Politics in Chile 1913–2005," *Enterprise and Society*, vol. 11, no. 2 (2010): 350–99: 357.

125. Philip, *Oil and Politics*, p. 192.

126. Philip, *Oil and Politics*, p. 185.

127. Philip, *Oil and Politics*, p. p. 197.

128. Bucheli, "Energy Politics," p. 371.

129. "Memorandum of the Oil Companies," April 3, 1939, FO (Foreign Office) 371 22774 [A3723/4/26], Public Record Office, London.

130. Raymond Daniell, "No Retreat on Oil, Cardenas Pledges: Mexico Inferentially Rules Out a Treaty-Guaranteed Deal with Americans," *New York Times*, February 28, 1939.

131. Castillo to Welles, March 21, 1939 and July 5, 1939, 812.6363/5636, Record Group 59, NA.

132. Daniels to Secretary of State, March 11, 1939, 812.6363/5569, Record Group 59, NA.

133. Memorandum of a conversation between Welles and Castillo, August 10, 1939, 812.6363/6014, Record Group 59, NA, and Roosevelt to Cárdenas, August 31, 1939, in the Josephus Daniels Papers #203, Southern Historical Collection, Wilson Library, University of North Carolina at Chapel Hill. See also Jayne, *Oil*, pp. 111–12.

134. Hackworth to Farish, February 6, 1940, Farish to Secretary of State, February 6, 1940, and Farish to Secretary of State February 13, 1940, 812.6363/6502 1/2 and 6504 1/2, Record Group 59, NA. See also the text of the General Treaty of Inter-American Arbitration, in *American Journal of International Law*, vol. 23, no. 2, Supplement: Official Documents (April 1929), pp. 82–88.

135. Jayne, *Oil*, p. 116.

136. Jayne, *Oil*, p. 153.

137. Petróleos de México, "Rendición."

138. Pemex, "Rendición de la deuda petrolera en pesos M.N.," *El Petróleo* (Mexico, 1970), p. 174. Payments converted to dollars at the prevailing market exchange rate.

139. Jersey Standard first entered the Mexican market when it purchased the Transcontinental Petroleum Company for $2.5 million in 1917. Transcontinental production declined precipitously after 1923. It fell from 21.4 million barrels in 1923 to 1.7 million in 1930. Transcontinental then basically exited the Mexican market, closing its Tampico refinery and transferring its remaining production and transportation facilities to Mexican Petroleum. Ironically, Jersey Standard would buy back the assets that remained when it bought Mexican Petroleum in 1932. See Jonathan Brown, *Oil and Revolution* (Berkeley: University of California Press, 1993), pp. 152, 160–61, and Jonathan Brown, "Why Foreign Oil Companies Shifted Their Production from Mexico to Venezuela during the 1920s." *American Historical Review*, vol. 90, no. 2 (1985), pp. 362–85: 372.

140. *Wall Street Journal*, "N. J. Standard '32 Net 1Cent a Share," May 19, 1933.

141. The interest rate on long-term corporate bonds was 5.1%. Lawrence Officer, "What Was the Interest Rate Then?" MeasuringWorth, 2008. http://www.measuringworth.org/interestrates/.

142. In 1938, U.S. corporate income tax brackets ran as follows: $0–$5,000, 12.5%; $5,001–$15,000, 14%; $15,001–$25,000, 16%, and 19% for all income over $25,000. See Jack Taylor, "Corporation Income Tax Brackets and Rates,1909-2002." Working Paper, Internal Revenue Service, 2002, p. 287.

143. Gainer to Foreign Office, January 17, 1941, FO (Foreign Office) 371 26061 [A364/47/26], Public Record Office, London.

144. Scott, Minute, May 12, 1941, FO (Foreign Office) 371 26062 [A3341/47/26], Public Record Office, London.

145. Jayne, *Oil*, p, 167.

146. Eden, Minute, January 15, 1941, FO (Foreign Office) 371 26061 [A218/47/26], Public Record Office, London.

147. Jayne, *Oil*, p. 174.

148. Bateman to Foreign Office, January 23, 1943, FO (Foreign Office) 371 33980 [A930/113/26], Public Record Office, London.

149. Lorenzo Meyer, "The Expropriation and Great Britain," in *The Mexican Petroleum Industry in the 20th Century*, ed. Jonathan Brown and Alan Knight (Austin: University of Texas Press, 1992), pp. 154–72: 164.

150. Antonio Bermúdez, *The Mexican National Petroleum Industry* (Palo Alto: Institute of Hispanic American and Luso-Brazilian Studies, Stanford University, 1963), p. 177.

151. Meyer, "Great Britain," p. 169.

152. Michael Adamson, "'Must We Overlook All Impairment of Our Interests?' Debating the Foreign Aid Role of the Export-Import Bank, 1934–41," *Diplomatic History*, vol. 29, no. 4 (September 2005), pp. 589–623: 604–5.

153. Adamson, "Foreign Aid," p. 608.

154. Adamson, "Foreign Aid," p. 612–13, and Frederick Adams, *Economic Diplomacy: The Export-Import Bank and American Foreign Policy, 1934–1939* (Columbia: University of Missouri Press, 1939), p. 202.

155. Bryce Wood, *The Making of the Good Neighbor Policy* (New York: W.W. Norton, 1961), p. 189.

156. Cited in Smith, *Talons*, p. 76.

157. Cited in Wood, *Making*, p. 190.

158. Cited in Wood, *Making*, p. 192.

159. Ingram, *Expropriation*, p. 119. This position would presage the creation of the International Centre for the Settlement of Investment Disputes, which would institutionalize the creation of arbitration panels along the lines desired by Jersey Standard.

160. Ingram, *Expropriation*, p. 119.

161. Carmen Sandoval, *Santa Cruz: Economía y Poder, 1952–93* (La Paz: Fundación PIEB: 2003), p. 24.

162. The term of the loan was for eight years. Frank Keller, "Institutional Barriers to Economic Development—Some Examples from Bolivia," *Economic Geography*, vol. 31, no. 4 (October 1955), pp. 351–63: 361.

163. Philip, *Oil and Politics*, pp. 452–53.

164. Keller, "Bolivia," p. 362.

165. Author's calculations.

166. *FRUS, 1952–54*, vol. 4: *The American Republics*, pp. 490–93, 510.

167. "Bolivia Nationalizes Tin Mines, Sets Tentative Indemnity Figures," *Wall Street Journal*, November 1, 1952, p. 2.

168. *FRUS, 1952–54*, vol. 4, p. 492.

169. Secretary of State to the Embassy in Bolivia, September 25, 1952, *FRUS, 1952–54*, vol. 4, p. 507.

170. Secretary of State to the Embassy in Bolivia, September 25, 1952, *FRUS, 1952–54*, vol. 4, p. 507.

171. Memorandum of Conversation by the Secreatary of State, October 7, 1952, *FRUS, 1952–54*, vol. 4, p. 510.

172. Memorandum by the Deputy Assistant Secretary of State for Interamerican Affairs (Mann) to the Undersecretary of State (Bruce), December 17, 1952, *FRUS, 1952–54*, vol. 4, p. 516. Italics added.

173. Secretary of State to the Embassy in Bolivia, December 23, 1952, *FRUS, 1952–54*, vol. 4, pp. 516–18.

174. *FRUS, 1952–54*, vol. 4, pp. 527–28; Bryce Wood, *The Dismantling of the Good Neighbor Policy* (Austin: University of Texas Press, 1985), p. 151.

175. Ingram, *Expropriation*, p. 132; *FRUS, 1952–54*, vol. 4, p. 526; "Bolivia Sets Scale for Tin Investors," *New York Times*, June 13, 1953, p. 3.

176. "Holders to Weigh Patino Settlement," *New York Times*, July 28, 1961, p. 29. The payments lasted until 1962.

177. Wood, *Dismantling*, pp. 146–52.

178. *FRUS, 1952–54*, vol. 4, p. 498.

179. *FRUS, 1952–54*, vol. 4, pp. 503–4.

180. *FRUS, 1952–54*, vol. 4, p. 501.

181. *FRUS, 1952–54*, vol. 4, p. 548.

182. *FRUS, 1952–54*, vol. 4, p. 563.

183. *FRUS, 1952–54*, vol. 4, pp. 566–67.

184. *USAID Green Book*, http://gbk.eads.usaidallnet.gov/, accessed February 21, 2013.

185. *FRUS, 1952–54*, vol. 4, p. 539.

186. *FRUS, 1952–54*, vol. 4, p. 535.

187. Ingram, *Expropriation*, p. 132–33.

188. Wood, *Dismantling*, p. 150.

189. *FRUS, 1952–54*, vol. 4, pp. 505, 509.

190. U.S. Department of State, *FRUS, 1945–50, Emergence of the Intelligence Establishment*, document 292, National Security Council Directive on Office of Special Projects, NSC 10/2, Washington, D.C., June 18, 1948, http://www.state.gov/www/about_state/history/intel/290_300.html.

191. U.S. Department of State, *FRUS, 1945–50, Emergence*, document 292.

192. Stephen Krasner, *Sovereignty: Organized Hypocrisy* (Princeton, N.J.: Princeton University Press, 1999), p. 207.

193. Tim Weiner, "F. Mark Wyatt, 86, C.I.A. Officer, Is Dead," *New York Times*, July 6, 2006.

194. Zachary Karabell, *Architects of Intervention: The United States, the Third World, and the Cold War, 1946–1962* (Baton Rouge: Louisiana State University Press, 1999), pp. 37–49.

195. Krasner, *Sovereignty*, p. 207.

196. Mostafa Elm, *Oil, Power, and Principle: Iran's Oil Nationalization and Its Aftermath*, Contemporary Issues in the Middle East (Syracuse, N.Y.: Syracuse University Press, 1994), pp. 161–65.

197. Stephen Kinzer, *All the Shah's Men: An American Coup and the Roots of Middle East Terror* (Hoboken, N.J.: J. Wiley & Sons, 2003), pp. 150–53.

198. *FRUS, 1952–54, Iran*, pp. 689–91.

199. *FRUS, 1952–54, Iran*, pp. 711–14.

200. Kinzer, *All the Shah's Men*, pp. 162–64.

201. Kinzer, *All the Shah's Men*, pp. 167–88.

202. *FRUS, 1952–54, Guatemala*, pp. xxv–xxvi.

203. *FRUS, 1952–54, Guatemala*, p. 73.

204. *FRUS, 1952–54, Guatemala*, pp. 73–74.

205. *FRUS, 1952–54, Guatemala*, pp. 74–75.

206. *FRUS, 1952–54, Guatemala*, p. xxv.

207. Nicholas Cullather, *Operation PBSUCCESS: The United States and Guatemala, 1952–1954*, CIA History Staff document, 1994, p. 99, http://www.gwu.edu/~nsarchiv/NSAEBB/NSAEBB4/. The party was called the "Partido Guatemalteco del Trabajo" in Spanish.

208. Robert L. Beisner, *Dean Acheson: A Life in the Cold War* (Oxford: Oxford University Press, 2006), pp. 580–85.

209. Don Coerver and Linda Hall, *Tangled Destinies: Latin America and the United States* (Albuquerque: University of New Mexico Press, 1999), p. 113.

210. Larry Tye, *The Father of Spin: Edward L. Bernays and the Birth of Public Relations* (New York: Henry Holt, 2002), pp. 167–68.

211. Cullather, *Operation PBSUCCESS*, pp. 97–104, http://www.gwu.edu/~nsarchiv/NSAEBB/NSAEBB4/cia-guatemala5_20.html and http://www.gwu.edu/~nsarchiv/NSAEBB/NSAEBB4/cia-guatemala5_27.html, accessed March 21, 2011.

212. Arindrajit Dube, Ethan Kaplan, and Suresh Naidu, "Coups, Corporations, and Classified Information," working paper, June 26, 2009.

213. Mary Ann Heiss, *Empire and Nationhood: The United States, Great Britain, and Iranian Oil, 1950–1954* (New York: Columbia University Press, 1997), p. 196.

214. *FRUS, 1952–54, Iran*, p. 789n2.

215. *FRUS, 1952–54, Iran*, p. 1009.

216. Heiss, *Empire and Nationhood*, pp. 200–201.

217. *FRUS, 1952–54, Iran*, pp. 949–50.

218. Heiss, *Empire and Nationhood*, p. 205.

219. *FRUS, 1952–54, Iran*, pp. 968–69.

220. Heiss, *Empire and Nationhood*, pp. 206–7.

221. Heiss, *Empire and Nationhood*, pp. 214–15.

222. Elm, *Oil, Power, and Principle*, pp. 324–25.

223. Heiss, *Empire and Nationhood*, pp. 203–4.

224. Elm, *Oil, Profit, and Principle*, pp. 326–26; Kinzer, *All the Shah's Men*, p. 196.

Chapter 8: The Empire Trap and the Cold War

1. Herbert L. Matthews, "Cuban Rebel Is Visited in Hideout," *New York Times*, February 24, 1957, p. 1.

2. U.S. Department of State, *FRUS, 1958–60, Cuba*, ed. John P. Glennon, vol. 6 (Washington, D.C.: GPO, 1958–60), pp. 298–99.

3. Lars Schoultz, *That Infernal Little Cuban Republic: The United States and the Cuban Revolution* (Chapel Hill: University of North Carolina Press, 2009), p. 80.

4. Schoultz, *Infernal*, p. 84.

5. Fundamental Law of 1959, Article 24, Biblioteca Virtual Miguel de Cervantes Saavedra, Universidad de Alicante, http://cervantesvirtual.com, accessed January 26, 2011.

6. Sigmund, *Nationalization*, p. 95.

7. *FRUS, 1958–60, Cuba*, p. 476.

8. Sigmund, *Nationalization*, p. 94.

9. Schoultz, *Infernal*, p. 95.

10. Schoultz, *Infernal*, p. 99. It is not clear why the Cubans wanted the bonds to be nontransferable.

11. Sigmund, *Nationalization*, p. 99.

12. Robert Caro, *The Years of Lyndon Johnson: The Path to Power* (New York: Knopf, 1982), pp. 213–14, and Schoultz, *Infernal*, p. 95–96.

13. Sigmund, *Nationalization*, p. 101.

14. *FRUS, 1958–60, Cuba*, pp. 539–41.

15. *FRUS, 1958–60, Cuba*, p. 552n1.

16. Sigmund, *Nationalization*, p. 98. There is no direct evidence that Florida sugar interests backed the quota suspension in order to insulate their own Floridian production from competition.

17. *FRUS, 1958–60, Cuba*, pp. 605–11.

18. Schoultz, *Infernal*, pp. 103–4.

19. Schoultz, *Infernal*, pp. 110–12.

20. *FRUS, 1958–60, Cuba*, pp. 739–40.

21. Schoultz, *Infernal*, p. 110.

22. Sigmund, *Nationalization*, p. 102.

23. Calculated from data in Jorge Domínguez, *Cuba: Order and Revolution* (Cambridge, Mass: Belknap Press, 1978), p. 163.

24. Sigmund, *Nationalization*, p. 104.

25. Willard Radell, "Cuban-Soviet Sugar Trade, 1960–1976: How Great Was the Subsidy?" *The Journal of Developing Areas*, vol. 17, no. 3 (April 1983), pp. 365–82.

26. *FRUS, 1958–60, Cuba*, p. 792.

27. United States, *Executive Sessions of the Senate Foreign Relations Committee (Historical Series)*, vol. 12, 86th Congress, 2nd session, 1960 (Washington, D.C.: GPO, 1982), p. 105.

28. United States. *Executive Sessions*, pp. 119–20.

29. *FRUS, 1958–60, Cuba*, pp. 794–800.

30. *FRUS, 1958–60, Cuba*, pp. 546–51.

31. *FRUS, 1958–60, Cuba*, p. 615.

32. *FRUS, 1958–60, Cuba*, p. 694.

33. CIA- Special National Intelligence Estimate 85–60, "Communist Influence in Cuba," March 22, 1960, Secret, OSANSA-NSC Briefing Notes, box 6, Eisenhower Presidential Library, Abilene, Kansas.

34. *FRUS, 1958–60, Cuba*, pp. 862, 902.

35. Schoultz, *Infernal*, pp. 119–20. The dollar ceased to be legal tender in Cuba in 1951. See Siegfried Stern, *The United States in International Banking* (New York: Columbia University Press, 1951), p. 168.

36. *FRUS, 1958–60, Cuba*, pp. 934–35.

37. Schoultz, *Infernal*, pp. 120–21.

38. Schoultz, *Infernal*, pp. 120–21.

39. *Cong. Rec.*, 86th Congress, 2nd session, June 29, 1960, p. 14967.

40. *Cong. Rec.*, 86th Congress, 2nd session, June 30, 1960, pp. 15,247–48.

41. *Cong. Rec.*, 86th Congress, 2nd session, July 2, 1960, p. 15,664.

42. Public Law 86-592, 74 Stat. 330 (1960); "President's Statement," *New York Times*, July 7, 1960, p. 8.

43. Eric Roorda, "McCarthyite in Camelot: The 'Loss' of Cuba, Homophobia, and the Otto Otepka Scandal in the Kennedy State Department," *Diplomatic History*, vol. 31, no. 4 (September 2007), pp. 723–54.

44. R. Hart Phillips, "Castro Attacks Sugar Quota Cut as 'Imperialism,'" *New York Times*, July 8, 1960, p. 1.

45. Sigmund, *Nationalization*, p. 109.

46. "Cuba and Latin America," *New York Times*, July 8, 1960, p. 20.

47. *Soviet News*, no. 4304 (July 11, 1960), pp. 28–29.

48. Ernesto Guevara, *Venceremos! The Speeches and Writings of Ernesto Che Guevara*, ed. John Gerassi (New York: Simon and Schuster, 1969), p. 110.

49. Sigmund, *Nationalization*, pp. 110–11.

50. Richard Goodwin, *Remembering America: A Voice from the Sixties* (Boston: Little, Brown, 1988), p. 174.

51. Paul Kennedy, "U.S. Helps Train an Anti-Castro Force at Secret Guatemalan Air-Ground Base," *New York Times*, January 10, 1961, p. 1.

52. Vernon Loeb, "Soviets Knew Date of Cuba Attack," *Washington Post*, April 29, 2000, p. A4.

53. House of Representatives, 88th Congress, 2nd session, *Hearings before the Subcommittee on Inter-American Affairs of the Committee on Foreign Affairs, July 28, 29, and August 4, 1964*, "Claims of U.S. Nationals against the Government of Cuba," pp. 144, 151.

54. As a constant share of U.S. national income, $1 billion in 1962 would be the equivalent of $24 billion in 2009. For comparison

purposes, the American Insurance Services Group estimated that Hurricane Katrina—rather less destructive than a nuclear strike—was responsible for $41 billion of insured losses in 2005, or $46 billion in 2009 dollars. Richard Knabb, Jamie Rhome, and Daniel Brown, "Tropical Cyclone Report: Hurricane Katrina, 23–30 August 2005," National Hurricane Center, working paper, August 10, 2006.

55. Juan de Onis, "Brazilians Seize U.S. Phone System," *New York Times*, February 17, 1962, p. 1.

56. Ruth Leacock, *Requiem for Revolution: The United States and Brazil, 1961–1969* (Kent, Ohio: Kent State University Press, 1990), pp. 85–86.

57. Leacock, *Requiem*, pp. 85–86; U.S. Senate, Committee on Foreign Relations, *Hearings on S. 2996 before the Senate Committee on Foreign Relations*, 87th Congress, 2nd session, pp. 417–18; "Brazilians Seize U.S. Phone System," p. 1. This section is also informed by Richard Lillich, "The Protection of Foreign Investment and the Foreign Investment Act of 1962," *Rutgers Law Review*, vol. 17 (1963), pp. 405–23.

58. U.S. Senate, Committee on Foreign Relations, *Hearings on S. 2996*, pp. 417–18. See also Donna McInnis, "The American Congress and Foreign Policy Making: A Case Study of the Hickenlooper-Adair Amendment," M.A. thesis, McGill University, 1973, p. 22.

59. Leacock, *Requiem*, pp. 85–86; U.S. Senate, Committee on Foreign Relations, *Hearings on S. 2996*, pp. 417–18; "Brazilians Seize U.S. Phone System," p. 1. This section is also informed by Richard Lillich, "The Protection of Foreign Investment and the Foreign Investment Act of 1962," *Rutgers Law Review*, vol. 17 (1963), pp. 405–23.

60. Leacock, *Requiem*, p. 86.

61. John Gunther, *Inside South America* (New York: Harper & Row, 1967), p. 39.

62. Leacock, *Requiem*, p. 83 and 271n11, citing CIA Current Intelligence Memorandum, September 27, 1961, National Security Council Files, Country: Brazil, John F. Kennedy Presidential Library, Boston, Mass. The Special National Intelligence Estimate of December 7, 1961, a joint report of American intelligence agencies reproduced in *FRUS, 1961–63*, vol. 12, document 219, pp. 453–54, was less certain about the spread of communism in Brazil under Goulart, stating "it is unlikely that Communist infiltration of the government will go so far as to give the Communist Party a significant influence on the formulation and execution of policy within the period of this estimate."

63. Leacock, *Requiem*, p. 83.

64. "Brazil: Investors Beware," *Time Magazine*, July 12, 1963.

65. Leacock, *Requiem*, p. 90.

66. Gunther, *Inside South America*, p. 39.

67. Leacock, *Requiem*, p. 84.

68. Leacock, *Requiem*, 86 and 272n27, citing Geneen to Rusk and Geneen to President, February 17, 1962.

69. "Brazilians Seize U.S. Phone System," p. 1.

70. Leacock, *Requiem*, 87 and 272n29, citing Secretary of State Rusk to U.S. Ambassador to Brazil Gordon, March 3, 1962, National Security Council Files, Country: Brazil, John F. Kennedy Library.

71. Cited in Kenneth Rodman, *Sanctity Versus Sovereignty: The United States and the Nationalization of Natural Resource Investments* (New York: Columbia University Press, 1988), p. 172.

72. Robert Pastor, *Congress and the Politica of U.S. Foreign Economic Policy* (Berkeley: University of California Press, 1980), p. 290.

73. *Cong. Rec.*, July 2, 1959, p. 12,586.

74. Pastor, *Congress*, p. 290.

75. Congressional Quarterly, *Almanac*, 1959, p. 159.

76. Cited in Richard Lillich, "The Protection of Foreign Investment and the Hickenlooper Amendment," *University of Pennsylvania Law Review*, vol. 112, no. 8 (June 1964), pp. 1116–31: 1118.

77. Pastor, *Congress*, p. 291.

78. 76 Stat. 260–61 (1962), 22 U.S.C. sec. 2370(e) (Supp. IV, 1962). The President shall suspend assistance to the government of any country to which assistance is provided under this chapter when the government of such country or any governmental agency or subdivision within such country *on or after January 1, 1962* (1) has nationalized or expropriated or seized ownership or control of property owned by any United States citizen or by any corporation, partnership, or association not less than 50 per centum beneficially owned by United States citizens, or (2) has imposed or enforced discriminatory taxes or other exactions, or restrictive maintenance or operational conditions, which have the effect of nationalizing, expropriating, or otherwise seizing ownership or control of property so owned, and such country, government agency or government subdivision fails within a reasonable time (not more than six months after such action or after August 1, 1962, whichever is later) to take appropriate steps, which may include arbitration, to discharge its obligations under international law toward such citizen or entity, including equitable and speedy compensation for such property in convertible foreign exchange, as required by international law, or fails to take steps designed to provide relief from such taxes, exactions, or conditions, as the case may be, and

such suspension shall continue until he is satisfied that appropriate steps are being taken and *no other provision of this chapter shall be construed to authorize the President to waive the provisions of this subsection.* [Italics added.]

79. *Cong. Rec.,* Senate, February 11, 1963, p. 2163.

80. Gene Smith, "I.T.&T. Chief Asks Ban on Aid to Nations Seizing Investments," *New York Times,* May 10, 1962, p. 51.

81. Lipson, *Standing Guard,* 209 and 301n21.

82. Cited in Pastor, *Congress,* p. 292.

83. *Cong. Rec.,* 87th Congress, 2nd session, October 2, 1962, pp. 21615–16.

84. A CPS opinion poll in the fall of 1960 reported 52% support for the statement "The United States should give economic help to the poorer countries of the world even if those countries can't pay for it." William Mayer, *The Changing American Mind: How and Why American Public Opinion Changed between 1960 and 1988* (Ann Arbor: University of Michigan Press, 1992), p. 427.

85. *Cong. Rec.,* 87th Congress, 2nd session, June 5, 1962, p. 9681.

86. *Cong. Rec.,* 87th Congress, 2nd session, June 5, 1962, p. 9942.

87. *Cong. Rec.,* 87th Congress, 2nd session, July 11, 1962, p. 13169.

88. "Soviet Offers Oil at Cut-Rate Price," *New York Times,* June 25, 1960, p. 24.

89. "West Protesting Ceylon Oil Move," *New York Times,* January 13, 1961, p. 39.

90. "Ceylon: Petroleum Corporation Act," *International Legal Materials,* vol. 1 (1962), pp. 126–59.

91. "Ceylon to Set Up Own Oil Concern," *New York Times,* May 6, 1961, p. 3.

92. "West Protesting Ceylon Oil Move," *New York Times,* January 13, 1961, p. 39

93. Ellen Collier, "Expropriation of American-Owned Property by Foreign Governments in the Twentieth Century," House Committee on Foreign Affairs, 88th Congress, 1st session, July 19, 1963, p. 23.

94. Lipson, *Standing Guard,* 206–7.

95. Lipson, *Standing Guard,* 208 and 300n17, Memorandum for McGeorge Bundy from the Department of State, April 5, 1963, President's Office Files, Countries, Ceylon, 1963, John F. Kennedy Library.

96. Lipson, *Standing Guard,* p. 208.

97. "U.S. Warns Ceylon on Aid," *New York Times,* July 8, 1962, p. 64; "Ceylon: Miss Willis Regrets," *Time,* August 3, 1962.

98. Dean Rusk, "Case Study—Effect of the Hickenlooper Amendment on U.S.-Ceylonese Relations," p. 3, John F. Kennedy Presidential Library and Museum, Ceylon: General 1961–1963 folder, accessed via http://www.jfklibrary.org/Asset-Viewer/Archives/JFKPOF-113-012.aspx.

99. Felix Belair, Jr., "U.S. Firm on Halt in Aid to Ceylon," *New York Times*, January 12, 1963, p. 9.

100. Lipson, *Standing Guard*, 87 and 300n16, Memorandum for the President from Dean Rusk, Secretary of State, May 27, 1963, pp. 4–5, President's Office Files, Country: Ceylon, 1963, John F. Kennedy Library.

101. Collier, "Expropriation," p. 23.

102. "United States: Suspension of Aid to Ceylon: Statements of United States Government and Government of Ceylon," *International Legal Materials*, vol. 2 (1963), pp. 386–91: 390–91.

103. Richard Olson, "Expropriation and International Economic Coercion: Ceylon and the West, 1961-65," *Journal of Developing Areas*, vol. 11, no. 2 (1977), pp. 205–26: 213.

104. Olson, "Ceylon," p. 210.

105. Jackson Hearn, "Ceylon Has a New Look: New Government Has Given Business a Decided Turn for the Better," U.S. Department of Commerce, *International Commerce* 72 (September 19, 1966), pp. 7–9.

106. *New York Times*, April 19, 1964, p. 15.

107. Olson, "Ceylon," p. 217.

108. Rusk, "Case Study," p. 1.

109. Soviet credits to Ceylon began to be paid back in 1967. The bilateral capital flow turned in the direction of the Soviet Union in 1967 and remained so until 1973. Calculated from data in *Balance of Payments Yearbook* (Washington, D.C.: International Monetary Fund), vol. 16 (January 1965), vol. 19 (November 1967), and vol. 24 (August 1973).

110. Rusk, "Case Study," p. 1.

111. Calculated from data in Alex Hunter, "The Indonesian Oil Industry," *Australian Economic Papers*, vol. 5, no. 1 (June 1966), pp. 59–106: 62, 70, and 97.

112. Mirza Karim and Karen Mills, "Disputes in the Oil and Gas Sector: Indonesia," *Journal of World Energy Law & Business*, vol. 3, no. 1, pp. 44–70.

113. Hunter, "Oil Industry," p. 66.

114. Hunter, "Oil Industry," p. 60.

115. Max Frankel, "U.S. Urges Sukarno to End Threat on Oil," *New York Times*, May 29, 1963, p. 1.

116. A. M. Rosenthal, "U.S. and Sukarno Begin Oil Parley," *New York Times*; May 30, 1963, p. 2.

117. Frankel, "Threat," p. 1.

118. "Indonesia and Caltex Pacific Oil Co., P.T. Shell Indonesia, and P.T. Stanvac Indonesia: Heads of Agreement for Petroleum Working Contracts," *International Legal Materials*, vol. 3, no. 1 (January 1964), pp. 81–85.

119. U.S. Department of State, Bureau of Intelligence and Research, "Nationalization, Expropriation, and Other Takings of United States and Certain Foreign Property since 1960," Research Study RECS-14, November 30, 1971.

120. U.S. Department of State, Bureau of Intelligence and Research, "Nationalization.

121. *New York Times*, May 29, 1963, p. 1.

122. H. W. Brands, *The Wages of Globalism: Lyndon Johnson and the Limits of American Power* (New York: Oxford University Press, 1997), p. 158.

123. Brands, *Globalism*, p. 160.

124. *FRUS*, 1961–63, vol. 23, *Southeast Asia*, http://dosfan.lib.uic.edu/ERC/frus/summaries/950306_FRUS_XXIII_1961–63.html, accessed August 14, 2012.

125. Brands, *Globalism*, p. 164.

126. Brands, *Globalism*, p. 164.

127. Brands, *Globalism*, p. 165.

128. Brands, *Globalism*, p. 166.

129. CIA, "G-1 Recommendations for Tightening Indonesian Internal Security, Including the Seizure of American Oil Companies and Expelling Some U.S. Officials," *Intelligence Information Cable*, March 2, 1965, http://www.foia.cia.gov/docs/DOC_0000105887/DOC_0000105887.pdf, accessed August 14, 2012.

130. CIA, "Prospects for and Strategic Implications of a Communist Takeover in Indonesia," Special National Intelligence Estimate no. 55–65, September 10, 1965, p. 1.

131. CIA, "Communist Takeover," p. 2.

132. Department of State to U.S. Embassy in Jakarta, March 3, 1964, vol. 1: Cables, box 246, Country File, National Security File, Lyndon B. Johnson Library, Austin, Tex.

133. U.S. Embassy in Jakarta to Department of State, March 6, 1964, vol. 1: Cables, box 246, Country File, National Security File, Lyndon B. Johnson Library.

134. U.S. Embassy in Jakarta to Department of State, January 21, 1965, vol. 1: Cables, box 246, Country File, National Security File, Lyndon B. Johnson Library.

135. Memorandum of Conversation between Secretary of State Rusk, and U.K. Ambassador Sir Patrick Dean, July 20, 1965, *FRUS*, 1964–68, vol. 26, p. 272.

136. Cited in Geoffrey Robinson, "The Post-Coup Massacre in Bali," in Daniel Lev and Ruth McVey, eds., *Making Indonesia: Essays on Modern Indonesia in Honor of George McT. Kahin* (Ithaca, N.Y.: Cornell University Press, 1996) p. 126.

137. U.S. Embassy in Jakarta to Department of State, November 4, 1965, vol. 1: Cables, box 246, Country File, National Security File, Lyndon B. Johnson Library.

138. U.S. Embassy in Jakarta to Department of State, December 1, 1965, vol. 1: Cables, box 246, Country File, National Security File, Lyndon B. Johnson Library.

139. U.S. Embassy in Jakarta to Department of State, November 28 and December 3, 1965, and Department of State to U.S. Embassy in Jakarta, December 8, 1965, vol. 1: Cables, box 246, Country File, National Security File, Lyndon B. Johnson Library.

140. Ambassador Green to Assis. Sec. of State Bundy, "Telegram From the Embassy in Indonesia to the Department of State," December 2, 1965, Department of State, INR/IL Historical Files, Indonesia, 1963–1965, http://www.namebase.org/gifs/indo01.gif, accessed August 14, 2012.

141. Editorial note, http://www.namebase.org/gifs/indo02.gif, accessed August 14, 2012. See also Kathy Kadane, "Ex-agents say CIA Compiled Death Lists for Indonesians," *San Francisco Examiner*, May 20, 1990, http://www.namebase.org/kadane.html, accessed August 14, 2012.

142. U.S. Department of State, Bureau of Intelligence and Research, "Nationalization."

143. U.S. Department of State, Bureau of Intelligence and Research, "Disputes Involving U.S. Private Foreign Direct Investment: March 1, 1977, through February 29, 1980," Report No. 1441, August 18, 1980.

144. Aluminum Limited, *Annual Report for the Year 1961* (Montreal: Alcan, 1962), p. 8.

145. World Bank, "Engineering Loan for Boke Infrastructure Project, Republic of Guinea," Projects Department Report no. TO-506c, March 14, 1966, p. 1.

146. See U.S. Department of State, Bureau of Intelligence and Research, "Disputes Involving U.S. Foreign Direct Investment: February 1,

1975, through February 28, 1977," INR Report no. 855, September 19, 1977.

147. See Pierre Bonte, "Multinational Corporations and National Development: Miferma and Mauretania," *Review of African Political Economy*, vol. 2, no. 2 (1975), pp. 89–109

Box 2: Ethiopia and Nicaragua

1. Peter Schraeder, *United States Foreign Policy toward Africa: Incrementalism, Crisis, and Change* (Cambridge: Cambridge University Press, 1994), p. 148.

2. Memo, Henze to Brzezinski, March 1978, "3/78" folder box/special: 2, NSA Staff Material, Jimmy Carter Library, Atlanta.

3. Schraeder, *Policy toward Africa*, pp. 148–49.

4. Schraeder, *Policy toward Africa*, pp. 149.

5. There is some evidence that the Somali were surprised by the Soviet decision: at the time of the invasion, Somalia was under a Marxist government and loosely allied to the USSR.

6. Thomas Ofcansky and LaVerle Berry, eds., *Ethiopia: A Country Study* (Washington, D.C.: Federal Research Division, Library of Congress, 1991), section "Foreign Military Assistance," http://memory.loc.gov/frd/etsave/et_05_03.html, accessed August 19, 2012.

7. Schraeder, *Policy toward Africa*, pp. 149.

8. Mark Kantor, Michael Nolan, and Karl Sauvant, eds., *Reports of Overseas Private Investment Corporation Determinations* (Oxford: Oxford University Press, 2011), pp. 582–84.

9. Kantor, Nolan, and Sauvant, *Determinations*, pp. xxxiv–xxxv.

Chapter 9: The Success of the Empire Trap

1. "Memorandum of Conversation," December 29, 1972, Central Files 1970–73, PET 17 US-SAUD, Record Group 59, NA.

2. Figures from *Survey of Current Business*, various issues. The numbers for adjusted income were converted into 2011 dollars using the GDP deflator.

3. CIA, Office of National Estimates, "Implications of Economic Nationalism in the Poor Countries," Memorandum of Conversation, June 29, 1971, pp. 22–23.

4. Calculated from data in CIA, Memorandum of Conversation, p. 375.

5. *Gulf Oil Corporation Annual Report—1974*, p. 12, and *Gulf Oil Corp. v. C.I.R.*, 914 F.2d 396 (1990); and United States Court of Appeals, Third Circuit, argued June 28, 1990, p. 7. The latter is available at http://www.leagle.com/xmlResult.aspx?page=7&xmldoc=19901310914 F2d396_11236.xml&docbase=CSLWAR2-1986-2006&SizeDisp=7#, accessed August 4, 2012.

6. *Gulf Oil Corp. v. C.I.R.*, p. 7.

7. Tax and royalty rates from Benjamin Shwadran, *The Middle East, Oil and the Great Powers* (New York: John Wiley and Sons, 1973), pp. 369–70 and 415–16, and Benjamin Shwadran, *Middle East Oil Crises since 1973* (Boulder, Colo.: Westview Press, 1986), pp. 78–79. Total costs for the Kuwait Oil Company were estimated using data in Gulf Oil's annual reports, under the assumption that all Eastern Hemisphere income derived from Kuwait. This assumption biases upward the estimates of Gulf Oil's earnings per barrel before the price run-up.

8. Gulf Oil received $56 million for a 40% stake in its operations in 1974. Kuwait nationalized the remainder in 1975.

9. If you exclude the $56 million above, then compensation came to only $302 million—but including windfall profits in 1973–74 takes compensation back up up to $422 million.

10. *Gulf Oil Corporation Annual Report—1980*, p. 2.

11. CIA, Memorandum of Conversation, p. 375.

12. Paul Reynolds, "U.S. Ready to Seize Gulf Oil in 1973," BBC, January 2, 2004, http://news.bbc.co.uk/2/hi/middle_east/3333995.stm, accessed August 5, 2012.

13. See U.S. Congress, Committee on International Relations, Special Subcommittee on Investigations, *Oil Fields as Military Objectives: A Feasibility Study*, report prepared by the Congressional Research Service, 94th Congress, 1st session, August 21, 1975 (Washington, DC: GPO, 1975), parts 1 and 2, pp. 1–39.

14. When market values were unavailable, valuation was considered against the net present value of future cash flows evaluated at the interest rate on high-quality ten-year corporate bonds.

15. The consortium consisted of Equity Funding (23.75%), Bell Oil and Gas (23.31%), Ada Oil (17.89%), Phillips (5.0%), OKC (15.83%), American Ultramar (11.05%), and General Exploration (3.17%). For details of the dispute, see U.S. Department of State, Bureau of Intelligence and Research, "Disputes Involving U.S. Foreign Direct Investment: July 1, 1971, through July 31, 1973," Research Study RECS-6, February 28,

1974; "Disputes Involving U.S. Foreign Direct Investment: August 1, 1973, through January 31, 1975," Research Study RS-240, March 20, 1975; "Disputes Involving U.S. Foreign Direct Investment: February 1, 1975, through February 28, 1977," INR Report no. 855, September 19, 1977; "Disputes Involving U.S. Private Foreign Direct Investment: March 1, 1977, through February 29, 1980," Report no. 1441, August 18, 1980; and "Disputes Involving U.S. Private Foreign Direct Investment: January 1, 1985, through May 1, 1987," IRR no. 102, July 6, 1987.

16. John Martz, *Politics and Petroleum in Ecuador* (New Brunswick, N.J.: Transaction, 1987), pp. 57–58 and 191.

17. Ingram, *Expropriation*, p. 132; *FRUS, 1952–54*, vol. 4, p. 526; "Bolivia Sets Scale for Tin Investors," *New York Times*, June 13, 1953, p. 3.

18. New York price for Grade A Straits (Malaysian) tin (99.85% pure), in *E&MJ* Metal and Mineral Markets.

19. Ingram, *Expropriation*, p. 133.

20. The company's value fell to $11.0 million by October, when Bolivia announced the nationalization.

21. In the United States, in the words of a contemporary Texaco publication, the depletion allowance "recognizes that an oilman's barrel of oil is his capital and merchandise rolled into one. When he sells it, he sells away part of his capital." Cited in Ingram, *Expropriation*, p. 167.

22. Ingram, *Expropriation*, pp. 167, 170, and 173.

23. Memorandum From the President's Assistant for National Security Affairs (Kissinger) to President Nixon, Washington, October 17, 1969, Nixon Presidential Materials, NSC Files, box 770, Country Files, Bolivia, vol. 1, 1969–70, NA.

24. Telegram 7658 From the Embassy in Bolivia to the Department of State, October 23, 1969, 1605Z, Central Files 1967–69, POL 15-1 BOL, Record Group 59, NA.

25. Memorandum Prepared in the Department of State, Washington, April 7, 1970, Nixon Presidential Materials, NSC Files, box 770, Country Files, Latin America, Bolivia, vol. 1, 1969–70, NA.

26. Ingram, *Expropriation*, p. 177.

27. Airgram A-76 From the Embassy in Bolivia to the Department of State, March 26, 1970, Central Files 1970–73, POL 1 BOL–US, Record Group 59, NA.

28. Bolivia, "Agreements Concerning Indemnification for the Nationalization of Bolivian Gulf Oil Properties," *International Legal Materials*, vol. 10, no. 6 (November 1971), pp. 1113–22.

29. Ingram, *Expropriation*, pp. 179–80, and p. 209n119.

30. U.S. Department of State, "Report on Nationalization, Expropriation, and Other Takings of U.S. and Certain Foreign Property since 1960," *International Legal Materials*, vol. 11, no. 1 (January 1972), pp. 84–118: 90.

31. Calculated from data in Instituto Nacional De Estadística, *Valores De Exportación De Petróleo Por País De Destino, 1950–1996*.

32. Ingram, *Expropriation*, p. 168.

33. There are additional reasons to believe that these estimates represent upper bounds. Independent oil companies (operating within the United States) generally traded at P/E ratios well *below* the 9.9 enjoyed by Gulf Oil—in fact, they traded at roughly half that level. These companies faced political risk, but less than Gulf's subsidiary in Bolivia. Unless Gulf expected Bolivian output to increase dramatically in the future (and there is no evidence of this), then its subsidiary should be valued less than Gulf Oil in general.

34. Sigmund, *Nationalization*, pp. 184–85; Richard Goodwin, "Letter from Peru," *The New Yorker*, May 17, 1969, pp. 44–46.

35. Sigmund, *Nationalization*, pp. 186–87.

36. The IPC's tax exemptions were due to expire in 1972.

37. The account appears in a *New Yorker* article by Richard Goodwin, a journalist and a former special assistant to President Johnson. Goodwin, "Letter from Peru," p. 60.

38. Goodwin, "Letter from Peru," p. 60.

39. Sigmund, *Nationalization*, pp. 188–89; Philip, *Oil and Politics*, pp. 252–53; Goodwin, "Letter from Peru," pp. 80–82.

40. Goodwin, "Letter from Peru," pp. 82–88.

41. Sigmund, *Nationalization*, pp. 190–91.

42. Philip, *Oil and Politics*, pp. 254–55.

43. Sigmund, *Nationalization*, p. 365n8.

44. Goodwin, "Letter from Peru," p. 43.

45. "Peruvians and Soviet Sign Their First Trade Accord," *New York Times*, February 18, 1969, p. 1.

46. *FRUS, 1969–76*, vol. E-10, *Documents on American Republics, 1969–72*, document 577, Memorandum From the President's Assistant for National Security Affairs (Kissinger) to President Nixon, Washington, February 6, 1969.

47. CIA, "Peru and the US: The Implications of the IPC Controversy," *Special National Intelligence Estimate*, March 6, 1969, pp. 3 and 13–14.

48. *FRUS, 1969–76*, vol. E-10, *Documents on American Republics, 1969–72*, document 576, Briefing Memorandum Prepared in the Depart-

ment of State for the President's Assistant for National Security Affairs (Kissinger), Washington, January 28, 1969.

49. CIA, "Peru and the US," p. 25.

50. "Transcript of the President's News Conference on Foreign Affairs and His Trip," *New York Times*, March 5, 1969, p. 8.

51. *FRUS, 1969–76*, vol. E-10, *Documents on American Republics, 1969–72*, document 581, Study Memorandum Prepared by the National Security Council Interdepartmental Group for Inter-American Affairs, Washington, March 7, 1969.

52. Sigmund, *Nationalization*, pp. 192–93.

53. *FRUS, 1969–76*, vol. E-10, *Documents on American Republics, 1969–72*, document 589, Transcript of Telephone Conversation Between President Nixon in Key Biscayne, Florida and the President's Assistant for National Security Affairs (Kissinger) in Washington, April 5, 1969, 9:45 a.m.

54. *FRUS, 1969–76*, vol. E-10, *Documents on American Republics, 1969–72*, document 604, Memorandum From the President's Assistant for National Security Affairs (Kissinger) to President Nixon, Washington, July 1, 1969.

55. *Cong. Rec.*, 91st Congress, 1st session, June 25, 1969, pp. 17355–6.

56. *FRUS, 1969–76*, vol. E-10, *Documents on American Republics, 1969–72*, document 604, Memorandum From the President's Assistant for National Security Affairs (Kissinger) to President Nixon, Washington, July 1, 1969.

57. President Richard Nixon's Daily Diary, April 6, 1969, accessed via http://www.nixonlibrary.gov/virtuallibrary/documents/dailydiary.php.

58. Sigmund, *Nationalization*, p. 193.

59. *FRUS, 1969–76*, vol. E-10, *Documents on American Republics, 1969–72*, document 607, National Security Decision Memorandum 21, Washington, July 22, 1969.

60. Sigmund, *Nationalization*, pp. 193–94.

61. Eighteen months later, in July 1975, Peru nationalized the Marcona iron mines. CIA, "Peru and the US."

62. Victor Arnold and John Hamilton, "The Greene Settlement: A Study of the Resolution of Investment Disputes in Peru," *Texas International Law Journal*, vol. 13, no. 263 (1977–78), p. 281.

63. Arnold and Hamilton, "The Greene Settlement," p. 278.

64. In retrospect, inflation would have cut that significantly—even at 1972's inflation rate of 3.3%, the net present value would have come to $133 million. At the inflation rates the United States actually wound up

experiencing over the next decade, the net present value of the deal would have fallen to $109 million.

65. U.S. Senate, 94th Congress, 1st session, Staff Report of the Select Committee to Study Governmental Operations with Respect to Intelligence Activities, December 18, 1975, *Covert Action in Chile, 1963–1973* (Washington, D.C.: GPO, 1975), pp. 15–16. (Hereafter, Church Report.)

66. Anthony Sampson, *The Sovereign State of ITT* (New York: Stein and Day, 1973), pp. 273–75; Church Report, p. 58.

67. Sampson, *Sovereign State of ITT*, p. 276; Church Report, p. 58.

68. Sampson, *Sovereign State of ITT*, pp. 278–81; Church Report, pp. 58–59.

69. Arindrajit Dube, Ethan Kaplan, and Suresh Naidu, "Coups, Corporations, and Classified Information," *Quarterly Journal of Economics*, vol. 126, no. 3 (2011), pp. 1375–1409.

70. The Ford administration brokered a similarly successful settlement for the Marcona Mining Company, which Peru nationalized in 1975. Marcona received a cash settlement and preferential access to Peruvian iron ore for a period of several years. See David Gantz, "The Marcona Settlement: New Forms of Negotiation and Compensation for Nationalized Property," *American Journal of International Law*, vol. 71, no. 3 (July 1977), pp. 474–93.

71. Osmel Manzano and Francisco Monaldi, "The Political Economy of Oil Contract Renegotiation in Venezuela," Harvard Kennedy School working paper, 2009, pp. 14–15.

72. Manzano and Monaldi, "Political Economy," pp. 14–15.

73. Philip, *Oil and Politics*, p. 475.

74. Manzano and Monaldi, "Political Economy," p. 23n37.

75. The Texas Railroad Commission controlled the output of Texan producers without taking any equity stakes.

Chapter 10: Escaping by Design?

1. Albert Bushnell Hart, *The Monroe Doctrine: An Interpretation* (Boston: Little, Brown, and Company, 1916), pp. 262–64.

2. *Convention Respecting the Limitation of the Employment of Force for the Recovery of Contract Debts*, October 18, 1907, 36 Stat. 2241, Treaty Series 537, http://avalon.law.yale.edu/20th_century/hague072.asp, accessed on February 23, 2011.

3. V. V. Veeder, "The Lena Goldfields Arbitration: The Historical Roots of Three Ideas," *The International and Comparative Law Quarterly*, vol. 47, no. 4 (October 1998), pp. 747–92.

4. Veeder, "Lena Goldfields." Most British records surrounding the Lena Goldfields case were destroyed in the blitz; however, enough evidence remains from the accounts in *The Times* of London and other sources to show considerable official interest in the arbitration settlement. Even the popular press commented on the ties between the settlement and the British state; for example, *Time* (September 15, 1930, "Foreign News: Millions for Lena") led its story with "In London last week a famed German professor of metallurgy and *an English lawyer of such distinction that he sits upon His Majesty's Privy Council* resolutely announced this awful decision" (italics added).

5. "Decision in the Arbitration Case between Radio Corporation of America versus the National Government of the Republic of China," *American Journal of International Law*, vol. 30, no. 3 (July 1936), pp. 535–51.

6. Jill Hills, *The Struggle for Control of Global Communication: The Formative Century* (Urbana: University of Illinois Press, 2002), pp. 197–98.

7. *FRUS*, 1933, *The Far East*, p. 389.

8. "Permanent Court of Arbitration. Circular Note on the Secretary General," *The American Journal of International Law*, vol. 54, no. 4 (October 1960), pp. 933–41: 937.

9. W. Mark Weidemaier, "Contracting for State Intervention: The Origins of Sovereign Debt Arbitration," *Law and Contemporary Problems*, vol. 73, no. 4 (Fall 2010), pp. 335–55: 351.

10. "Foreign Seizure of Investments: Remedies and Protection," *Stanford Law Review*, vol. 12, no. 3 (May 1960), pp. 606–37: 614.

11. Karl-Heinz Bockstiegel, "Arbitration of Disputes between States and Private Enterprises in the International Chamber," *American Journal of International Law*, vol. 59, no. 3 (July 1965), pp. 579–86: 582–83.

12. David Yackee, "*Pacta Sunt Servanda* and State Promises to Foreign Investors before Bilateral Investment Treaties: Myth and Reality," *Fordham International Law Journal*, vol. 32, no. 5 (2008), pp. 1576–82.

13. Yackee, "*Pacta Sunt Servanda*," pp. 1576–82.

14. I. M. Aboul-Enein, "Arbitration of Foreign Investment Disputes: Responses to the New Challenges and Changing Circumstances," in *New Horizons in International Commercial Arbitration and Beyond*, ed. Albert

Jan van den Berg, International Council for Commercial Arbitration (The Hague: Kluwer Law International, 2005), , pp. 181–91: 188.

15. "Organisation for Economic Co-operation and Development: Draft Convention on the Protection of Foreign Property," *International Legal Materials*, vol. 2, no. 2 (March 1963), pp. 241–67.

16. Clement Henry Moore, *Tunisia since Independence: The Dynamics of One-Party Government* (Berkeley: University of California Press, 1965), p. 206.

17. President John Kennedy had vocally and loudly favored Algerian independence from his time as a senator.

18. "World Bank May Form Agency to Help Settle International Disputes," *Wall Street Journal*, September 20, 1961, p. 9.

19. Scott Barrett, *Conflict and Cooperation in Managing International Water Resources*, World Bank Policy Research Working Paper 1303, May 1994, pp. 11–12.

20. Aron Broches, "Development of International Law by the International Bank for Reconstruction and Development," *American Society of International Law: Proceedings*, vol. 59 (1965), pp. 33–38: 34–35.

21. Christoph Schreuer, *The ICSID Convention: A Commentary* (Cambridge: Cambridge University Press, 2001), pp. 2–3.

22. Paul C. Szasz, "The Investment Disputes Convention and Latin America," *Virginia Journal of International Law*, vol. 11 (1971) pp. 256–65: 256–57.

23. *Convention on the Settlement of Investment Disputes between States and Nationals of Other States*, Chapter 4, Article 63, http://www .jus.uio.no/lm/icsid.settlement.of.disputes.between.states.and.nationals. of.other.states.convention.washington.1965/, accessed August 4, 2012.

24. "Each contracting State shall recognize an award rendered pursuant to this Convention as binding and enforce the pecuniary obligations imposed by that award within its territories as if it were a final judgment of a court in that State. . . . Execution of the award shall be governed by the laws concerning the execution of judgments in force in the State in whose territories such execution is sought." *Convention*, Chapter 4, Article 53 and 54.

25. *Convention*, Chapter 4, Article 55.

26. The Latin American group—Argentina, Bolivia, Brazil, Chile, Colombia, Costa Rica, the Dominican Republic, Ecuador, El Salvador, Guatemala, Haiti, Honduras, Mexico, Nicaragua, Panama, Paraguay, Peru, Uruguay, and Venezuela—and the Philippines dissented from the board

of directors' opinion. The Latin American group and Iraq voted against the resolution. Szasz makes the interesting point that the Latin American board members were bankers, not lawyers. Szasz, "Investment," p. 257; "International Bank for Reconstruction and Development: Resolution on Convention for the Settlement of Investment Disputes," *International Legal Materials*, vol. 3, no. 6 (November 1964), pp. 1171–76: 1175; International Centre for Settlement of Investment Disputes, *Documents Concerning the Origin and the Formulation of the Convention* (Washington, D.C.: ICSID, 2001), vol. 2, p. 606.

27. U.S. Senate, Committee on Foreign Relations, Hearing held Before Committee on Foreign Relations, Nomination of Joseph Palmer, II To Be an Assistant Secretary of State, Convention on the Settlement of Investment Disputes, Report of Proceedings, March 29, 1966, p. 48.

28. U.S. Senate, Committee on Foreign Relations, Hearing, March 29, 1966, pp. 51–52.

29. *Cong. Rec.*, 89th Congress, 2nd session, May 16, 1966, pp. 10611–17.

30. *Cong. Rec.* 89th Congress, 2nd session, July 19, 1966, p. 16176.

31. U.S. House of Representatives, 89th Congress, 2nd session, Hearing before the Subcommittee on International Organizations and Movements of the Committee on Foreign Affairs on H.R. 15785, Convention on the Settlement of Investment Disputes, June 28, 1966, p. 17.

32. *Cong. Rec.*, 89th Congress, 2nd session, August 1, 1966, pp. 17747–48.

33. U.S. House, Committee on Foreign Affairs, Convention on the Settlement of Investment Disputes, June 28, 1966, pp. 21–22. Gross: "Of course, we don't use the Oxford Dictionary around here. At least I don't. Maybe some of the rest of them do."

34. *Cong. Rec.*, 89th Congress, 2nd session, August 1, 1966, pp. 17747–48.

35. Japan started an investment guarantee program in 1956 for essentially the same reasons—its government had no way to protect the overseas investments of its citizens without upending the entire Cold War order. William Miller, "Protection of United States Investments Abroad: The Investment Guarantee Program of the United States Government," *George Washington International Law Review*, vol. 32, no. 288 (1963–64), p. 296.

36. These nations could not protect their investors by military means—either because they lacked the capability, like Switzerland and Sweden, or because they once had the capability but could no longer effectively

exert it after the end of their colonial empires, like the Netherlands and Belgium. The Low Countries (like West Germany) were additionally limited in their ability to use economic sanctions by the European Economic Community—unless all six governments of the EEC agreed to them, trade sanctions would be practically ineffective unless a country withdrew from the Common Market.

37. Patricia Robin, "The BIT Won't Bite: The American Bilateral Investment Treaty Program," *American University Law Review*, vol. 33 (1984), pp. 931–58: 957.

38. U.S. Department of State, Egypt Bilateral Investment Treaty, http://www.state.gov/e/eeb/ifd/43255.htm

39. Kenneth Vandevelde, "The Bilateral Investment Treaty Program of the United States," *Cornell International Law Journal*, vol. 21, no. 201 (1988).

40. Vandevelde, "Treaty Program," p. 212.

41. Vandevelde, "Treaty Program," p. 235.

42. Vandevelde, "Treaty Program," pp. 265–66.

43. Vandervelde, "Treaty Program," p. 210.

44. Kenneth Vandervelde, "A Brief History of International Investment Agreements," *UC Davis Journal of International Law & Policy*, vol. 12, no. 157 (2005), p. 175.

45. "Intergovernmental Agreements under the United States Investment Guarantee Program," *Indiana Law Journal*, vol. 43, no. 429 (1967–68), p. 430. The word "areas" was deliberately used in order to allow the program to apply to European overseas colonies. Algeria was covered by the French agreement, along with the overseas departments of Guadeloupe, Martinique, and French Guiana.

46. *Second Report to Congress on the Mutual Security Program* (Washington, D.C.: GPO, 1952), pp. 43–44.

47. United States, *Mutual Security Program, Non-Regional Programs, Fiscal Years 1957*, p. 269.

48. The uptick in pending applications for developed nations in 1956 was entirely due to the program's expansion to cover war risk. War insurance applications consisted mostly of applications in France (55%), Turkey (21%), West Germany (14%), and Taiwan (7%). South Korea was not eligible for war insurance, since it was technically still at war with North Korea and the People's Republic of China.

49. United States, *Mutual Security Program*, p. 270.

50. Fees for convertibility and war insurance were identical. If a company wished to purchase all three, its premium would be 1.5%. Miller, "Protection," p. 301.

51. The investor would need to pay a fee of 0.25% on the balance, so this type of temporary reduction in coverage was not costless. Miller, "Protection," p. 301.

52. The Foreign Assistance Act of 1961, 75 Stat. 429–32 (1962).

53. U.S. Senate, Committee on Foreign Relations, "Investment Guarantee Program," *Hearings on S. 2996,*, pp. 605–9, and Agency for International Development, "TIAS Document Accession List of Investment Guaranty Agreements and Amendments," January 20, 1963, p. 281.

54. "Intergovernmental Agreements," p. 434.

55. Marina von Neumann Whitman, *Government Risk-Sharing in Foreign Investment* (Princeton, N.J.: Princeton University Press, 1965).

56. "The Investment Guaranty Program: Problems of Administration," *Columbia Law Review*, vol. 64, no. 315 (1964), p. 317.

57. "The Investment Guaranty Program," p. 324.

58. "Government Guaranties of Foreign Investments," *Harvard Law Review*, vol. 66, no. 514 (1953), p. 518.

59. Bruce Clubb and Verne Vance, Jr., "Incentives to Private U.S. Investment Abroad under the Foreign Assistance Program," *Yale Law Journal*, vol. 72, no. 3 (January 1963), pp. 475–505: 476.

60. "Intergovernmental Agreements," p. 435.

61. *Cong. Rec.*, 91st Congress, 1st session, May 28, 1969, pp. 14162–63.

62. *Cong. Rec.*, 89th Congress, 2nd session, July 18, 1966, p. 16067.

63. *Cong. Rec.*, 90th Congress, 2nd session, 1968, pp. 24,510–18.

64. *FRUS, 1969–76, vol. 4, Foreign Assistance, International Development, Trade Policies, 1969–72* (Washington, D.C.: GPO, 2002), pp. 253–54.

65. *Cong. Rec.*, 91st Congress, 1st session, December 12, 1969, p. 38696.

66. Pastor, *Congress*, p. 276.

67. *Cong. Rec.*, 91st Congress, 1st session, December 12, 1969, p. 38709.

68. Richard Nixon, "Statement on Signing the Foreign Assistance Act of 1969," December 31, 1969, John Woolley and Gerhard Peters, The American Presidency Project [online], Santa Barbara, Calif., http://www.presidency.ucsb.edu/ws/?pid=2391, accessed March 31, 2011.

69. Marshall Mays, "The Overseas Private Investment Corporation," *Lawyer of the Americas*, vol. 5, no. 3 (1973), pp. 471–79: 471.

70. U.S. Congress, House, Committee on Foreign Affairs, 1973, *The Overseas Private Investment Corporation: A Critical Analysis*, 93rd Congress, 1st session, p. 2.

71. There is no historical evidence that this occurred, but companies that received guarantees often lobbied local governments to nationalize money-losing investments. Whitman, *Risk-Sharing*, p. 77.

72. Lipson, *Standing Guard*, 247.

73. The IDA was a subsidiary of the World Bank directed at reducing extreme poverty.

74. *Cong. Rec.*, 92nd Congress, 1st session, October 19, 1971, p. 36815.

75. *Cong. Rec.*, 92nd Congress, 1st session, October 19, 1971, p. 36818.

76. *Cong. Rec.*, 92nd Congress, 1st session, October 19, 1971, p. 36820.

77. *Cong. Rec.*, 92nd Congress, 1st session, October 20, 1971, pp. 37031–32.

78. *Cong. Rec.*, 92nd Congress, 1st session, October 20, 1971, p. 37043.

79. Sec. 21 of the Inter-American Development Bank Act, Public Law 92-246; Sec. 18 of the Asian Development Bank Act, Public Law 92-245; and Sec. 12 of the International Development Association Act, Public Law 92-247.

80. Einhorn, *Expropriation Politics*, pp. 87–89.

81. Einhorn, *Expropriation Politics*, p. 89 note c.

82. *Cong. Rec.*, 92nd Congress, 2nd session, February 1, 1972, p. 2039.

83. *Cong. Rec.*, 92nd Congress, 2nd session, February 1, 1972, p. 2019.

84. Einhorn, *Expropriation Politics*, pp. 86–87.

85. *Cong. Rec.*, 92nd Congress, 2nd session, February 1, 1972, p. 2039.

86. *Cong. Rec.*, 92nd Congress, 2nd session, February 1, 1972, pp. 2031–32.

87. *Cong. Rec.*, 92nd Congress, 2nd session, February 1, 1972, pp. 2037–38.

88. *Cong. Rec.*, 92nd Congress, 2nd session, February 1, 1972, p. 2046.

89. Morgan Guaranty Trust Company, *World Financial Markets*, various issues.

90. Rex Hudson and Dennis Hanratty, eds., *Bolivia: A Country Study* (Washington, D.C.: GPO for the Library of Congress, 1989), p. 68, http://countrystudies.us/bolivia/69.htm, accessed August 20, 2012.

91. Jeffry Frieden, *Debt, Development, and Democracy: Modern Political Economy and Latin America, 1965–1985* (Princeton, N.J.: Princeton University Press, 1991), pp. 63–65.

92. Paul Krugman, "U.S. Policy on Developing-Country Debt," in *American Ecomnomic Policy in the 1980s*, ed. Martin Feldstein (Chicago: University of Chicago Press, 1994), p. 693, http://www.nber.org/chapters/c7762.pdf, accessed August 20, 2012.

93. "HNG Write-Off Set on Peru Oil Assets," *New York Times*, December 30, 1985.

94. Arturo Porzecanski, "Dealing with Sovereign Debt: Trends and Implications," in *Sovereign Debt at the Crossroads*, ed. Chris Jochnick and Fraser Preston (New York: Oxford University Press, 2004), pp. 267–96: 280.

95. Kenneth Hansen, "Investment Promotion and Political Risk Insurance," paper for the "Encouraging Capital Flows into Africa" conference, Johannesburg (September 29–30, 2004), p. 2.

96. Adeoye Akinsanya, "International Protection of Direct Foreign Investments in the Third World," *International and Comparative Law Quarterly*, vol. 36, no. 1 (January 1987), pp. 58–75: 67.

97. *National Union Fire Insurance Company of Pittsburgh v. Belco Petroleum Corporation*, 88 F.3d 129 (3d Cir. 1993).

98. "HNG Write-Off."

99. *National Union v. Belco.*

100. Clyde Farnsworth, "Insurer Offers Peru Proposal on Oil Claim," *New York Times*, June 12, 1989.

101. "American International Group and Other Parties Reach Settlement with Peru in Belco Petroleum Expropriation Case," *PRNewswire*, December 23, 1991.

102. Stephen Kobrin, "Expropriation as an Attempt to Control Foreign Firms in LDCs: Trends from 1960–1979," *International Studies Quarterly*, vol. 3 (September 1984), pp. 29–48; and Michael Minor, "The Demise of Expropriation as an Instrument of LDC Policy, 1980–1992," *Journal of International Business Studies*, vol. 25, no. 1 (1st Quarter 1994), pp. 177–88.

103. Krugman, "Developing-Country Debt," p. 719.

104. Quoted in Wolfgang Peter, Jean-Quentin de Kuyper, and Bénédict de Candolle, *Arbitration and Renegotiation of International Investment Agreements* (The Hague: Kluwer Law International, 1995), p. 369.

105. Ibrahim Shihata, *MIGA and Foreign Investment: Origins, Operations, Policies and Documents of the Multilateral Investment Guarantee Agency* (Dordrecht: M. Nijhoff, 1988), p. 179.

106. Ibrahim Shihata, "Towards a Greater Depoliticization of Investment Disputes: The Roles of ICSID and MIGA," *ICSID Review*, vol. 1, no. 1 (1986), pp. 1–25: 13 and 15.

107. Shihata, "Depoliticization," p. 21.

108. Shihata, "Depoliticization," p. 23.

109. Jack Tate to James McGranery, May 19, 1952, *Department of State Bulletin*, 24.

110. Tate to McGranery, May 19, 1952, *Department of State Bulletin*, 24. Italics in the original.

111. Tom McNamara, *A Primer on Foreign Sovereign Immunity* (Denver: Davis Graham & Stubbs, March 8, 2006).

112. Tate to McGranery, May 19, 1952, *Department of State Bulletin*, 24.

113. John O'Brien, *International Law* (London: Routledge-Cavendish, 2001), p. 290.

114. http://conventions.coe.int/Treaty/Commun/ChercheSig.asp?NT=074&CM=8&DF=&CL=ENG.

115. Robert von Mehren, "The Foreign Sovereign Immunities Act of 1976," *Columbia Journal of Transnational Law*, vol. 17 (1978), pp. 33–66: 38.

116. McNamara, *Primer*.

117. Patrick Wautelet, "Immunity of Foreign Central Banks Assets in Belgium," published on the official blog of the *Journal of Private International Law*, http://conflictoflaws.net/2008/immunity-of-foreign-central-banks-assets-in-belgium/, accessed August 23, 2012.

118. Federico Sturzenegger and Jeromin Zettlemeyer, *Debt Defaults and Lessons from a Decade of Crises* (Cambridge, Mass: MIT Press, 2007), p. 65.

119. *Republic of Argentina v. Weltover, Inc.*, 504 U.S. 607 (1992).

120. *ICSID Convention, Regulation and Rules* (April 2006), Articles 9 and 10, pp. 14–15.

121. Noel Maurer and Gustavo Herrero, "YPF—The Argentine Oil Nationalization of 2012," Harvard Business School case no. N1-000-000, June 20, 2012, p. 8.

122. Anthony Sinclair, Louise Fisher, and Sarah Macrory, "ICSID Arbitration: How Long Does It Take?" *Global Arbitration Review*, vol. 4, no. 5 (October 2009), http://www.goldreserveinc.com/documents/ICSID%20arbitration%20%20How%20long%20does%20it%20take.pdf, accessed August 23, 2012.

123. Final award in *Mobil Cerro Negro, Ltd. v. Petróleos de Venezuela, S.A. et al.* (ICC Case no. 15415/JRF, December 11, 2011), part B, pp. 459–66.

124. *Michele Colella and Denise Dussault v. The Republic of Argentina*, F.Supp.2d, 2007 WL 1545204 (N.D.Cal.).

125. Arrêt n° 867 du 28 septembre 2011 (09-72.057)—Cour de cassation—Première chambre civile. Demandeur(s): La société NML Capital Ltd; Défendeur(s): La République Argentine.

126. E. Gaillard and J. Younan, eds., *State Entities in International Arbitration*, IAI Series on International Arbitration (New York: Juris, 2008) pp. 190–91.

127. J. E. Anzola, "Venezuela Clashes with Investment Arbitration," Transnational Dispute Management (October 2011), p. 10. http://eanzola.com/images/uploads/Venezuela_clashes_with_Investment_Arbitration.pdf, accessed February 22, 2013.

128. James Berger, "International Dispute Resolution Update: Foreign Sovereign Immunity," *StayCurrent* (June 2010), pp. 10–11, http://www.paulhastings.com/assets/publications/1629.pdf, accessed August 23, 2012.

129. "Hay 10 socios para invertir en Vaca Muerta," *La Mañana de Neuquén*, May 31, 2012.

130. "Argentina Invites Russia's Gazprom to Consider Investing in YPF Operations," *MercoPress*, June 19, 2012, http://en.mercopress.com/2012/06/19/argentina-invites-russia-s-gazprom-to-consider-investing-in-ypf-operations.

131. The complaint accused Argentina of violating its pledge to tender for all Class D shares of YPF if it ever took back control of the company: "Argentina's failure to launch a tender offer despite having retaken control over YPF constitutes a breach of its contractual obligations to other shareholders." Quoted in "Repsol Sues Argentina over YPF in NY Court and Also Takes the Case to World Bank Arbitration," *MercoPress*, May 16, 2012, http://en.mercopress.com/2012/05/16/repsol-sues-argentina-over-ypf-in-ny-court-and-also-takes-the-case-to-world-bank-arbitration.

132. Jude Webber and Miles Johnson, "Repsol Warns Rivals over Investing in YPF," *Financial Times*, May 7, 2012, http://www.ft.com/intl/cms/s/0/a401e746-9860-11e1-8617-00144feabdc0.html#axzz1yjJKfF2u.

133. Quoted in Maurer and Herrero, "YPF," p. 11.

134. "La Justicia española admite la demanda de Repsol contra Chevron por el 'caso YPF'," *El Mundo*, November 11, 2012, http://www.elmundo.es/elmundo/2012/11/19/economia/1353350342.html, accessed February 22, 2013.

135. "Repsol sues Chevron in U.S. court over YPF deal," Reuters, December 4, 2012, http://www.reuters.com/article/2012/12/04/repsol-chevron-ypf-uscourt-idUSL1E8N4CZ120121204, accessed February 22, 2013.

136. Taos Turner, "Chevron Embargo Is Setback for YPF, Argentina," *Wall Street Journal*, February 4, 2013, http://online.wsj.com/article/SB1000 142412788732444590457828429398964824.html?mod=googlenews_ wsj, accessed February 22, 2013.

137. John Crook, "U.S. Response to Venezuelan Nationalizations," *American Journal of International Law*, vol. 101, no. 3 (July 2007), pp. 645–47.

138. For an excellent account of events leading up to the coup, as well as the coup itself and the aftermath of its failure, see Brian Nelson, *The Silence and the Scorpion: The Coup against Chávez and the Making of Modern Venezuela* (New York: Nation Books, 2009).

139. See Noel Maurer, "Old Evil Vendepatria PDVSA Saves New Socialist PDVSA!" *Power and the Money*, January 5, 2012, and "Is Venezuelan Heavy Oil Less Risky Than French Nuclear Power?" *Power and the Money*, February 17, 2012, http://noelmaurer.typepad.com/aab/2012/01/ old-evil-vendepatria-pdvsa-saves-new-socialist-pdvsa.html and http:// noelmaurer.typepad.com/aab/2012/02/is-venezuelan-heavy-oil-less-risky-than-french-nuclear-power.html, accessed August 24, 2012.

140. Susan Franck, "Empirically Evaluating Claims about Investment Treaty Arbitration," *North Carolina Law Review*, vol. 86 (2007), pp. 1–88.

141. Data through 2010 from UNCTAD, http://archive.unctad.org/iia-dbcases/cases.aspx and the Investment Treaty Arbitration database, http:// www.italaw.com/awards/by-claimant.

142. Clint Peinhardt and Todd Allee, "The International Centre for Settlement of Investment Disputes: A Multilateral Organization Enhancing a Bilateral Treaty Regime," paper prepared for the 2006 Annual Meeting of the Midwest Political Science Association, Chicago, April 14, 2006, p. 9. Kazakhstan delayed paying a 2003 judgment worth $9.9 million to AIG Capital Partners, but it eventually settled.

143. Alan Alexandroff and Ian Laird, "Compliance and Enforcement," in *The Oxford Handbook of International Investment Law*, ed. Peter Muchlinski, Federico Ortino, and Christoph Schreue (Oxford: Oxford University Press, 2008), p. 1183.

144. Alexandroff and Laird, "Compliance," p. 1184.

145. See Abrahm Lustgarten, "Shell Shakedown," *Fortune*, February 1, 2007, http://money.cnn.com/magazines/fortune/fortune_archive/2007/ 02/05/8399125/index.htm, accessed August 24, 2012.

146. OECD (2012), p. 30.

Chapter 11: The Empire Trap in the Twenty-first Century

1. José Pablo Ferrándiz, "Expropiación injustificada," *El País*, Apirl 22, 2012, http://blogs.elpais.com/metroscopia/2012/04/tres-de-cada-cuatro-espa%C3%B1oles-77-consideran-totalmente-injustificada-la-expropiaci%C3%B3n-de-la-petrolera-ypf-filial-argenti.html, accessed August 31, 2012.

2. The details of the poll are available at http://www.realinstitutoel cano.org/wps/portal/rielcano/contenido?WCM_GLOBAL_CONTEXT=/ elcano/elcano_es/barometro/oleadabrie30, accessed August 31, 2012.

3. For the Brazilian case, see William Summerhill, *Order against Progress: Government, Foreign Investment, and Railroads in Brazil, 1854–1913* (Stanford, Calif: Stanford University Press, 2003). For the Mexican case, see John Coatsworth, *Growth against Development: The Economic Impact of Railroads in Porfirian Mexico* (DeKalb: Northern Illinois University Press, 1981).

4. Louis Wells, "The Backlash to Investment Arbitration: Three Causes," in *The Backlash against Investment Arbitration: Perceptions and Reality*, ed. Michael Waibel (Austin, Tex.: Wolters Kluwer Law & Business, 2010), p. 343.

5. Gus Van Harten, *Investment Treaty Arbitration and Public Law* (Oxford: Oxford University Press, 2008), p. 4.

6. Susan Franck, "Empirically Evaluating Claims about Investment Treaty Arbitration," *North Carolina Law Review*, vol. 86 (2007), p. 1.

7. U.S. Embassy, Buenos Aires, *2009 Report on Investment Disputes and Expropriation Claims: Argentina*, WikiLeaks cable 09BUENOS-AIRES846, http://wikileaks.org/cable/2009/07/09BUENOSAIRES846. html, accessed September 1, 2012.

8. "U.S. Supreme Court Rules in Favour of Argentina and Unfreezes Funds," *MercoPress*, June 26, 2012, http://en.mercopress.com/2012/06/26/ us-supreme-court-rules-in-favour-of-argentina-and-unfreezes-funds, accessed September 1, 2012.

9. Luisa Corradini, "Pedirá Francia que se anule el embargo," *La Nación*, April 8, 2009, http://www.lanacion.com.ar/1116436-pedira-francia-que-se-anule-el-embargo, accessed September 1, 2012.

10. David Glovin, "Argentina Bondholders Lose Bid to Seize State Airline," *Bloomberg*, August 20, 2009, http://www.bloomberg.com/apps/new s?pid=newsarchive&sid=a.3p5n6GcstM, accessed September 1, 2012. For

the details behind the voluntary transfer of the money-losing airline from Spanish-owned Marsans to the Argentine government, see "The Nationalization of Aerolíneas Argentinas and Austral: Will the Government Set Them Straight?" *Universia Knowledge Wharton*, August 6, 2008, http://www.wharton.universia.net/index.cfm?fa=viewfeature&id=1563&language=english, accessed September 1, 2012.

11. Matt Moffett, "Besting Argentina in Court Doesn't Seem to Pay," *Wall Street Journal*, April 20, 2012.

12. "US Will Vote against Loans to Argentina in World Bank and IDB," *MercoPress*, September 29, 2011, http://en.mercopress.com/2011/09/29/us-will-vote-against-loans-to-argentina-in-world-bank-and-idb, accessed June 11, 2012.

13. U.S. Embassy, Buenos Aires, "GSP Fact Sheet," http://argentina.usembassy.gov/gsp2.html, accessed June 11, 2012.

14. See Maurer and Guerrero, "YPF," exhibits 2, 3, and 4.

15. Jude Webber, "Repsol Keeps Seat on YPF Board," *Financial Times*, June 5, 2012, http://www.ft.com/intl/cms/s/0/29e3655a-ae92-11e1-b842-00144feabdc0.html#axzz1yb9GUqow.

16. Maurer and Guerrero, "YPF," p. 7.

17. The reason for the high dividends was to allow the Eskenazis to repay the loans that they had contracted in order to purchase their share. The Eskenazis financed the entire purchase with debt fully collateralized by the family's shares in YPF; 40% of the loans came from Repsol itself. Maurer and Guerrero, "YPF," pp. 5.

18. Martin Roberts, "Spain Targets Argentine Biodiesel in YPF Reprisal," Reuters, April 20, 2012, http://www.reuters.com/article/2012/04/20/us-spain-argentina-idUSBRE83J1DY20120420, accessed June 11, 2012.

19. "Spain, on the Edge of a Financial Cliff, Cancels All Development Aid to Latin America," *MercoPress*, May 23, 2012, http://en.mercopress.com/2012/05/23/spain-on-the-edge-of-a-financial-cliff-cancels-all-development-aid-to-latin-america, accessed June 11, 2012.

20. Fiona Govan and Emily Gosden, "European Parliament Calls for Sanctions against Argentina," *The Telegraph*, April 20, 2012.

21. See "EU Brings WTO Dispute against Argentina," *International Law Prof Blog*, May 29, 2012, http://lawprofessors.typepad.com/international_law/2012/05/eu-brings-wto-dispute-against-argentina.html, and "EU Agrees to File a Trade Suit with WTO against Argentina's Import Restrictions," *MercoPress*, May 15, 2012, http://en.mercopress.com/2012/05/15/eu-agrees-to-file-a-trade-suit-with-wto-against-argentina-s-import-restrictions, accessed June 30, 2012.

22. See Seattle to Brussels Network, "Call for an Alternative Investment Model," November 6, 2011, http://www.s2bnetwork.org/fileadmin/dateien/downloads/Statement-ENG.pdf, accessed September 1, 2012.

23. Luke Peterson, "Out of Order," *fDi Magazine*, October 7, 2008, http://www.bilaterals.org/spip.php?article13779, accessed June 30, 2012.

24. "863 Citizen Groups Call on World Bank President to Respect Bolivia's Withdrawal from Arbitration Court," Common Dreams press release, January 16, 2008, http://www.commondreams.org/news2008/0116-10.htm, accessed September 1, 2012.

25. Skadden, Arps, Slate, Meagher & Flom, LLP, "Nicaragua Advocates Withdrawal from ICSID: Implications for Investors," April 24, 2008, http://www.skadden.com/Index.cfm?contentID=51&itemID=1391.

26. "Venezuela Submits a Notice under Article 71 of the ICSID Convention," ICSID news release, January 26, 2012.

27. Bretton Woods Project, "ICSID in Crisis: Straight-jacket or Investment Protection?" *Bretton Woods Update* 66, July 10, 2009, http://www.brettonwoodsproject.org/art-564878, accessed April 5, 2011.

28. On October 5, 2012, an ICSID panel awarded Occidental $1.77 billion in damages, including interest dated back to the May 16, 2006, expropriation event. See *Occidental Petroleum Corporation and Occidental Exploration and Production Company v. The Republic of Ecuador*, ICSID Case no. ARB/06/11, p. 317, http://www.italaw.com/sites/default/files/case-documents/italaw1094.pdf, accessed October 14, 2012.

29. Yaraslau Kryvoi, *The International Centre for Settlement of Investment Disputes* (Alphen aan den Rijn, the Netherlands: Kluwer Law International, 2010), pp. 83–86.

30. "Of Coups and Coverage: Political Turmoil Is Costly Unless You Are Fully Insured," *Economist*, April 7, 2007.

31. "How to Become Politics-proof," *Economist*, March 31, 2011.

32. The People's Republic still hews to the principle of absolute sovereign immunity.

33. Qianru Song and Rodrigo Wagner, "How Can China Invest in Countries Where Others Are Expropriated?" Tufts University Department of Economics working paper (May 10, 2012), p. 11.

34. "Why Brazil Gave Way on Itaipú Dam," BBC.com, July 26, 2009, http://news.bbc.co.uk/2/hi/americas/8169139.stm, accessed April 5, 2011.

35. "Brazilian Congress Set to Approve This Week Compensation for Paraguayan Power," *MercoPress*, April 2, 2011, http://en.mercopress.com/2011/04/02/brazilian-congress-set-to-approve-this-week-compensation-for-paraguayan-power, accessed April 5, 2011.

36. "Under the conflict hypothesis the Green Country (allegedly Brazil) and the Yellow Country (allegedly Paraguay) are forced into conflict. Social unrest, populist speeches, emptying of fuel resources cause serious energy problems in the Yellow country which then threatens and challenges the Greens. The Green country with support from United Nations declares war and a strategic battle begins with simulation of air bombings to eliminate the enemy Air force. In the middle of the conflict the bi-national hydroelectric complex 'Itá' jointly belonging to the Green and Yellow countries becomes an objective, since it supplies a significant percentage of the Green energy demand, particularly to its main cities and industrial hubs." See "Brazilian Military Launch Operation Lasso with the Itaipú Dam in Mind," *MercoPress*, November 16, 2009, http://en.mercopress.com/2009/11/16/brazilian-military-launch-operation-lasso-with-the-itaip-dam-in-mind, accessed April 5, 2011.

37. "Brazilian Military," *MercoPress*, November 16, 2009.

38. Raúl Zibechi, "Is Brazil Creating Its Own 'Backyard' in Latin America?" *Upside Down World*, February 16, 2009, http://upsidedownworld.org/main/brazil-archives-63/1720-is-brazil-creating-its-own-qbackyardq-in-latin-america, accessed April 5, 2011.

39. Cable reproduced in "Paraguay Fearful of 'Brazilian Dominance' Reveals Wikileaks Cable," *MercoPress*, February 18, 2011, http://en.mercopress.com/2011/02/18/paraguay-fearful-of-brazilian-dominance-reveals-wikileaks-cable, accessed April 5, 2011.

40. U.S. Embassy, Brasília, "Brazil—Uncertain Response to Bolivian Oil and Gas Nationalization," document 06BRASILIA876, May 5, 2006, http://wikileaks.vicepresidencia.gob.bo, accessed April 5, 2011.

41. U.S. Embassy, Brasília, "Uncertain Response."

42. U.S. Embassy, Brasília, "Brazilian Foreign Ministry Says 'No Crisis Yet' with Bolivia, but Two Potential Flashpoints Are Brewing," Document 06BRASILIA888, May 8, 2006, http://wikileaks.vicepresidencia.gob.bo, accessed April 5, 2011.

43. U.S. Embassy, Brasília, "Uncertain Response."

44. George Gray Molina, "Global Governance Exit: A Bolivian Case Study," paper prepared for the 2nd Annual GLF Colloquium, May 3–4, 2010, mimeo, pp. 7–8, and Ana Paula Ribeiro, "Acordo com Bolívia garante rentabilidade para Petrobras, diz Silas," *La Folha*, October 29, 2006.

45. Walter Brandimarte, "Brazil Petrobras Upbeat about Bolivia Refinery Deal," Reuters, April 28, 2007, and "Bolivia to Buy 2 Petrobras Refineries for $112 Mln," Reuters, May 10, 2007.

46. Clare Ribando, "Bolivia: Political and Economic Developments and Relations with the United States," Congressional Research Service report, January 26, 2007, p. 14.

47. "Protests Threaten Oil Pipes," *Washington Times*, September 9, 2008, http://www.washingtontimes.com/news/2008/sep/09/protests-threaten-oil-pipes/?page=1.

48. Stephan Kueffner and Joshua Goodman, "Ecuador May Default on Brazil Loan Tied to Odebrecht," *Bloomberg*, September 24, 2008.

49. Zibechi, "Is Brazil Creating Its Own 'Backyard' in Latin America?"

50. "Brazil Envoy Returns to Ecuador; Disputed Hydro Payments Never Stopped," *HydroWorld.com*, January 14, 2009, http://www.hydroworld.com/index/display/article-display/articles/hrhrw/News/Brazil_envoy_returns_to_Ecuador_disputed_hydro_payments_never_stopped.html, accessed April 5, 2011.

51. Petrobras, *2008 Financial Analysis and Statements* (Rio de Janeiro: Petrobras, 2009), p. 96.

52. Calculated from data in Petrobras, *2008 Financial Analysis*, p. 96; Petrobras, *2010 Financial Analysis and Statements* (Rio de Janeiro: Petrobras, 2011), p. 65; Petrobras, *2008 Annual Report* (Rio de Janeiro: Petrobras, 2009), p. 83; Mercedes Alvaro, "Ecuador Expects June Asset Accord with Petrobras," *Wall Street Journal*, May 24, 2012, http://www.marketwatch.com/story/ecuador-expects-june-asset-accord-with-petrobras-2012-05-24, accessed September 1, 2012; "Ecuador Begins Takeover of Petrobras Fields," *Latin American Herald Tribune*, November 23, 2010; and Ministerio de Economía y Finanzas, "Participación del 50% del Estado por Excedentes de los Precios de Petróleo no Pactados y no Previstos," mimeo, 2008.

53. Alvaro, "Ecuador."

INDEX

Page numbers in italic type indicate a figure, map, or table on that page. The letter *b* following a page number indicates a box at that location. Entries for U.S. presidents may refer to the individual, the administration, or both.

Argentina, 435, 437–44; 1990s privatizations and, 437–38; arbitration and, 437; arbitration cases against since 2001, *439–41*; Calvo Doctrine and, 438, 444; debt default of, 421; ICSID claims and, 438; ICSID enforcement and, 424; investor-versus-state arbitration and, 441–42; moral hazard and, 442–43; navy of, 77; oil expropriations of 2012 and, 443; oil pipline to Bolivia and, 261; service contracts" and, 355n1; sovereign debt default and, 437–38; success in arbitration and, 438; U.S. and Europe state sanctions and, 442; YPF company (Repsol) and, 425–27

Argentine Republic v. Weltover (1992), 387, 421–22

Arias, Arnulfo, 252

Arias, Desiderio, 99, 100–101

Armond, David de, on the Lodge bill, 42

Arosemena, Otto, 362

Arrelano, Rodolfo, 228

Asian Bank Bill, 411

Asociación de Industriales Mineros de Bolivia, 178–79

Asphalt Company of America, 83

Atlantic Monthly, 307

Aurelio, Marco, 447

Bacon, Robert, 50

Báez, Buenaventura, 60

Báez, Ramón, 99

Balmelli, Carlos Mateo, 447

Banco Nacional de Cuba, 323

Bandaranaike, Sirimavo, 332–33, 334; political vulnerability and, 336

Bank of British West Africa, 133–34

Bank of the Philippine Islands, 52

Banque Nationale de Saint Domingue, 61

Barber, Amzi Lorenzo, 83

Barings crisis of 1890, 77

Barr, Joseph, 397

Bass, W. L., 64

Bateman, Charles, 290

Bates, Robert H., 16

Batista, Fulgencio, 234, 236, 315, 316

Bayh, Birch on Hickenlooper Amendment to the Foreign Aid Act, 340

Belaúnde, Fernando, 368, 369

Belco Petroleum (Enron), 415–16

Bello, Clemente Vazquez, 226

Benguet Consolidated Mining Company, 51–52

Berle, Adolf, 233–34

Berlin Airlift of 1948–49, 302

Bermúdez, Antonio, 291

Bernays, Edward, 307

Biato, Marcel, 449

bilateral investment treaties (BITs), 399–404, 424; Brazil and, 447; chronological list of, 1959–65, *401*; depoliticization of investment disputes and, 403–4; Federal Republic of Germany and, 400; military capabilities and, 524n36; U.S., 1982–2012, *403*; U.S. and, 402

BITs. *See* bilateral investment treaties (BITs)

Black, Eugene, 395, 396

Blanco, Antonio Guzmán, 82

Board of Education, Brown v., 411

Bobo, Rosalvo, 122

Boliívar, Simon, 172

Bolivia, 184–85; Alianza Popular Revolucionaria Americana (APRA) and, 195–96; American interests in, 180; arbitration and, 263–64, 299; central government revenue and tin prices, 1922–32, *195*; Comisión Fiscal Permanente (CFP) and, 175–76, 177–78, 480n126, 481n11; default and,

13, 194; Definitive Agreement on Retentions and, 299; government revenues, 1905–31, *176–77*; graft and corruption in, 175, 180; Gulf Oil nationalizations of 1969 and, 363–64; Kemmerer and, 181; low-cost carrots and, 311; mining and, 178; Movimiento Nacional Revolucionario (MNR) and, 297–98; oil industry and, 260–64; oil production and gross revenues, 1926–41, *295*; Standard Oil of New Jersey (Jersey Standard) and, 292–96; tax reform and, 176–77; tin industry nationalizations and, 175–78, 363–64; U.S. Army plans and, 193, 481n10; U.S. embassy on, 365; U.S. Export-Import (Exim) Bank and, 293; U.S. intervention in, 174–81; U.S. politics of scarcity and, 243; U.S. pressure and, 263; U.S. sanctions and, 364

bond spreads: circum-Caribbean nations, 1900–1910, *76*; circum-Caribbean nations, 1906–7, *79*; collapse of Cuba and, *88*; Latin American nations, 1905–28, *81*; U.S. interventions and, *80*

Bonilla, Manuel, 80
Bonsall, Philip, 316, 319, 321, 324
Borah, William, 153
Bordas, José, 98
Borno, Louis, 164, 167–68
Bosnia, 494n4
Bosque, Pio Romero, 204
Bowen, Herbert, 85
Brache, Rafael, 200
Brady Plan, 417–18
Brazil: bilateral investment treaties (BITs) and, 447; BITs and, 447; Bolivia and, 448–49; Ecuador and, 449–50; empire trap and, 449–50; expropriation of Companhia Telefonica Nacional (CTN), 327–28; ICSID and, 447; navy of, 77; Operation Laçador

and, 448, 535n36; Paraguay and, 447–48; U.S. anticommunism and, 328–29
Bridges, Styles, 330
British-Aluminum Company, 357n10
Brizola, Leonel, 328, 329; expropriations and, 329
Broches, Aron, 395
Brock, Bill, 411
Broe, William, 380–81
Broomfield, William, 340
Brown Brothers and Seligman, 111, 113, 114–15
Brown v. Board of Education, 411
Bryan, William Jennings, 37, 98, 114; Haiti and, 120; port of Tampico, "neutral zone" and, 147b
Burgos, Juan Bautista Vicini, 165
Burns, Arthur, 408
Busch, Germán, 261, 262, 293
Bush, George W., 427
Butler, Smedley, 125
Byrd, Harry, 411

Cabot, John, 300
Cáceres, Ramón, 62, 94
Cadell, R. Mackay, 130
Caffery, Jefferson, 207, 234, 236
Caltex, 333
Calvo, Miguel, 226
Calvo Doctrine, 18, 389, 395, 396, 438; Argentina and, 444
Cannon, Lee Leroy, 108
Caperton, William, 101
Caracoles, 179
Cárdenas, Lázaro, 272–73, 286; on oil companies, 275
Carner, Ambrose, 82–83, 84
Carranza, Venustiano, 139b–40b; mining and, 145b–46b, 474n31
Carter, Calvin, 158–59, 186
Carter, Jimmy, 4; Ethiopia and, 14, 347b, 349b
Carvalho Siqiera, José Elito, 448
Castle, William, 154

Castro, Cipriano, 1–2, 60, 80–81, 83–85, 362, 363
Castro, Fidel, 4, 14, 315; Decree 188, 323; expropriation of American properties and, 325; on foreign investments, 313; Law 851 and, 324; U.S sugar quota cut and, 324
Central America: General Treaty of Peace and Amity and, 206, 210; U.S. politics of scarcity and, 243
Central Dominican Railroad Company, 65
Central Intelligence Agency (CIA), 302–3; Bay of Pigs operation and, 326; Bolivia and, 300; Brazil and, 329; Chile and, 380–81; Cuba and, 315–16, 320, 322–23; Czechoslovakia and, 304, 305; expropriations and, 345–46; Guatemala and, 307, 322–23; Indonesia and, 341; Iran and, 305; Operation Ajax and, 305; Operation PBSUCCESS and, 307. See also specific regions and operations
Cerro de Pasco Corporation, 174–75, 376, 520n64
Céspedes, Carlos Manuel de, 233
Ceylon (Sri Lanka): capital flight and, 336; Ceylonese-Soviet oil agreement and, 333–34; Hickenlooper Amendment to the Foreign Aid Act and, 332; official loans and grants from Western and Communist sources, 1960–67, 335; Soviet Union and, 332, 513n109; success and failure of U.S. sanctions and, 337; U.S. sanctions and, 335–36
CFP. See Comisión Fiscal Permanente (CFP)
Chaco War, 261
Chamorro, Diego, 158
Chamorro, Emiliano, 115, 158, 159–61
Chamorro-Weitzel Treaty, 113–15

charter cities, 20–21
Chase National Bank, 220, 221; Cuban loan payments and, 223; Cuban loan terms and, 222–23, 229; Machado loans and, 228
Chávez, Hugo, 1–2, 427, 436; Morales and, 449
Chicago Tribune, 73
Chile, 77, 379; American orbit and, 197; ITT and, 328, 381–82; navy of, 77; OPIC and, 409. See also Allende, Salvador
China, 43–44; absolute sovereign immunity and, 425; expropriation responses and, 446–47; expropriations and, 446–47; Hawaii and, 34; Indonesia and, 385; Philippines and, 43–44; radio traffic and, 391–92; W. Wilson and, 118–19. See also Radio Corporation of America v. China
China, Radio Corporation of America v., 391–92
Chivas, Antonio, 225–26
chronological list of bilateral investment treaties, 1959–65, 401
Church, Frank, 409–10
Churchill, Winston, 49
circum-Caribbean nations: American empire in, 11, 59; average bond spreads, 1900–1910, 76; average bond spreads, 1905–28, 79; defined, 59; Dominican Republic and, 70; Platt Amendment (Cuban Constitution) and, 78; protection of investors in, 184; securities and, 75–76; sovereign debt and, 183–84
Clark, J. Reuben, 151, 192, 250, 475n12
Clark, James "Champ," 44
Clark, Reed Paige, 131, 132
Clausen Tom, 418
Cleveland, Grover: Dominican Republic and, 62; on Hawaii, 26–27; Hawaii and, 31–32

Dulles, John Foster, 300; Anglo-Iranian Oil Company and, 309; United Fruit and, 306–7
Dye, Alan, 212

Eastern States Petroleum Company, 281
economic imperialism, U.S., periodization of, 23
Ecuador, 197–98, 361–63, 517n14; ADA consortium and, 517n15; Brazil and, 449–50; compensation and, 356n6; default and, 197–98
Eden, Anthony, 289–90
Edwards, Jack, 374
Einhorn, Jessica, 17
Eisenhower, Dwight, 4, 297, 301, 310; Cuba, investor pressure and, 318; economic retaliation on Cuba and, 321; investor disputes and, 307–8; Iranian policy of, 304–5; leniency towards Bolivia and, 299
El Salvador, 481n11; American investments in, 203–4; chaos in, 207–8; communism and, 207–8; debt restructuring and, 209–10; default and, 203, 208–9; external debt, customs revenue, sugar prices and 1921–35, 204; Great Depression and, 205–6; Socorro Rojo Internacional and, 205; U.S. control in, 204, 483n53
Eldredge, Alberto Ruiz, 370
empire trap: annexation of Hawaii and, 33; Cold War and, 14–15, 345; containing communism and, 312; correlation of political forces and, 186; Cuban franchises and concessions and, 53–54; cycles of empire and, 10–22; defined, 8–10; depoliticizing of investment disputes and, 15–16, 18–19; Dominican Republic and, 96–97; Eisenhower and, 310; enforce-

ment and, 410; FDR and, 434; first American empire and, 184, 296; foreign aid, covert action and, 13–14; Good Neighbor policy and, 311–12; governmental structures of foreign nations and, 246, 494n4; Great Depression and, 244; Harding and, 149; Hispaniola and, 164–66; independence of national foreign policy and, 450–51; interventionism and, 433; investor-state arbitration and, 7, 15–16, 18–19; late 1930s version of, 246, 296; mechanisms for the escape from, 410; Nicaragua and, 113–17; Philippine Organic Act of 1902 and, 240; politics of scarcity and, 312; second American empire and, 434; supercession of, 387
Engineering and Mining Journal, 146b
Enron. *See* Belco Petroleum (Enron)
Eskenazi family, 533n17. *See also* Repsol, Argentina and
Esso, 323, 333
Estrada, Juan José, 108, 110, 111
Estrada. Tomás, 78
Ethelburg Syndicate, 109
Ethiopia, 345; 1974 nationalizations and, 347b; Brooke-Alexander Amendment and, 347b; Carter, J. and, 14; Cold War position and, 347b–48b; the Derg and, 345
European Convention on State Immunity, 421
European Organisation for Economic Co-operation and Development (OECD), 394
expropriations, 344–45, 355n, 431; 1980s and, 414, 417, 431–32; BITs and, 402; Congressional definition of, 406; noncommunist Asia and, 355n. *See also specific instances of*
ExxonMobil, 2, 426, 427–28

Farnham, Roger, 120
FDI. *See* foreign direct investment (FDI)
Feis, Herbert, 250, 292
Ferrara, Orestes, 215
findings, basic, 2–8; domestic interests *versus* strategic imperatives and, 3–4; empire trap and, 8–10; U.S. interventions, 1890s to 1980s and, 3; U.S. interventions, property rights and, 4–7; U.S. interventions, technology and, 6–7
Finot, Enrique, 262
Firestone, Harvey, 50, 154, 155–56
Firestone Tire and Rubber Company, 49–50, 152. *See also* United States Trading Company (Firestone)
first American empire, *185*; debt enforcement and, 251; extrication from, 187; preferntial tariffs and, 186
fiscal receiverships, U.S., 21–22
Fish, Hamilton, 284
Fleming, Ian, 350
Food for Peace, 334
Foraker, Joseph, 53–54
Foraker Amendent, 1899, 52, 53–54; annexation of Cuba and, 55; circumvention of, 54–55
Ford, Gerald, 382
Fordney-McCumber Tariff Act, 214–15
Foreign Assistance Act of 1961, 407
Foreign Assistance Act of 1962, 330–31, 334; public opinion and, 512n84
Foreign Assistance Act of 1966, 408
Foreign Assistance Act of 1969, 409
Foreign Bondholders Protective Council (FBPC), 249–51, 495n8
foreign direct investment (FDI), 3–4, 22; 1980s and, 418; foreign portfolio investment and, 4; Great Depression and, 13, 189; Nicaragua and, 109–10; Peru and, 197; sovereign debt and, 247, 296

Foreign Sovereign Immunities Act of 1976 (FSIA), 387, 388, 406–7, 421, 421–22
Foreman, Ed, 411
France: Argentina and, 424, 441; Dominican Republic and, 61–62; Haiti and, 119, 123; Hawaii and, 456n7; Liberia and, 131, 134; sovereign immunity and, 419; sub-Saharan Africa and, 394; Tunisia and, 394
Franck, Susan, 429, 441
Fraser, Donald, ICSID and, 398
Frieden, Jeffrey, 19
Frondizi, Arturo, 355n1
FSIA. *See* Foreign Sovereign Immunities Act of 1976 (FSIA)
Fujimori, Alberto, 416–17
Fulbright, J. William, 330, 408–10

Galbraith, Frances, 340
Galván, Jesús, 65
García, Alan, 19, 415, 416, 417
Garner, John Nance, 218–19
Garrity, Ned, 381
Geneen, Harold, 328, 329, 331, 380–81
General Treaty of Inter-American Arbitration, 287
George, Walter, 409–10
George Emery Company, 105
Germany: BITs and, 400; Dominican Republic and, 65–66; Haiti and, 119; Hispaniola and, 121; Liberia and, 132; Southern Cone countries and, 77; Venezuela and, 85. *See also* chronological list of bilateral investment treaties, 1959–65
Ghana, 357n10
Gilson, J. Lawrence, 209
Gold Stabilization Act of 1934, 283
Gómez, Juan Vicente, 277
Gonzales, William, 169
González, Henry, 411; on ICSID, 413

Act and, 339; Johnson and, 17; official loans and grants to, 1955–68, *341*; oil concessions and, 337; Soviet Union and, 385

Ingram, George, 17

Instituto Cubano de Petróleo, 323

Insular Cases, Supreme Court and, 7

Inter-American Bank Bill, 411–12

International Bank for Reconstruction and Development (IBRD), 301

International Centre for Settlement of Investment Disputes (ICSID), 2, 387, 395; annual cases filed, 1972–2011, *423*; annulments and, *424*; boycotts and, *425*; cases and, *422*; default rules and, 396; "El no de Tokio" and, 396, *422*; Mareva injunctions and, *425*; numbers of member nations by region, 1965–81, *399*; procedures and, *423–30*; pullouts and, 445–46; ratification process and, 396; secretary general as gatekeeper of, 396; time and costs and, *423*; U.S. domestic legislation and, 397–98; U.S. ratification process and, 397; World Bank and, *399*

International Chamber of Commerce (ICC), 392; arbitrated disputes of, 392–93

International Court of Justice, 391

International Development Bill, 411

International Monetary Fund (IMF), 415; 1980s and, 417; Peru and, 379

International Petroleum Company (IPC), 172–73, 367–69; annual earnings of, 1969–72, *379*; Peruvian assets of, 375; Peruvian settlements and, 375–79; tax rates and returns on assets, 1916–30, *174*

International Telephone and Telegraph (ITT), 328, 329; Brazil and, 327–28, 329; Chilean politics and,

380–81; lobbying of, 330–31; use of nontraditional channels and, 379–82

International Tribunal at the Hague, 2

interventions, U.S., 59; alignment of interests and, 11, 85–86, 108–9; alignment of investors and, 59–60; Bolivia and, 174–81; Cold War and, 313–14, 361; communism and, 297, 301–10; covert actions and, 297; the Depression and the withdrawal from formal empire and, 236–41; domestic opposition to, 151–52; domestic political costs and, 314, 327; early 1950s and, 297; effectiveness of, 90–91, 182–83; expropriation insurance and, 387, 431; FDR administration and, 313; first American empire and, 92; Haiti, fiscal and political stability and, 123–25; Haiti and, 121–22; Harding and, 92; Hickenlooper Amendment to the Foreign Aid Act and, 314; interventions, bond spreads and, 80; invasion of Northern Mexico and, 140b; investor alignment, pressure and, 80; investor-versus-state arbitration and, 389; Liberia and, 131–34; Mexico, plans for the invasion of, 140b–42b; Nicaragua and, 110; Nicaraguan receivership and, 111–12; Panama and, 128–29; Peru and, 172–75; political stability and, 135; power of the executive branch and, 386–87; revenue and, 182; second American empire and, 247–48; sphere of, 88; tax revenue and, 135; technologies and, 247; Wilson and, 91–92

Investment Guaranty Program (IGP), 404–6, 430–31; fees and, 406, 525n50, 525n51; guarantees

costs, adjusted for maturity, 127; default wave in, 195–203; defaults, constitutional democracy and, 203; lending to, 1980s, 414–15; revenue regressions and, 1900–1931, *183*; stability and, 89–90. *See also specific regions and nations*

Latin American and Sub-Saharan African natural resource investment disputes, 1946–80, *352–57*

Lechín Oquendo, Juan, tin mine nationalization and, 298

Lee, Higginson and Company, 200–201

Leguía, Augusto, 168–70, 173, 195

Lena Goldfields Limited v. SR, 390, 391, 522n4

Levi, Margaret, 16

Liberia, 184, 345; boundary disputes and, 130–31; customs receivership and, 131–34; empire-trap dynamics and, 129–30; Firestone loan and, 152–57; government revenues, 1900–31, 132; Harding and, 152–53; Kru rebels and, 132

Libya: compensation and, 350, 358; expropriation and, 425; oil company output and, 385; Qaddafi and, 453n2

Liliuokalani, Queen, 31

Lindberg, Irving, 116

Lipson, Charles, 410; *Standing Guard*, 18

Llosa, Mario Vargas, 416

Lodge, Henry Cabot, 38, 45, 247

Long, Boaz, 120

Long, John, 35

Long, Russell, 330

Loomis, Francis, 84

López Contreras, Eléazar, 277

Lowenfeld, Andreas, ICSID and, 398

Machado, Gerardo, 13, 215, 220, 221, 223, 243; debt service and, 229; default and, 228; loan

negotiations and, 222; management of government expenses and, 230; reelection of, 223; resignation of, 233; sugar production limits and, 215–16; sugar tax and, 230; support from U.S. bankers and, 227; suspension of constitutional guarantees, repression and, 223–24, 227; on threat of U.S. intervention, 231, 232; U.S support of, 229

Mackay Radio and Telegraph Company, 391

Madero, Francisco, 137b

Madriz, José, 108

Mann, Thomas, 298–99, 318, 323, 368

Mansfield, Mike, 330

Mantilla, Pico, 362

Manufacturer's Chatham Bank, 207

Manzano, Osmel, 383

Marcantonio, Vito, 256–57, 496n27

Marcona Mining Company, 521n70

Marroquín, José Manuel, 82

Marshall Plan: IGP and, 404; Italy and, 304

Martí, Agustín Farabundo, 205

Martínez, Maximiliano "El Brujo" Hernández, 206, 208, 209, 210

Mauratania, 357n14

McAdoo, William, 133

McCafferty, Frank, 207

McCone, John, 379

McDermott, Allan, on the Lodge bill, 41

McIlhenny, John Henry, 166

McKinley, William: on Cuba, 35; on George Dewey, 34; Hawaii and, 26, 32; imperial expansion and, 27; Philippines and, 35

McNutt, Paul, 242

McReynolds, Samuel, 284

Mellon, Andrew, 149

Mena, Luis, 112

Mendieta, Carlos, 223, 236

Mene Grande Company, 278

Mossadegh, Mohammad, 304, 305
Muccio, John, 263–64
Multilateral Investment Guarantee Agency (MIGA), 417–19, 445
Mutual Security Act of 1951: "areas" and, 525n45; IGP and, 404; war risk and, 525n48

Naidu, Suresh, 308, 382
Nasution, General, 342
Nation, The, 307
National City Bank of New York, 126, 132, 151, 154, 166, 167
National Industrial Recovery Act of 1934, 292
National Lead Company, 179
natural resources, investment in, 3, 14, 19, 20
navies, 77, 464n75
Nelson, Samuel, 387
Neptune Mining Company, 348b
Neutrality Act, U.S., 110
New York and Bermúdez Company (NY&B), 80–81, 82–83, 84
New York Convention of 1958, 387, 393–94. *See also* Convention on the Recognition and Enforcement of Foreign Arbitral Awards (New York Convention); *under* interventions, U.S.
New York Herald-Tribune, 307
New York Times, 153, 208, 218, 279, 307; on Bay of Pigs operation, 326; on Brazilian expropriations, 329; Castro, Fidel, and, 315; on Cuban sugar quota cut, 324; on Indonesian oil, 338
New York World, 138b
Newlands, Francis, 32
Newsweek, 307
Nicaragua: arbitration and, 349; civil war in, 160; customs receivership, results of, 104; fiscal revenues of, 1892–1916, *112*; government revenues, 1916–35,

116; invasion of Honduras and, 80; nationalizations and, 348b–49b; revolution of 1979 and, 348b; Sandanista nationalizations and, 348b; U.S. continuing involvement in, 116–17; U.S. receivership and, 111; S *Denver* peace talks and, 161; World War I and, 115, 117
Nixon, Richard, 4, 372–73, 408; on Cuba, 316; expropriation of American assets and, 372; on F. Castro, 317; Hickenlooper Amendment to the Foreign Aid Act and, 364; Peru and, 14, 367; settlement of Peru-IPC dispute and, 379
Norris, George, 153
Northwest Ordinace of 1784, 29
Nouel, Adolfo, 96, 97
Nowell, R. I., 257

Obama, Barack, 442
Obregón, José Emilio, 228
O'Brien, Robert, 255
Odría, Manuel, 368
OECD. *See* Organisation for European Economic Co-Operation (OECD)
Office of Strategic Services (OSS), 302–3. *See also* Central Intelligence Agency (CIA)
Oliver, William, 319
Onganía, Juan Carlos, 355n1
OPEC, 359
OPIC. *See* Overseas Private Investment Corporation (OPIC)
Oreste, Michel, 120
Organisation for European Economic Co-Operation (OECD), 394
Orinoco Steamship Company, 84–85
Osmeña, Sergio, 241
Ovando, Alfredo, 364, 365
Overseas Private Investment Corporation (OPIC), 387, 388, 407–10; IMF and, 415–16

pine Independence Act of 1934
and, 241, 494n238; U.S. banking
system and, 45; U.S. direct investment in, *44*; U.S. establishment of
civil government in, 37–38; U.S.
tariff legislation and, 240; war of
the insurgency and, 37
Pike, H. H., 216
Pinochet, Augusto, 381
Pittman, Key, 283
Platt Amendment (Cuban Constitution), 55; abrogation of by U.S.
and Cuba, 236, 254; Article 2 of,
220; second and third clauses of,
251–52
political risk insurance, 16–17, 416,
419–20, 435; AIG and, 415–16;
Enron and, 415–16; OPIC and,
408–10; private market for, 445.
See also Multilateral Investment
Guarantee Agency (MIGA)
political science, imperialism and, 17
Pond, Charles, 101–2
Porras, Belisario, 126, 128
Porter Convention of 1907, 389
Prado, Manuel, 367–68
Pratt, Ruth, 217, 218; 17th District
and, 487n116; Garner and,
218–19
private political risk insurance, OPIC
and, 416
property rights of investors: Cold
War and, 313–14; FDR administration and, 313; mobilization
of state power and, 312. *See also*
expropriations; *specific instances
of nationalization and expropriation*
Puerto Rico, 36; citizenship and,
493n235; Jones Act of 1917
and, 238; Jones-Shafroth Act of
1917, 496n24; sugar industry
and, 256–57, 497n28; U.S. and,
455n4
Puig, José Maria, 232–33
Pullium, William, 199

Quadros, Jânio, 329
Quezon, Manuel, 51, 237, 242; on
dominion status, 242
Quintanilla, Carlos, 293

racism: Asiatic Barred Zone Act and,
238, 239; Dominican Republic
and, 60; Hawaii and, 26–27;
Japan and, 27; Liberian interven-
tion and, 131; Liberian loan and,
153; Philippines and, 34, 56;
U.S.politics and, 26–27, 60; Wat-
sonville, California, and, 238–39;
Wilson administration and, 131
*Radio Corporation of America v.
China*, 391–92
Ramsey, Henry, 319–20
Rawlins, Joseph, on the Lodge bill,
43
Reagan, Ronald: BITs and, 402;
Strategic Petroleum Reserve and,
415
Reciprocal Trade Agreement of 1934
(U.S.), 260
Reconstruction Finance Corporation
(RFC), 233, 234; Bolivian tin and,
299–300
Reed, Thomas, 32
Repsol, Argentina and, 425–27,
443–44, 530n131, 533n17
Requena, José Luis, 465n99
Revenue Act of 1913, 46–47
Revere, 356n9
Riter-Conley Manufacturing Com-
pany, 106
Rivas, Alfredo, 158–59
Roa, Rail, 319
Robbins, Warren, 204
Robertson, J. L., 65
Robinson, John, on the Lodge bill,
41–42
Roddy, William, 197
Rodríguez, Abelardo, 272
Rodríguez, Demetrio, 65–66, 93–94
Rogers, William, 371, 374
Romer, Paul, 20–21

277; Oil Act of 1943 and, 382; oil nationalization and, 23; operating income per barrel of private oil companies, 1948–80, *384*; United Kingdom and, 288

Verizon, 427–28

Victoria, Alfredo, 94

Victoria, Eladio, 94

Villa, Francisco "Pancho," 139b–40b, 143b–45b

Villistas: metal smelting and, 144b–45b, 473n26; revenue and, 473n26

Volcker, Paul, 414–15

W. R. Grace Company, 174–75

Wadsworth, Eliot, 199

Wagner, Rodrigo, 446–47

Wang, Frank, 253–54

Warner, Charles, 84

Warner-Quinlan Asphalt Company, 83

Warren, Charles, 46

Warwick, Walter, 128

Washington Convention of 1965, 395–96, 523n24; Latin American group and, 523n26; ratification of, 398–99. *See also under* interventions, U.S.

Watsonville, California, 238–39

Weingast, Barry R., 16

Weintraub, Sidney, 17

Weitzel, George, 112

Welles, Sumner, 165, 209–10, 231, 232–33, 264, 292–93; on Cuban default, 233; on Good Neighbor policy in Bolivia, 263; on moratorium for Cuban principal payments, 230; on threat of Cuban anarchy, 232

Weltover, Argentine Republic v. (1992), 387, 421–22

Westendorps & Co., 61

White, Francis, 128–29, 250

White, Harry Dexter, 284, 293

White-Weld, 171

Wieland, William, 321–22, 324

Williams, John on the Philippines, 25

Willis, Frances, 334

Wilson, Henry Lane, 138b

Wilson, Woodrow, 4; anti-interventionism and, 91–92, 103; Dominican Republic and, 12, 99; early disengagement and, 118–19; election of 1912 and, 117; on foreign policy and national interest, 117, 118; on imperialism, 97; military intervention in Mexico and, 137b–40b; Nicaragua and, 117

Wolfe, Joseph, 362

Wood, Bryce, 245–46, 299

Wood, Leonard, 49, 54, 89; Cuba annexation and, 53; Philippines and, 237

World Bank, 388, 395; ICISD and, 399; Multilateral Investment Guarantee Agency (MIGA) and, 418–19

World Trade Organization, 444

World War I: Haiti and, 121–22; ICC and, 183, 392; Latin American revenue and, *183*; Nicaragua, European markets and, 115; Nicaragua and, 115; Panama and, 128; U.S. plans for the invasion of Mexico and, 141–42

World War II: Bolivia and, 294; covert action, U.S. public opinion and, 10; expropriation of America property and, 355n; spread of communism and, 297; U.S. development of covert action capabilities and, 7, 302

Woss y Gil, Alejandro, 63, 64

Wright, Mark, 19

Wyatt, F. Mark, 303

Yacimientos Petrolíferos Fiscales Argentinos (YPF), 262–63

Yacimientos Petrolíferos Fiscales Bolivianos (YPFB), 263, 295–96

Young, Arthur, 150
Young, Charles, 131
YPF company (Repsol), 425–27, 443–44; opinion polls and, 436

Zamor, 120
Zelaya, José Santos, 104; American interests and, 105–7; planters and, 107–8
Zevada, Manuel, 287